M000086906

SAGE was founded in 1965 by Sara Miller McCune to support the dissemination of usable knowledge by publishing innovative and high-quality research and teaching content. Today, we publish over 900 journals, including those of more than 400 learned societies, more than 800 new books per year, and a growing range of library products including archives, data, case studies, reports, and video. SAGE remains majority-owned by our founder, and after Sara's lifetime will become owned by a charitable trust that secures our continued independence.

Los Angeles | London | New Delhi | Singapore | Washington DC | Melbourne

Handbook of
TRIBAL POLITICS
IN INDIA

Handbook of
TRIBAL POLITICS
IN INDIA

LIBRARY OF
CONGRESS
SURPLUS
DUPLICATE

Edited by
Jagannath Ambagudia • Virginius Xaxa

Los Angeles | London | New Delhi
Singapore | Washington DC | Melbourne

Copyright © Jagannath Ambagudia and Virginius Xaxa, 2021

All rights reserved. No part of this book may be reproduced or utilized in any form or by any means, electronic or mechanical, including photocopying, recording or by any information storage or retrieval system, without permission in writing from the publisher.

First published in 2021 by

SAGE Publications India Pvt Ltd
B1/I-1 Mohan Cooperative Industrial Area
Mathura Road, New Delhi 110 044, India
www.sagepub.in

SAGE Publications Inc
2455 Teller Road
Thousand Oaks, California 91320, USA

SAGE Publications Ltd
1 Oliver's Yard, 55 City Road
London EC1Y 1SP, United Kingdom

SAGE Publications Asia-Pacific Pte Ltd
18 Cross Street #10-10/11/12
China Square Central
Singapore 048423

Published by Vivek Mehra for SAGE Publications India Pvt Ltd. Typeset in 10/12 pt Times by Zaza Eunice, Hosur, Tamil Nadu, India.

Library of Congress Control Number: 2020950791

ISBN: 978-93-5388-458-1 (HB)

SAGE Team: Rajesh Dey, Syed Husain Naqvi, Parul Prasad, Madhurima Thapa and Rajinder Kaur

Dedicated to the tribal communities of India
and their persistent political struggle

Thank you for choosing a SAGE product!
If you have any comment, observation or feedback,
I would like to personally hear from you.

Please write to me at **contactceo@sagepub.in**

Vivek Mehra, Managing Director and CEO, SAGE India.

Bulk Sales

SAGE India offers special discounts
for purchase of books in bulk.
We also make available special imprints
and excerpts from our books on demand.

For orders and enquiries, write to us at

Marketing Department
SAGE Publications India Pvt Ltd
B1/I-1, Mohan Cooperative Industrial Area
Mathura Road, Post Bag 7
New Delhi 110044, India

E-mail us at **marketing@sagepub.in**

Subscribe to our mailing list
Write to **marketing@sagepub.in**

This book is also available as an e-book.

Contents

List of Figures

List of Tables

List of Abbreviations

AAPTL	All Assam Plains Tribal League
ABSSS	Akhil Bharatiya Samaj Sewa Sansthan
ABSU	All Bodo Student Union
ADC	Autonomous District Council
ADSS	Adivasi Dalit Samara Samithi
AFSPA	Armed Forces (Special Powers) Act
AGMS	Adivasi Gotra Maha Sabha
AGP	Asom Gana Parishad
AHTU	Assam Hills Tribal Union
AITC	All India Trinamool Congress
AIIC(T)	All India Indira Congress (Tiwari)
AIUDF	All India United Democratic Front
AJSU	All Jharkhand Students Union
AJSUP	All Jharkhand Students Union Party
ALCP	Assam Legislative Council Proceedings
AMAMS	Aikya Mala Araya Maha Sabha
ANSAM	All Naga Students Association Manipur
APCC	Assam Pradesh Congress Committee
APHLC	All Party Hill Leaders Conference
ASDC	Autonomous State Demand Committee
ATMAMS	Akhila Thiruvithamkoor Mala Araya Maha Sabha
ATTF	All Tripura Tiger Force
BC	Backward Class
BJA	Bharat Jan Andolan
BJD	Biju Janata Dal
BJP	Bharatiya Janata Party
BJS	Bharatiya Jan Sangh
BLT	Bodo Liberation Tigers
BNP	Bharatiya Navshakti Party
BOPF	Bodaland Peoples Front
BPF	Bodoland's Progressive Front
BPPF(H)	Bodo People's Progressive Front (Hagrama Faction)
BPPF(R)	Bodo People's Progressive Front (Rabiram Faction)
BPPF	Bodo People's Progressive Front

BSS	Bodo Sahitya Sabha
BTAD	Bodoland Territorial Autonomous District
BTC	Bodoland Territorial Council
BTP	Bharatiya Tribal Party
BVA	Bahujan Vikas Aaghadi
CA	Constituent Assembly
CAD	Constituent Assembly Debates
CFR	Community forest rights
CHT	Chittagong Hill Tracts
CM	Chief Minister
CNTA	Chotanagpur Tenancy Act
CNUS	Chotanagpur Unnati Samaj
CPI	Communist Party of India
CPI(M)	Communist Party of India (Marxist)
CPI(ML)	Communist Party of India (Marxist–Leninist)
CRESP	Commission for Review of Social and Environmental Sector Policies, Plans and Programmes
DAN	Democratic Alliance of Nagaland
ECI	Election Commission of India
EITU	Eastern Indian Tribal Union
EMRS	Ekalavya Model Residential School
FRA	Forest Rights Act
GAC	Gorkha Apex Committee
GDCT	Gurjar Desh Charitable Trust
GER	Gross Enrolment Ratio
GGP	Gondwana Gantantra Party
GNC	Garo National Council
GOI	Government of India
GPHDI	Gram Panchayat Human Development Index
HAC	Hill Areas Committee
HSPDP	Hill State People's Democratic Party
ICS	Indian Congress (Socialist)
IFR	Individual Forest Rights
INC	Indian National Congress
INC(I)	Indian National Congress (Indira)
INC(U)	Indian National Congress (U)
IND	Independent
INPT	Indigenous Nationalist Party of Twipra
IPFT	Indigenous Peoples Front of Tripura
JADS	Jagrit Adivasi Dalit Sangathan
JAYS	Jai Adivasi Yuva Shakti
JCC	Jharkhand Coordination Committee
JD	Janata Dal

JD(G)	Janata Dal (Gujrat)
JD(S)	Janata Dal (Secular)
JD(U)	Janata dal (United)
JMM	Jharkhand Mukti Morcha
JKD	Jharkhand Party
JNP	Janta Party
JP	Janata Party
JPC	Joint Parliamentary Committee
JRS	Janadhipathya Rashtriya Sabha
JSS	Janashiksha Samiti
JSS-GMP	Janashiksha Samiti-Gana Mukti Parishad
KHAM	Kshatriya, Harijan, Adivasi and Muslim
KHNAM	Khun Hynniewtrep National Awakening Movement
KJHDCC	Khasi and Jaintia Hills District Congress Committee
KMD	Kerala Model of Development
LSD	Lok Sabha Debates
MCC	Maoist Communist Centre
MCLA	Member of Council of Legislative Assembly
MDC	Member of District Council
MFP	Minor Forest Produce
MGNREGA	Mahatma Gandhi National Rural Employment Guarantee Act
MLA	Member of Legislative Assembly
MLPC Act	Mizoram Liquor (Prohibition and Control) Act
MNF	Mizo National Front
MNFF	Mizo National Famine Front
MoS	Memorandum of Settlement
MP	Madhya Pradesh
MP	Member of Parliament
MPF	Mizoram Peoples Forum
MU	Mizo Union
NAC	National Advisory Committee
NBCC	Nagaland Baptist Church Council
NCP	Nationalist Congress Party
NDA	National Democratic Alliance
NDFB	National Democratic Front of Boroland
NEDA	North-East Democratic Alliance
NEFA	North-East Frontier Agency
NGO	Non-governmental Organizations
NGT	National Green Tribunal
NLFT	National Liberation Front of Tripura
NNC	Naga National Council
NOC	No Objection Certificate

NOTA	None of the Above
NPEP	Naga People's Party
NPF	Naga People's Front
NPP	Naga People's Party
NPP	National People's Party
NSCN	National Socialist Council of Nagalim
NTFP	Non-timber Forest Produce
OBCs	Other Backward Classes
OSATIP	Orissa Scheduled Areas Transfer of Immovable Property
OTFD	Other Traditional Forest Dweller
PCDR	People's Coordination for Democratic Rights
PDA	People's Democratic Alliance
PDF	People's Democratic Front
PDS	Public Distribution System
PESA Act	Panchayats (Extension to Scheduled Areas) Act
PRI	Panchayati Raj Institution
PRISM	Peoples Right to Information and Development Implementing Society of Mizoram
PSP	Praja Socialist Party
PSSS	Paryavaran Sanrakshan Sangharsh Samiti
PTC	Plains Tribals Council of Assam
PTCA	Plain Tribal Council of Assam
PTG	Primary Tribal Group
PVTG	Particularly Vulnerable Tribal Group
PWG	People's War Group
RJAM	Rabha Jatiya Aikya Manch
RJD	Rashtriya Janata Dal
RSP	Revolutionary Socialist Party
RSS	Rashtriya Swayamsevak Sangh
SBSP	Suheldev Bahujan Samaj Party
SC	Scheduled Caste
SDCM	Schedule Demand Committee Manipur
SDF	Sikkim Democratic Front
SHS	Shivsena
SJAM	Sanmilita Janagosthiya Aikya Mancha
SKM	Sikkim Krantikari Morcha
SLA	Sikkim Legislative Assembly
SLTTJAC	Sikkim Limboo Tamang Tribal Joint Action Committee
SP	Samajwadi Party
SP	Socialist Party
SPTA	Santhal Pargana Tenancy Act
SRC	States Reorganisation Commission

SSD	Sardar Sarovar Dam
ST	Scheduled Tribe
SWA	Swatantra Party
TAC	Tribal Advisory Council
TDP	Telugu Desam Party
TICI	Tribal Intellectual Collective India
TJAM	Tiwa Jatiya Aikya Manch
TJMK	Tripura Jatiyo Mukti Parishad
TRS	Telangana Rashtriya Samiti
TSP	Tribal Sub-Plan
TUJS	Tripura Upajati Juba Samiti
UDF	United Democratic Front
UDP	United Democratic Party
UMFO	United Mizo Freedom Organisation
UP	Uttar Pradesh
UPA	United Progressive Alliance
UPP	United People's Party
UPPL	United People's Party Liberal
YSRCP	Yuvajana Sramik Rythu Congress Party
YMA	Young Mizo Association

Preface

Over the period of our research on tribal issues, we encountered a scanty literature on tribal politics in India as compared to other marginalized groups, such as the Dalits, women and religious groups. This is probably due to the fact that the academic arena has not given due attention to various issues of tribal communities in general and their engagement in democratic politics in particular. However, the political science departments of various universities have recently begun to symbolically include tribal communities in their educational curriculum. Despite the location of tribal communities at the margin, anthropology has been studying tribes since the inception of universities in eastern and north-eastern India. The recent trend indicates an academic upsurge and a resurgence of research interests on tribal issues in general and tribal politics in particular in Indian universities due to the entry of tribal academics and researchers into higher educational institutions. In teaching tribal politics, we felt the paucity of published materials and, hence, the need for a comprehensive volume on understanding various dynamics of tribal politics in India. We discussed such requirement at various platforms during our stint at the Tata Institute of Social Sciences (TISS), Guwahati Campus, albeit with little success. The need of a concise book on the topic under consideration resurfaced when Jagannath Ambagudia offered the thematic course, *Democracy, Rights and Tribes in India* to scholars pursuing MPhil in social sciences at TISS, Guwahati Campus. Challenges and anxieties experienced while teaching this course compelled us to have frequent discussions and encouraged us to work more meaningfully on tribal politics and to develop a network to collectively bring out a comprehensive volume on tribal politics in India.

Diversity and accommodation are integral part of democratic processes in the contemporary world. Such practices are conspicuous in a multicultural society like India, which is seen as a complete grid of caste, ethnicity, gender and religion. Such distinctiveness can also be used to differentiate and exclude certain social categories from mainstream social life. The distinct ethnic identities of tribal communities were/are largely used to exclude them from various spheres of life. Against this backdrop, post-colonial India debated the location of tribal communities in 'mainstream' society and developed modalities via constitutional provisions of preferential considerations in politics, government employment and education.

Turning towards politics, institutional arrangements were made by the framers of the Indian Constitution, who realized that there should be an adequate representation of tribal communities in decision-making bodies. As a consequence, there is a provision of political reservation for tribes under Articles 330 and 332 of the Indian Constitution. However, bringing tribal communities into modern democratic institutions has largely undermined their traditional political system and exposed them to the competitive power politics of modern democracy. Such integration has led to different levels of political development among tribal communities of India.

The uneven political development among tribal communities has resulted in various forms and degrees of engagement with modern democratic politics. This has helped us in problematizing the idea of tribe as a homogenous group in India. The heterogeneity of tribal communities facilitates the process of their interaction with democratic politics at their corresponding levels, thereby leading to various degrees of political articulation and influence over the political system. Political integration of tribes, through preferential consideration, has essentially provided the ground for the emergence of tiny political elites in tribal society. Within this backdrop, it can be seen that the tribal communities of north-eastern India are more politically articulative in comparison to their central Indian counterparts. Tribal communities of India have developed different forms of relationship with political parties and a larger political structure.

Within this backdrop, the *Handbook of Tribal Politics in India* traces the location of the tribes in modern democracy. It explores the relationship between tribal communities and electoral politics at the centre and state levels by considering quantitative (election data) and qualitative data (field data). It looks at the engagement of tribes in mainstream democratic politics and focuses on patterns, conditions and challenges that lie before the participation of tribal communities in electoral politics in India. While doing so, this volume provides state-by-state analysis of tribal politics. It explores the changing relationship between tribal communities and political parties, the performance of the latter in ST-reserved constituencies and the various factors responsible for such performances. The book discusses the role of tribal political representatives in policymaking, especially issues related to tribal communities. The book helps us locate gender in tribal politics in India. It raises issues and concerns of tribal politics with greater implications over policy and research in India.

Acknowledgements

Working on an ambitious project has never soiled through an easy path. During the course of this journey, we met with numerous individuals on various academic platforms, discussed, debated, disagreed and resolved a myriad of issues that are critical to understand tribal politics in India. It may not be possible for us to acknowledge each one of them individually, but all of them left their marks in the various pages of this volume. At the outset, we would like to take this opportunity to thank all the contributors who trusted us and agreed to be part of this pains-taking journey by contributing chapters. We are grateful to the International Work Group for Indigenous Affairs, the *Economic & Political Weekly*, the Indian Institute of Dalit Studies and the *Journal of Social Inclusion Studies* for giving permission to reprint chapters of Samar Bosu Mullick, Ramachandra Guha, Suryasikha Pathak and Jagannath Ambagudia.

Colleagues and friends at TISS, Guwahati Campus; Tezpur University; Institute for Human Development, New Delhi, helped us in several ways during our stint in these institutions. Their regular enquiry about the status of the volume compelled us to put extra efforts to bring the work to the light of the day. We are also thankful to Sujata Buragohain, Medusmita Borthakur and P. Lalpekhlui, PhD scholars at TISS, Guwahati Campus, for their help in proofreading the initial versions of the reprinted chapters. We would also like to thank Kamal Azad, another PhD scholar at TISS, Guwahati Campus, for redrawing the maps used in this book.

The acknowledgements, in fact, remain incomplete without endorsing the contributions of our family members, Sasmita Mohanty, little angel Jiyana Jigyansha Ambagudia, Chameli Xaxa and Aashish Khakha. Despite their professional commitments and family responsibilities, they eased the volume by creating space for us to devote the time that this volume required at various stages.

Finally, we would like to thank Rajesh Dey, Managing Editor-Commissioning, SAGE, who constantly monitored the progress of the volume and the entire SAGE team for their interest and continuous support in bringing out this book.

About the Editors and Contributors

EDITORS

Jagannath Ambagudia is Dean, School of Social Sciences and Humanities (2020–), and Associate Professor at the Centre for Peace and Conflict Studies, School of Social Sciences and Humanities (2014–), Tata Institute of Social Sciences, Guwahati Campus, Assam, India. He was also the Chairperson, Unit for Research and Development, Tata Institute of Social Sciences, Guwahati Campus, Assam, India (2016–2020). Previously, he taught at the Department of Political Science, Rajdhani College, University of Delhi (2009–2014); National Law School of India University, Bangalore, Karnataka (2008–2009); and ARSD College, University of Delhi (2006–2008). He obtained MA, M. Phil. and Ph. D. in Political Science from Jawaharlal Nehru University, New Delhi. He is the author of *Adivasis, Migrants and the State in India* (Routledge, 2019). His area of interest lies on issues of Adivasi society, social exclusion and inclusion, development and deprivation, marginalisation, preferential treatment, distributive justice and community conflict. He is currently working on the role of tribal MPs in Indian Parliament within the broader relationship between scheduled tribes and democracy in India.

Virginius Xaxa is currently visiting Professor at the Institute for Human Development (IHD), New Delhi. Prior to joining IHD, he was Professor of Eminence and Bharat Ratna Lokapriya Gopinath Bordoloi Chair at Tezpur University (2016–2018). He was also Professor and Deputy Director of the Tata Institute of Social Sciences, Guwahati Campus (2011–2016). He taught Sociology at the Delhi School of Economics, University of Delhi (1990–2011), and North-Eastern Hill University, Shillong (1978–1990). He obtained MA in Sociology from Pune University and Ph.D. from the Indian Institute of Technology (IIT), Kanpur. He is the author of *Economic Dualism and Structure of Class: A Study in Plantation and Peasant Settings in North Bengal* (Cosmo, 1997) and *State, Society and Tribes: Issues in Post-Colonial India* (Pearson, 2008), co-author of *Tea Plantation Labour in India* (Friedrich Ebert Stiftung, 1996) and co-editor of *Social Exclusion and Adverse Inclusion: Development and Deprivation of Adivasis in India* (OUP, 2012), *Work, Institutions and Sustainable Livelihood: Issues and Challenges of Transformation* (Palgrave, 2017) and *Employment and Labour Market in North-East India: Interrogating Structural Changes* (Routledge, 2019). He was also the Chairman of the *High Level Committee on Socio-Economic, Health and Educational Status of Tribal Communities of India*, Government of India (2014).

CONTRIBUTORS

A. K. Verma is Honorary Director, Centre for the Study of Society and Politics (CSSP), Kanpur, Uttar Pradesh, India. He is the former Chair, Political Science, Christ Church College. He is also the Editor of *Shodharthy*, a social science Journal in Hindi. He specialises in the Politics of Uttar Pradesh. He was invited by Harvard University in 2008 for his theories of Social Osmosis and Reverse Social Osmosis that explained identity politics and transition to *inclusive* politics.

Abhilash T. is currently working as Assistant Professor in Centre for Development Studies, Thiruvananthapuram, Kerala. Before joining this Centre, he was a faculty at Gokhale Institute of Politics and Economics, Pune. His area of research mainly focuses on political economy, social exclusion and tribal studies. He had undertaken research projects on vulnerable and nomadic tribal communities in southern western ghat.

Ashvin Vasava is a doctoral student at the Centre for the Study of Society and Development, School of Social Sciences, Central University of Gujarat, Gandhinagar, Gujarat. His ongoing research work focuses on Forest Rights Movement amongst the Adivasis of Gujarat. He is also associated with Aadi Seva Mandal-Vadava, an organisation working for social welfare of Adivasis in Narmada district, Gujarat.

Bipin Jojo is a Professor at the Centre for Social Justice and Governance, School of Social Work, Tata Institute of Social Sciences, Mumbai. He was awarded Research Fellowship from University Grant Commission for PhD, and prestigious Commonwealth Fellowship of British government at School of Oriental and African Studies, London University. He has been involved in teaching, research and training in various issues of tribal society, such as governance, land, forest, social work with tribal perspective, tribal education, etc. among others. He has written several academic articles and reports for government and non-government organisations in these areas. He has also been associated with several academic and development organisations nationally and Internationally.

Bodhi S. R. is an Assistant Professor at the Centre for Social Justice and Governance, School of Social Work, Tata Institute of Social Sciences, Mumbai. He is also the National Convener of the Tribal Intellectual Collective India. His areas of interest are tribal epistemology, dialogical history and Navayana Buddhist studies.

H. Beck is a Professor at the Centre for Community Organization and Development Practice, School of Social Work, Tata Institute of Social Sciences, Mumbai. He has been teaching since last 29 years. Besides teaching, he is also engaged in wide variety of academic activities like, training, research on areas like electoral process and participation of people in governance, displacement, rehabilitation and resettlements, manual scavengers, budget outcome studies in infrastructure and development sectors, etc. He was also part of the Expert committee on *Tribal Health in India: Bridging the Gap and Roadmap for the Future*, constituted by Ministry of Health and Family Welfare and Ministry of Tribal Affairs, Government of India, 2018.

Himani Ramchiary is currently working as an Assistant Professor in the Department of Anthropology, M.C College, Barpeta, Assam. She is also pursuing her PhD on the broader issues of struggle of Bodo communities for a separate homeland at Tata Institute of Social

Sciences, Guwahati Campus. Her area of interest involves understanding the social, cultural and political transitions of tribal communities in the contemporary society.

Jelle J. P. Wouters is a social anthropologist, who teaches in the Department of Social Sciences at Royal Thimphu College, Bhutan. He has written about political lifeworlds, democracy and elections, kinship and identity and social history in Northeast India for *Hau: Journal of Ethnographic Theory, Contributions to Indian Sociology, Studies in History, Economic and Political Weekly, Journal of Cambridge Anthropology,* and other journals. He is the author of *In the Shadows of Naga Insurgency* (OUP, 2018), *Nagas as a Society Against Voting and Other Essays* (Highlander Books, 2019) and the co-editor of *Democracy in Nagaland: Tribes, Traditions, Tensions* (Highlander Books 2018) and *Nagas in the 21st Century* (Highlander Books, 2017).

Joseph Riamei is teaching at the Centre for Community Organisation and Development Practice, School of Social Work, Tata Institute of Social Sciences, Guwahati Campus. He did his PhD from Tata Institute of Social Sciences, Mumbai. His interest areas include federalism, ethnicity and conflict studies in South East Asia, state, democracy and tribes, social work with a special focus on indigenous people's epistemic and human rights.

Kamal Nayan Choubey teaches Political Science at Dyal Singh College, University of Delhi, New Delhi. He has done his Ph.D on Tribal Forest Land Rights in India and published a book on *Jungle ki Haqdari: Rajneeti Aur Sangharsh* (CSDS-Vani Prakashan, 2015).

Mini Pathak Dogra is an Assistant Professor at the Department of Political Science, Himachal Pradesh University, Shimla, Himachal Pradesh. She did her PhD on Khampa tribe of Himachal Pradesh. She has contributed several articles on different aspects of Indian politics in various peer reviewed journals.

Moses Kharbithai is currently teaching in the Department of Political Science, Assam University, Silchar, Assam. His areas of interest are political theory, democratic institutions and processes, regional politics and political institutions and processes in Northeast India, Indian regional diaspora and politics of migration.

N. Rajaram was a former Professor and Dean, School of Social Sciences, Central University of Gujarat, Gandhinagar, Gujarat. His area of research interest is sociology of development, especially in Gujarat. He has researched and published extensively on cooperatives, politics, gender and health, and transnational migration from Gujarat.

Nani Bath, a recipient of Indian Political Science Association Young Political Scientist Award, is Professor in the Department of Political Science, Rajiv Gandhi University, Itanagar, Arunachal Pradesh. His area of interest is international relations and society and politics in India's North East. He is the author of *Electoral Politics in Arunachal Pradesh* (Pilgrims Publishing, 2009), *Party Politics in Arunachal Pradesh* (2016) and *Voices from Border: Responses to Chinese Claim over Arunachal Pradesh* (Pentagon Press, 2015) edited with Gurudas Das and CJ Thomas.

Nilamber Chhetri is Assistant Professor of Sociology at the School of Humanities and Social Sciences, India Institute of Technology, Mandi, Himachal Pradesh. His work explores the growth and proliferation of ethnic associations in Darjeeling hills and their demands for recognition as scheduled tribes. His research interests include politics of social and cultural identities, scheduling of tribes and practices of state classification in India, and issues related to ethnic minorities and the politics of recognition in South Asia. He regularly contributes research papers and book reviews to reputed national and international journals and is currently exploring the impact of infrastructural development on tribal population of Himachal Pradesh.

P. Lalpekhlui is a PhD scholar in Social Sciences, Tata Institute of Social Sciences, Guwahati Campus. She completed her MPhil in Social Sciences from Tata Institute of Social Sciences, Guwahati Campus. She has worked in the area of civil society and its role in electoral politics with special reference to Mizoram.

Pandurang Bhoye is an Assistant Professor at the Department of Politics and Public Administration, Savitribai Phule Pune University, Pune, Maharashtra. His research interests include tribal political history, movements and politics in Western India. He has 12 research papers to his credit published in national and regional professional journals. He has also contributed a number of chapters in edited volumes.

Pradeep Ramavath J. is Assistant Professor and Assistant Director with Institute of Public Policy (IPP), Centre for the Study of Social Exclusion and Inclusive Policy (CSSEIP) of National Law School of India University (NLSIU), Bengaluru. His areas of specialization include Public Policy & Social Justice. Previously he worked with Azim Premji University where he taught courses in Educational Policy and Governance. Pradeep is also the coordinator for Dr. B.R.Ambedkar Studies Centre and Centre for Study of Marginalized Communities. Presently he is involved in policy studies relating to selected most deprived SCs and STs in the state of Karnataka.

R. K. Debbarma currently teaches at the Centre for Peace and Conflict Studies, School of Social Sciences and Humanities, Tata Institute of Social Sciences, Guwahati Off-Campus. He completed his PhD in Political Science from University of Hyderabad. He writes on issues of space, place and politics in Northeast India.

Ramachandra Guha is a historian and biographer based in Bengaluru. He has taught at the Universities of Yale and Stanford, held the Arné Naess Chair at the University of Oslo, and served as the Philippe Roman Professor of History and International Affairs at the London School of Economics. He is the author of a number of books including a pioneering environmental history, *The Unquiet Woods* (University of California Press, 1989). His most recent book is a two volume biography of Mahatma Gandhi: *Gandhi Before India* (Knopf, 2014), and *Gandhi: The Years That Changed the World* (Knopf, 2018).

Rupak Kumar is a doctoral researcher at the Centre for the Study of Law and Governance, Jawaharlal Nehru University, New Delhi. His research interest lies in political institutions and their political processes, government and politics. He has worked on the interface between Parliamentary Committees and the Indian Parliament. Presently, he is working on the Nature of Parliamentary Opposition in India after independence. Earlier, he has worked as a researcher at the Election Commission of India.

Samar Bosu Mullick, also known as Sanjay, has been engaged in the Adivasi struggle for autonomy, identity and rights to economic and cultural resources since a very young age of 17. He
has published books and papers on these issues and has made presentations in many renowned
universities of the world. He has been connected to many indigenous peoples' movements in
the country and abroad. He was a leading person in the Jharkhand separate state movement and
presently engaged in the forest rights movement in the country. He was a faculty member of the
Xavier Institute for Social Service, Ranchi.

Sanghamitra Choudhury is a senior faculty in the Department of Peace and Conflict Studies
and Management, Sikkim University, Gangtok, Sikkim. She has completed her PhD from
Jawaharlal Nehru University, New Delhi and Post-Doctoral Studies from University of Oxford
(2016). She is the recipient of Charles Wallace India Fellowship (Queen's University) and
International Law Fellowship by United Nations (Hague Academy of International Law, The
Netherlands) for the year 2011. She is the author of *Women and Conflict in India* (Routledge,
2016) and co-author of *Human Rights in the Indian Armed Forces: An Analysis of Article 33*
(Vij Books, 2019).

Sasmita Mohanty is an Assistant Professor of Political Science, Rajdhani College, University
of Delhi, New Delhi. She is also doing PhD on various dynamics of Indian Diaspora in Africa
from Jawaharlal Nehru University, New Delhi. Her area of interest focuses on migration, diaspora, gender, state politics and human rights.

Subeno Kithan works as Assistant Professor in the Department of Social Anthropology at the
Centre for Sociology and Social Anthropology, School of Social Sciences and Humanities, Tata
Institute of Social Sciences, Guwahati Campus. Her area of specialisation is anthropology of
religion, culture and communication and pastoral nomadic communities. She has worked on the
Religion of the Gujjars of Jammu and Kashmir for her doctoral research and has engaged with
the community between 2009–2011.

Sudha Pai retired as Professor at the Centre for Political Studies, and as the Rector of Jawaharlal
Nehru University, New Delhi. She was National Fellow, Indian Council of Social Science
Research, New Delhi (2016–2017) and Senior Fellow at the Nehru Memorial Museum and Library,
Teen Murti, New Delhi (2006–2009). Some of her well known books include *Developmental
State and the Dalit Question in Madhya Pradesh: Congress Response* (Routledge, 2010);
Everyday Communalism: Riots in Contemporary Uttar Pradesh (OUP, 2018) and more
recently *Constitutional and Democratic Institutions in India: A Critical Analysis* (edited)
(Orient Blackswan, 2020).

Sujit Kumar works as Assistant Professor in the Department of Political Science at St. Joseph's
College, Bengaluru. His areas of interest are land acquisition in scheduled areas of Jharkhand
and adivasi politics. He has published research papers in journals like *Studies in Indian Politics*
and *Studies in Humanities and Social Sciences*. He is the co-editor of *India's Scheduled Areas:
Untangling Governance, Law and Politics* (Routledge, 2020).

Suryasikha Pathak is a faculty at the Centre for Tribal Studies, Assam University, Diphu
Campus. Earlier, she taught history in Assam University, Silchar. She was awarded Fulbright

Senior Fellow (2008–2009) and Schlesinger Research Awardee, Harvard University (2013). Her research interests include tribal identity politics, gender and missions in northeast India. She has published on these areas.

Tikendra K. Chhetry is a Guest Faculty at the Department of Peace and Conflict Studies and Management, Sikkim University, Gangtok, Sikkim. He was a National Doctoral Fellow of the Indian Council of Social Science Research (2014–16) and a National Post-Doctoral Fellow of the Indian Council of Social Science Research (2019–2021). He is selected for DR. APJ Abdul Kalam National Award 2020 by International Institute for Social and Economic Reforms (Bangaluru). He has published several research articles in peer-reviewed journals.

Valerian Rodrigues has taught at Mangalore University, Karnataka, India (1982–2003), and Jawaharlal Nehru University, New Delhi, India (2003–2015). He was National Fellow of Indian Council of Social Science Research, New Delhi (2015–2017) and Ambedkar Chair, Ambedkar University, New Delhi (2017–2018). His recent books include *The Essential Writings of B. R. Ambedkar* (OUP, 2002), *The Indian Parliament: A Democracy at Work* (OUP, 2011, co-authored with B. L. Shankar), *Speaking for Karnataka* (Bengaluru University Press, 2018, co-authored with Rajendra Chenni, Nataraj Huliyar and S. Japhet). He has edited *Conversations with Ambedkar: 10 Ambedkar Memorial Lectures* (Columbia University Press, 2019).

Venkatesh Vaditya teaches in the Department of Social Exclusion Studies, School of Interdisciplinary Studies, The English and Foreign Languages University, Hyderabad. He obtained MA in Political Science from University of Hyderabad, Hyderabad and M. Phil. and Ph. D. in Political Science from Jawaharlal Nehru University, New Delhi. His areas of interest include human rights, exclusion studies, methods and methodologies in exclusion studies and epistemic justice.

Introduction:
Situating Tribal Politics in India

Jagannath Ambagudia and Virginius Xaxa

Diversity, recognition and redistribution are integral parts of liberal democratic processes in the contemporary world. The relationship between democracy and diversity is more significant in a socially stratified society where different social groups are placed at various levels of the social ladders. The framers of the Indian Constitution realized that equal citizenship in terms of equality before the law is inadequate to ensure the representation of socially and politically excluded groups, such as the Scheduled Tribes (ST),[1] in decision-making processes that affect them on a daily basis and define their relationship with the larger society. The members of the Constituent Assembly recognized these critical issues, which led them to engage in extensive debates on the place of tribals in the framework of the Indian nation and their adequate representation in decision-making bodies to protect and promote their interests (Ambagudia, 2011).

The 'Introduction' begins with a brief discussion on the rationale for group representation of tribal communities in India. It then

moves to focus on tribal situation in India, followed by an overview of tribal politics[2] in India. It looks at tribal engagement with mainstream democratic politics and explores the patterns, conditions and challenges of participation of tribal communities in electoral politics and policy framing and functioning in India. It also provides an overview of the chapters.

RATIONALE FOR COMMUNITY REPRESENTATION

The philosophical foundation of tribal politics in India is essentially embedded in a group representation which again is intertwined with the collective rights of communities. The practice of group representation makes a significant contribution to procedural democracy and thereby results in substantive outcomes. Since liberal democratic states operate with the aim of promoting and preserving diversity

---

[1] The concepts of tribe, Adivasis, ST and indigenous people are used interchangeably in this book, except in presenting the case from the Northeast India, especially Assam. We are aware about the fact that Adivasis of Northeast India are not recognized as ST by the Indian state. For a detailed discussion on these concepts, see Xaxa (2008) and Ambagudia (2019a).

[2] The book uses the concept of politics in a wider sense and does not confine itself only to a narrow understanding by limiting itself to political processes, party politics, elections and electoral statistics. The wider notion of politics includes articulation, debates, discussion, social and political movements, protests and various platforms used by tribal communities to express their consent and satisfaction, and more often to register their discontent and disenchantment with the state and established structure.

through the means of fair and equal treatment, it is perhaps important to address centuries of discrimination and marginalization emerging out of ethnic and cultural differences that precede the granting of group rights. Group rights would enable equal participation of all citizens within the national polity.

Group representation in politics argues for the readjustment of rules for electoral competition so that the outcome would be more representative. In politics, it is believed that their own community members would be in a better position than other legislators to comprehend the problems faced by tribal communities if they were represented as a group. As John Burnheim puts it, 'Our interests are better protected when we are represented by those who share our experience and interests and that this similarity of condition is far better indicator than whether people might share our rather shaky opinions' (cited in Phillips, 2003, p. 2). James Mill also maintains that 'The benefits of the representative system are lost in all cases in which the interests of the choosing body are not the same with those of the community' (cited in Jayal, 2006, p. 6). So Burnheim and Mill believe that the representatives shall share and bear similar issues and concerns of those represented. While strengthening the symbiotic relationship between representatives and representees, Pettit (2009) explores three significant relationships: simulative, enactive and interpretive, roughly corresponding to standing for someone, acting for someone and speaking for someone. Presenting the ideal-type models of the US and British governments, he contends that the representatives speak for the represented.

Kymlicka (1995) draws a link between historical injustice and group representation and advocates for a more vocal form of group representation. The historical injustices meted against certain ethnic communities make them more vulnerable, contributing to the difficulties of effective political participation. Group representation, for him, is essential to avoid further exclusion from political processes. Rawls (1971) points out that there must be a balance between the principle of equal liberty and the principle of difference. While the first principle is concerned with the dispensation of citizenship rights of equality and liberty, the second principle takes care of the minority rights and social justice for the disadvantaged. The second principle postulates a differential treatment of groups that are unequally placed in the socio-economic and political conditions. Phillips (1995, p. 5) advocates group representations and distinguishes between 'politics of presence' and 'politics of ideas'. Politics of presence believes in democratic equality and endorses the equal and balanced political presence of various communities. It believes in the principle of democratic inclusion and invokes the political inclusion of ethnic communities that are excluded. On the other hand, the politics of ideas represents what is or should be the basis of representation, even though it inadequately deals with the issues and concerns of politically excluded communities. Hence, the politics of ideas and the politics of presence should work towards ensuring an adequate representation of politically excluded communities.

The existing theoretical underpinnings strongly advocate group representation and contend that 'others' cannot represent marginalized and excluded groups, such as the STs. Since tribal communities have hitherto been excluded from the political sphere, there is a strong endorsement for their group representation. In order to meet the objective of the celebrated principle of democracy, 'one man one vote, one vote one value', there is a need to extend the group rights to the tribals in India. Kymlicka (1995, p. 141) insists that others would not be able to represent minorities in politics. McMillan (2005, p. 5) underlines that group representation for the tribals tends to be justified in the context of persistent political exclusion and past discrimination perpetuating separate community identities. Some may still argue that community representation through preferential considerations stands diametrically opposite to individual or citizenship rights.

The discourse on community rights versus individual rights, however, shall not take a dichotomous form. Individual rights and community rights must not be seen as antithetical to each other, or community rights would replace individual rights, because group rights never intend to do so. However, group rights complement individual rights. Thus, the democratic inclusion argument appears to advocate group representation for tribal communities in India.

TRIBAL SITUATION IN INDIA

As per the 2011 census, the tribal population is estimated at 104 million, forming 8.6 per cent of the total population of the country. In 1961, the population in comparison was 30.1 million, constituting 6.9 per cent of the total population. The increase in tribal population has been due to natural growth as well as the inclusion of many groups and communities into the fold of the STs that were left out of the earlier list.

Although the tribal population is spread over the country, their distribution is far from uniform. Broadly speaking, they are concentrated in two distinct geographical regions of the country. One of them is broadly referred to as Central India. The other is Northeast India. More than three-fourths of the tribal population live in Central India, that is, Madhya Pradesh (14.69%), Chhattisgarh (7.5%), Jharkhand (8.29%), Andhra Pradesh (5.7%), Maharashtra (10.08%), Odisha (9.2%), Gujarat (8.55%), Rajasthan (8.86%) and West Bengal (5.6%). The north-eastern region of Assam, Arunachal Pradesh, Manipur, Meghalaya, Mizoram, Nagaland, Sikkim and Tripura comprises about 13 per cent of the total tribal population in the country. The remaining about 6 per cent is located in southern and northern India combined with the Andaman and Nicobar Islands. However, the share of the tribal population in respect of the total population of the different states and

Table I.1 State- and Union Territory-wise ST Population, 2011 (in Descending Order)

State/Union Territory	% to the Total Population
Lakshadweep	94.8
Mizoram	94.4
Nagaland	86.5
Meghalaya	86.1
Arunachal Pradesh	68.8
Dadra and Nagar Haveli	52.0
Manipur	35.1
Sikkim	33.8
Tripura	31.8
Chhattisgarh	30.6
Jharkhand	26.2
Odisha	22.8
Madhya Pradesh	21.1
Gujarat	14.8
Rajasthan	13.5
Assam	12.4
Jammu and Kashmir	11.9
Goa	10.2
Maharashtra	9.4
Andaman and Nicobar Islands	7.5
Andhra Pradesh	7.0
Karnataka	7.0
Daman and Diu	6.3
West Bengal	5.8
Himachal Pradesh	5.7
Uttarakhand	2.9
Kerala	1.5
Bihar	1.3
Tamil Nadu	1.1
Uttar Pradesh	0.6

Source: Government of India (2013, p. 126).

union territories tells a different demographic story. This is presented in Table I.1.

Table I.1 indicates that the highest concentration of tribal population (94.8%) can be found in Lakshadweep followed by hill states of Mizoram (94.4%), Nagaland (86.5%), Meghalaya (86.1%) and Arunachal Pradesh (68.8%), Manipur, Tripura (31.8%) and Sikkim (33.8%). In the rest of India, Chhattisgarh is the only state that crosses over 30 per cent of the tribal population in proportion to the total population of the state. The other states with a substantial population are Jharkhand (26.1%), Odisha (22.8%) and Madhya Pradesh (21.1%). The lowest concentration of tribal population in proportion to the total population of the state can be found in northern India (Uttar Pradesh [0.6%], Bihar [1.3%] and Uttarakhand [2.9%]) and southern India (Kerala [1.5%], Tamil Nadu [1.1%]). The distribution of tribal population with respect to states is important for the understanding of tribal electoral politics in India, as the electoral constituencies at the national and state levels are contingent on the size of tribal population in the states and their geographical distribution.

TRIBES AND POLITICAL ENTANGLEMENT

The political engagement of tribal communities during the pre-colonial period largely depended on their relationship with the larger Indian society. Tribal communities remained outside the Hindu civilization (Ambagudia, 2019a, p. 47; Beteille, 1986, p. 316). Initially, they were not part of the state system that had developed in the larger Indian society. Having remained outside the state system, they had developed their own systems of administration and governance, usually carried out either by village headmen or by hereditary tribal chiefs.

During the pre-colonial period, the political life of some tribal communities revolved around the formation of the state. The need for a state system was not well received by the Kolarian tribes, who showed little interest towards state formation. However, the curiosity of state formation was more pronounced in the case of Dravidian tribes such as Doms, Bears and Gonds. Singh (1985, pp. 37–38) attributes to these tribes four reasons for the emergence of state formation. One, settled agriculture and the correspondingly organized tribal village community. The extension of cultivation through a network of irrigation schemes was necessary for building and sustaining states. This was visible in the context of the Kachari tribes of Assam. The second factor was what N. K. Bose (1941) considers the Hindu method of absorption, or the process of acculturation, or what Xaxa (2008) calls the process of Hinduization. The third factor was the determined, acculturated and powerful tribal elite that wanted to rule over their own people. Fourth, once the state had come into being, they were subjected to a spat of external invasions, which, together with their own urge for expansion, strained their resources, weakened them and hastened their end.

Sachidananda (1993, p. 142) underlines that the continuous interaction between tribal and non-tribal communities has also influenced the political processes in tribal society, though the interaction has been one of tensions and conflicts. He further mentions that the tribes made an unsuccessful attempt to establish their dominant position, which led them to undergo considerable adjustment and accommodation. Interaction between tribals and non-tribals also exposed tribals to the larger world, which practised discrimination, exploitation and oppression towards tribal communities. Hence, Sinha (1987, p. xxiv) argues that tribal regions have gone through cycles of evolution and devolution in response to the pressures and pulsations they have received from the state system of the plains.

The tribal model of democracy, governance and autonomy did not last for long and soon succumbed to the wrath of the British administration. The colonial administration forcefully integrated tribal society into the colonial political regime by suppressing the retaliation from tribal communities. As a result, they became part of the colonial political system, and the Government of India Act, 1935 (Government of India, 1935), for the first time introduced the tribes to electoral politics in 1935 (Ambagudia, 2019b, p. 46). The tribes continued to be part of the modern political system in the post-colonial period.

After centuries of exclusion from the social, economic and political realms, a ray of hope emerged for the tribes in post-colonial India. This was reflected in the design of a democratic structure in a more inclusive manner, which not only recognized diversities but also provided adequate democratic rights through differential citizenship. Thus, diversities, recognition and redistribution emerged to define the nature of democracy in independent India within the larger framework of community representation. The discourse on group representation emerged under the theoretical underpinnings of representation based on who should represent the tribals in post-colonial India? Should tribal interests be protected and promoted by non-tribals? The Constituent Assembly critically engaged with these questions as part of its mandate to draft the Constitution for independent India by considering the claims and demands of the different competing social groups. As a consequence, the Indian Constitution adopted the provision of political reservation for ensuring the adequate voices of tribal communities in representative institutions (Galanter, 1984).

The contemporary practice of reserved constituencies in India is the product of an impasse between Mahatma Gandhi and B. R. Ambedkar in the early 1930s, which led to the emergence of a joint electorate in an electoral system, rather than latter's insistence to separate electorate for the marginalized communities, especially the Dalits. Under the Indian Constitution, seats are reserved for socially marginalized communities such as the SCs and the STs so that their community voices can be represented in the highest decision-making bodies such as the assemblies and the Parliament. This proposition is based on the guiding principle that any successful electoral system cannot offer to ignore the underrepresentation or lack of representation

of ethnically minority communities. As the existing literature indicates the correlation between proportional representation and the success of an electoral system (Gallagher, 1991; Grofman & Lijphart, 1986), India has made every attempt to ensure the proportionate representation of tribes in representative political institutions under Articles 330 and 332 of the Constitution.[3]

With a view to translate the proportionate representation of the tribes, India has evolved a system of reserved constituency for parliamentary and assembly elections. Table I.2 presents a profile of the parliamentary constituencies in India.

Table I.2 deals with the number and types of parliamentary constituencies in India, where each social group was allocated a

Table I.2   Number and Types of Parliamentary Constituencies in India

Year	Unreserved	SC	ST	Total
1951	481	0	8	489
1957	478	0	16	494
1962	385	79	30	494
1967	406	77	37	520
1971	406	76	36	518
1977	426	78	38	542
1980	422	79	41	542
1984	401	75	38	514
1989	412	78	39	529
1991	407	76	41	524
1996	423	79	41	543
1998	423	79	41	543
1999	423	79	41	543
2004	423	79	41	543
2009	412	84	47	543
2014	412	84	47	543
2019	412	84	47	543

Source: Compiled from various reports of the Election Commission of India.

---

[3] Articles 330 and 332 deal with the provision of political reservation for tribes in the Lok Sabha and state assemblies in accordance with the percentage of their population to the total population. However, such a reservation does not deprive the tribes to contest from unreserved Parliamentary and assembly constituencies in India.

proportionate number of seats on the basis of their population strength. It is important to mention that the first two elections were conducted under the provision of dual-/multi-member constituencies (Ambagudia, 2019a, p. 159). Under this, 8 out of 489 and 16 out of 494 seats were allocated to the tribes in India. However, these two elections did not appear to have followed the population strength formula. There was an increase and decrease in terms of seat allocation to the tribes in proportion to the population strength between 1952 and 1989. The seats for tribes in

the Lok Sabha were increased to 41 in 1991, which continued till 2004. Due to the implementation of Delimitation of Parliamentary and Assembly Constituencies Order, 2008, the seats were further increased from 2009 general election. Table I.2 indicates that there are 47 seats reserved for tribes in the Lok Sabha at present. Similarly, with the impact of the Delimitation of Parliamentary and Assembly Constituencies Order, 2008, the seats for the tribes in state assemblies have also been increased from 532 to 554 at present (Ambagudia, 2019b, p. 55).

Table I.3   ST Population in ST-reserved Parliamentary Constituencies in India in Descending Order (2001 Census)

Sl. No	State	Name of the Constituency	Total Population	ST Population	% of ST Population
1.	Lakshadweep	Lakshadweep	60,650	57,321	94.51
2.	Mizoram	Mizoram	888,573	839,310	94.46
3.	Meghalaya	Shillong	1,448,870	1,257,164	86.77
4.	Meghalaya	Tura	869,952	735,698	84.57
5.	Gujarat	Dahod	1,895,923	1,374,627	72.50
6.	Madhya Pradesh	Ratlam	2,091,716	1,497,428	71.59
7.	Rajasthan	Banswara	2,328,707	1,639,416	70.40
8.	Chhattisgarh	Bastar	1,786,283	1,257,341	70.39
9.	Jharkhand	Lohardaga	1,711,288	1,123,650	65.66
10.	Gujarat	Valsad	1,926,715	1,234,603	64.08
11.	Gujarat	Bardoli	1,951,194	1,236,247	63.36
12.	Dadra & Nagar Haveli	Dadra and Nagar Haveli	220,490	137,225	62.24
13.	Maharashtra	Nandurbar	1,976,290	1,164,897	58.94
14.	Odisha	Mayurbhanj	1,762,803	1,015,042	57.58
15.	Jharkhand	Singhbhum	1,782,774	1,013,827	56.87
16.	Rajasthan	Udaipur	2,358,501	1,313,407	55.69
17.	Odisha	Nabarangpur	1,777,950	988,218	55.58
18.	Chhattisgarh	Surguja	1,972,094	1,076,669	54.60
19.	Gujarat	Chhota Udaipur	2,013,627	1,075,219	53.40
20.	Odisha	Koraput	1,763,760	915,048	51.88
21.	Madhya Pradesh	Mandla	2,322,709	1,202,017	51.75
22.	Andhra Pradesh	Araku	1,732,218	893,017	51.55
23.	Jharkhand	Khunti	1,982,479	996,101	50.25
24.	Odisha	Sundargarh	183,0673	918,903	50.19
25.	Madhya Pradesh	Khargone	2,105,534	1,055,377	50.12
25.	Madhya Pradesh	Dhar	2,044,692	1,016,761	49.73
27.	Chhattisgarh	Kanker	1,868,514	894,280	47.86
28.	Odisha	Keonjhar	1,796,484	844,003	46.98
29.	Chhattisgarh	Raigarh	2,008,689	917,656	45.68

Sl. No	State	Name of the Constituency	Total Population	ST Population	% of ST Population
30.	Jharkhand	Dumka	1,808,185	808,077	44.69
31.	Madhya Pradesh	Shahdol	2,066,121	893,518	43.25
32.	Maharashtra	Palghar	2,035,075	829,725	40.77
33.	Tripura	Tripura East	1,553,003	619,455	39.89
34.	Madhya Pradesh	Betul	2,113,163	801,255	37.92
35.	Andhra Pradesh	Mahabubabad	1,854,953	659,447	35.55
36.	Maharashtra	Dindori	2,024,688	677,239	33.45
37.	Maharashtra	Gadchiroli-Chimur	1,925,588	589,142	30.60
38.	West Bengal	Jhargram	1,882,209	492,828	26.18
39.	Rajasthan	Dausa	2,059,329	533,161	25.89
40.	West Bengal	Alipurduar	1,967,325	495,590	25.19
41.	Andhra Pradesh	Adilabad	1,736,306	369,802	21.30
42.	Karnataka	Bellary	1,791,796	322,629	18.01
43.	Karnataka	Raichur	1,917,293	327,326	17.07
44.	Assam*	Autonomous District	NA	NA	
45.	Assam*	Kokrajhar	NA	NA	
46.	Jharkhand	Rajmahal	NA	NA	
47.	Manipur*	Outer Manipur	NA	NA	

Source: Final Paper 7 of respective states developed by the Delimitation Commission of India.

Note: *Delimitation exercise was not carried out in these states.

Table I.3 shows the tribal situation in the ST-reserved parliamentary constituencies in India. Table I.3 reflects that Lakshadweep Lok Sabha constituency has the highest percentage (94.51%) of the tribal population in proportion to the constituency population and the lowest in Raichur constituency (17.07%) of Karnataka. The comparison suggests that though Lakshadweep has the highest tribal population in proportion to the constituency population, it has the lowest tribal concentration in relation to the tribal population of other constituencies. The constituency-wise highest concentration of tribal population can be found in Banswara constituency of Rajasthan. The location of ST parliamentary constituencies has been presented in Figure I.1.

The delimitation exercise was not carried out in Assam due to the stay orders of the Guwahati High Court in the case of *Shri Ram Prasad Sarmah and Ors. v. Union of India and Others* (PIL No. 62/2007). In addition, some of the other factors, such as sentiments of people concerning the break-up of affiliations between the public and their representatives, alienation of different tribal groups because of change of boundary, representations from Assam state to postpone the process till the completion of the National Register of Citizens updating process, potential law and order problems, opposition to the anticipated curtailment of three constituencies from upper Assam, etc., did not favour the delimitation process in Assam (Government of India, 2008b). However, the government has recently notified to carry out the delimitation process in Assam. Similarly, the process of readjusting the division of each state and union territory into territorial constituencies for the purpose of election of Lok Sabha and assembly constituencies was not carried out in the state of Manipur due to more or less similar reasons attributed to the state of Assam (Government of India, 2008b).

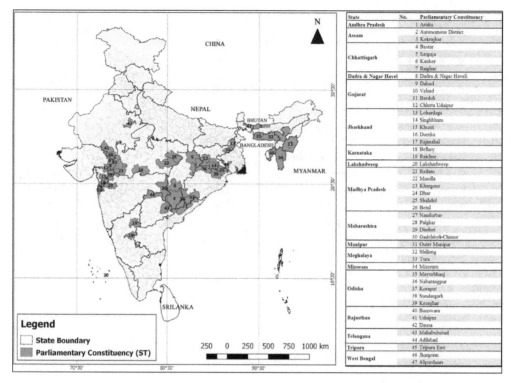

State	No.	Parliamentary Constituency
Andhra Pradesh	1	Aruku
Assam	2	Autonomous District
	3	Kokrajhar
	4	Bastar
Chhattisgarh	5	Surguja
	6	Kanker
	7	Raigbar
Dadra & Nagar Haveli	8	Dadra & Nagar Haveli
	9	Dahod
Gujarat	10	Valsad
	11	Bardoli
	12	Chhota Udaipur
	13	Lohardaga
	14	Singhbhum
Jharkhand	15	Khunti
	16	Dumka
	17	Rajmahal
Karnataka	18	Bellary
	19	Raichur
Lakshadweep	20	Lakshadweep
	21	Ratlam
	22	Mandla
	23	Khargone
Madhya Pradesh	24	Dhar
	25	Shahdol
	26	Betul
	27	Nandurbar
	28	Palghar
Maharashtra	29	Dindori
	30	Gadchiroli-Chimur
Manipur	31	Outer Manipur
Meghalaya	32	Shillong
	33	Tura
Mizoram	34	Mizoram
	35	Mayurbhanj
	36	Nabarangpur
Odisha	37	Koraput
	38	Sundargarh
	39	Keonjhar
	40	Banswara
Rajasthan	41	Udaipur
	42	Dausa
Telangana	43	Mahabubabad
	44	Adilabad
Tripura	45	Tripura East
West Bengal	46	Jhargram
	47	Alipurduars

Figure I.1 ST Parliamentary Constituencies of India
Source: Adopted and redrawn by Kamal Azad.

Note: Map not to scale. It represents the political map of India that existed prior to the abrogation of Article 370, by which Jammu and Kashmir lost state status.

GENDER AND TRIBAL POLITICS

The gender relationship in tribal society has its unique feature which struggles between the traditional practices of tribal communities and the aspirations of the modern democratic system. Although tribal communities are relatively egalitarian, gender inequality remains an issue especially in the sphere of public domain. Hence, the gender issue has been introduced in the discussion on tribal politics.

Table I.4 deals with the gender-wise representation of tribal MPs in Lok Sabha. Table I.4 indicates that the representation of tribal women in the Lok Sabha has always been neglected since 1952 until the recent Lok Sabha (2019). The 2019 general election witnessed a relatively better representation of tribal women MPs, where there are 10, constituting 21.27 per cent of the total tribal MPs. However, the number of tribal women MPs is slightly increasing since the 2009 general election. Between 1952 and 2019, out of 629 tribal MPs, 51 women MPs (8.10%) have been able to reach the highest decision-making bodies in India.

The trend questions the credibility of the very tribal society on the basis of respect, toleration and egalitarian values. Jaipal Singh and J. J. M. Nichols-Roy had once raised in the Constituent Assembly debates that independent India should adopt the idea of equality and real democracy that tribal communities had achieved (Government of India, 1949a, p. 143; 1949b, pp. 1021–1023). There has also been an instance of opposing mechanisms to increase the representation of women via reservation at the local level of decision-making bodies in Northeast India. Such an instance, however, discredits the tribal society for which it was once known for.

Table I.4 Gender-wise Tribal MPs in India, 1952–2019

Year	Total	Men	Women
1952	8	7	1
1957	16	16	0
1962	30	29	1
1967	37	34	3
1971	36	34	2
1977	38	37	1
1980	41	38	3
1984	38	36	2
1989	39	37	2
1991	41	36	5
1996	41	37	4
1998	41	39	2
1999	41	38	3
2004	41	40	1
2009	47	42	5
2014	47	41	6
2019	47	37	10
Total	629	578	51

Source: Retrieved from http://loksabhaph.nic.in/Members/lokprev.aspx

ST-RESERVED CONSTITUENCIES AND POLITICAL PARTIES

Different political parties compete for reserved and unreserved parliamentary and assembly constituencies in India. They do so by making competing claims to garner the support of the voters in different elections. As a result, considering the promises and the likelihood translation of their promises into reality, voters express their support or disapprove the claims during different elections over the period, which eventually lead to the performance of political parties in electoral constituencies in India.

Table I.5 reflects on constituency-wise performance of political parties in India. Table I.5 shows that no political party has been able to register its consistent winning in various constituencies over the period. Most of the ST constituencies were shared between two national parties, such as the Congress and the BJP. The BJP, however, has retained some

of the ST constituencies, such as Bellamy, Khargone and Betul since 2009, when they were converted into ST-reserved constituencies. It seems to be too early to predict the continuous retaining of these seats by the BJP.

Table I.6 shows the performance of political parties in ST-reserved constituencies in terms of seat share (not vote share) since the 1980 general election in India. The BJP, which emerged in 1980, made its debut in the tribal-reserved constituencies in 1989 by securing six parliamentary seats. Tables I.5 and I.6 demonstrate that the BJP won 3, 11, 14, 21, 15, 14, 27 and 31 ST parliamentary constituencies in 1991, 1996, 1998, 1999, 2004, 2009, 2014 and 2019 elections, respectively. What is more intriguing is that though the BJP alone secured a clear-cut majority of 282 seats in the 2014 general election, it did not, however, secure even a single ST-reserved constituency from Northeast India (Table I.5).

However, it won a total of eight unreserved seats from Northeast India in 2014. The BJP won the Autonomous District and Tripura East tribal parliamentary constituencies of Assam and Tripura in 2019 election. The unsuccessful contest of the BJP from the ST-reserved parliamentary constituencies of Northeast India in 2014 depends on the nature of the relationship it maintains with the tribal people. The BJP, however, fought successfully in 8 out of 16 ST-reserved constituencies in the 2016 state assembly election of Assam. The success of the BJP in the tribal assembly constituencies of Assam can perhaps be explained, among others, as a result of the anti-incumbency factor and the projection of a tribal candidate as a chief ministerial face. Similarly, the Congress party won 30, 32, 20, 29, 21, 18, 9, 14, 20, 5 and 4 seats in 1980, 1984, 1989, 1991, 1996, 1998, 1999, 2004, 2009, 2014 and 2019 elections, respectively.

Table I.7 shows the party-wise representation of tribal MPs during the 2019 general election. In the 2019 election, the BJP performed extremely well in tribal reserved constituencies, where it won 31 out of 47 seats.

Table 1.5 Performance of Political Parties in ST-reserved Parliamentary Constituencies, 1980–2019

Name of the Reserved Constituency	1980	1984	1989	1991	1996	1998	1999	2004	2009	2014	2019
Parvathipuram/Adilabad	INC(U)	ICS	INC	INC	INC	TDP	TDP	INC	TDP	TRS	BJP
Bhadrachalam/Aruku	INC(I)	CPI	INC	INC	CPI	CPI	TDP	CPM	INC	YSRCP	YSRCP
Mahabubabad	NA	NA	NA	NA	NA	NA	NA	NA	INC	TRS	TRS
Autonomous District	NA	NA	NA	ADC	ASDC	ASDC	CPI(ML)(L)	INC	INC	INC	BJP
Kokrajhar	NA	NA	PTC	IND	IND	IND	IND	IND	BOPF	IND	IND
Surguja	INC(I)	INC	BJP	INC	INC	BJP	INC	BJP	BJP	BJP	BJP
Raigarh	INC(I)	INC	BJP	INC	BJP	INC	BJP	BJP	BJP	BJP	BJP
Bastar	INC(I)	INC	INC	INC	IND	BJP	BJP	BJP	BJP	BJP	INC
Kanker	INC(I)	INC	INC	INC	INC	BJP	BJP	BJP	BJP	BJP	BJP
Dahod	INC(I)	INC	INC	INC	INC	INC	BJP	BJP	INC	BJP	BJP
Chhota Udaipur	INC(I)	INC	JD	JD(G)	INC	INC	BJP	INC	BJP	BJP	BJP
Mandvi/Bardoli	INC(I)	INC	INC	INC	INC	INC	BJP	INC	INC	BJP	BJP
Bulsar/Valsad	INC(I)	INC	JD	INC	BJP	BJP	BJP	INC	INC	BJP	BJP
Rajmahal	INC(I)	INC	JMM	JMM	INC	BJP	INC	JMM	BJP	JMM	JMM
Dumka	IND	INC	JMM	JMM	JMM	BJP	BJP	JMM	JMM	JMM	BJP
Singhbhum	JNP	INC	INC	JMM	BJP	INC	BJP	INC	IND	BJP	INC
Khunti	JKD	INC	BJP	BJP	BJP	BJP	BJP	INC	BJP	BJP	BJP
Lohardaga	INC(I)	INC	INC	BJP	BJP	INC	BJP	INC	BJP	BJP	BJP
Raichur	NA	NA	NA	NA	NA	NA	NA	NA	BJP	INC	BJP
Bellamy	NA	NA	NA	NA	NA	NA	NA	NA	BJP	BJP	BJP
Jhabua	INC(I)	INC	INC	INC	INC	INC	INC	INC	NA	NA	NA
Sindhi	INC(I)	INC	BJP	INC	AIIC(T)	BJP	BJP	BJP	NA	NA	NA
Shahdol	INC(I)	INC	JD	INC	BJP	BJP	BJP	BJP	INC	BJP	BJP
Mandla	INC(I)	INC	INC	INC	BJP	BJP	BJP	BJP	INC	BJP	BJP
Ratlam	NA	NA	NA	NA	NA	NA	NA	NA	INC	BJP	BJP
Dhar	INC(I)	INC	INC	INC	BJP	INC	INC	BJP	INC	BJP	BJP
Khargone	NA	NA	NA	NA	NA	NA	NA	NA	BJP	BJP	BJP
Betul	NA	NA	NA	NA	NA	NA	NA	NA	BJP	BJP	BJP
Nandurbar	INC(I)	INC	INC	INC	INC	INC	INC	INC	INC	BJP	BJP
Dahanu/ Gadchiroli-Chimur	INC(I)	INC	INC	INC	BJP	INC	BJP	INC	INC	BJP	BJP
Malegaon/Dindori	INC(I)	INC	JD	INC	BJP	INC	JD(S)	BJP	BJP	BJP	BJP
Dhule/Palghar	INC(I)	INC	INC	INC	BJP	INC	BJP	INC	BVA	BJP	SHS
Outer Manipur	INC(I)	INC	INC	INC	INC	CPI	NCP	IND	INC	INC	NPF
Shillong	NA	NA	NA	NA	NA	NA	NA	NA	INC	INC	INC
Tura	NA	NA	NA	NA	NA	NA	NA	NA	NCP	NPEP	NPEP
Mizoram	IND		INC	INC	INC	IND	IND	MNF	INC	INC	MNF
Sundargarh	INC(I)	INC	JD	INC	INC	BJP	BJP	BJP	INC	BJP	BJP
Keonjhar	INC(I)	INC	JD	JD	INC	BJP	BJP	BJP	BJD	BJD	BJD
Mayurbhanj	INC(I)	INC	JD	INC	INC	BJP	BJP	JMM	BJD	BJD	BJP
Nabarangpur	INC(I)	INC	INC	INC	INC	INC	BJP	BJP	INC	BJD	BJD
Koraput	INC(I)	INC	INC	INC	INC	INC	INC	INC	BJD	BJD	INC

Name of the Reserved Constituency	1980	1984	1989	1991	1996	1998	1999	2004	2009	2014	2019
Sawai Madhopur/Dausa	INC(I)	INC	BJP	BJP	INC	INC	BJP	INC	IND	BJP	BJP
Salumbar/Udaipur	INC(I)	INC	BJP	INC	INC	BJP	INC	BJP	INC	BJP	BJP
Banswara	INC(I)	INC	JD	INC	INC	BJP	INC	BJP	INC	BJP	BJP
Tripura East	CPM	CPM	INC	INC	CPM	CPM	CPM	CPM	CPM	CPM	BJP
Alipurduar	RSP	RSP	RSP	RSP	RSP	RSP	RSP	RSP	RSP	AITC	BJP
Jhargram	CPM	CPM	CPM	CPM	CPM	CPM	CPM	CPM	CPM	AITC	BJP
Dadra & Nagar Haveli	INC(I)	IND	IND	INC	INC	BJP	IND	BNP	BJP	BJP	IND
Lakshadweep	INC(U)	INC	INC	INC	INC	INC	INC	JD(U)	INC	NCP	NCP

Source: Compiled from Government of India (1980, 1984, 1989, 1991, 1996, 1998, 1999, 2004, 2009, 2014, 2019).

Note: NA means not applicable.

Table I.6 ST Lok Sabha Seats Won by Some Major Political Parties, 1980–2019

Year	BJP	Congress	CPI	CPI(M)	IND	Total ST Constituencies
1980	0	30	0	2	2	41
1984	0	32	1	2		38
1989	6	20	0	1	1	39
1991	3	29	0	1	1	41
1996	11	21	1	2	9	41
1998	14	18	2	2	2	41
1999	21	9	0	2	6	41
2004	15	14	0	3	5	41
2009	14	20	0	2	2	47
2014	27	5	0	1	1	47
2019	31	4	0	0	1	47

Source: Compiled from Government of India (1980, 1984, 1989, 1991, 1996, 1998, 1999, 2004, 2009, 2014, 2019).

Table I.7 ST Lok Sabha Seats Won by Political Parties in 2019 Election

Political Parties	No. of Seats
Bharatiya Janata Party	31
Indian National Congress	4
Community Party of India	0
Community Party of India-Marxist	0
Independent	2
Biju Janata Dal	2
Yuvajana Sramika Rythu Congress Party	1
Telangana Rashtra Samithi	1
Nationalist Congress Party	1
Jharkhand Mukti Morcha	1
Naga People's Front	1
Mizo National Front	1
Shiv Sena	1
National People's Party	1
Total	47

Source: Government of India (2019).

The Congress secured four seats, the BJD won two seats. Two independent candidates also got elected to the 17th Lok Sabha. The Left parties did not register any victory from the tribal reserved constituencies. Yuvajana Sramika Rythu Congress Party, Telangana Rashtra Samithi, Nationalist Congress Party, Jharkhand Mukti Morcha, Mizo National Front, Naga People's Front, Shiv Sena and National People's Party secured one tribal seat each in the 2019 general election.

These figures suggest that there is a gradual shift of the social support base from the 'catch-all party' (the Congress) to the 'ideological party' (the BJP). Consequently, the Congress party, once considered the preferred political party by the tribal communities (Bose, 1990, p. 71; Weiner & Field, 1975), is losing its grip over its social support base and the BJP is gradually expanding its traditional narrow social base over the period. Tribal voters, therefore, switch between parties and are attracted, albeit temporarily, by competing parties mobilizing on renewed claims to represent them.

The electoral success of the BJP in the tribal belt, especially in Central India, cannot be attributed to the appeal made by the party alone. Success has been facilitated quite substantively by different auxiliary organizations which are affiliated or at least ideologically synchronized with the BJP. Persistent efforts of establishing Vanavasi Kalyan Ashram, Ekal Vidyalaya, Seva Bharati, Vivekananda Kendra, Bharat Kalyan Pratishthan, Friends of Tribals Society, etc., and providing various services to improve the social, economic, educational and health conditions of tribal communities by some of the affiliated organizations such as Rashtriya Swayamsevak Sangh have made a substantive difference in widening the social support of the BJP (Jayal, 2006, p. 113; Thachil, 2011, 2014). The affiliated organizations entered the arena of 'competitive proselytization' in the 1950s and launched an agenda of the alternative welfare system in non-state sectors primarily to dismantle the evangelical works of Christian missionaries in tribal areas, prevent conversions (Kanungo, 2008, p. 17; Sundar, 2012, p. 246) and initiate the process of reconversion among the converted Christian tribals.

The success rate of Left parties (CPI, CPM) and independent candidates is marginal (Tables I.5 and I.6). The Left parties failed to secure even a single ST seat in the Naxal-affected states of Odisha, Jharkhand, Chhattisgarh, etc., in 2009, 2014 and 2019 elections (Tables I.5–I.7). The Left parties did not win even a single tribal parliamentary constituency in the 2019 election. The marginal success of the CPI and the CPM in the ST-reserved constituencies runs counter to the established argument that tribal areas are a fertile ground for Naxalite politics, and that tribals are a support base for the Naxalites (Government of India, 2008a, p. 44). To put it differently, whatever the nature of the support that the Naxalites have gained from tribal communities, they have not been able to translate it into electoral outcomes. Parties driven by Marxist ideology reduce tribals into a class society and make themselves part of

the countrywide revolutionary movement, sabotaging their distinct tribal identities (Bosu Mullick, 2001, p. 109; Prasad, 2016, p. 317).

It has been observed that sometimes political parties fill tribal candidates in unreserved constituencies. For instance, the Congress and the BJP gave an equal number of party tickets of three and six to ST candidates to contest from unreserved constituencies in the 2009 and 2014 elections, respectively. Political parties issue tickets to ST candidates where there is a high concentration of ST population. For instance, the Arunachal East and West constituencies are unreserved, the Congress and the BJP, however, filled the ST candidates in the 2009 and 2014 elections due to the high concentration of tribal population in these constituencies. All the candidates contested from Arunachal East and West constituencies in 2019 were from tribal communities. The filling of ST candidates in unreserved constituencies does not suffice that they are incrementally ready to part political power with marginal groups. In contemporary Indian democratic practices, the election of the Rajya Sabha has merely reduced to the nomination process of political parties and elections are conducted only to meet the constitutional requirements. Consequently, there is a negligible representation of tribals in the Rajya Sabha, which also plays a significant role in the policymaking process. In short, the changing relationship between political parties and tribals has been incompatible. The distribution of tickets, however, became the strategy of the political parties to win parliamentary seats.

The internal dynamics of political parties reflect less concern in addressing the issues of marginalization, deprivation and dispossession that tribals endured in their everyday lives. Political parties succeeded in integrating tribals through a structural rearrangement of power because of electoral reservation rather than co-opting tribal leaders into different national political parties (Weiner & Field, 1975, p. 116). Different political organizations, such as the Indian National Trade Union Congress, the Hind Mazdoor Sangh, the All India Trade Union Congress and the Centre of Indian Trade Unions experienced marginal, though not absent, representation of tribals. Hence, political parties maintain trade-off relationship with tribals in the sense that parties symbolically incorporate them. This is because the catch-all or the Congress party and the ideological parties, such as the BJP and the Left, depend on group representation and patronage to retain their support base (Farooqui & Sridharan, 2014, p. 90). The parties' upper class and upper caste leadership would be, however, recognized as legitimate and representative of the masses (Yadav & Palshikar, 2006, p. 80). To put it differently, the system is structured/designed in such a way that tribals find it extremely difficult to rise to positions of power and prominence (Ambagudia, 2019a, p. 166; Bailey, 1960, p. 129).

The representation of tribals is marginal not only in the formal political institutions but also in the rank of party leadership. Existing data show that both at the state and the union levels, the tribals have never been given proportionate representation in various ministries (Ambagudia, 2019a, p. 166; Jayal, 2006, p. 10; Panigrahi, 1998, p. 90). Meanwhile, whatever the marginal ministerial berth is extended to tribals, they are largely confined to the Ministry of Tribal Affairs. In other words, democracy still provides multiple means to reinforce the dominance of certain groups in a range of contexts. The prevalence of such dominance increasingly questions the nature of 'inclusive democracy' and leads to a crisis in a democratic state (Waylen, 2015, p. 496).

CONTEMPORARY DEVELOPMENTS

In the contemporary period, a number of interesting developments have been taking place in the arena of tribal politics in India. Tribes experience incompatibility not only with political parties but also with the established democratic system that provides a ground

for their continuous demand for autonomy and self-determination. Political parties have failed to address tribal issues, and tribals are exploring alternative means of protecting and promoting their interests. In Kerala, tribals are moving away from political parties such as the CPI and have formed their own social organization, Adivasi Gotra Maha Sabha (AGMS), to articulate their problems and fight for their rights.

Sporadic attempts were made by tribal communities to revive their traditional way of politics and provide alternative politics to party politics in India. The tribals have been the valued parties of Bharat Jan Andolan (Indian People's Movement), formed under the leadership of Dr B. D. Sharma (former Chairman, National Commission for Scheduled Castes and Scheduled Tribes). It mobilized people under the slogan 'our village, our rule' and emphasized Gaon Ganraj (village republic), which highlighted the significant role of the community in deciding the candidate. It promoted the idea of selecting candidates by consensus by the community who could contest the election. During the 2005 state assembly election, all the Gaon Ganraj candidates of Jharkhand and Chhattisgarh were selected by the village republic by consensus after due deliberations. Although none of the candidates won the election, they gave stiff competition to the winners (Jojo, Beck, Toppo, & Renne, 2008, p. 95).

On the other hand, Northeast India has been able to revive as well as continue to uphold its traditional democratic practices amid modern politics. This is primarily because of different geographical terrains, distinct culture, traditions, customary laws, etc., which compelled the framers of the Indian Constitution to make special administrative arrangements in the form of the Sixth Schedule of the Indian Constitution for Northeast India. The Sixth Schedule has the provision for an autonomous district council that allows tribals residing in the Sixth Schedule Areas of Assam, Meghalaya, Mizoram and Tripura to run their civil affairs according to their customary laws. Guided by this administrative framework, the tribals of some of the non-Sixth Schedule Area states, such as Nagaland and Manipur, demanded similar opportunities. As a consequence, Articles 371A and 371C were introduced into the Indian Constitution in 1963 and 1972, respectively, allowing the tribals of Nagaland, Manipur and Mizoram to govern along the lines of their customary laws.

Tribals are increasingly articulating their political identity along resource relationship (Ambagudia, 2019a). However, various state governments have made organized attempts to disarticulate their political identity. For instance, the Gujarat government de-notified Rathvas as tribals through an official order in October 2013 (Rathva, Rai, & Rajaram, 2016). The Odisha government amended the Orissa Scheduled Areas Transfer of Immovable Property (by Scheduled Tribes) Regulation, 1956, in 2010 to allow the transfer of tribal land to non-tribals, and this was also approved by the governor and sent for the president's assent. The president of India, however, did not give the assent. As a result, the state government reconstituted an Inter-Ministerial Committee to look into the matter again (Barik, 2015).

Quota system has produced an educated elite among tribal communities. The emergence of Tribal Intellectual Collective India (TICI) is one such example that has been organizing annual conferences on various tribal issues since 2015. The members of TICI also regularly meet with tribal political representatives to put forward issues that are critical to tribal communities (Ambagudia & Mohanty, forthcoming/2020). In addition, certain issues, such as land alienation, extraction of resources from resource-rich tribal areas, erosion of culture, language domination, discrimination, dispossession, deprivation, marginalization, migration, educational disadvantage, human rights violation and poverty, continue to govern contemporary tribal politics in India.

FUTURE OF TRIBAL POLITICS IN INDIA

The future of tribal politics seems to be more complicated and uncertain. This is primarily not attributed to questioning the continuation of political reservation for the STs. However, this concerns the substantial notion of such a provision. Although it demands a detailed research on the role of tribal political elites at both the national and state levels, the nature and patterns of their political behaviour and the level of their participation in the decision-making process of the highest houses, such as the Parliament and state assemblies, the general impression is that they have not come up to the expectations of the very people to whom they claim to represent. The role of tribal political representatives has become a mockery at the hands of the most powerful section of the political elite in Indian democracy.

One of the emerging trends in Indian politics has been the emergence of different ethnic-based political parties. The effectiveness of ethnic-based political parties has confined to the region of origin with limited success for a limited period of time. At the national level, tribal MPs from ethnic-based political parties have proved to be ineffective in their influence over policymaking. This does not mean to articulate that they are incapable of addressing tribal issues. They have been articulative and effective, per se, at the regional level in tilting public policies in favour of their communities, especially in Northeast India. Their sorry state of affairs at national level is due to the existing structural constraints that imposed undue restriction while raising individual voices. Parliamentary democracy, however, emphasizes on their party affiliation, which has been reflected through allocating time along the line of party affiliation for participating in debates.

Due to the limited success of ethnic political parties, it appears that the future of tribal politics lies not in the formation of various tribal political parties, but in how effectively they place their issues and concerns in the larger discourse of democratic politics. Although the formation of ethnic/tribal political parties would relieve them from the experience of discriminatory practices in formal and informal institutional arrangements and pressurize the government for the enactment of welfare policies for tribal communities, they still have a long way to go. Due to the numerical disadvantage in a democratic state functioning along the lines of politics of number, tribal MPs' influence on policy outcomes remained to be minimum. Guha (2007) emphasizes that the issues and concerns of tribals remain at the margins of political discourse because political parties find little incentive in addressing such issues as they are insignificant in number. On the contrary, Xaxa (2008) argues that tribals have remained at the periphery and have failed to articulate their grievances through democratic and electoral processes because of the lack of committed political parties to represent them at national level. The tribal leadership crisis too has contributed to the dismal issues further.

It appears that ethnic political parties are more loyal and committed to the problems of their communities. They are large enough to alter the political arrangement at the regional level. For instance, 59 out of 60, 55 out of 60, 39 of out 40, 59 out of 60 assembly seats are reserved for the tribes in Arunachal Pradesh, Meghalaya, Mizoram and Nagaland, respectively. These are highly pleasing statistics at the state levels that can tilt public policies in favour of tribal communities with ease, if all tribal representatives show their commitment to tribal cause and act as 'a block' in policy discourses irrespective of their party affiliations. On the contrary, experiences show that the government (e.g., Jharkhand) headed by a tribal chief minister has not been able to halt any policy that displaced tribals, and the tribals of Jharkhand continue to struggle for survival at the margins of the society. This can perhaps be explained by the fact that major decisions concerning different developmental projects are taken at the central level and the states have little say in them.

The numerically minority status of the tribes does not make decisive impacts on the electoral process at national level. Proportional representation of tribes in the Parliament is insufficient to make representation meaningful as well as insignificant to influence parliamentary discourse and to ensure that rights and interests of tribals are addressed effectively. Unless the entire Parliament draws its attention towards tribal issues and problems, no major breakthrough can be experienced in the process of policy-making (Mahajan, 1998, p. 123). The nature of tribal representation in the Parliament is dubbed as virtual, especially prior to the 1980s (Shankar & Rodrigues, 2014, p. 219). Due to their minority status in demographic arithmetic, the popularly elected government is less likely to target tribals concerning policy outcomes (Pande, 2003). This can be demonstrated by underlining the role of different tribal political parties in some of the important public policies/acts designed to appropriate tribal problems. The enactment of the Panchayats (Extension to Scheduled Areas) Act, 1996, and the Scheduled Tribes and Other Traditional Forest Dwellers (Recognition of Forest Rights) Act, 2006, was not the product of initiatives of tribal political parties or tribal MPs, but rather of a protracted organized political movement of the tribal people coupled with support from tribal sympathizers (Chemmencheri, 2015; Choubey, 2016). Hence, it appears to some extent that the future of tribal politics in India lies in the role of civil society.

FUTURE DIRECTION IN RESEARCHING TRIBAL POLITICS

Future research on tribal politics shall focus, though not exclusively, on the following dimensions. First, though electoral reservation has ensured the numerical representation of tribal communities in the Parliament and state assemblies, there is, however, a dearth of study supported by strong empirical evidence on the legislative behaviour of tribal representatives in these bodies. The nature, degree and level of participation of tribal representatives in the Parliamentary/assembly deliberations to a large extent have remained unexplored. How do tribal representatives address issues of the development, deprivation and marginalization of tribal communities in India? Second, the relative experience of tribal political leaders with non-ethnic political parties (especially national and regional) has attracted no or less attention from the academia. Third, the gender dimension of tribal politics has largely been neglected in political studies. Fourth, the contextualization of tribal representation in politics, government jobs and education demonstrates that politics is the only sphere where tribals have been representing 100 per cent of the prescribed quota.

However, stiff resistance against reservation in India is less about the continuation of political reservation and more towards the practice of reservation in spheres of education and government employment. It is, however, important to mention that politics was the only sphere where reservation was initially adopted for 10 years and other spheres were excluded from such time limit clause. The need of the day is to explore why there is less resistance to political reservation than to reservation in education and employment. This is primarily because the continuation of political reservation has demonstrative effects over other spheres. Last but not least, the various chapters in this volume suggested that tribal representatives contributed very little to the advancement of the communities they represented. Such a notion opens up the scope for debating on the nature of representation that would be more effective in addressing the issues and problems of communities for which the Constitution has adopted the institutional mechanism of the quota system.

STRUCTURE OF THE BOOK

Politics is a process through which different groups raise demands, articulate their interests and influence the groups holding power to make decisions in their favour. In the due process, they experience success as well as formidable challenges. In the case of India, tribal communities have remained mostly ineffective in influencing political elites and policymakers. Various factors, such as demography, socio-economic conditions, geographical location and marginal presence of the middle class, poor educational attainment, exploitation, discrimination and prejudice of the mainstream society against tribals, explain such state of affairs. Tribal politics is also affected by many issues such as identity, ethnicity, culture, movement, social organization and resource relationship. Considering the thickness of the book, it was extremely challenging to include all issues that are critical to tribal society in a single volume, but largely focused on various issues having political implications. In addition, scholars have written extensively on many of such issues. However, there is a dearth of literature on tribal communities and electoral politics, or this issue has not been adequately addressed. Notwithstanding, the *Handbook* explores the nature and dynamics of tribal participation in contemporary Indian politics. The *Handbook* aims to understand the relationship between tribal communities and electoral politics at central and state levels by considering quantitative (election) data and qualitative (field) data.

Within this backdrop, the *Handbook* consists of 31 chapters, divided across three sections, excluding the 'Introduction'. Section I focuses on the genealogy of tribal politics in India. The initial stage of tribal politics emerged in the form of struggle and resistance against the alien state with a view to overthrowing the imposed colonial rules and regulations on tribal communities. This section focuses on the transition from the community-led tribal movement to the mass movements organized by the national leadership to the institutionalized politics of the modern state. This section also focuses on how tribal communities joined hands with others and became part of larger social movements in which tribal and non-tribal communities participated. It addresses with the changing relationship not only with the colonial state but also with the non-tribal population. This section analyses and underlines the role of tribals as evolving political actors, creating conditions to emerge tribal leadership and their entry into different political parties, including their own ethnic-based political parties.

Section II engages with the nature and dynamics of tribal politics at the national level, especially in the post-independence period. In independent India, the political integration of tribal communities took place in two forms. One, because of the isolated position of the tribals, the Indian state integrated them into mainstream society to accelerate the process of nation-building. Second, as a part of the modern nation state, tribal communities were also entitled to citizenship rights. As a consequence, Indian democratic politics has given a space to tribal communities for participation at two important levels: national and state, besides at the local level in which they have traditionally been participating. Section II, however, is confined to tribal politics at the national level. It may be noted, as the demographic picture indicates, tribals not only formed a small minority but were also scattered across the country. Consequently, there has been no pan-tribal identity. Given this dynamic, it is worth exploring tribal engagement with politics at the national level. In this context, this section discusses issues such as tribal leadership, national political parties and tribes, preferences and modes of nominating tribal candidates, including women, electoral behaviour of tribal communities, participation in decision-making bodies and the role of tribal political representatives in influencing and framing policies revolving around tribal issues.

Section III is devoted to tribal politics at the state level. Tribals are mainly a territorial community, and hence, unlike the Dalits scattered over villages and cities in different parts of India, tribals are generally concentrated in a distinct locality/territory. At the state level, where tribal presence is relatively stronger in terms of demography, there has been relatively a greater space for active participation in state politics through the articulation of demands and movements, thereby influencing political parties or state leadership by acting as important interest groups. This has often led to the formation of their own political parties. Given the significant departure from national politics, this section of the *Handbook* explores tribal politics in different states having reserved constituencies with respect to issues raised in the previous section, such as tribal leadership, regional political parties and tribes, preferences and modes of nominating tribal candidates, including women, electoral behaviour of tribal communities, participation in the decision-making bodies and the role of tribal political representatives in influencing and framing policies revolving around tribal issues. This section is aimed to represent all states, where there are ST-reserved constituencies both at the state and national levels, or at the state level. However, there are no representations from the states of Bihar, Rajasthan, Tamil Nadu and Uttarakhand, where there are ST-reserved constituencies in assemblies and/or the Parliament. Such absence is driven by the unavoidable circumstances in which scholars initially agreed but could not contribute within the tight schedule of the volume.

The 'Introduction' draws the contours of the context. It provides an overview of tribal politics in India. It looks at the engagement of tribes in mainstream democratic politics and explores the patterns, conditions and challenges of tribal participation in electoral politics and within the policy process functioning in India. It also provides an overview of the chapters.

In Section I, Virginius Xaxa's chapter focuses on the nature and dynamics of tribal politics during pre-colonial period, especially in the context of governing the society through self-rule, the impact of the intervention of colonial forces in the tribal lifeworld. He argues that the intrude of the British into tribal society has invariably led to the erosion of the tribal form of self-rule in India. He also discusses the responses of tribes to the erosion of tribal lifeworld via various movements and counter-response of the British, which provided the window for interfacing between tribes and modern democratic practices. The entry of tribes into modern democratic political institutions was not an easy journey, and they had to travel through the zigzag path to carve their space in democratic institutions.

Section II begins with the chapter of Jagannath Ambagudia, where he emphasizes that the political marginalization of the STs due to historical injustices has compelled the Indian state to explore alternative means to ensure an adequate representation for them by adopting a provision of political reservation. Political reservation has, therefore, become their primary means of political empowerment, wherein it has ensured the redistribution of political resources in favour of tribal communities. Against this backdrop, he briefly explores the location of tribal communities within the colonial political system, the reasons for their disproportionate representation, the nature and dynamics of the ST-reserved constituency and the effects of the political reservation on these communities. He argues that the political reservation has brought both hope and despair among the STs.

Valerian Rodrigues explores the extent to which Adivasis have succeeded in marking their distinctive presence in the representational and participatory politics of Indian democracy and the challenges before their leadership today. He emphasizes that there were two sets of issues much in contention in the constitutional and representational outlay for the STs in the early years of India's

independence: autonomy versus inclusion on the one hand, preferential considerations versus equality of citizenship on the other. The challenge the Adivasi question threw up had few precedents elsewhere, but it was believed that Indian democracy would be able to rise up to this challenge. However, the representational politics and policy architecture that directed the course of India led to the confinement of Adivasi leadership and its co-option. In turn, Adivasis closed their ranks behind ethnic markers, asserting their distinctiveness rather than the thick concerns they shared in common. He argues that Adivasi leadership played a second fiddle to these developments, often employing conceptual baggage to justify ethnic closures, rather than reorienting Adivasi futures with a redefinition of Indian democracy.

Samar Bosu Mullick's chapter begins by discussing the relationship between indigenous people (tribal/Adivasis) and the state, and looks at the linkages between tribes and different political parties. It also focuses on trends in voting patterns among tribal communities in India. Regional analysis of electoral politics has also been provided. He argues that the relationship between the tribes and the various political parties has been of an incompatible nature.

Sasmita Mohanty explores the changing relationship between gender and politics in the context of tribal society in India. Representative democracy in India facilitates the equal participation of all communities, irrespective of their language, culture, caste, ethnicity, gender, etc. The representation of women in the highest decision-making body has always remained a debatable topic and a matter of concern. While underlining that the representation of tribal women in politics is highly negligible, she focuses on the relationship between political parties and tribal women in an established political structure, issues of their political representation and recent trends that have been taking place among some of the regional political parties concerning the nomination of tribal women in ST-reserved constituencies. She argues that wherever the opportunities are given to tribal women elected representatives, they have performed with commitment and responsibilities than their male counterparts. She raises one of the pertinent questions: why is there so much of politics *on* tribal women and politics *for* tribal women and not politics *of* tribal women?

Ramachandra Guha traces the relationship between Adivasis, Naxalites and democracy in India and argues that Adivasis have not gained much from decades of democratic practices in India. He compares the position of tribes with Dalits and Muslim communities and discusses the reasons for the minimal impact of tribes on Indian politics. Juxtaposing Adivasis, Dalits and Muslims, he underlines that Adivasis are lagging behind the other two marginalized communities (Dalits and Muslims) in terms of their share of modern democratic politics. Unlike the Dalits, tribes have been unable to effectively articulate their grievances through democratic and electoral processes. The failures of the state and the formal political system have provided a space for Maoist revolutionaries to move into.

Kamal Nayan Choubey's chapter raises one of the pertinent questions: do national political parties give prominence to Adivasis concerning their development, ownership over their natural resources and autonomy to live their lives according to their customs? What kind of differences and similarities exist among the election manifestos of different political parties vis-à-vis the Adivasi issues? Do these promises mentioned in the election manifestos really make an impact on the electoral performances of different political parties? He attempts to probe these questions. In this context, while evaluating the election manifestos of three national parties, such as the Congress, the BJP and the CPI(M), by considering two general elections of 2014 and 2019, he analyses the continuities and ruptures in the promises of these political parties regarding tribal issues in their election manifestos. The chapter proposes that one can find a continuity and consensus among all political parties on certain issues related to the life of Adivasis.

Rupak Kumar's chapter focuses on the role of tribal MPs in the formulation of public policies, especially related to tribal communities in India. It examines the substantive aspect of the representation of these MPs, going beyond the idea of representation as microcosm of the larger population. The purpose is to understand the changes that can be brought into these policies with the intervention of tribal MPs. This aspect was considered in the context of the Forest Rights Act, 2006, which is one of the most progressive legislations concerning tribal communities in India. He emphasizes that tribal MPs played a crucial role in the entire stage of policymaking, legislation and scrutiny. However, it is not an attempt to essentialize the role of tribal MPs as someone only meant to raise community-specific issues and questions. The interventions of tribal MPs are discussed in the form of participation in parliamentary debates, standing committees, asking questions in the house, demanding accountability from the executive, etc.

Turning towards Section III, Venkatesh Vaditya's chapter emphasizes that the political sociology of electoral politics in the erstwhile Andhra Pradesh state was the story of domination of two principle dominant castes ruling the state, most of the time alternatively. This political duet was disturbed with the creation of Telangana and the emergence of alternative dominant caste as the ruling political class in Telangana. Constitutional safeguards necessitate the representation of the tribal community in state politics through reservation. However, when it comes to electoral politics, tribes of Telugu states, such as Andhra Pradesh and Telangana, have failed to raise their autonomous voices, rather they have always depended upon the patronage of the dominant political parties in the state. Tribal electoral politics in both Andhra Pradesh and Telangana states are not beyond the logic of client and patron relationship. This situation prevents tribal leaders to raise their autonomous voices on behalf of their own communities.

Nani Bath examines the process of transformation of traditional tribal society into participatory democratic politics in Arunachal Pradesh. He narrates the history of political evolution and the intricacy of electoral politics, starting from the understanding of democratic elements in traditional sociopolitical institutions; the introduction of statutory Panchayati Raj Institution, which laid the political foundation of the state; the statistical analysis of the different assembly elections and the voting behaviour of tribes in Arunachal Pradesh. He also focuses on some of the critical issues of tribal politics in the state. The Chakma-Hajong issue has remained unresolved since the 1960s, which has placed indigenous communities in collision with outsiders and the Government of India. The history of settlement and the positions of different stakeholders have been placed objectively. Finally, he examines the possible political implications of the presence of large numbers of outsiders, constituting the third largest ethnic group in the state.

Suryasikha Pathak's chapter on Assam examines tribal politics in the state during the colonial period. She deals with the larger concern of constructing tribal identity within the broader discussion on the precarious condition of tribal communities during the colonial period. She also looks at various reasons for the backwardness of the tribes and attempts made by different tribal political leaders to develop, uplift and improve the conditions of the tribes. This chapter traces the emergence of plains tribal in the political map of Assam and shows how it came to be defined partly in opposition to other competing social categories and partly in terms of internal markers of identity.

Himani Ramchiary's chapter underlines that it is pertinent for any minority linguistic community within a majority linguistic state to find expression in their political institutions and organizations. Assam is one such linguistic state, home to many minor communities, some of which are tribal communities and some of which are non-tribal communities. The Bodos of Assam are one of the tribal communities of the state accounting to possess the highest number of tribal population as per the census report of 2011. Of late, the Bodos are seen to take part actively in politics. The social mobility of the Bodos in terms of their political institution is seen to be very recently emerging as one of the strong fields in which the Bodos have begun to express their dissension or favour. The Bodo tribes have their own political party, the Bodoland People's Front. Within this backdrop, the chapter discusses the history of the entry of the Bodos into the realm of Indian politics before independence. The chapter then deals with the participation of the Bodos in the politics of Assam in the post-independence period.

Bipin Jojo and H. Beck's chapter deals with the political assertion of tribal communities in the context of the state of Chhattisgarh. The chapter argues that due to incompatible experiences with modern democracy and the larger political system, tribal communities of Chhattisgarh are exploring alternative sites of assertion where they can (possibly) revive their tradition of taking decisions on the basis of a consensus to have their representatives in decision-making bodies.

N. Rajaram and Ashvin Vasava's chapter analyses tribal politics in Gujarat over the last seven decades, between 1947 and 2019, which has been seen through three phases: the Nehruvian era (from 1947 to 1964) when the present areas of Gujarat were part of the multilingual Bombay state; the post-Nehruvian Congress rule (from about 1964 to 1990) as Nehru passed away in May 1964 and the rule of the BJP (from 1998 onwards). They also focus on various issues of tribal politics, such as tribal development, reservation and education, and health, and provide brief attention to the emergence of the Bharatiya Tribal Party in Gujarat. Mini Pathak Dogra's chapter focuses on the participation of tribal communities of

Himachal Pradesh in electoral politics. She explores the various critical issues that shape tribal politics in the state and the contemporary challenges of tribal politics.

Subeno Kithan's chapter underlines that the state's role in the development of pastoral nomads is evident in a number of policy interventions, especially through the inclusion of Gujjars in the ST categories of Jammu and Kashmir. Despite the lucrative prospect that comes with such a policy, the community has been struggling for genuine representation in sociopolitical spheres. The alienation and marginalization of Gujjars are still at large, even though the state boasts of addressing the needs of the community. Even in a representative democracy, we find disparity with regard to mobile communities left at the margins compared to sedentary communities in terms of representation and participation in the political process. Being a Gujjar in the state of Jammu and Kashmir has its benefits as well as apprehensions. Therefore, it is important to understand what does being a Gujjar mean in the present political context? What is the way forward for this community, which is juggling between their tradition and the modern ways of life; their expectations and apprehensions, and the way forward in the light of the present sociopolitical context? Drawing data from ethnographic research, she attempts to address these questions and documents the nature of the struggle that Gujjars have been going through over the years.

Sujit Kumar's chapter captures the political behaviour of the tribal communities in Jharkhand by locating them in their specific culture, history and society. He uses the 'state-in-society' framework to understand the evolving perceptions about the state among the tribals. He further analyses the 'fault lines' in the project of discovering and asserting the common use of Adivasi identity as a tool of politics. The chapter also explicates the myriad ways in which the Adivasi community expresses its political choice and the reasons behind it. In Jharkhand, it has been observed

that the manner in which the political socialization of the Adivasi community has happened is quite diverse. One can sense the influence of factors such as missionary education, rebellion against the British authorities, state jobs, resistance movements against neoliberal capitalism and interaction with religions determining their voting behaviour to a large extent. At present, the community stands at a crossroads where the well-wishers are searching for a reasonable approach to 'integration' in the mainstream as well as 'autonomy' in their political self-determination.

Pradeep Ramvath J.'s chapter emphasizes that the understanding of political characters of tribal communities with respect to their relative bargaining power in Karnataka requires multiple approaches, including political demography. This, along with the political intersectionality method, is very useful to examine microscopic invisible tribal communities along with politically dominant macroscopic tribal groups. As of now, we have not developed constitutional tools and methodologies for a comparative understanding of subgroups within the larger ST categorization. Intersectionality and political demography will help us to device inclusive methods of policy analysis. The available election and population data on tribals till 2018 assembly election are used to understand intra- and inter-group inequalities created through policy formulation processes, such as providing political reservation in legislative constituencies. The field-based evidence is presented in order to collate the discourse of the political scenarios offered to different categories of tribal communities by the policy elites after the reorganization of the state through an act of political reservation. Finally, a typology comprising tribal regions and zones of political manoeuvring has arrived that classifies STs as microscopic minority tribes that are politically voiceless living in the 'zone of silent exclusion', mesoscopic significant tribes living in the 'zone of negotiation' and finally macroscopic politically dominant tribe living in the 'zone of domination' with powerful control over entire tribal politics of the state.

Abhilash T.'s chapter examines the political articulation of Adivasis in Kerala with special reference to AGMS, the home-grown indigenous collective and its ideological contents. The crystallization of the land rights movement under the AGMS puts forth a fundamental critique, not only of the known equations of national modernization in the post-colonial context, but also challenges the wisdom of modernity in South Asia. Beginning with an analysis of the Kerala model of development and exclusion of Adivasis, with a brief evaluation of the colonial roots of Adivasi marginality, he articulates the positions of the different political parties on the larger Adivasi cause. He further evaluates the factors behind land alienation and landlessness, the most pertinent issues associated with Kerala's Adivasis, and the role played by the state and its agencies with unimplemented rules and regulations designed to protect Adivasi land livelihoods and later factors that led to the emergence of a fresh political consciousness among Adivasis, which culminated into the formation of the AGMS. He argues that the land rights movement initiated under the AGMS refurbished the collective Adivasi identity assertion along with a systematized effort for democratic bargaining, which empowered different Adivasi groups and organizations in the state to assert their rights later.

Considering the socioeconomic condition and demographic picture of tribal communities of Madhya Pradesh, Sudha Pai's chapter focuses on the growing political consciousness of the tribes, which has been phenomenal since the 1990s. She argues that the political sphere has become an important arena for the tribes of Madhya Pradesh to express their consent and satisfaction, but more often to register their discontent and disenchantment with the state, which seems to have become less sensitive and less ignorant towards the 'core values' of tribal society. She also focuses on the attempts of the two national political parties, such as the Congress and the BJP, to appropriate the tribal support base, often plugged in by their own political organizations. Despite the presence of such a scenario, the articulation and voices of tribes, as the chapter indicates, remain relatively weak in contemporary tribal politics in Madhya Pradesh.

Pandurang Bhoye's chapter begins with the tribal situation in Maharashtra. He then explores various organizations and social and political movements, led by both tribals and non-tribals, working towards the advancement of tribal communities. He also focuses on contestations between different political parties to appropriate tribal votes and reserved constituencies and reflects the trends in tribal politics in Maharashtra. Joseph Riamei's chapter underlines that political instability and peoples' resistance, especially the tribal groups' clamours against the state and dominant politics, have been never-ending issues in the state of Manipur. Peoples' experiences and their responses to the undemocratic reality have given birth to many secessionist movements in the state by tribal communities. The decentralization and self-governance framework for tribal communities sanctioned by the state is a drastic failure and, thus, remains a state of contested terrain. The disparities in development between the hills and the valley have also resulted in the antagonization of the rigid political elites. He reflects on the politics of representation and unravels the experiences of tribal communities of Manipur. He critically looks at the representation of tribal people in the state legislative assembly and the governance framework for hill areas.

Bodhi S. R.'s chapter reads statehood in the context of Khasi's political reality. It provides the historical anecdotes and processes that took place before Meghalaya attained full statehood and its implications over tribal politics in the state. It also focuses briefly on the post-statehood scenario of Meghalaya. Moses Kharbithai's chapter emphasizes on changing political narratives and tribal politics in Meghalaya. This aspect of tribal politics has been done by taking the 2018 assembly election as the special reference point. He focuses on the campaign trail of the various political parties and the means employed by them during election campaigns. The chapter brings interesting insights that are almost absent in the tribal politics of Central India. He also focuses on the vote and seat sharing of the various political parties in a 60-member assembly, where 55 seats are reserved for the STs.

P. Lalpekhlui's chapter focuses on the fact that elections are an important mechanism for citizens to elect their representatives. Non-state actors in Mizoram promise to escort and correct the deteriorated electoral system, which was controlled by structural biases, such as inclination towards a particular party system and money driving the process that impedes the quality of electoral system as a whole and the status quo of a peaceful state. In this scenario, non-state actors used the available spaces to mobilize the masses along ethnic-religious lines, resulting in substantial changes in the democracy system. The intense mobilization of the masses along the ethnic-religious identity in electoral politics has resulted in a substantial increase in the turnout of the voters, which has, in turn, enhanced the political system and, at the same time, cemented the principles of democracy that rest upon the representative form of government. She looks at various issues, contexts, patterns and actors that influence electoral politics in the context of tribal communities of Mizoram.

Jelle J. P. Wouters asks what the winds of liberal democracy have done to Naga society? What is/has turned Naga society into? But equally, what happens in the meeting between liberal democracy and home-grown Naga political theory and praxis? What hybrids are produced by the collusion of divergent sets of political practices and principles, ethics and mores, ethos and telos? What have Nagas done to liberal democracy by applying their agency and cultural creativity to retailor it to their own uses and lifeworlds? It is this double investigation, he argues, of how democracy

changes the community and how the community changes democracy that leads to a number of insights into the contemporary character of Naga tribal politics. In other words, he explores the unsettled relationship between the traditional practices of the Naga community and the modern democratic aspirations in the context of Nagaland.

Jagannath Ambagudia's chapter begins by exploring the proportionate relationship between the tribal population and the assembly and the parliamentary seat allocation to them in Odisha. He analyses the parliamentary election data between 1991 and 2019 concerning tribal and non-tribal constituencies in terms of voter turnout, the competitive nature of politics, the vote and seat share among the Congress, the BJP and the Left parties, gender and tribal politics, etc. State-level election data are also analysed; however, such analysis is confined to the ST-reserved constituencies only. It also explains the reasons for the shifting trend of tribal support base to different political parties, in addition to reflecting on issues that are critical to tribal politics in Odisha.

Tikendra K. Chhetry and Sanghamitra Choudhury's chapter emphasizes that the politics of tribalization and the struggle for contested space among various communities in Sikkim are not new. In fact, Sikkim has witnessed a number of political transitions and upheavals in relation to sharing of seats among various communities in the legislative assembly till date. They argue that the contested space has become more visible with the decision to declare Bhutia-Lepcha, Limboo and Tamang as STs in different times and to grant political reservations only to the Bhutia-Lepchas. It was clear that Bhutia-Lepchas constitute approximately 22 per cent of the total population of state having a reservation of 12 out of 32 seats in the state legislative assembly, whereas Limboo and Tamang of Gorkha/Nepali sub-ethnic communities are not yet provided any right of seat reservation despite being recognized as STs under the framework of the Indian Constitution. Moreover, after due recognition of Limboo and Tamang, 11 other sub-ethnic groups of the same Gorkha/Nepali fold are still excluded from ST status despite the fact that the Roy Burman Committee recommended for their immediate inclusion in the ST list. Such kind of a complicated trajectory has created resentment in the political space among the communities with the demands of Limboo and Tamang seat reservation in the state legislative assembly and ST status for the 11 left out groups of the Gorkha/Nepali fold. They capture these contested issues in relation to the sharing of political space along with the politics of tribalization in Sikkim.

R. K. Debbarma's chapter begins by discussing tribal politics in Tripura premised on two interrelated themes of demographic transformation and subsequent land alienation of the indigenous population. He evaluates the political implications of this way of thinking about tribal politics and demands a critique of politics itself. What makes it possible to think and do tribal politics of certain kind? It argues that the category called 'tribal politics' in Tripura is the product of the history and ideology of creating a settler society in Tripura. The chapter teases out this history and ideology, and provides an account of tribal politics. A. K. Verma's chapter begins with formidable challenges of tribal identity in Uttar Pradesh, which have emerged in the form of constitutional, administrative and political assaults supported by wrong census. He raises three critical concerns, such as social exclusion, political deprivation and economic exploitation, which grapple with tribal communities in Uttar Pradesh and their potential implications over politics.

Considering the nature of tribal politics unfolding in the state of West Bengal, Nilamber Chhetri's chapter explores the multivariate ways in which tribes deal with the state and its functionaries. He discusses the nature of the tribal population in the state while focusing more on electoral politics unfolding in the tribal constituencies in the state.

The chapter provides a crucial reading of the changing political relationship in the region, while suggesting a changing trend of political affiliation in the state. He also draws upon the empirical study conducted in Darjeeling to unravel the demands for recognition as STs unfold among the 10 ethnic groups in the region. In this regard, the chapter details the interphase between the regional demand and the rising aspiration for the coveted ST status. Considering these various facets of tribal politics, he argues that the politics of the tribes in West Bengal shows a hybrid of the struggle for recognition and redistribution. The chapter highlights how politics of recognition is unfolding both within and outside the category of STs.

The contemporary dimensions of tribal politics in India are largely grappling with various issues. Some of the prominent issues that are pointed out in the different chapters are migration, identity, struggle for the share in legislative assembly, land alienation, rights over natural resources, the destruction of their indigenous political system, the dominance of non-tribals over tribal communities, etc. Wherever there is any sign of violation of tribal rights over natural resources, the tribes have resisted and fought to reinstate their rights over resources. The issue of migration in the states of Odisha, Assam, Mizoram, Arunachal Pradesh and Tripura, among others, has raised the eyebrows of tribal communities. The recently passed Citizenship Amendment Act, 2019, which grants citizenship to illegal migrants from Hindu, Sikh, Buddhist, Jain, Parsi and Christian religious minorities who migrated from Pakistan, Bangladesh and Afghanistan prior to December 2014, will also have greater implications over tribal politics in India in due course. To put it differently, all these issues have their implications over tribal politics at their corresponding levels.

Contributors range from senior scholars working on tribal issues to early career academics who have focused on a myriad of intriguing aspects of tribal politics based on their recent empirical research. Since the book follows an interdisciplinary approach, it will be of interest to a vast canvas of scholars drawn from the disciplines of history, sociology, social and cultural anthropology, political science as well as administrators, policymakers and social activists. We hope that this *Handbook* will encourage scholars to further explore the complex dynamics of tribal politics in India.

REFERENCES

Ambagudia, J. (2011). Scheduled tribes and the politics of inclusion in India. *Asian Social Work and Policy Review, 5*(1), 33–43.

Ambagudia, J. (2019a). *Adivasis, migrants and the state in India*. London: Routledge.

Ambagudia, J. (2019b). Scheduled tribes, reserved constituencies and political reservation in India. *Journal of Social Inclusion Studies, 5*(1), 44–58.

Ambagudia, J., & Mohanty, S. (forthcoming/2020). Adivasis, integration and the state: Experiences of incompatibilities. *International Review of Social Research*.

Bailey, F. G. (1960). Traditional society and representation: A case study in Orissa. *European Journal of Sociology, 1*(1), 121–141.

Barik, S. (2015). Odisha may allow tribals to sell their land to non-tribals. *The Hindu*, 9 November. Retrieved from https://www.thehindu.com/news/national/other-states/odisha-may-allow-tribals-to-sell-their-land-to-nontribals/article7859466.ece

Beteille, A. (1986). The concept of tribe with special reference to India. *Journal of European Sociology, 27*(2), 296–318.

Bose, N. K. (1941). The Hindu method of tribal absorption. *Science and Culture, 7*(2), 188–194.

Bose, P. K. (1990). Congress and the tribal communities in India. In R. Roy & R. Sisson (Eds.), *Diversity and dominance in Indian politics, vol. 2: Division, deprivation and the Congress* (pp. 58–80). New Delhi: SAGE Publications.

Bosu Mullick, S. (2001). Indigenous peoples and electoral politics in India: An experience of incompatibility. In K. Wessendorf (Ed.), *Challenging politics: Indigenous peoples experience with political parties and elections* (pp. 94–144). Copenhagen: International Workgroup for Indigenous Affairs.

Chemmencheri, S. R. (2015). State, social policy and subaltern citizens in Adivasi India. *Citizenship Studies, 19*(3–4), 436–449.

Choubey, K. N. (2016). The state, tribals and law: The politics behind the enactment of PESA and FRA. *Social Change, 46*(3), 355–370.

Farooqui, A., & Sridharan, E. (2014). Incumbency, internal process and renomination in Indian parties. *Commonwealth & Comparative Politics, 52*(1), 78–108.

Galanter, M. (1984). *Competing equalities: Law and the backward classes in India*. New Delhi: Oxford University Press.

Gallagher, M. (1991). Proportionality, disproportionality and electoral systems. *Electoral Studies, 10*(1), 33–51.

Government of India. (1935). *Government of India Act, 1935*. New Delhi: Government of India.

Government of India. (1949a). *Constituent assembly debates* (vol. I). New Delhi: Lok Sabha Secretariat.

Government of India. (1949b). *Constituent assembly debates* (vol. IX). New Delhi: Lok Sabha Secretariat.

Government of India. (1980). *Statistical report on general elections, 1980 to the seventh Lok Sabha*. New Delhi: Election Commission of India.

Government of India. (1984). *Statistical report on general elections, 1984 to the eighth Lok Sabha*. New Delhi: Election Commission of India.

Government of India. (1989). *Statistical report on general elections, 1989 to the ninth Lok Sabha*. New Delhi: Election Commission of India.

Government of India. (1991). *Statistical report on general elections, 1991 to the tenth Lok Sabha*. New Delhi: Election Commission of India.

Government of India. (1996). *Statistical report on general elections, 1996 to the eleventh Lok Sabha*. New Delhi: Election Commission of India.

Government of India. (1998). *Statistical report on general elections, 1998 to the 12th Lok Sabha*. New Delhi: Election Commission of India.

Government of India. (1999). *Statistical report on general elections, 1999 to the thirteenth Lok Sabha*. New Delhi: Election Commission of India.

Government of India. (2004). *Statistical report on general elections, 2004 to the 14th Lok Sabha*. New Delhi: Election Commission of India.

Government of India. (2008a). *Report of an export group on development challenges in extremist affected areas*. New Delhi: Planning Commission.

Government of India. (2008b). *The Gazette of India, extraordinary, part-ii, section 3-sub-section-(ii)* (No. 187). Retrieved from https://dipp.gov.in/sites/default/files/ExplosivesRules_2008_0%20%281%29.pdf

Government of India. (2009). *Statistical report on general elections, 2009 to the 15th Lok Sabha*. New Delhi: Election Commission of India.

Government of India. (2013). *Statistical profile of Scheduled Tribes in India, 2013*. New Delhi: Ministry of Tribal Affairs.

Government of India. (2014). *Statistical report on general elections, 2014 to the 16th Lok Sabha*. New Delhi: Election Commission of India.

Government of India. (2019). *General election, 2019*. New Delhi: Election Commission of India. Retrieved from https://eci.gov.in/files/category/1359-general-election-2019/

Grofman, B., & Lijphart, A. (Eds.). (1986). *Electoral laws and their political consequences*. New York, NY: Agathon Press.

Guha, R. C. (2007). Adivasis, Naxalites and Indian democracy. *Economic & Political Weekly, 42*(32), 3305–3312.

Jayal, N. G. (2006). *Representing India: Ethnic diversity and the governance of public institutions*. New York, NY: Palgrave Macmillan.

Jojo, B. K., Beck, H., Toppo, E., & Renee, D. S. (2008). *Tribal empowerment and electoral politics* (Research Project Report). Mumbai: Tata Institute of Social Sciences.

Kanungo, P. (2008). Hindutva's fury against Christians in Orissa. *Economic & Political Weekly, 43*(37), 16–19.

Kymlicka, W. (1995). *Multicultural citizenship: A liberal theory of minority rights*. Oxford: Oxford University Press.

Mahajan, G. (1998). *Identities and rights: Aspects of liberal democracy in India*. New Delhi: Oxford University Press.

McMillan, A. (2005). *Standing at the margins: Representation and electoral reservation in India*. New Delhi: Oxford University Press.

Pande, R. (2003). Can mandate political representation increase policy influence for disadvantaged minorities? Theory and evidence from India. *The American Economic Review, 39*(4), 1132–1151.

Panigrahi, P. K. (1998). *Political elite in tribal society*. New Delhi: Commonwealth Publishers.

Pettit, P. (2009). Varieties of public representation. In I. Shapiro, S. C. Stokes, E. J. Wood, & A. S. Kirshner (Eds.), *Political representation* (pp. 61–89). Cambridge: Cambridge University Press.

Phillips, A. (1995). *The politics of presence: The political representation of gender, ethnicity and race*. New York, NY: Oxford University Press.

Prasad, A. (2016). Adivasis and the trajectories of political mobilization in contemporary India. In M. Radhakrishnan (Ed.), *First citizens: Studies on Adivasis, tribals and indigenous peoples in India* (pp. 307–336). New Delhi: Oxford University Press.

Rathva, A., Rai, D., & Rajaram, N. (2014). Denotification of the Rathvas as Adivasis in Gujarat. *Economic & Political Weekly, 49*(6), 22–24.

Rawls, J. (1971). *A theory of justice*. Delhi: Oxford University Press.

Sachidananda. (1993). Politics and political processes in tribal India: Then and now. In M. K. Raha, & I. A. Khan (Eds.), *Polity, political processes and social control in South Asia: The tribal and rural perspective* (pp. 141–163). New Delhi: Gyan Publishing House.

Shankar, B. L., & Rodrigues, V. (2014). *The Indian parliament: A democracy at work*. New Delhi: Oxford University Press.

Singh, K. S. (1985). Tribal society in India: An anthropo-historical perspective. New Delhi: Manohar.

Sinha, S. (1987). Introduction. In S. Sinha (Ed.), *Tribal polities and state systems in pre-colonial eastern and north eastern India* (pp. ix–xxvi). Calcutta: K. P. Bagchi and Company.

Sundar, N. (2012). Adivasi politics and state responses: Historical processes and contemporary concerns. In S. Das Gupta & R. S. Basu (Eds.), *Narratives from the margins: Aspects of Adivasi history in India* (pp. 237–254). New Delhi: Primus Books.

Thachil, T. (2011). Embedded mobilization: Nonstate service provision as electoral strategy in India. *World Politics, 63*(3), 434–469.

Thachil, T. (2014). *Elite parties, poor voters: How social services win votes in India*. Cambridge: Cambridge University Press.

Waylen, G. (2015). Engendering the 'crisis of democracy': Institution, representation and participation. *Government and Opposition, 50*(3), 495–520.

Weiner, M., & Field, J. O. (1975). How tribal constituencies in India vote. In J. N. Bhagwati, P. Desai, J. O. Field, W. L. Richter, & M. Weiner (Eds.), *Electoral politics in the Indian states: Three disadvantaged sectors, volume 2: Studies in electoral politics in the Indian states* (pp. 79–120). New Delhi: Manohar Book Service.

Xaxa, V. (2008). *State, society and tribes: Issues in post-colonial India*. New Delhi: Pearson.

Yadav, Y., & Palshikar, S. (2006). Party system and electoral politics in the Indian States, 1952–2002: From hegemony to convergence. In P. R. deSouza, & E. Sridharan (Eds.), *India's political parties* (pp. 73–115). New Delhi: SAGE Publications.

Genealogy of Tribal Politics in India

Tribal Politics in India: From Movement to Institutionalism

Virginius Xaxa

Politics is about access to power of decision-making at different levels of society. In modern times, politics in generally discerned at four levels. These are relations among nation states, nature and role of states within societies, organization of political movements and parties and participation of individuals in politics (Abercrombie, Stephen & Turner, 1984). The attempt here is to understand the nature and type of tribal politics in India dating from the beginning of the British rule to the present times. In the context of the four levels mentioned above, this falls broadly in the category of organization of political movements and parties. One of the key concerns of politics at the collective level is to wield power or wrest power if it is eroded and taken away. It is a form of self-rule which exists at different levels such as village, caste, tribe, region, nationality and nation. It is an agenda to determine and regulate their own lives. The tribal politics in India is primarily centred on this agenda. To recover this, tribal politics has taken different routes and strategies. In post-independent India, it has made transition to institutional politics but movements continue to play critical role in its politics. This points to the structural limitation

of institutional politics in modern India as far as tribes are concerned.

Question of self-rule especially in respect of a community or collective identity as belonging to the region emerges in the context of domination of one group by another. Domination of one entails the subjugation of the other. Domination and subjugation are, thus, tied with the use and exercise of power. 'Power' in Weberian sense is the ability of individuals or groups to pursue a course of action even against the will and opposition of others. Power, thus, can be seen from the two perspectives—one from the perspective of those who exercise power and the other from those over whom power is exercised and who do not hold power (Gerth & Mills, 1970, p. 193). The articulation or demand for self-rule invariably emanates from the latter.

Individuals and groups under subjugation submit to power due to a variety of reasons. Fear of the power holders could be one of them. The other could be convergence or overlapping of interest. There could even be third, namely, the voluntary submission. Broadly, then submission to power is of two types. One is voluntary submission which Weber terms as domination and power exercised as authority. The other is non-voluntary submission, Weber terms it as coercion. The use of power then broadly takes two forms—coercion and domination. Coercion, in contrast to domination, is characterized by negation of voluntary submission and hence it suffers from legitimacy (Gerth & Mills, 1970, p. 195). Rule or regime so characterized tends to be unacceptable and hence is resisted and opposed. However, even in case of the rule or regime, which is characterized by voluntary submission and hence as legitimate, legitimacy tends to be far from stable and hence precarious leading to resistance and opposition to the rule. Articulation of self-rule emerges out of such context.

SELF-RULE AND ITS EROSION UNDER THE BRITISH

By virtue of the fact that tribes lived in relative isolation from the dominant community, they enjoyed autonomy of governance over the territory they occupied. They held control over the land, forest and other resources. The advent of the British rule, however, drew and incorporated them into the larger economic, political and social framework. This is not to say that tribes did not have such encounter earlier. Many tribes in different parts lived under alien political suzerainty at some point or other. The suzerainty ranged from symbolic gesture of loyalty to the payment of tribute/tax to the political authority. However, despite being under such political authority, they enjoyed autonomy in respect of their lands, forests and other resources. They also governed themselves in terms of their own rules and regulations. However, by the 18th century, such social arrangement including the ownership and control of tribal land had begun to be eroded (Dasgupta, 2011, pp. 62–88; Streumer, 2016, pp. 81–139; Thapar & Siddiqi, 2003, pp. 40–46).

The advent of the British rule was different in the sense that it extended its administration

in tribal areas also. It introduced new laws and regulations—civil as well as criminal. It had set up an administrative structure that was alien. Like in many other parts of India, the British imposed upon the tribes the notion of the private property and landlordism in place of lineage or community-based ownership of land. The revenue collectors/administrative officials were converted into owner and landlords, which they were not. This led to a large-scale eviction of tribes from their land and encroachment of non-tribes in their land. In due course, land assumed a form of commodity which began to be bought and sold. The British also opened tribal areas to the outside world through extension of roads and railways. This led to an exodus of movement of the population from the plains to tribal areas in search of land for cultivation and opportunity for trade and commerce. The latter opened a space for market, to begin with for commodity and credit and later for labour. The rise of the different forms of commodity has led to increasing monetization of the economy. The payment of revenue to the state in cash led to increasing demand for cash, giving rise to the business of money lending at exorbitant rate of interest. The commodity market further heightened the demand for cash. This gave rise to credit market which played havoc in tribal society. The indebtedness of tribal people to moneylenders, traders and others swelled. Credit was provided only against the security of land, the most important asset of the tribal people. The rate of interest being exorbitant, tribes were unable to repay the loan. The result was the massive alienation of land from tribes to non-tribes.

Besides this, the transfer of land from tribes to non-tribes also took place through measures such as fraud and deceit. Since tribes had no practice of record keeping, as they did not have the knowledge of reading and writing, non-tribes took advantage of forging evidence and documents in their favour. The local administration, which was manned by the non-tribes, worked hand in hand with their ethnic kinder men to ensure smooth transfer of land from tribes to non-tribes. The court language was alien to tribes and they had absolutely no idea of what was happening in the court. Over and above, the colonial state took upon itself the right over the forest, thereby denying tribes the right to collect fuel and other daily necessities of life for which they were so heavily dependent on forest (Bosu Mullick, 1993; Singh, 2002). These processes at work caused havoc in tribal society. Tribes lost autonomy or their control over land and forest. They lost autonomy over the way they governed and regulated themselves as a society. In short, they lost all autonomy or self-rule they enjoyed prior to the advent of the British.

RESPONSE TO EROSION OF SELF-RULE

The response of the tribes to the loss of self-rule/swaraj invariably took the form of armed struggle. In fact, the late 18th and 19th centuries encounter of the British with groups/communities (which later came to be described as tribes) was characterized by series of revolt and rebellion. Prominent among the revolts at this early phase were the revolt of Pahariya Sirdars (1778), the Tamar Revolt (1789, 1794–1795), the Tribal Revolt (1807–1808), the agrarian tribal revolts (1811, 1817, 1820) and so on. However, it was the revolts that took place after the Great Kol Insurrection of 1831–1832 that have received wide attention. The prominent among these revolts are the Bhumij Revolt (1832–1833), the Santhal rebellion (1855–1857), the Kherwar/Sardari movement (1858–1895), the Birsa Munda movement (1895–1990) and so on. (Bosu Mullick, 1993; Raghavaiah, 1979).

These early struggles of tribes had primarily to do with the issue of overthrowing the colonial rule and administration. Hence, it would not be altogether out of context to describe these early struggles as a kind of struggle for self-rule. Of course, self-rule as it has come to be articulated

in the post-independence era has been different in a very substantive sense from the ones under the British rule. Yet there has been much overlapping at least in spirit if not in letter, that this has been so can be inferred from the way struggles of the time had come to be described in colonial administration. Terms broadly used to describe the struggles were revolt, resistance, insurrection and so on. Even the scholarly historical works have adhered with such description of the struggles. An interesting aspect of the tribal struggles of the period is that, in the post-colonial official history, these have come to be seen as a part of the freedom struggle movement. Such characterization of the struggles tends to equate the struggles of the tribes with the struggle of the people at large against the British rule. In the process, it is often forgotten that tribal struggles were not only against the British but also against the non-tribal people who were engaged marginalizing tribals in different forms.

The non-tribals were invariably seen as ones who took advantage of the administrative and other structures created by the British and squeezed out tribes from their lands and other resources by fraud, coercion, debt and bondage. In fact, tribal struggle was more intensely fought against the non-tribes as they were seen as the immediate exploiters and oppressors of the tribes. In fact, whereas the rule of the British ended after India attained independence, the rule of the dominant group over the tribals continued even after India became independent. Self-rule demand in the form of a separate state which caught the imagination of the tribal people in the post-independent India in different parts of the country has in fact its roots in such structure of the tribal society.

All revolts/rebellion had their main roots in their grievances against loss of land and forest by the tribals. The grievances, however, did not acquire the form of land- or forest-based movement as the issues were intricately connected with overall destabilization of society brought about by the colonial rule and alien administration. After all, land was not mere source of livelihood for tribals but something connected with every institution of the tribal social structure. In fact, tribal kinship structure, religious beliefs and practices, social organization, their collective life, all hinged around their relationship with land. Since those usurped tribal land were outsiders including the British administration, the movement took the form of a revolt against the British rule and the aliens especially the landlords, moneylenders and the traders. Discontent during the period was over the whole system of rule and administration, which besides bringing them under alien authority caused havoc in their lives that they had never experienced before.

Hence, the resistance at this phase aimed at total or complete autonomy. It aimed at overthrowing the alien structure that had brought along with it pervasive coercion, exploitation and domination. It was, thus, aimed at restoration of their traditional social structure, a structure that was as noted earlier relatively egalitarian, democratic and where there was no constraint on their civil and economic rights if one were to use those terms. The autonomy underlying the struggles was diffused and this was to do with the nature of society itself. After all, in tribal society, it was very difficult to draw boundary between different institutions of the tribal social structure. All institutions such as economy, kinship, polity, religion and so on were enmeshed with each other. Further, the struggle aimed at autonomy not only from the system that was built but also from those who run the system. The struggle challenged not only the system but also the agency. It was, thus, a struggle of tribals against all alien forces and symbols and to that extent aspect of autonomy running through the struggles has strong ethnic dimension.

RESPONSE OF BRITISH TO TRIBAL POLITICS

In response to resistance, the British administration toyed with the idea of suitable administrative set up which provided some space for self-rule for tribals. Accordingly, they came up after much experiment with arrangements which were different from those in the non-tribal areas. This was evident in framing of distinct legislative and executive measures for tribes, which aimed primarily at protecting and safeguarding the interests of the tribes. Thus, tribes or tribal areas since 1874 came to be governed by the Scheduled District Act. As per this act, laws enacted by the Governor-General in Council or Governor in Council were not extendable tribal areas. It could be extended to those areas only if the executive authority (governor-general/governor) deemed it fit. In other words, the executive authority was required to notify as to what laws were to be in force in the scheduled areas/districts. Such provision continued under the Government of India Act 1919, which gave power to Indians on self-governance on certain subjects. It may be noted that enactment made by legislature/legislatures was not directly applicable to tribal areas unless so desired by the executive authority. Even under the Government of India Act 1935, tribal areas declared as excluded and partially excluded areas were not brought under the direct purview of federal or provincial legislatures (Misra, 2012). The arrangements made for the administration of the tribal areas during the British period were continued with some form in the post-independence era. Nowhere is this better reflected than in provisions made in the Indian Constitution for administration of areas inhabited by the tribes in the form of fifth and sixth schedules of the Indian Constitution (Verma, 1990). There was some space for self-rule for tribals in the colonial rule. Yet these provisions turned out to be ineffective and inadequate and the plight tribals suffered at the early phase of the colonial rule and administration continued unabated. Side by side these tribal struggles continued but it tended to take different forms.

TRIBES IN FREEDOM STRUGGLE MOVEMENT

With the momentum of freedom struggle movement since 1920s, agrarian and forest issues came to the forefront of the movement among the tribes but with a difference. This time, the movements were parts of the larger mobilization process of civil disobedience or non-cooperation movements launched by the Congress or the other nationalist leadership. Agrarian movement not only took the form of non-cooperation and civil disobedience against the colonial state but also took the form of struggle and resistance against the exploitation and oppression of the landlords. The latter were mobilized primarily by the left wing political parties both in the colonial and post-colonial period. Such struggles were aimed broadly at security of tenure, reduction of rent, increased share of produce and so on. In these struggles, tribals aligned with other exploited classes of the agrarian society. The struggles were directed at the colonial rule as well as the exploited section of the India society (Iyer & Mahajan, 1986; Singh, 1986; Singh, 1983, Tirkey, 2002). Autonomy envisaged was one which provided tribes freedom from oppression of the state and exploitation of the landlords. Indeed the idea of autonomy from state oppression and zamindari exploitation was so strong that other form of domination exercised by non-tribals over tribals was glossed over (Tirkey, 2002, p. 59). That explains as to why these movements never articulated the demand for greater autonomy for tribals. Even in the post-independence period, this remained unarticulated for a long period of time. The problem with these movements was that they treated the movements primarily as land and forest based movements. Hence, tribes were treated not more than peasant and forest dwellers. Hence, the concerns came to be exclusively addressed in terms of economic livelihood. Where such movements did take place they have invariably been led by outside agencies such as political parties, activists, social workers and so on. Where tribals on their own have taken to such issues, they have invariably been part of the wider issues such as demand for political autonomy or general control over land, forest and other resources by the tribals. This has been the case with movements both in pre-independent and post-independent India.

TRIBES' ENTRY INTO MODERN POLITICS

The tribal struggles barring the struggles of the 19th century as noted earlier have been apparently issue oriented. This was much more the case with struggles organized from outside such as the nationalist leadership or political parties or interest group organizations. In contrast, tribal led resistance or struggles invariably directed at the totality. The 19th-century struggles such as the Kol insurrection, Santhal revolt, Birsa Munda movement and so on. bear witness to it. Yet the 19th-century struggles were reactive and aimed at restoring earlier social structure. Most of them had millenarian feature and aimed at leading tribes to its past glory. Unlike these earlier movements, which were aimed at restoring the past, the movement that began in late 1930s onwards among various tribal groups in the form of autonomy movement had for the first time showed an element of future looking. Like the earlier tribal struggles, the struggle in reference was not issue-oriented but aimed at reorienting the tribal society in a new mould. This new mould was articulated in the form of the demand for a separate state for the tribals. The stirring of autonomy movement by tribes in the form of separate state could be traced to the period preceding the end of the British rule. However in its nascent form, it had already begun to be talked about in 1910s. The Naga Club in Nagaland and the Chotangpur Unnati Samaj in Jharkhand were formed during this period to protect the interests of the tribes.

The tribal leadership in Jharkhand as well as Nagaland had already made reference to it at the visit of the Simon Commission in India. The difference being that while tribal leadership in Jharkhand was articulating separate state within India, the Naga leadership was referring to sovereign state (Tirkey, 2002, p. 29; Vashum, 2000, p. 65). After India became independent, movements for separate states both in Jharkhand and Nagaland assumed intense mobilization and mass participation. The movement in Nagaland turned out to be violent and the Indian Government had to deploy the army. Simultaneously, soon as a part of the strategy to contain the movement, the Nagas in 1963 were granted separate statehood within the Indian Union. The Nagas were however unhappy with the limited autonomy and the struggle for sovereignty continues till this day though in a much truncated form. In Jharkhand, the demand was not given serious consideration and the struggle as in case of Nagaland continued.

Autonomy movements in mainland India have been confined to certain pockets of eastern, central and western India. In Gujarat, there was a stir for autonomy among tribes living in the southern part of the state. Similarly, in Madhya Pradesh, there was demand in 1950s for a separate state of Gondwana for Gond tribes. Yet both in Gujarat and Madhya Pradesh, the demand failed to get translated into an organized movement (Desai, 1983; Singh, 1983). In fact, the only autonomy movement worth its name in the mainland India has been the movement for a separate state of Jharkhand. The movement has been one of longest fought struggles and has passed through many historical ups and downs.

The movement has also been one of the longest struggles of autonomy movement in India. There was intense mobilization for the demand in the years after independence. In fact, in the very first legislative assembly election held after independence, the Jharkhand Party has bagged a large number of seats in the Bihar assembly. In fact, it was major opposition party. Now the spectacular success of the Jharkhand Party in the assembly election was largely due to their demand for a separate state for the tribals. There was also massive participation of the people at the visit of the States Reorganization Committee to Ranchi (Bosu Mullick, 2003; Tirkey, 2002). The committee however found the demand untenable and the demand was rejected. This not only demoralized the leadership but also dampened the spirit and enthusiasm of the people. The Jharkhand party formed to spearhead the movement got disintegrated into a number of splinter groups. There was lull in the movement but the demand was kept alive. Soon, other organizations emerged and began to aggressively articulate the demand for a separate state of Jharkhand. Prominent among these organizations have been the Jharkhand Mukti Morcha (JMM) and All Jharkhand Students Union (AJSU). In the process, however, the movement has undergone a considerable change in its character, organization, strategy, mobilization and so on. Indeed, the change has been such that the movement has since 1970s shifted from its ethnic character to a regional character accommodating the interests of diverse segments of the population inhabiting the region. There was now a greater acceptability to the demand for a separate state. This was partly conceded when Jharkhand was granted autonomous regional council status with some legislative as well as executive functions. By this time, the separate state of Jharkhand has become an important electoral issue and national political parties just could not ignore it. In a sense, it was the constraints of electoral politics, which set into motion the formation of the separate state of Jharkhand. The constraint itself was the result of long-drawn struggles carried out by the tribals and at a later phase also by the Jharkhand non-tribals.

In contrast, the movement for autonomy among tribes of Northeast India has not only been pervasive but has also been carried forward with single-minded dedication and massive support of the people. Movements on the whole were democratic and within constitutional framework barring a few exception. It assumed armed struggle only with the failure of democratic process of negotiation. The formation of states often referred to as tribal states and autonomous district and territorial councils under the sixth schedule of the Indian Constitution among some other states of the region are result of such movements of the people (Xaxa, 2008).

EMERGENCE OF TRIBAL POLITICAL PARTIES

The movements for autonomy in the form of the state have invariably been led by the regional political formation that aimed to address the aspiration of the people. This was manifested in a birth of organization. Most of them later turned into the political parties or took its role. The formation of such parties/organizations could be traced to the period nearing independence or after independence. The Adivasi Mahasabha was formed in 1938 after merging various existing organization to fight for the cause of the tribes. In 1949, the same was christened as the Jharkhand Party. The demand for the separate state of Gondwana was launched in the 1940s under the auspice of Gondwana Adivasi Seva Mandal. The State Reorganisation commission rejected the demand for a separate state on the same ground as in the case of Jharkhand. This gave a setback to the movement (Singh, 2003; Tirkey, 2002). Since the late 1980s, there has been further momentum in the demand leading to the formation of distinct of political party known as Gondwana Ganatantra Party in 1991.

The Jharkhand Party and JMM were the key regional formations in what was erstwhile Bihar and Jharkhand today. The Jharkhand Party in course of time split into a number of factions based on specific tribal identity and have almost disappeared from the scene today. The JMM that has emerged in 1970 took the role of erstwhile Jharkhand Party and continues to be an important regional player today. The Gondwana Prajatantrik Party has been the other tribal based regional party in mainland India. Like the Jharkhand Party, it articulated the demand for a separate state of Gondwana. Of late, there has been some sign of the revival of the party which is evident from their participation in electoral politics especially in Madhya Pradesh and Chhattisgarh. Its influence, however, remains very limited (Poyam, 2015). In more recent times, a new political party has emerged in the name of the Bhartiya Tribal Party. It emerged in the state of Gujarat in 2017 but has begun to make dent in the neighbouring states of Rajasthan and Maharashtra. It has been participating in electoral politics and has been successful in wining some seats in the assembly elections in Gujarat and Rajasthan. It has not been successful in parliamentary election so far (Bordia, 2019).

The formation of the political parties had been more of a phenomenon after independence in Northeast India. Earlier, there were organizations which articulated the interest of tribes and even took the role of political parties. The Naga club had emerged as early as 1918 to protect the interests of the Nagas, and so was the concern of the Mizo Union in Mizoram. There was a similar concern in Meghalaya and other parts of tribal regions of Northeast India. However, soon after independence, it took distinct political turn in Nagaland. The Naga National Council and later the Nationalist Socialist Council of Nagaland spearheaded the political movement which took the form of armed struggle later. In other parts of the region, tribal political parties emerged following the autonomy movement by the hill tribes dating late 1960s. The All People Hill Leaders Conference (APHLC), under which the autonomy movement took shape in the region, was the precursor of the regional party in Mizoram and Meghalaya. Of these, the Hill

State Peoples Democratic Party in Meghalaya has been notable. Soon thereafter, there has been rise of other political formations in different parts of the region. The United Tribal Nationalist Front, the Assam Tribal Leagues in Assam, Tripura Upajati Juba Samiti, Tripura National Volunteers in Tripura, Naga National Democratic Party, Nagaland Peoples Party, Nagaland People Council, Arunachal Pradesh People's Party and so on. Some of the parties of the earlier phase are still a force to reckon with, some have become redundant and their places have taken by different ones. In fact, many more tribal parties are visible today in Northeast (Chaube, 1973; Kumar, 1995). The regional political formation has combined the electoral democratic politics with larger democratic movements in addressing the issues of the people. As to why such tribal politics has succeeded in Northeast and not in Central India is a different story which has not been explored except by Surajit Sinha but on a synoptic manner (Sinha, 1972).

POLITICAL SPACE AND ELECTORAL POLITICS: RESERVED CONSTITUENCY

Participation of tribes in modern political institutions such as the state is traced to the Government of India Act 1935. The participation has, however, been marginal. The nationalist leadership took cognizance of it and aimed at addressing these limitations. Accordingly, it made a special provision for their representation in the Parliament and state legislatures under Articles 330 and 332 of the constitution. The share of representation was worked out in proportions to size of the tribal population. It is in keeping with this principle that seats have been reserved for them at different levels of legislative bodies such as Parliament, state legislature, municipality and gram panchayats. Such reservation has been worked out in terms of reserved constituencies. As seats reserved in

the Parliament and state legislatures are determined on the size of the population, reserved seats/reserved constituencies are allocated to each state for Parliament and state legislatures in keeping with size of the tribal population in the respective states. The same principle was followed for state legislature, namely, representation of tribes in proportion to the populations of tries in the concerned states (Xaxa, 2019a). In 1991, there were 41 tribal representatives in the Parliament constituting 7.5 per cent share of the total seats. In state legislatures the percentage of seats earmarked for them varies corresponding to size of their respective population in the concerned state. Interestingly, at the state, level their share has been as large as 13.2 per cent of the total seats. The larger share of tribes has been mainly due to the existence of tribal states of Nagaland, Meghalaya, Mizoram and Arunachal Pradesh (Government of India, 2000).

The reserve constituencies for the Parliament has been worked out in keeping with size of the tribal population for the country as a whole as per the national census and the same is distributed among different states as per the size of the tribal population in different states. Following this, reserved constituencies are worked out keeping in mind the geographical concentration of tribal population in the states. Based on this principle, the reserved constituencies are drawn by the Delimitation Commission, instituted by the Parliament as per the Delimitation Act. Delimitation literally means the act or process of fixing limits or boundaries of territorial constituencies in the country having legislative body or bodies. The job of Delimitation is assigned to higher body known as the Delimitation Commission. In India such, Delimitation Commission has been constituted four times, in 1952 under the Delimitation Commission Act 1952, in 1963 under the Delimitation Commission Act of 1962, in 1973 under the Delimitation Commission Act of 1972 and in 2002 under the Delimitation Commission Act of 2002 (Ambagudia, 2019; Xaxa, 2019b).

The latest Delimitation Commission, set up under the Delimitation Act, 2002, was entrusted with the task of readjusting all parliamentary and assembly constituencies in the country in all the states of India, except the state of Jammu and Kashmir, on the basis of population ascertained in 2001 Census. Government of India under provision 10B of the Delimitation Act, 2002, nullified the final order of the delimitation commission for the state of Jharkhand. Similarly, the government passed four separate orders under provision 10A of the Delimitation Act, 2002, deferring the delimitation exercise in the four North-eastern states of Assam, Arunachal Pradesh, Manipur and Nagaland. Elections in these states were held as per the delimitation of parliamentary and assembly constituencies order 1976 (Xaxa, 2019b).

As per the order issued by the Delimitation Commission in 2008, of the 543 seats in the Parliament, 412 are general seats, 84 reserved for scheduled castes (SCs) and 47 for the scheduled tribes (STs). The 47 parliamentary constituencies reserved for tribal population constitutes 8.65 per cent of the total parliamentary constituencies of 543. It is important to note that though the Parliament has frozen the addition of additional constituencies till 2026, it has made internal arrangement to address the tribal population strength and reserved some additional seats for the tribals from the existing seats of 543 without increasing the total elected seats of the Lok Sabha. As per the earlier Delimitation of Parliamentary and Assembly Constituencies Order 1976, tribes had only 41 seats out of the total of 543 elected seats in the lower house of the Parliament. For the assembly, the share of tribes is contingent on the size of the tribal population of the concerned state.

Whereas the principle underlying reservation is by and large clear and consistent, the same is not clear and consistent with states such as Nagaland, Mizoram, Meghalaya and Arunachal Pradesh, generally referred as tribal states. Since tribals in these states form numerical majority, it is assumed that tribal would invariably be elected even if the constituency remains unreserved. Yet there are anomalies. In Mizoram and Meghalaya, the two numerical tribal dominant states, the three parliamentary constituencies are reserved for tribes. In contrast, the other two tribal dominated states of Nagaland and Arunachal Pradesh with three parliamentary seats are general constituencies. In theory, the general constituency opens up the same for anyone to contest. Interestingly, as per the Parliament and Assembly Constituency Order 1976, the two parliamentary seats in Meghalaya were general but were converted into reserved constituency as per the Parliamentary and Assembly Constituencies Order, 2008. Paradoxically, however, all assembly seats excepting one are reserved for tribes in Arunachal Pradesh. Similarly except one seat each, all seats in Nagaland and Mizoram are reserved seats. In case of Meghalaya, 55 out of 60 seats are reserved for tribes and five for the general population. It is also interesting to note that Nagaland with much higher population than that of Arunachal has only one parliamentary seat as against two for the Arunachal Pradesh. Thus, there are certain anomalies and reasons for it are far from clear.

To understand the anomaly, one may have to fall back on the principle of allocation of parliamentary reserved constituency. When states compete for ST-reserved constituencies, they do so on the basis of their share to the total tribal population in the country (Ambagudia, 2019, p. 48). The tribal population in North-eastern states constitute very small size of the total tribal population of the country. Hence, it is possible that the small North-eastern states in population terms are exempted from the application of population criteria while allocating the Lok Sabha seats (Ambagudia, 2019, p. 49). In Meghalaya, as per the Delimitation of Parliamentary and Assembly Constituencies Order, 1976, the parliamentary seats were general but as per the Delimitation of Parliamentary and

Assembly Constituencies Order 2008, they have been turned into the reserved constituencies. Paradoxically, however, all assembly seats, except one, are tribal seats in Arunachal Pradesh. Similarly, except one seat each, all seats in Nagaland and Mizoram are ST-reserved seats. In Meghalaya, 5 seats are general and 55 are reserved. It is also interesting to note that Nagaland has much higher population than that of Arunachal Pradesh but it has only one parliamentary as against two for the Arunachal Pradesh (Xaxa, 2019b).

POLITICAL REPRESENTATION AND TRIBAL ISSUES

The representation of tribes in the Parliament and state assemblies has been largely through the political parties. Though their representation is visible across tribes, they have formed the strong support base of certain political parties. Tribes have been for a very long period rallied solidly behind the Indian National Congress. They have also been the part of the left political parties. Since the last two decades, however, there has been a major shift in favour of the Bhartiya Janata Party (BJP). Their representation through the regional parties too has been growing. However, the representation especially at the state level beside mediation through other parties is also being mediated through the parties formed by tribals themselves. The Jharkhand Party in erstwhile state of Bihar has been one such example. In the first general election of post-independent India, the party has won as many as 25 out of 35 seats reserved for tribes in the Bihar assembly. In addition it has won five seats from the general and two from the SC reserved constituencies. In fact, with 32 seats, it was the main opposition party in the Bihar assembly (Tirkey, 2002). The support base, however, gradually dwindled and got split into a number of a number of different factions. Since then the tribal political parties

have declined. It recent years, however, there seems to be a sign of revival of tribal political parties. The Gondwana Prajatantrik Party referred above is an example. In contrast, the representation through regional parties formed by tribes themselves is strong in the Northeast region. Here too, the tribal political parties have either got split into different groups. In addition, there has been formation of new political parties. The tribal regional parties in Northeast India have come to stay. They have been running governments in many states for quite some times. In fact, the national parties like the BJP have been trying to make space as junior partners in the government. Barring the Eastern and North-eastern region, the presence of tribal regional parties have been absent in the past but have begun to emerge as referred above in western India

Despite their share and participation in the Parliament and state legislatures due to reservation, tribes have not been able to make their presence felt at the national and even at state level except the Northeast India. This is so even in states where their numerical strength is larger than Dalits. Madhya Pradesh, Odisha and Gujarat may be taken as illustrations. It is difficult to identify one national-level leadership of some significance from among the tribes. Of course at the state level, barring the northeast tribal states there have been Chief Ministers from among the tribes in states like Gujarat and Odisha and more recently in Jharkhand and Chhattisgarh. Notwithstanding that, place of tribals in over all political articulation, state agenda making and share in office remain weak and tenuous. This is so due to both weak political mobilizations of the tribals on the one hand and discrimination against them by the dominant community on the other. They have remained excluded from the highest level of decision-making bodies both at the level of government and political parties. Hence, wherever there has been a strong political awareness and mobilization among them, the political mobilization has invariably assumed the form of demand for some kind of autonomy.

Unlike in services and education, where the participation of tribes is examined in respect of their share in proportion to size of the population, there arises no such problem in respect of participation in political institution. Generally, there exists congruence between what is stipulated as the share and what is actually held. However, this merely points to formal equality, namely, equality of opportunity at the level of entry. However, there are two questions which remain to be explored. One is the extent of their participation in the more substantive structure of the political institution such as governments in the form of council of ministers, rank of minister, types of the ministry or membership of committees and subcommittees formed by the Parliament and state legislatures. The other is the issue of their performance in Parliament and state legislature and as well as the offices they hold as ministers or other positions either in the government or the legislatures. Over the question on what should be the dimensions of performances on which they are to be evaluated, there has hardly been any concern and systematic discussion. The appointments to position mentioned above may be contingent on the nature of their participation, articulation and mobilization process. Hence, they may be taken as the dimensions on which the relative performance of the ministers and legislators may be assessed. There are, however, no data at our disposal on the aspect corresponding to the ones we have on service and education

TRIBES AND LOCAL LEVEL POLITICS

Tribes at the national level form a tiny minority. At the state level, the numerical position is relatively better as compared to the national level. Nevertheless, they form a minority. Hence, structurally they have a little space to push their agenda. Of course, there are states like Mizoram, Meghalaya, Nagaland and Arunachal Pradesh in North-eastern India who do not suffer from this problem. However,

at the level of local governance, tribes do form a majority in large number of districts, blocks and villages. Hence, at the level of local self-government, they may have a better chance to take up their agenda. However, even at this level, they constitute minority in a large number of districts, blocks and villages. India has a long history of village self-governance. This had been an integral feature of tribal self-governance too.

Under the colonial rule, tribes were allowed to govern themselves as per their traditional system. Even when the British introduced the local self-government institutions following the Government of India Act 1919, this was not extended into backward tribal tracts. Rather tribes were allowed to govern as per their customary practices. This had been no longer the case in post-independence India. As a consequence, the traditional institution of local governance has been witnessed to much change. Changes have mainly been due to factors coming from outside and for these two they have been the most critical. One is the role of the state and the other is that of Christianity and Hinduism. Both these have affected the traditional social system including traditional institution in a significant way. The presence of Christianity and Hinduism led to much acculturation among the tribes and paved the way for division of the same people along religious lines. Members of the same tribe are thus today divided into as Christians, Hindus or Sarnas on the basis of their religious affiliation and practices. Needless to say that change in religious affiliation led to some changes in the mode of their social organizations as well as social norms. Those converted to Christianity or acculturated to Hinduism abandoned many of their tribal customs, norms and values. They became part of organization, which has wider social base. Segregated community life became one of the entrenched practices. This led to a regulation of life in the village not in terms of common norms and values as was the case earlier but in terms of norms and values specific to each religion. Notwithstanding such changes, there was still some continuity with the tradition. However, division of the people along religious lines did pose a serious problem to the traditional institution of local governance.

The other powerful factor of change has been the state intervention through its laws, rules and policies, especially in respect of land and forest, the life support system of the tribal people. Not only in the context of land and forest but even in the context of local governance there has been an intervention by the state in tribal people who inhabited areas through the introduction of the Panchayati Raj System. Of course, some tampering with traditional institution of local governance did take place under the British, though the overall ethos was to allow it to function it as per the traditional customary practices. Thus, the most serious jolt to the traditional institution of governance came from the state created institution of the Panchayati Raj in the post-independent India. This deeply impacted the traditional institution of governance prevailing among the tribal people. With the introduction of the Panchayati Raj Institution (PRI) by the state, a new institution of local governance was created side by side the traditional institution of governance. Since the former had state resources at its disposal for development programmes in the village, its presence undermined the traditional institution. Yet it faced manifold hurdles and the overall development programmes in general suffered. One of the reasons as to why the PRI failed is that tribal people took it as an alien institution. They did not identify themselves with it. There is no doubt that there has been a recognition of the distinct practice of traditional system of governance among the tribal people. There was also an attempt to incorporate traditional elements into it. However, such attempt was mere symbolic. The net result is that in the presence of state mandated PRIs, the traditional system has not been able to stand and it has slowly slipped away from the public domain. This, of course, does not mean that they have withered

away. They do exist but the sphere of their jurisdiction is now very limited. It is mainly confined to social and cultural practices. It plays little role in development initiatives and activities.

Unlike the special constitutional provision of representation for STs and SCs in the Parliament and state legislature, there was no such provision in case of local self-government institutions prior to the enactment of 73rd Constitutional Amendment Act. It was left to the states to enact laws and regulations as they deemed fit. The result was that hardly any state in India, with Maharashtra as an exception, made provision for reservation for SCs and STs in local self-governing institutions. Other states extended this benefit only after the amendments to their PRIs Acts following the 73rd Amendment to the constitution. The 73rd Amendment Act makes reservation of seats for the STs, the SCs and women in the PRIs mandatory. Reservation of seats both at the level of the legislative bodies and the office was made obligatory. The reservations in various bodies were earmarked in proportion to the respective size of the population of the SCs and the STs in a particular panchayat area. Further, such seats are to be allotted by rotation to different constituencies in a panchayat and one-third of the seats from within the categories are being reserved for women. The access to the rural power structure for the people from the weaker section of the society including the tribes enlarged the social base of the PRIs. The experience prior to the 73rd Amendment Act has shown that the members of the dominant communities had controlled the local power structure. The members of the weaker section could hardly make any dent into the power structure. The reservation has made the PRIs representative of the village community at the level of panchayats.

The 73rd Constitution Amendment Act came into effect from 24 April 1993. Hence, in keeping with this amendment, the provincial states either came up with new Acts or brought about necessary amendments to the existing Acts. In case of the tribal population, these state Acts were in force only in those areas which were outside the provision of the fifth and sixth schedule of the Indian Constitution. In the sixth schedule area, there was already a provision of local self-governance in the form of the Autonomous District Council. However, there has been no such provision (viz. local self-governance) in the sixth schedule areas. The 73rd Constitutional Amendment exempted the fifth schedule areas from the mandatory provisions of Part IX of the Constitution with a hope that these areas could be left free for evolution of their own system of self-governance or continuation of their traditional panchayats or similar bodies. Accordingly, the provision of the Panchayats (extension to the Scheduled Areas) Act, 1996 came into force in fifth schedule areas from 24 December 1996.

For participation of tribal people at national-, state- and local-level politics, the provision of reservation has been made for the tribal people in the constitution. This is a pointer to the fact that representation through reservation is critical for political participation of communities on the margin of society such as the tribes. Hence, it becomes worth exploring if they would have been able to participate if there were no such provisions. The answer is very unlikely. It is the constitutional compulsion that constrains most of the political parties and governments to provide space from people from tribal communities. Interestingly, however, once basic minimum has been put in place, tribes on the whole have often been deprived of position of importance in the government as well as political parties. Such situation cuts across political parties of all persuasions. This is not to argue that only tribes can represent the interests of the tribes. Even non-tribes can do and probably they can do more effectively than tribes because of their better articulation, network and mobilizing and manoeuvring capacity.

More often than not, however, there has been wedge (social, political, economic and cultural) between tribes and non-tribes and the interests of tribes have often been sacrificed in the interest of others or the general interest. Even in case of the panchayat in the fifth scheduled areas, the provisions of Panchayat (Extension to Schedule Areas) Act at the state level has been framed by almost all the states in such a way that very provisions of the Act and its spirit have been completely diluted. In short, the state Acts without exception defeat the very purpose of the Central Act.

CONCLUSION

Reservation was extended to tribes with a view to integrate them in the so-called mainstream of Indian life. The Indian state has been greatly successful in this mission. Tribes too have made some gains but not so much in the direction of protecting their rights over land, forest and other resources or in making substantive contribution in the decision-making process but in the direction of raising the political aspiration of the tribal people. The political empowerment has been the major gain of the policy of reservation in politics. This was not an intended consequence but arose as an unintended consequence. Indeed provisions laid down in PRIs through 73rd Amendment and the Panchayat Act 1996, especially the latter has been an outcome of this process of political empowerment at work among the tribes. It is not at all surprising that the working of the provisions in those Acts have led to intense conflicts and tensions between tribes and non-tribes at the grass root politics. In short, unlike in pre-independence era when tribes were thought as unable to represent themselves, tribes today have come to a stage where they are not only able to represent but probably able to do so even without the provision of reservation.

REFERENCES

Abercrombie, N., Stephen, H., & Turner, B. S. (1984). *The penguin dictionary of sociology*. Harmondsworth: Penguin Books.

Ambagudia, J. (2019). Scheduled tribes, reserved constituencies and political reservation in India. *Journal of Social Inclusion Studies, 5*(1), 44–58.

Bordia, R. (2019, April 27). Ground report: How the Bharatiya Tribal Party Is making Its mark in Rajasthan. *The Wire*. Retrieved from https://thewire.in/politics/elections-2019-bharatiya-tribal-party-rajasthan.

Bosu Mullick, S. (1993). Jharkhand movement: A historical analysis. In M. Miri (Ed.), *Continuity and Change in Tribal Society*. Shimla: Indian Institute of Advanced Study.

Bosu Mullick, S. (2003). Introduction. In R. D. Munda & S. Bosu Mullick (Eds.), *The Jharkhand Movement: Indigenous Peoples' Struggle for Autonomy in India* (pp. iv–xvii). Copenhagen: International Work Group for Indigenous Affairs.

Chaube, S. K. (1973). *Hill politics of north-east India*. New Delhi: Orient Longman.

Das Gupta, S. (2011). *Adivasis and the raj: Socio-economic transition of the Hos, 1820–1932*. New Delhi: Orient Black Swan.

Desai, I. P. (1983). The Tribal autonomy movement in South Gujarat. In K.S. Singh (Ed.), *Tribal Movements in India. Vol.1* (pp. 243–259). New Delhi: Manohar.

Gerth, H. & Mills, C. W. (1970). *Character and social structure (from Max Weber: Essays in sociology)*. London: Routledge& Kegan Paul.

Government of India. (2000). *Tribes in India (A data sheet)*. New Delhi: Planning Commission.

Iyer, G. K. & Maharaj, R. N. (1986). Agrarian movements in tribal Bihar (Dhanbad) 1972–80. In A. R. Desai (Ed.), *Agrarian Struggles in India after Independence* (pp. 330–361). New Delhi: Oxford University Press.

Iyer, G. K. & Maharaj, R. N. (1986). Agrarian movements in tribal Bihar (Dhanbad) 1972–80. In A. R. Desai (Ed.), *Agrarian Struggles in India after Independence* (pp. 330–361). New Delhi: Oxford University Press.

Kumar, B. B. (1995). *Tension and conflict in north east India*. New Delhi: Cosmo Publications.

Misra B. P. (2012, November 22–24). *Keynote address: Draft at national seminar on governance, socio-economic disparity and unrest in the 'scheduled areas' of India*. Tata Institute of Social Sciences, Guwahati Campus.

Poyam, A. (2015, December 18). 10 Things you need to know about 'Gondwana State' demand. *Adivasi Resurgence*. Retrieved from http://adivasiresurgence.com/2015/12/18/10-things-you-need-to-know-about-gondwana-state-demand/.

Raghavaiah, V. R. (1979). Tribal revolts in chronological order, 1778–1971. In A. R. Desai (Ed.), *Agrarian Struggles in India after Independence* (pp. 12–22). New Delhi: Oxford University Press.

Singh, K. S. (1983). Tribal autonomy movements in Chotanagpur. In K. S. Singh (Ed.), *Tribal Movements in India* (Volume II, pp. 1–29). New Delhi: Manohar.

Singh, K. S. (1986). Agrarian dimension in tribal movements. In A. R. Desai (Ed.), *Agrarian Struggles in India after Independence* (pp. 145–167). New Delhi: Oxford University Press.

Singh, K. S. (2002). *Birsa Munda and his movement, 1872–1901: A study of a millenarian movement in Chotanagpur*. Kolkata: Seagull Books.

Sinha, S. (1972). Tribal solidarity movements in India: A review. In K. S. Singh (Ed.), *Tribal Situation in India*. Shimla: Indian Institute of Advanced Study.

Streumer, P. (2016). *A land of their own. Samuel Richard Tickell and the formation of the autonomous Ho country in Jharkhand 1818–1842*. The historian's edition. Houten: Wakkamqn.

Thapar, R. & Siddique, H. M. (2003). Chotanagpur: The pre-colonial and colonial situation. In R. D. Munda & S. Bosu Mullick (Eds.), *The Jharkhand Movement: Indigenous Peoples' Struggle for Autonomy in India* (pp. 31–72). Copenhagen: International Work Group for Indigenous Affairs.

Tirkey, A. (2002). *Jharkhand movement: A study of its dynamics*. New Delhi: All India Coordinating Forum of the Adivasi/Indigenous Peoples.

Vashum (2000). *Nagas' right to self determination*. New Delhi: Mittal Publications.

Verma, R. C. (1990). *Indian tribes through the ages*. New Delhi: Ministry of Information and Broadcasting.

Xaxa, V. (2008). *State, society and tribes: Issues in post-colonial in India*. Delhi: Pearson Education.

Xaxa, V. (2019a). Tribal politics in Jharkhand. *Economic and Political Weekly, 54* (28), 10–11.

Xaxa, V. (2019b, September 26). Tribals in India have been unseated by a breach of trust. *The Telegraph*. Retrieved from https://www.telegraphindia.com/opinion/tribals-in-india-have-been-unseated-by-a-breach-of-trust/cid/1707296

Tribal Politics
at the National Level

Scheduled Tribes, Reserved Constituencies and Political Reservation in India*

Jagannath Ambagudia

INTRODUCTION

In recent times, studies on the tribal population in India have attracted scholarly attention from academic circles (Pati, 2011; Radhakrishnan, 2016; Shah, 2010; Sundar & Madan, 2016; Xaxa, 2008). However, most of the studies focus on the historical, sociological and anthropological perspectives, paying little heed to the political dynamics of the tribal communities. This does not mean that such accounts are overtly polemical, there are exceptions like the contributions of Galanter (1984), McMillan (2005), Xaxa (2005), and so on. Galanter (1984), for instance, conceded that the enactment and practice of political reservation have led to the emergence of political elites among the tribal communities, which otherwise would not have been possible. McMillan (2005), on the other hand, focused on various dynamics of electoral reservations that have had ramifications on

the tribal communities in India. Xaxa (2005) traces the sociological understanding of the political dynamics of the tribal society by addressing the incompatible experiences of tribal people in the context of political reservation. Nonetheless, the existing curriculum of Indian politics in different universities, and some of the fundamental readings on Indian politics such as Jayal and Mehta (2011), have paid little or no attention to tribes in comparison to other social groups.

The chapter begins by focusing on the tribes' location and their representation in the colonial political system, the paradoxes embedded in the colonial pattern of representation, and their implications on the tribal people. It explores the criteria employed for reserving a constituency and describes the journey from a multi-member constituency to a single-member constituency. It also briefly discusses constitutional provisions by narrowing down to political reservation, impact of

* This chapter was previously published in *Journal of Social Inclusion Studies*, 5(1), 2019, 44–58.

Delimitation of Parliamentary and Assembly Constituencies Order, 1976, and changes that occurred because of the enforcement of the Delimitation of Parliamentary and Assembly Constituencies Order, 2008, at the national and state levels with statistical evidence.

TRIBES IN COLONIAL POLITICAL SYSTEM

The tribal society has a long history of self-governance, own conception of democracy, autonomy and tribal lifeworld. It was structured around communitarian and egalitarian democratic values, thereby facilitating the tribal lifeworld. This was probably one of the most important reasons why the tribal representatives in the Constituent Assembly, such as J. J. M. Nichols Roy and Jaipal Singh, apparently advocated a 'tribalized' form of democracy in post-colonial India. The advent of Britishers in India challenged their autonomy, patterns of governance, and notion of democracy by total disregard of their lifeworld. As a result, many tribal communities launched insurrections against the British. The colonial forces, however, followed the confrontational path and suppressed tribal revolts by military means and brought them under a single political regime through coercion, war and conquest. This authoritative integration of the tribals into the mainstream political system not only undermined the tribal practice of democracy but also imposed new political settings that were hitherto alien to them (Wessendorf, 2001, p. 10). Subsequently, the tribal communities became the part of the colonial political system.

Due to the exclusionary nature of colonial political system, Indians persistently demanded popular participation in the decision-making process to ensure that they got adequate representation in the executive councils of the governor-general and the governors along with an expansion of the central and provincial councils (Saksena, 1981, p. xi).

Under the Morley-Minto reforms (1909), the British introduced group representation of various interests as identified by them through nominations/elections. Each measure in the direction of a popular government and representative institutions was accompanied by corresponding reservations to protect the rights and interests of minorities (Saksena, 1981, p. xiii–xiv). It is interesting to note that the British treated Sikhs, Anglo-Indians, Indian Christians, the depressed classes and the backward tribes as minorities. The protective frameworks enacted for these minorities included separate representation in legislatures and reserved quotas in public services, among others.

The British introduced the tribes to electoral politics for the first time under the Government of India (GOI) Act, 1935 (Bosu Mullick, 2001, p. 104). While granting provincial autonomy to India in 1935, the British recognized the need for protecting 'depressed communities' via reserved seats in assemblies. As a result, the Act reserved a certain number of seats for different categories of people. Under the fifth schedule of the GOI Act, 1935, seats were reserved for Muslims, Christians and Europeans in the provincial legislative councils. While there were no reservations for the scheduled castes (SCs) and backward tribes in the provincial legislative councils (GOI Act, 1935, p. 246), the provincial legislative assemblies had some seats reserved for them. Table 2.1 shows that 24 out of 1,585 seats were reserved for the backward tribes in the provincial legislative assemblies. Despite their share of 2.45 per cent of the total population by 1931 (Maharatna, 2015, p. 196), only 1.51 per cent of the seats were reserved for the tribes, thereby indicating their disproportionate representation in the decision-making bodies of the colonial political system.

The colonial pattern of representation led to a paradoxical situation in Indian politics. On the one hand, it appears that seat allotment to the backward tribes was influenced by the concentration of tribal communities in certain pockets, such as the erstwhile provinces of

Table 2.1   Reservation of Seats in Provincial Legislative Assembly

Provinces	Total Seats	General Seats Reserved for Scheduled Castes	Seats for Representatives of Backward Areas and Tribes
Madras	215	30	1
Bombay	175	15	1
Bengal	250	30	—
United Provinces	228	20	—
Punjab	175	8	—
Bihar	152	15	7
Central Provinces and Berar	112	20	1
Assam	108	7	9
North Western Frontier Province	50	—	—
Odisha	60	6	5
Sindh	60	—	—
Total	1585	151	24

Source: Government of India Act (1935, p. 245).

Bihar, Assam and Odisha, where seven, nine and five seats, respectively, were reserved for them under the GOI Act, 1935. On the other hand, colonial pattern of proportional representation was far from tenable. For instance, the backward tribes of the Central Provinces and Berar constituted as much as 20 per cent of the population (Ghosh, 1987, p. 2), but only one seat was reserved for them. Similarly, only one seat each in Madras and Bombay provincial legislative assemblies was allocated for the tribes. In the Federal Assembly, there was no reservation for backward tribes.[1] Though reservation for minorities accompanied every stage of a decision-making process, this was not the case for the tribes. The British considered the demonstrative capabilities of the tribal communities as the basis for ensuring tribal representation in the decision-making processes (Xaxa, 2005, p. 120). They developed a stereotype approach towards the tribal people, which attributed to the non-availability of capable tribal people from some areas such as Odisha to represent them (McMillan, 2005, p. 117). In short, the tribal communities were disproportionately represented in the political sphere during the colonial period. Their underrepresentation apparently provided a ground for debating the proportional representation of the indigenous people and indicated the need for reserved constituencies in independent India.

TRIBES IN POST-COLONIAL POLITICAL SYSTEM

During the colonial period, neither the British nor the national leadership recognized tribal politics as a distinct political formation, thereby opening the window for the question of difference in the post-colonial India (Kapila, 2013, p. 106). After Independence, therefore, the Indian state began to negotiate with tribal communities as a distinct category. The negotiation process emerged on a discourse on what should be the basis of tribal political representation in India. The discourse arose on the theoretical underpinning of representation grounded in who should represent the tribes in post-colonial India. The Constituent

[1] In the Federal Assembly, out of 250 seats, 105 were general, 19 were SCs, 6 were Sikhs, 82 were Muslims, 8 each were Europeans and Indian Christians, 11 were representatives of commerce and industry, 7 landholders and 10 were representatives of labour (GOI Act, 1935, p. 220).

Assembly deliberated on these critical questions as a part of the mandate in order to draft the constitution for independent India. In the process, it considered the claims and demands of different competing social groups to protect and promote their interests (Bajpai, 2015; Jha, 2003, 2004; McMillan, 2005; Rao, 1967, 1968; Saksena, 1981). At the end of a long-drawn debate in the Constituent Assembly, it was resolved that only the tribal people would protect and promote the rights and interests of their communities. Thus, it adopted various provisions for group representation in the constitution.

DEMARCATING THE RESERVED CONSTITUENCY

The nature of group representation in the post-Independence period changed with the declaration of certain constituencies as reserved ones. In Indian politics, declaring reserved constituencies has always been a matter of concern since Independence. The Parliament, mainly through the Delimitation Commission, demarcates the reserved constituencies. The first decade of democratic practices, however, began with confusion and uncertainty concerning the nature of tribal representation in India because of the practice of double-/multi-member constituency that affected the electoral system between 1952 and 1961 (Ambagudia, 2019, p. 160).

The Delimitation Commission, thus, adopted distinct standards to declare a single- or double-member constituency. A single-member constituency having more than half of the tribal population was declared as an scheduled tribe (ST)-reserved constituency. Nonetheless, the constituency, which had a substantial number of tribal population but less than a majority, was declared as a double-member constituency, with one seat reserved for the tribes. The size of a double-member constituency was twice as large as single-member constituency. The electoral process followed the block vote or distributive vote system in a double-member constituency, where each voter had two votes but could not cast more than one vote for a single candidate. The double-member constituency, however, did not reflect two independent contests. In a double-member constituency, a candidate securing the highest vote under the first-past-the-post system among the tribal contestants was first declared as the winner. Other tribal candidates were also eligible for general seats, and in fact, many of them were elected from time to time (Weiner & Field, 1975, pp. 87–88). For instance, 1 and 4, 3 and 11 ST candidates were elected to the Parliament and state assemblies in 1952 and 1957 elections, respectively (Prasad, 2001, p. 77).

However, the Election Commission of India saw the overlapping representation of tribal people from the double-member constituency as a threat to the political representation of non-tribal people (McMillan, 2005, p. 195). Hence, the practice of double-member constituency came to an end with the enactment of the Two Member Constituencies (abolition) Act, 1961, which emphasized that India should opt for single-member constituencies due to the size of the double-member constituency and the overlapping representation of the tribals (Jensenius, 2012, p. 378). As a result, India adopted a unique method of defining or drawing the reserved constituency. The drawing of an ST-reserved constituency was relatively more straightforward than the SC-reserved constituency.[2] The former was determined on the basis of the compact inhabitation of the tribal population in certain tracts.

---

[2] The SC-reserved constituency was determined on the basis of two criteria: higher concentration of SC population and geographical dispersion of seats. The second criterion was applied due to relatively less compact nature of SC population, which invoked severe criticism against the Delimitation Commission due to the use of its discretionary power to define the dispersal criteria (Alam, 2015; McMillan, 2005, 2008, p. 76).

Formula 1: Entitlement of ST seats in the Lok Sabha

$$= \frac{\text{Total tribal population of the country}}{\text{Total population of the country}}$$
$$\times \text{Total elected seats of the Lok Sabha}$$

Formula 2: Entitlement of ST seats for the state

$$= \frac{\text{Total tribal population of the state}}{\text{Total tribal population of the country}}$$
$$\times \text{Total ST seats of the Lok Sabha}$$

Formula 3: Entitlement of ST seats in the Assembly

$$= \frac{\text{Total tribal population of the state}}{\text{Total population of the state}}$$
$$\times \text{Total seats of the Assembly}$$

Formula 4: Entitlement of ST seats for the district

$$= \frac{\text{Total tribal population of the district}}{\text{Total tribal population of the state}}$$
$$\times \text{Total ST seats of the Assembly}$$

As a standard procedure, the Delimitation Commission determines the entitlement of ST seats based on the proportion of tribal population to the total population of the country according to the preceding census against the backdrop of the existing number of constituencies. The number of ST-reserved parliamentary constituencies in India can be determined by following Formula 1. Based on the population strength (2001 census), 47 parliamentary seats are reserved for STs in India. The 47 seats are to be distributed among the states as per the proportion of ST population of the state to the total ST population of the country (Formula 2). However, on the flip side, this has denied tribal parliamentary constituencies to some of the highest tribal concentrated states in proportion to state population. For instance, Nagaland has 89.1 per cent of the tribal population in proportion to state population (2001 census) but they do not have any ST parliamentary constituency. This perhaps can be explained that though they have the highest concentration of tribal

population in their respective states in a competition for ST-reserved assembly seats, they lag behind other states in the competition for reserved parliamentary seats due to the lack of a substantial percentage of tribal population in proportion to the total tribal population of the country. For instance, according to the 2001 census, the tribal people of Nagaland constitute only 2.1 per cent of the total tribal population, respectively, but the figures are far lower than other states. However, some of the small north-eastern states are exempted from the application of population criteria pertaining to their seat allocations in the Lok Sabha (McMillan, 2008, p. 77).

Similar formulae have also been adopted to distribute ST seats in state assemblies. The entitlement of assembly seats can be determined by following the principle of proportion of ST population to the total population of the state multiplied by total seats in the legislative assembly (Formula 3). Further, entitlement of ST seats for a district is determined by the principle of proportion of ST population of the district to the total tribal population of the state multiplied by the total ST assembly seats (Formula 4). After determining the entitlement of reserved seats for the state at the parliamentary level and for the district at the assembly level, constituencies having the highest number of tribal population are declared as ST-reserved constituencies.

However, Parliament has frozen the equalization of constituency population since 1971, which has further been extended up to 2026 under the 84th Constitution Amendment Act, 2002, and will be effective only after the 2031 census. Such initiative has eventually affected the quantum of ST-reserved constituencies in India (Lublin, 2014). Based on the fast decadal growth rate of the tribal population (Table 2.2),[3] the reapportionment of constituencies between states has eventually denied the highest tribal concentrated states to have

---

[3] The decadal growth rate was 24.39, 23.18 and 20.01 per cent in 1991; 23.25, 18.40 and 17.86 per cent in 2001; and 21.30, 15.70 and 17.64 per cent in 2011 among the STs, SCs and total population, respectively (Table 2.2).

Table 2.2   Decadal Growth Rate of Population in India

Year	ST	SC	Total
1991	24.39	23.01	20.01
2001	23.25	18.40	17.86
2011	21.30	15.70	17.64

Source: Rangacharyulu & Kanth (2017, p. 444).

some additional ST-reserved constituencies. However, steps have been undertaken to allocate proportionate seats to tribes based on the 2001 census by readjusting the constituencies within each state under the Delimitation of Parliament and Assembly Constituencies Order 2008 without allocating additional seats to states (Tables 2.3 and 2.5).

CONSTITUTIONAL PROVISIONS AND POLITICAL RESERVATION

Democratic rights have been extended to tribes by granting equal citizenship status. Nonetheless, the framers of the Indian constitution realized that considering the history of social discrimination and marginalization, a mere extension of citizenship rights to the indigenous people would not ensure their adequate representation in the political sphere. Hence, institutional mechanisms were developed to ensure their adequate representation in democratic politics. Consequently, the Indian state adopted the 'quota system' for the STs in the form of reserved seats in politics in proportion to their numerical strength to the total population as per the latest preceding census. According to Article 330, seats shall be reserved for the STs in the lower house of

the Indian Parliament (Lok Sabha). Further, under Article 332 of the Indian constitution, seats are reserved for STs in the legislative assembly of every state. The number of seats reserved shall be based on the principle of proportionality.

The provision of electoral reservation addresses discrimination emerging out of their exclusion from formal political institutions in order to accommodate differences within the political sphere. It not only aims to widen the base of Indian democratic politics by assuring adequate representation of STs but also enables establishing an inclusive political system. Political reservation is prevalent in India through the prism of 'joint electoral system', as opposed to Dr B. R. Ambedkar's demand for 'separate electorate' for marginalized communities.[4] In the joint electoral system, the contending candidate must belong to the reserved category. The entire electorate, however, participates in the process of electing candidates so qualified. Conforming to the single policy rule that applies to all states, Articles 330 and 332 of the Indian constitution provide for political reservation for STs in the Lok Sabha and State Assemblies, respectively.

The provision of political reservation, however, does not restrict the tribal people from contesting elections from unreserved seats. For instance, 136 tribal candidates contested the 2009 general elections from unreserved constituencies, out of which six even emerged victorious (Government of India, 2009). Similarly, six tribal candidates were elected to the Lok Sabha from unreserved constituencies in the 2014 general election (Government of India, 2014). Electoral reservation, however, has not been extended to the upper houses of the Parliament (Rajya Sabha) and State Assemblies (legislative councils)

---

[4] The notion of separate electorate was one of the most contentious provisions during the 1930s. The GOI Act, 1909 provided separate electorate to the Muslims. The SCs were assured separate electorate under the GOI Acts, 1919 and 1935. Such provisions prompted Ambedkar to demand a separate electorate for the Dalits, where only the Dalits would participate to elect their representatives. This was, however, stiffly resisted by Mahatma Gandhi who took to fast unto death. Consequently, Ambedkar reconsidered his demand and the separate electorate was replaced by a joint electorate with a provision electoral reservation (Galanter, 1984, pp. 18–40).

Table 2.3   State/Union Territory-wise Seats in the Lok Sabha and Their Reservation Status

States and Union Territories	No. of Seats in the House as Constituted in 2004 on the Basis of the Delimitation of Parliamentary and Assembly Constituencies Order, 1976 as Amended from Time to Time				No. of Seats in the House as Subsequently Constituted as per the Delimitation of Parliamentary and Assembly Constituencies Order, 2008		
	Gen.	SC	ST	Total	Gen.	SC	ST
I. States							
Andhra Pradesh	34	6	2	42	32	7	3
Arunachal Pradesh	2	—	—	2	2	—	—
Assam	11	1	2	14	11	1	2
Bihar	33	7	—	40	34	6	—
Chhattisgarh	5	2	4	11	6	1	4
Goa	2	—	—	2	2	—	—
Gujarat	20	2	4	26	20	2	4
Haryana	8	2	—	10	8	2	—
Himachal Pradesh	3	1	—	4	3	1	—
Jammu & Kashmir	6	—	—	6	6	—	—
Jharkhand	8	1	5	14	8	1	5
Karnataka	24	4	—	28	21	5	2
Kerala	18	2	—	20	18	2	—
Madhya Pradesh	20	4	5	29	19	4	6
Maharashtra	41	3	4	48	39	5	4
Manipur	1	—	1	2	1	—	1
Meghalaya	2	—	—	2	—	—	2
Mizoram	—	—	1	1	—	—	1
Nagaland	1	—	—	1	1	—	—
Odisha	13	3	5	21	13	3	5
Punjab	10	3	—	13	9	4	—
Rajasthan	18	4	3	25	18	4	3
Sikkim	1	—	—	1	1	—	—
Tamil Nadu	32	7	—	39	32	7	—
Tripura	1	—	1	2	1	—	1
Uttar Pradesh	63	17	—	80	63	17	—
Uttarakhand	4	1	—	5	4	1	—
West Bengal	32	8	2	42	30	10	2
II. Union Territories							
Andaman & Nicobar Island	1	—	—	1	1	—	—
Chandigarh	1	—	—	1	1	—	—
Dadra & Nagar Haveli	—	—	1	1	—	—	1
Daman & Diu	1	—	—	1	1	—	—
Delhi	6	1	—	7	6	1	—
Lakshadweep	—	—	1	1	—	—	1
Pondicherry	1	—	—	1	1	—	—
Total	423	79	41	543	412	84	47

Source: Government of India (2008, pp. 4–5).

Table 2.4 Social Category-wise Seats in the Lok Sabha and Their Reservation Status

Election	Year	ST	SC	Others[a]	Total[a]
1st Lok Sabha	1952–1957	38 (7.12)	90 (16.88)	405 (75.98)	533
2nd Lok Sabha	1957–1962	36 (6.89)	79 (15.13)	407 (77.96)	522
3rd Lok Sabha	1962–1967	34 (6.46)	87 (16.53)	405 (76.99)	526
4th Lok Sabha	1967–1970	38 (6.92)	85 (15.48)	426 (77.59)	549
5th Lok Sabha	1971–1977	41 (7.45)	84 (15.27)	425 (77.27)	550
6th Lok Sabha	1977–1979	43 (7.74)	82 (14.77)	430 (77.47)	555
7th Lok Sabha	1980–1984	43 (7.62)	87 (15.42)	434 (76.95)	564
8th Lok Sabha	1984–1989	42 (7.43)	84 (14.86)	439 (77.69)	565
9th Lok Sabha	1989–1991	40 (7.51)	80 (15.03)	412 (77.44)	532
10th Lok Sabha	1991–1996	44 (7.97)	81 (14.67)	427 (77.35)	552
11th Lok Sabha	1996–1997	42 (7.65)	81 (14.75)	426 (77.59)	549
12th Lok Sabha	1998–1999	42 (7.72)	80 (14.70)	422 (77.57)	544
13th Lok Sabha	1999–2004	42 (7.42)	83 (14.66)	441 (77.91)	566
14th Lok Sabha	2004–2009	42 (7.19)	83 (14.21)	459 (78.59)	584
15th Lok Sabha	2009–2014	48 (8.60)	84 (15.05)	426 (76.34)	558
16th Lok Sabha	2014	46 (8.64)	83 (15.60)	403 (75.75)	532

Source: Government of India (2020).

[a]Nominated members are excluded.

due to different nature of representation,[5] and the Rajya Sabha was created for maintaining the centre–state relations rather than accommodating diversities.

Electoral reservation is an ad hoc arrangement that ensures adequate representation of tribes in formal political institutions. Initially, it was adopted for 10 years with the rationale that the time frame would help in implementing preferential considerations more effectively, thereby making it easier to evaluate the impact after 10 years. However, in reality, the tenure of political reservation has

continuously been extended since then. It is worthwhile to mention that the time limit was applied to politics only (Article 334) and was not meant for other spheres of reservation such as government employment and education. This can perhaps be explained that once political reservation ceases to exist, the Parliament may amend the constitution easily and strike down the provision of reservation.

Table 2.3 demonstrates that due to the delimitation of constituencies, the quantum of seats reserved for tribes has increased from 41 to 47 in the Lok Sabha. Andhra Pradesh and

[5] It is pertinent to mention that both the houses of Parliament are created for two different purposes. The Lok Sabha (lower house) is created to maintain, protect and promote diversity by representing different social groups in India. The Rajya Sabha (upper house) is, however, created to maintain balance between the centre and states because of the lesser power of states in matters of national importance, thereby maintaining, preserving and promoting the federal character of India state. Accordingly, the electoral processes for both the houses are designed differently corresponding to their contexts of establishment. Consequently, members of Parliament (MPs) of the Lok Sabha and the member of legislative assemblies (MLAs) of the Vidhan Sabhas are directly elected by the people. The Rajya Sabha, however, consists of representatives of states and union territories and members nominated by the president. Unlike the Vidhan Sabha (legislative assembly), the members of the Vidhan Parishad (legislative council) are elected by the members of municipalities, district boards and other local authorities, graduates of universities, persons engaged in teaching and other educational institutions, MLAs and members nominated by the governor. In short, the representatives of the lower houses are more directly responsible to the people than the upper houses.

Madhya Pradesh have gained one additional tribal constituency each, while Karnataka and Meghalaya have benefitted from two tribal seats each. Table 2.4 demonstrates an election-wise representation of social categories in Lok Sabha. Further, Table 2.4 indicates that, during the initial elections, the representation of the tribal people was relatively higher than their numerical strength. This could be due to the practice of double-member constituencies, whereby many tribal candidates were elected from unreserved seats (Prasad, 2001, p. 77; Weiner & Field, 1975, pp. 87–88).

Table 2.5 shows that after delimitation, the number of tribal reserved constituencies has increased from 532 to 554 in State Assemblies. The tribes in Odisha, Tamil Nadu, Uttarakhand and West Bengal have lost one seat each, while Chhattisgarh has lost five ST-reserved constituencies that have now been converted into non-tribal constituencies. On the contrary, 13, 6, 4 and 3 seats have been converted to ST-reserved constituencies in Karnataka, Madhya Pradesh, Andhra Pradesh and Maharashtra, respectively. Gujarat, Kerala and Rajasthan have gained one additional ST-reserved constituency each. The general and SC people have lost one seat each to the tribal people in Bihar. Successive delimitation of constituencies orders have unevenly affected tribal communities at the state level. Although the Delimitation of Parliamentary and Assembly Constituencies Order, 2008 increased the aggregate number of tribal representatives in state assemblies, STs have experienced hope and despair at respective state levels.

Hope and despair of tribal communities have further been aggravated by ineffective performance of tribal political representatives in democratic politics due to various reasons.

Despair is also supplemented by the relatively restricted political choices of ST candidates to contest from reserved constituencies located outside their states. In recent times, it has, however, been observed that candidates have been contesting elections in unreserved constituencies located outside their states. This is primarily done in the form of contesting election from two parliamentary constituencies under Section 33 of the Representation of People Act, 1951, one is located in their own state, and other is outside the state.[6] The relatively restricted political choice of ST candidates can perhaps be explained on the ground that the ST lists are state-specific lists and STs cannot claim the status outside their states.[7]

CONCLUSION

The article began with the experiences of tribal communities in the colonial political system and moved to the need for ST-reserved constituencies in independent India and engagement of tribal communities with the state in the political sphere. The democratic practices suggest that India has become politically 'inclusive' by accommodating the tribes under its ambit at least at the theoretical level. The political situation of tribal communities has experienced changes with the enactment of political reservation, which in turn has led to the emergence of a tiny section of political elites among tribal communities. The contextualization of tribal representation in politics, government jobs and education demonstrates that politics is the only sphere where the tribes have been representing 100 per cent of the prescribed quota. Therefore, political reservation for tribal communities has ensured

---

[6] Sonia Gandhi, Akhilesh Yadav, Mamata Banerjee, Lalu Prasad Yadav, Narendra Modi, and so on, have contested from two constituencies in different elections.

[7] The geographical identification of a tribe is justified under Article 341(1) of the Indian constitution, which states that in order to get the benefits of being a member of an ST in the matter of public employment, the person claiming it should be a member of such tribe in relation to the particular area or state where he is residing and where he seeks employment.

Table 2.5   State/Union Territory-wise Seats in the Assembly and Their Reservation Status

States and Union Territories	No. of Seats in the House as Constituted in 2004 on the Basis of the Delimitation of Parliamentary and Assembly Constituencies Order, 1976, as Amended from Time to Time				No. of Seats in the House as Subsequently Constituted as per the Delimitation of Parliamentary and Assembly Constituencies Order, 2008		
	General	SC	ST	Total	General	SC	ST
I. States							
Andhra Pradesh	240	39	15	294	227	48	19
Arunachal Pradesh	1	—	59	60	1	—	59
Assam	102	8	16	126	102	8	16
Bihar	204	39	—	243	203	38	2
Chhattisgarh	46	10	34	90	51	10	29
Goa	39	1	—	40	39	1	—
Gujarat	143	13	26	182	142	13	27
Haryana	73	17	—	90	73	17	—
Himachal Pradesh	49	16	3	68	48	17	3
Jammu & Kashmir[a]	80	7	—	87[a]	—[a]	—[a]	—[a]
Jharkhand	44	9	28	81	44	9	28
Karnataka	189	33	2	224	173	36	15
Kerala	126	13	1	140	124	14	2
Madhya Pradesh	156	33	41	230	148	35	47
Maharashtra	248	18	22	288	234	29	25
Manipur	40	1	19	60	40	1	19
Meghalaya	5	—	55	60	5	—	55
Mizoram	1	—	39	40	1	—	39
Nagaland	1	—	59	60	1	—	59
Odisha	91	22	34	147	90	24	33
Punjab	88	29	—	117	83	34	—
Rajasthan	143	33	24	200	141	34	25
Sikkim[b]	18	2	12	32[b]	17[b]	2[b]	12[b]
Tamil Nadu	189	42	3	234	188	44	2
Tripura	33	7	20	60	30	10	20
Uttar Pradesh	314	89	—	403	318	85	—
Uttarakhand	55	12	3	70	55	13	2
West Bengal	218	59	17	294	210	68	16
Total	2936	552	532	4020	2789	590	554
II. Union Territories							
Delhi	57	13	—	70	58	12	—
Puducherry	25	5	—	30	25	5	—

Source: Government of India (2008, p. 6–7).

[a]Under the constitution of Jammu and Kashmir, the number of seats in the legislative assembly of that state excluding the 24 seats earmarked for Pakistan occupied territory is 87 out of which seven seats have been reserved for the SCs in persuasion of the Jammu and Kashmir Representation of the People Act 1957.

[b]Reserved one seat for Sangrias and 12 seats for Bhutia-Lepcha Community.

quantitative representation, without which even that would have been lacking. Their qualitative representation, however, remains highly questionable. Hence, the above analysis suggests that political reservation has brought hope and despair to tribal communities in India. The democratic assertion of marginalized communities in the contemporary period appears to suggest the continuation of political reservation in India.

REFERENCES

Alam, M. S. (2015). Selection of reserved seats: Laws, procedures, practices and implications for equality of political opportunity. In M. S. Alam & K. C. Sivaramakrishnan (Eds.), *Fixing of Electoral Boundaries in India: Laws, Processes, Outcomes and Implications for Political Representation* (pp. 148–166). New Delhi: Oxford University Press.

Ambagudia, J. (2019). *Adivasis, migrants and the state in India*. London and New York, NY: Routledge.

Bajpai, R. (2015). *Debating difference: group rights and liberal democracy in India*. New Delhi: Oxford University Press.

Bosu Mullick, S. (2001). Indigenous peoples and electoral politics in India: An experience of incompatibility. In K. Wessendorf (Ed.), *Challenging Politics: Indigenous Peoples Experience with Political Parties and Elections* (pp. 94–144). Copenhagen: International Workgroup for Indigenous Affairs.

Galanter, M. (1984). *Competing equalities: Law and the backward classes in India*. New Delhi: Oxford University Press.

Ghosh, S. (1987). *Law enforcement in tribal areas*. New Delhi: APH Publishing House.

Government of India Act, 1935. Retrieved from http://www.legislation.gov.uk/ukpga/1935/2/pdfs/ukpga_19350002_en.pdf

Government of India. (2008). *Delimitation of parliamentary and assembly constituencies order, 2008*. New Delhi: Delimitation Commission of India.

Government of India. (2009). *Statistical report on general elections, 2009 to the 15th Lok Sabha*. New Delhi: Election Commission of India.

Government of India. (2014). *Statistical report on general elections, 2014 to the 16th Lok Sabha*. New Delhi: Election Commission of India.

Government of India. (2020). *All members of Lok Sabha (since 1952)*. New Delhi: Lok Sabha. Retrieved from http://164.100.47.194/Loksabha/Members/lokprev.aspx

Jayal, N. G. & Mehta, P. B. (Eds.) (2011). *The Oxford companion to politics in India*. New Delhi: Oxford University Press.

Jensenius, F. R. (2012). Political quotas in India: Perceptions of constituent political representation. *Asian Survey, 52*(2), 373–394.

Jha, S. (2003). Rights versus representation: Defending minority rights in the constituent assembly. *Economic and Political Weekly, 38*(16), 3175–3180.

Jha, S. (2004). Representation and its epiphanies: A reading of constituent assembly debates. *Economic and Political Weekly, 39*(39), 4357–4360.

Kapila, K. (2013). Old differences and new hierarchies: The trouble with tribes in contemporary India. In S. S. Jodhka (Ed.), *Interrogating India's Modernity: Democracy, Identity and Citizenship* (pp. 99–116). New Delhi: Oxford University Press.

Lublin, D. (2014). *Minority rules: Electoral systems, decentralization and ethnoregional parties*. New York, NY: Oxford University Press.

Maharatna, A. (2015). On the demography of India's broad social stratification. In R. Saenz, D. G. Embrick, & N. P. Rodriguez (Eds.), *The International Handbook of the Demography of Race and Ethnicity* (pp. 189–217). Dordrecht: Springer.

McMillan, A. (2005). *Standing at the margins: Representation and electoral reservation in India*. New Delhi: Oxford University Press.

McMillan, A. (2008). Delimitation in India. In L. Handly & B. Grofman (Eds.), *Redistricting in a Comparative Perspective* (pp. 75–95). New York, NY: Oxford University Press.

Pati, B. (Ed.) (2011). *Adivasis in colonial India: Survival, resistance and negotiation*. New Delhi: Orient BlackSwan.

Prasad, A. (2001). *Reservation policy and practice in India: A means to an end*. New Delhi: Deep and Deep Publications.

Radhakrishnan, M. (Ed.) (2016). *First citizens: Studies on adivasis, tribals and indigenous peoples in India*. New Delhi: Oxford University Press.

Rangacharyulu, S. V. & Kanth, G. R. (2017). *Rural development statistics 2016–2017*. Hyderabad: National Institute of Rural Development and Panchayati Raj.

Rao, B. S. (1967). *The framing of India's constitution: Selected documents, Vol. II*. New Delhi: Indian Institute of Public Administration.

Rao, B. S. (1968). *The framing of Indian constitution: Selected documents, Vol. IV.* New Delhi: Indian Institute of Public Administration.

Saksena, H. S. (1981). *Safeguards for scheduled castes and tribes: Founding fathers view.* New Delhi: Uppal Publishing House.

Shah, A. (2010). *In the shadows of the state: Indigenous politics, environmentalism and insurgency in Jharkhand, India.* New Delhi: Oxford University Press.

Sundar, N. & Madan, T. N. (Eds.) (2016). *The scheduled tribes and their India: Politics, identities, policies and work.* New Delhi: Oxford University Press.

Weiner, M. & Field, J. O. (1975). How tribal constituencies in India vote. In J. N. Bhagwati, P. Desai, J. O. Field, W. L. Richter, & M. Weiner (Eds.), *Electoral Politics in the Indian States: Three Disadvantaged Sectors, Studies in Electoral Politics in the Indian States* (volume 2, pp. 79–120). New Delhi: Manohar Book Service.

Wessendorf, K. (2001). Introduction. In K. Wessendorf (Ed.), *Challenging Politics: Indigenous Peoples Experience with Political Parties and Elections* (pp. 10–19). Copenhagen: International Workgroup for Indigenous Affairs.

Xaxa, V. (2005). Electoral reservations for scheduled tribes: The legitimisation of domination. In S. Tawa Lama-Rewal (Ed.), *Electoral Reservations, Political Representation and Social Change in India: A Comparative Perspective* (pp. 119–135). New Delhi: Manohar.

Xaxa, V. (2008). *State, society and tribes: Issues in post-colonial India.* New Delhi: Pearson.

Democracy's Ghettos: Adivasi Leadership in India

Valerian Rodrigues

In the last 50 years, historiographical research has brought home the fact that Adivasis across India have been in the forefront of some of the most militant movements aimed at securing a set of assorted objectives directed against non-usurpation and alienation of land, exorbitant land rent and other exactions, extortion by moneylenders, self-serving outsiders, cultural domination and seeking access to forests and its resources, remunerative price for their produce in the market, defence of their culture and identity and so on.[1] Some of these movements were led by traditional leaders, while many others were led by charismatic individuals by tapping the cultural resources of their respective communities and/or reconstructing the new tidings they encountered in the wider world and making them speak to their concerns.[2] Many Adivasi social movements have been preceded by churnings from within to weld the community together through internal reforms, broadly termed Bhagat movements in Central, Northern and Eastern India

(Fuchs, 1966–1967, pp. 15–33). From the second decade of the 20th century, we have movements that have been planned and led by a vanguard drawn from the concerned communities themselves to clearly serve certain modernist ends such as the Naga movement and the Jharkhand movement. There have also been movements whose social composition has been primarily Adivasi but led by ideological currents and leadership not drawn from them. This would be the case with the Godavari Parulekar led Warli movement (Parulekar, 1975) or the Maoist movement in Dandakaranya today (Shah, 2018). Apart from such movements, there are imperatives of the reproduction of everyday social existence which calls for a distinct brand of leadership. Adivasis in India today are settled communities, mainly agrarian, and many of them have been so for generations. Their internal affairs and their relationship with other communities are governed by community leadership, generally headed by chiefs, with varied titles

---

[1] For brief accounts of these movements, see Kothari (2009) and Kothari, Savyasaachi and George (2010).
[2] One of the good examples in this regard is Sarkar (1985, pp. 136–164).

across different tribes. Such leadership generally tends to resort to customary laws and practices in deciding and arbitrating over community affairs. Further, India's national movement and democratic politics has thrown up its distinct brand of leadership among tribal communities.

On the basis of the reports and critical studies on movements, modes of community reproduction and political participation of Adivasis, we can develop a typology of Adivasi leadership in India. We can also test to what extent categories of leadership such as the ones proposed by Max Weber or W. H Morris-Jones could be adopted to classify the prevailing leadership among the Adivasis (Morris-Jones, 1963; Weber, 1978, pp. 32–94). This chapter, however, does not intend to pursue any such classification. It seeks to assess the extent to which Adivasi leadership has succeeded in asserting its presence in the representational and participatory politics of Indian democracy, its distinct contribution to such politics, the issues that Adivasis have put upfront through their movements as their key concerns and the challenges before this leadership today. While the category 'indigenous' is highly problematic in the Indian context,[3] and the legal term 'scheduled tribe' (ST) has acquired a life of its own, several concerned spokespersons of tribal communities have argued and employed 'Adivasi' as their apt self-description. Together they form one of the largest concentration of such peoples in any country in the world today. The homologous condition of indigenous peoples elsewhere in the world and that of the Adivasis in India is reflected in some of the key concerns they share in common. If direction, *direzione*, is a key element of leadership, then the direction the Adivasi public takes in India would have much wider repercussions in shaping the lives of the indigenous and akin people worldwide. I have employed the term 'leadership' to denote the collective agency at work among Adivasis directing the course of their common concerns.

ADIVASI POLITICS AT THE TURN OF INDIA'S INDEPENDENCE

As is well known, colonial rule employed a very paternalistic approach towards Adivasi communities in India while subjecting them to the agrarian order instituted by it. It placed them at the primitive/backward point on the axis of reason and enlightenment, as it did similar people in its other colonies as well. Political and strategic considerations too played no small a role in the colonial cartography of tribes. The India Act, 1935 demarcated three types of habitats of Adivasis in India: The excluded areas, the partially excluded areas and the non-excluded areas. The excluded areas located in the frontier regions were primarily inhabited by Adivasis and people regarded as 'backward' and were wholly excluded from the jurisdiction of provincial assemblies under the Act. Such exclusion was based on 'strict necessity' and was 'as limited as possible' in scope. Such areas were few in number and, following partition of India in 1947, included the Laccadive group of islands in the West Coast of Madras province, the Chittagong Hill tracts in Bengal, wazirs of Spiti and Lahaul in the Panjab, the North-East Frontier, the Naga Hills District and the surrounding areas, the Lushai Hills district and the North Cachar Hills subdivision of the Cachar District. The partially excluded areas were those having a 'preponderance of aborigines' or 'very backward people' that were contiguous and of sufficient size and recognizable boundaries to make possible the application of special legislation to them. At the same time, they came under assorted policy measures and administrative arrangements common to the concerned province as a whole. Generally,

---

[3] For a discussion on the controversy surrounding the term 'indigenous' in general and with reference to India in particular, see Karlsson (2016, pp. 109–133).

such areas were located in hilly tracts. They included the East Godavari Agency and the Polavaram Taluk of West Godavari Agency in Madras Province, parts of West Khandesh, East Khandesh, Nasik, Thana, Broach and Panch Mahal district of Bombay Province, the Mandla District of Central Provinces, the Khondmals of the former Angul district and the Sambalpur District of Orissa, the Chota Nagpur division and the Santhal Parganas district of Bihar, parts of Dehradun and Mirzapur districts of United Provinces, Darjeeling district and parts of Mymensingh district of Bengal, the Garo Hills district, the Mikir Hills and the British portion of the Khasi and Jaintia of Assam except Shillong. It is important to point out that the majority of the Adivasis lived in non-excluded areas. In many Princely States, there were areas primarily inhabited by Adivasis and there was no special consideration meted out to them qua Adivasis.

Meanwhile, Adivasis had begun to throw up their distinct organizations in several parts of the country. Some of the most significant among them was the Adivasi Mahasabha formed in 1936 and the Naga National Council (NNC) in 1946. The Adivasi Mahasabha was a successor to a number of organizations that emerged in the Chota Nagpur region and encompassed most of them including the Chotanagpur Unnati Samaj (CNUS), formed in 1916. The CNUS strove to weld together concerns of a region alongside those of the tribes who inhabited there. Invariably, it was susceptible to contending pressures: As a region it included, apart from over 30 tribes, inhabitants belonging to other castes and communities native to the place, as well as those who migrated to this mineral rich and fast industrializing tract from other parts of the country, particularly Bihar. As an Adivasi habitat, it included several major tribes such as the Mundas, the Santhals, the Oraons and

the Hos who spilled over into the surrounding parts of Bihar as well as Bengal, Orissa and Central provinces. Besides, the tea plantations of Assam had heavily drawn their labour from the tribal communities of Chota Nagpur region and Santhal Parganas. These two-fold contentions, whether to accord primacy to Adivasi concerns or those of the region, were to bedevil genuine political leadership here continuously. The CNUS, supported by different organizations of the region, pressed the demand for a separate state before the Simon Commission in the name of the region as well as of its Adivasis. While the Commission rejected the demand of statehood, it recommended the status of a 'partially excluded area' to it. With the formation of Adivasi Mahasabha, led by Jaipal Singh, while a united Adivasi habitat came to be focussed, its opponents stroke fears of the non-Adivasi inhabitants of the Area. In 1949, the Adivasi Mahasabha renamed itself as the Jharkhand Party, narrowing its scope from being a representative of Adivasi interests at large while striving to be inclusive of diverse regional interests. The party made an appeal for a separate state for the region before the State Reorganization Commission (SRC).[4] However, it was rejected, as a 'minority demand' (Bosu Mullick, 2003, p. XV). The NNC considered itself as the legatee of the Naga Club, formed in 1918 as the first 'common organization of the Nagas' by the initiative of demobilized army men after World War I, that aimed to foster a common identity across several scattered Naga tribes (Ao, 2002, pp. 40–41). The Club submitted a memorandum to the Simon Commission in 1929 that suggested that as and when the British left India for good, the political order prior to their conquest should be restored as far as the Nagas were concerned. The NNC asserted the solidarity of all Naga tribes,

---

[4] The original demand was for greater Jharkhand with an area of 63,859 sq miles with a population of 16,367,177 which included 18 districts of Bihar, 3 districts of West Bengal, 4 districts of Odisha and 2 districts of Madhya Pradesh. See the Memorandum presented to State Reorganization Commission by Jharkhand Party dated 22 April 1954.

sought self-determination in February 1947 prior to the British withdrawal from India and argued for the same before the constitutional subcommittee on North-East Frontier (Assam) Tribal and Excluded Areas. It declared Naga independence on 14 August 1947 at Kohima and Mokokchung and in the plebiscite held on 16 May 1951 found an overwhelming endorsement to its stand.

It is important to point out that there emerged a large number of Adivasi organizations across India, most of them specific to a tribe, from early part of the 20th century. The chiefs of tribes at times came together, often in defence of their traditional privileges, by forming their own organizations such as the Chief's Council of Mizoram formed in 1939. Gandhi as an exemplar charts a distinct trail among many Adivasi communities (Hardiman, 1987; Sarkar, 1985, pp. 136–164). A few non-Adivasi leaders of the Indian National Congress (INC) too were actively involved in reaching out to the tribes, such as A. V. Thakkar.[5] Several Christian sects were active among Adivasis across India, particularly in the Northeast and Chota Nagpur regions and the institutions they ran had a profound impact on Adivasis who came in contact with them.

THE CONSTITUENT ASSEMBLY AND MODE OF INCLUSION OF THE ADIVASIS

The Constituent Assembly constituted two bodies to closely investigate the conditions of Adivasis in India: The first was North-East Frontier (Assam) Tribal and Excluded Areas subcommittee, chaired by G. N. Bordoloi. The other members of this Committee were J. J. M. Nichols-Roy, Rup Nath Brahma and A. V. Thakkar. The Committee adopted a very painstaking method of eliciting the views of the different tribes and areas falling within its ambit that included holding hearings at the district and the subdivisional headquarters and documenting the responses of the representatives of different groups through critical probing visiting select villages for on-the-spot inquiry and examining closely all the documents concerning a case in point with the officials concerned. Except for the frontier tracts, the Committee co-opted two members from the tribes of each one of the districts visited, who signed the minutes of the meeting as well.[6] While the account and recommendations of this Committee are complex and detailed,[7] some of its observations are worth taking note of. It felt that there was much unevenness across different Adivasi communities of the region. While some of them had long interaction with people of the plains, a few others such as the Nagas and the Lushais had little such contact. The Committee appreciated the traditions of representation and collective decision-making prevailing among most of the tribes and felt that there was no reason to deny extension of franchise that would be available to the rest of the citizen community, to them as well. At the same time, the Committee was cautious of the claims to representation made by some members and organizations such as the Lushai District Conference and NNC. It

---

[5] A.V. Thakkar chaired the Committee that eventually led to the provisions of fifth schedule of the constitution. He was also a member of the Bordoloi Committee.

[6] Mr. Kezehol, a representative of the NNC, who submitted his resignation during the final hearing in Shillong did not sign the proceedings. There were two members, Mr Kelhoushe and Mr Aliba Imti, who signed expressing their dissent on some observations of the subcommittee.

[7] For the summary, see Government of India, 1949a, pp. 100–142. Apart from the observations and recommendations of the committee contained in volume I, part I and part II of volume II on 'Evidence' provide a detailed account of the working of the subcommittee, *Constituent Assembly of India, North-East Frontier (Assam) Tribal and Excluded Areas Sub-Committee, vol. II (Evidence) Part I: Lushai, North-Cachar, Garo, Mikir and Naga Hills* (henceforward *Bordoloi Committee Report*) (Government of India, 1949c).

took note of the varied and often conflicting claims of different tribes and their supposed representatives. While some wanted all power, except defence, external affairs and communication, to be vested in their respective councils, others made more modest demands. However, there was unanimity with regard to exercising control over land, local customs, administration of justice and regulating access to outsiders. The NNC representatives, however, demanded self-determination for Nagas under a guardian power for 10 years and be left free afterwards.

The concern and empathy of the Committee for the Adivasis in question are writ large across its report even when it disagreed with some of the demands placed before it. It felt that assimilation of these people cannot be forced by 'breaking up tribal institutions', but only be through 'evolution or growth on the old foundations', something that 'should come as far as possible from the tribe itself' (Government of India, 1949a, p. 110). It recommended that they should have powers of 'legislation over occupation or use of land' (Government of India, 1949a, p. 110), other than 'reserved forest' and land for public purposes and to 'regulate money-lending'. It felt that with regard to forest management and policy the susceptibilities of the Hill people should be taken into account. It recommended that the tribes should have full power of administering their own social laws, codifying or modifying them. It thought that 'all criminal offences except those punishable with death, transportation or imprisonment for five years and upwards should be left to be in accordance with local practice' (Government of India, 1949a, p. 111). Primary education should be left to the local councils and if they have the necessary resources they could manage secondary schools as well. In such matters as 'management of dispensaries or construction of roads', the local councils could work under the 'executive direction of the corresponding provincial department'. The Committee disagreed with the demand of the tribal representatives 'that all powers of taxation should rest

on the National Councils' and felt it proper 'to allocate certain taxes and financial powers to the Councils'. While management of mineral resources might have to be centralized, the Committee felt, local councils needed to be consulted in leasing out and a fair share of the proceeds should be assigned to them.

The Excluded and Partially Excluded Areas (other than Assam) Subcommittee was chaired by A. V. Thakkar and had Jaipal Singh, Devendra Nath Samanta, Phul Bhanu Shah, Jagjivan Ram, Profulla Chandra Ghosh and Raj Krushna Bose as members. They also co-opted Khetramni Panda (Phulbani area), Sadashiv Tripathi (Orissa P.E. areas), Kodanda Ramiah (Madras P.E. areas), Sneha Kumar Chakma (Chittagong Hill Tracts) and Damber Singh Gurung (Darjeeling district) as members. This Committee did not restrict its observations merely to the excluded and partially excluded areas but commented on the constitutional and political arrangements for Adivasis as a whole. The Committee (Government of India, 1949a, p. 145) argued that 'the whole tribal population should be treated as a minority community for the welfare of whom certain special measures are necessary'. Taking a close look at the tribal conditions in the different provinces, it felt that the colonial policy of both exclusion and partial exclusion has not yielded tangible results in the economic and educational betterment of Adivasis. They face the threat of alienation of land and 'virtual serfdom' under the moneylender. The Committee felt that Adivasi representatives who made submissions before it had sought better educational facilities but there was a dearth of good teachers.

Further the committee (Government of India, 1949a, p. 157) argued, 'it is necessary to provide that in certain areas laws of the provincial legislature which are likely to be based largely on the needs of the majority of the population should not apply automatically, if not generally, at least in certain specified subjects' to Adivasi areas. It would be helpful, it felt, to demarcate certain special areas for specific considerations to be known as 'scheduled areas' (Government of India, 1949a, p. 157). It recommended Tribes Advisory Councils, with 'strong representation of tribal element' 'to exercise special supervisory functions', with regard to the concerns that it had highlighted, in such provinces as 'Madras, Bombay, West Bengal, Bihar, Central Provinces and Orissa'. The Committee recommended that in subjects such as social matters, occupation of land including tenancy laws, allotment of land and setting apart of land for village purposes and village management including village panchayats the advice of the Tribes Advisory Council was necessary. Even in other subjects, the provincial governments 'should have the power to withhold or modify legislation on the advice of the Tribes Advisory Council' (Government of India, 1949a, p. 158).

A close scrutiny of the reports of these two subcommittees suggests that both of them shared much in common with regard to their understanding of the tribal world, their stress on respecting their cultural autonomy and ways of life, the need to create appropriate institutions for the purpose and making room for their greater participation in the political institutions of India's democracy. However, there is a major difference. The Bordoloi Committee was much more deferential to the autonomy demands of Adivasis,[8] while the Thakkar Committee laid stress on enabling Adivasi access to wider national life and promoting temperance movement among them. The latter also stressed on reservation in representation under the joint electorate and 'due proportion' of recruitment in government services (Government of India, 1949a, p. 183).[9] It is important to point out that Jaipal Singh, a member of the Committee and the leader of the Jharkhand Party, expressed his dissent with its report for not including districts of Manbhum,

Hazaribagh and Palamau, in the 'scheduled area' of Chota Nagpur. He also wanted to include (Government of India, 1949a, pp. 182 and 188) the tribal tract in Mirzapur district in the 'scheduled area' of Chota Nagpur and wanted the Government of India to claim the Chittagong Hill Tracts, against the recommendations of the Radcliff Award of division of India into India and Pakistan. The rejoinder of A. V. Thakkar (Government of India, 1949a, pp. 182 and 188), the Chairman of the Committee, to this dissent shows not merely a substantive disagreement between him and Jaipal Singh but a difference in perspective on the Adivasi question in India: While the former stressed the inclusion of Adivasis in national life, the latter was concerned about their autonomy and identity.

The debate on the Adivasi question in the Constituent Assembly demonstrates the great divide between those who argued for a level-playing field for them in national life and those who argued for sustaining their difference and autonomy. Rohini Kumar Chaudhury pitted himself against the recommendations of the Bordoloi Committee and argued,

> We want to assimilate the tribal people. We were not given that opportunity so far...The autonomous district is a weapon whereby steps are taken to keep the tribal people perpetually away from the non-tribals and the bond of friendship which we expect to come into being after the attainment of independence would be torn asunder. (Government of India, 1949b, p. 1,017)

Speaking against the Thakkar Committee Report, Babu Ramnarayan Singh argued,

> We wanted that there ought to be one and one administration only in every part of the country. We all ashamed of such things as backward tract or excluded area or partially excluded areas. Now Sir, it pains me and I think it must be paining

---

[8] In the recorded hearings of the Bordoloi Committee, we often find the Chairman Bordoloi prodding the representatives to spell out their autonomy demands, just to be reined in by Sir B. N. Rau, the Constitutional Adviser, to point out the limited mandate of the Committee that has no authority over wider political questions.
[9] It is important to point out that most of these recommendations were very close to the Congress policy and were formulated during and after the Poona Pact of 1932. For the Pact and its implications for affirmative policies in India, see Vundru (2018, pp. 41–64).

everybody in this country to find that we have begun to do things now against which we have protested so long during the British rule. (Government of India, 1949b, pp. 986–987)

Listening to the debate on sixth schedule, Jaipal Singh was forced to retaliate that he was 'shocked by the amount of venom that has been poured forth' (Government of India, 1949b, p. 1,019) against the tribal people of Assam. While these disagreements and contentions mirrored the wider anthropological approach to the tribal question at the time,[10] in the Constituent Assembly Debates (CADs), they took on the hue of very distinct ideas of India as a nation and the kind of constitutional democracy it sought.

It is important to note that the contentious and diverse demands of the Adivasis in India came to be organized in very innovative ways by the constitutional order of India breaking away from the colonial legacy in decisive ways. While some of these measures were embraced in the constitutional framework right from the beginning, others were incorporated into it later: (a) All Adivasis came under a regime of preferential consideration in legislative representation, public employment and higher education and affirmative public policies. (b) The excluded and partially excluded areas and agency tracts were brought under an asymmetrical federal arrangement, granting significant autonomy to Adivasi areas under the category 'District Councils' and 'scheduled areas' as expressed in fifth and sixth schedules of the constitution respectively. These arrangements were meant to protect the autonomy of tribal clusters, their customary law, language and cultural practices. (c) As religious, linguistic and cultural minorities, Adivasis were entitled to the same claims that other minorities enjoyed. (d) A significant section of Adivasis found the idea of federation attractive and rallied to carve out separate states under Indian federation. (e) Considerations of specific

autonomy that certain Adivasi-dominated states enjoyed was protected under Article 371 of the constitution. (f) Some measures such as the Forest Rights Act (FRA)[11] and Panchayat (Extension to Scheduled Areas) (PESA) Act[12] carried further the constitutional vision with regard to Adivasis. However, in all these very impressive initiatives, the tension between inclusion of Adivasis in national life and their autonomy persisted.

ADIVASI LEADERSHIP IN THE REPRESENTATIONAL AND PARTICIPATORY POLITICS OF INDIAN DEMOCRACY

The constitutional frame for Adivasis called for a distinct type of leadership which could direct Adivasi futures in the deeply contentious and multi-pronged political space of India. In the first general election to the Lok Sabha in 1952, organized Adivasi political expression was fragmented and there was no all-India Adivasi organization, leave alone a political party. The Adivasi Mahasabha which started with much promise came to be effectively confined to a regional outfit, the Jharkhand Party. While representational reservation had ensured a predictable proportion of ST members in the Parliament, many of them had little or no education. In the first Lok Sabha, they included Shri Hembrom Lal from Santhal Parganas cum Hazaribagh, Shri Kherwar Jethan from Palamu cum Hazaribagh cum Ranchi, Shri Birendranath Katham from Jalpaiguri, Shri Rupaji Bhavji Parmar from Panch Mahals cum Baroda East, Shri M. G. Uikey from Mandla, all of them from the INC, Shri Randaman Singh from Shahdol-Sidhi of Kisan Mazdoor Praja Party, Shri Girdhari Bhoi from Kalahandi of Ganatantra Parishad; Shri Ram Chandra Majhi from Mayurbhanj

---

[10] For the debate in India on the tribal question in 1940s, see Guha (1999).
[11] Scheduled Tribes and Other Traditional Forest Dwellers (Recognition of Forest Rights) Act, 2006.
[12] Panchayat (Extension to Scheduled Areas) Act, 1996.

of Jharkhand Party and independents such as Shri Muchaki Kosa from Bastar and Shri Gam Malludora of Visakhapatnam. However, ST members of the first Lok Sabha who were educated, particularly from the Northeast, had relatively higher qualifications from better-known educational institutions (Government of India, 2003; Shankar & Rodrigues, 2011, pp. 70–104) compared to their peers.

The ST members of the second Lok Sabha, on an average, were even less qualified as compared to that of the first Lok Sabha. Shri P. B. Bhogji Bhai from Banswara, Shri Kankipathi Veeranna Padal from Golconda, Shri Mardi Selku from West Dinajpur and Shri M. G. Uikey from Mandla, all of them were from INC, Shri Shambhu Charan Godsora of Singhbhum and Shri Ramachandra Majhi of Mayurbhanj, both from Jharkhand Party, and Shri Kalo Chadramani from Sundargarh of Ganatantra Parishad, had little or no education. Even those who were better qualified among them, except those from the Northeast, hailed from less known educational institutions. Closer reading of the profiles and performances of the representatives of Adivasi's in the Parliament demonstrates that in the first 15 years after independence India's Adivasi public came to be marked by the following debilities: (a) There was no unified expression of an Adivasi policy by seriously engaging the Adivasis themselves and in all instances of a such a policy, the Congress Party spoke for them. (b) There was a clear split between the Adivasis of Northeast India and the rest. The ST representatives hailing from the former, many of them very articulate, spoke for their region or tribe, rather than Adivasis as a whole. (c) There was a disconnect between educated Adivasi representatives and the rest. Minutes of parliamentary proceedings demonstrate that very few Adivasi members raised the concerns of Adivasis on the floor of the House. (d) There was an absence of an All-India Adivasi bloc of shared concerns and sympathies. (e) There was much changeover in Adivasi representation, indicating weakly

founded leadership. (f) The overall voter turn-out of STs remained low and there was a wide margin between male and female voter-turn-out (Alam, 2004, pp. 26–44). Comparatively, most of the scheduled caste (SC) members of the Lok Sabha during this period had fairly high qualifications and made common cause when concerns of untouchability came to be voiced.

There was a ray of hope in the ghetto to which Adivasi politics was confined in early 1970s, when STs across India, including the women-folk, turned up at the hustings equally, if not more, compared to the average voter-turn-out. This development was in tune with the response of other vulnerable sections too. Paradoxically, however, the ST representatives, alongside those of the SCs, were further marginalized as the language of populism and development increasingly dwarfed the significance of the Parliament. In 1977 election to the Lok Sabha, Adivasis overall shed their hitherto pronounced tilt towards the INC. Yet, there was a little change in the standing of Adivasi leaders in the representative spectrum of Indian polity. The creation of Adivasi dominated provinces in 1970s such as Meghalaya and after the Rajiv Gandhi–Laldenga Accord granting statehood to Mizoram in 1987, threw up a few autonomy spaces for Adivasis without redefining Indian polity in any significant ways to mark their presence. In the 1990s, when there was a significant educational and occupational diversification among the members of the Lok Sabha, there was no comparative similar developments among representatives of STs, although in comparison to the first two Lok Sabha, they were better qualified and educationally diverse (Shankar & Rodrigues, 2011, pp. 94–95). It is also important to note that the remarkable strides of the Bharatiya Janata Party among Adivasis in 2000s resulted in confining Adivasi representatives belonging to the party interest themselves in the affairs of the Adivasi communities they hailed from rather than in the wider affairs of the polity as a whole (Shankar & Rodrigues, 2011, p. 233, table 5.7).

At the state level, Adivasi representation could have redefined the political space in Central and Eastern India—Bihar, Central Provinces, Orissa and West Bengal and in the Northeast—, Assam, North East Frontier Agency and Tripura, as India went to the hustings in 1951–1952. However, in the former cluster of provinces only in Bihar, Adivasi politics in the form of Jharkhand Party held its own for a while. In the latter, it took a very different turn, leading to both fragmentation and localization. The Jharkhand Party formed in 1949 did comparatively well in the first general elections of 1952, securing 33 out of 352 seats in Bihar assembly. The Party also registered its presence in the surrounding tribal belt of West Bengal, Orissa and Central Provinces. But the demand for a separate Jharkhand state was rejected by the State Reorganization Commission. The opposition of the INC to the Jharkhand Party led to its electoral setback and in 1962 election, the latter secured only 20 seats in the Bihar assembly. In 1963, Jaipal Singh, the leader of the Party, decided to merge it with the INC, a decision that came to be opposed by many other party leaders. It resulted in the emergence of not less than nine tribal based Jharkhand parties and groups out of its remnants (Ghosh, 1998, p. 46) that included Hul Jharkhand Party, Rajya Hul Jharkhand Party, Birsa Sewa Dal and All India Jharkhand Party, each claiming themselves as the real Jharkhand Party.

In 1970s, Sibu Soren led a militant mass movement against the alienation of Adivasi lands and the domination of Dikhus or outsiders for securing employment for Adivasis in the Coal mines and other public sector undertakings and in defence of Adivasi culture which led to the formation of Jharkhand Mukti Morcha (JMM). In the early stages, the JMM reflected convergence of the militant movement of workers in collieries led by A. K. Roy, the Adivasi movement led by Sibu Soren and the movement of local people against the domination of outsiders led by Binod Bihari Mahato. This alliance of social forces soon got disintegrated, largely due to the machinations

of the INC, the JMM eventually played a muted role in the formation of Jharkhand State in 2000 (Corbridge, Jewitt, & Kumar, 2004; Kumar, 2008; Prakash, 2001). The new state carved out from Bihar included the Chota Nagpur division of Bihar and Santhal Parganas and involved shedding claims to the neighbouring Adivasi regions which were integral to the imagination of Jharkhand.

While there was much in common between Adivasi demands expressed in the Northeast and in Jharkhand, eventually India's national politics and differing Adivasi priorities in these regions led to very different outcomes. The Naga social imaginary of being a distinct nationality led to the demand for self-determination, which the Indian state attempted to contain and co-opt under a federal format. The federal format was also employed to carve out separate states of Meghalaya and Mizoram which were predominantly composed of Adivasis. In the rest of the Northeast, in areas with Adivasi concentration, the idea of Autonomous District Councils, under sixth schedule of the constitution, proved attractive. Elections in the Northeast too have registered very high voter turn-outs and state-based parties, often in coalition with national parties, have succeeded in offering political stability. The National People's Party established by P. A. Sangma has, however, reached out to the Northeast as a whole and, apart from Meghalaya, has carved out significant electoral support base in Manipur, Nagaland and Arunachal Pradesh. The Election Commission of India has recognized it as a National Party in 2019. It is too early, however, to say to what extent exclusive focus on elections and resultant outcomes is the best way of directing the future of Adivasis in India, be it in the Northeast or elsewhere.

Social construction of ethnicity as nationalism has had its own attraction in the Northeast. As in all such instances, the boundaries of ethnicity remained porous. Discursively it has drawn the line between 'we' and the tribal-others on the one hand, and non-tribal-others, on the other hand, and reinforced the outer boundaries of such delineation through civic and political action. The Nagas, for instance, divided into several Naga tribes have forged a common identity and politically remained very adroit about it.[13] They have even reached out to traditional enemies such as the Kukis, at times, stressing shared beliefs and social practices. However, they have sharply demarcated themselves from other tribes such as the Mikirs and the Cacharies. The work of Phizo in welding Nagas as a nationality has been of enormous significance. Phizo's concept of nationalism as independent political existence informed by sovereignty erased all markers of differences within the Naga tribes and across the space of their inhabitation. Therefore, any departure from such ideal or even negotiation with regard to political independence became a betrayal (Steyn, 2002). Probably, Phizo's self-exile in Britain following his departure from Nagaland in December 1956 symbolized it more than anything else. Similarly, while the Mizos have forged a common bond among themselves, they have othered the Brus and the Chakmas and the role that the Young Mizo Association (YMA), Mizo Hmeichhe Insuihkhawm Pawl (MHIP) and Mizo Students' Union (MSU) have played is not inconsiderable in this regard (Sailo, 2014, pp. 176–204).

Ethnicity as nationalism has made Adivasis to close ranks behind their imputed identities, preventing them from reaching out to others of their kind in shared concerns. We can mark certain characteristics of the Adivasi leadership that unfolded in the representational politics in India: (a) It remained confined to the margins and had little scope to define the polity as a whole. Even when such leadership seemed to be more competent than of its epigones, at times, it was much weaker relative to the non-Adivasi representational leadership. (b) The political endeavour to make the idea of the nation inclusive of Adivasis resulted in absorbing Adivasi leadership within the INC which in turn confined them to the Adivasi enclaves. (c) The constitutional provisions of autonomy eventually turned out to be limiting Adivasi reach to their habitats rather than enabling them to direct the course of the nation as a whole.

ADIVASI LEADERSHIP AND GOVERNMENT POLICY INITIATIVES

In the early years after independence, government was cautious to assertions of difference—be it linguistic, ethnic or religious—although some exception was made to the tribal question, particularly in the Northeast, while employing a heavy hand to suppress secessionist tendencies. While the approach of the government to the demands of the NNC (Ao, 2002, p. 80; Steyn, 2002, pp. 88–99) and later to that of the Mizo National Front (Lalrintluanga, 2008, pp. 45–73) was a reflection of the latter, and the government's response to the criticisms of tribal representatives was an indication of the former. For instance, Rishang Keishing (Outer Manipur, ST reserved) raised the problems the North East faced in the first Lok Sabha itself and this intervention led to the expression of regret by the government for not taking necessary measures for the development of Adivasis (Government of India, 1952, pp. 283–288). Such a stance of regret, however, was to become feeble over the years.

The tribal question, however, became an important concern particularly with the outbreak of Naga militancy drawing attention to the neglect and autonomy of tribal communities. At the same time, there were others in policymaking circles who pointed out the impact Adivasi unrest has had on law and order and security considerations and sought

---

[13] The Bordoloi Committee confronted such assertive unity in its deliberations with the NNC representatives and even its suggestion of internal cleavages within Naga society was rebuffed by them.

reinforcing the same.[14] There were Congress leaders such as Jawaharlal Nehru who thought that while eventually Adivasis have to be 'mainstreamed', it has to be done gradually enabling them to decide the course of things for themselves. This disposition of 'enabling' could, however, run into an entire spectrum: from respecting the autonomy of the Adivasis to preparing the groundwork for enablement which was strongly stamped by the ideas of economic development. The bureaucracy, as a rule, was heavily tilted towards the latter. There were a few Adivasi leaders who, however, thought that the journey of the Adivasis is not necessarily towards a specific kind of mainstream but choosing the kind of life they wish to live. Whether it would lend itself to a mainstream, or the mainstream itself would be redefined in the process, could not be pre-empted in advance![15]

Given this ambivalence, the INC had its long rule at the Centre and in that capacity held a commanding position for Adivasis, although a certain state government might have charted a different course in details, pursued an assorted sort of policy measures towards Adivasis. It respected the formal autonomy of the auton-omous districts and scheduled areas but most of its leaders by paying lip-service to such canon behaved as if they knew what was good for the Adivasis. On the ground, they patron-ized their own chain of clientele. Even when Adivasi-dominated states were carved out, they were under close watch and ward. The Congress also drew within its fold some of the most important leaders of the Adivasis such as Jaipal Singh. However, once they joined the party then their concern became largely secur-ing offices and positions rather than fighting as representatives of their people. There were frequent splits among leaders rebelling against the agreement reached by one set of leaders. This took place in 1963 in Chota Nagpur when

Jaipal Singh joined the INC (Kujur, 2003, pp. 16–30) as well as among Nagalin partisans following the Shillong Accord between Naga underground and Government of India (Steyn, 2002, pp. 211–212).

The cartography that the INC and the regimes that followed it at the Centre, employed to reach out to Adivasi autonomy demands invariably led to leaving out certain sections that sought inclusion, while bringing in those who did not fit in there. For instance, a significant section of Nagas was excluded when Nagaland was created in 1963, but the Brus and Hmars had little option but to be included under the dominance of the Mizos when Mizoram became a state in 1987. Similarly, when Jharkhand state was carved out, significant sections of Adivasis who identified themselves with Jharkhand as their homeland came to be excluded. At times, such cartography pitted a section of a tribe against another section or a grouping of tribes against another such grouping.

This policy resulted in the creation of a tribal elite from among the leading Adivasi communities. The justification for the same was drawn from the constitutional provisions of reservation. The same constitutional pro-visions could have been employed to benefit Adivasis as a whole although they need not have succeeded wholly in avoiding the rise of a stratum of elite. But there is no evidence to suggest that such a policy approach was even considered. There was also no serious attempt to enable Adivasi languages as a whole. Eventually, the linguistic policy employed towards Adivasis resulted in concentrating resources to develop a few Adivasi languages and ignore others. Incidentally, in Jharkhand, out of 32 Adivasi languages, only Santhali, Mundari, Ho, Kuruk and Kharia have found some state support.

---

[14] This conflict resurfaced as development versus security under the INC led UPA II (2009–2014), in its approach towards the Communist Party of India (Maoists) in the Dandakaranya belt.

[15] For an interesting discussion in this regard, see Viswanathan (2006).

The strategy of development that the government has carried out has led to the further marginalization of the Adivasis. Adivasis have borne the brunt of displacement in the name of development more than any other community. This strategy of development has also targeted and often devastated the most important resources of Adivasi livelihood—land, forests and water bodies.[16] The tinkering in their belief systems that different religious bodies have pursued, has led to the further fragmentation of Adivasis. Christian Missions came to focus on Adivasis more than any other community in India from early 19th century and eventually succeeded in enlisting a significant number of adherents from among them into their fold, particularly in the Northeast and Chota Nagpur. But for the past 50 years or so, Hindu organizations, mainly affiliated to the Sangh Parivar, have not merely resisted the advance of these Missions in the Adivasi areas, but also promoted religious practices, festivals and rituals to testify them as Hindus. This strife for redrawing religious boundaries has not merely ignited communal passions but has also disenabled the Adivasis to collectively take stock of their religious social capital.

It is this shrinking space of their habitats that has spawned Adivasi action and led to the rise of a militant leadership in several walks of life. It is this leadership that has succeeded in agitating for some of the most radical legal measures in recent years such as the FRA and PESA Act. Sometimes measures, such as the PESA, have led to imaginative new modes of community-grounded political action such as the Niyamgiri struggle against Sterlite Industries (India) Limited, a subsidiary of Vedanta Alumina Limited.[17] Adivasis have been in the forefront of struggles against projects that involve largescale denudation of forests big dams that call for extensive acquisition of land and replacement of communities that inhabit it, resumption of land for mines, industry transport and communication without eliciting their consent, hazardous modes of extraction and transportation of minerals and disposable of waste and bureaucratic and corporate arrogance. They have rallied to protect water bodies, flora and fauna and sites and symbols dear to them. It is the support of the Adivasi communities that has sustained a rich human rights agenda in India and much of the NGO endeavour is located there. Adivasi activists have also challenged age-old notions such as 'eminent domain'[18] which in the name of public purpose has played havoc with Adivasi land and their habitations. Sometimes, Adivasis have combined arguments of sixth schedule of the constitution with provisions of PESA to spread movements. The Pathalgadi movement[19] is an apt illustration for the same. The Communist Party of India (Maoists) have found in the grievances of the Adivasis of Jharkhand, Chhattisgarh, Odisha, Maharashtra and Telangana, an apt base to entrench themselves.

Today, much of Adivasi India bristles with an array of social movements. Such movements have also nurtured a militant stratum of Adivasi activists. But few of them speak for Adivasi India as a whole. It is generally the non-Adivasi social activists who speak for Adivasis as a whole. Adivasi activists are primarily confined to their tribe, community or region. Further, hardly anyone of them have proposed a frame in which Adivasis can be themselves, living with others markedly different from them, but sharing a life in common.

---

[16] For a brief account, see Bhaduri (2009).

[17] In this decade of long struggle, the Gram Sabhas (Village Councils) of the affected areas eventually employed the provisions of PESA to deny to a multinational company's, Vedanta, permission to mining bauxite, even though the company had obtained clearance for the same even from the concerned departments of the Government of India and that of the Odisha state.

[18] For the idea of 'eminent domain', see Bhattacharya (2015, pp. 45–53).

[19] For the state of the movement, as well as a poser to its opponents, see Xaxa (2019, pp. 10–12).

DISTINCT CONTRIBUTION OF ADIVASIS TO DEMOCRATIC POLITICS IN INDIA

At the time of independence, many perceptive observers of the Indian national life realized that there was a strong state and a weak public that characterized Indian polity and unless this relationship was changed, independence would not mean much.[20] The opposition in the Indian Parliament and in most of the state legislatures was also very weak and the kind of representatives that the leading party, the INC, selected from among the Adivasis was not on par with the other representatives in their ability to shape nationalist discourse. Therefore, we need to look at the contribution of Adivasis to democratic politics in India outside the institutional complex and much more in the social arena.

The following features stand out in their discourses, submission before authorities and in their political action: (a) They rejected a homogenous conception of Indian nation. There was no mainstream. They demanded autonomy, not merely in the organization and exercise of power but also with regard to their customary practices, forest rights and language use. (b) The Thakkar Committee and Bordoloi Committee reports bring home the fact that Adivasis across India were deeply conscious of their belonging as distinct from the rest of the population, although many tribes had assimilated the social and ritual practices of their neighbouring communities. Further, such distinctiveness marked many facets of their life. (c) Across much of the Adivasi world in India, we find a faultline emerging in the 19th century, that was reinforced across the 20th century, between 'we' and the hostile outsider. In the Jharkhand region, the later was denoted as 'dikhu'. It was a generic category that included moneylenders, merchants, contractors, political leaders and a variety of people with certain skills, who employed them to trick people and eventually reduced them to subservience. (d) Inter-tribal conversation was weak and, wherever found, was mediated by an agency external to the tribe. There was some change in this regard under the colonial context when a section of Adivasis across the tribes came into contact with one another at the administrative level, educational institutions and the army. (e) In contact with nationalist movements not merely in India but elsewhere too, Adivasis came to widely employ the language of nationalism and rights. The term 'socialism' and 'republicanism' too found some currency as in the National Socialist Council of Nagaland (NSCN). From the latter part of 1970s, Adivasi groups have widely embraced the language of 'human rights'. Socialists and Communists resorted to categories of class—worker, peasant, and so on—to denote segments of Adivasis. These terms and categories, however, are sometimes suspect to grapple with the Adivasi dispositions and orientations and need closer scrutiny.[21] (f) In the post-independent period in India, there have been a wide array of social movements with Adivasis at the vanguard. These movements have been critical of the working of Indian democracy, but at the same time drawn millions to engage with it. (g) There has been, sometimes, a romantic onrush to denote the mode of functioning of Adivasi collectives as democratic. While many Adivasi communities regulate their affairs through consensus factoring in consultation, such a mode of living the common is markedly different from a modern democratic polity. A modern democratic polity is an associational bond of free and equal members, extending over a determinate territory, who regulate their collective affairs in the indefinite future through mutual debate and discussion accepting certain codes

---

[20] The writings of Jayaprakash Narayan and Ram Manohar Lohia bear witness to it.
[21] The stories of Mahasweta Devi sometimes help us to grapple with these realities than a conceptual reading of these terms.

and norms. However, response of Adivasis to the working of democracy in India has demonstrated that there is a homologous relationship between the way most of them have conducted their community affairs and such an idea of democracy. Adivasis bring to democracy in India certain distinct inputs, but it also throws open new opportunities and challenges before them.

CHALLENGES BEFORE ADIVASI LEADERSHIP TODAY

The Adivasi repertoire outlined above provides a profile of the place and position of the Adivasis in India and normatively suggests a course of political action. There was an originary moment when India came to grapple with the concerns of Adivasis—the Bordoloi Committee Report, the Thakkar Committee Report and the CADs—and, in spite of the disagreements and contentions they were caught in, there was much convergence across them. We can boldly say that these committees and debates faced the challenge before them squarely and with a sense of urgency never seen afterwards. There were two sets of issues much in contention: autonomy versus inclusion on one the hand and preferential considerations versus equal citizenship on the other. It was also recognized, admittedly with many ifs and buts, that these contentions were the burdens of Indian democracy and could be resolved only through its resources and there were no precedents for the same elsewhere.

The representational politics that unfolded in India, however, led to confinement of Adivasi leadership, further fragmentation and dispersal of the Adivasi public and snapped its capacity of providing a distinct orientation to the Indian democracy. The policies that the different regimes in India pursued with regard to the Adivasis attempted to either co-opt them or split them up. These policies, including reservation measures, led to the creation of a tribal elite who easily fell a prey to share the couch with prevailing modes of dominance. Paradoxically, all of it happened by invoking the language of autonomy, inclusion, egalitarian considerations and development. The constitutional and representational vectors led Adivasis to close ranks behind ethnic markers asserting their distinctiveness rather than the thick concerns they shared in common. Adivasi leadership played second fiddle to such tendency and often employed a conceptual baggage to justify the ethnic closures rather than redefine Adivasi futures with a redefinition of Indian democracy. The latter kind of leadership would have placed it at the head of the central concerns of indigenous peoples across the world, particularly in the post-colonial context. Fortunately, social movements of Adivasis in the last 30 years have thrown up a stratum of militant leadership at the grassroots and this leadership has succeeded in exerting decisive pressure in enacting a series of radical legislation such as the FRA and PESA and teasing out new radical possibilities out of them. However, as yet, this leadership is confined to the grassroots. The challenge before it is to seize the initiative and assert shared Adivasi concerns across India as a whole as its domain of political action, explore the meeting ground with other marginalized sections and rewrite the basic contours of India's democratic dispensation.

REFERENCES

Alam, J. (2004). *Who wants democracy?* Hyderabad: Orient Longman.

Ao, A. L. (2002). *From Phizo to Muivah: The Naga national question in north-east India.* New Delhi: Mittal.

Bhaduri, A. (2009). *The face you were afraid to see.* New Delhi: Penguin.

Bhattacharya, D. (2015). History of eminent domain in colonial thought and legal practice. *Economic and Political Weekly, 50*(50), 45–53.

Bosu Mullick, S. (2003). Introduction. In R. D. Munda & S. Bosu Mullick (Eds.), *The Jharkhand Movement:*

Indigenous People's Struggle for Autonomy in India (pp. iv–xvii). Copenhagen: International Work Group for Indigenous Affairs.

Corbridge, S, Jewitt, S., & Kumar, S. (2004). *Jharkhand: Environment, development, ethnicity*. New Delhi: Oxford University Press.

Fuchs, S. (1966–1967). Messianic movements in tribal India. *The Journal of the Asiatic Society of Bombay, 20*(1–2), 15–33.

Ghosh, A. (1998). *Jharkhand movement: A study in the politics of regionalism*. Calcutta: Minerva Associates.

Government of India. (1949a). *Constituent assembly debates* (volume VII). New Delhi: Lok Sabha Secretariat.

Government of India. (1949b). *Constituent assembly debates* (volume X). New Delhi: Lok Sabha Secretariat.

Government of India. (1949c). *Constituent assembly of India, north-east frontier (Assam) tribal and excluded areas sub-committee, Vol. II (evidence) Part I: Lushai, North-Cachar, Garo, Mikir and Naga hills*. New Delhi: Government of India.

Government of India. (1952). *Parliamentary Debates, Volume 1, Part II*. New Delhi: Lok Sabha Secretariat.

Government of India. (2003). *Indian parliamentary companion: Who's who of members of Lok Sabha (first to thirteenth Lok Sabha)*. New Delhi: Lok Sabha Secretariat.

Guha, R. (1999). *Savaging the civilized: Verrier Elwin, his tribals and India*. New Delhi: Oxford University Press.

Hardiman, D. (1987). *The coming of the devi: Adivasi assertion in western India*. New Delhi: Oxford University Press.

Karlsson, B. G. (2016). Anthropology and the 'indigenous slot': Claims to and debates about indigenous peoples' status in India. In N. Sundar (Ed.), *The Scheduled Tribes and Their India* (pp. 109–133). New Delhi: Oxford University Press.

Kothari, S. (2009). *Social movements in India: A calendar of resistance*. New Delhi: Intercultural Resources.

Kothari, S., Savyasaachi, & George, PT. (Eds.). (2010). *Dissent, self-determination and resilience: Social movements in India*. New Delhi: Intercultural Resources.

Kujur, I. (2003). Jharkhand betrayed. In R. D. Munda & S. Bosu Mullick (Eds.), *The Jharkhand Movement: Indigenous Peoples' Struggle for Autonomy in India* (pp. 16–30). Copenhagen: International Work Group for Indigenous Affairs (IWGIA).

Kumar, B. (2008). *Ethnicity, regionalism and the Jharkhand movement* (M. Phil Dissertation). Jawaharlal Nehru University, Centre for Political Studies, School of Social Sciences, New Delhi.

Lalrintluanga. (2008). Separatism and movement for statehood in Mizoram: An historical overview. In J. K. Patnaik (Ed.), *Mizoram: Dimensions and Perspectives: Society, Economy and Polity* (pp. 45–73). New Delhi: Concept Publishing Company.

Morris-Jones, W. H. (1963). India's political idioms. In C. J. Philips (Ed.), *Politics and Society in India*. London: George Allen and Unwin.

Parulekar, G. (1975). *Adivasi revolt: The story of Warli peasants in struggle*. Calcutta: National Book Agency.

Prakash, A. (2001). *Jharkhand: Politics of development and identity*. Hyderabad: Orient Longman

Sailo, M. L. (2014). *Associational life and political stability: The rise of voluntary groups in Mizoram* (Ph.D. Thesis). New Delhi: Jawaharlal Nehru University, Centre for Political Studies, School of Social Sciences.

Sarkar, T. (1985). Jitu Santal's movement in Malda, 1924–1932: A study in tribal protest. In R. Guha (Ed.), *Subaltern Studies IV* (pp. 136–164). New Delhi: Oxford University Press.

Shah, A. (2018). *Nightmarch: Among India's revolutionary guerrillas*. Chicago, IL: The University of Chicago Press.

Shankar, B. L. & Rodrigues, V. (2011). *The Indian parliament: A democracy at work*. New Delhi: Oxford University Press.

Steyn, P. (2002). *ZAPUPHIZO: Voice of the Nagas*. London: Kegan Paul.

Viswanathan, S. (2006). The tribal world and imagination of the future. *Verrier Elwin lecture*. Retrieved from http://www.indiatogether.org/2006/nov/.

Vundru, R. S. (2018). *Ambedkar, Gandhi and Patel: The making of India's electoral system*. New Delhi: Bloomsbury.

Weber, M. (1978). Politics as a vocation. In G. Roth & C. Wittich (Eds.), *Economy and Society* (pp. 39–94). Berkeley and Los Angeles: University of California Press.

Xaxa, V. (2019). Is the Pathalgadi movement in tribal areas anti-constitutional? *Economic and Political Weekly, 54*(1), 10–12.

Indigenous Peoples and Electoral Politics in India: An Experience of Incompatibility*

Samar Bosu Mullick

INTRODUCTION

India is the ancestral home of the largest number of indigenous peoples in the world and, incidentally, is currently the largest democracy in the world with the largest number of political parties. However, the Anglo-Saxon form of democracy that determines Indian polity today is quite different from the indigenous peoples' notion of participation in the decision-making process and governance.

The indigenous peoples of India have a long history of interaction with alien political systems. In the past, they entered into political conflicts with the tribal oligarchy of the early Aryan aggressors (circa 1500–500 BC), the autocracy of the early empires (600 BC–500 AD), the feudalism of the Hindus (500–1100 AD), the Muslim monarchy (1200–1700 AD)

and the British colonial rule (1757–1947 AD). The conflicts were resolved either by the retreat of the indigenous peoples into more inhospitable terrain beyond the pale of aggressing political power and reconstruction of their old society (Thapar, 1980, p. 10) or through acceptance of the paternalistic rule of the state whilst, at the same time, keeping a relative distance from it. In the absence of both these options, their gradual submergence into the mainstream composite culture was inevitable (Chatterji, 1951; Chattopadhyaya, 1959; Zide & Zide, 1973). With the passage of time and the never-ending process of expansion of the state's political power, the first option ended at a point when there was no such space left to fall back into. In the presence of a gradually expanding condition of dispossession and powerlessness in the peripheral areas of the indigenous habitat, submergence

* This chapter was previously published in K. Wessendorf. (Ed.) (2001). *Challenging politics: Indigenous peoples experience with political parties and elections* (pp. 94–144). Copenhagen: International Workgroup for Indigenous Affairs.

or 'sanskritization' of the indigenous communities remained a constant feature. In the core regions, characterized by high concentrations of indigenous peoples and geographical inhospitability, the second option remained effective until the end of British rule.

The current feature of incompatibility of political ideology with the dominant society is, thus, a continuation of the past experience of the indigenous peoples of India. While indigenous peoples acknowledged the overall sovereignty of the state, 'the medieval state system sought to preserve tribal autonomy' (Singh, 1985, p. 124). During the Mughal period, the indigenous peoples developed a strategy of accommodation and coexisted with the stratified caste society in exchange for some irregular contributions (tribute) to the state (as was the case in Jharkhand, for instance) (Sinha, 1987, p. xvii). In some cases, they themselves developed a sort of tribal oligarchy (as was observed among the Boro-Kacharis in Assam and Southern Gonds of Adilabad in Andhra Pradesh) (Haimendorf, 1985). Yet, in a few other cases, a primary state emerged out of the indigenous matrix (among the Raj Gonds of Madhya Pradesh, Andhra Pradesh and Maharashtra and Bhumijs of Bengal and part of Jharkhand, for instance) (Sinha, 1962; Singh, 1987). The hunter-gatherers among the indigenous peoples, however, remained distanced from such compulsion and existed rather as independent and free peoples in hilly and inhospitable terrain.

The advent of the British colonialism shook the indigenous peoples' social systems by their roots and brought to an end all the previous political equations between the peoples and the state at local level. The 100 years of bloody resistance that the indigenous peoples launched against colonial and feudal rule forced the British Raj to come to certain agreements with them here and there and to enact a number of laws to stop submergence. In order to maintain at least some of their distinctive characteristics, the Scheduled District Act of 1874 came into operation. According to this Act, the tribal areas were treated as separate entities for the purpose of administration. This small concession was, however, just another part of the process of the total subjugation of the indigenous peoples. This process was almost complete by the turn of the last century, when an era of compromise began to appear within the politics of the indigenous peoples, replacing the earlier strategy of accommodation (Bosu Mullick, 1993). The indigenous peoples had now almost given up their millenarian dreams of regaining their lost land and autonomy and had adopted many of the traits of the colonial institutions in social as well as political terms in order to save their pitiable existence from tragedy. They adopted Christianity on a large scale, enrolled their children in western educational institutions and, above all, adopted the colonial political institutions. Even before Independence they, along with the rest of the people, were exposed to the first provincial election in 1937 under the provisions of the Government of India Act, 1935. Their representatives returned from the seats reserved for them and participated in the provincial assemblies. At the same time, they continued to participate in municipal elections in the urban areas (Sachchidananda, 1976). Their initiation into this new system of decision-making obviously took place on a very low scale, but it was nevertheless the humble beginnings of a process that was to humble them even more in the near future.

By the time of independence in 1947, the process of political subjugation of the indigenous peoples of the subcontinent was almost complete, except for a small section of people in the eastern-most fringe of the modern Indian nation state. However, the imminent end of colonialism encouraged the indigenous peoples to aspire to the restoration of pre-colonial political conditions. This was not only in India. At the end of colonialism, there was a global phenomenon of indigenous peoples, who constituted the mosaic of postcolonial nation state societies, stressing their identity and staking claim to a share in the state resources (Singh, 1990). On the issue of autonomy, there emerged three types of

demands: continuation of the relative autonomy enjoyed by the peoples in the princely
states[1] during the colonial periods; separate
statehood within the Indian union; and sovereignty or restoration of pre-colonial political
power enjoyed by the peoples as their natural
right. The new state was, thus, confronted with
the question of formulating a general policy to
satisfy its own interests as well as to pacify the
indigenous peoples.

In the colonial situation, the indigenous
communities (labelled as tribes on the basis
of their backwardness) sought protection
through isolation. Various theories, such as
those of isolation, assimilation and integration were formulated to define the relationship of the tribes, non-tribes and the state. A
good number of colonial officers and anthropologists came out in favour of isolation, the
nationalist and social workers (upper caste
Hindu) were in favour of assimilation and,
ultimately, constitutional arrangements were
worked out in favour of integration. However,
the assimilationist theory did not fade away
(Singh, 1990).

In the post-colonial situation, the adoption
of the integrationist approach, as was propounded in the Tribal Panchsheel (five principles of tribal policy), created a space for the
indigenous peoples to retain their cultural identity. However, their political integration within
the new nation state became a big problem and
continues to be so to this day. They largely
opposed the merger of the princely states into
one or other of the provinces. In many cases,
police resorted to violence, killing thousands
of people throughout the country (especially
in the areas of the Gonds of Baster and Santals
of Mayurbhanj) (Praharai, 1988). The liberal
policies of the princely states allowed the
indigenous peoples to retain their cultural life
and control over their ancestral resources. In
many cases, the kings themselves were from
the indigenous communities (as in the case of

the Gonds) and they understood the indomitable spirit of freedom inherent in the culture
of the people (Haimendorf, 1985). There was
a fear that the merger would rob them of their
relative autonomy. In the central tribal belt,
the demand for statehood became fiercer in
the face of state oppression. With the departure of the British, the Northeastern region of
the country, where most of the hilly areas had
actually never fully become a part of British
India, aspired to independence. The Indian
Government's disregard of these demands led
to an armed conflict claiming innumerable
lives and a conflict, which has still not been
resolved.

The integrationist approach of the state
in the realm of politics entailed bringing the
indigenous peoples into the general political process of the country (with a safeguard)
while providing different forms of political
autonomy at the local and regional levels,
which, however, fell far short of popular
aspirations. The constitution provided for the
provision of seats reserved at both Parliament
and Assembly levels for the scheduled tribes
(STs) to ensure their participation in the representative form of democracy. Accordingly,
it declared some tribal dominated parts of the
old Assam of the Northeastern India as the
sixth schedule area and those of the mainland
as the fifth scheduled areas. While in the sixth
scheduled areas, the traditional village councils of the indigenous peoples were allowed to
function, albeit with many constraints, in the
fifth scheduled areas, the peoples were given
the right to form advisory councils by which
to guide the state governments in implementing the developmental activities of the state
in the scheduled areas. Thus, the people were
left with virtually only one choice of political intervention through which to shape their
future and protect their identity; they were
encouraged to enter into electoral politics, so
alien to their tradition.

[1] The princely states were those pre-colonial kingdoms that the British left to be administered by the families of
the erstwhile rulers under an agreement of the payment of regular taxes.

However, a sense of suspicion and mistrust preoccupied the minds of the indigenous peoples from the very beginning of the existence of the largest democracy in the world. Some of their leaders on the floor of the Constituent Assembly pointed out that there was no need for the tribal peoples to learn democracy from others, rather others should learn to adopt democratic values from the tribal peoples in order to make democracy functional in the country. Indigenous peoples did not even require safeguards or protection from the rest of the people. They required 'protection from the ministers!' 'We do not ask for any special protection. We want to be treated like every other Indian' (Saksena, 1981, p. 7).

During the last half century of functioning of the western model of democracy in India, the indigenous peoples have been exposed to a new set of institutions and political Ideas. Their interaction with these has appeared quite inconsistent and erratic. They found themselves playing an insignificant role in the political drama that was gradually unfolding before them. Their dissatisfaction could not be suppressed. The tribal state relationship was flooded with accords and agreements, but in vain. Problems arising out of the basic issues of identity and autonomy of the indigenous peoples could not be resolved in democratic terms and, ironically, the state frequently resorted to violent means to force people to enter into democratic forms of governance!

Electoral politics has never been the only method of achieving the social and economic goals of the indigenous peoples in India. Of the many avenues, however, it has remained the most accessible and available one, particularly in terms of achieving economic benefits.

But there has been a marked unevenness in the exposure of the indigenous peoples to this method. The degree of intensity of interest and willingness to participate in the electoral process varies widely from tribe to tribe and from time to time. An overview of the fact sheet from Rajasthan in the west to Manipur in the extreme north east of the country exemplifies this; the more we travel east, the less we find the level of participation. This unevenness is also observed in the case of the party affiliation of the people. The level of competitiveness among the national, regional and tribal political parties is not the same all over the country.

This chapter seeks to assess the indigenous peoples experience of electoral politics in the midst of such unevenness since 1952, the year the first general elections took place in the country. The aim is to see whether the cherished aspiration of the indigenous peoples to break with political subjugation of the past has been achieved within the political space provided by the modern Indian nation state. The chapter gives a general background to the all-India scenario while focusing in more detail on the Jharkhand region, located on the eastern side of the central Indian tribal belt. The struggle of the indigenous peoples for autonomy and identity finds its typical expression in this region and, thus, gives us a glimpse of all the dimensions of the issue.

For the sake of convenience, in this chapter, India has been divided into seven zones on the basis of dominance of the respective indigenous community or group of communities from an electoral point of view and the data has been analysed accordingly. The zones are defined in the Annex to this chapter. Trends have also been measured in terms of the core and peripheral habitats of the peoples. Owing to lack of time, I have not been able to examine the assembly poll results and have based my research solely on the results of the parliamentary elections.

INDIGENOUS PEOPLES AND THE STATE

The Indian nation state does not recognize the existence of indigenous peoples in the country. The constitution, however, categorizes 461 indigenous communities as STs, with a population of 51,628,638 according to the census report of 1981,[2] without defining the term 'indigenous'. The basis of identification has obviously been the social 'backwardness' of the notified communities, the objective being the protection of their interests and promotion of their welfare. This arrangement is considered to be perfectly in tune with the constitutional commitment to a socialist, secular and democratic order.

Owing to continuous popular agitation and to political consideration, as in the case of the Banjaras for instance, a few additional communities have, from time to time, been included in the list. As a result of this, the percentage of STs in relation to the total population of the country has continued to increase. While they constituted 7.8 per cent of the total population in 1981, by 1991 the figure had increased to 8 per cent.

SCHEDULED TRIBES

Most of the country's national level indigenous peoples' organizations have accepted the ST list as a workable list (though not exhaustive) of the indigenous peoples of India for the time being. These organizations do not usually accept membership from the communities that have been left out. Some of the larger indigenous communities, like the Kudmis of Jharkhand who were de-scheduled in 1931, resent the national indigenous organizations position very strongly and continue

demanding their inclusion within these organizations, particularly those who regularly represent India's indigenous peoples in international form, including those of the United Nations. The scheduled castes[3] also claim to be the indigenous peoples of India. However, their proposal to form a single representative body with the STs has been turned down by the ST organizations. For the present purpose of our analysis of the main trends and to arrive at a general assessment, we have also considered the ST list as a workable one because whilst not exhaustive it covers the core of indigenous India.

SCHEDULED AREAS

The STs are found in all the states of the country with the exception of the states of Punjab and Haryana and the union territories of Chandigarh, Delhi and Pondicherry. The identity of the STs is related to the scheduled areas (the identification of these areas is based on the excluded and partially excluded areas[4], and the tribal areas were originally notified during British rule. The Government of India Act, 1935 and the Acts before it contained special provisions for the administration of all such areas) which are supposed to be their ancestral homelands. Each community is related to a specific location beyond which the members of it lose their ST status. There is, however, a flaw in this arrangement. The

[2] The Constitution of India states: 342. Scheduled Tribes. (1) The President may with respect to any State [or Union Territory] and where it is a State, after consultation with the Governor thereof, by public notification, specify the tribes or tribal communities or parts of or groups within tribes or tribal communities which shall for the purposes of this Constitution be deemed to be Scheduled Tribes in relation to that State [or Union Territory, as the case may be]. (2) Parliament may by law include in or exclude from the list of Scheduled Tribes specified in a notification issued under clause (1) any tribe or tribal community or part of or part of or group within any tribe or tribal community, but save as aforesaid a notification issued under the said clause shall not be varied by any subsequent notification.
[3] The scheduled castes are the Hindu 'untouchable' communities.
[4] These areas were characterized by the concentration of the indigenous peoples and their resistance movements against colonial aggression. The British government partially excluded these areas from the general administrative system of the colony and brought them under the direct control of the Governor General of India. These areas were administered by his agents.

tribes in Jharkhand who live in Assam and whose members work as tea garden and ex-tea garden labourers are not considered as STs. Similarly, the hundreds of thousands of members of the ST communities living in cities like Delhi are not considered either as members of the STs or as permanent residents of the city. In many instances, it has been observed that a ST in one state is not considered to be so in the neighbouring state. This situation not only restricts mobility on the part of the peoples in question but also deprives them of their rightful place in the political system of the country. In Assam alone, approximately 500,000 people have been denied political representation through reserved constituencies.

Most STs are located in the Central and Northeastern areas of India of which 63.4 per cent live in hilly terrain. Their size varies widely. Most of the tribes are too small in number to make any significant impact on the electoral process. But a few of them are large enough to influence the political situation of their respective region. The largest tribes, like the Gonds in Madhya Pradesh, the Bhils in Gujarat and the Santals and Oraons in Bihar and Orissa, are indispensable in shaping the political present and future of their respective states (Table 4.1).

RESERVATION OF CONSTITUENCIES

The Constitution of India provides for a policy of reservation of constituencies in the elections for the STs to both Parliament (Lok Sabha) and the assemblies in the provinces (normally called the states) in order to ensure their political representation within the highest decision-making bodies of the country (Article 330, pp. 1b and c). In these constituencies, only the members of the STs are eligible for (filing nomination for contesting) elections. Given the uneven development of the different categories of population and given the competitive nature of politics, it was felt necessary to make such special provision for this weaker section of Indian society (Oomenn, 1977, p. 161). This constitutional provision, commonly known as 'protective discrimination', is actually a continuation of the arrangements under the 1935 Act but with a difference: now seats are reserved in proportion to the size of population. On the eve of the adoption of the constitutional provision, Jaipal Singh, one of the most vocal leaders of the indigenous peoples, pointed out the significance of this provision in the Constituent Assembly,

[...] I have come to say a few words on behalf of the Adivasis of India in so far as they are affected by the recommendations of the Minorities Sub-Committee. [...] Our stand point is that there is a tremendous disparity in our social, economic and educational standards and it is only by some statutory compulsion that we can come up to the general population level [...] Our point now is that you have got to mix with us. We are willing to mix with you and it is for that reason [...] that we have insisted on a reservation of seats as far as the Legislatures are concerned [...] Under the 1935 Act, throughout the Legislatures in India, there were altogether only 24 Adivasi (Indigenous) MLAs out of a total of 1,585, as far as the provincial legislatures were concerned and not a single representative at the Center. Now in

Table 4.1   The Largest Tribes in India

Tribe	Population	States of Residence
The Gond	7,449,193	Madhya Pradesh and Maharashtra
The Bhil	7,367,973	Gujarat and Rajasthan
The Santhal	4,270,842	Bihar, Orissa and West Bengal
The Mina	2,087,075	Rajasthan
The Oraon	1,865,995	Bihar, Orissa and Madhya Pradesh

Source: Singh (1994).

this adult franchise system of one member for one lakh (100,000) of the population you can see the big jump. It will be ten times that figure when I speak of Indians. (Saksena, 1981, p. 156)

The constitutional provision for the reservation of tribal constituencies is, however, not a permanent arrangement. It was originally provided up to 1960. Since then it has been extended every 10 years, for another decade. The assumption behind the fixing of a time limit has been that, within that period of time, the STs will have made sufficient progress in social, economic and political fields to be able to successfully compete with other people for election.

Reserving seats for certain parts of the state in the electoral process is often viewed as promoting underdevelopment (Oommen, 1977, p. 163). But, considering the basic situation in which this policy was formulated and recognizing the inherent aspirations of the STs, this can be viewed differently. The state's policy with regard to the STs has two rather contradictory aspects: (a) to draw them into the concourse of national life through a process of successive approximation to the wider society and at the same time and (b) to maintain at least some of their distinctive characteristics (Oommen, 1977, p. 156). Thus, it aims to strike a fine balance between isolation and assimilation and promoting integration. But, on the one hand, under the strong pull of the dominant society, the balance tends to tilt towards assimilation and adversely affect the peoples' urge to protect their identity and, on the other hand, the peoples' apprehension of losing their identity if unprotected pulls the balance down towards isolation. It is generally agreed that neither isolation nor assimilation can ensure development of the STs. In a plural society such as India, it is possible only through a balanced integration. Jaipal Singh rightly pointed out the very premise of the integrationist approach in the Constituent Assembly: 'We do not want protection, we want equality with you' (Saksena, 1981, p.

156). A successful democracy can only be built on equality.

In the valedictory session of the same forum, however, Dr B. R. Ambedker, the Chairman of the Constituency Assembly, himself sounded a note of caution. He said,

> On the 26th January 1950, we are going to enter into a life of contradictions. In politics, we will have equality and in social and economic life we will have inequality. In politics, we will be recognizing the principle of 'one man one vote' and 'one vote one value'. In our social and economic life, we shall, by reason of our social and economic structure, continue to deny the principle of 'one man one value' [...] If we continue to deny it for long, we will do so only by putting our political democracy in peril. (quoted by Jaipal Singh cited in Iyer, 1984)

Thus, the political equality sought by Jaipal Singh is possible only when economic and social equality become a reality. At the moment, Indian society is far from achieving this goal. It is still ridden with caste hierarchy and class divisions, privileges and disabilities. Equality of opportunity is a far cry. On the occasion of the completion of 25 years of democracy in India, Professor T. K. Oommen observed,

> It is extremely unlikely that soon after the termination of reservation of seats, the STs will be able to get elected to as many numbers of seats as at present [...] it is (also) unlikely that others will support the candidates drawn from these categories (such as the STs) if they contest general constituencies. (Oommen, 1977, p. 163)

Basically, nothing changed over the next quarter of a century. In this kind of scenario, the continuation of the policy of reservation appears to be the only means of providing some opportunity for indigenous peoples to vent their grievances as well as to articulate their demands.

Forty-one parliamentary and 530 assembly constituencies are currently reserved for the STs out of a total of 543 and 2,980 constituencies, respectively.[5]

---

[5] Due to the implementation of the Delimitation of Parliamentary and Assembly Constituencies Order, 2008, 47 out of 543 parliamentary constituencies and 554 out of 4,109 assembly constituencies are reserved for the STs

POLITICAL PARTIES

Political parties emerged for the first time in India during the last phase of British colonial rule. Their aim was to press the demand for freedom from imperialism and to establish democracy in the country. In spite of political parties being the most vital institution for the functioning of democracy, it was an absolutely new institution for the peoples of India in general and for the indigenous peoples in particular, who were at home with their village-level non-party democracy. The indigenous peoples, along with the rest of the people of the country, were for the first time introduced to electoral politics in 1935 (in British India). Between 1935 and 1952 (the year the first general election was held in independent India), many elections were held including municipal ones. The indigenous peoples participation in those elections was, however, negligible. Only a few educated and aware individuals took part in them. But they soon realized that they were in most cases left with only one way of venting their aspirations and demands through this alien institution in the new liberal democratic set up in independent India. In most cases, they were brought into the fray through political parties formed and led by non-indigenous people. In a few places, like Jharkhand and Assam, they tried to intervene through political parties they themselves formed.

The non-indigenous political parties have different ideological approaches to the issues of the indigenous peoples. Whereas some, such as the Congress Party and the Socialists, stand for integration others, like the Bharatiya Jan Sangh (BJS)/Bharatiya Janata, the Hindu Nationalist Party and the Communist Party of India (CPI) (Marxist), propagate their assimilation into mainstream Indian society. Some parties of the Left, like the CPI and Forward Block, hold an ambiguous position. Only in recent times have some underground communist parties agreed with indigenous peoples issues of concern, such as identity and autonomy. They, however, influence the electoral process in constituencies dominated by the indigenous peoples by calling for a boycott of the elections. We shall briefly discuss the ideological positions of the major political parties with regard to the indigenous peoples.

THE CONGRESS

Way back in 1885, A. O. Hume, a British citizen, formed the Indian National Congress with a group of leading members of the Indian elite, educated in colleges in England. Gradually the Congress developed into a broad forum of nationalist forces imbibed with western liberal political ideas. The second generation leadership, however, tried to integrate the Fabian Socialism of Nehru and reformed Hinduism of Gandhi on the eve of independence.

Gandhi's approach towards the Adivasis, as he called the indigenous peoples, was in favour of their Hinduization on a reformed level. His ideal of Ram Rajya (The Kingdom of Lord Rama), where truth and justice prevail, certainly had a place for the loyal Hanuman (the monkey-god), supposedly the ancestor of the Adivasis, though never articulated in such terms. He preached non-violence, vegetarianism and cleanliness among the Adivasis. He motivated many reform movements among the indigenous peoples, such as the Safa Hor (clean men) among the Santals and the Tana Bhagats cult among the Uraons.

> While giving a political message to the tribal peoples, the Mahatma was also able to communicate some of the basic tenets of Hinduism. Moreover, in their simple mind, by and large, they considered him to be a 'Hindu leader' and generally felt inspired to emulate the Hindu model of life, which Mahatma represented. (Sahay, 1980, p. 62)

---

in India (Note of this volume editors).

Mahatma Gandhi's promotion of non-violence, however, robbed the indigenous peoples of their heroic spirit for fighting oppressive forces, both feudal and colonial. The militancy of the Bhils, for instance, took a back seat in the national movement under Gandhi and the Bhils, known for the value they placed on and for their courage, were confused and found their customs and traditions incompatible with the non-violent spirit of the national movement (Singh, 1995, p. 168).

Gandhian intervention in the indigenous peoples' movements also discouraged the people from continuing their struggle against the feudal moneylenders (Hardiman, 1987) and zamindars (landlords) (MacDougal, 1985). In the garb of Gandhian reformism, some Gandhians even went to the extent of converting the indigenous peoples to Hinduism. The leading congressmen of Bihar encouraged the Santals to convert to Hinduism by wearing the sacred thread[6] (Singh, personal conversation). However, in many cases where they had no other option but to choose between the British and Gandhi, they opted for the latter, particularly in western and central India. Their participation in the non-cooperation movement and *Praja Mandal* (Peoples' Council) politics demonstrated this trend. But, as we move towards the east, to Jharkhand and Northeast India, Gandhi's popularity wanes. In Orissa, the indigenous peoples were not interested in the Congress. The Santals and the Kols (Ho-Mundas) continued their struggle even in the year of independence (Paik revolt in 1947) and immediately after that (anti-merger struggle of 1948) (Praharai, 1988). In Bihar also, Gandhi and the Congress were popular only in pockets. In the northeastern hills, except for Jadonang and Rani Gaidinliu's movements (1930–1932), which were inspired by Mahatma Gandhi and the Congress and in this sense had an Indian national dimension, most of the tribes wanted to be free from the control of the government of the plains following the departure of the British (Kabui, 1990).

After independence, the Gandhian Congress took a back seat and the Nehruvian Congress took over with a different approach towards meeting the demands of the indigenous peoples. Nehrus *Tribal Panchsheel* (five principles for the tribal peoples) recognized the indigenous aspirations for autonomy and identity and, as opposed to the Gandhian way of gradual assimilation, adopted a secular means of integration. But problems emerged over the issue of autonomy. Congress stood for a ridiculously low degree of autonomy and persuaded those formulating the constitution of India to enshrine its views under the fifth and the sixth schedules. Nehru wanted to win the hearts of the indigenous peoples by providing economic and political concessions. But, where he failed, the Congress turned to crude violence. The Congress forced its entry into the Northeast, the Jharkhand region and into the southern hilly ranges of central India including Telangana. In the rest of the indigenous regions, where the sharpness of the peoples organized strength was already blunted, the policy of giving concessions paid dividends.

By the 1960s, the Congress had established itself as the most successful political party among the indigenous peoples. It turned its support base in the indigenous regions into a bank of votes and made steady profit for the next three decades until being seriously challenged by the Bharatiya Janata Party (BJP). Today, the Congress Party has been losing in many constituencies and is engaged in a neck-and-neck fight with the BJP in the rest.

THE RIGHT-WING PARTIES

The parties that very ardently uphold Hindu national chauvinism today are the BJP

---

[6] Sacred threads are threads worn by the Hindu upper castes across the chest to symbolize their initiation into the caste hierarchy and, by extension of this, their superiority and power.

and the Shiv Sena. Whereas the latter has recently emerged as a regional party based in Maharashtra, the former has a long history. The Hindu chauvinist forces, one of whose members killed Gandhi, had a very bad name during the early years of independence. Their mother body, called the Rashtriya Swayamsevak Sangh (RSS), ideologically and organizationally in tune with the Nazis of Germany, was banned. But its political wing, called the BJS, continued to participate in elections with the aim of establishing a Hindu India, scoring negligible success. During the time of the Emergency (1975) instigated by the then Prime Minister Indira Gandhi,[7] the BJS became part of the Janata Party, formed of a coalition of centrist opposition parties in order to fight the Congress. This event gave the party a rare opportunity to gain all-India access and some degree of prestige. When the Janata Party became defunct, the party was rechristened the Bharatya Janata Party (BJP).

With regard to the policy towards indigenous peoples, the RSS has from the very beginning been overtly promoting assimilation. It could not accept the reformist approach of Gandhi, let alone the integrationist approach of Nehru. For this party, the indigenous peoples are simply the *vanavasi* (the forest dwellers). One of the founders of the organization tried to make people believe that the *vanavasi* were Hindus of an ancient type. Because of their relative isolation they remained purer than the rest of the Hindus (Golwalker & Madhav, 1980) and practiced ancient Hindu religion (Sanatan Dharm). Following the footsteps of this Guru, many sociologists and anthropologists also denied the existence of the tribe as an entity independent of the dominant social system. This view is manifested best in Professor Ghurye's refusal to allow any separate definition of tribe and caste. For him, tribes were only backward castes (Ghurye, 1963). The fact ignored by this position is that

'the confrontation between the tribals and the non-tribals is not of recent origin. The long history of their interaction has been one of tension and conflict [...]. In the process there was considerable adjustment and accommodation. The emergent dominant ethos bore unmistakable evidence of having absorbed elements from the country's tribal heritage. In the reverse direction, the tribal ethos also did not remain uninfluenced by the pan-Indian pattern of life that was gradually consolidating itself. But the fusion of the two ways of life was never complete: some tribal groups were assimilated and lost their tribal identities; others determinedly sought to retain their diacritical marks and worked for the preservation of their cultural self-image. (Dube, 1972, p. 29)

However, it was only natural that the BJP would adopt a program of converting the indigenous peoples to orthodox (Brahmanic) Hinduism, but what has been most shocking to many Indians is its effort to support sister organizations to reconvert indigenous peoples who embraced Christianity a century or more ago in order to get rid of the inhuman oppression of the Hindu landlords, contractors and moneylenders. The party has taken on an extensive programme of supplanting the Christian educational and other philanthropic organizations in the tribal areas. In the political sphere, it has taken full advantage of the indigenous peoples' growing dissatisfaction with the Congress and, of late, has emerged as the second largest party in ST-reserved constituencies.

THE LEFT-WING PARTIES

The CPI entered the indigenous regions with an agenda of land reform immediately after its formation in 1921. In eastern India, particularly in the undivided Bengal extending to Assam, it successfully mobilized the indigenous peoples under the great Tebhaga

---

[7] Prime Minister Indira Gandhi proclaimed an Emergency in India on the grounds of external and internal threats to the sovereignty of the country, banning all opposition political parties and intending to establish a dictatorial rule.

(one-third share in produce) Movement. In Telangana and the neighbouring hilly ranges of northern Andhra Pradesh, it consolidated its strength among the Girijans (the mountain dwellers, as they called the Indigenous peoples there) on similar agrarian issues. However, the party never recognized questions of identity and autonomy of the indigenous peoples. For them, indigenous peoples remained as the forest dwellers, a remnant of primitive communism. After independence, the party became divided over the issue of entering into parliamentary democracy. The section opposed to it and in favour of carrying on armed struggle, accepted the majority opinion of leaving the bullet and embracing the ballot after an initial resistance, only to be resurrected in the late 1960s and progressively strengthened in the following years. Three major communist parties emerged from this process: the CPI, the Communist Party of India-Marxist (CPI-M) and the Communist Party of India Marxist-Leninist (CPI-ML). The CPI-ML emerged out of a long-standing agrarian movement organized by revolutionary communists among the Santals, a very consolidated and heroic indigenous people (Duyker, 1987). Later on, the Party developed its strong bases mainly among the indigenous communities in Bengal, Assam and Andhra Pradesh. Its extra-parliamentary revolutionary agenda and its programme of restoration of land rights attracted the freedom-loving indigenous peoples. In recent years, however, a section of the party has joined electoral politics.

The Marxist parties are both internally and among themselves divided ideologically in their approach to the question of the indigenous peoples and their aspirations. Marx had very little to say about indigenous peoples' society in India. His general observation, based on secondary information, of Indian society and his attempts to develop a model of an Asiatic mode of production touched the life of these peoples only partially. However, they are still the people who have interacted most with the Marxists in the course of their economic and political movements rather than the followers of Gandhi or Lohia. The Marxists endeavour to follow the words of Marx rather than to use the basic principles of Marxism that has always turned out to be a misfit in the context of the indigenous peoples' movement. However, this has neither deterred the Marxists nor the peoples from continuing to try to find a Marxist solution to the stagnant tribal movement for liberation in the country.

Among the Marxist, the debate has centred around the question of characterization of the indigenous peoples' society and indigenous movements and thereby on the issue of their incorporation into the countrywide revolutionary movement. For the peoples, the problem remains one of being associated with the communist revolutionary movements as peasants and workers, or as components of emerging nationalities, at the cost of their distinct indigenous identity. The most common and conventional practice has been to define indigenous peoples, commonly called tribes in Marxist parlance, as part of the class society. A slight distinction is, however, made between the settled and nomadic tribes when it is said that,

> All the major tribes of India are actually peasant societies existing within the broad political economy of the state. Their existence and motion can only be understood in terms of a class analysis of these societies and the articulation of the different modes of production within their structure. (Pathy, 1984, p. 43)

In support of his argument, Pathy refutes the prevalent anthropological notion of the tribal society's isolation, homogeneity and so-called static state of being. He clarifies his position, however, by saying that 'it is true that even now a few small, acephalous tribal communities have little specialization and division of labour, but that description cannot be generalized for the majority of the tribal societies in India, covering at least 85 per cent of the tribal population' (Pathy, 1984, p. 23). Besides, among the advanced STs, the rich households exploit not only the poor fellow tribals and those belonging to backward tribes but also, to a lesser extent, the dispossessed non-tribal communities (Pathy, 1984, p. 24).

This kind of analysis naturally cannot truly perceive the nature of tribal movements centred either on political autonomy and identity or on the issue of displacement. For a section of the Marxists, the autonomy movement appears to be a retrogressive and reactionary endeavour. They tend to equate it with the nationalist movement of the Slaves, which was used to defeat the Austrian and Magyar progressive movements in the multi-national Hapsburg Empire during the 19th century. This was something which Marx and Engels could not forgive the Slavs. Engels referred to such national groups as non-historic nations who lacked national vitality and were condemned to disappear or prone to being de-nationalized (Engels, 1973, 1974).

Marxists of another hue discard the over-emphasis placed on the fact of economic differentiation observed in the tribal societies and consider them as nationalities or sub-nationalities. Both anthropologists and sociologists have supported this position (Sharma, 1993). In the Indian context, the Marxists describe indigenous peoples movements as anti-neocolonial. But there still remains a problem when they describe the regional movements like the Jharkhand, Chhattisgarh, Vidarbha, and so on, as the movements of oppressed nationalities. These nationalities are conceived of as social groups that emerged out of a composite of both indigenous and non-indigenous peoples. The indigenous peoples, however, strongly resent the Marxist design to club them together with others as one people. In response to this opposition, the Marxists retreated a little, coming up with the theory of emerging nationalities. It is propounded that in many tribal regions during the course of the state formation in the feudal period, many ethnic communities were forged into one economic and political system and together they evolved a common culture and common language. But the British colonial invasion thwarted this process of nationality formation in these regions (Keshari, 1982). The tribes and non-tribes of Jharkhand, for instance, instead of being assimilated into the neighbouring nationalities, as earlier predicted (Bose, Ghurye etc.), have shown a definite trend towards a differentiated trans-ethnic unity, claiming the status of a nationality (Orans, 1968; Roy Burman, 1960).

The theory of internal colonialism is presented in this context. A. K. Roy highlighted the operation in Jharkhand, arguing that social inequality and regional unevenness, in terms of political development and regional economic disparity, have created numerous internal colonies in India, of which Jharkhand is the biggest and most important. Tribal areas such as Jharkhand have become the colonies of the developed areas within India.

The view with the strongest potential to attract tribal peoples into the Marxist fold has been a rejection of the inevitability of tribal society going through various stages of history before it is liberated. This position, therefore, negates the call of other Marxists for the peasantization and proletarianization of the tribes.

While observing anti-colonial movements in India, Marx certainly come across the 'Choar rebellion and the Santal Hur' (Marx. Notes). But he did not consider them specifically as indigenous movements. They were looked at as a part of the countrywide rebellion against the destruction of the earlier agrarian relations of the feudal period caused by the East India Company. The Marxists, therefore, identified them as a part of the spontaneous peasant uprisings, which flared up against the land and taxation policy of the company (Kaviraj, 1981, p. 137). It is certainly correct to see these tribal movements as the outcome of the introduction of the permanent settlement in the Jharkhand region and it is wrong to seek to prove that they were directed against the local landlords and moneylenders alone. 'Any attempt to divorce the permanent settlement from the British colonial policy, or to trace the disintegration of the tribal village community without reference to British colonial rule, is bound to be a futile intellectual exercise that will hardly convince anyone' (Kaviraj, 1981, p. 139). But it is equally a faulty analysis if the tribes of Jharkhand, for instance, are not distinguished from the peasants of Bengal in terms of their relationship with the land, which was destroyed by the British. Under the Mughal rule, the peasantry enjoyed the rights of occupancy and could not be ejected from the land as long as they paid revenue. But a tribal was not a *ryot* (a tenant) because he did not pay revenue. He held the ancestral land collectively with his lineage brethren. Although the new system turned both of them into tenants-at-will, the cause and demand of their struggle were different. The peasantry resented the loss of their earlier rights over land and the tribals demanded restoration of their ancestral right to land. Thus Professor Sushebhan Sarkar very rightly observed,

> Marx did not leave behind any systematic presentation of the history of India, that was never his main preoccupation. He set down his observation on certain current Indian questions, which attracted public attention, or drew materials from India's past and present conditions to illustrate parts of his more general arguments. These passing reflections cannot therefore be taken as a finished study of the subject in any dogmatic sense. (Sarkar, 1969, p. 93)

The conventional Marxist understanding of the Indian reality failed to recognize the indigenous peoples as a separate entity, one that can be seen neither as simply classes nor as nationalities. This weakness is reflected in the failure of the Marxist parties to address the issues of the peoples in their totality. It is only in recent times that some of the underground Marxist parties, engaged in armed struggles mostly in the hilly and forested areas of Central and eastern India, have realized this fact and supported the aspirations of the peoples. Those who are engaged in parliamentary politics, such as the CPI, CPI (M) and CPI (ML), have fared very badly in the electoral fray in constituencies

dominated by the indigenous peoples throughout the country. Similarly, the electoral boycott, called for by the underground parties, has not been able to secure the response of the people to any considerable extent. But these are still the only organizations that have the potential to attract the most oppressed section of the indigenous peoples.

OTHER SMALLER PARTIES

The socialists (social democrats), under Ram Manohar Lohia, realized the difference between caste and tribe. But their basic tragedy has been their inability to remain united. Several varieties of socialist parties, such as the Socialist Party (SP), Praja Socialist Party (PSP), Samyukta Socialist Party (SSP), the Revolutionary Socialist Party (RSP) and so on, have entered into electoral politics and have had some sporadic success. The socialists received a shot in the arm after the Emergency in 1976 and then in 1989 under the Janata Dal (JD). But their all-India success was not similarly reflected in the constituencies dominated by the STs. Although the party stood for tribal identity, on the issue of autonomy, it adopted a vague position, the majority opposed the tribal peoples' demand for more autonomy beyond the inadequate provisions of the fifth and the sixth schedules. Neither did it take up the agrarian issues affecting the indigenous peoples nor did it address their acute problem of displacement due to mining, industrialization and urbanization. The party remained confined to the issue of reservation for the other backward classes (OBCs) in government services. However, the RSP in Bengal has continued to remain a popular party among the tea garden labourers consisting mainly of indigenous peoples from Jharkhand. In general, the party is engaged in trade union movements and in relation to tribal autonomy, it does not want to go beyond the existing constitutional provisions.

In the early years following independence, a group of people made up largely of members of the royal families of the princely states formed the Swatantra Party (SWA). The Indigenous peoples of these princely states did not initially want to merge their territories with the states run directly by the British. They were motivated to vote for their erstwhile kings, queens and princes or people nominated by them to represent them in the Parliament and the state assemblies. But when they realised the futility of this effort, they abandoned the party and gradually the party ceased to exist as it lost its only support base.

Recently the Bahujan Samaj Party has entered the indigenous areas to contest elections. The party's ideological understanding of the Indian social reality is based on achieving the plurality of Indian society and continuing the oppressive caste hierarchy. Only 10 per cent of Brahmins (priestly class), Rajputs (royal caste), Banias (traders) and other upper castes have been ruling the 90 per cent of Dalit, tribals and Shudras (including the Muslims who were converted to Islam from these castes). Hence, the liberation of these bahujan (plural majority) is possible only by the destruction of the age-old caste system under the leadership of these oppressed people. Although the party has not yet been able to secure any seats either in the Parliament or in assemblies from the indigenous areas, it has registered its presence there with some degree of success.

ELECTORAL POLITICS

Although the STs constitute only about 8 per cent of the Indian population, their concentration in certain areas of Central and Northeastern India enables them to determine the electoral results of not only the reserved constituencies but also the contiguous non-reserved ones. The 1961 census does provide a district-wise breakdown by STs. Matching this data with the distribution of reserved seats by district shows that in every district in which the tribal population exceeds 50 per cent of the total, more than 50 per cent of the seats are reserved for tribal candidates. Indeed, virtually every district in the country with a substantial tribal population there appears to be a close fit between the proportion of tribals within the district and the proportion of seats that are reserved (Weiner & Field, 1975, p. 86). The distribution of the ST population by state and Parliamentary and Assembly seats reserved for them shows their dominance in the electoral politics of the states (Table 4.2).

The four most turbulent states of Mizoram, Nagaland, Meghalaya and Arunachal Pradesh in the North-east of India, along with Lakshadweep and Dadar and Nagar Haveli, clearly show the overwhelming dominance of the STs in the electoral politics of the states. The other two Northeastern states of Manipur and Tripura, with a little more than 30 per cent of ST population, reserve 50 per cent of their parliamentary seats. However, in the case of their assemblies, the percentage of reservation roughly corresponds to the percentage of population of the STs.

In the central tribal belt, the states of Madhya Pradesh, Orissa and Gujarat, where the majority of the ST population is located, reserve about the same percentage of seats (i.e., 22.5, 23.8 and 15.4) as the strength of the population of the tribes. In these three states, ST communities hold the key to the balance of power in the governments. In Sikkim, the STs enjoy the same position.

In the Northeastern state of Assam, although the official percentage of STs is only 12 per cent, a huge number of tribes of Jharkhand origin live there who influence the political scene in the state either through their individual votes or together with the indigenous communities of the state. In Rajasthan, Maharashtra and Bihar, the STs usually have very little say in electoral politics and governance. In the rest of the states, the influence of the STs is virtually negligible.

Table 4.2 Distribution of ST Population by State and Parliamentary and Assembly-Reserved Constituencies

SI. No.	State	1981% of Total Population	1991 % of Total Population	No. of Parliamentary Seats	No. of Assembly Seats
1.	Mizoram	93.5	94.8	1 out of 1	39 out of 40
2.	Nagaland	84.0	87.7	—	59 out of 60
3.	Meghalaya	80.6	80.5	—	55 out of 60
4.	Arunachal Pradesh	69.8	63.7	—	59 out of 60
5.	Manipur	27.3	34.4	1 out of 2	19 out of 60
6.	Tripura	28.4	30.9	1 out of 2	20 out of 60
7.	Madhya Pradesh	23.0	23.3	9 out of 40	75 out of 320
8.	Sikkim	23.3	22.4	—	12 out of 32
9.	Orissa	22.4	22.2	5 out of 21	34 out of 147
10.	Gujarat	14.2	14.9	4 out of 26	26 out of 182
11.	Assam	—	12.8	2 out of 14	16 out of 126
12.	Rajasthan	12.2	12.4	3 out of 25	34 out of 200
13.	Maharashtra	9.2	9.3	4 out of 48	22 out of 288
14.	Bihar	8.3	7.7	5 out of 54	28 out of 234
15.	Andhra Pradesh	5.9	6.3	2 out of 43	15 out of 294
16.	West Bengal	5.6	5.6	2 out of 42	17 out of 294
17.	Karnataka	4.9	4.3	—	2 out of 224
18.	Himachal Pradesh	4.6	4.2	—	3 out of 68
19.	Kerala	1.0	1.1	—	1 out of 140
20.	Tamil Nadu	1.1	1.0	—	3 out of 234
21.	Uttar Pradesh	0.2	0.2	—	1 out of 425
	Union Territories				
1.	Lakshadweep	93.8	93.1	1 out of 1	—
2.	Dadra and Nagar Haveli	78.8	79.0	1 out of 1	—
3	Daman and Diu	—	11.5	—	—
4.	Andaman and Nicobar Island	4.8	9.5	—	—
	All India	7.8	8.0	41 out of 543	530 out of 4072

Source: Census Reports, Government of India—Arrangement: Author.

For the first two general elections in 1952 and 1957, the Delimitation Commission, the commission that demarcated the area of the reserved seats, reserved a seat for an indigenous representative if the ST population within a constituency amounted to more than half of the total population. Where the STs were substantial but less than a majority, the commission created double member constituencies (as distinct from single-member constituencies elsewhere) in which one of the seats was reserved for a ST candidate and the other one was open to any candidate, ST or non-ST. In these constituencies, each voter had two votes and the constituency was twice as large as other constituencies. By the 1962 general election, this distinction between single- and double-member constituencies had been eliminated and the Election Commission had dropped double-member constituencies.

THE EMERGING TRENDS[8]

The electoral results of the last 50 years reveal an uneven pattern of voting behaviour on the part of the STs (indigenous peoples) of the country. Since the Congress remained in power for the first 25 years following independence without a break and continued its hold until 1998 with a few brief breaks, it remained powerful all over the country, including the ST areas. But, it has not shown any steady increase in success. While it constantly remained powerful among the Meenas in Rajasthan and the Gonds of the northern part of Madhya Pradesh, it gradually lost its support base among the Bhils in Gujarat, Maharashtra and among the Gonds of the southern part of Madhya Pradesh. Similarly, in Orissa, it developed a solid base among the Khonds and Sabars in the west but a less steady relationship with both the Santals and the Ho-Munda-Oraon combined in the Northeastern part of the state. In Bihar, among the same tribes, it could never establish itself with strong roots. In the North-east in the state of Assam and in its six sister states, Meghalaya, Mizoram, Manipur, Nagaland, Arunachal Pradesh and Tripura, the party has always faced uncertainty. For many STs, the Congress has been the ruling party of an aggressive and oppressive state and, for others, it has been a party combining tribal elites and alien migrants.

The BJP, the strongest opponent of the Congress in the ST areas, emerged in the electoral arena only after 1984. Like the Congress, it has not been able to influence all ST constituencies uniformly. Among the Meenas in Rajasthan, it is visible only in the peripheral seats.

Among the Bhils in Gujarat, it has just made an entry by starting to gain followers. Among the Bhils in Maharashtra and Madhya Pradesh, it is not a powerful force at all. With the tribes in Andhra Pradesh, it has not yet made any inroads. Among the Khonds and Shabar-dominated seats in western Orissa, it won three out of five seats only in the last elections in 1999. Among the Gonds of the northern part of Madhya Pradesh, it has fared very well and, in neighbouring Bihar, it has been on a winning run. But it has not been able to make progress in Eastern and Northeastern India. The parties of the Left have registered only sporadic success in Andhra Pradesh, Maharashtra, Bihar and Assam. In West Bengal, however, they have established strong roots among the STs.

ASPIRATIONS AND EXPERIENCES

The indigenous peoples of India have retained their cultural and social identity to varying degrees but they have virtually lost their political autonomy. A 100-year-long struggle, beginning in the later part of the 18th century and ending of the late 19th century, to retain the traditional political identity of the people, resulted in an arrangement under the Government of India Act, 1935. It reflected the paternalistic colonial policy, veering towards the isolationist approach. The Gandhians and the Nationalists did not approve when Ambedkar, the most respected leader of the Hindu uncountable communities, proposed its continuation in independent India (Thakkar & Ambedkar, 1945). Enlightened indigenous leaders such as Mr Jaipal Singh demanded the inclusion of indigenous peoples in the general political framework of the country, with the constitutional provision of reservation of constituencies to ensure their political representation. In independent India, a new and alien political system was imposed

---

[8] For a more detailed study of the emerging trends in the voting behaviour of indigenous peoples in different regions and for a definition of the core and peripheral areas, see the Annex to this chapter.

on the indigenous peoples. They were neither prepared for it nor capable of handling it. Now they were forced to take political decisions, not separately anymore but together with the rest of the people of the country. Now they were to elect their own people along with their non-tribal neighbours and they were exposed to powerful political lobbies consisting mostly of their oppressors who controlled the new political process. The voter turnout in reserved constituencies as compared to the general turn-out in the non-tribal rural constituencies in the first six general elections clearly revealed a lack of interest in this new political system among indigenous peoples (Table 4.3). This observation was particularly conspicuous in the areas where movements for autonomy were strong. In the case of Bihar, for instance, where the demand for a separate Jharkhand state consistently dominates the political scene, the falling percentage of tribal voter turnout reflects their frustration at unfulfilled aspirations (Weiner & Field, 1975, p. 90).

It is true that if the STs acted together as a block, they would be a formidable political force. They could not only control the smaller states of Nagaland, Mizoram, Meghalaya and

Arunachal Pradesh, but also play a powerful role in Orissa, Madhya Pradesh and even Gujarat and Assam. But this did not happen. The marked unevenness in the level of political aspirations and political consciousness of the indigenous peoples of India has kept them divided politically. Some authors identified three major political tendencies among them on the eve of independence.

In the hill areas of the northeast, some tribals were *secessionist*. Amongst the Naga and Mizo tribes in particular there were those who argued that their differences from other Indians were sufficiently great to justify the creation of a separate independent state [...] Many of the Ho, Munda, Oraon and Santal tribes of southern Bihar and neighbouring Orissa and Madhya Pradesh (and also West Bengal) were separatists who supported the Jharkhand Party's demand for the separation of the tribal areas from these three (four) states and formation of a tribal state within the Indian political system. Separatist politics also emerged among the Garo, Khasi and Jaintia tribes of the southwestern districts of Assam.

In Assam secessionist and separatist politics permeated nearly all tribes as a backlash response to the growth of strong cultural nationalism among the Assamese-speaking people of the state [...] In the princely areas of Rajasthan, Madhya Pradesh

Table 4.3   Turnout[14] in Tribal and Non-Tribal Rural Constituencies in Selected States

Year	Assam[a] Non-T Rural %	Tribal %	Bihar Non-T Rural %	Tribal %	Madhya Pradesh[b] Non-T Rural %	Tribal %	Orissa Non-T Rural %	Tribal %
1952	53	44	43	47	41	36	39	29
1957	51	40	44	39	40	35	43	28
1962	51	41	45	34	42	32	36	25
1967	59	49	50	32	51	38	44	28
1969	—	—	51	34	—	—	—	—
1971–72	61	57	54	32	54	41	42	27

Source: Weiner & Field (1975).

Note: [a]The Assam figures for 1972 do not include the areas that are now part of Meghalaya and Mizoram.

[b]The Madhya Pradesh figures for 1952 also pertains to the territories of Madhya Bharat, Bhopal and Vindya Pradesh, newly included in the state.

[14] The figures shown refer to valid turnout. The rural figures for 1952 and 1957 pertain to single member constituencies only.

and Orissa tribal peoples were *loyalist* in their politics. Some of the maharajas (kings) had created a paternalistic and personalized relationship with the tribes-men that was often reinforced by real or mythical agnatic relationships. In several princely states nationalist organizations, affiliated to the Indian national Congress, became politically active in the late 1930s and 1940s, but by and large these did not win the support of tribals or their leaders. (Weiner & Field, 1975, p. 82)

This kind of categorization, however, has its problems. The so-called loyalist tribes, as the election results show, though initially apprehensive of the merger of the princely states with the existing states (provinces) under the direct rule of the British Raj, did not remain loyal to their previous masters following independence and supported the Congress instead of the SWA formed of the princes and their lackeys. Among the Meenas in Rajasthan, the SWA only once won a core seat in its short lived presence from 1962 to 1971. In each of the Bhil-dominated constituencies, it secured one core seat in the 1962 and 1967 elections, and among the Gonds in Madhya Pradesh, it could not even win a single seat during this period of its existence. In Orissa, too, it could win only one core seat during its lifetime. Thus, in the erstwhile princely states it was not the loyalty of the indigenous peoples to the feudal aristocracy that guided their political decisions but quite clearly the dominant ideology of the Gandhian Congress. However, many scions of the ex-princely states joined the Congress to perpetrate their rule over the tribes. In recent years, In many such areas, such as Chhattisgarh, Vidarbha and Telangana, separate state movements have emerged. On the other hand, the fine line of difference between the separatist and secessionist tendencies has always remained unstable. The original demand of Jharkhand was to become a Crown's Colony. At one point in time, Jaipal Singh, the supreme leader of the indigenous peoples of Jharkhand, talked to Jinnah, the creator of Pakistan, about keeping Jharkhand in the proposed corridor between the east and the west parts of Pakistan. Again in the late

1980s, the Hos of Kolhan demanded a sovereign Kolhan. In recent times the 'separatists' of the 1970s have become 'secessionists' in Assam. The quiet Tripuris of the past have become secessionist as well.

These tendencies actually reflect varying degrees of aspiration for autonomy. Their roots can be traced back to the varying degrees of disintegration of the indigenous peoples traditional social systems. The gradual erosion of their identity and autonomy from west to east, from the coast of the Arabian Sea to the hills of Burma (officially called Myanmar) reveals the fact of their uneven historical exposure to the ever expanding power of the Brahmanic Hinduism and the Hindu state, the spread of Islam and the Islamic state and the advent of Christianity and British colonialism. While the Bhils and allied peoples were the earliest victims of such exposure, the Nagas and other Northeastern peoples have been the latest ones to face state aggression. The Gonds held their spirit of independence high for quite some time but finally had to compromise with the Mughals and Marathas by adopting some feudal elements in the peripheral areas. The Santa ls, the Munda-Hos and the Uraons retained their autonomy until the advent of British colonialism, while the Bodos and Kacharis of the Brahmaputra valley lost their autonomy at about the same time. The indigenous peoples living in the hills never actually surrendered to the British.

Thus, the prospect of departure of the British evoked a mixed reaction in the minds of the people. While the Nagas and other hill peoples of the North-east developed a hope of regaining their lost sovereignty, the Bhils at the other end of the scale aspired, at most, to retrieve their lost land. While the Jharkhand peoples hoped to revive their lost autonomy within a framework of a symbiotic relationship with the state, the Gonds hoped to receive a share of the emerging political power under the leadership of the Congress. On the other hand, the demands of mainstream society's nationalist leadership were quite uniform. It wanted the people to be integrated into main-stream Indian society and politics by giving up their demand for political identity beyond the limit of the constitutional provisions and to be happy with limited recognition of social identity.

Since the Congress had emerged as the leading national force, the indigenous peoples were forced to negotiate with it. The process of such negotiations was never peaceful nor was it fruitful in most cases. The indigenous peoples entered into the process of negotiation in three ways, depending on their historical and political conditions and consciousness. The Meenas, the Bhils and the Gonds, as well as other small peoples in western-central India, joined the Congress, the Jharkhand peoples in the eastern-central region and the Bodos and Karbis in the plains of Assam formed their own political parties and the Nagas and the Mizos in the Hills established their own governments. With the passage of time, the process of negotiation with the Indian government took many dramatic twists and turns.

THE NORTH-EAST

This part of the Indian Union has remained politically turbulent since the time of independence. While the plains of the river Brahmaputra remained comparatively docile during the initial years, the hills declined to be a part of India. Understanding the indomitable urge of the indigenous peoples for independence, those who drew up the Indian constitution formulated a provision for limited local autonomy at the district level under the sixth schedule of the constitution, but the arrangement fell far short of the peoples' demand. Their resentment over the last half a century has found its expression in either a rejection of the electoral process and the party system, or entry into the system by forming their own political parties. An overview of three typical cases of political expressions, that of the

Bodos, the Nagas and the Kokborok people of Tripura, will suffice to gain an appreciation of the peoples' experiences of the electoral process and political parties.

The Nagas in India are the inhabitants of the easternmost part of the north-east, covering the state of Nagaland, the hills of Manipur and adjoining parts of Assam. The Nagas aspired to gain back the freedom they lost to the British and to be united with their brethren across the border in Burma after the withdrawal of the colonial rulers. But this hope remained unfulfilled. The government of India under Nehru and his Congress party rejected outright the Nagas and appealed to come to the negotiating table. Instead the Indian Army was employed to unleash a reign of terror in Naga country.

The Nagas boycotted the first general election of 1952 as a practical demonstration of their non-acceptance of the Indian constitution. A letter addressed to the President of India dated 18 September 1954 on behalf of the Nagas from the Kilonsers (administrating elders), the Government of Free Nagaland set the tone for future action amongst the Nagas. It read,

The influence of Mahatma Gandhi was so great that the people of Free Nagaland have been calmly tolerating the Indian troops for all these years hoping that the truth will ultimately prevail [...] Since the doctrine of 'non-violence' is now fast running out to the Indian Government and the troops alike, 'Ahimsa' has become a mockery, the synonym of cowardice in our Free Nagaland; and the free Naga people have no patience left just to stand by and see the Indian officers and troops shooing, beating, slapping and kicking the Nagas as if we are their slaves. Women are being so often molested and raped that the depravity and lustfulness of the Indians now in Free Nagaland would certainly shame you and the Indian nation. (Government of Nagaland, 1968)

The formation of the state of Nagaland in order to provide greater autonomy to the people after a long period of bloodshed and humiliation did not solve the problem. The insurgency went on unabated. The National

Socialist Council of Nagaland clearly disapproved of the participation of the Nagas in the Indian multi-party political system. It declared,

Party politics proceeds in the main, from party interests and as party politics in any form is obviously affording opportunities to the opponents in many ways to have hold on some of the antagonistic parties, it is dangerous and unwarranted in times of national emergency [...] In a country like Nagaland, particularly at the present time, the party system could never accomplish any thing except leading her to ruination [...] Hence the dictatorship of the people through a single political organization and the active practice of democracy within the organization is unquestionable for the salvation of Nagaland. (National Socialist Council of Nagaland, 1980)

Thus, the Nagas never participated wholeheartedly in the electoral process. Electoral turnout in Nagaland and Manipur has always been low. In many polling booths, nobody turns up to cast their votes. In some places, the abnormal percentage of polling is reported to be the handiwork of the army. For instance, in Nagaland, 33.8 per cent of votes were cast in the parliamentary elections of 1996, but this increased to 76.2 per cent in 1999. If this is compared with the results of other states, the abnormality becomes conspicuous. One of the government's strategies to win the hearts of the Nagas has been to pump huge amounts of money into the state. But this has not only corrupted the bureaucracy but essentially degraded the ministers and political leaders. The easy money culture has taken its toll on democratic processes in the state. 'The money culture has been destroying the Nagas. This has numbed our people; their initiatives and political consciousness', said MLA Mr Hasuka Sumi. Mr R Paphino, another MLA, says, 'For an assembly constituency of hardly 6,000 to 12,000 voters, the ruling party candidates are given ₹50 to 60 lakh [100,000] or even one core [10 Million]' (National Campaign Committee against Militarization and Repeal of Armed Forces (Special Power) Act, 1997). The Congress' victory in the Naga areas, therefore, should not be taken at face value. Although a few Naga political parties regularly contest elections, none of them has alone been able to form a government in recent years.

The Bodos form one of the major indigenous peoples of Assam. They inhabit the plains of the Brahmaputra river valley. The Government of India Act, 1935 recommended the provision of reserved seats for the plain tribe of Assam. As a result of this, in the 1937 elections, a few Bodo leaders were returned to the provincial assembly by contesting the elections under the banner of their only party, the Tribal League. Since then, the Bodos have been taking part in elections through their own parties and other all India or regional parties as well. By the 1960s, the people realized the futility of achieving the much sought after autonomy through the provisions of the sixth schedule of the constitution. They demanded a Bodo-dominated state under the Plain Tribal Council of Assam (PTCA). The government paid no heed to it. But in the meantime, the PTCA mobilized people politically and replaced the Congress in the only parliamentary-reserved constituency that they were allotted. In the assembly elections also, the party fared well.

In the following years, however, the party considerably lost its spirit and determination to fight for the cause it stood for. Its leaders were accused of drifting into corrupt practices. The All Bodo Students Union (ABSU), the student unit of the party founded in 1967, now took the lead after 20 years of existence in order to strengthen the demands for Bodo autonomy and to protect Bodo identity. Under the leadership of the ABSU, the movement became ever more militant. Violence erupted all over Bodoland. The Union called for a boycott of elections during the late 1980s and early 1990s. In 1991, the Bodoland Accord was signed. The government agreed to provide an autonomous council for Bodoland under the state of Assam. One section of the agitators did not agree to it on the grounds that it gave no power to the people to shape their future.

The government refused to give more political power to the Council. Now the Congress played a dirty trick to weaken the agitation. It developed a rift between the tea labourers in Jharkhand and the Bodos. The Bodos expected them to vote for their candidates but the Santals supported the Congress, which falsely promised them ST status in Assam. This rift led to a bloody conflict between the Santals and the Bodos. In the following riots, hundreds of people lost their lives and thousands were rendered homeless. The Bodoland movement now demanded a sovereign country for the Bodos.

The political experiences of the last few decades have made it evident that under the present political and administrative set-up, the Bodos are not able to safeguard their interests (Daimari, 1997). Today the Bodos are divided into several political groups and parties following contradictory strategies to achieve their dream of political autonomy.

Tripura has been a classic case of displacement of indigenous peoples by the huge and incessant migration of the Bengalis from the neighbouring country Bangladesh. This has turned the demography of the state upside down. Today, the indigenous peoples of Tripura have not only become a small minority in their own land but have also at the same time lost a considerable part of their source of livelihood. During the period between 1931 and 1951 alone, while the population of the Bengalis grew by about three lakhs that of the indigenous peoples saw an increase of just 30,000. The indigenous peoples, who accounted for 95 per cent of the population of Tripura in the 1931 census, have now been reduced to a mere 31 per cent, according to the 1991 census.

In 1967, the Borok indigenous people of Tripura established a socio-cultural non-political organization called the Tripura Upajati Juba Samiti (TUJS) with the aim of strengthening existing social, cultural and religious bonds between the state's Borok communities. In 1968, it made a demand for the sixth schedule of the constitution to provide a series of safeguards for the indigenous peoples. This became a source of controversy between itself and the non-indigenous immigrants over the next decades. As the tension between the two groups mounted, by 1978, the TUJS had gathered enough support to win 4 seats in the 60 member Legislative Assembly. In mid-1979, when the Tripura Tribal Areas Autonomous District Council Bill was discussed in the Communist Party of India (Marxist) (CPM) led Left Front state assembly (which remained in power until 1988), it was strongly opposed by the Amra Bangali (We Bengalis) party and by the Congress party. The Bill was, however, passed in the assembly and received the President's assent in July 1979.

But now the Congress used a dirty trick to win over the sympathy of the Bengalis. Along with the Amra Bangali, it instigated a communal riot that left 350 people dead, 500 seriously injured and almost 300,000 people homeless. As a result, the TUJS split in two, forming the Tripura Volunteer Force, which later became known as the Tripura National Volunteer Force. It led an armed revolt to re-establish the autonomy of the Borok people.

In Tripura, the Congress and the CPM have played on the sentiments of the people and now they are paying dearly for that. After Manipur, Tripura has become the most violent state in the northeast. The indigenous peoples have virtually relinquished electoral politics and are fighting tooth and nail to protect their ancestral land.

JHARKHAND

Jharkhand is the ancient abode of the Austro-Asiatic language speaking Mundari group of indigenous peoples. The Dravidian language-speaking Uraons also constitute one of the numerous indigenous peoples living in this region. It covers roughly Zones 5 and 6 according to our categorization (see Annex).

The indigenous peoples of Jharkhand had organized themselves to demand autonomy even before the British decided to leave India. They made a representation to the Simon Commission.[9] They formed the Adivasi Mahasabha (the Great Council of the Indigenous Peoples) in 1935, which coincided with the adoption of the Government of India Act partially recognizing the demand of autonomy. They, thus, had no problem in responding to the political challenges immediately following independence. The Jharkhand Mahasabha was converted into the Jharkhand Party under the leadership of the unchallenged leader, Jaipal Singh, an Oxford blue and the captain of the Indian hockey team that, for the first time, won Olympic gold. The party had a spectacular success in the 1987 parliamentary elections by winning five core and two peripheral seats (in Zones 5 and 6) on the issue of the formation of a separate state (province) of Jharkhand with an overwhelming majority of indigenous peoples. In the following assembly election in Bihar, it secured 35 seats and became the second largest party after the Congress in the Bihar assembly. But the Congress did not pay one iota of respect to this popular verdict, it played all kinds of tricks and deceits to frustrate the aspirations of the people. Jaipal Singh himself became a victim of this dirty game and betrayed the cause of his people. When the members of the State Reorganizing Commission visited Ranchi to feel the peoples' pulse on the spot, Mr Singh did not turn up to meet them.

However, 100,000 people gathered in Ranchi to register their demand. In its recommendation, the Commission clearly undermined the electoral verdict of the peoples and betrayed democratic values by rejecting the popular demand on faulty and flimsy grounds. In the first place, it did not agree to form a

ST-dominated state carved out of the four contiguous states of West Bengal, Bihar, Orissa and Madhya Pradesh, on the grounds that the peoples living there had no common language with which to communicate. Then it showed that, in Bihar, part of the proposed Jharkhand, the STs were in minority. And to counter the same demands of the non-ST indigenous communities, who were also for a Jharkhand state but for different reasons, it said that the formation of such a state would create a regional economic imbalance. The loss of popularity and growing discontent among the masses owing to the failure of the Jharkhand Party leadership to force the government to create Jharkhand and constant efforts of the Congress Party's top political leadership for its merger with the Congress paved the way for the Jharkhand Party leaders to believe that, once in government, they would be able to pursue policies of tribal welfare effectively as well as strengthen their demand for a separate state (Mandal, 1986, p. 24).[10]

Jaipal Singh merged the Jharkhand party with the Congress in 1962. He was given a place in the Central Ministry and a few of his close associates were made ministers in the Bihar government. In the ensuing years, however, they had to pay heavily for their decision to merge. Jaipal Singh was dropped from the ministry and his lieutenant, Mr S. K. Bage, was made a minister in the new ministry. In the fourth general elections, in 1967, most of the leaders who merged with the Congress suffered the blast of this anti-merger wind. Jaipal Singh narrowly escaped while Mr Bage succumbed to it, forfeiting even his security deposit (Sachchidananda, 1976, p. 18). The Congress then made another move to break the backbone of the movement by creating a rift

[9] The Simon Commission was a seven member commission sent to India in 1927 by the Imperial Government in London to prepare a report on political reforms in India with a view to amending the Government of India Act. It was headed by Sir John Simon and six other members of the British Parliament. It was boycotted by the Indian National Congress.

[10] In the meantime, three new states, namely Uttaranchal, Chhattisgarh and Jharkhand, have been created. Unfortunately Jharkhand only partially fulfils the demands of the indigenous peoples because it does not include the areas lying in West Bengal, Orissa and now Chhattisgarh (former Madhya Pradesh) (note of the editor).

between the Christian and the non-Christian indigenous peoples. The Party projected a non-Christian leader, Mr K. Oraon, who demanded the removal of the Christians from the ST list on the grounds that, by converting to Christianity, they had lost their indigenous characteristics. His second argument was that the Christians had reaped the benefits of the constitutional privileges because they were already educated and so now the benefits should go to the non-Christians. During the visit of the Canada Committee to Ranchi in November 1968, he presented these points to the members. Later on, he also prepared a bill asking for the removal of the Christian STs from the ST list, a dramatic change in the political situation of the country with the promulgation of the Emergency in 1975, how- ever, frustrated his efforts (Sachchidananda, 1976, p. 18). But the Congress took advan- tage of this, a section of the Christian com- munity, especially the members of the Roman Catholic Church and the Anglican Church, joined Congress to safeguard their privileges.

Despite these developments, the autonomy movement did not die. Second-level leaders came forward to revive the Jharkhand Party immediately after the merger. Since then several parties have emerged in the name of Jharkhand and occupied centre stage of the electoral politics in the region. Even in the darkest days of the movement, the reorganized Jharkhand party continued to win one or two core seats and scored the first runner-up posi- tion in many seats.

The Jharkhand movement received a shot in the arm with the emergence of the Jharkhand Mukti Morcha (JMM) in 1973 in the coal fields of Dhanbad. A number of Marxist cadres from the CPM defected from the party under the leadership of a very popular trade union leader, Mr A. K. Roy and a Kudmi leader, Mr B. B. Mahato, in order to address the ethnic issue of autonomy along with eco- nomic demands. The party received the spon- taneous support of not only the Santals and the Kudmis but also a section of the non-tribal

coal miners. This development led to the erup- tion of a bloody struggle between the JMM and the Congress-supported coal mafias. The JMM emerged victorious but at the cost of many tribal and non-tribal lives. Very soon the party spread all over the proposed Jharkhand state, covering the four existing states.

A new wave of the Jharkhand movement began. Shibu Soren emerged as a charismatic leader of the Santals. His party declared a crusade against the coal mafias, land mafias, moneylenders and corrupt government officers who usurped the money earmarked for tribal development. The Congress gov- ernment in Bihar, where the epicentre of the movement lay, responded with bullets for the people and jail for the leaders. Shibu Soren went underground. Organizationally, the party was not strong enough to face such a level of state terrorism and, ideologically, it had just entered into the process of develop- ing a new premise of ethnic and class unity. A. K. Roy's theory of internal colonialism in Jharkhand, and other similar tribal dominated areas of the county, was yet to be developed. The Congress took advantage of these weak- nesses and hatched a conspiracy to destroy the unity of the people. It used the internal con- tradictions of the Kudmis and the Santals and the political contradiction between Marxist thought and tribal elitist individualism. Shibu Soren was contacted and taken to Delhi. Indira Gandhi, the Prime Minister of India, assured him of a withdrawal of all court cases against him and promised that all kinds of support would be provided in the forthcom- ing elections, but on condition that he would have to sever all connection with the Marxists. Shibu Soren accepted the offer and came back to Jharkhand to prepare his base on a divided ground for the coming elections. He played the ethnic card and the Congress opened its coffers.

In the parliamentary election of 1980, the Congress made a comeback by winning four core and two peripheral seats in the Ho-Munda and Uraon Zone and 2 core and 3 peripheral seats in the Santal zone. JMM (Soren) was duly rewarded; Shibu Soren won the Dumka seat. In the 1984–1985 Assembly election in Bihar, the Congress party bagged 14 ST reserved seats and the JMM secured 6. During this period, the JMM members of the legislative assembly in Bihar kept 'selling' their votes to support the Congress. They started amassing wealth and developing relationships with the mafias, big contractors and industrialists of the region. This gradually led to their alienation from the people. At one point in time, Shibu Soren realized this and openly said, 'I was a tiger in Tundi [where he developed his base first] and now have become a dog of Delhi'.[11] But it was too late to undo the wrongs that he had done.

The simmering discontent among the people found a space for political expression when a group of Santal and Kudmi students organized to form the All Jharkhand Students Union (AJSU) in 1986. The Union received the tacit support of the President of the JMM, Mr Nirmal Mahato, who gradually drifted away from the Congress fold. Around the same time, a group of dissident JMM second-level leaders took an initiative to reorganize the Jharkhand movement.

The initiative received support from the most enlightened sections of the Jharkhand intelligentsia and some Marxist groups. They formed the Jharkhand Coordination Committee (JCC) in 1975 with 53 social, cultural and literary organizations, trade unions and two political parties, including the Binod Bihar Mahato group of the divided JMM, the Jharkhand Party under the old guard Mr N. E. Horo, the Marxist Coordination Committee of A. K. Roy and the Santosh Rana Faction of the CPI-Marxist-Leninist. The AJSU became the leading group in the JCC. The autonomy movements of the Gorkhas and the Bodos inspired the leaders of AJSU. In its first convention, there was a unanimous decision to adopt a strategy of boycotting the elections until the Jharkhand state was created. The JMM strongly opposed the decision. But immediately after that, the Congress hatched a conspiracy to Kill Nirmal Mahato, a strong supporter of the AJSU movement. He was fired at point blank by a known Congressman in the presence of Sibu Soren. His killing created a stir throughout Jharkhand. The AJSU declared the other JMM leaders, including Shibu Soren and Suraj Mandal, Secretary and Vice-President, respectively, in whose presence the killing took place, as traitors and stooges of the Congress and began a militant movement in association with the JCC.

With the growing militancy of the AJSU, supported by all sections of the indigenous peoples of Jharkhand, a new phase of the Jharkhand movement began. The movement compelled the central Congress government to begin a series of negotiations first with the AJSU and then with the JCC. The Committee on Jharkhand Matters, formed by the union government, described the cultural unity of the area proposed under the Jharkhand state and recommended autonomy for the region. It was a moment of great victory for the indigenous peoples of the region. But the following period undid the gains. With high hopes of achieving Jharkhand, as promised by the central Congress party, the AJSU withdrew its call to boycott elections and entered into the fray itself. In the 1990 Bihar assembly elections, the Congress lost 6 (total 8) ST seats, whereas the JMM gained 4 (total 10) and AJSU got only 1 seat. In the following election of 1995, the Congress lost further three seats and the Jharkhandi parties together secured 14 seats (JMM - 11, JPP-AJSU - 2 and JKP - 1). This was reflected at the negotiation table. The Congress, back in central power in 1990, initially agreed to form the state of Jharkhand but only by dividing Bihar where, naturally, the indigenous peoples would become a minority.

---

[11] Personal communication with Shibu Soren.

However it did not implement this but, on the contrary, bribed the four JMM members of Parliament to save its government from a no confidence motion. The AJSU disclosed this underhand dealing and, later on, the Central Bureau of Intelligence took up the case and framed charge sheets against Shibu Soren and three other JMM MPs. They were put behind bars on charges of corruption. The Jharkhand movement received a second series of setbacks.

During the period of decline of the Jharkhand parties, the BJP gradually widened its area of influence. It presented an alternative to Jharkhand in the name of Vananchal (the forestland).[12] The frustrated and humiliated non-Christian indigenous peoples slowly shifted their allegiance to the BJP in ever greater numbers. In the 1998 parliamentary election, it won in all three core seats and four out of six peripheral seats in the Santal-dominated constituencies (Zone 6) and three out of six core seats and one out of two peripheral seats in the Ho-Munda and Uraon-dominated constituencies (Zone 5). In the 1999 parliamentary election, these figures increased further. In Zone 5, it gained all six core seats. However, in Zone 6, it lost one core and one peripheral seat. In the Bihar assembly election of 2000, it secured 14 out of 28 ST-reserved seats. These electoral results clearly indicate the indigenous peoples' frustration and loss of faith in their own parties, on the one hand and on attempt to achieve their age-old demand of ridding themselves of the misrule of Bihar and exploitation of the Biharis, on the other. But there is going to be a high price to pay. The BJP has been spreading the venom of communalism in Jharkhand for quite a long time. It has been convincing the non-Christian indigenous peoples that they are Hindus and the Christians to reconvert to Hinduism. Its Vananchal is not going to uphold the aspiration of autonomy of the indigenous peoples of Jharkhand. Its allegiance to those with financial power goes naturally against the economic interests of the indigenous peoples. Thus, the party is not going to help the people from either an ethnic or an economic point of view. The Congress and BJP have been successful in dividing the people along political and religious lines.

THE BHILS AND THE GONDS

In terms of states, Gujarat is the heartland of the Bhils. The Bhils joined the Congress movement under the leadership of Gandhi. The Gandhization of the Bhils was almost complete in his lifetime. The heroic Bhils changed their old way of revolting against oppressive forces and submitted to the Gandhian way to achieve their objective of attaining their freedom and protecting their identity. Thus, no party other than the Congress could enter into their area. The Bhils also showed an inclination to cut across the ethnic barrier and during the colonial period, under the leadership of Motilal Tejawat, they formed a joint organization called the Eka (Unity) with the peasants of Bijotia, who belonged to the Dhakra caste. In this case, caste and ethnicity merged under economic compulsion. This strategy of uniting with the lower ranking sections of the population in the state continued even after independence. The Bhils united with other communities to form KHAM, consisting of the Kshatriya-Baxi Panch caste (a combination of two backward castes), Harijan (untouchable castes), Adivasi (indigenous peoples) and Muslims.

This political alliance of numerous communities had constituted a solid support

---

[12] The Hindu fundamentalist organizations, including BJP, their political organ, used Vananchal to substitute the idea of Jharkhand. For them, the term Jharkhand stood for Christian conspiracy of separatism. The move was obviously politically motivated and attempted to create a social division between the Christians and the Muslims on the one side and the Hindus on the other. More dangerously, it tried to create a rift between the Christian and the animist indigenous peoples by promoting the thesis that the latter are Hindus.

structure for the Congress. When the powerful farming communities withdrew their support from the Congress, KHAM stood by it from 1975 onwards.

It [...] stood the Congress in good stead during the powerful anti-reservation stirs and the elections from 1975 to 1989. After the 1989 Lok Sabha polls, however, the Congress leadership alienated these supportive caste groups. Such a trend helped the JD to carve its base among the Adivasis and the Muslims. The Congress base in the reserved seats was significantly eroded. Whereas in 1985 assembly poll, it won all the 26 ST seats, in the 1990 poll, it won only 7 ST seats. The JD jumped from 1 seat in 1985 to 6 and the BJP opened its account by winning 6 seats in 1990. The entropy of KHAM as the social base of the Congress can be traced to the elitist attitude of the Congress leaders toward the respective mass base of these numerically strong groups [...]. What had actually happened was the cornering of the fruits of power, patronage and development by the new KHAM elite to the negligence of the KHAM masses. The average voters of these backward groups, perceiving this elitist trend, felt alienated from the leaders who reaped the advantages of the Congress rule in the name of the masses. The communal riots of the mid-1980s and the Ram Shila Pujan (the Hindutwa drive of the BJP) helped them reorient their religious and political affiliation to the BJP. The callous disregard of the Congress in looking after the Muslim masses prompted the Muslim masses to move towards Mr. V.P. Singh's JD.[13] During the period of the Coalition government (until November 1990) the BJP expanded its base amongst the OBCs and the Adivasi communities by inducting their leaders into the Government Boards and Corporations. (Seth, 1992)

The Gonds of central India have a long history of exposure to the state and civilisation of the northern plains. Apart from certain densely forested and inhospitable tracts, most of the Gond territory was brought under the indirect rule of the Mughals through the numerous feudal principalities, some of which were headed by the Gonds themselves. The British did not disturb this arrangement to any extent

and the authorities of these princely states allowed the indigenous peoples to continue to maintain their traditional practices of making decisions on the basis of their customary laws. The Congress evoked a new spirit of optimism among the Gonds and other smaller tribes in the region. The aristocracy of the princely states expected to be free of the British yoke in the independent India and the people expected to live in the Ram Rajya (the kingdom of god) as propagated by the Congress. This led the region to become a strong support base for the Congress. Until 1989, no party (except the Bharatiya Lok Dal [BLD] in 1977) was able to make any dent in it. Only in the peripheral regions in the south and in northern Andhra Pradesh did the Communist Parties developed mass support.

The small section of Gond oligarchy received a prestigious position in the Congress leadership hierarchy and positions in the ministry. However, the prestige, power and privileges gradually made them yes-men of the ruling party leadership and also of the forces of the industrialists and feudal elements. Their gradual alienation from popular issues like the industrial labourers' movement in Bhopal, the movement against the construction of big dams on the Narmada, the sacred river of the Gonds, or the movements for restoration of land rights in Baster started to be reflected in the electoral results. The inclusion of the Banjaras in the ST list for purely political reasons, which unbalanced the Gond domination in many areas such as Adilabad in Andhra, was strongly resented by the people (Haimendorf, 1985). The random exploitation of the mineral and forest resources of the indigenous peoples' habitats created wealth for outsiders and generated poverty for the people.

All these factors led to the mobilization of popular opinion in three directions: regional autonomy movements in Chhattisgarh in Madhya Pradesh, Vidarbha in Maharashtra

---

[13] The Janata Dal Party was formed in 1989 and led by V. P. Singh in order to oppose the Congress Party, particularly on the issues of the Bofors gun deal and reservation for the OBCs.

and Telangana in Andhra Pradesh started to gain popularity. The Congress fast began to lose its support base to the BJP and the extra-parliamentary-armed revolutionary movements of the Marxists gained immense popularity by addressing issue of land reform. The formation of the separate state of Chhattisgarh is being shaped. In the last parliamentary election of 1999, the BJP established itself as a dominating political force by winning three out of five core seats and two out of nine peripheral seats in Zone 3. The Telugu Desam Party (TDP) of Andhra Pradesh and the Biju Janata Dal (BJD), Orissa, its allied parties, also altogether gained one core and four peripheral seats. In Zone 4, the BJP routed the Congress by gaining three out of four core seats and four out of five peripheral seats.

CONCLUSION

In India, none of the existing political parties has ever shown any interest in understanding and appreciating the cultural values of the indigenous peoples. They have looked at ethnic differences as an obstacle to development and national integration. Thus, even after half a century of a democratic polity in India, the indigenous peoples continue to find their aspirations unfulfilled. The integrationist policy of the state, as well as a majority of the ruling and powerful political parties, turned a small section of the educated and privileged indigenous peoples into a domesticated species and alienated from the rest of the state system. The growing demand for ever more autonomy suggests the lessening confidence of the people in the goodwill of the ruling parties. The mounting exploitation of the indigenous peoples habitats and consequent impoverishment of the peoples have time and again forced the people to revolt against the state. More and more indigenous peoples have been following the path of the Nagas and the Mizos in the Northeast and that of

the Communist revolutionaries (the so-called Naxalites) in the rest of the country.

The present electoral process and party politics have remained considerably alien to the people. Indigenous peoples find it difficult to make their voice heard at the centre and in state decision-making bodies for two reasons: first, they find it very difficult to adjust themselves to the demands of a modern representative democracy in a multiparty system, which has replaced their traditional participatory democracy or, as some authors prefer to call it, 'subject political culture' (Mishra, Prasad, & Sharma, 1982). This substitution has compelled the indigenous peoples to imbibe new political values, attitudes and beliefs, which may not be congenial to their political health (Sachchidananda, 1976). The growing importance of money and muscles in the elections has compelled the leaders to corruption and their close associates to becoming goons. Thus, the true voice of the people can be neither articulated nor conveyed properly. Second, the multi-party system of democracy has divided the peoples from within. The indigenous peoples, with no traditions of elections but of decision-making by consensus, have now been forced to choose one among many of their own contesting brothers by casting votes. It is generally observed that a voter seldom votes for a candidate in cognition of the virtue of voting. He votes under pressure from the village mukhia (headman), influential persons, tribal or caste leaders, faction leaders, etc. He or she sometimes government order to cast their votes (Chandra & Maheddin, 1990). The elected members of the peoples cannot act jointly either in the Parliament or in the state assemblies for the common cause of their communities because of their affiliation with the different political parties (Haimendorf, 1985, p. 163).

In general, the turnout among ST voters has always remained much lower than among non-tribal voters. Between tribal and rural constituencies, the difference in percentage turnout was calculated at an average of about

10 per cent (Weiner & Field, 1975, p. 93). Our data on the core and peripheral constituencies of the last three parliamentary elections shows an approximate 5 per cent gap between them in mainland India consisting of states other than those of the Northeast. The Northeast situation is now completely different. Rigging on a large scale and boycotting at an alarming rate mark the polling process in a considerable number of the tribal dominated polling booths of the reserved constituencies.

But still the indigenous peoples have been casting their votes in progressively greater numbers with the passage of time. Because, for the majority of them, despite all its shortcomings, it is the only way left to vent their political opinion.

While the non-indigenous political parties address only class/economic issues, the indigenous political parties raise the ethnic/cultural demands of the indigenous peoples. Thus, the lack of a holistic approach to the indigenous question marks the electoral politics of the country. This has to be developed on the part of the extra-parliamentary revolutionary political forces in recent years. The failure of the Congress to keep a tight hold on the indigenous voters and the inability of the indigenous parties to maintain and increase their support base amongst their own people must be considered within this context. The BJP's growing popularity in recent times in the indigenous peoples' areas has been the direct outcome of this.

It is gradually becoming a reality in Indian politics that the days of one party rule have come to an end. In the changed political situation, with the emergence of regional political parties and state governments run by them and the coalition governments at the centre running with their support, the importance of the STs in electoral politics has increased considerably. The political parties are now being forced to recognize their demands. The stakes, however, have become very high. If the indigenous leadership misses this opportunity now, their hope of fulfilling their demands through peaceful electoral democracy will remain no more than a distant dream and ever more people will join and swell the ranks of the parties with extra-parliamentary strategies by which to achieve the same demands.

REFERENCES

Bosu Mullick, S. (1993). Jharkhand movement: A historical analysis. In M. Miri (Ed.), *Continuity and Change in Tribal Society*. Shimla: Indian Institute of Advanced Study.

Chandra, R., & Maheddin, A. (1990). Tribals in election process in a Rajasthan village. In

Chatterji, S. K. (Ed.) (1951). *Kirata-Jana-Kriti: The Indo-Mongoloids: Their Contribution to the History and Culture of India*. Calcutta: The Asiatic Society.

Chattopadhyaya, D. (1959). *Lokayata: A study in ancient Indian materialism*. Bombay: People's Publishing House.

Daimari, A. (1997). *The plight of the Boros of north east India*. mimeo.

Dube, S. C. (1972). Inaugural address. In K. S. Singh (Ed.), *The Tribal Situation in India*. Shimla: Indian Institute of Advanced Study.

Duyker, E. (1987). *Tribal guerrillas: The Santals of West Bengal and the Naxalite movement*. New Delhi: Oxford University Press.

Engels, F. (1973). *Magyar struggle in Marx: The revolutions of 1848*. London: Lawrence & Wishart.

Engels, F. (1974). What have the working class to do in Poland? In K. Marx (Ed.), *The First international and After*. London: Penguin Books.

Ghurye, G. S. (1963). *The scheduled tribes*. Bombay: Popular Prakashan.

Golwalker, G., & Madhav, S. (1980). *A bunch of thoughts*. Bangalore: Jagran Prakashan.

Government of Nagaland (1968). *A brief historical background of Naga independence*. Federal Government of Nagaland, Second Edition.

Haimendorf, C. V. F. (1985). *Tribes of India: The struggle for survival*. New Delhi: Oxford University Press.

Hardiman, D. (1987). *The coming of the Devi: Adivasi assertion in western India*. New Delhi: Oxford University Press.

Iyer, V. R. K (1984). *Human rights and the law*. Indore: Vedpal Law House.

Kabui, G. (1990). Political development in tribal North East India. In B. Chaudhuri (Ed.), *Tribal Transformation in India. Vol. III: Ethnopolitics and Identity Crisis*. New Delhi: Inter-India Publications.

Kaviraj, N. (1981). Spontaneous peasant risings as a problem of historiography. In D. Chattopadhyaya (Ed.), *Marxism and Indology*. New Delhi: K. P. Bagchi & Company.

Keshari, B. P. (1982). *Jharkhand andolan ki vastavikta*. Ranchi: Chetna Prakashan.

MacDougal, J. (1985). *Land or religion*. New Delhi: Manohar.

Mandal, B. B. (1986). *Tribals at the polls*. New Delhi: Uppal Publishing House.

Mishra, S. N., Prasad, L. M., & Sharma, K. (1982). *Tribal voting behaviour: A study of Bihar tribes*. New Delhi: Concept Publishing Company.

National Campaign Committee against Militarization and Repeal of Armed Forces (Special Power) Act (1997). *Where "peace keepers" have declared war: A report on violation of democratic rights by security forces and the impact of the Armed Forces (Special Powers) Act on civilian life in the seven states of the north east India: 1997*. New Delhi: National Campaign Committee against Militarization and Repeal of Armed Forces (Special Power) Act.

National Socialist Council of Nagaland. (1980). *Free Nagaland manifesto*. Oking: National Socialist Council of Nagaland.

Oomenn, T. K. (1977). Scheduled castes and scheduled tribes. In S. C. Dube (Ed.), *India since Independence: Social Report on India, 1947–1972* (pp. 153–193). India: Vikas Publishing House Pvt. Ltd:

Orans, M. (1968). *The Santal: A tribe in search of a great tradition* (pp. 113 and 52–55). Detroit: Wayne State University Press.

Pathy, J. (1984). *Tribal peasantry dynamics and development*. New Delhi: Inter-India Publications.

Praharai, D. M. (1988). *Tribal movements and political history in India: A case study from Orissa (1803–1949)*. New Delhi: Inter-India Publications.

Roy Burman, B. K. (1960). Basic concepts of tribal welfare and integration. In L. P. Vidyarthy (Ed.), *Anthropology in Action*. Ranchi: Council for Social and Cultural Research.

Sachchidananda (1976). *The tribal voters of Bihar*. New Delhi: National Publishing House.

Sahay, K. N. (1980). The transformation scene in Chotanagpur: Hindu impact on the tribals. In P. Dash Sharma (Ed.), *The Passing Scene in Chotanagpur* (pp. 25–71). Ranchi: Maytryee Publications.

Saksena, H. S. (1981). *Safeguards for scheduled castes and tribes: Founding fathers' view: An exploration of the constituent assembly debates*. New Delhi: Uppal House, Publishing House.

Sarkar, S. (1969). Marx on Indian history. In P. C. Joshi (Ed.), *Homage to Karl Marx*. New Delhi: People's Publishing House.

Seth, P. (1992). The 1990 poll and politics: A western Indian perspective. In S. Mitra, & J. Chriyankandath (Eds.), *Electoral Politics in India*. New Delhi: Segment Books.

Sharma, K. L. (1993). The question of identity and sub-nationality: A case of Jharkhand in Bihar. In M. Miri (Ed.), *Continuity and Change in Tribal Society*. Shimla: Indian Institute of Advanced Studies.

Singh, C. S. K. (1995). *The sound of drums: Tribal movement in Rajasthan, 1881–1947*. New Delhi: Manak Publications.

Singh, H. D. (1998). *543 faces of India*. New Delhi: Newsmen Publishers.

Singh, K. S. (1985). *Tribal society in India*. New Delhi: Manohar Publications.

Singh, K. S. (1987). Chhotanagpur raj: Mythology, structure and ramifications. In S. Sinha (Ed.), *Tribal Polities and State Systems in Pre-colonial Eastern and North Eastern India* (pp. 51–72). Calcutta: K P Bagchi & Company.

Singh, K. S. (1990). *Ethnicity, identity and development*. Delhi: Manohar Publications.

Singh, K. S. (1994). *The scheduled tribes*. New Delhi: Oxford University Press.

Sinha, S. (1962). State formation and Rajput myth in Tribal Central India. *Man in India*, 42(1), 36–80.

Sinha, S. (Ed.) (1987). *Tribal politics and state system in pre-colonial eastern and north eastern India*. Calcutta: K. P. Bagchi and Company.

Thakkar, A. V., & Ambedkar, B. R. (1945). *Aboriginals' cry in the wilderness*. Bombay: Servants of India Society.

Thapar, R. (1980). *From lineage to state*. Bombay: Oxford University Press.

Weiner, M., & Field, J. O. (1975). How tribal constituencies in India vote. In J. N. Bhagwati, P. Desai, J. O. Field, W. L. Richter, & Weiner, M. (Eds.), *Electoral Politics in the Indian States: Three Disadvantaged Sectors* (Vol. 2): Studies in Electoral Politics in the Indian States (pp. 79–120). New Delhi: Manohar Book Service.

Zide, N. H., & Zide, A. R. K. (1976). Proto-Munda cultural vocabulary: Evidence for early agriculture. In P. N. Jeuner, L. C. Thompson, & S. Slarosta (Eds.), *Austroasiatic Studies*, Part II (pp. 1295–1334). Hawaii: University of Hawaii Press.

ANNEXURE: AN ANALYSIS OF VOTING PATTERNS

For the sake of analysis, I have divided the ST-dominated constituencies, both those with reserved seats and those with no reserved seats, into two categories, namely, the core and the periphery, according to their strength of population. The core constituencies are those that have around 50 percent or more ST population out of the total population of the constituency and the peripheral constituencies are those that have less than 50 per cent but at least 15 per cent of the population. This arrangement pushes even some reserved constituencies into the category of periphery. In the case of the parliamentary constituencies, out of 41 reserved constituencies 8 seats register less than 50 per cent, 21 seats between 50 per cent and 70 per cent, and 12 seats above 70 per cent ST population. Actually, among the eight seats with less than 50 per cent ST population, only one has 48 per cent and the rest all have less than 35 per cent ST population. Since the purpose of this categorization is to see how the ST voting pattern emerges in the ST-majority seats as compared to the ST-minority seats, we have kept this 48 per cent ST-populated seat within the core area. The logic behind keeping the ST-minority-reserved constituencies in the periphery category is that even if the candidates are members of the STs, they are dependent on the decisions of the non-STs for their chances of winning and, later on, the winning candidate has to take into consideration the interests of the non-ST voters more than those of their own people.

Second, I have divided the entire ST reserved seats into seven zones on the basis of the concentration of the STs instead of analysing the data by state. The purpose is to see whether the STs' electoral behaviour is determined by ethnicity or by state politics. For instance, although the majority of the Santals of Bihar support the Congress, behaviour is determined by ethnicity or by state politics.

For instance, although the majority of the Santals of Bihar support the Congress, do their kinsmen and women behave the same way across the state border in Orissa and West Bengal, or are they guided by the dominant politics of the respective states? This would help us to see the role of ethnicity as well as the pragmatism of the people in electoral politics. The second purpose is to see the voting pattern of individual STs.

The following analysis is based on 41 (Table 4.4) reserved constituencies and 31 (Table 4.5) unreserved parliamentary constituencies since 1977 when new states were carved out of Assam. They have been categorized as 38 core constituencies and 34 peripheral constituencies. Earlier, between 1952 and 1971, the numbers of reserved seats were less and the number progressively increased over this period owing to factors such as the carving up of the double-member constituencies, division of existing constituencies and scheduling of new constituencies. I have also taken these constituencies into consideration. The analysis, thus, shows the trends of ST voting from 1952 until the last general elections held in 1999. The approximate electoral results by zone is as follows.

ZONE 1: MEENA-DOMINATED CONSTITUENCIES IN RAJASTHAN

The Meenas are concentrated in Rajasthan alone. Therefore, Zone 1 has only one state. It has two parliamentary reserved seats and four seats with substantial tribal population. However, there is only one seat, called Salumber, where more than 50 per cent of the population are STs. In the other reserved seat, called Sawai Madhopur, only 25 per cent of its total population are STs. Generally, the Meenas have been supporters of the Congress since 1952, except for in 1977 and 1989. Apart from these two elections, the party has kept its

Table 4.4   Distribution by State of Lok Sabha (Parliament) Reserved Constituencies since 1977

State	Constituency	State	Constituency	State	Constituency
Andhra Pradesh	1. Parvatipuram	Lakshadweep	15. Lakshdweep	Manipur	29. Outer Manipur
	2. Bhadrachlam	Madhya Pradesh	16. Sindhi	Mizoram	30. Mizoram
Assam	3. Autonombus District		17. Shahdol	Orissa	31. Mayurbhanj
	4. Kokrajhar		18. Sarguja		32. Koraput
Bihar	5. Rajmahal		19. Raigarh		33. Nowrangpur
	6. Dumka		20. Kakar		34. Sundargarh
	7. Lohardaga		21. Bastar		35. Keonjhar
	8. Khunti		22. Mandla	Rajasthan	36. Sawai Madhapur
	9. Singhbhum		23. Dhar		37. Banswara
Dadra & Nagar Haveli	10. Dadra & Nagar Haveli		24. Jhabua		38. Salumber
Gujarat	11. Dohad	Maharashtra	25. Dahnu	Tripura	39. Tripura-East
	12. Chhota Udaipur		26. Malegaon	W. Bengal	40 Alipurduar
	13. Mandavi		27. Dhulia		41. Jhargram
	14. Bulsar		28. Nandurbar		

Source: Compiled from the reports of the Election Commission of India.

Table 4.5   Distribution by State of Lok Sabha (Parliament) Non-Reserved Constituencies having 15% or more ST Population since 1977

State	Constituency	State	Constituency	State	Constituency
Andhra Pradesh	1. Adilabad	Madhya Pradesh	12. Mahasamund	Orissa	23. Berhampur
	2. Warangal		13. Betul		24. Phulbani
Arunachal Pradesh	3. Arunachal East – 1		14. Chindwar		25. Kalhandi
	4. Arunachal West		15. Seoni		26. Balasore
Assam	5. Lakhimpur		16. Bilaspur	Rajasthan	27. Jhalawar
			17. Satna		28. Chittorgarh
Bihar	6. Ranchi	Maharashtra	18. Chandrapur		29. Udaipur
	7. Jamshedpur		19. Yotmal		30. Dausa
	8. Godda	Meghalaya	20. Shillong	Tripura	31. Tripura West
	9. Giridh		21. Tura		
Gujarat	10. Sabarkantha	Nagaland	22. Nagaland		
	11. Godhra				

Source: Compiled from Singh (1998).

hold on the single core seat of Salumber the whole time. In the peripheral seats, too, it has been able to keep on average more than 50 per cent of the seats within its fold. The party faced challenges from only two opponents, the SWA and the BJS/BJP. Although the ST-dominated areas remained under the princely states, the former could not gather enough ST votes to overthrow the Congress. It remained alive only until 1971 and gained two peripheral seats in 1962, the same number in 1967 and one core seat in 1971. The BJS could likewise make little inroads into the Congress support base although it registered its presence from 1962. It secured one peripheral constituency in 1962 and 1967 and two in 1971 until its merger with the BLD. The BLD was formed as an unsuccessful experiment on the part.

Bharatiya Lok Dal, SP and Indian National Congress (Organization). The 1977 elections were dominated by the BLD, winning all the core and peripheral seats of the zone. The Congress won the next two elections in 1980 and 1984, losing only one peripheral seat in 1980 to the JD. But in the next election in 1989, the party lost all its seats to BJP, which emerged as an apparently formidable force by cleverly playing its Hindu card. This was the time of the demolition of Babri Masjid and the proposed construction of Ram Janmabhoomi Temple (the temple on the supposed birthplace of the Hindu deity lord Rama). However, this sudden fundamentalist frenzy was short lived and Congress recovered the core seat and two out of the five peripheral seats in the next elections in 1991. It further consolidated its position in 1996 by adding one more peripheral seat to its previous gains. These seats, one core and three peripheral, it retained until the last elections in 1999, while the BJP retained two peripheral seats in each election over the same period. Thus, although the Congress is still a dominant force, it has been facing a serious challenge from the BJP.

The Meenas are actually fully sedentarized agriculturists and a considerably alienated section of the Bhils. While the Bhils were known for their love of freedom and spirit of revolution, the Meenas remained closed to the Hindu Rajput landed gentry during the colonial period. After independence, they took full advantage of the protective discriminative provisions and produced a strong elite group while the literacy rate and the general level of education. These education increased at a much higher pace among them than the Bhils. These factors are most probably responsible for their overwhelming support for the Congress. But the BJP's entry into this traditional stronghold of the Congress is significant. It is apparent that the non-indigenous voters have been shifting their allegiance to the BJP, whereas the ST voters are still with the Congress.

ZONE 2: BHIL-DOMINATED CONSTITUENCIES IN MAHARASHTRA, RAJASTHAN AND MADHYA PRADESH

The zone had 6 core seats in 1952, which was increased to 9 in 1957 and remained so until 1962; it was further increased to 10 in 1967. The number of peripheral seats was two in 1952 and this was increased to four in 1957.

The Bhils had been no less ardent supporters of the Congress than the Meenas until 1998. In 1999, it faced a serious debacle when the BJP registered its dominance over 5 out of 10 core seats and 2 out of 4 peripheral seats. However, the Congress considers this defeat to be another passing phenomenon as in the previous years of 1977 and 1989. In 1977, the BLD wrested three core and one peripheral seat from the Congress' previous tally of eight and three, respectively, in 1971. Similarly, in 1989, the Congress lost three core and two peripheral seats to the Janata Party. However, the nature of the BJP threat is much more serious than past threats. The Swatantra Parties' influence among the Bhils was never of any significance. It surfaced in 1962 with one core seat and kept it only up to the next 1967 elections. In the periphery, however, it snatched two seats from the Congress but could retain only one until the next election in 1971. Then, in 1977, it merged with the BLD. The Socialist and Communist parties made an entry into the scene only nominally between 1957 and 1977, that being in one constituency called Dahanu in Maharashtra.

ZONE 3: GOND AND KHOND-DOMINATED CONSTITUENCIES IN ANDHRA PRADESH, ORISSA, MADHYA PRADESH AND MAHARASHTRA

The concentration of the Gonds in central India is divided between two distinct areas. Although in ancient times they were contiguous, they are now connected by an area thinly populated by Gonds, lying between them. The division is not only geographical but also to some extent cultural, whereas the Northern Gonds are heavily Hinduized the Southern ones still retain many of their traditions. Zone 3 lies in the southern Gond area. Here, the habitats of the two major indigenous communities, the Khonds and the Gonds, overlap each other. Whereas Gonds are found in all three contiguous states of Andhra Pradesh, Orissa and Madhya Pradesh, the Khonds live mostly in Orissa, a minor indigenous community known as the Koyas is in Andhra Pradesh. There are many other smaller communities in the zone, such as the Sugalis, the Konda Dora, the Bagata in Andhra Pradesh, the Bhattodas, Parojas, Saura and Sabar in Orissa, the Pradhans, Kolams, Andha in Maharashtra, and the Bhumias, the Halbas and the Kawars in Madhya Pradesh. The zone had four core constituencies from 1952 to 1964 and five thereafter. It had eight peripheral constituencies in 1952 and nine thereafter.

The Congress was the dominant party in the zone until 1996. In the following two general elections of 1998 and 1999, the party for the first time faced a serious debacle when the BJP, along with its electoral ally the TDP, robbed it of its traditional voters in this indigenous area. Barring the exceptional elections in 1977, when the BLD won two core and three peripheral seats, the Congress only occasionally lost one core seat each to either the CPI or to the independent candidates. The SWA was restricted to the periphery with three and two seats, respectively, in 1967 and 1971. Similarly the JD paid a short visit by winning only three peripheral seats in 1989. The BJP, which was for quite a long time trailing behind the Congress, emerged victorious in two core and two peripheral seats in 1998 and further encroached upon the Congress base by winning one more core seat in addition to that. Its ally, TDP, which entered the area through the peripheral seats in 1998, in the 1999 elections won one core seat for the first time and retained three peripheral seats that it secured

in the 1998 elections. Its other ally BJD made its entry into the zone by securing one peripheral seat each in the 1998 and 1999 elections.

However, an analysis of the results by state shows the growing popularity of the regional parties such as the TDP in Andhra Pradesh and BJD in Orissa. The Congress lost to these parties because they raised the regional issues and promised to fulfil regional interests, which the Congress had failed to consider. These issues have attracted the ST voters too. The CPI is present in Andhra Pradesh alone and that too in only one constituency because of its long involvement in the peasant movement in the area. Thus, the Congress' base in Madhya Pradesh and Maharashtra has been challenged by the BJP alone. In Madhya Pradesh, it lost both the core seats to the BJP in 1998 and 1999 elections and the one peripheral seat in 1998, which it recovered in 1999. In Maharashtra, it retained both its peripheral seats but was followed very closely by the BJP.

ZONE 4: GOND-DOMINATED CONSTITUENCIES IN MADHYA PRADESH

The zone has four core constituencies (in 1952 the number was three, this was increased to four thereafter) and five peripheral seats. All the core seats are also reserved seats. The election results of this zone show the overwhelming support the Congress received from the Gonds and also the extent of the disgrace it has suffered at their hands. Except for the elections of 1977 when the BLD caught the imagination of the people by securing the four core and four out of five peripheral seats, the Congress retained its unquestionable sway over the area until 1984. In 1986, it lost two core and four peripheral seats to the BJP and one core to the JD. This shock was overcome by regaining all of them in the next election of 1991. But the party failed to retain the voters confidence after that. The BJP emerged as the main winner. It secured two core and two peripheral seats in 1996, four core and three peripheral in 1998 and three core and four peripheral seats in the 1999 elections.

ZONE 5: HO-MUNDA AND URAON-DOMINATED CONSTITUENCIES IN MADHYA PRADESH, ORISSA, BIHAR AND WEST BENGAL

The zone had three core and one peripheral constituency in 1952. The number of core constituencies was increased to six in 1957 and that of the periphery to two in 1971. This has historically been an anti-Congress zone. Barring 1971, 1980 and 1984 elections, the party never fared well. The Jharkhand parties, despite all kinds of bickering and even a merger with the Congress in 1962, continued to win the core seats until 1980 and when they failed, the BJP took over from 1989 and won all seats in the zone in 1999. The Congress had its heyday only in the intervening year of 1984, when it won all core seats and one peripheral seat. As in 1999, the Congress lost all seats in 1977, also because of the emergence of the BLD, which cornered five core seats. During the second revival of the Jharkhand movement, the JMM once won one core seat only in 1991. In the geographically isolated Alipurduars seat, the RSP established an unchallenged authority and has continuously won the seat from 1977, when the constituency was formed, until the last elections in 1999.

Two interesting observations can be made about the zone: first, the same tribe behaves differently in different states and, second, the Congress failed to address the autonomy issue of the indigenous peoples, which was raised initially by the Jharkhand Parties and was later taken up by the BJP. In Orissa and Madhya Pradesh, the Jharkhand parties were never able to win a parliamentary seat (although in Orissa, the Jharkhand parties

were constantly winning Assembly seats). In the 2 core seats of Orissa, out of 13 general elections held so far, the Congress has won only six times in each constituency. Different anti-Congress parties came and went with little success, such as the AIJP, the GP, the SWA, the BLD and the JD. The Congress, however, ruled over the lone core seat in Madhya Pradesh until being seriously challenged by the BJP since 1984.

ZONE 6: SANTAL-DOMINATED CONSTITUENCIES IN ORISSA, BIHAR AND WEST BENGAL

The zone had one core and one peripheral constituency in 1952, which was increased to three each in 1957. In 1962, the number of peripheral seats was further increased to six. This zone has also largely been a non-Congress dominated one, like Zone 5. Out of 13 general elections, the opponents have been the Jharkhand parties and the BJP. During the last two elections in 1998 and 1999, it was wiped out of the area.

In this zone also, like in Zone 5, the ST voters are influenced more by the nature of state politics than by their ethnic solidarity. While in Bihar, the ethnic issues are stronger, in Orissa and in West Bengal, other factors—mostly economic ones—play a determining role. In Orissa, the Congress and the opposition parties fight neck and neck and win the seats intermittently. But in West Bengal, the CPM and its Left Front ally the Forward Block have established permanent dominance in the two peripheral seats since 1971 and 1977, respectively. In the Bihar part of the zone, the ethnic issue of political autonomy and cultural identity has heavily dominated the electoral politics. After the initial set back in 1962, the Jharkhand groups under the JMM held a strong presence in the area from 1989 to 1991. But then the demand for political separation from Bihar was hijacked by the more powerful BJP, which made landslide victories in 1998 and 1999. The socialists were never really able to enter the area. The PSP, the JP and the JD have been able to win only one peripheral seat each so far.

ZONE 7: NORTH-EAST INDIA

This zone covers the land of the rebellious indigenous peoples. Its connection with mainstream electoral politics is comparatively weaker than in mainland India. Owing to the strong demand for autonomy, several new states were carved out of the former Assam, thereby increasing the number of core constituencies. The number rose from two in 1952 to three in 1971 and eight in 1977. The number of peripheral seats, however, remained at two the whole time.

The Congress had a very tough time until 1977, when it created the three new states of Arunachal Pradesh, Meghalaya and Mizoram. In the elections of 1952, 1957 and 1971, it won only one core seat each time, while in the 1962 and 1967 elections, it scored a duck. It is mostly the tribal parties who have challenged the Congress party. Except for the Communists and the Socialists (only once in 1952), no other all-India parties have so far been able to secure a seat in the zone. The CPI and the CPI-M, however, continued to win in Tripura alone not on the basis of ST votes but on the basis of the migrant Bengalis from neighbouring East Pakistan, later re-christened as Bangladesh. The independent winners are actually the representatives of small tribal parties.

Gender and Tribal Politics in India

Sasmita Mohanty

INTRODUCTION

Representative politics not only determines the nature and dynamics of representative democracy but also ensures the effective role of diverse communities and groups in the decision-making process. The role of different groups in politics can be measured through the structural arrangement of power and by ensuring their effective participation in India. Representative democracy not only ensures active participation of all groups/communities irrespective of their identities but also creates a platform for them to protect their rights, identity and dignity to live as a free citizen of the country and access to the political institutions to represent, deliberate and articulate on various issues that are critical to their communities.

The study of politics goes beyond the narrow focus on those holding formal offices and the politics of distribution. It now encompasses many new groups espousing 'gender trouble' as well as new ideas about masculinity and femininity across a range of contexts, from home to the houses of Parliament (Celis

et al., 2013, p. 2). Comprehending the relationship between gender and politics always remains a challenging task for the academicians and policymakers and social activists in contemporary India. Without understanding such relationship, any attempt to glimpse the status of women in India in general and tribal women in particular becomes extremely difficult because of the complex political realm and the established structure driven by patriarchy. Hence, Celis et al. (2013) argue that gender is crucial to politics and gender inequalities are embedded in both the study and practice of politics.

The democratic structure of our country provides a platform to each and every citizen of the country irrespective of their ethnic, religious, cultural and gender identities. But in reality, the participation of women remains minuscule or negligible when it comes to decision-making bodies. Within this backdrop, the participation and representation of tribal women are not up to the mark in politics. The existing literature has not focused much on various issues of political representation of tribal women in the highest decision-making bodies, which largely determines their political status as compared to their socioeconomic and cultural status.

The relationship between tribal women and politics raises certain pertinent questions. Why is there so much of politics *on* tribal women and politics *for* tribal women and not politics *of* tribal women? Who will address the vulnerabilities of tribal women and children if the tribal women do not have the opportunity to represent their voices at the highest decision-making bodies such as State Assemblies and Parliament in India? Why are the tribal women often been the victims of politics? Within this backdrop, the chapter looks at the nature and dynamics of participation of the tribal women in politics which largely determines their fate as an active participant of the political community.

Tribal politics in India revolves around the protection of tribal rights in relation to cultural identity, issue of survival and livelihood, right to health and the issue of development. Tribal women's representation in politics has relatively increased only after the implementation of the Constitutional (73rd Amendment) Act 1992, albeit at the grassroots level. Prior to that, although 7.5 per cent seats are reserved for the scheduled tribes (STs) in politics, the representation of tribal women was quite negligible in the political realm. The gender bias is existed in relation to the representation of tribal women in politics. Despite their greater concerns towards socioeconomic issues, it appears that women are always pushed aside or denied important portfolios/positions (decision-making role) as compared to their male counterparts.

SOCIOECONOMIC STATUS OF TRIBAL WOMEN

The journey of tribal women to political realm is incomplete without understanding their socioeconomic status which provides base for political nourishment, participation and empowerment. It has been largely accepted by the tribal societies that women have low status compared to their male counterparts. But Dhebar Commission Report (1961) emphasized that tribal women play very important role in family matters. This is something significant to understand the nature of participation and decision-making skill of the tribal women at large. Tribal women enjoy higher socioeconomic status specifically in the matriarchal, matrilineal and polyandrous societies with some exception (Thakur & Thakur, 1994, p. 5).

Study on the socioeconomic status of the tribal women reveals that the tribal women are in a better position as compared to the scheduled caste (SC) and 'mainstream' Hindu women. This can be attributed to their distinct culture and traditions, where the tribal women face relatively less discrimination than the SC and 'mainstream' Hindu women. The relatively better position of tribal women is also because of the way the tribal society was located, where it seems to be distanced and isolated by the Hindu society. Although G. S. Ghurye discredited the distinction between caste society and tribes and considered the tribes as 'backward Hindus' (Ambagudia, 2019a, p. 47; Ghurye, 1963, p. 19; Oommen, 2011, p. 236), the tribal communities continue to practice and maintain their distinct culture, traditions and languages and remained outside the Hindu civilization (Ambagudia, 2019a, p. 47; Beteille, 1986, p. 316). Tribal women play an important role in all the socioeconomic and cultural activities. They also have a much higher work participation rate than non-tribal women (Mitra, 2008, p. 1203).

Freedom of choice, freedom of movement and freedom to take major decisions for the family largely exercised by the tribal women where the Hindu women are mostly denied of such rights and are subject to many restrictions in Indian society. The tribal women no doubt face many hardships in terms of physical labour and fighting against poverty but they do enjoy more freedom compared to the other mainstream women. Divorce and widowhood are not a stigma/taboo in tribal society. Bride price considered as a mark of respect or value to the women in their society. In nutshell, we can say that a tribal woman's social space is not curtailed, which appears to be more prominent in the case of a Hindu women (Thakur & Thakur, 1994, pp. 5–6).

The socioeconomic status of tribal women cannot be measured by employing a homogenous yardstick because of the internal differentiation among the tribes, which is the result of their attainment of different stages of socioeconomic, cultural and political developments. Various tribal communities of India have also been integrated into the mainstream society at various levels (Ambagudia, 2019a, p. 54). They are also undergoing change while coming in contact with adjacent non-tribal communities. In addition, they are located at different geographical terrain, exhibiting different lifestyles, social habits, religious beliefs and cultural patterns (Mitra, 2008, p. 1,204). The existing literature suggests that the tribal women, especially the Naga women, exercise significant decision-making power within their societies (Mitra, 2008, p. 1206; Xaxa, 2004). Economically, the North-eastern tribal women are more active as compared to the Central Indian tribal women (Xaxa, 2004).

SEX RATIO

The credibility of a society depends on the equal treatment of individuals irrespective of their gender identities, and thereby indicating the equal treatment of both male and female members of the society. The (un)equal treatment between women and men sometimes depends on the larger orientation of a society towards the 'other' gender. Considering the case of India, the established social structure functions in such a way that the male members appear to get priority as well as differential

treatment in comparison to the female counterpart. This probably affect the sex ration (number of females for 1,000 males) of a particular country. The sex ratio of tribals was 978 in 2001 census, out of which rural and urban areas experienced 981 and 944 female members, respectively, for 100 males. However, the sex ration has changed during the 2011 census, where there is slight increase and is now 990, indicating 991 and 980 for rural and urban areas (Government of India, 2013, p. 129). The state and union territory-wise data indicate that the union territory, Dadra and Nagar Haveli, had the highest sex ration of 1,028, followed by Kerala (1,021). In 2011, most of the states have improved the sex ration among the tribal communities, and Goa topped the figure with 1,046, followed by Kerala with 1,035 (Government of India, 2013). Interestingly, though both the states topped in terms of sex ration among the tribes, they, however, have insignificant tribal population.

LITERACY

Amartya Sen (2000) considers that education is one of the important means of empowerment and enlargement of freedom of the individual. Hence, there is a positive relationship between education and making choices, and thereby indicates that the political choices can be made more effectively when individuals attained education (Ambagudia, 2019a). It has, however, observed that the tribal women lag behind their male counterparts in terms of attaining education, which also affects their capacity to make independent political choices. For instance, the 2001 census indicates that the tribal male and female literacy rate stands at 57.39 and 32.44 per cent, respectively, and thereby indicating the literacy gap of 24.95 per cent. As per the 2011 census, the male and female literacy rate was 66.8 and 46.9 per cent, respectively, with a literacy gap of 19.9 per cent.

GENDER AND POLITICS IN THE CONTEXT OF TRIBAL SOCIETY

Politics, as a practice, has experienced changes drastically over a period of time in India which encompasses many issues and challenges. Among those, the issue of women representation in general and tribal women representation in particular has not taken up very seriously so far except some initiatives taken by some of the political parties at the state level such as the Biju Janata Dal (BJD) in Odisha and All India Trinamool Congress in West Bengal. Tribal women always remained in the forefront as far as their participation in political movements is concerned, and take peace-building measures in conflict prone areas. Naga mothers association, Nagaland, is consistently addressing the issues of conflict and peace. The tribal women fought with all courage and enthusiasm along with their male counterparts which could be witnessed from the writings of Maheswata Devi and other academia who have been working on these issues. From Chipko to Pathalgadi movement, the tribal women largely participated. Their representation in Parliament and State Assemblies, however, is negligible. Effective and vibrant democracy is possible only through the participation of diverse sections of people in decision-making process, including tribal women, which can happen through making the political institutions accessible to all including tribal women.

The enactment of laws and their implementation largely depend on the political will of the parliamentarians. We have witnessed in last 70 years from the adoption of this constitution, every single law to give justice to women and empower them has taken much longer time than they were expected. Even some of the important bills are still hanging because of the lack of political will. The hindrances are very much rooted in the patriarchal structure and composition of the legislature/Parliament, where is the dominance of male members. Hence, it is very crucial to explore the mechanisms through which the representation

of tribal women can be ensured and their voices can be accommodated and heard at the decision-making level.

TRIBAL WOMEN AND POLITICAL PARTIES

Over the period, the relationship between tribal women and political parties has become a continuous concern in Indian politics. It appears that gender issue in politics has been unable to draw the attention of various political parties, and thereby the increase in marginalization and discrimination of tribal women is visible in political parties. Such practices against tribal women have been carried out by not recognizing their political significance and political leadership. The tribal women are denied of spaces not only in the process of ticket distribution to contest elections but also in party organizations. The phenomenon can perhaps be partially understood by looking at the organizational structure of political parties. The close observation indicates that most of the political parties are headed by male political leaders, who appear to have neither understood the women issues nor interested to address them. There are some exceptions in some of the political parties such as the Congress, Trinamool Congress, Bahujan Samaj Party, and so on, where the parties are led by women. Needless to mention that none of them are from tribal backgrounds. Such scenario in the political circle not only reflects the incompatible relationship between tribal women and political parties but also the larger dissatisfaction of tribal communities with political parties.

The practice of modern electoral system does not provide a pleasing statistics on tribal women representation in politics. Jena (2009) draws on the electoral statistics concerning the state of Odisha to locate the tribal women in the larger political system in general and in the party structure in particular. She points out that during the 2009 Assembly and Parliamentary elections, out of 157 and 1,397 contested candidates, only 6 and 10 per cent, respectively, were women. Sometimes, political parties respond positively to the possibility of nominating women candidates in elections (Tables 5.3 and 5.4). Whenever they have been given the opportunity, the success rate has been relatively higher than their male counterparts. The political parties sometimes adopt face-saving approach by giving tickets to tribal women candidates and, with their winning, sometimes they also get accommodated in the ministerial berth. For instance, Saraswati Hembrum, a tribal women, who represented Kuliana constituency of Mayurbhanj district of Odisha between 1980 and 2000 with a Congress ticket, was accommodated in the ministry, and became the first tribal women Member of the Legislative Assembly (MLA) to shoulder the responsibility of a minister of textile, handlooms and handicraft in 2009. Frida Topno successfully contested the 1991 and 1996 Lok Sabha elections from Sundergarh. Sushila Tiriya successfully contested the Lok Sabha election of 1996. Even the regional parties like the BJD, which showed its commitment to address issues of women and tribal communities, nominated only 8 women out of 130 candidates for the Assembly election of 2009 (Jena, 2009).

Sometimes, male members of the family also push the tribal women to enter into politics. Jena (2009) beautifully crafts the political journey of Ms Hema Gamang. Hema Gamang's entry has much credit to her husband, Giridhar Gamang. She acknowledged, 'I was acquainted with politics and knew grassroots party workers well, having campaigned for my husband. But I was not keen to jump into the thick of the fray at that point' (Jena, 2009). However, Giridhar Gamang was the Chief Minister of Odisha and wanted to keep his Koraput Lok Sabha constituency intact where he had represented the constituency for six consecutive terms. Giridhar Gamang bargained to retain the Lok Sabha ticket for the Koraput constituency, which invariably led to the emergence of scuffle

between the husband–wife duo. The Congress party supported Giridhar Gamang and offered the Koraput Lok Sabha ticket. However, the Congress also offered her a party ticket to contest the Gunupur Assembly Constituency. Meanwhile, she was also denied the Gunupur Assembly Constituency during the 2009 election, and was compelled to shift her constituency to Laxmipur.

Hema Gamang accepted the humility and uttered, 'The men try to push a woman around in politics as well' (Jena, 2009). Hundreds of tribal women suffered from similar situation in different parts of the country over the period. Such scenario reflects two aspects: one, the nature of struggle that the tribal women have to go through for making their presence in politics, and, second, the deep entrenched patriarchal values in politics is not only visible in the larger political structure but also work at the family level. In short, irrespective of family's political background, tribal women's political journey has been filled with rocky thorny path and myriad unnecessary stopovers at every stage.

Jensenius (2016, p. 454) explores the relationship between political parties and ST women candidate nomination in two different phases: pre- and post-1996 phases and the data has been provided in Table 5.1. During pre-1996 period, the Congress and the BJP nominated 3.6 and 3.1 per cent of women candidates, respectively, in ST-reserved Assembly constituencies. Similarly, the Congress and the BJP nominated 9.1 and 9.3 per cent of tribal women candidates in constituencies in the post-1996 phase, resulting the difference of 5.5 and 6.2 per cent between the pre- and

Table 5.1 Parties' Nomination of Women Candidates in ST-Reserved Assembly Constituencies before and after 1996 (in %)

	Before 1996	After 1996	Change
Congress	3.6	9.1	5.5
BJP	3.1	9.3	6.2
Other Parties	2.4	7.3	4.9

Source: Jensenius (2016, p. 454).

Table 5.2 Parties' Nomination of Women Candidates in ST-Reserved Parliamentary Constituencies before and after 1996 (in %)

	Before 1996	After 1996	Change
Congress	9.5	14.8	5.3
BJP	4.2	6.7	2.6
Other Parties	2.9	7.9	5.1

Source: Jensenius (2016, p. 454).

post-1996 period, respectively. Similarly, other political parties nominated 2.4 and 7.3 per cent women candidates in ST-reserved Assembly constituencies, resulting a difference of 4.9 per cent between pre- and post-1996 period. While exploring the relationship between tribal women and political parties, Table 5.3 indicates that both the national political parties, the Congress and the BJP, outnumbered the combination of all other parties in nominating women candidates in ST-reserved Assembly constituencies.

The party nomination of women candidates in ST-reserved Parliamentary constituencies indicates that the Congress party nominated 9.5 and 14.8 per cent during the pre- and post-1996 period (Table 5.2). Similarly, the BJP's nomination stands at 4.2 and 6.7 per cent during the pre- and post-1996 phase, respectively. The other political parties' nomination of women candidates in ST-reserved Parliamentary constituencies stands at 2.9 and 7.9 per cent during the pre- and post-1996 period. The difference of nominated women candidates in ST-reserved Parliamentary constituencies between pre- and post-1996 period was 5.3, 2.6 and 5.1 per cent for the Congress, the BJP and other political parties, respectively.

Table 5.2 reflects that the Congress has outnumbered both the BJP and all other parties in terms of nominating women candidates in ST-reserved Parliamentary constituencies. Interestingly, unlike the state election, all other parties have outnumbered the BJP while nominating women candidates to the ST-reserved Parliamentary constituencies after 1996. The presented data in Tables 5.1

and 5.2 hint at intriguing inferences that all political parties have increased their nomination of women candidates in ST-reserved Assembly and Parliamentary constituencies, and thereby, to some extent, it seems to appear that various political parties are gradually showing their interest in giving relatively more tickets to women candidates, at least in reserved constituencies. Hence, Jensenius (2016, p. 1) underlines that that many women are entering Indian Parliament at the cost of SC and ST men.

TRIBAL WOMEN AND POLITICAL REPRESENTATION

The practice of political reservation under articles 330 and 332 has entitled the tribal communities of India to 554 out of 4,109 Parliament seats and 47 out of 543 Parliamentary seats (Ambagudia, 2019b, pp. 51–52, 54–55). Since the enacted political reservation at the state and national level has not been gender-centric or it does not consider gender identity as the basis of reserving seats, women from the tribal communities are also the equal competitors for the ST-reserved Assembly and Parliamentary constituencies.

Table 5.3 shows the percentage of women candidates who contested the election between

Table 5.3   Women Candidates in ST-Reserved Assembly Constituencies, 1961–2015 (in %)

1961–1967	1.2
1968–1973	1.1
1974–1979	2.5
1980–1985	3.3
1986–1990	3.4
1991–1995	4.4
1996–1999	6.8
2000–2005	6.5
2006–2010	8.9
2011–2015	9.1

Source: Jensenius (2016, p. 453).

1961 and 2015 in ST-reserved Assembly constituencies. The percentage of their candidature has increased from 1.1 per cent during 1968–1973 to 2.5 per cent in 1974–1979, which has further increased to 3.3 per cent in 1980–1985, to 3.4 per cent in 1986–1990, to 4.4 per cent in 1991–1995, to 6.8 per cent in 1996–1999, to 8.9 per cent during 2006–2010 and to 9.1 per cent during 2011–2015. However, the percentage of women candidature in ST-reserved Assembly constituencies has decreased in two occasions, from 1.2 per cent in 1961–1967 to 1.1 per cent during 1968–1973 and 6.8 per cent in 1996–1999 to 6.5 per cent during 2000–2005 (Table 5.3).

Table 5.4 demonstrates that the women candidates have chequered history in relation to their percentage in contesting the ST-reserved Parliamentary constituencies. Table 5.4 indicates that 3.0 per cent of the tribal women contested the ST-reserved Parliamentary constituencies in 1962 election, which has increased to 5 per cent during 1967 election. However, their per cent decreased to 3.6 per cent in 1977 election. The women candidature has witnessed lowest ever in 1984 election, which was confined to 2.4 per cent. Other elections experienced ups and downs in terms

of tribal women candidature in ST-reserved Parliamentary constituencies. In short, Tables 5.3 and 5.4 do not present pleasing statistics in terms of women candidates in ST-reserved Assembly and Parliamentary constituencies. However, the quantum of women candidates in ST-reserved constituencies largely depends on the orientation of political parties towards nominating women candidates. Since party affiliation provides various kinds of opportunities that range from securing cadre support to financial and material benefits and enhances the chances of winning the elections, ST women as independent candidates may not always come forward to contest elections.

Table 5.5 deals with the tribal women Members of Parliament (MPs) of India between 1952 and 2019. Between 1952 and 2019, there are a total of 713 women MPs, out of which 118 (16.54%) and 51 (7.15%) are from SC and ST categories, respectively. The tribal women representation began with a representative (Bonily Khongmen) from the

Table 5.4 Women Candidates in ST-Reserved Parliamentary Constituencies, 1962–2014 (in %)

1962	3.0
1967	5.0
1977	3.6
1980	4.9
1984	2.4
1984	4.4
1991	7.5
1996	6.9
1998	6.2
1999	10.0
2004	8.9
2009	7.5
2014	10.4

Source: Jensenius (2016, p. 453).

Table 5.5 Tribal Women MPs in India, 1952–2019

Year	Total	SC	ST
1952	24	5	1
1957	24	6	0
1962	37	5	1
1967	33	3	3
1971	28	6	2
1977	21	1	1
1980	32	4	3
1984	45	5	2
1989	28	3	2
1991	42	5	5
1996	41	10	4
1998	44	12	2
1999	52	10	3
2004	52	11	1
2009	64	12	5
2014	68	13	6
2019	78	7	10
Total	713	118	51

Source: Compiled from Government of India (2020).

autonomous district of Assam during the first Lok Sabha. The following Lok Sabha (second Lok Sabha, 1957), however, failed to have any representation from the tribal women. The 1962, 1977 and 2004 elections had one each tribal woman representatives. Two women MPs each were there during 1971, 1984, 1989 and 1998 elections. During 1967, 1980 and 1999, there were three tribal women MPs each. Similarly, there were four tribal women MPs during 1996 election and five each were there in 1991 and 2009 elections. Though there were ups and downs in terms of numerical representation of tribal women MPs in Lok Sabha, the curve of tribal women representation is moving forward since the last three elections (2009 to 2019) having 5, 6 and 10 in 2009, 2014 and 2019 elections.

Table 5.6 shows the party-wise representation of tribal women MPs between 1952 and 2019. Table 5.6 demonstrates that the Congress party has the highest number of tribal women MPs, consisting 30 (58.82%) out of 51. The BJP followed the Congress in terms of having tribal women MPs and settled at 12 in number at the present. Two tribal women represented

Table 5.6 Party-wise Tribal Women MPs in India, 1952–2019

Congress	30
BJP	12
CPI	1
BJD	2
NCC	1
NPP	1
TRS	1
TDP	1
AITC	1
YSR Congress	1
Total	51

Source: Compiled Government of India (2020).

AITC, All India Trinamool Congress; BJD, Biju Janata Dal; BJP, Bharatiya Janata Party; CPI, Communist Party of India; NCC, Nationalist Congress Party; NPP, Naga People's Party; TDP, Telugu Desai Party; TRS, Telangana Rashtriya Samiti; YSR Congress, Yuvajana Sramika Rythu Congress

the regional party of Odisha, the BJD, having sent Chandrani Murmu, the youngest MP of India, in 2019 election. One tribal woman MP each represented the Communist Party of India (CPI), Nationalist Congress Party, Naga Peoples' Party (NPP), Telangana Rashtriya Samiti (TRS), Telugu Desam Party (TDP), All India Trinamool Congress and Yuvajana Sramika Rythu Congress Party. The analysis suggests that the national political parties such as the Congress and the BJP are having relatively better tribal women representation in the Lok Sabha than the regional political parties.

The highest number of tribal women MPs from the Congress Party can perhaps be explained by the fact that the party has governed the country for the maximum years after independence. Between 1952 and 1996, all 24 elected tribal women MPs were from the Congress, having highest number of tribal women MPs in 1996 (four). Consider the domination of the Congress at the national politics, there was a high chance of getting elected whenever the party nominated the tribal women candidates during various elections. Turning towards the BJP, it had the first tribal women MP during the period when it had the full-term government for the first time (1999–2004). The BJP had two, three and six tribal women MPs during the 2009, 2014 and 2019 elections, respectively. The CPI had the only woman representative from Outer Manipur constituency of Manipur in 1998 election so far. The analysis also suggests that most of the regional political parties began to send their tribal women MPs, albeit less in number, to the Parliament recently, as the first tribal women MP from a regional party (TDP) was recorded during the 1999 election.

Table 5.7 demonstrates that the state of Madhya Pradesh has topped the table in terms of having the tribal women MPs between 1952 and 2019. It had a total of 12 tribal women MPs between 1952 and 2019; however, it did not have a single tribal women MPs during the last election (2019). Eight tribal women MPs each represented the states

Table 5.7 State-wise Tribal Women MPs in India, 1952–2019

Madhya Pradesh	12
Andhra Pradesh	8
Odisha	8
Bihar	3
Maharashtra	3
Rajasthan	3
Chhattisgarh	2
Gujarat	2
Jharkhand	2
Meghalaya	2
Assam	1
Karnataka	1
Manipur	1
Telangana	1
Tripura	1
West Bengal	1

Source: Compiled from Government of India (2020).

of Andhra Pradesh and Odisha, three each represented the states of Bihar, Maharashtra and Rajasthan. Similarly, two tribal women MPs each represented the states of Chhattisgarh, Gujarat, Jharkhand and Meghalaya, and one tribal woman MPs each were from Assam, Karnataka, Manipur, Telangana, Tripura and West Bengal. The state-wise representation of tribal women MPs depends on the commitment of political parties to gender issue, which facilitates the process of nominating women candidates in ST-reserved Parliamentary constituencies. As has been stated earlier, women are actively contesting elections, albeit most of them are contesting the elections as independent candidates, and the party nomination of tribal women candidates is negligible.

Table 5.8 demonstrates the representation of tribal women MPs in the most recent Lok Sabha (17th Lok Sabha, 2019–2024). There are 10 tribal women MPs in the present Lok Sabha. Out of 10 tribal women MPs, 6 are from the ruling party, the BJP, and 1 each from four parties such as the Congress, BJD, NPP and TRS. Out of 10, 2 tribal women MPs each are from Maharashtra and Chhattisgarh, and 1 each from Gujarat, Jharkhand, Madhya Pradesh, Meghalaya, Odisha and Telangana.

If we see the trend of women representation in the Indian Parliament, the women MPs in the 10th Parliament (1994) were largely middle-class professionals, mostly from upper and middle castes, and predominantly Hindu. This position did not change significantly over the next 20 years, although the proliferation of caste-based parties led to some broadening of the class and caste base of India's women MPs (Rai & Spary, 2019, p. 125).

The issue of tribal women and political representation has also been debated at the regional level. The case of Naga women

Table 5.8 Tribal Women MPs in 2019 Election

Name	Party Affiliation	Name of the Constituency	Name of the State
Heena Vijaykumar Gavit	BJP	Nandubar	Maharashtra
Geeta Kora	Congress	Singhbhum	Jharkhand
Kavitha Malothu	TRS	Mahabubabad	Telangana
Chandrani Murmu	BJD	Keonjhar	Odisha
Bharti Pravin Pawar	BJP	Dindori	Maharashtra
Gitaben Vajesingbai Rathva	BJP	Chhota Udaipur	Gujarat
Gomati Sai	BJP	Raigarh	Chhattisgarh
Agatha K. Sangma	NPP	Tura	Meghalaya
Renuka Singh Saruta	BJP	Surguja	Chhatisgarh
Himadri Singh	BJP	Shahdol	MP

Source: Compiled from Government of India (2020).

BJD, Biju Janata Dal; BJP, Bharatiya Janata Party; NPP, Naga People's Party; TRS: Telangana Rashtriya Samiti.

struggle for 33 per cent reservation at the urban district council and the State Assembly which they were promised to be given through an amendment act and later on denied of, has brought in to the surface of many hidden facts about the patriarchal and hegemonic role of the male members of the Legislative Assembly and lack of their political will. Surprisingly, this is happening with the women of a particular tribal group where women are socially and economically enjoying higher status compared to the women of other tribal groups in India. The male members cite the practice of Naga tradition as the reason for the denial of 33 per cent reservation to women.

According to the male members of the Assembly, Naga society does not have any tradition of giving reservation to women. Patriarchally structured deliberations, consultation and decision-making procedures adopted by the government of Nagaland and the judiciary have failed to accord equal participation and effective voice to women (Hausing, 2017, p. 36). They also argued that it is against the provisions of the Article 371(A) of the constitution (Sankar, 2019, p. 1). Such position of the male members of the Assembly irrespective of their party affiliation is just an indication of the continued practice of patriarchal democracy or otherwise egalitarian Naga society. The denial of political reservation to Naga women at the local level reinforced the unsettled conflict and interface between the tradition and practices of larger tribal society and the modern democratic values that refuse to accept tradition as the basis of political representation.

This patriarchal perspective against the political right of women to become integral part of the state decision-making bodies, equally contributing to the legislation process opened up a new debate in the discourse of gender and tribal politics in India. The question arising here is, should the tradition undermine the values of the liberal and democratic politics which ensures equal participation of all, irrespective of their caste, class, sex, ethnicity, race, etc.? does not it underestimate and

question the intrinsic values of Naga society which is being considered as 'egalitarian' in nature? Because the champions (thekedar) of tradition believe that the 'politics is a very difficult task which is left to be handled by the men'. This is a clear case of patriarchy which downplays the importance of equal rights for women by intercepting the latter by false notion and customs (Sankar, 2019, p. 1). The high social and economic status of women is necessary but not sufficient without ensuring their political empowerment, and, at the moment it seems, political empowerment of Naga women could be possible only through reservation. Because till now their representation is quite negligible at the state legislative assemblies and even in local representative bodies. Hence, there is a need to initiate the process of dialogue between the advocates of political reservation for Naga women and the protagonists of traditional practices of Naga society. This shall be done through balancing the two.

IMPACT OF TRIBAL WOMEN LEADERSHIP

The changing relationship between gender and politics essentially raises the question of representation in the context of tribal women in India. Representative or deliberative democracy focuses on equal opportunities irrespective of gender identity. Political representation of women not only makes them realize their inner potential to provide leadership, articulate on various political issues coincided with the issues of women and the art of political deliberation and debate but it also gives them confidence to come out of social complexities and take decisions at the critical situation in the political realm. Many tribal women leaders are working at the grassroots level and their remarkable contributions not only benefit the tribal communities but also the non-tribals of their areas. The policies and programmes which took years together to be implemented by their male counterparts because of the lack of commitment and political will, the women local leaders achieved those targets in a few years. Thanks to the 73rd Constitutional Amendment Act of 1992, which showed the path to the women to get in to local politics in large number and make their mark.

Despite hurdles based on patriarchal values as well as structural arrangement of power, tribal women have managed to reach the decision-making bodies. The existing writings narrate the struggles of tribal women that they encountered over the period. The cases of Sandhya Rani Chakma, Sabitri Debbarma and Madhumati Debbarma of Tripura, Mukta Jhodia and Sumoni Jhodia of Odisha can be demonstrated here.

Sandhya Rani Chakma was a member of the executive council of the Tribal Area Autonomous District Council, and handled the social education and health. Sabitri Debbarma was also elected to the council as well as State Assembly in 2008. Madumati Debbarma was also elected to the council. The commitment of these tribal women representatives from Tripura was phenomenal in terms of addressing various issues and problems that the tribal communities encounter on a regular basis. These women representatives gave utmost importance to women's welfare and empowerment, including economic spheres. These women spoke of language of development. Sandhya Rani Chakma was committed to work towards affordable medical care to rural areas (Hanghal, 2013). They emphasized on the need for an adequate representation of tribal women in decision-making bodies through various means, including reservation and nomination of more women in elections by various political parties. They realized that institutional support base shall be created to encourage and facilitate women to come to politics. Sandhya Rani Chakma pointed out that 'If institutionally women are given more

support, then many more will come forward to contest elections' (Hanghal, 2013).

Jena (2009) brought out similar stories from the state of Odisha, where women have come forward and provided leadership services despite their unequal political opportunities. Mukta Jhodia mobilized tribal people to protect their lands and discouraged them to not fall under the wrath of the bauxite mining in Kashipur areas of Rayagada district in Odisha. As a token of appreciation and recognition of her work towards tribal empowerment, she was conferred Chingari Award,[1] primarily instituted for women fighting against corporate crime. Sumoni Jhodia was the unofficial advisor on tribal development between 1993 and 1995 to the then Chief Minister of Odisha, Mr Biju Patnaik (Jena, 2009). She was closely associated with the tribal development policies and programmes and offered valuable suggestions towards materializing them.

CONCLUSION

Political history of India witnessed gender bias and discrimination in political realm. The prima facie position suggests that mostly all the political parties and political leaders are ready to speak on issues that are critical to women from different social groups. Everybody loves the number game but when it comes to the question of actual empowerment of women by increasing their participation in the decision-making bodies, they differ. There is a stiff resistance from within the political circle to any move that gives political opportunity to women in general. Though the Indian constitution has adopted numerous positive provisions towards gender equality, the Indian state so far has failed to translate this procedural equality and justice to substantive reality because of the lack of political will.

---

[1] The Chingari Award is instituted by the Chingari Trust located in Bhopal.

Women from the marginalized groups such as the tribal women are worst sufferers of this patriarchal mindset and they continue to experience exclusion from the decision-making process. Various political parties have been engaging tribal women during the political rallies and election campaigning. However, they look down upon tribal women during the nomination process and deny party tickets for contesting elections.

Study reveals that there is a strong resistance to tribal women participation at the top-level decision-making process (Parliament) as compared to the lower level, although it was not easy for women to get in to the decision-making process at the lower level. In this era when money and muscle powers play important role in winning elections, how a tribal woman can think of winning assembly or Parliamentary elections without party support. Becoming an MLA or MP is not just a matter of winning one seat at the highest decision-making bodies but it means a lot for a tribal woman. It brings development to the most backward and poverty-prone tribal populated constituency which she represents. Her representation ensures health, education, sanitation, livelihood and socioeconomic empowerment of people of that particular area. Along with that she is also becoming inspiration for thousands of women at the rural area as well as for the community she belongs to. Tribal women have already demonstrated commendable examples through their contributions as sarpanches at the local/panchayat level and they can also achieve the same when they get opportunities at the state- and national-level politics; however, there is an ample scope for ensuring an adequate representation of tribal women at the state and national politics. Even though there is lack of consensus on political reservation for women at the state and national politics among the parliamentarians, the numerical representation of tribal women can be ensured in the Assemblies and Parliament by nominating more tribal women candidates during elections. Some political parties such

as the BJD and the TMC have already robust initiatives in this direction and other political parties should follow them.

REFERENCES

Ambagudia, J. (2019a). *Adivasis, migrants and the state in India.* London and New York: Routledge.

Ambagudia, J. (2019b). Scheduled tribes, reserved constituencies and political reservation in India. *Journal of Social Inclusion Studies, 5*(1), 44–58.

Beteille, A. (1986). The concept of tribe with special reference to India. *Journal of European Sociology, 27*(2), 296–318.

Celis, K., Kantola, J., Waylen, G., & Weldon, S. L. (2013) (Eds.). *The Oxford handbook of gender and politics.* Oxford: Oxford University Press.

Feminism in India (FII) (n.d.). Feminism in India. Retrieved from https://feminisminindia.com.

Ghurye, G. S. (1963). *The scheduled tribes.* Bombay: Popular Prakashan.

Government of India. 2013. *Statistical profile of scheduled tribes in India, 2013.* New Delhi: Ministry of Tribal Affairs.

Government of India. (2020). All members of Lok Sabha (since 1952): Members biographical sketches. Retrieved from http://loksabhaph.nic.in/Members/lokprev.aspx

Hanghal, N. (2013). Fantastic tribe of women leaders. Retrieved from https://www.thehindubusinessline.com/news/variety/fantastic-tribe-of-women-leaders/article23031776.ece

Hausing, K. K. S. (2017). 'Equality as tradition' and women's reservation in Nagaland. *Economic and Political Weekly, 52*(45), 36–43.

Jena, M. (2009, May 16). Where are tribal women in Indian politics? *India Together.* Retrieved from http://www.indiatogether.org/tribals-society.

Jensenius, F. R. (2016). Competing inequalities? On the intersection of gender and ethnicity in candidate nominations in Indian elections. *Government and Opposition, 51*(3), 440–463.

Mitra, A. (2008). The status of women among the scheduled tribes in India. *The Journal of Socio-Economics, 37,* 1202–1217.

Oommen, T. K. (2011). Scheduled castes, scheduled tribes and the nation: Situating G. S. Ghurye. *Sociological Bulletin, 60*(2), 228–244.

Rai, S. M., & Spary, C. (2019). *Performing representation: Women members in the Indian Parliament*. New Delhi: Oxford University Press.

Sankar, D. V. (2019). From emancipation to representation: Women's reservation in Nagaland, an unending struggle for equality. *Global Journal of Political Science*, *7*(1), 1–7.

Sen, A. (2000). *Development as freedom*. New York: Alfred A. Knopf.

Thakur, D., & Thakur, D. N. (1994). *Tribal women* (Tribal Life in India-6). New Delhi: Deep and Deep Publications.

Xaxa, V. (2004). Women and gender in the study of tribes in India. *Indian Journal of Gender Studies*, *11*(3), 345–367.

Adivasis, Naxalites and Indian Democracy*

Ramachandra Guha

On 13 December 1946, Jawaharlal Nehru moved the Objective Resolution in the Constituent Assembly of India. This proclaimed that the soon-to-be-free nation would be an independent Sovereign Republic. Its constitution would guarantee citizens 'justice, social, economic and political; equality of status; of opportunity and before the law; freedom of thought, expression, belief, faith, worship, vocation, association and action, subject to law and public morality'.

The resolution went on to say that 'adequate safeguards shall be provided for minorities, backward and tribal areas and depressed and other backward classes...'. In moving the resolution, Nehru invoked the spirit of Gandhi and the 'great past of India', as well as modern precedents such as the French, American and Russian Revolutions.

The debate on the Objective Resolution went on for a whole week. Among the speakers were the conservative Hindu Purushottam Das Tandon, the right wing Hindu Shyama Prasad Mukherjee, the scheduled caste leader B. R. Ambedkar, the liberal lawyer M. R. Jayakar, the socialist M. R. Masani, a leading woman activist, Hansa Mehta and the communist Somnath Lahiri. After all these stalwarts had their say, a former hockey player and lapsed Christian named Jaipal Singh rose to speak. 'As a jungli, as an Adibasi', said Jaipal in the Constituent Assembly,

I am not expected to understand the legal intricacies of the Resolution. But my common sense tells me that every one of us should march in that road to freedom and fight together. Sir, if there is any group of Indian people that has been shabbily treated it is my people. They have been disgracefully treated, neglected for the last 6,000 years. The history of the Indus Valley civilisation, a child of which I am, shows quite clearly that it is the newcomers—most of you here are intruders as far as I am concerned—it is the newcomers who have driven away my people from the Indus Valley to the jungle fastness... The whole history of my people is one of continuous exploitation and dispossession by the non-aboriginals of India punctuated by rebellions and disorder, and yet I take Pandit Jawahar Lal Nehru at his word. I take you all at your word that now we are going to

* This chapter was previously published in *Economic and Political Weekly*, *42*(32), 2007, 3305–3312.

start a new chapter, a new chapter of independent India where there is equality of opportunity, where no one would be neglected (Government of India, 1946, pp. 143–144).

Sixty years have passed since Jaipal took Nehru and all the others at their word. What has been the fate of his people, the Adivasis, in this time? This essay will argue that, in many ways, the tribals of peninsular India are the unacknowledged victims of six decades of democratic development. In this period, they have continued to be exploited and dispossessed by the wider economy and polity. (At the same time, the process of dispossession has been punctuated by rebellions and disorder.) Their relative and oftentimes absolute deprivation is more striking when compared with that of other disadvantaged groups such as Dalits and Muslims. While Dalits and Muslims have had some impact in shaping the national discourse on democracy and governance, the tribals remain not just marginal but invisible.

I

There are some 85 million Indians who are officially classified as scheduled tribes (STs). Of these, about 16 million live in the states of North-eastern India. This essay, however, focuses on the roughly 70 million tribals who live in the heart of India, in a more-or-less contiguous hill and forest belt that extends across the states of Gujarat, Rajasthan, Maharashtra, Madhya Pradesh, Chhattisgarh, Jharkhand, Andhra Pradesh, Orissa (Odisha), Bihar and West Bengal.

The tribes of the Northeast differ from their counterparts in other parts of India in several crucial ways. First, they have, until the recent past, been more or less untouched by Hindu influence. Second, they have, in the

recent past, been exposed rather substantially to modern (and especially English) education; as a consequence, their literary rates and, hence, their chances of being advantageously absorbed in the modern economy, are much higher than that of their counterparts elsewhere in India. Third, unlike the tribals of the mainland, they have been largely exempt from the trauma caused by dispossession; till recently, their location in a corner of the country has inhibited dam builders and mine owners from venturing near them.

There are, of course, many different endogamous communities—more than 500, at last count—that come under the label STs. However, despite this internal differentiation, taken as a whole, the tribes of central and eastern India share certain attributes—cultural, social, economic and political—that allow us to treat them as a single segment, distinct not only from North-eastern tribals but also from all other Indians. In everyday language, this commonality is conveyed in the term Adivasi. It is not a word that can be or is used to describe a Naga or a Mizo. However, it comes easily to one's lips when speaking of a Gond or a Korku or a Bhil or an Oraon. For these (and other) individual tribes are nevertheless unified, in the Indian imagination, by some common characteristics. Usually, what they share is denoted in cultural or ecological terms—namely, that these Adivasis generally inhabit upland or wooded areas, that they generally treat their women better than caste Hindus, that they have rich traditions of music and dance and that while they might occasionally worship some manifestation of Vishnu or Siva, their rituals and religion centre around village gods and spirits.

The basis for these everyday understandings of the Adivasi lies in a series of ethnographic monographs written over the years.[1] From the perspective of Indian democracy, however, what unites the Adivasis is not their

---

[1] On anthropological constructions of the tribe in India, see, among other works, Elwin (1939, 1964); Ghurye (1959); Singh (1972); Haimendorf (1982); Singh (1985); Béteille (1991); Guha (1999) and Sundar (2007).

cultural or ecological distinctiveness, but their economic and social disadvantage. As a recent book by the demographer Arup Maharatna demonstrates, when assessed by the conventional indicators of development, the Adivasis are even worse off than the Dalits. For example, the literacy rate of Adivasis is, at 23.8 per cent, considerably lower than that of the Dalits, which stands at 30.1 per cent. As many as 62.5 per cent of Adivasi children who enter school dropout before they matriculate; whereas this happens only with 49.4 per cent of Dalit children. While a shocking 41.5 per cent of Dalits live under the official poverty line, the proportion of Adivasis who do so is even higher, that is, 49.5 per cent.

With respect to health facilities, too, the Adivasis are even more poorly served than the Dalits. Among the tribals, 28.9 per cent have no access whatsoever to doctors and clinics; for Dalits the percentage is 15.6 per cent. Among tribal children, 42.2 per cent have been immunized; as compared to 57.6 per cent of Dalit children. Again, 63.6 per cent of Dalits have access to safe drinking water, as against 43.2 per cent of tribals.[2]

On the one hand, by not providing them with decent education and healthcare, the government of India has dishonoured its constitutional guarantee to provide the Adivasis equal opportunities for social and economic development. On the other hand, the policies of the government have more *actively* dispossessed many Adivasis of their traditional means of life and livelihood. The tribals of the mainland live amidst India's best forests, alongside many of its fastest-flowing rivers and on top of its richest mineral resources. Once, this closeness to nature's bounty provided them the means for subsistence and survival. However, as the pace of economic and industrial development picked up after independence, the Adivasis have increasingly had to make way for commercial forestry, dams and mines. Often, the Adivasis are displaced because of

the pressures and imperatives of what passes as development; sometimes, they are displaced because of the pressures and imperatives of development's equally modern other, namely, conservation. Thus, apart from large dams and industrial townships, tribals have also been rendered homeless by national parks and sanctuaries (Rangarajan & Shahabuddin, 2006).

How many Adivasis have lost their homes and lands as a result of conscious state policy? The estimates vary—they range from a few million to as many as 20 million. Even if we cannot come up with a precise reliable number to the question, how many tribals have been involuntarily displaced by the policies of the government of India, the answer must be too many. The sociologist Walter Fernandes estimates that about 40 per cent of all those displaced by government projects are of tribal origin. Since Adivasis constitute roughly 8 per cent of India's population, this means that a tribal is five times as likely as a non-tribal to be forced to sacrifice his home and hearth by the claims and demands of development and/ or conservation (Fernandes, 2006).

Adivasis were displaced from their lands and villages when the state occupied the commanding heights of the economy, and they continue to be displaced under the auspices of liberalization and globalization. The opening of the Indian economy has had benign outcomes in parts of the country where the availability of an educated workforce allows for the export of high-end products such as software. On the other hand, where it has led to an increasing exploitation of unprocessed raw materials, globalization has presented a more brutal face. Such is the case with the tribal districts of Orissa (Odisha), where the largely non-tribal leadership of the state has signed a series of leases with mining companies, both Indian and foreign. These leases permit, in fact encourage, these companies to dispossess tribals of the land they own or

---

[2] Maharatna's estimates are based on studies and surveys conducted in the 1990s (Maharatna, 2005).

cultivate, but under which lie rich veins of iron ore or bauxite.

II

The sufferings of the Adivasis as a consequence of deliberate state policy have been underlined in a series of official reports down the decades. A decade after independence, the home ministry constituted a committee headed by the anthropologist Verrier Elwin to enquire into the functioning of government schemes in tribal areas. It found that the officials in charge of these schemes 'were lacking in any intimate knowledge of their people [and] had very little idea of general policies for tribal development'. Worse, there was 'a tendency for officials to regard themselves as superior, as heaven-born missionaries of a higher culture. They boss the people about; their chaprasis abuse them; in order to "get things done" they do not hesitate to threaten and bully. Any failure is invariably placed at the tribal door;... the Block officials blaming everything on the laziness, the improvidence, the suspiciousness, the superstitions of the people'.

After studying 20 blocks spread across the country, the committee concluded that 'of the many tribal problems the greatest of all is poverty'. Much of the poverty and degradation they saw, said the committee, was

> the fault of us, the 'civilised' people. We have driven [the tribals] into the hills because we wanted their land and now we blame them for cultivating it in the only way we left to them. We have robbed them of their arts by sending them the cheap and tawdry products of a commercial economy. We have even taken away their food by stopping their hunting or by introducing new taboos which deprive them of the valuable protein elements in meat and fish. We sell them spirits which are far more injurious than the home-made beers and wines which are nourishing and familiar to them and use the proceeds to uplift them with ideals. We look down on them and rob them of their self-confidence and take away their freedom by laws which they do not understand (Government of India, 1960, pp. 20, 192).

Not long afterwards, the senior congressman (and former Congress president) U. N. Dhebar was asked to chair a high-powered committee to look into the situation in tribal areas. Its members included six members of Parliament (among them Jaipal Singh) and some senior social workers. The committee identified land alienation, the denial of forest rights and the displacement by development projects as among the major problems facing the Adivasis (Government of India, 1961). Sometimes, state policy had come to the rescue of tribals; at other times, it had only worked to impoverish them further. The state machinery had been unable to prevent the loss of land to outsiders, or to check the exploitative activities of moneylenders. Meanwhile, the major power projects and steel plants set in motion by the Five-Year Plans had 'resulted in a substantial displacement of the tribal people'. The committee was concerned that this form of industrial development would 'sweep [the tribals] off their feet... We have to see that the foundations of tribal life are not shaken and the house does not crash'. Because of the dams and mills already built, the tribals were dislodged from their traditional sources of livelihood and places of habitation. Not conversant with the details of acquisition proceedings they accepted whatever cash compensation was given to them and became emigrants. With cash in hand and many attractions in the nearby industrial towns, their funds were rapidly depleted and in course of time they were without money as well as without land. They joined the ranks of landless labourers but without any training, equipment or aptitude for any skilled or semi-skilled job.

The Dhebar Committee's most eloquent passages concerned the suppression of tribal rights in the forest. As a consequence of the forest laws introduced by the British and continued by the governments of independent India, 'the tribal who formerly regarded himself as the lord of the forest, was through a deliberate process turned into a subject and placed under the forest department'. The officials and their urban conservationist supporters claimed that in order to protect the forests, the Adivasis had to be kept out. The Dhebar Committee commented,

> There is constant propaganda that the tribal people are destroying the forest. We put this complaint to some unsophisticated tribals. They countered the complaint by asking how they could destroy the forest. They owned no trucks; they hardly had even a bullock cart. The utmost that they could carry away was some wood to keep them warm in the winter months, to reconstruct or repair their huts and carry on their little cottage industries. Their fuel needs for cooking, they said, were not much, because they had not much to cook. Having explained their own position they invariably turned to the amount of destruction that was taking place all around them. They reiterated how the ex-zamindars, in violation of their agreements and the forest rules and laws, devastated vast areas of forest land right in front of officials. They also related how the contractors stray outside the contracted coupes, carry loads in excess of their authorised capacity and otherwise exploit both the forests and the tribals.

There is a feeling amongst the tribals that all the arguments in favour of preservation and development of forests are intended to refuse them their demands. They argue that when it is a question of industry, township, development work or projects of rehabilitation, all these plausible arguments are forgotten and vast tracts are placed at the disposal of outsiders who mercilessly destroy the forest wealth with or without necessity.

Already, by the 1960s, reports commissioned by the government of India were demonstrating the utter failure of the state in providing a life of dignity and honour to its tribal citizens. Nor was this a generalized critique; rather, the specific problems faced by the Adivasis were identified—namely, callous and corrupt officials, the loss of land, indebtedness, restrictions on the use of the forest and large-scale displacement. The evidence offered in these (and other reports) should have called for a course correction, for the formation and implementation of policies that ensured that India's industrial and economic development was not to be at the cost of its Adivasi citizens.

These reports and their recommendations would be met with a deafening silence that had not been unanticipated. As the Elwin Committee noted, past reports on tribal problems had been 'ignored in practice'. It 'is extraordinary', it commented, 'how often... a recommendation sinks into the soulless obscurity of an official file and is heard of no more' (Government of India, 1960, pp. 191–192). Or at least not for another 20 or 30 years. For in the 1980s, another series of official reports commented strongly on the continuing deprivation of the Adivasis. These were written by the then Commissioner for Scheduled Castes and Scheduled Tribes, B. D. Sharma, a civil servant with wide experience of working with and alongside tribals. As documented by Sharma, the major problems faced by tribals were still land alienation, restrictions on their use of forests and displacement by dams and other large projects. He pointed out that 'the tribal people are at a critical point in their history...'. They were 'losing command over resources at a very fast rate but are also facing social disorganisation which is unprecedented in their history', and yet the 'tales of woes from tribal areas are hardly heard outside. And when they come they are not taken seriously...'. What was worse, 'the State itself sometimes tends to adopt a partisan role and become a privy even for actions not quite legal simply because the matter concerns voiceless small communities' (Government of India, 1988 and 1990).

This time, the government's response to these well documented and soberly worded indictments was to refuse to table the reports in the Parliament.

III

Those are some facts about the neglect and exploitation of the Adivasis in independent India. Let me turn now to the history of rebellion and disorder. In the colonial period, there were major rebellions in tribal areas, as for example, the Kol and Bhumij revolts of the early 19th century, the Santhal 'Hool' of 1855, the Birsa Munda-led 'Ulugulan' in the 1890s, the uprising in Bastar in 1911, the protests in Gudem-Rampa in the 1920s and the Warli revolt of 1945–1946. Most often, these protests had to do with the alienation of land or the expropriation of forests. They were quelled only with the use of force, often very substantial force.[3]

The first two decades after independence were, comparatively speaking, a time of peace in tribal India. Perhaps, like Jaipal Singh, most Adivasis took the government at its word that with freedom a new chapter would begin, where 'there is equality of opportunity, where no one would be neglected'. However, as the evidence mounted that the benefits of development were unevenly distributed and that the costs were borne disproportionately by tribal communities, discontent began to grow. Thus, for example, there was a major uprising of Adivasis in Bastar in 1966, led by their recently deposed Maharaja, Pravir Chandra Bhanj Deo. Then, in the 1970s, a militant movement took shape in the tribal districts of Bihar, demanding an end to the exploitation by moneylenders and the forest department and also asking for the creation of a separate state to be named 'Jharkhand'. In the same decade, tribals in Maharashtra were organized in defence of their land and forest rights by groups such as the Bhoomi Sena and the Kashtakari Sanghatana. Also in the 1970s, there were the protests against the Koel-Karo projects in Bihar. Then, beginning in the 1980s and coming down to the present day, the plight of tribals ousted by development projects (and by large dams in particular) has been highlighted by the Narmada Bachao Andolan. Most recently, Adivasis threatened by mining projects in Orissa (Odisha) have organized a series of processions and boycotts to reassert their rights over land handed over by the state government to mining companies.[4]

Above and beyond these various protests, Maoist revolutionaries have been active in tribal areas. The village Naxalbari, which gave the Naxalites their name, itself lies in a part of West Bengal which has a substantial tribal population. Another major centre of Naxalite activity in the late 1960s was the tribal districts of Andhra Pradesh. In the 1970s, the Maoists spread their influence in two main areas—the caste-ridden districts of central Bihar and the tribal districts of the southern parts of the state. In recent decades, as the Maoist insurgency has spread, its major gains have been in tribal districts—in Maharashtra, in Orissa (Odisha), in Jharkhand, but above all in Chhattisgarh.[5]

Over the past four decades, the Adivasis of central India have often expressed their public and collective discontent with the policies and programmes of the state. Their protests have sometimes (as in Bastar in 1966 or in Jharkhand in the late 1970s) taken recourse to traditional means and traditional leaders. At other times (as in Maharashtra in the 1970s, or in the Narmada Andolan), Adivasis have been mobilized by social activists from an urban, middle-class background. More recently, however, tribal disaffection has been largely expressed under the leadership of armed Maoist revolutionaries.[6]

---

[3] See, among other works, Jha (1964, 1967); Desai (1979); Arnold (1982); Guha (1983); Singh (2002); Hardiman, (1987) and Skaria (1999).

[4] For a general overview, see Desai (1986); Sundar (2002); Devalle (1992); Sengupta (1982); Baviskar (2004). The mining conflicts in Orissa (Odisha) are the subject of a forthcoming book by Felix Padel.

[5] The early phase of the Maoist movement in India is ably treated in Banerjee (1980). There is, as yet, no comparable work on Maoism as it has evolved in the 1990s and beyond.

[6] In the remainder of this essay I use tribal and Adivasi interchangeably, as also Maoist and Naxalite.

IV

Section I briefly compared the economic and social situation of the Dalits to that of Adivasis. When the comparison is extended to the domain of politics, one finds that Adivasis appear to be even more disadvantaged. The weakness and vulnerability of Adivasis is made even more manifest when one further extends the comparison to include a third marginalized minority, namely, the Muslims.

Consider, for example, the constitution of various union cabinets from 1947 to 2007. In this time, there have often been Dalits and Muslims who have held important portfolios. Dalits and/or Muslims have served, sometimes for long periods, as Home Minister, Defence Minister, Agriculture Minister and External Affairs Minister in the government of India. On the other hand, no major portfolio in the Union Cabinet has ever been assigned to an Adivasi politician.

Likewise, both Dalits and Muslims have held high constitutional posts. One Dalit and three Muslims have held the highest office of all—that of President of the Republic. One Dalit and three Muslims have served as Chief Justice of India. No tribal has ever been made President or Vice President or Chief Justice. So far as I know, no Adivasi has been appointed a judge of the Supreme Court, and many more Dalits and Muslims have served as Governors of states than have tribals.

These facts are manifestations of the much wider invisibility of tribals from the political process. Muslims and Dalits have been able to constitute themselves as an interest group on the national stage—they are treated in popular discourse as communities that are pan-Indian. On the other hand, tribal claims remain confined to the states and districts in which they live. Unlike the Dalits and the Muslims, the Adivasis continue to be seen only in discrete, broken-up, fragments.

The Dalits, in particular, have effectively channelized their grievances through constitutional means. They have successful political parties, such as the Bahujan Samaj Party, which

is (was) now (then) in power in Uttar Pradesh and which is rapidly extending its influence and appeal in other states. Dalits also have nationally known leaders, such as the (then) Uttar Pradesh Chief Minister, Mayawati, who is now being spoken of as a possible future Prime Minister of India. On the other hand, the Adivasis have neither a successful political party nor a well-known political leader. Back in the 1940s, a Jharkhand Party was formed under Jaipal Singh's leadership. While it did reasonably well in the first general elections, in 1952, it remained a regional party. It fought 60 years for a separate state, but its effectiveness was undermined by a series of splits. In any case, when the state of Jharkhand was created in 2000, it consisted only of the tribal districts of Bihar, rather than being, as Jaipal had hoped, a much larger province consisting of the contiguous tribal districts of Bengal, Orissa (Odisha), Madhya Pradesh and Andhra Pradesh as well as Bihar. As finally constituted, this 'moth-eaten' Jharkhand has an overwhelming majority of non-tribals.

If, as is commonly (and justly) acknowledged, Dalits and tribals are the two most disadvantaged sections of Indian society, why have the former been more effective in making their claims heard by the formal political system? This contrast is, I believe, largely explained by aspects of geography and demography. The tribals of central India usually live in tribal villages, in hills and valleys, where they outnumber the non-tribals among them. However, in no single state of peninsular India are they in a majority. In Andhra Pradesh, for example, Adivasis constitute 6 per cent of the state's population. In Maharashtra, the proportion is 9 per cent; in Rajasthan, 12 per cent. Even in states professedly formed to protect the tribal interest, such as Jharkhand and Chhattisgarh, roughly two-thirds of the population is non-tribal.

The Dalits too are a minority in every state, but unlike tribals they live in mixed villages, alongside other castes and communities. This means that when election time comes, they can have a decisive impact even in constituencies not reserved for them. In most states of the union and in most districts in these states, they command between 10 per cent and 20 per cent of the vote. Therefore, political parties have to address the Dalit interest in a majority of Lok Sabha and Assembly constituencies. Tribals, on the other hand, can influence elections only in the few, isolated districts where they are concentrated. In a general election, for example, the tribal vote may matter only in 50 or 60 constituencies, whereas the Dalit vote matters in perhaps as many as 300.[7]

Dalit mobilization on a provincial and national scale is also enabled by the structural similarities in the ways they experience oppression. The caste system operates in much the same manner across India. In villages in Tamil Nadu as in Uttar Pradesh, Dalits are allotted the most degrading jobs, made to live away from upper-caste hamlets, allowed access only to inferior water sources and prohibited from entering temples. It is, therefore, possible for them to build links and forge solidarities horizontally, across villages and districts and states. On the other hand, there are many variations in the forms in which tribals experience oppression. In one place, their main persecutors are forest officials; in another place, moneylenders; in a third, development projects conducted under the aegis of the state; in a fourth, a mining project promoted by a private firm. In the circumstances, it is much harder to build a broad coalition of tribals fighting for a common goal under a single banner.

The Dalits have also been helped by the posthumous presence of B. R. Ambedkar. He has been for them both example and inspiration, a man of towering intellect who successfully breached the upper-caste citadel and who, long after he is gone, encourages his fellows to do likewise. Indeed, the figure of Ambedkar is a rallying point for Dalits across the land.

The tribals, on the other hand, have never had a leader who could inspire admiration, or even affection, across the boundaries of state and language. Birsa Munda, for example, is revered in parts of Jharkhand; but he is scarcely known or remembered in the Adivasi areas of Andhra Pradesh or Maharashtra. One advantage that Ambedkar enjoys over tribal icons is that he was a builder of modern institutions as well as a social activist. He burnt copies of the Manusmriti and formed labour unions; but he also founded schools and political parties and, above all, directed the drafting of the Indian constitution. Ambedkar has become an all-India figure in part because of the similarities in the way his followers experience oppression, but also because they can follow him both in protesting injustice and in building a better future.

One might say that the weak literacy rates among Adivasis have been accompanied by a weak articulation ratio. They do not have national leaders; while such men as do represent them are not conversant enough with the languages and discourses of modern democratic politics. On the other hand, in the case of the Dalits, the presence of Ambedkar in the past and of Mayawati in the present, has been complemented by an articulate second rung of activists, who know how to build political networks and lobby within and across parties.

As argued above, at a *national* level another minority that has had an significant political impact is the Muslims. Outside the Kashmir valley, Muslims, like Dalits, live in villages and towns alongside Indians of other creeds. As their depressed economic situation shows, the state has not been especially attentive to their material interest. However, politicians have necessarily to be attentive to their votes. In the last Bihar elections, one leader

---

[7] These estimates are not offered on the basis of a scientific study, but are an educated guess. A detailed statistical analysis of individual constituencies would, of course, revise these figures upwards or downwards, but I suspect by not very much.

promised to appoint a Muslim Chief Minister if his party won. No such promise has ever been made by politicians to tribals, even in states such as Madhya Pradesh where they form as much as one-fifth of the population.

Also relevant to this discussion is the history of Indian nationalism and in particular the history of the Indian National Congress. Even before Gandhi assumed its leadership, the Congress had to face the charge that it was essentially an upper-caste, Hindu party. To combat this criticism, it had to reach out to Muslims and low castes. This imperative became even more pronounced in the Gandhian era, when the Mahatma's claim that the Congress represented all of India was strongly challenged by M. A. Jinnah, presuming to speak on behalf of the Muslims and by B. R. Ambedkar, who sought to represent the lowest castes. The rhetoric of Congress nationalism, before and after independence, always had space within it for the special interests of Muslims and Dalits. (The operative word here is 'rhetoric': what happened in practice was another matter.) On the other hand, the Congress has never really understood the distinctive nature of the tribal predicament. Down the decades, matters concerning Adivasis have rarely been given prominence in meetings of the All India Congress Committee or the Congress Working Committee.

The contrast between a relative Dalit and Muslim visibility, on the one hand, and tribal invisibility, on the other, can also be illustrated with reference to the mainstream media. Both newspapers and television give a fair amount of coverage to the continuing victimization of Dalits and the continuing marginalization of

the Muslims. It is sometimes argued that the coverage of Dalit and Muslim issues in the media is not nearly as nuanced, nor as substantial, as it should be. These criticisms are not without merit. However, in comparison with their Adivasi compatriots Dalits and Muslims are actually quite well served by the media. In real life, the tribals are unquestionably as victimized and as marginal; yet they rarely have their concerns discussed or highlighted in talk shows, editorials, reports or feature articles.

V

The increasing presence of Naxalites in areas dominated by Adivasis has a geographical reason, namely, that the hills and forests of central India are well suited to the methods of roaming guerrilla warfare. But it also has a historical reason, namely, that the Adivasis have gained least and lost most from 60 years of political independence.[8]

In fact, the two are connected. For the state's neglect of the Adivasis is in many respects a product of the terrain in which they live. In these remote upland areas, public officials are unwilling to work hard and often unwilling to work at all. Doctors do not attend the clinics assigned to them; school teachers stay away from school; magistrates spend their time lobbying for a transfer back to the plains. On the other hand, the Maoists are prepared to walk miles to hold a village meeting and listen sympathetically to tribal grievances. As a senior forest official was recently constrained to admit: 'In the absence of any government

---

[8] Notably, while they have made major gains in states such as Jharkhand and Chhattisgarh, the Naxalites have no real influence in the western Adivasi belt—that is, in the states of Gujarat and Rajasthan, where the populations are more closely integrated with caste peasant society and where the terrain is much less suited to guerrilla action. Of course, it is not merely in tribal areas that the Naxalites are active. For instance, they have a strong presence in the Telangana region of Andhra Pradesh and in central Bihar. In both areas, they work chiefly with sharecroppers and agricultural labourers of low-caste origin, mobilizing them in opposition to the upper-caste moneylenders and landlords (Bhatia, 2005). However, in recent years, their greatest gains appear to have been in districts where Adivasis are in a majority. In any case, this essay's focus on the tribal predicament means that it necessarily has to give short shrift to Naxalite activity in areas where the principal axes of social identification are caste and class.

support and the apathetic attitude of the forest management departments towards the livelihood of forest-dependent communities, the Naxalites have found fertile ground to proliferate...' (Mukherji, 2005).

The Maoists live among and in the same state of penury as the tribals is unquestionable. Some of their actions that have sometimes helped the Adivasis can also be conceded. This is especially the case with rates for the collection of non-timber forest produce, such as tendu patta, which have gone up by as much as 200 per cent in areas where the Naxalites are active and the contractors fearful of their wrath. However, the principal aim of the Maoists is not the social or economic advancement of the Adivasis, but the capture of power in Delhi through a process of armed struggle. In this larger endeavour, the tribals are a stepping stone—or, as some would say, merely cannon fodder.

From its origins, the Naxalite movement was riven by internal discord, by sharp and often bloody rivalries between different factions, each claiming itself to be the only true Indian interpreter of Mao Zedong's thought. However, by the end of the last century the People's War Group (PWG) and the Maoist Communist Centre (MCC) had emerged as the two groups which still had a functioning organization and a devoted cadre of revolutionary workers. The PWG was very active in Andhra Pradesh, whereas the MCC's base was principally in Bihar.

The Naxalite movement gathered force after the merger in 2004 of the PWG and the MCC. The new party called itself the Communist Party of India (Maoist). That its abbreviation (CPI-M) mimicked that of a party that had fought and won elections under the Indian constitution was surely not accidental. We are the real inheritors of the legacy of revolutionary Marxism, the new party was saying, whereas the power-holders in Kerala and West Bengal are merely a bunch of bourgeois reformists.

The new, unified party has been a mere three years in existence, but in that time, it has rapidly expanded its influence. The erstwhile MCC cadres have moved southwards into Jharkhand and east into West Bengal. Those who were once with the PWG have travelled into Orissa (Odisha) and Chhattisgarh. This last state is where the Maoists have made the most dramatic gains. Large parts of the district of Dantewada, in particular, are under their sway. On one side of the river Indravati, the Indian state exercises an uncertain control by day and no control at night. On the other side, in what is known as Abujmarh, the state has no presence by day or by night.

Dantewada forms part of a forest belt which spills over from Chhattisgarh into Andhra Pradesh and Maharashtra. The region was known in mythical times as 'Dandakaranya', a name the Maoists have now adopted as their own. Under the Special Zonal Committee for Dandakaranya operate several divisional committees. These, in turn, have Range committees reporting to them. The lowest level of organization is at the village, where a committee of committed workers is known as a 'Sangam'.

According to a senior functionary of the party, the Sangams in Dantewada seek to protect people's rights over '*jal, jangal, zameen*' (water, forest and land). At the same time, the Maoists make targeted attacks on state officials, especially the police. Raids on police stations are intended to stop them harassing ordinary folk. They are also necessary to augment the weaponry of the guerrilla army. Through popular mobilization and the intimidation of state officials, the Maoists hope to expand their authority over Dandakaranya. Once the region is made a liberated zone, it is intended to be used as a launching pad for the capture of state power in India as a whole.[9]

---

[9] These paragraphs are based on an interview conducted in Bastar in the summer of 2006, with a Maoist leader calling himself Sanjeev.

How many Maoists are there in India? The estimates are imprecise and widely varying. There are perhaps between 10,000 and 20,000 full-time guerrillas, many of them armed with an AK-47. These revolutionaries are also conversant with the use of grenades, landmines and rocket-launchers. They maintain links with guerrilla movements in other parts of South Asia, exchanging information and technology with the Liberation Tigers of Tamil Eelam and, at least before their recent conversion to multiparty democracy, with the Nepali Maoists.

What we know of the leaders and cadres suggests that most Maoists come from a lower-middle-class background. They usually have a smattering of education and were often radicalized in college. Like other communist movements, the leadership of this one too is overwhelmingly male. No tribals are represented in the upper levels of the party hierarchy.

The general secretary of the now unified party, the Communist Party of India (Maoist), calls himself Ganapathi. He is believed to be from Andhra Pradesh, although the name he uses is almost certainly a pseudonym. Statements carrying his name occasionally circulate on the Internet—one, issued in February 2007, reported the successful completion of a party Congress 'held deep in the forests of one of the several Guerrilla Zones in the country...'. The party Congress 'reaffirmed the general line of the new democratic revolution with agrarian revolution as its axis and protracted people's war as the path of the Indian revolution...'. The meeting 'was completed amongst great euphoria with a call to the world people: *Rise up as a tide to smash Imperialism and its running dogs! Advance the Revolutionary war throughout the world!*'

In pursuit of this protracted people's war, the Maoists have conducted daring attacks on artefacts and symbols of the state. In November 2005, they stormed the district town of Jehanabad in Bihar, firebombing offices and freeing several hundred prisoners from jail. In March 2007, they attacked a police camp in Chhattisgarh, killing 55 policemen and making off with a huge cache of weapons. At other times, they have bombed and set fire to railway stations and transmission towers.

However, the violence promoted by the revolutionaries is not always aimed at the state. A landmine they set off in Gadchiroli in May 2006 killed many members of a wedding party. The Maoists have also maimed and murdered those they suspect of being informers.

VI

How can a democratic state fight the rise of Maoist extremism in the tribal areas? It might do so, on the one hand, by bringing the fruits of development to the Adivasi and on the other hand by prompt and effective police action. However, the policies currently being followed by the government of India are the antithesis of what one would prescribe. Instead of making tribals partners in economic development, they marginalize them further. State governments, themselves run and dominated by non-tribals, are signing away tribal land for mining, manufacturing and energy generation projects. Moreover, instead of efficient police action, we have the outsourcing of law and order, as in the Salwa Judum campaign in Chhattisgarh, where the state government has set up a vigilante army that runs a parallel administration in the region.

In the most peaceful of times, the state has often failed to uphold the law in tribal areas. Fifth and sixth of the constitution provide for a substantial degree of self-governance in districts where Adivasis are in a majority. Yet their clauses protecting tribal rights in land and forests, curbing the activities of moneylenders and mandating the formation of village and district councils have been honoured only in the breach. These schedules provide for local councils to share in the royalties from minerals found on tribal land; what happens in practice is that the Adivasis do not get to see or spend a paisa from mining, whose proceeds are shared between the contractors and the state-level (and usually non-tribal) politicians. Meanwhile, the criminal justice system is in a state of near collapse, as witness the murder of Shankar Guha Niyogi, the one who selflessly strived for the rights and dignity of Adivasi workers in Chhattisgarh. It was widely believed that Guha Niyogi was killed by assassins hired by capitalists; yet those who planned and executed the murder have gone scot-free.

Even with this kind of record, Salwa Judum marks a new low. In the past, the state failed to sincerely uphold the law of the land in tribal areas, but now it has gone so far as to actively promote disorder and lawlessness. The impact of Salwa Judum in the Dantewada district of Chhattisgarh has been studied by several fact-finding committees composed of activists, academics, journalists and retired civil servants. Their reports have demonstrated that the campaign has led to an escalation of violence. On the one side, Salwa Judum cadres have burnt villages and abused women; on the other hand, Naxalites have attacked and killed those they see as working in the service of the state. An atmosphere of fear and insecurity pervades the district. Families and villages are divided, some living with or in fear of the Maoists, others in fear of or in roadside camps controlled by the Salwa Judum. As many as 50,000 people have been displaced from their homes. These tribal refugees live in a pitiable condition, in tents exposed to the elements and with no access to healthcare or gainful employment. Thousands of others have fled across the border into Andhra Pradesh.[10]

In the district of Dantewada, a civil conflict is under way, which threatens to turn into a civil war. With a veil of secrecy surrounding the operations of the state and the revolutionaries and with the Adivasis too scared to file First Information Reports, there are no reliable estimates of the casualties in this war.

Perhaps between 500 and 1,000 people have died of unnatural deaths in Dantewada in the past year alone. Among those killed or murdered, some are security personnel and others are Naxalites. However, the vast majority are tribals caught in the crossfire.

Ironically, by arming civilians, the state has merely reproduced the methods of the other side. The Tribal boys in their teens have joined Salwa Judum for much the same reason as other boys had previously joined the Naxalites. Educated just enough to harbour a certain disenchantment for labouring in field and forest, but not enough to be absorbed with honour in the modern economy, these boys were enticed by the state into a job which paid them a salary (albeit a meagre one—₹1,500 a month) and gave them a certain status in society. Gun in hand, they now strut around the countryside, forcing those without weapons to fall in line.

In this manner, the machismo of revolution is being answered by the machismo of counter-revolution. Call them Sangam Organizer or Special Police Officer, the young men of Dandakaranya have been seduced by their new-found—and essentially unearned—authority. In the Dantewada district alone, there are now several thousand young males punch-drunk with the power which, as Mao said, flows from the barrel of a gun.

There is, thus, a double tragedy at work in tribal India. The first tragedy is that the state has treated its Adivasi citizens with contempt and condescension. The second tragedy is that their presumed protectors, the Naxalites, offer no long-term solution either.

Can the Communist Party of India (Maoist) come to power in New Delhi through armed struggle? I think the answer to this question must be in the negative. Corrupt and corroded though it is, the Indian state, c 2007, cannot be compared to the Chinese state, c 1940s. It is highly unlikely that a revolution based on Maoist principles will succeed in India. In

---

[10] See, among other works, People's Union for Democratic Rights (2006) and Independent Citizens' Initiative (2006).

fact, I would say it is impossible. In dense jungle, the Maoists can easily elude a police force that is poorly trained, poorly equipped and running scared to boot. It is not inconceivable that they will, at some stage, manage to establish a liberated zone in some part of Dandakaranya. But once they seek to expand their revolution into more open country, they will be mowed down by the Indian army.

Of the commitment of the Maoists to their cause, there should be no doubt. These are young men (and occasionally women) who have lived for years on the end in the most difficult circumstances, in pursuit of their dream of a successful revolution. I believe that, in military terms, this dream is a fantasy. The Maoists will never be able to plant the Red Flag on the Red Fort. The tragedy is that it might take them years to come to this conclusion. While the Maoists will find it difficult to expand outside their current areas of operation, the Indian state will not be able to easily restore order and legitimacy in the tribal areas that have passed out of its grasp. A war of attrition lies ahead of us, which will take a heavy toll of human life—lives of policemen, of Maoists and of unaffiliated civilians.

Such is the prospect in the short term. From the longer-term perspective of the historian, however, the Maoist dream might be seen not as fantasy but as nightmare. For the signal lesson of the 20th century is that regimes based on one-party rule grossly violate human dignity and human welfare. By common consent, the most evil man of the modern age was Adolf Hitler. The holocaust he unleashed and the wars he provoked cost some 30 million lives. But in the mass murder stakes, Stalin and Mao are not far behind. In fact, some estimates suggest that revolutionary communism has claimed even more human lives than fascism and the extremist ideologies of the right (Service, 2007).

The multiparty democracy is, if not the best, certainly the least harmful political system devised by humans and appreciated by some Adivasis themselves. On a visit to Dantewada in the summer of 2006, I had a long conversation with a Muria tribal. He was the first generation literate, who had been sent to study in an ashram school across the river. After graduation, he returned to his native village, to teach in the school there. At the same time, he obtained a BA degree through correspondence. A teacher, if he does his job well, is among the most respected men in rural India. This Muria teacher was that, but when the Maoists came to his village, he experienced an abrupt fall in status and authority. In their eyes, he was an official of the Indian state and thus, subject to harassment and extortion.

Last year, at the age of 25, the Muria teacher fled the village of his forefathers and crossed the Indravati into the Sarkari side of the district. His qualifications allowed him to get a job in a still functioning school. He lived near where he worked, at first in a tent and then in a house built by himself on government land. In fact, I first came across the Muria teacher while he was painting the walls of his home, pail in one hand, brush in the other.

A slim, dark man with a moustache, clad in a simple lungi, the Muria teacher talked to me while his two little children played around him. He told me that when the Maoists had first come to the district, they were full of idealism and good intentions. Over time, however, they had been corrupted, turning from defenders of the tribals to their tormentors. I answered that we could say the same of the Salwa Judum. It may have once been a people's movement, but it had since been taken over by contractors and criminals, these are mostly non-tribal. We argued the point, back and forth, while a crowd of interested parties gathered. Finally, the Muria teacher said that while he could contest what I was saying in public and in front of other people, among the Maoists, such free exchange of views was simply impermissible. As he put it: '*Naxalion ko hathiyar chhodné aur janta ké samné baath-cheeth karné ki himmat nahin hai*'. Indeed, the Indian Maoists do not have the courage to put down their arms and state their case openly before the people.

How then might the Maoist insurgency be ended or at least contained? On the government side, this might take the shape of a sensitively conceived and sincerely implemented plan to make Adivasis true partners in the development process by assuring them the title over lands cultivated by them, by allowing them the right to manage forests sustainably and by giving them a solid stake in industrial or mining projects that come up where they live and at the cost of their homes.

On the Maoist side, this might take the shape of a compact with bourgeois democracy. They could emulate the CPI and the CPM, as well as their counterparts in Nepal, by participating in and perhaps even winning elections. Comrade Prachanda appears to recognize that the political ideology most appropriate to the 21st century is multiparty democracy. A reconciliation of extremism with electoral democracy seems even more urgent and necessary in a country like India, which is much larger and much more diverse than Nepal.

As things stand, however, one cannot easily see the Indian Maoists give up on their commitment to armed struggle. Nor, given the way the Indian state actually functions, can one see it so radically reform itself as to put the interests of a vulnerable minority—the Adivasis—ahead of those with more money and political power.

In the long run, perhaps, the Maoists might indeed make their peace with the Republic of India and the republic come to treat its Adivasi citizens with dignity and honour. Whether this denouement will happen in my own lifetime, I am not sure. In the forest regions of central and eastern India, years of struggle and strife lie ahead. Here, in the jungles and hills they once called their own, the tribals will continue to be harassed on one side by the state and on the other by the insurgents. As one Bastar Adivasi put it to me, '*Hummé dono taraf sé dabav hain, aour hum beech mé pis gayé hain*'. It sounds far tamer in English, 'Pressed and pierced from both sides, here we are squeezed in the middle'.

NOTE

The arguments in this essay were first presented in a series of talks across the country in the first months of 2007—in the 'Challenges to Democracy' series organized by and at the Nehru Centre, Mumbai (January); as the seventh ISRO-Satish Dhawan lecture at the Jawaharlal Nehru Centre for Advanced Scientific Research in Bangalore (also in January); as the annual lecture of the Raja Rammohun Roy Foundation in Jaipur (February); and as the first Rajiv Kapur Memorial Lecture at the India International Centre, New Delhi (March). I am grateful to the audience at these lectures for their questions and comments. The present text has also benefited from the comments and criticisms of Rukun Advani, David Hardiman, Sujata Keshavan, J. Martinez-Alier, Mahesh Rangarajan and Dilip Simeon. I am especially indebted to Nandini Sundar, from whose work on Adivasis I have learnt a great deal over the years. The usual disclaimers apply.

REFERENCES

Arnold, D. (1982). Rebellious hillmen: The Gudem Rampa risings, 1839–1924. In R. Guha (Ed.), *Subaltern Studies-I*. Delhi: Oxford University Press.

Banerjee, S. (1980). *In the wake of Naxalbari: A history of the Naxalite movement in India*. Calcutta: Subarnarekha.

Baviskar, A. (2004). *In the belly of the river: Tribal conflicts over development in the Narmada valley*. New Delhi: Oxford University Press.

Béteille, A. (1991). *Society and politics in India: Essays in a comparative perspective*. London: Athlone Press.

Bhatia, B. (2005). The Naxalite movement in central Bihar. *Economic and Political Weekly, 40*(15), 1536–1549.

Desai, A. R. (Ed.) (1979). *Peasant struggles in India*. New Delhi: Oxford University Press.

Desai, A. R. (1986). *Agrarian struggles in India since independence*. New Delhi: Oxford University Press.

Devalle, S. B. C. (1992). *Discourses of ethnicity: Culture and protest in Jharkhand*. New Delhi: SAGE Publications.

Elwin, V. (1939). *The Baiga*. London: John Murray.

Elwin, V. (1964). *The tribal world of Verrier Elwin: An autobiography*. New York: Oxford University Press.

Fernandes, W. (2006). Development-induced displacement and tribal women. In G. C. Rath (Eds.), *Tribal development in India: The Contemporary Debate*. New Delhi: SAGE Publications.

Ghurye, G. S. (1959). *The scheduled tribes*. Bombay: Popular Prakashan.

Government of India. (1946). *Constituent assembly debates, volume-I*. New Delhi: Lok Sabha Secretariat.

Government of India. (1960). *Report of the committee on special multipurpose tribal blocks*. New Delhi: Manager of Publications.

Government of India. (1961). *Report of the scheduled areas and scheduled tribes committee*. New Delhi: Manager of Publications.

Government of India. (1988 and 1990). *The 28th and 29th reports of the commissioner for scheduled castes and scheduled tribes*. New Delhi: Government of India Press.

Guha, R. (1983). *Elementary aspects of peasant insurgency in colonial India*. New Delhi: Oxford University Press.

Guha, R. (1999). *Savaging the civilised: Verrier Elwin, his tribals and India*. New Delhi: Oxford University Press.

Haimendorf, C. V. F. (1982). *The tribes of India: Struggle and survival*. Berkeley, CA: University of California Press.

Hardiman, D. (1987). *The coming of the Devi: Adivasi assertion in western India*. New Delhi: Oxford University Press.

Independent Citizens' Initiative. (2006). *War in the heart of India: An enquiry into the ground situation in Dantewada district, Chhattisgarh*. New Delhi: Independent Citizens' Initiative.

Jha, J. C. (1964). *The Kol insurrection of Chhota Nagpur*. Calcutta: Thacker, Spink & Co.

Jha, J. C. (1967). *The Bhumij revolt 1832–33*. New Delhi: Munshiram Manoharlal.

Maharatna, A. (2005). *Demographic perspectives on India's tribes*. New Delhi: Oxford University Press.

Mukherji, D. (2005, June, 28). If you look after forest people, you kill Naxalism. *The Asian Age*.

People's Union for Democratic Rights. (2006). *When the state makes war on its own people: A report on the violation of people's rights during the Salwa Judum campaign in Dantewada, Chhattisgarh*. New Delhi: People's Union for Democratic Rights.

Rangarajan, M., & Shahabuddin, G. (2006). Displacement and relocation from protected areas: Towards a biological and historical synthesis. *Conservation and Society, 4*, 359–378.

Sengupta, N. (1982). *Fourth world dynamics, Jharkhand*. New Delhi: Authors Guild Publications.

Service, R. (2007). *Comrades: A world history of communism*. London: Macmillan.

Singh, K. S. (1985). *Tribal society in India*. New Delhi: Manohar.

Singh, K. S. (2002). *Birsa Munda and his movement 1872–1901: A Study of a millenarian movement in Chotanagpur*. Kolkata: Seagull Books.

Singh, K. S. (Ed.) (1972). *The tribal situation in India*. Shimla: Indian Institute of Advanced Study.

Skaria, A. (1999). *Hybrid histories: Forests, frontiers and wildness in western India*. New Delhi: Oxford University Press.

Sundar, N. (2007). *Subalterns and sovereigns: An anthropological history of Bastar, 1854–2006*. New Delhi: Oxford University Press.

Adivasi Issues and Election Manifestos of National Political Parties

Kamal Nayan Choubey

In all contemporary democratic systems, whether parliamentary, presidential or any other, election is an inevitable mechanism to determine the mandate of the voters. In elections, every party presents its agenda for the next term, it underlines its understanding of different national and international issues and also expresses its programmes for different sections of the electorate. Undoubtedly, election manifestos are crucial documents to understand the policies and programmes of different political parties. Tribal population of India constitute 8.6 per cent of total population (Government of India, 2013, p. 25). They are also among the most marginalized section of the country. Though there are many protective provisions in the constitution of India for the Adivasis,[1] they are still the most marginalized section of India. In this context, it could be asked that how various political parties treated Adivasis in their policies and

programmes? More specifically, what kind of understanding emerges from the study of the election manifesto of various political parties? What kinds of agendas were presented by them for the one of the most deprived sections of the Indian society?

During colonial rule in India, the rulers tried to implement the mechanisms of parliamentary system in India with a limited franchise. The Union Constitution Committee of the Constituent Assembly (1946–1950) under the chairmanship of Jawaharlal Nehru recommended the parliamentary type of government based on the English model. The Constituent Assembly accepted the colonial provisions of 'wholly excluded areas' and 'partially excluded areas' in the form of sixth schedule and fifth schedule, respectively. It also made provision of the reservation of seats for the scheduled tribes (STs) in Lok Sabha and state legislative assemblies according to proportion

---

[1] The chapter uses scheduled tribes (STs), tribal population, tribe and Adivasis interchangeably.

of their population. In the current Lok Sabha, 47 out of 543 elected seats are reserved for STs.[2]

During the debate in constituent assembly, Mahavir Tyagi highlighted the importance of the political parties, their manifestos and the mandate of the people. He observed that 'The Cabinet...has to be loyal to the majority party which has the mandate of the people to run the government on their behalf. The administration shall be run on the lines of the manifesto which has been approved by the general electorate' (Tiwari, 2018, p. 3). Manifestos offer several important things in a parliamentary democracy: one, a standard of performance against which subsequent achievements can be measured; two, authoritative statement of the party's clarity on policy; and, three, articulation of the popular consensus on major themes (Tiwari, 2018, p. 3).

This chapter evaluates the core Adivasi issues in the parliamentary elections of India. In this context, it evaluates the election manifestos of three national parties (i.e. Indian National Congress (INC), Bhartiya Janata Party (BJP) and Communist Party of India-Marxist (CPI-M) in last two general election (2014 and 2019). The chapter analyses the continuities and ruptures in the promises of these political parties regarding tribal issues in their election manifestos. It also focuses on the relationship between the promises of these parties and their actual performance regarding these issues. The chapter emphasizes that one can find a consensus about the larger tribal issues in all prominent 'national parties', however, in practice, most of the governments have been following the policies that are detrimental to the interests of tribal people.

I

GENERAL ELECTION OF 2014 AND ADIVASI ISSUES IN ELECTION MANIFESTOS

In election manifesto of every party, there are certain sections and promises which are related to common masses, and, in this sense, they also belong to Adivasi communities too. For example, the INC promised Nyuntam Aay Yojana (i.e. minimum income guarantee scheme) in 2019 election, which was related to ensure basic minimum income for all families, including Adivasi families (Indian National Congress, 2019). This chapter, however, focuses on the specific promises related to Adivasis in the election manifestos of three national parties.

2014 ELECTION MANIFESTO OF THE BJP AND ADIVASI ISSUES

The BJP fought 2014 election by declaring Narendra Modi as its prime ministerial candidate. As the chief minister of Gujarat, Modi always tried to present himself as a pro-tribal leader. In 2014 election, the BJP promised many crucial things to Adivasi voters. The BJP manifesto underlined that till now governments had not adopted any serious and honest approach for developments of tribals. It insisted on the necessity of the long term plan for the comprehensive development of tribal communities. It promised that it would give primacy to tribal development while preserving their 'unique identities'. It also emphasized that the governments of BJP ruled states like Gujarat, Madhya Pradesh and Chhattisgarh had worked with full dedication

---

[2] It is important to note that the Indian constitution makes a clear provision for the reservation of seats for scheduled castes (SCs) and STs in the Lok Sabha on the basis of their proportion in population. In state legislative assemblies, the reservation is based on the population of these communities in a particular state (Choubey, 2015a, pp. 10–11).

for the betterment of tribal live and created a net of welfare and development schemes for them. The BJP took a pledge to initiate a van bandhu kalyan yojna at the national level, which would be monitored by a tribal development authority. Through this proposed programme, it aimed to establish a well-planned network of schools for tribals, and provide them better facilities of housing, water, health etc. (Bhartiya Janata Party, 2014, p. 16). In the section of decentralization and people's participation, the BJP promised to give more power and importance to the Gram Sabha for the development of Adivasis (Bhartiya Janata Party, 2014, p. 9).

The party also promised certain crucial measures for SCs, STs and Other Backward Classes (OBCs) and underlined that it would create an ecosystem for education and entrepreneurship and ensure proper use of funds and implementation of programmes related to these marginalized sections. It pledged to fulfil the needs of education, health, housing and skill development of these sections, and give special attention to the needs of girl child (Bhartiya Janata Party, 2014, p. 16).

Though the BJP manifesto promised many initiatives to make the lives of Adivasis better it did not mention anything on the Panchayat (Extension to Scheduled Areas) Act (PESA)[3] or the Scheduled Tribes and Other Traditional Forest Dwellers (Recognition of Forest Rights) Act, 2006, commonly known as Forest Rights Act (FRA)[4] in its manifesto. However, it clearly mentioned about decentralization of power and during election campaign, the BJP leaders, particularly Narendra Modi, focused on the need for giving rights to forest dwelling communities.

2014 ELECTION MANIFESTO OF THE INC AND ADIVASI ISSUES

In its 2014 election manifesto the INC mentioned several legislations for the welfare of marginalized sections including Adivasis and it promised that it would do more in its next tenure. It pledged to enact a central legislation on the SCs and STs sub-plans so that the development of SCs and STs can be accelerated to

---

[3] The PESA was passed by the Parliament in 1996. Many grassroots organizations played a crucial role in the mobilization for PESA. Bharat Jan Andolan led by Dr Brahm Dev Sharma was one such organization. This law is crucial for the rights of Adivasis in fifth schedule areas because it gives them right over natural resources near their villages and makes a provision for consultation with Gram Sabha (village assembly) before land acquisition or mining it these areas. To understand the various aspect of PESA and struggle for its enactment and implementation, see (Bijoy, 2012; Choubey, 2014b; 2016; Government of India, 1996; 2006; Sharma, 1998; 2005; 2010) Many scholars including Nandini Sundar has argued that the PESA is not making any provision for the rights of non-ST minority groups in the villages of fifth schedule areas. Also, giving STs right to live their life according to their own customs could give legitimacy to those customs which are against individual rights and autonomy (Sundar). It is also true that the implementation process of PESA has been less than satisfactory. In many fifth schedule areas, however, Adivasis (STs) have used the provisions of this law to assert their rights (Choubey; 2014b; 2015b; 2015c, 2016; Sundar, 2009).

[4] The FRA gives forest dwelling communities individual forest rights (IFR) and CFR to STs and other traditional forest dwelling communities (OTFDs), who are living in or dependent on forest land and its resources. The OTFD category was created by this law which is applicable on those communities who are not part of the category of STs, but they are dependent on forest land and its resources. IFR is related to giving the ownership rights over forest land and CFR gives them rights to use and protect forest land and its resources. The IFRs are related to giving property rights on the forest land used by these communities. The law was enacted as a result of a systematic grassroots mobilization by many tribal organizations but it was not implemented properly in most of the places, particularly the CFRs have been denied to forest dwelling communities. And larger proportion of OTFDs have not been able to get either IFRs or CFRs. To understand the enactment of the FRA, its various provisions and the experience of implementation, see (Choubey, 2013a; 2013b; 2014a; 2014b; 2015a; 2016; 2017; Government of India, 2007; 2010; 2019).

become at par with other communities (Indian National Congress, 2014, p. 21–22).

Congress also promised many measures for the better opportunities for Adivasi students, researchers and other youths of different marginalized sections. It took the pledge to establish one Navodaya Vidyalaya type of school in each and every block of the country to provide high standard school for the marginalized sections of the society. It announced to give Rajiv Gandhi research fellowship for all enrolled SC and ST students and establish a new scholarships to study in foreign universities for 1000 students annually. It also promised to give ₹10,000 to every unemployed SC or ST graduate or post graduate for skill development course (Indian National Congress, 2014, p. 21–22).

Congress also made clear its intention to initiate and accelerate development activities and more opportunities for STs and stringent implementation of PESA, 1996 and the FRA, 2006. Apart from these measures, it promised to give all kind help to small and medium scale enterprises of SC and ST and support them through easy access to credit and other measures to establish and develop their own business (Indian National Congress, 2014, p. 21–22). It also underlined that it would work to create a national consensus on affirmative action for SCs and STs in the private sector. It promised to identify different communities within SCs, STs and OBCs who could not get the benefit of affirmative programmes, including reservation and give them special attention (Indian National Congress, 2014, p. 21–22).

Though the manifesto of INC promised many things to STs, however, it could be easily underlined that most of the promises were not more than lip service. For example, it promised to make consensus regarding the affirmative action for SCs and STs in private sector. It made the same promise in its 2009 election manifesto, but UPA government did not make any serious attempt to do this in its ten years long tenure (2004–2014) (see Indian National Congress, 2009). Similarly, it never tried to overcome the many crucial limitations of the PESA and the FRA.

2014 ELECTION MANIFESTO OF THE CPI-M AND ADIVASI ISSUES

In its 2014 manifesto, the CPI-M also promised many measures for the betterment of the life of Adivasis. It emphatically asserted that all vacancies of ST-reserved posts in all government services would be fulfilled within a legally mandated time framework and there would be reservation in the private sector too.

It promised many crucial things for the protection and restoration of Adivasis land rights, which were alienated from them. In the context of FRA 2006, it asserted that it would nullify the unjust cut-off year provision for other traditional forest dwellers (OTFDs) through an amendment and ensure the proper implementation of each and every provision of the FRA.[5] In the context of PESA, it showed and intention to implement it outside the boundary of Schedule V areas and promised to include all areas of tribal concentration in the purview of this law. Interestingly it also emphasized the need to make and implement similar protective provisions for the tribal urban areas (Communist Party of India-Marxist, 2014).

It gave assurance to setting up a national commission for determination the minimum support price for minor forest produce and undertaking procurement of minor forest produce with adequate financial provisions. It also promised to ensure recognition, protection and development of tribal languages and scripts. Tribal languages such as Bhili and Gondi, etc. to be included in the eighth schedule of the constitution; the concerned state governments

---

[5] According to existing provisions of the FRA, the cut of date for OTFDs is three generations and 75 years before 13 December 2005, the date when the Forest Rights Bill was first introduced in the Parliament (Choubey, 2015a).

must recognize the language of Adivasis as the state's official language (Communist Party of India-Marxist, 2014).

The manifesto of CPI-M also focused on some other crucial issues related to the life of Adivasis. The Adivasis who migrate from one state to another state face many problem regarding their inclusion in the STs list. The CPI-M supported the automatic inclusion of migrated STs from one state to another state in the declared domicile list of the state government. It promised to ensure basic amenities like drinking water, health centre, schools and so on, for all tribal communities (Communist Party of India-Marxist, 2014).

Though CPI-M's election manifesto included many progressive measures, it did not work systematically for many of these issues earlier. The issue of reservation for STs and other marginalized sections were not raised systematically and seriously by the CPI-M during their outside support to the UPA-I and an opposition party after 2009 Lok Sabha elections. Similarly, the party had done nothing to implement PESA in non-scheduled areas district.

Certain points, however, are clear from the study of the manifestos of 2014 of these three national parties: first, in comparison to the INC and CPI-M, the BJP gave less space to the tribal issues; second, one can find that there was a commitment for giving more rights to the tribal communities in the form decentralization or Panchayati Raj; third, INC and the CPI-M explicitly mentioned some progressive laws for Adivasis. However, the BJP leaders also claimed that they would work for the better implementation of these laws for Adivasis (particularly PESA and FRA). What is crucial is that none of these parties seems to be concerned about the clear contest between the prevailing development model and rights of Adivasis.

II

2019 GENERAL ELECTION AND ADIVASI ISSUES IN ELECTION MANIFESTOS

In 2019, the BJP was the incumbent party and its manifesto, it tried to present itself as the true saviour of Adivasis, not only from the Maoist violence, but also from all kind of socio-economic problems. The Congress specifically focused on different measures for the progress of the Adivasi communities. Similarly, the CPI-M also presented a vast set of future planning in its manifesto.

2019 ELECTION MANIFESTO OF THE BJP AND ADIVASI ISSUES

The BJP projected the control of Maoists as one of its most important successes and underlined that it is committed to eliminate left-wing extremism in the next five years. It also argued along the line of its achievement in relation to ensuring the development of economic and social infrastructure such as roads, mobile towers, schools and medical facilities in the tribal areas affected by left-wing extremism, and it promised to continue to make efforts in this direction (Bharatiya Janata Party, 2019, p. 12).

Though the BJP did not mentioned the laws like PESA and FRA specifically in its manifesto, but it pledged to work for gram swaraj and visualized Mahatma Gandhi's vision of gram swaraj to ensure everyone's equitable access to resources (Bharatiya Janata Party, 2019, p. 16).[6]

Under the sub-heading forest and environment of its manifesto, the BJP claimed that it

---

[6] In this connection, the BJP promised to ensure a *pucca* house to every family who are living in a *kuchha* house by 2022; ensure piped water connection to every household by 2024; every gram panchayat will be connected through a high speed optical fibre network by 2022; connect centres of education, healthcare centres, and

ensured the effectiveness in issuing forest and environmental clearances for eligible projects due to which the forest cover was increased by around 9000 Sq. Kms. The BJP manifesto also claimed that the Narendra Modi government continuously protected and promoted the interest of forest dwellers particularly the tribal communities and endeavoured to provide basic amenities, such as roads, telephone connectivity and cooking gas connection, in addition to houses and toilets, at the doorstep of people living in remotest forest areas. It promised to work continuously in this direction (Bharatiya Janata Party, 2019, p. 26).

The BJP manifesto was, however, silent on the issue of the proper implementation of the FRA. Many grassroots organizations and activists criticized the government's proposal to amend Indian Forest Act of 1927, which could create a negative impact on the rights of forest dwelling communities. It was also emphasised by many commentators that issuing forest and environmental clearances and increasing forest cover were two inherently contradictory things.

2019 Election Manifesto of the INC and Adivasi Issues

In 2019 election manifesto, the INC clarified its stand on many contentious and important issues related to Adivasis and promised to ensure their rights on the basis of laws passed by the Parliament. In the context of North-Eastern states, it acknowledged the importance of autonomous district councils within these states and promised to enhance financial assistance to these councils (Indian National Congress, 2019, p. 42).

In the case of Maoists problem in Adivasi area of central India, the INC (like BJP) underlined its clear intention to 'fight (their)

violent activities'. However, unlike BJP, it asserted that it would address developmental challenges in the areas concerned and enlist the support of the people and win over the Maoist cadres (Indian National Congress, 2019, p. 27). The INC also pledged to ensure that the authority of the Gram Sabha would be respected and laws like PESA and FRA would be implemented in letter and spirit (Indian National Congress, 2019, p. 35).

The INC promised to set up an equal opportunities commission, which would recommend affirmative action strategies and policies to achieve equality—and equity—in education, employment and in economic opportunities. It also promised to restore the original purpose and intent of the 200-point roster system and implement it by considering the institution as a single unit. It also claimed that it would fill all backlog vacancies reserved for SCs, STs and OBCs in government, semi-government and central public sector organizations within 12 months and to amend the constitution to provide reservation in promotion for these categories (Indian National Congress, 2019, p. 40). It also resolved to pass a law in relation to extending reservation in private higher education institutions for SCs, STs and OBCs.

The INC also mentioned about land distribution to SCs and STs and insisted that it would acquire and distribute lands to SCs and STs. It promised to ensure the availability of basic amenities like water, sanitation, electricity and internal roads in every SC and ST village or habitation. It also underlined that it would work with state governments to review the curriculum of schools and include texts on the history and culture of SCs and STs and the contributions made by leaders belonging to these marginalized communities (Indian National Congress, 2019, p. 41).

---

markets with hinterlands to promote rural growth. (BJP, 2019, p. 16). The BJP also promised many programmes for the welfare of peasants, and Adivasis can also be included in the category of peasants (Ibid, pp. 13–14).

The INC not only promised to implement FRA properly, but it also aimed to ensure the time bound review of all rejected cases of individual forest rights (IFR) and community forest rights (CFR) under FRA, and dispose all such matters within six months. It took pledge to establish a national commission for non-timber forest produce and offer minimum support prices for such produce to improve the livelihood and income of Adivasis. It also asserted that it would pass a law to bring transparency in budget allocations to SCs and STs under the special component plan for SCs and tribal sub-plan for STs and to prohibit diversion of such funds (Indian National Congress, 2019, p. 41).

Undoubtedly, the Congress manifesto comprehensively covered the crucial issues related to Adivasis. It could be argued, however, that many aspects of the Congress manifesto were nothing but rhetoric. Many promises are repetition of 2014 manifesto and INC never tried seriously to work on these issues when it was leading UPA government for 2004–2014.

2019 Election Manifesto of CPI-M and Adivasi Issues

The CPI-M had also made some very crucial promises to the Adivasis. Followings are the main points of its promises: filling all vacancies for ST reserved posts in all government services within a legally mandated time framework; protecting land rights of Adivasis and restoring land illegally alienated from them; withdrawal of amendments to Land Acquisition, Rehabilitation and Resettlement Act, 2013, which in the name of ease of business removes all right of consent of Adivasi communities for land acquisition; withdrawal of national forest policy which advocates privatization of forests and replacement with an appropriate policy protecting tribal rights; implementing the FRA in full; amending the Act to include OTFDs with 1980 as the cut-off year; no eviction of Adivasis from their

habitat, etc. (Communist Party of India-Marxist, 2019, pp. 25–26).

Apart from these crucial promises, the CPI-M also pledged to removal all amendments and government circulars which dilute the role of gram sabhas and it promised to protect the rights under PESA and fifth schedule. One important aspect of CPI-M's manifesto was its promise to protect and encourage tribal languages like Bhili Gondi and Kokborok. Indeed it promised to include them in the eighth schedule of the constitution and making these languages official language in their respective states (Communist Party of India-Marxist, 2019, p. 25–26).

The CPI-M also promised automatic inclusion of Adivasis in the declared domicile list of the state governments with their ST identity and rights irrespective of their migration from one state to another. It pledged to increase the scholarships for Adivasi students. It declared that it would distribute five acres of arable land for cultivation to landless family from SC and ST communities; and enact a central legislation to provide reservations in the private sector for SCs and STs. It also promised for the enactment of a central legislation for the better implementation of Tribal Sub-Plan at centre and state level and Scheduled Castes and Scheduled Tribes (Prevention of Atrocities) Act, 1989 (Communist Party of India-Marxist, 2019, p. 25).

If we compare and contrast the space and importance of Adivasi issues in the above mentioned manifestos of these three national parties, it can be easily concluded that the BJP had given less space and importance to different dimensions of Adivasi issues. Though the INC and the CPI-M discussed various Adivasi issues comprehensively, their stand on many issues could be termed as rhetoric, as they never tried to implement these things in those states where they had their governments. However, it cannot be denied that if we study the promises for Adivasis, the manifesto of the CPI-M was far better than the BJP and the INC.

III

COMMON AGENDA AND COMMON PRACTICES: CONTINUED NEGLECT OF FUNDAMENTAL QUESTIONS

The previous two sections of the chapter presented the promises of three main national parties regarding the Adivasi issues. From the above description, it is clear that there were several repetitions and rhetoric in the manifestos of these parties. This section analyses a detailed analysis of various tendencies emerged from the manifestos of all three selected national parties.

First, largely there has been a consensus among different parties about crucial measures related to tribal areas. So, one can find that all three parties have been expressing their support for proper implementation of PESA (in fifth schedule areas) and FRA (in the whole country). Though the BJP did not mention them in its manifesto of 2014 and 2019, but it did promise to create a situation of gram swaraj. As the chief minister of Gujarat, Narendra Modi tried to project himself as a leader who was serious about giving rights to forest dwelling communities (Choubey, 2015, pp. 250–251). It is also true, however, that in post-2014 years, the Modi government did not take any concrete step to ensure the proper implementation of the PESA and FRA. But in election rallies in the tribal areas, the BJP leaders, including prime minister, have been continuously expressing their full commitment for security of Adivasis concerning *jal, jangal and zameen* (water, forest and land).[7] It is worth noting that he Akhil Bhartiya Vanvasi Kalyan Ashram, the tribal wing of Rashtriya Swayamsewak Sangh prepared a comprehensive report on the status of tribal communities and demanded proper implementation of the PESA and FRA, (Akhil Bhartiya Vanvasi

Kalyan Ashram, 2015), but Modi government did not give importance to these demands. Indeed, the Modi government ensured the enactment of Compensatory Afforestation Fund Act, 2016 which undermines the role of Gram Sabha and gives lots of power to bureaucracy (Agarwal, 2018). There was a proposal to amend the Indian Forest Act, 1927 and most of the amendments were detrimental to the rights of forest dwelling communities given by the FRA (Pandey, 2018). The Modi government, however, did not go ahead with these amendments due to compulsions of electoral politics.

Similarly, the Modi government did not try to ensure the better implementation of the PESA. The INC and CPI-M, on the other hand, not only promised the implementation of the PESA and FRA, but also accepted the need to amend or extend these laws. Particularly, the CPI-M focussed on the extension of PESA in urban areas and amendment the FRA to bring a drastic change in the cut-off date for the OTFDs. However, one can find that the implementation process of these laws is not satisfactory in the states ruled by these parties. So, the implementation of the FRA in INC ruled states (Andhra Pradesh till 2014, Rajasthan till 2014, etc.) was less than satisfactory, and particularly the CFR were not granted, and even in the case of private forest rights, many claims were rejected. In BJP ruled states, the STs and OTFDs faced the same problem and in CPI-M ruled West Bengal (till 2011), the implementation of the FRA was less than satisfactory (Choubey, 2015a). This is the case with PESA too, which has not been implemented properly in any state, whether it was ruled by the Congress or the BJP, the CPI-M is not an influential force in any state with fifth scheduled areas). The Congress prepared a proposal to amend the PESA and make it more effective in the last year of UPA-II but it

---

[7] For example, Jharkhand Assembly election of 2019 Narendra Modi promised Adivasi voters that BJP is committed to protect their '*Jal, Jangal and Zameen*' (water, forest and land) (*The Economic Times,* 2019).

could not introduce that Bill in the Parliament (Choubey, 2015b, 2015c). The Narendra Modi led government did nothing to ensure the better implementation of the law.

Second, 'development' has been a crucial issue of contention in tribal areas. Though political parties have been talking about total opposition of any kind of forced displacement, one can easily find various examples of forced displacement for 'development' project in most of the tribal dominated areas, ruled by different political parties. The basic problem is that most political parties have faith on a specific conception of 'development', which is based on the extraction of natural resources by the corporate capital and establishment of big industries. When constitutional provisions or the laws like PESA and FRA became an obstacle to this conception of development, most governments (both central and states) violated them indiscriminately and at least two principal parties (the BJP and the INC) have consensus on the issue of economic policies and development model based on the extraction of natural resources and giving corporate sector primary role in this. And experiences clearly show that constitutional provisions of tribal rights have been clearly violated by the governments led by both these parties (Choubey, 2015a, pp. 248–314). Though CPI-M (and Communist Party of India i.e. CPI) is not unequivocal supporter of this stand and on many occasions, they led struggle for the rights of Adivasis, but the experiences of the previous West Bengal government have also showed that a Left government can also be very repressive for the sake of industrial development (Roy, 2018).

Third, both the BJP and the INC have emphasised on the need to control Maoist movement. Indeed, one can find that there was a cooperation between the leaders of the BJP and the Congress regarding Salwa Judum in the South Bastar region of the Chhattisgarh. The Congress leader Mahendra Karma played pivotal role in the beginning of this violent movement and the BJP's Chhattisgarh state government provided him all kind of support. The Salwa Judum campaign violated most of the constitutional rights of the Adivasis and laws like PESA and FRA in this region. Indeed the whole episode of Salwa Judum underlined that there has been a clear contradiction between implementation of laws related to tribal rights and support for the anti-Maoist movement, and both the Congress and the BJP were unsuccessful in creating a balance between the two (Choubey, 2018). Most of the non-violent movements questioning this conception of development have also been termed as 'anti-national' or the threat to the 'national security'.[8] The CPI-M has not mentioned this issue clearly, but obviously the party has always taken a stand against the violent activities of the Maoists. However, in its 2014 manifesto, it promised to make an attempt to free innocent Adivasi people, who were put in jail on the basis of false allegations (Communist Party of India-Marxist, 2014).

Fourth, one can also find that there has been a consensus among all political parties in providing 'state help' to Adivasi people. The Congress and the CPI-M clearly mentioned about their proposed policies and programmes for Adivasi youths, and the BJP presented it in the framework of larger programmes mentioned for the all sections of population. However, in practice, there is no concrete progress in the life of tribal communities in many parts of the country. They are facing severe challenges from corporate houses, who want to exploit natural resources and there are ample examples that almost all state governments have been taking sides of corporate houses rather than Adivasi people.

---

[8] For example, between July 2017 to July 2018 the Raghubar Das led BJP government of Jharkhand imposed sedition cases against 10,000 tribal people for supporting Pathalgadi movement, which was largely related to the demand of the implementation of constitutional provisions related to tribal areas (Sharma, 2019).

Fifth, it could be argued that there are many promises in the manifestos of these national parties, which are nothing but rhetoric. For example, the INC manifestos of 2014 and 2019 mentioned that it would work for creating a consensus for the reservation in private sector for STs (and also for SCs and OBCs). The CPI-M also mentioned the similar points in its manifesto. However, both the parties have not made any serious or systematic attempt to create a consensus on this issue. Similarly, the BJP mentioned a contradictory thing in its 2019 election manifesto. Abhay Xaxa rightly argued that even while there have been hundreds of Adivasi and forest dwellers agitating against forced eviction, displacement and forest and land alienation, in the name of development projects, the BJP manifesto, however, promises speedy environmental and forest clearances for projects as they have done in the past five years in government. They claim this has increased the forest cover by 9,000 Sq km. How can both be possible (Choudhury, 2019)? Similarly, the BJP, in its 2014 manifesto, had even promised an extensive educational network in tribal areas under the Vanbandhu scheme, but surprisingly this promise had disappeared from its 2019 manifesto. Any kind of transformative change in Adivasi communities can only happen when there is a special focus on public education systems in Adivasi areas. The NDA government had curtailed the budget of tribal sub-plan from ₹32,387 crore in 2014–2015 to ₹20,000 crore in 2015–2016. However, there was a slight increase to ₹24,005 crore in 2016–2017. Even though it increased to ₹31,920 crore in 2017–2018, what the NDA has done is added non-targeted (generic/administrative) expenditure (such as grants towards infrastructure maintenance, farm loan waivers, good governance fund, sports authority of India allocations, etc.) as TSP specifically to inflate figures (Choudhury, 2019).

It should also be noted that, it seems, at least in the general elections of 2014 and 2019, the election manifestos and their promises did not play the pivotal role in determining the results. In both the elections, the BJP won majority of seats reserved for STs. Of the 47 seats reserved for candidates from STs, in 2019 elections, BJP won 31 seats (65.95%), while the INC won only four seats. The remaining seats were won by independent leaders and regional parties such as Telangana Rashtra Samithi, Yuvajana Sramika Rythu Congress Party, Jharkhand Mukti Morcha (JMM), Nationalist Congress Party, Shiv Sena, Naga Peoples Front, Biju Janata Dal, National Peoples Party, and Mizo National Front. In the 2014 elections, BJP had won 27 (57.44) of the 47 seats, while Congress had won five of them (Aggarwal, 2019).

The results of 2014 and 2019 elections in ST constituencies underline that in existing political spectrum the Adivasis also chose to vote according to the prevailing electoral environment, which worked on the basis of the idea of a strong leader (i.e. Narendra Modi) and strong sentiment of nationalism (particularly in 2019 general elections).[9] In state legislative assembly elections, however, the Adivasis voted on the basis of their day to day concerns and the issues related to their livelihood and ownership over resources. The assembly election of Jharkhand (2019) could be mentioned as one such instance where the issues related to Adivasis livelihood got centre stage during campaign.[10]

---

[9] It has been accepted by most of the prominent analysts that the Narendra Modi factor made huge impact on the results of 2019 Lok Sabha election (Chatterjee, 2019; Palshikar, Kuamar & Shastri, 2019; Singh & Venkatesth, 2019).

[10] In Jharkhand election, held in December 2019, JMM-Congress-RJD alliance primarily focused on local issues and the expressed their commitment to ensure the constitutional rights of the Adivasis and the implementation of various laws, including PESA and FRA. The BJP, however, tried to raise national issues like Citizenship

IV

CONCLUSION

After a critical evaluation of the election manifestos of three national parties, it could be argued that the manifesto of CPI-M is far better than other two parties, because it comprehensively covers the issues of rights over natural resources, and also clearly articulates issues of land rights. But then we should remember that the party is not the main political force in most tribal areas. The CPI-M is followed by the manifesto of the Congress for raising issues of forest rights and powers of Gram Sabha. I would say the BJP's manifesto is the most problematic for statements such as the one related to speedy clearances of the proposal of the diversion of forest land for non-forest use, which would directly affect tribals. Further, most of the commitments towards Adivasis which the BJP promised in 2014 have disappeared in their 2019 document. The INC promised many things but it did not show seriousness about the implementation of most of its crucial promises during UPA-I or UPA-II rule.

Obviously, there is a clear distinction between the manifesto promises of the political parties and their actual behaviour. Adivasis can at least expect that parties should promise to follow constitutional provisions and procedure established by law before expropriating their resources for the 'national' development. The dual behaviour of parliamentary parties, particularly the Congress and the BJP has given strength to the Maoist's criticisms against parliamentary democracy. However, it is obvious that rejection of democratic procedures is not a viable or acceptable option.

Many theorists have underlined the limitations of procedural representative democracy, where people got very limited opportunities to question parties and their leaders about the promises in the elections. It has been argued by the supporters of participatory and deliberative democracy that there should be more participation of citizen in the decision-making processes.[11] In this context making citizens aware about the agenda of different political parties and creating opportunities to question ruling party about its election manifesto would be crucial aspect to make Indian democracy more vibrant. In this context it is imperative to formulate certain structural mechanisms so that citizen could get opportunity to question their representative in the mid-term (or every year). Indeed, Indian electoral experiences, particularly the experiences of Adivasi areas, show that most of the time parties do not bother to fulfil their promises and raise some emotive issues during elections. So, it is necessary to give common masses more knowledge about their rights. When it comes to promises made to Adivasis, unfortunately, there is very little awareness created by candidates or political

---

Amendment Act, Ram mandir and so on. However, its leaders also claimed at various political rallies that they would protect the Adivasis rights on *jal jangal and zameen* (water, forest and land) (Priyam, 2019).

[11] For example C. M. Macpherson, a prominent participatory democracy theorist, has argued that representative governments of western societies are not giving actual participation of citizens. He accepts that existence of diverse interests is inevitable and it gives rise to political parties. The competition between parties will ensure that government remains responsive to people. It is necessary, Macpherson emphasises, to reorganize parties on non-hierarchical principles and political administrators and managers should be more accountable to the persons within organizations they represent. These genuinely participatory parties can function within a parliamentary system complemented and checked by fully self-managed organizations in the work place and local community (Macpherson, 1965; 1973). The idea of deliberative democracy emphasises that there should be full deliberation with a specified target of consensus and the essential conditions for deliberation is freedom and equality of citizens and the deliberation must include cultural plurality and social complexities of modern mass democracy. Obviously, it argues that representative democracy is not sufficient and deliberation among citizens on different issues related to their life is necessary to create a vibrant democracy. Many thinkers presented their ideas about this kind of democracy (Bohman & Rehg, 1997).

parties among Adivasi voters. Therefore, there remains a huge gap between what Adivasis need and aspire for, what is promised to them, and what actually gets delivered.

REFERENCES

Agarwal, S. (2018). *Green fund rules notified: some hits, major mises*. Retrieved from https://www.down-toearth.org.in/news/forests/green-fund-rules-noti-fied-some-hits-major-misses-61381

Aggarwal, M. (2019). Despite controversies on tribal issues, BJP wins in tribal constituencies. Retrieved from https://india.mongabay.com/2019/05/despite-con-troversies-on-tribal-issues-bjp-wins-in-tribal-constit-uencies/

Akhil Bhartiya Vanvasi Kalyan Ashram (ABVKA). (2015). *Bharat ki janjatiyon hetu ek drishtipatra*. Mumbari: Akhil Bhartiya Vanvasi Kalyan Ashram and Ramabhau Malgi Prabodhini.

Bhartiya Jantaa Party. (2014). *Ek Bharat shrestha Bharat, sabka saath sabka vikas: Election Manifesto 2014*. New Delhi: Bharatiya Janata Party.

Bhartiya Janata Party. (2019). *Sanklpit Bharat, sashakt Bharat: Bhartiya Janata Party sankalp satra Lok Sabha 2019*. New Delhi: Bhartiya Janata Party.

Bijoy, C. R. (2012). *Policy brief on panchayat raj (exten-sion to scheduled areas) act of 1996*. Delhi: UNDP.

Bohman, J., & Rehg, W. (1987). *Deliberative democ-racy: Essays on reason and politics*. Massachusetts, London: The MIT Press.

Chatterjee, P. (2019). Populism plus. *The India Forum: A Journal-Magazine on Contemporary issues*, June 3. Retrieved From https://www.theindiaforum.in/article/populism-plus.

Constitution of India. (2008). Fourth edition. Allahabad: Central Law Publications.

Choubey, K. N. (2013b). *Jangal ka sangharsh, 'pragtish-eel' kanoon aur rajya, samyik prakashan*, Samaj aur Itihas, Naveen Shrinkhla 3. Delhi: Nehru Samarak Sanghralya aiyam Pustakalya.

Choubey, K. N. (2014a). *The forest rights act and the politics of marginal society*. NMML Occasional Paper: Perspectives in Indian Development, New Series 31, Nehru Memorial Museum and Library.

Choubey, K. N. (2014b). *Law as site of contestation between state and the margin: A comparative study of the experiences of two progressive laws (PESA and FRA)* (Unpublished Final Report of the Post-Doctoral

Project Submitted to Nehru Memorial Museum And Library). New Delhi: Teen Murti House.

Choubey, K. N. (2015a). *Jungal ki haqdari: Rajneeti aur sangharsh*. Delhi: CSDS-Vani Prakashan.

Choubey, K. N. (2015b). Enhancing PESA: The unfin-ished agenda. *Economic and Political Weekly*, *50*(8), 21–23.

Choubey, K. N. (2015c). The public life of a "progressive" law: PESA and gaon ganarajya (village republic). *Studies in Indian Politics*, *3*(2), 247–260.

Choubey, K. N. (2016). The state, tribals and law: The politics behind the enactment of PEA and FRA. *Social Change*, *46*(3), 355–370.

Choubey, K. N. (2017). Turning the tide in forest rights. *Economic and Political Weekly*, *52*(1), 21–23.

Choubey, K. N. (2018). Salwa judum: Rajya, Maowad aur Hinsha ki anthin dastan. *Pratiman: Samay Samaj Sankriti*, *6*(12), 188–208.

Choudhury, C. (2019). All political parties have treated adivasis as disposable people. Retrieved from https://www.indiaspend.com/all-political-parties-have-treat-ed-adivasis-as-disposable-people/)

Communist Party of Indian (Marxist). (2014). *Manifesto for the 16th lok sabha election 2014*. New Delhi: Communist Party of India (Marxist).

Communist Party of Indian (Marxist). (2019). *Manifesto for the 17th lok sabha election 2019*. New Delhi: Communist Party of India (Marxist).

Dandekar, A., & Choudhury C. (2010). *PESA, left-wing extremism and governance concerns and challenges in India's tribal districts*. Anand: Institute of Rural Management.

Government of India. (1996). *The provisions of panchayats (extension to the scheduled areas) act, 1996, No 40 of 1996*. New Delhi: Government of India.

Government of India. (2006). *Report of the sub-committee appointed by the ministry of panchayati raj to draft model guidelines to vest gram sabhas with powers as envisaged in PESA*. New Delhi: Ministry of Panchayati Raj.

Government of India. (2007). *Scheduled tribes and other traditional forest dwellers (recognition of forest rights) act 2006*. New Delhi: Ministry of Law and Justice.

Government of India. (2008). *Development challenges in extremist affected areas: Report of an expert group to planning commission*. New Delhi: Planning Commis-sion of India.

Government of India. (2009). *Third report of the stand-ing committee on inter-sectoral issues relating to tribal development on standards of administration and governance in scheduled areas (Chairman:*

Dr. Bhalchandra Mungerkar, Member, Planning Commission). New Delhi: Ministry of Tribal Affairs.

Government of India. (2010). *Manthan: Report of national committee on forest rights act, December 2010*. A Joint Committee of Ministry of Environment and Forest and Ministry of Tribal Affairs, New Delhi.

Government of India. (2013). *Statistical Profile of Scheduled Tribes of India 2031*. New Delhi: Ministry of Tribal Affiars, Statistics Divison.

Government of India. (2019). *Status report on implementation of scheduled tribes and other tradition forest dwellers (recognition of forest rights act) 2006* [for the period ending at 31.10.2019 Ministry of Tribal Affairs. Retrieved from *https://tribal.nic.in/FRA/data/MPROct2017.pdf*

Indian National Congress. (2009). *Lok Sabha Election 2009: Manifesto of the Indian National Congress*. New Delhi: Indian National Congress.

Indian National Congress. (2014). *Your voice, our pledge: Lok sabha election 2014 manifesto, Indian National Congress*. New Delhi Indian National Congress.

Indian National Congress. (2019). *Congress will deliver: Manifesto to lok sabha election 2019*. New Delhi: Indian National Congress.

Machpherson, C. B. (1965). *The life and times of liberal democracy*. London: Oxford University Press.

Machpherson, C. B. (1973). *Democratic theory: Essays in retrieval*. Oxford: Clarendon Press.

Plashikar, S., Kumar S., & Shastri, S. (2019). Post-poll survey: Modi all the way in 2019. Retrieved from https://www.thehindu.com/elections/lok-sabha-2019/modi-all-the-way/article27297266.ece.

Pandey, S. (2018). The amendment to the Indian forest act 1927 will create new markets and jobs for poor communities. Retrieved from https://www.downtoearth.org.in/news/forests/the-indian-forest-act-1927-amendment-will-create-new-markets-generate-millions-of-jobs-for-poor-communities-59712

Priyam, M. (2019). Jharakhand is a mandate of the poor, for their rights. Retrieved from https://www.hindustantimes.com/analysis/jharkhand-is-a-mandate-of-the-poor-for-their-rights/story-Wun2wiOSP-6wE8BYim8twcL.html.

Roy, D. (2018). Politics at the margin: A tale of two villages. In S. S. Jodhka (Ed.), *A Handbook of Rural India* (pp. 424–436). Delhi: Orient Blackswan.

Savyasaachi. (1998). *Tribal forest-dwellers and self-rule: The constituent assembly debates on the fifth and sixth schedules*. New Delhi: Indian Social Institute.

Sharma, B. D. (1998). *The little lights in tiny mud-pots defy 50 years of anti-'panchayat' raj*. New Delhi: ShayogPustakKutir.

Sharma, B. D. (2010). *Unbroken history of broken promises: Indian state and the tribal people*. New Delhi: Freedom Press and SahyogPustakKuteer.

Sharma, B. D. (2005). *Adivasi khetra kis or? Savinthanik sansodhan bhuria samiti report aur uske aage*. New Delhi: Sahyou Pustak Kuteer.

Sharma, S. (2019). 10,000 people charged with sedition in one Jharkhand district. What does democracy mean here? Retrieved from https://scroll.in/article/944116/10000-people-charged-with-sedition-in-one-jharkhand-district-what-does-democracy-mean-here

Singh, A., & Venkatesh, M. (2019). Pratap Bhanu Mehta says this election results boils down to two words 'Narendra Modi'. Retrieved from https://theprint.in/thought-shot/pratap-bhanu-mehta-says-this-election-result-boils-down-to-two-words-narendra-modi/240500/.

Sundar, N. (2009). Framing the political imagination: Custom, democracy and citizenship. In N. Sundar (Ed.), *Legal grounds: Natural resources, identity, and the law in Jharkhand* (pp. 188–215). New Delhi: Oxford University Press.

Sundar, N. (2016). *The burning forest: India's war in Bastar*. New Delhi: Juggernaut Book.

The Economic Times. (2019). Congress, allies driven by lust of power: PM Modi tells Jharkhand poll rally. Retrieved from https://economictimes.indiatimes.com/news/politics-and-nation/bjp-govt-to-protect-jharkhands-jal-jungle-jameen-pm-modi/articleshow/72220701.cms?from=mdr.

Tiwari, A. K. (2018). *Political parties, party manifestos and elections in India, 1909–2004*. Routledge: New York.

Political Representation and Policymaking: Role of Tribal MPs in Indian Parliament

Rupak Kumar

INTRODUCTION

The question of effectiveness of represent-atives in a political system is central to the parliamentary democracy. The building block or the basic unit of representative democracy that India envisioned and continue to embark upon is the acceptance of a system in which people vote in a free and fair electoral process to elect representatives who would eventually, not only speak but would assert the needs, demands and public causes of their respective electorates in the Parliament. Any society is replete with various forms of oppression and exploitation. The maladies against specific caste categories or ethnic communities prev-alent in the social fabric of India threaten the very existence of a democratic system. Similarly, the tribal communities of India are left neglected and treated as pariah since ages. Where there is a rampant inequality, not only in economic arena but also in social status and indignity practiced against fellow beings, substantive democracy could never be rooted

deeply. The deeply rooted maladies would hinder the flourishing of any impartial insti-tutions through which the defining features of a democracy, that is, justice, equality, free-dom, rights, and so on, are ensured to each and every fellow human. Democratic institutions constitute together various virtues which lead to the emergence of a vibrant and substantive democracy. Keeping in view, not only the question of representation becomes important but the issue of representativeness occupies a pivotal place as well. It becomes imperative to study what role these representatives play and how effectively they represent the voices and concern of their electorates in making laws, formulating policies and legislating on the issues which make their lives good.

The Constituent Assembly of India, while writing the constitution, faced a para-dox. Arguably it was about how to reconcile the proposed political equality with that of social inequality. Certainly, the attempt was to annihilate the rampant graded inequality and at the same time to compensate for the historical wrongdoings. One of the measures they devised was to introduce a system of reservation of seats for the scheduled castes and scheduled tribes (STs) in Lok Sabha (Article 330).[1] The idea behind was to ensure at least a minimum number of representatives from SCs and STs separately in the legislative body. The rationale behind ensuring a minimum number of representatives had to address the issues and demands of that particular community as both the communities remained historically marginalized and socially excluded. Jaipal Singh Munda, a tribal representative in the Constituent Assembly argued that

> It is for the majority community to atone for their sins of the last six thousand odd years. It is for them to see whether the original inhabitants of this country have been given a fair deal by the late rulers...[] What has happened in the past, let it be a matter of the past. Let us look forward to a glorious future, to a future where there shall be justice and equality of opportunity. (Government of India, 1949, p. 650)

Munda spoke for the reservation of seats because 'the fact is that any section of our society that is economically and politically backward must have safeguards and provisions which will enable it to come up to the general level' (Government of India, 1949, p. 653). For Munda, 'Reservation is very necessary for the backward people whether they are Adivasis or whether they are Scheduled Castes, or Jains or Muslims'(Government of India, 1949, p. 654). Most importantly, Jaipal

Munda believed that reservation of seats to the SCs and STs would compel them 'to come into the inner circle and do their best and contribute their share for the betterment of this country' (Government of India, 1949, p. 655). Thus, he supported the motion moved by none other than Dr B.R. Ambedkar.

The chapter explores the role of tribal MPs in the policymaking for the advancement of STs in India. What role do these MPs play in the formulation and legislation of such policy[2] in the Parliament? What role do they play during parliamentary debates on such policy, at committee deliberations and policy enactment? Do they play an instrumental role in bringing, enacting and legislating such policymaking for the tribal communities? These are some of the questions that the chapter answers while exploring substantive representation of tribal MPs in policymaking for tribal communities.

The warning at the beginning is that it is not an attempt to essentialize the role of tribal MPs as only meant to raise community specific issues and questions. The underlying assumption is, of course, that legislature as a whole makes policy. The aim is to understand the role of a particular group of MPs because as per institutional arrangements, they happen to represent those communities who have been subject to historical injustices and marginalization, namely, the tribal communities. The interventions of tribal MPs can be discussed in the form of participation in

---

[1] Article 330—Reservation of seats for Scheduled Castes and Scheduled Tribes in the House of the People (1) Seats shall be reserved in the House of the People for (a) the Scheduled Castes; (b) the Scheduled Tribes except the Scheduled Tribes in the autonomous districts of Assam; and (c) the Scheduled Tribes in the autonomous districts of Assam.

[2] A policy outlines the goals and principles of any government it hopes to achieve for the good of the people, for some specific groups or even for the betterment of economic scenario of a country. It states the goals such as industrial policy, economic policy, agriculture policy, education policy that a government aspires to achieve over the time. A policy document is not necessarily an Act of the Parliament but in order to achieve the goals of a policy, it needs certain rules, regulations, procedures, and monetary resources enacted by the Parliament to give it a legal sanction. An Act is a Bill that has been approved by both the Houses, that is, Lok Sabha and Rajya Sabha and been given assent by the President. Some of the Acts can be substantive in nature such as MGNREGA, FRA which are meant to fulfill the policy aims of a government at the socioeconomic level. In this chapter, the Forest Rights Act 2006 was also referred as 'policy', sometimes interchangeably as this particular Act aimed to address the redistribution of resources.

parliamentary debates, in standing committees, their involvement in asking questions in
the Parliament, or demanding accountability
from the executive. The MPs also play critical role outside the Parliament. However, the
primary focus of this chapter is to understand
the 'inside' aspect of Parliament, especially in
the context of the STs and Other Traditional
Forest Dwellers (Recognition of Forest
Rights) Act, 2006, commonly known as the
Forest Rights Act (FRA), 2006. Currently
47 Lok Sabha constituencies are reserved for
STs. In 2019 Lok Sabha, there are 52 ST MPs,
out of which 5 have been elected from general
constituencies.

THE CONTEXT

The population of STs in India is 10.45 crore
as per 2011 census. It constitutes 8.6 per cent
of the total population. Even after seven decades of independence and self-government,
the socioeconomic situations of tribal communities remain dismal. Despite various
government policies, the concerns for their
upliftment are abysmally low. Even recent
standing committee report stated that

> The performance audit of Tribal Sub Plan (hence-
> forth TSP) by the CAG in 2015 found out that
> the funds allocated for Tribal Sub Plan[3] were
> mostly released at the end of the year and state
> government hardly release utilisation certificates
> for funds that have been utilised under TSP.
> (Government of India, 2018, p. 20)

The same audit report also highlighted the
fact that the TSP funds are being diverted

for minority institutions between 2010–2011
and 2013–2014 and these funds are spent
for ineligible states like Punjab and Haryana
(Government of India, 2018, p. 10). Even the
Ministry of Tribal Affairs was not involved in
the process of finalization of annual plan of
central ministries (Government of India, 2018,
p. 11). This is just one anecdote of a policy
which is considered to be overarchingly
applicable in all the wings of the government
meant for the welfare of the tribal communities. Besides, the role of forest department in
alienating the tribal is a perennial problem.
The everyday harassment faced by the tribal
people by the forest officials has created a
wall of separation between the government
and tribal communities. Hence, the policy
goal never reached the intended target group.
    The bulldozing of over bureaucratized
structures and functions of the policy and
planning involving tribes led to the failure
of the targeted achievements of policies. The
benefits hardly reached the targeted population, nor it led to the constructive engagement
of the tribal representatives as they continuously sidelined the voices from the grassroots.
The failure of various policies and plan lies
in the utter disregard to the primary voices of
the community. Such blatant application of
the state power without taking the lifeworld
of tribal communities into consideration made
them pariah in their own country in terms of
social, economic and educational developments. In this context, it becomes pivotal to
understand the representation of tribes by the
leaders of their own communities in order to
defend their demands and needs.

---

[3] The Tribal Sub-Plan (TSP) was introduced in the fifth five year plan (1974–1979), which is renamed as scheduled
tribes component in national democratic alliance (NDA) I government led by the Bharatiya Janata Party (BJP). It
is a strategy for the rapid socioeconomic development of tribal people. It is meant to bridge the gap between
the STs and the general population with respect to all socioeconomic development indicators in a time-bound
manner. It forms a part of annual plan of a state/union territory. The benefits given to the tribals and tribal areas
of a state or union territory from the TSP are in addition to what percolates from the overall plan of a state/union
territory. The funds provided under the TSP have to be at least in proportion to the ST population of each state/
union territory.

THE GENESIS

The success of decision-making in a parliamentary system has to do with the consideration and assumption that the collective decision-making and policy formulation lead to better success and implementation. Whenever the policymaking is amplified by the experiences and voices for which is it supposed to make, the voices of the representatives propel a policy which has the potential to bring some change in the lives of the people under consideration.

The approach of the government has been mainly to mainstream the tribal population. The plans and policies remained a subject of particular gaze even by the legislators. Any plan for tribal communities primarily focused on the 'twin objective of socio-economic development of STs and [the] protection of tribal[s] against exploitation' (Government of India, 2012, p. 1.4). Tribal were largely seen as intruders or encroachers of the land and forest and the state tried to mend its way against the existing practices of tribal communities such as shifting cultivation. For example, government adhered the tribal groups involved in the shifting cultivation should do away with it. In successive erstwhile existing five year plans, '6 lakh tribal families involved in shifting cultivation were provided with alternative source of livelihood to wean them away from practicing shifting cultivation' (Government of India, 2012, p. 2.6). The purpose behind formulating any policy is either to reduce poverty and unemployment, or to sustain growth and development, or is targeted to improve the human development by focusing on health and education or to strengthen the economic well-being of the citizens or to safeguard the people against oppression and exploitation.

The policy and plan should address the issues and concerns of affected groups for which it is made and these concerns have time and again been brought to the forefront in different government reports. One such report on the evaluation of the TSP clearly writes that

If the quality of lives of the marginalised Tribal have to improve and if they are to be brought above poverty line and if basic livelihood resources are to be provided to them, the schemes/programmes formulated should specifically attend to the felt needs of the Tribal...[] involvement of local people and elected representatives, local bodies, etc. (Government of India, 2012, p. 2.24)

The committee emphasized on the degree of serious involvement by the affected representatives as it observed that in contrary to the guidelines which clearly stipulates involvement of elected members such as MPs, MLAs, panchayat members and other prominent leaders in the districts in monitoring of [TSP], 'it has become routine affair for the government planners, administrators and political leaders ever since its inception, devoid of local people participation as well as elected representatives of the people' (Government of India, 2012, p. 2.24).

THE POLICY

One of the rights based policy for tribal communities that was formulated in the 21st century is the FRA, 2006, which ensures the land ownership in forest areas. In hindsight, looking at the processes of policy formulation and flourishing of plan since its inception, various MPs, specifically coming from the ST-reserved constituencies played an indispensable role, be it the writing of the Bill, in the Joint Committee, during the debate in the Parliament till it became a law and thereafter also, in raising and posing questions to the government in relation to its implementation. This policy is the 'outcome of a prolonged struggle and represents a milestone in Indian legislative history, with radical provisions for major reforms in tenure and forest governance' (Sarin, 2016, p. 402). Though the nodal agency for implementation of this Act is the Ministry of Tribal Affairs, the primary responsibility of implementation, however, vests with the state governments. The central government has to facilitate and monitor the execution of the Act. This policy was intended to fulfil the mandate of the directive principles as stated in articles 39(a), 39(b) and 46, so it deserves protection under the Ninth Schedule of the Indian constitution to prevent any sort of dilution.

There was a consensus in various parliamentary committees, as against the government's position, that there is a dire need to address the tribal issues with some seriousness going beyond piecemeal measures such as minuscule number of scholarships, fee relaxation, school uniforms, and so on. Scrutinizing various policies made for the welfare of STs and SCs between 1994 and 1999, 18th Report of committee on the welfare of SCs and STs (submitted in 2006) minced no word by expressing, 'government should take suitable steps...[] and Tribals should be conferred with the right of upkeeping and protecting the plantation so as to prevent future destruction' (Government of India, 2006b, p. 2.41). The committee desired that 'the States should educate the tribals, by organizing camps regarding the importance of regeneration and protection of forest for their own good' (Government of India, 2006b, p. 2.54). Another perturbing issues that the same committee noted, 'the land allotted to tribals was not suitable as it did not yield much and because of which the tribals prefer to go back to shifting cultivation' (Government of India, 2006b, p. 2.74).

The same committee underlined that it is

Pained to note that the National Policy on Resettlement and Rehabilitation of tribals was under consideration since 1987 but during the course of time a decision to prepare a comprehensive National Policy on the Resettlement and Rehabilitation of Projects Affected Persons/Families for large Projects-Displacing 1000 families or more, which includes the Resettlement and Rehabilitation of tribals also, has been taken.

The committee further stated that

The reason why the earlier policy which was specifically meant for resettlement and rehabilitation of tribals was not pursued, but made to fit in the larger canvas is definitely a ploy to delay justice to the affected tribal people. (Government of India, 2006b, p. 2.294)

Though the Scheduled Tribes (Recognition of Forest Rights) Bill, 2005 seems to have based on the issues and concerns of tribal communities raised in this report, but the demand has been galvanized by the civil society organizations and tribal leaders. The committee report reflects the reality of the policies made for tribal communities before this period.

THE PROCESS

The Scheduled Tribes and Other Traditional Forest Dwellers (Recognition of Forest Rights) Bill, 2005, which originally tabled in the Lok Sabha as the Scheduled Tribes (Recognition of Forest Rights) Bill, 2005, was examined, scrutinized and evaluated by a Joint Parliamentary Committee (JPC),[4] known as the Joint Committee on the Scheduled Tribes (Recognition of Forest Rights) Bill, 2005, commonly known as the JPC, consisting total of 30 MPs (20 from the Lok Sabha and 10 from the Rajya Sabha). The JPC was headed by a Lok Sabha MP, V. Kishore Chandra S. Deo, elected on a ST seat from Parvathipuram

---

[4] The JPC was constituted on 26 December 2005 with a purpose to carve out alternative spaces of direct participation by legislators of both the houses of the Indian Parliament to legislate on bills, demand for grants, to inquire, to investigate, to oversight issues involving irregularities, misconduct or violations of government bodies, offices or for that matter to make rules and regulations in bipartisan manner. The proceedings of JPC in India is not open for public or broadcasted unlike countries such as the UK and the United States. Hence, the JPC submits the final report. If there is any dissent by any member, it is published as a note at the end of the report. Hence, it seems to be extremely difficult to have a glimpse of the position taken by the members of the JPC on the bill during their meetings.

(ceased to exist after delimitation in 2008). Out of the total 20 Lok Sabha MPs, 10 were ST MPs. Besides, Babu Lal Marandi was also a member of the committee who was elected from an unreserved constituency of Kodarma, Jharkhand. In total, there were 11 ST MPs out of 20 Lok Sabha MPs in the JPC, who were representing the voices of the tribal communities in order to come up with robust legislation which would have made a lasting impression on millions of lives across India.

The STs MPs were Shingada Damodar Barku from Dahanu seat in Maharashtra, Mahaveer Bhagora from Salumbar in Rajasthan, Giridhar Gamang from Koraput in Odisha (Orissa), Dr P. P. Koya from Lakshadweep, Hemlala Murmu from Rajmahal in Jharkhand, Jual Oram from Sundargarh in Odisha, Baju Ban Riyan from Tripura East, Nand Kumar Sai from Surguja in Chhattisgarh, Dr Babu Rao Mediyam from Bhadrachalam (ceased to exist after delimitation in 2008) in Andhra Pradesh (became a member of the JPC from 21 February 2006), and Babu Lal Marandi from Kodarma in Jharkhand.

The JPC held 14 sittings before submitting its final report on 23 May 2006 to the Lok Sabha. On an average, 11 out of 20 Lok Sabha MPs attended the 14 sittings. Mr V. Kishore Chandra S. Deo as the chairman[5] of the JPC chaired all the 14 sittings. Baju Ban Riyan who represented Tripura East actively participated and deliberated in 13 sittings followed by Mahaveer Bhagora from Salumbar and P. P. Koya from Lakshdweep who attended 12 sittings in total. Babu Rao Mediyam from Bhadrachalam who became the part of JPC with effect from 21 February 2006 attended 11 sittings followed by Giridhar Gamang from Koraput who attended 10 sittings. Other members like Babu Lal Marandi and Jual Oram attended only four sittings of the committee deliberations. Hemlal Murmu attended merely

three sittings followed by Damodar Barku Shingada who participated in two sittings and Nand Kumar Sai took part in one committee discussion.

The JPC played an instrumental role in crafting the Bill from altogether a new angle. In fact, most of the essential provisions were inducted in the Bill during the committee deliberation which was eventually accepted by the government before tabling the Bill for the debate and enacted by the Parliament. Since the JPC was headed by a member who belongs to the tribal community and there were more than one-third of the members of the committee from the tribal community, it could successfully bring a real experience of the needs, demands and grievances of the tribal communities.

The purpose is to situate the committee report with the reality of the composition of the committee. The committee minutely thought on each and every clause. The recommendations were serious in nature and had to do with the reality of the tribal communities. The outcome reflected the solidarity of the marginalized communities. The JPC submitted a unanimous report to the Parliament after discussing clause by clause provisions of the Bill. Some of the important recommendations and suggestions can be thematically categorized.

Re-Crafting the Bill

The JPC deliberations and discussions not only redefined the Bill but broadened its horizon as well. It brought in several crucial provisions in the Bill which had the potential to address the utmost concern of correcting the historical injustices. The committee recorded that

---

[5] The way a committee tilt, much depends on the chairman. It is the steering potential of the chairman which decides whether to go for a minority report or consensual report by all the members. This tendency is often observed in the Westminster system where the burden of the success or the failure of committee is left to the leadership. It is one of the reasons due to which government keeps the chairmanship with itself.

People have also been victims of historical injustice as they have lived on forest land from ancient times. Non-recognition of their rights would not only pose a threat to their livelihood but also lead to their eviction from the forests. (Government of India, 2006a, p. 25)

JPC showed a strong sense of solidarity with other traditional forest dwellers (OTFD) as well in ensuring their rights along with the tribal community as 'these people have lived in forest in close harmony with the STs community in the forest…[] or in close proximity of the forest or forest land for generations and primarily depend on forest land or forest resources for their bona fide livelihood' (Government of India, 2006a, p. 25). One of the defining moments during consideration of the Bill was the fact that committee unanimously decided to change the entire face of the Bill by adding the term 'other traditional forest dwellers'.

The JPC in its report observed during the sittings and deliberations that 'a large number of forest dwelling STs not only reside in forest but also in the close proximity of the forest land who mainly depend on forest for their bona fide livelihood needs'(Government of India, 2006a, p. 21). Therefore, the JPC strongly recommended that the

Need is to expand the definition of 'forest dwelling Scheduled Tribes' to include such STs who reside in or in the close proximity of the forest land to protect their rights to livelihoods and other rights and also to the 'other traditional forest dwellers. (Government of India, 2006a, p. 21)

Above recommendation changed the entire positioning of the Bill as it revolutionized the content of the proposed policy in ensuring the rights over land to millions of people who have traditionally safeguarded it along with using it sustainably. It was the JPC members' experience among their electorates which further propelled the need to add such recommendations as they were already exposed to the vulnerability of the tribal community among whom many were not formally fall

under the governmental category of STs, but were traditionally the forest-dwelling community.

Another outstanding recommendation given by the JPC which further broadened the ambit and scope of the Bill was to extend the cut-off date for the claim. In the original draft, the cut-off date was 25 October 1980 for the recognition of rights. The committee commented that

Such a cutoff date in the distant past will take away the right of many people who have migrated or been displaced or shifted from their original location during this period. Furthermore, it will make it very difficult for the forest dwellers to prove and establish their claims for rights. (Government of India, 2006a, p. 40)

The original cut-off date of 1980 in the draft was against the very spirit and object of the Bill as the motive of the policy is, as JPC observed was to 'undo the historic injustice towards forest dwelling STs and other traditional forest dwellers' (Government of India, 2006a, p. 40). Reasoning behind such a recommendation was the fact that between 1980 and 2005, a complete generation has passed and almost 10 lakh hectares of forest land have been diverted for non-forest use for mines, industry and development projects. So, the earlier cut-off date would lead to 'eviction and denial of right to millions of forest dwellers who depend on forest land for their bona fide livelihood' (Government of India, 2006a, p. 40). Therefore, The JPC recommended a recent cut-off date as of 13 December 2005, which was later accepted by the government. The committee was also against the government putting a ceiling to the land rights. In the original Bill, it was 2.5 hectares but the committee recommended removal of any ceiling altogether. But the original Act has ceiling of 4 hectares. The JPC also defined the meaning of 'community forest resources' which was left open to explanation and exaggeration and misinterpretation in the original Bill.

Ambit of Authority and Ownership

The JPC recommended that 'the authority determining the forest rights and for deciding any disputes in relation to any forest right recognized and vested under the act shall be the Gram Sabha' (Government of India, 2006a, p. 18) and not any other ambiguously used term as 'competent authority' in the Bill. The committee suggested giving significance to traditional institutions in tribal community such as Padas, Tolas or elected village committees. The JPC recommended that the right of ownership should include the right to collect, transport and dispose of minor forest produce which have been traditionally collected within and outside village boundaries. The committee suggested that these should be included in the right of ownership access (Government of India, 2006a, p. 30) along with expanding the 'meaning of the rights to include all forest villages, old habitations and unsurveyed villages and other villages in forest, whether recorded, notified or not into revenue villages to make it more comprehensive and clear' (Government of India, 2006a, p. 32).

The committee recommended and later accepted by the government was one of the important provisions that 'Gram Sabha should be made the primary authority for determination and recognition of rights as it is completely public and open forum...'(Government of India, 2006a, p. 51). The logic was that 'Gram Sabha brings together the persons who have the most direct knowledge of the ground situation' (Government of India, 2006a, p. 51). After this, any aggrieved person can go to the subdivisional level committee. The Gram Sabha will consider the recommendations of the sub-divisional committee. If the recommendation is not accepted, then again the affected person can approach the district-level committee followed by state-level monitoring committee. At the same time, the JPC advocated that at least one-half of its members should be from the forest-dwelling STs with the inclusion of elected representatives and disadvantaged communities and one-third of the non-official members shall be women (Government of India, 2006a, p. 51).

Provisions for Rehabilitation

The JPC clearly acknowledged that 'displacement is one of the most severe threats to the livelihood and dignity of forest dwelling communities. Displacement and eviction have been taking place across the country without the settlement of rights and mostly without the provisions of rehabilitation' (Government of India, 2006a, p. 36). So, the committee has felt that there should be provisions in the 'Bill to recognize the rights of such displaced people, thereby, the people so displaced should have the right to *in situ* rehabilitation and alternative land' (Government of India, 2006a, p. 36). The committee recommended a strong provision in case of displacement and advocated for prompt rehabilitation policy as well.

Reconciling Development

The committee went ahead recognizing some of the 'provisions for developmental requirements of food, fibre, education, health, communication and facilities like schools, hospitals, roads etc. by way of diversion of forest land which may involve felling of trees not exceeding seventy five trees per project' (Government of India, 2006a, p. 38). The JPC advocated that the clearance of development projects where the requirement of land is less than one hectare in each case is recommended by the Gram Sabhas.

Besides, these specific recommendations, the JPC also strongly recommended that once this Bill is enacted, it should be placed in the Ninth Schedule[6] of the constitution as the Bill

---

[6] The Ninth Schedule of the Indian Constitution consists a list of central and state laws which cannot be challenged in courts and are shielded from the purview of judicial review. Ninth Schedule was inserted in the constitution in

was 'an urgent measure intended to address a historical injustice done to a large section of some of the weakest and most marginal communities...[] and in particular the Scheduled Tribes' (Government of India, 2006a, p. 60). The JPC was right in observing that implementation would delay in the wake of various litigations which proved to be right in some states later.

The JPC recommendations were blunt and straight forward. It reflects serious deliberations among themselves, with civil society and NGOs. No opportunity was left to reinterpret the provisions by the United Progressive Alliance (UPA)-I government led by the Congress party. It was a successful attempt to come up with a robust report which was also accepted by the entire Parliament wholeheartedly. The UPA-I did not accept few recommendations, which was later introduced in 2012 amendment as discussed later.

THE DEBATE

The final Bill was introduced in the Lok Sabha on 15 December 2006 for debate in which seven members representing the ST seats actively participated in the debate. These MPs were Rameshwar Oraon from Lohardaga, Baju Ban Riyan from Tripura East, Bapu Hari Chaure from Dhule, Jual Oram from Sundargarh, Sansuma Khunggur Bwiswmuthiary from Kokrajhar, Mahaveer Bhagora representing Salumbar and Babu Rao Midiyam from Bhadrachalam.

P. R. Kyndiah, the then Minister of Tribal Affairs introduced the Bill in the Lok Sabha. The motive of the Bill was to 'vest the forest rights and occupation in forest land in forest dwelling Scheduled Tribes and OTFD who have been residing in such forest for generations but whose rights could not be recorded...' (Lok Sabha Debates [LSD], 15 December 2006). Sundargarh MP, Jual Oram from BJP, supported the Bill. However, he did raise his concerns and apprehensions against some of the steps of the government as they brought the Bill in haste. Oram said that government should have first brought the JPC report in the Parliament in order to debate on the suggestions and recommendations. It is important to remember that Oram was also one of the members of the JPC. He was clueless whether cabinet accepted those recommendations or not. In fact, his concern was right as another member, Sansuma Khunggur Bwiswmuthiary, who was elected from Kokrajhar Lok Sabha constituency as an independent candidate, vehemently complained and even protested as the Bill was not circulated before moving the motion in the Lok Sabha.

Jual Oram's complaint was that the government is bringing the Bill as they have no other choice, but compelled to move it. It is the pressure of the opposition which left no other way for the government but to Act in haste even without discussing the JPC report in the house or circulating the final Bill. However, reiterating his stand again, he strongly advocated that the Act must be put under ninth schedule to protect it from any future infringements. Even JPC in its 13th sitting in which Jual Oram was present and had also recommended it; however, this particular recommendation was unanimously decided by the committee. Another significant aspect of the tribal livelihood was also raised by Oram, when he demanded that the definition of minor forest produce must be broadened by bringing products like bamboo, stones and so on. Besides,

---

1951 during first constitutional amendment. The legal strength behind this is article 31A and 31B. Although the courts have observed previously that even laws under this schedule would be open to scrutiny if they are violating the fundamental rights or the basic structure of the constitution. It is in this context, the FRA was proposed to put under this schedule so that it could be protected from tinkering and hampering by future governments. There are currently 284 such laws placed under this schedule including one that provides 69 per cent reservation in the state of Tamil Nadu.

Oram brought attention to one important aspect that could lead to rejection of claims of tribal by the gram panchayats because they have no revenue records. Oram argued that 'unfortunately large area of forest is marked as Reserved Forest or Sanctuary due to which there are no revenue records of those inhabitants who are living since 30–40 years' (LSD, 15 December 2006). Jual Oram responded to the critique of this Bill by saying, 'it is important to save the Tribal than the tigers' (LSD, 15 December 2006). He was responding to those who were lobbying against the passing of the legislation. For Oram, the security of the tribal is paramount.

Another MP from Tripura East, Baju Ban Riyan of CPM supported the Bill. He was also one of the members of JPC. He spoke about the longstanding demand of the STs over land rights. He said that most of the people living below the poverty line are STs. Riyan reiterated Oram's point that 'tribals cannot prove that they are living there for long as they do not have any revenue records' (LSD, 15 December 2006). Riyan continued that 'all they (tribals) have to show as proof are their small huts, some trees and other valuable timber in the forests, there is nothing to prove that they are living since long' (LSD, 15 December 2006).

Mahaveer Singh Bhagora, a BJP MP from Salumbar wholeheartedly supported the Bill and assured the house that this legislation would bring some relief to the lives of 'Adivasis'. Babu Rao Mediyam, a CPM MP from Bhadrachalam (ceased to exist after delimitation in 2008) demanded that the 'Gram Sabha should be given the full and final authority to decide the beneficiaries…'(LSD, 15 December 2006). Moreover, he asserted that 'at the Committee level, there should be adequate representation of the STs'(LSD, 15 December 2006). Lohardaga MP from Congress, Rameshwar Oraon brought to the notice of the house the adversities the tribals have faced time and again as they have been displaced multiple times, but this Bill would be the first step when efforts have been made

to give land rights to the tribal community. He also advocated for the role of the Gram Sabha as it is the democracy from below in true sense for the tribal society.

Most importantly, Sansuma Khunggur Bwiswmuthiary opposed some of the provisions of the Bill. He raised certain specific points about North East states. According to Bwiswmuthiary, the earlier version of the Bill was good, but the JPC had inserted many such provisions which could be detrimental to the tribal communities of North-east. He complained saying that only three out of eight North-east state's representatives were part of the committee. His anxiety was that the people of North-east were not taken into confidence. Also, opinions of autonomous district councils' representatives were not sought. Therefore, he moved an amendment, which later, of course negatived, that some of the provisions must not be applied to these states. Otherwise, such 'unholistic move tantamount to intending to create a lot of trouble and tension' (LSD, 15 December 2006). He was amazed to realize that 'under what consideration this Panchayati Raj System was brought into the provision, particularly in relation to the North-East regions wherein Autonomous District Council have been existing from 1952. So, these serious aspects have to be looked and taken into account while passing this Bill' (LSD, 15 December 2006). A total of 36 MPs have submitted a memorandum to the Prime Minister to consider the demands of the North-east states.

Bwiswmuthiary's apprehension came true in 2013, when the then Minister of Tribal Affairs, V. Kishore Chandra Deo, who was the chairman of the JPC to scrutinize and study the forest rights Bill back in 2005, accepted that

State Governments of Arunachal Pradesh, Nagaland, Manipur, Meghalaya and Sikkim have informed about the limitations of applicability of FRA-2006 in their States. The State Government of Arunachal Pradesh has informed that barring few pockets of land under wildlife sanctuaries and reserved forests, most of the land in the entire State is community land and therefore, FRA-2006 does not have much relevance in the State. The State Government of Manipur has informed that the tribal communities and tribal chiefs are already holding ownership of forest land and therefore, implementation of FRA is perceived minimal. The State Government of Meghalaya has informed that 96% of the forest land is owned by the clans/communities/individuals and therefore implementation of FRA has limited scope. The State Government of Nagaland has informed that the land holding system and the village system of the Naga people is peculiar in the sense that the people are the land owners, hence FRA per se may not be applicable to the State. However, a Committee has been constituted to examine the applicability of the Act as per the provisions of Article 371(A) of the Constitution. The State Government of Sikkim has informed that there are no forest dwelling Scheduled Tribes and Other Traditional Forest Dwellers in the true sense of the term as most of the Scheduled Tribes of Sikkim hold revenue land and are not solely dependent on forests for their livelihood (Unstarred question number 275, LSD, 15 March 2013).

However, all the amendments moved on the floor of the house by Jual Oram, Bwiswmuthiary, Babu Rao Midiyam were negatived followed by which Bwiswmuthiary walked out of the house in protest. Midiyam asserted the need to give full and final authority to decide the beneficiaries to the Gram Sabhas (LSD, 15 December 2006). Also, he moved an amendment to ensure 'adequate representation of the Gram Sabhas at the committee's level' (LSD, 15 December 2006).

The FRA was amended in 2012, followed by the issues it was facing during the implementation. Moreover, there were apprehensions since 2006 that some more safeguards needed to be added to shield the policy either from misuse or to evade the distribution of land to the tribal communities. The National Advisory Committee (NAC) during UPA-II also made detailed recommendations in March 2011 to revamp some of the provisions of the Act so that the 'legal regime' surrounding the FRA-2006 could be amended for smooth implementation (Rajya Sabha Debates, 29 March 2012). It was the NAC's recommendation which gave impetus to the 2012 amendment in the rules and the guidelines. The STs and OTFD (recognition of forest rights) amendment rules, 2012 was notified on 6 September 2012. Some of the provisions which were changed were related to the disposal of minor forest produce within and outside forest area, regarding collection of minor forest produce free of royalties and so on. It empowered the tribal communities to collect and use non-timber forest produce as well. It also amended the composition of tribal communities in forest rights committee by making it two-third. Also, representation of one-third women was made mandatory in Gram Sabhas.

THE ASSESSMENT

A standing committee on social justice and empowerment scrutinized the FRA-2006 and its implementation in 2010–2011 under the chairmanship of Dara Singh Chauhan, a BSP MP from Ghosi in Uttar Pradesh. Four tribal MPs, namely, Baliram Kashyap of BJP from Bastar, Basori Singh Masram of Congress from Mandla, Baliram Jadhav of Bahujan Vikas Aaghadi from Palghar and Manohar Tirkey of Revolutionary Socialist Party from Alipurduars, were the members of the standing committee. The only MP among the tribal MPs who was present in all the deliberations, discussions and sessions of the committee was Baliram Jadhav. He attended all the three detailed sessions of the scrutiny committee. Manohar Tirkey attended two sittings followed by Basori Singh Masram who attended one sitting, while Baliram Kashyap was absent from all the sitting which deliberated the issue of implementation of FRA, 2006.

The committee stated that 'forests provide sustenance in the form of minor forest produce, water, grazing ground and habitat for shifting cultivation'. It recognized the fact that for the STs and others,

Forest rights on ancestral lands and their habitat had not been adequately recognised in the consideration of State forests... [] in independent India resulting in injustice to the forest dwelling Scheduled Tribes and other traditional forest dwellers who are integral to the very survival and sustainability of the forest ecosystem (Government of India, 2010, p. 9).

So, the committee highlighted that it was the primary reason to

Address the long standing insecurity of tenurial and access rights of forest dwelling STs.

The review committee was of the view that FRA 2006 is 'an all encompassing Act' fulfilling the long felt needs and aspirations of STs. One of the concern was that, if the Act is implemented in 'letter and spirit', it would go a long way in 'redressing the historical injustice meted out to the Scheduled Tribes... (Government of India, 2010, p. 12).

The scrutiny committee while studying the implementation of FRA-2006 commented that states have 'progressed in varying degrees in the implementation of the Act' (Government of India, 2010, p. 13). States like Andhra Pradesh, Chhattisgarh, Gujarat, Madhya Pradesh, Maharashtra, Odisha, Rajasthan, Tripura and West Bengal have received a large number of claims for the forest land. However, states like Goa, Himachal Pradesh, Manipur, Uttarakhand were delaying the constitution of the committee authorized to scrutiny the application or the scope of the Act were very limited in states like Manipur or Meghalaya. By 2010, the committee noted that Bihar had not distributed 'a single title deed' whereas a total of 2,179 claims had received. Similar was the case with Tamil Nadu (due to stay order by Madras High Court) and Uttarakhand. It was startling to know that tribal dominated states like Jharkhand was performing very dismal in distributing the claims. In the case of North Eastern states, the context was different. As per the evidence, 'North East was a separate case...[] in the North East, most of the forests are community owned and rights have been specified....[] people know their rights' (Government of India, 2010, p. 21).

In order to deduce the reason for the rejection of large number of claims, the committee wanted to know the stage, that is, Gram Sabha, Sub-Divisional Level Committee or District Level Committee, at which the maximum numbers of claims were being rejected. It was found that largest number of rejection were taking place either at the Gram Sabha level or subdivisional level committee mainly because of non-availability of written records, non-possession of forest land, doubtful tribal status, multiple claimants, timeline-related clarity (Government of India, 2010, p. 25).

The Ministry of Tribal Affairs did not have any 'prescribed time limit' for the recognition and vesting of forest rights to the STs (Government of India, 2010, p. 27), whereas the presidential address in 2009 in UPA-II argued that 'need is to ensure the distribution of the title deeds to all the eligible claimants by the end of December, 2009'. Arguably, delay in many states was triggered by several factors such as in the states of Tamil Nadu, Andhra Pradesh and Odisha, it was the court cases in respective high courts (Government of India, 2010, p. 30). In general, there were 14 writ petitions—12 in various high courts and 2 in the supreme court, which challenged the FRA 2006.

The outcome of the policy was very dismal. By November 2010, a mere 32.36 per cent of total claims in all the states were actually distributed to the targeted groups across the country (Government of India, 2010, p. 31). Even the committee expressed its displeasure on the success rate of the policy. By the end of 31 May 2014, almost 14 lakhs titles were distributed among the claimants, submitted to the then Minister of State for Tribal Affairs, Mansukhbhai Dhanjibhai Vasava in the Lok Sabha in response to a question by B. S. Yeddurappa (Unstarred question number 1318, LSD, 18 July 2014).

The lacklustre and lethargic preparation of the government before the implementation was one of the major reasons behind tardy implementation and distribution of the land deeds. To begin with, government under estimated the number of claims to be received under this FRA as happened later in its implementation process. While testifying before the committee, a secretary to the Ministry deposed and seemed satisfied with 32 per cent success rate saying that 'originally when the Act came into operation, the Ministry had expected only about three to four lakh claims to be distributed' (Government of India, 2010, p. 31); whereas, the government had already distributed almost 10,00,000 claims (32%) which 'far exceeds the expectations' (Government of India, 2010, p. 32). One can understand the government's expectations and the seriousness behind the policy formulation. The difference between government expectation and reality was whopping more than 25 lakhs by the end of 2010 only. As of April 2019, out of approximately 42 lakhs claims, 19.5 lakhs titles were distributed[7] which is approximately around 46 per cent of the total claims.

On the other hand, the success of this Act precisely lies with the fact that it gives 'individual rights' over the forest land to tribal communities along with securing claims for the 'community rights' as well. That is the reason why a large number of claims were made in the capacity of individuals. Another difficulty behind high rate of claim rejection was the time period of three generations (equivalent to 75 years) stipulated for the OTFD. It was cumbersome for them to prove the residency period of three generations who are living and dependent on the forest land for their livelihood baked by documentary proofs.

Overall, the scrutiny committee was disappointed with the pace of implementation of the Act. It opined that 'it is still far from satisfactory' and have not even completed 50 per cent (Government of India, 2010, p. 36). The Committee are constrained to note that even after Prime Minister's direction emphasizing the need for such a synergy/coordinated approach and the establishment of the task force by the Ministry of Rural Development for convergence of programmes concerning education, health and agriculture sectors with Mahatma Gandhi National Rural Employment Guarantee Act (MGNREGA), coordination among ministries pertaining to tribal development programmes is hardly forthcoming/happening as ministries continue to work in total isolation to each other resulting in detachment of tribal pockets from developmental mainstream' (Government of India, 2010, p. 53). The committee deprecated the inaction on the part of the Ministry of Tribal Affairs in guarding the interests and rights of various primitive tribal groups like Dongoria Kandhas and the Kuti Kandhas in the Niyamgiri hills due to proposed bauxite mining project of the government (Government of India, 2010, p. 73).

The role of MPs in the wake of such irregularities and massive complaints specially in tribal dominated states failed to witness active involvement other than in committees or in some parliamentary questions. That is one of the reasons the implementation of FRA was questioned time and again.

THE ECHOES

This section explores the nature of questions related to FRA-2006 that was raised in the Lok Sabha. The FRA-2006 came to force on 1 January 2008 during the 14th Lok Sabha. Only three questions directly linked with the FRA were asked by the tribal MPs like Anandrao Vithoba, Madhusudan Mistry, Uday Singh, M. Jagannath and Mansukhbhai Vasava.

In the 15th Lok Sabha, as many as 28 questions were asked about the FRA in the Lok Sabha. These questions were around the issue of implementation of the policy, violations and claims. Out of these 28 questions, 9 questions were raised by those MPs who were elected on the ST seats.

---

[7] https://www.fra.org.in/document/FRA%20Status%20Replrt%20April%202019_India.pdf.

One of the active MPs was Yashbant Narayan Singh Laguri from Keonjhar, Odisha. According to a question asked by him along with other MPs like Arjun Munda (Unstarred question number 2981, LSD, 24 July 2009), the government replied that they are taking all necessary steps for expeditious implementation of the FRA. Responding to a question posed by Kowase Marotrao Sainuji, MP from Gadchiroli-Chimur, Kantilal Bhuria, Tribal Affairs Minister, responded that the government has not decided any time limit for the completion of the distribution of titles under the policy (Starred question number 195, LSD, 6 August 2010). However, it is worth noticing that between 24 July 2009 and 6 August 2010, government had already distributed almost 7 lakhs titles to the people. In total, they had distributed around 10 lakhs titles. On another occasion, Yashbant Narayan Laguri asked the Ministry about the steps taken to rectify the issue of 'critical wildlife habitat' (Unstarred question number 1912, LSD, 2 December 2011). As pointed out by different leaders that the forest department officials are the real bone of contention for the tribal communities as they have been violating the rights and dignity of the community by harassing and registering cases against them in many occasions. Yashbant Narayan Laguri asked the same question but the government categorically denied the reporting of any cases (Unstarred question number 4,447, LSD, 7 September 2012).

Other MPs who asked questions about the progress of the FRA were Vincent Pala from Shillong (Meghalaya), Ramsinhbhai Patalbhai Rathwa from Chhota Udaipur (Gujarat), and Harishchandra Deoram Chavan from Dindori (Maharashtra).

In the 16th Lok Sabha, at least 17 questions were asked by different MPs in the Lok Sabha directly pertaining to the FRA. Out of these 17 questions, 5 tribal MPs raised their questions on the implementation of the FRA. Shahdol MP Dalpat Singh Paraste asked whether there is any preparation to reinterpret the FRA and to dilute the requirement of consent of Gram Sabhas before the forests were cut down. The Ministry of Tribal Affairs categorically denied saying there is no such proposal (Unstarred question number 4,321, LSD, 20 April 2015). At another occasion, Sakuntala Laguri, Keonjhar MP and Jyoti Dhurve, Betul MP asked about the status report on the recommendations of the joint committee of the Ministry of Tribal Affairs and the Ministry of Environment and Forests (constituted in 2010) and what steps did the government undertake to remove the obstacles in the implementation of the FRA. The Ministry of Tribal Affairs replied that the recommendations of the committee were taken into account when the FRA was amended on 6 September 2012 in order to 'remove the impediments and ensure effective implementation on the ground' (Unstarred question number 2523, LSD, 14 December 2015). They also asked about the total number of claims disposed of in the name of women, for which the Ministry responded that though the claims are registered jointly in the name of both the spouses, but it has no specific record for women only.

On 21 December 2015, Laxman Giluwa from Singhbhum and Sakuntala Laguri again asked about the interface between the two ministries (Ministry of Tribal Affairs and Ministry of Environment, Forest and Climate Change) and their implications on FRA (Unstarred question number 3673, LSD, 21 Dec 2015). Again on 2 August 2016, Laxman Giluwa and Sakuntala Laguri addressed a question to the Ministry of Environment, Forests and Climate Change about the alleged interference by the department of forests in the implementation of forest rights which were detrimental for the tribal communities (Unstarred question number 2,688, LSD, 2 August 2016). However, the Ministry denied any interference from forest department. Arjunlal Meena, MP from Udaipur, enquired about mechanism or agency working with the government to monitor and implement the FRA, for which the Sudarshan Bhagat, Minister of State for Tribal Affairs replied that the progress is reported by different states to the central government on a monthly basis (Unstarred question number 301, LSD, 18 December 2017).

Other questions related to this policy was asked by MPs like B. S. Yeddurappa, Anurag Thakur, Om Birla, Srinivasa Reddy, Hansraj Gangaram Ahir, M. B. Rajesh, Anant Kumar Hegde, Rabindra Jena, Dharmendra Yadav, Shrirang Appa Barne, Shivji Patil, Pritam Gopinath Munde, Virendra Kashyap, K. V. Reddy and R. Vanaroja. The nature of questions oscillated between whether the government has any plan to amend the Act, or dilute the Act, or purported interference of Environment and Forest Ministry. The answers to these questions were in negative by the government. In this ongoing 17th Lok Sabha, in three sessions, questions pertaining to FRA implementation was raised at five different occasions by members like Bharati Pawar representing Dindori, Raju Bista representing Darjeeling, Sukhbir Singh Jaunapuria representing Tonk-Sawai Madhopur and Karti P. Chidambaram from Sivaganga.

It is important to keep in mind that most of the questions regarding the implementation of the policy were asked in the wake of the fact that it was facing lots of adversities on the ground like convening of Gram Sabha meetings at the panchayat level, exclusion of some minuscule communities among the tribes who were not a part of any village, non-recognition of absolute rights over the minor forest produce to the tribal community and forest dwellers, failure to curb the monopoly of state forest corporations in trade of high value minor forest produces, rejection of the claims without giving any justifications, claimants were not being informed about the rejection of their claims so, they failed to appeal within the deadline, bizarre requirements for certain specific documentary proof, and non-recognition of rights in national parks and sanctuaries.

THE FAILURES

Even after a decade of the implementation of the FRA 2006, more than 190 million forest dwellers are unrecognized (India Today, 2016). There were multiple protests across the country because of violations of FRA as activists and civil society organizations alleged that Gram Sabha's mandate were being disrespected and sidelined. Many attempts are made by the consecutive governments after 2009 to dilute the Act. The Ministry of Forest and Environment plays critical role in diluting the Act in the name of mining and development. However, during UPA-II government, the then Tribal Affairs Minister, S. Kishore Chandra Deo disagreed with it on many occasions. Similarly, in NDA-I government also, the Ministry of Tribal Affairs disagreed on several occasions with the proposal of Forest Ministry. Jual Oram, the Minister of Tribal Affairs in NDA-I, who was also a member of the JPC for FRA, ensured that this Act will not be diluted at the cost of tribal rights. The contention has always been the tribals' right over the forest land or whether the Forest Ministry is free to decide over it. The role of MPs who come from ST-reserved constituencies should have played an important role in delineating this, but one can hardly see any united or joint effort circumventing the party lines over the tribal issues. There are many tribal dominated states like Jharkhand where this policy was never implemented properly. However, the lawmakers failed to intervene constructively. By mid-2015, after nine years of the policy, Jharkhand government had awarded only 22,400 titles (Times of India, 2015).

The tribal MPs played indispensable role in formulating and enacting this particular Act. However, in ensuring the objective of this policy as stated in the Act itself to ensure 'forest rights on ancestral lands and their habitat were not adequately recognized in the consolidation of state forests during the colonial period as well as in independent India resulting in historical injustice to the forest dwelling

Scheduled Tribes and OTFD' (https://www.fra.org.in/) still unattainable and the role of these MPs in demanding this is questionable and rare. As Madhu Sarin writes 'the intensity of bureaucratic resistance to the radical mandate of the FRA became evident in the concerted efforts made to stall the implementation…' (Sarin, 2016, p. 390). Seldom, there is an attempt by these MPs to come together as a group surpassing the respective party ideologies to demand prompt and full-fledged implementation of FRA.

REFERENCES

Government of India (1949). *Constituency assembly debates, volume IX.* New Delhi: Lok Sabha Secretariat.

Government of India (2006a). *Joint committee on the scheduled tribes (recognition of forest rights) bill, 2005.* New Delhi: Lok Sabha Secretariat.

Government of India (2006b). *Report of the standing committee on the Welfare of Scheduled Castes and Scheduled Tribes (2006–2007), fourteenth Lok Sabha: Monitoring and implementation of recommendations of the committee on the Welfare of Scheduled Castes and Scheduled Tribes during the years 1994–95 to 1998–99, 18th Report.* New Delhi: Lok Sabha Secretariat.

Government of India (2010). *Report of the standing committee on social justice and empowerment (2010–2011), fifteenth Lok Sabha: Implementation of scheduled tribes and other traditional forest dwellers (recognition of forest rights) act, 2006-rules made thereunder, tenth report.* New Delhi: Lok Sabha Secretariat.

Government of India (2012). *Report of the standing Committee on the Welfare of Scheduled Castes and Scheduled Tribes (2012–13), fifteenth Lok Sabha: Working of Tribal Sub Plan, 25th Report.* New Delhi: Lok Sabha Secretariat.

Government of India (2018). *Report of the standing Committee on the Welfare of Scheduled Castes and Scheduled Tribes (2018–19), Sixteenth Lok Sabha: Monitoring of Scheduled Tribes Sub Plan (STSP) now called as Scheduled Tribe Component (STC).implementation for Development and welfare of STs, 26th Report.* New Delhi: Lok Sabha Secretariat.

Government of India (n.d.). FRA. Retreieved from https://www.fra.org.in/document/FRA%20Status%20Replrt%20April%202019_India.pdf

India Today (2016, December 13). Around 190 mn forest dwellers unrecognised 10 yrs after FRA. *India Today.*

Sarin, M. (2016). India's forest tenure reforms, 1992-2012. In N. Sundar (Ed.), *The Scheduled Tribes and Their India: Politics, Identities, Policies, and Work.* New Delhi: Oxford University Press.

Times of India. (2015, June 2). Jharkhand Wakes up to forest rights after 9 years. *Times of India.*

Tribal Politics
at the State Level

Political Accommodation and Tribal Electoral Politics in Andhra Pradesh and Telangana

Venkatesh Vaditya

INTRODUCTION

Historically, scheduled tribes (STs) are the disadvantaged communities. Their vulnerability continues even today, not because of their poverty but their general inability to negotiate and cope up with the mainstream economy, society, culture and political system, which were alien to them. In the present context, their vulnerability becomes worst due to unresolved issues like displacement, land alienation, indebtedness, shifting cultivation and deprivation of forest rights. The development activities undertaken by the state so far in India have displaced Adivasis in a large number. In majority of cases, these displaced people have still not been rehabilitated properly. There was a major shift in tribal development approach from 1997, shift from 'welfare' to 'development' to 'empowerment'. To make a sense of decent existence, following basic needs have to be taken care of by any modern nation state in the form of basic developmental rights, that is, shelter, health,

livelihood and education. Beyond this, interaction of new human rights problem might emerge from the consequences of integration of global markets with local markets, shrinkage of welfare states, increased transnational flow of goods, services and forced migration, spread of culture of intolerance and increased power of decision-making process of new or growing global institutions (Rai, 2006, p. 1).

STS IN UNDIVIDED ANDHRA PRADESH

For colonial state, the term tribe was to represent people with diverse physical, linguistic, demographic, ecological and social formation. Such a term was necessitated to construct vast diversity into a category for classificatory and administrative expediency. Xaxa (2014, p. 2) says, 'although tribe as a category and as a point of reference may be treated as a colonial construction, the image and meaning underlying the category was far from being a colonial construction'. The term ST is a politico-administrative description but socially tribal communities are not a homogeneous category and have their own distinct ways of life and worldviews. Tribes are treated as those groups enumerated in the Indian constitution in the list of STs. Indeed, the constitution defines an ST 'as such tribe or tribal community or part of or groups within such tribes or tribal communities as are deemed under Article 342 to be scheduled tribes' (Xaxa, 2014, p. 3). The ST population in the country is ever expanding due to inclusion of various communities from time to time. As a result, total ST population increased from 6.9 per cent in 1961 to 8.6 per cent in 2011 (Government of India, 2013, p. 2). The reorganization of states on linguistic basis in 1956 created some anomalous positions concerning tribal groups especially in states like Madhya Pradesh, Maharashtra and Andhra Pradesh (AP). The anomaly was that substantial parts of tribal population in these states were recognized only in some districts of the state. In 1976, this position was rationalized with the enforcement of the Constitution Order Scheduled Castes and Scheduled Tribes (Amendment) Act, 1976 and the Removal of Area Restrictions (Amendment) Act, 1976. These acts removed area restrictions on the recognition of STs, making lists applicable to entire states rather than blocks and districts within states. This has increased the Adivasi population in the country by about 30.80 lakhs at 1971 base level (Deogaonkar, 1994).

According to 2001 census, the undivided Andhra Pradesh state had 6.59 per cent of tribal population (Table 9.1). Khammam, Adilabad and Visakhapatnam districts had substantial number of tribal population. After bifurcation of AP, according to the 2011 census, the ST population constituted around 9.3 per cent in Telangana state. The major tribes in Telangana are Gonds, Koyas, Konda Reddys, Yerukala, Chenchus and Lambadas. The percentage of literacy is very low among the tribes in Telangana. According to 2011 census, only 49.51 are literates (Government

of India, 2018), it is the lowest among the tribal-dominated states in India. Indian constitution makers were aware about the pressing situation of inequalities in the society. Therefore, it incorporated the philosophy of 'social justice' provisions in the preamble and subsequent articles.

POPULATION IN TELANGANA

Telangana is the 12th largest state in terms of both area and size of population in the union of India. The population of the state consists predominantly of backward classes (BCs), scheduled castes (SCs) and STs. According to 2011 census, STs constituted 9.08 per cent of the total population of the state (Government of Telangana, 2017, p. 43). The inclusion and removal of area restriction of tribal communities enabled to increase a sudden jump in percentage of ST population from 2.81 per cent in 1961 to 8.19 per cent in 1981 and further to 9.08 per cent in 2011. The reorganization of districts in October 2016 has left Khammam way behind Bhadradri-Kothagudem in terms of ST population compared to the overall population in the district. Khammam, which had the maximum number of Adivasi population among the 23 districts of the then undivided AP, has now relegated to seventh position among the 33 districts in Telangana. The ST population in the state is 31.78 lakhs as per 2011 census. After reorganization of the districts, total ST population of nine scheduled area districts was 8.46 lakhs and that of 22 plain area districts was 23.31 lakhs. It is to note that the portion of the state in agency areas is covered under the provisions of fifth schedule of the constitution of India. In the state, the scheduled areas have extended over 13924.46 sq. kms. in nine scheduled area districts of Adilabad, Mancherial, Asifabad, Nagarkurnool, Warangal Rural, Mahabubabad, Bhupalapally, Khammam and Kothagudem covering 1,174 villages (Government of Telangana, 2018, p. 3).

Table 9.1   District-wise Basic Data of STs in Erstwhile Andhra Pradesh, 2001 Census

Sl. No	Name of the District	Total ST Population 2001 Census (%)	Literacy rate in percentage (1991 Census)	Number of Land Holdings (1995–1996)		No. of Medical Institutions Available in Tribal Areas
				Number	Percentage to Total	
01	Adilabad	416511 (16.74)	17.67	82158	10.89	176
02	Nizamabad	165735 (7.07)	12.22	25271	3.35	0
03	Karimnagar	90636 (2.60)	12.31	13291	1.76	0
04	Medak	134533 (5.04)	11.49	23652	3.13	0
05	Hyderabad	34560 (0.90)	44.91	1	0	0
06	Rangareddy	146057 (4.09)	17.30	18847	2.49	0
07	Mahabubnagar	278702 (7.93)	10.06	52063	6.90	7
08	Nalgonda	342676 (10.55)	14.50	61170	8.11	0
09	Warangal	457679 (14.10)	13.38	78702	10.43	133
10	Khammam	682617 (26.47)	15.80	117745	15.6	332
11	Srikakulam	151249 (5.96)	19.70	26517	3.5	47
12	Vizianagaram	214839 (9.55)	15.68	34075	4.5	105
13	Visakhapatnam	557572 (14.55)	16.58	81456	10.8	196
14	East Godavari	191561 (3.91)	22.04	31142	4.1	106
15	West Godavari	96659 (2.54)	24.06	15852	2.1	60
16	Krishna	107611 (2.57)	21.68	6983	0.92	0
17	Guntur	208157 (4.66)	20.89	14572	1.93	0
18	Prakasham	118241 (3.86)	21.17	9595	1.27	0
19	Nellore	242257 (9.08)	16.36	18603	2.46	0
20	Cuddapah	61371 (2.36)	22.89	5861	0.7	0
21	Kurnool	69635 (1.97)	24.86	5629	0.74	0
22	Anantapur	127161 (3.46)	26.73	17286	2.29	0
23	Chittoor	128085 (3.42)	21.06	13664	1.81	0
Total		76210007 (6.59)	17.15	754135	100	1162

Source: Government of Andhra Pradesh (2008).

Displacing Khammam, Mahabubabad has emerged as the top district accounting for 37.80 per cent of STs of the total population followed by Bhadradri-Kothagudem (36.66%), Adilabad (31.68%), Kumaram Bheem-Asifabad (25.91%), Jayashankar-Bhupalapalli (17.37%) and Warangal Rural (14.65%). Interestingly, Karimnagar (1.27%) was second from the bottom after Hyderabad (1.24%) as the district with the least ST population (Table 9.2). This is because the residual Karimnagar district after reorganization of

districts now remains an urban conglomeration. More than half of the tribal population (52.96%) lives in integrated tribal development agencies (ITDA) districts.

Major Tribal Communities in Telangana

There are 32 communities categorized as STs in the state.[1] The Lambada community is

---

[1] The 32 communities are: 1. Andh, Sadhu Andh 2. Bagata 3. Bhil 4. Chenchu 5. Gadabas, Bodo Gadaba, Gutob Gadaba, Kallayi Gadaba, Parangi Gadaba, Kathera Gadaba, Kapu Gadaba 6. Gond, Naikpod, Rajgond,

Table 9.2   ST Population and Sex Ratio in Telangana

Sl No	District Name	Percentage of STs to Total Population	Sex Ratio of STs	Sex Ratio of State Population
1	Adilabad	31.68	989	989
2	Kumuram Bheem Asifabad	25.91	1,029	998
3	Mancherial	7.06	972	977
4	Nirmal	11.36	1,026	1,046
5	Nizamabad	6.81	1,030	1,044
6	Jagityal	2.37	1,020	1,036
7	Peddapally	1.88	987	992
8	Jayashankar Bhupalapally	17.37	1,025	1,009
9	Bhadradri Kothagudem	36.66	1,017	1,008
10	Mahabubabad	37.80	976	996
11	Warangal Rural	14.65	954	994
12	Warangal Urban	3.08	928	997
13	Karimnagar	1.27	971	993
14	Rajanna Sircilla	4.16	1,027	1,014
15	Kamareddy	8.40	1,000	1,033
16	Sangareddy	5.68	930	965
17	Medak	9.50	978	1,027
18	Siddipet	2.47	980	1,008
19	Jangaon	11.06	971	997
20	Yadadri Bhuvanagiri	5.86	930	973
21	Medchal-Malkajgiri	2.26	947	957
22	Hyderabad	1.24	915	954
23	Rangareddy	5.70	912	950
24	Viakarabad	10.21	974	1,001
25	Mahabubanagar	8.89	961	995
26	Jogulamba Gadwal	1.54	983	972
27	Wanaparthy	7.97	957	960
28	Nagarkurnool	12.40	933	968
29	Nalgonda	12.93	915	978
30	Suyapet	12.85	964	996
31	Khammam	14.22	997	1,005
Total		9.08	977	988

Source: Government of Telangana (2017, p. 17).

Koitur, 7. Goudu (in the Agency tracts) 8. Hill Reddis 9. Jatapus 10. Kammara 11. Kattunayakan 12. Kolam, Kolawar 13. Konda Dhoras, Kubi 14. Konda Kapus 15. Kondareddis 16. Kondhs, Kodi, Kodhu, Desaya Kondhs, Dongria Kondhs, Kuttiya Kondhs, Tikiria Kondhs, Yenity Kondhs, Kuvinga 17. Kotia, Bentho Oriya, Bartika, Dulia, Holva, Sanrona, Sidhopaiko 18. Koya, Doli Koya, Gutta Koya, Kammara Koya, Musara Koya, Oddi Koya, Pattidi Koya, Rajah, Rasha Koya, Lingadhari Koya (ordinary), Kottu Koya, Bhine Koya, Rajkoya 19. Kulia 20. Manna Dhora 21. Mukha Dhora, Nooka Dhora 22. Nayaks (in the Agency tracts) 23. Pardhan 24. Porja, Parangiperja 25. Reddi Dhoras 26. Rona, Rena 27. Savaras, Kapu Savaras, Maliya Savaras, Khutto Savaras 28. Sugalis, Lambadis, Banjara 29. Thoti (in Adilabad, Hyderabad, Karimnagar, Khammam, Mahbubnagar, Medak, Nalgonda, Nizam abad and Warangal districts) 30. Yenadis, Chella Yenadi, Kappala Yenadi, Manchi Yenadi, Reddi Yenadi 31. Yerukulas, Koracha, Dabba Yerukula, Kunchapuri Yerukula, Uppu Yerukula 32. Nakkala, Kurvikaran.

Table 9.3 Population of Major Tribal Communities in Telangana

Sl No	Community	Population	% of STs in Total State ST Population	% of STs in Total State Population
1	Lambada	20,46,117	64.38	5.84
2	Koya	4,86,391	15.30	1.38
3	Gond, Naikpods	2,97,846	9.37	0.85
4	Yerukala	1,44,128	4.53	0.41
5	Pardhan	24,776	0.77	0.07
Total		29,99,258	94.37	8.56

Source: Government of Telangana (b).

largest one and is spread in all the districts of the state. They are concentrated in undivided Adilabad, Warangal, Khammam, Nalgonda, Mahabubnagar and Nizambad districts. The Koyas are the second largest community within the Adivasis in the state and they live predominantly in scheduled areas. There are exclusive Adivasi tracts in Telangana. In the agency areas, they are the victims of land alienation, indebtedness and bonded labour (Suri, 2002, p. 12). The population of major five communities is given in Table 9.3. These groups together constitute 94.27 per cent of the total ST population of the state and 8.56 per cent of total population of the state.

The ecological factors and habitats are closely associated with the economy and livelihood practices of the STs. Among the plain tribes, along with Lambadas, the Yerukulas are known as the ex-criminal tribe in the state and traditionally, they are the basket makers and swine herders. They usually live in village society and maintain a symbiotic relations with non-tribes. The Lambadas live in exclusive settlements known as Tandas. Their habitats are located in proximity with the caste-ridden village society nearer to hillocks and green postures to rear cattle. Earlier, the Lambadas were known to be nomads, but in modern times, they are becoming sedentary cultivators, and rearing of cattle has become their secondary occupation (Reddy & Kumar, 2010, p. 15). In Vaditya's (2017) opinion, present day Lambada community seems to be under a deep cultural crisis, emanating from leaving away their old egalitarian practices

and adopting the hierarchical Hindu culture. The Government of India has identified three communities such as Chenchus, Kolams and Konda Reddys as particularly vulnerable tribes in erstwhile Andhra Pradesh in 1975–1976 and 1980, respectively. In 1982–1983, Thotis, Khonds, Porjas, Gadabas, and Konda Savaras were recognized as particularly vulnerable tribes. Their habitats are located mostly on the hilltops and they largely depend on shifting cultivation and minor forest produce collection. Among these groups, the Chenchus are considered as the most primitive group as they are still struck at food gathering stage of history but they are progressing slowly towards food producing stage. Their traditional habitats are found in the proximate forest tracts of Nallamala hills as much of the area of the Nallamala hills through which the Krishna river flows is presently declared as tiger reserve project area (Rao, Reddy & Chathukulam, 2012). Kolams are found in Adivasi areas of Adilabad district; they live in exclusive settlements in interior forests and mountainous tracts. They speak their own dialect called 'Kolami'. Konda Reddis inhabit on the banks situated on either side of the Godavari river and in the hilly/forest tracts undivided Khammam district. Thotis are living in the erstwhile districts of Adilabad, Karimnagar and Nizamabad (Government of Telangana, 2018). The population size of these particularly vulnerable tribes is given in Table 9.4.

As per 2011 census, the literacy level of tribes is abysmally low compared to the

Table 9.4   Population of Particularly Vulnerable Tribal Groups in Telangana

Sl No	Community	Population	% of Total STs in the State	% of STs in Total State Population
1	Kolam	44,805	1.40	0.12
2	Chenchu	16,912	0.53	0.04
3	Konda Reddi	7,997	0.25	0.02
4	Thoti	4,811	0.15	0.01
Total		74,525	2.34	0.21

Source: Government of Telangana (a).

general population. Less than half of the Adivasis (49.80%) are literates. Out of which only 40.64 per cent females are literate against 61.02 per cent of male literate (Government of Telangana, 2018). It is obvious that there is a huge gap between all social groups and STs. However, the literacy rate of STs in Mahabubnagar district, which is considered as the most backward, is lower (42.29%) than the average literacy rate of tribes in the state (49.51%). Low level of literacy rate is one of the main reasons for their lack of awareness about various state sponsored development programmes.

EMERGENCE OF TELANGANA: THE POLITICAL CONTEXT OF ERSTWHILE ANDHRA PRADESH

The state of Telangana was part of the erstwhile Nizam's composite Hyderabad state, which comprised of eight Telugu-speaking, three Kannada-speaking and five Marathi-speaking districts. In Telangana region, given the historical specificity of the Nizam's dominion, the nature of socioeconomic changes and political trajectory took a different turn. The Nizam ruled over a cosmopolitan population over 16 million people, and over a land extending 82,698 sq. miles of a homogeneous territory. It was a multilingual state. Hyderabad, the biggest and wealthiest princely states during that time under the Nizam-VII, decided on 11 June 1947 through a *Firman* (official order), that he was entitled to declare independence

on 15 August. However, the Indian independence bill, which was introduced in the British Parliament on 9 July 1947, came as a shock to the Nizam when the bill envisaged Hyderabad as part of one of the two dominions of India or Pakistan. The Nizam insisted that Hyderabad should be a third domain (Rao, 1984).

The Indian government on 13 September began an army action on Hyderabad state from five directions as Muhammad Ali Jinnah died on 12 September. This army operation was called 'police action' and in the army nomenclature, it was called 'operation polo' as Hyderabad state had 17 polo grounds. Hyderabad forces without much resistance were defeated at the outskirts of Hyderabad city on 17 September 1948. The next day, the Prime Minister Jawaharlal Nehru informed the Nizam on telephone that Hyderabad had been declared an ally of Indian union and hence he is appointed as *Rajpramukh* (equivalent to Governor). Further, he was informed that he would be paid ₹50 lakh for his personal maintenance and ₹6 crore for the maintenance of his family. Major General J. N. Chaudhary was appointed as the military Governor on 18 September. In January 1950, M. A. Vellodi, a senior civil servant, was made the Chief Minister of the Hyderabad state. After the election of 1952, the first popular ministry headed by B. Ramakrishna Rao took charge of the state. The police action, Razakar's atrocities and Telangana armed struggle happened simultaneously with different designs. The armed struggle was mainly witnessed in the Telangana region and communal clashes occurred in the Kannada and Marathi-speaking areas of Hyderabad state.

In the state, a class of landed gentry, consisting of Muslim Jagirdars and Hindu Deshmukhs belonging to the Reddy, Velama and Brahmin castes, constituted the support base of the Nizam's rule. Although all sections of the Telangana countryside including peasants, artisan, service castes and the Dalits were mobilized around the issues of *vetti* (bonded labour) and 'land to the tiller' demand, it is sociologically instructive to note that it was the peasant castes of the Kapu-Reddys who dominated the leadership positions in the *dalam*s (armed squads) and panchayats. The redistribution of land belonging to Brahmin-Karanam, Reddy and Velama doras during the struggle was significantly influenced by the caste composition of the Panch Committee[2] assigned with this task. Thus, while the lands of these doras were distributed among the Kapu-Reddy farmers and tenants, the common pastures and wastelands went to the landless Dalits and other lower castes (Srinivasulu, 2002). In this situation, the Communist Party took a decision to take part in the general elections of 1951–1952. Since there was a ban on the party, it contested under the banner of People's Democratic Front, and joined hands with other political forces. Thus, it entered the parliamentary democracy in India. During this interregnum, Army and police returned as much as 1,000,000 acre of land to the doras, which was, captured from the, Deshmukh, Deshpande landlords by the armed Communist squads in the region (Tadakamall et al., 2008). The Congress tried to spread the message of Mahatma Gandhi across the Hyderabad state. Many ashrams were established as the part of this programme. The *Sarvodaya* (welfare of all) philosophy propagator Acharya Vinoba Bahve was invited to a Sarvodaya Sammelan in a village near Hyderabad city in April 1951. Vinoba Bhave realized the importance of land in driving away the peasants and labourers from the path of violence and requested his audience to come forward for *bhoodan* (land gift), and one landlord named Ramachandra Reddy came forward and donated 100 acres to the local Dalits. Later, Vinoba Bhave spread the *bhoodan* movement across the country. T. K. Oommen (1977, p. 169) rightly said, 'the Telangana peasant's struggle provided 'the womb to the non-violent *Bhoodan-Gramdan* movement'.

The region of coastal Andhra was far more developed than the other two regions of Andhra Pradesh, that is, Rayalaseema and Telangana. The reason behind the faster development of the Andhra region in general, and Guntur, Krishna, East and West Godavari districts in particular, were the consequence of construction of many irrigation projects across the Krishna and Godavari rivers in the mid-nineteenth century by the British colonial government. With a view to augmenting its revenue from agriculture, an extensive area was brought under cultivation: this led to the commercialization of agriculture and generation and accumulation of agrarian surplus. The impact of this could be witnessed in the urbanization in this region as centres of commerce and of education besides socio-cultural reform movements. The growth of towns such as Kakinada, Rajahmundry and Guntur in the coastal region has to be seen against this backdrop.

A significant aspect of rural transformation that has occurred since the late-nineteenth century is the differentiation of the peasant society and the emergence of an enterprising agrarian stratagem belonging predominantly to the Kammas, followed by the Reddys and to a lesser extent to the Kapus. The educated élites of these peasant castes were catalytic in the emergence of caste-specific assertive movements against Brahmin domination. They also played a leading role in the *kisan* (farmer) movement and the anti-zamindari struggles by rallying the lower strata of the

---

[2] The Panch Committee was administrative unit in more than 3,000 villages liberated by the armed squads of Communist Party during Telangana armed struggle.

agrarian classes. Because of these struggles, abolition of the zamindari system and the tenancy reforms were enacted in the early years of the post-colonial era; hence, the farmers and tenants gained access to most of the fertile lands.

What is sociologically significant about this trajectory of change, and of immediate relevance to our analysis, is the polarization of this class along the caste lines across mass organizations, political parties or factions therein. While the Reddys joined the ranks of the Congress Party and waged struggles against Brahmin leadership, the Kammas gravitated to the Communist Party of India and rose to positions of leadership (Srinivasulu, 2002, p. 5). The Telugu people in the Madras presidency were not only dominated by the Tamils but also humiliated by them. This situation provoked the Telugus to launch a Telugu identity based movement in the Madras presidency. They started demanding a separate province for the Telugu-speaking areas. The demand for a separate Andhra was not conceded easily, but due to a protracted struggle waged by the Telugus, and, in this regard, the contribution of Gandhian Potti Sri Ramulu's sacrifice had a special mention in the history of Andhra. He started a fast unto death on 19 October 1952 demanding carving out the Telugu-speaking areas in to a separate Andhra state from the Madras state.

Ultimately, Andhra state was materialized on 1 October 1953 without the city of Madras. Meanwhile, there was a demand for Vishalandhra, a metamorphosed state of Andhra Pradesh based on Telugu language. Even though the Telugu of Telangana was a language of the productive masses intermixed with the Urdu, the Telugu of Andhra was the language of Andhramu or Andhra bhasha, a Sanskritized language. During nationalist movement, the dominant castes of coastal Andhra including the Brahmins were drawn into the framework of Andhra bhasha. It was also being the nascent bourgeoisie, who visualized Andhra desam but not Telugu desam in its own image. In Ilaiah's words:

> The bourgeoisie elite formation around Andhra Bhasha from Brahmin, Reddy, Kamma and Raju castes in coastal districts was very powerful when compared to the Brahmin, Reddy and Velama leadership in Telangana, as it was still feudal and had not acquired any bourgeoisie characteristic (1997, p. 5).

After formation of Andhra state in October 1953, the demand for the creation of other linguistic states gained momentum. As a result, on 22 December 1953, the Government of India appointed the States Reorganization Commission (SRC) under the chairmanship of Sayed Fazl Ali to examine 'objectively and dispassionately' the whole question of the re-organization of the states of the Indian union. The Commission was of the view that language criteria only would not fulfil the aspirations of the people. Ambedkar also endorsed it and favoured smaller states. In his opinion, smaller states facilitate a greater voice to the various minority groups. He looked at the issue from the eyes of the depressed classes and warned that formation of linguistic provinces meant 'handing over of Swaraj to a communal majority' (Ambedkar, 1986). In his view, linguism is another name for communalism. While leaders from Andhra state were united in their call for a larger unified state, the Telangana leadership was for retaining its separate entity. Yet the state of Andhra Pradesh came into being through the unification of both these states, following gentlemen's agreement in 1956, despite the warning by the states Reorganization Commission against merger of Telangana with Andhra.

Since the formation of AP, two violent agitations namely Jai Telangana movement in 1969 and a counter Jai Andhra movement in 1972 rocked the state. The separate Telangana movement resurfaced during late 1990s and continued until the achievement of separate Telangana state in 2014. Apart from the inter-regional disparities, social and economic inequalities among different social groups led to the political dominance of region and castes in the state. Since formation of state, political leaders from Rayalaseema and coastal

Andhra regions have dominated politics. Between 1956 and 2010, both Rayalaseema and coastal Andhra together held the chief minister position for 42 years (former for 23.9 years and later for 18.11 years) whereas Telangana for 10.5 years, respectively, till 2010 (Government of India, 2010, p. 407). After a protracted struggle, the state of Telangana was created as the 29th state in the Indian union as per the Andhra Pradesh Reorganization Act, 2014 (No. 6 of 2014) of Parliament, which received the assent of the President of India on the 1 March 2014 and came into existence with effect from 2 June 2014. The Act was amended and it was called the Andhra Pradesh Reorganization (Amendment) Act, 2014 (No. 19 of 2014), transferring certain mandalas and villages (327) of Khammam district to residual Andhra Pradesh, enforcing this amendment with effect from 29 May 2014.

UNDERSTANDING ELECTORAL POLITICS IN ERSTWHILE ANDHRA PRADESH: CASTE AND CLASS COMPOSITION

Electoral process and political parties in a democracy have greater significance as they provide the dynamism for political mechanism; they act as the indicators of public opinion, and ultimately help in reviving state legitimacy. James Manor observed in 1990 that even after nine general elections, most of Indians are not liberal in any meaningful sense because Indian society is a society of castes, which predominantly emphasizes on ascription, hierarchy and compartmentalization. He says these 'predominant features, cannot directly generate the kind of liberal outlook that is usually associated with the working of an electoral system based on universal suffrage' (2016, p. 23). The Congress party in the state has always been under the leadership of the elite Reddy community and they have a complete dominance over it. N. Sanjeeva Reddy (1956–1960 and 1962–1964),

K. Brahmananda Reddy (1964–1971) and Y. S. Rajasekhara Reddy (2004–2009) who ruled the state were the most powerful chief ministers from the party. The composition of the State Assembly between 1957 and 2014 shows that the Reddys occupied the majority of the ministerial post for 248 times out of the total 888 times (comprising 28%) were the single largest group, whilst their share in the population is approximately 6 per cent. The Kammas, who occupied 116 Ministerial posts (13%), followed the Reddys and their population is just 4 per cent. Post-independence political change favoured the agrarian castes by replacing earlier Brahmin political domination and Brahmin's political decline at the state level is visible. After 1956, the reins of power changed completely and came under the Reddys' control. The OBCs constituted 50 per cent of the population but had approximate 13 per cent presence in the state assembly. There is a constitutional safeguard for the SCs and STs in the form of reservations that is why their representation has not been denied.

The governments and politics in Telugu states are dominated by the dominant castes like Reddys, Kammas and Velamas. For instance, from the inception of Andhra Pradesh state to 2018, there have been 888 ministerial posts. Out of these post Raddys occupied 248 (28%) post, Kammas 116 (13%), Velamas 45 posts (5%), Kapus 62 (7%), SCs 111 (12.5%) and STs 22 (2.48%). As of now, there is no ST chief minister in these two Telugu states. Reddys occupied the chief minister post for 14 times, Kammas 7 times, Velamas 3 times and SC, Brahman and Vysyas each one time as of now (Booker, 2018).

All mainstream political parties are under control of dominant castes, especially parties like Indian National Congress (INC) and Telugu Desham Party (TDP) (Table 9.5). A Dalit Congress leader from coastal Andhra Damodaram Sanjeevaiah was made Chief Minister of the state for a brief period between 1960 and 1962. He was the first Dalit chief minister anywhere in India. This opportunity came to Sanjeevaiah as an interim arrangement because of differences among Reddy

Table 9.5   Caste Composition of Andhra Pradesh Assembly, 2009

Party	OCs	BCs	SCs	STs	Minorities
INC	77	33	33	11	3
TDP	54	17	13	6	1
PRP	17	1		—	—
TRS	5	3	2	—	—
CPM	1	—		—	—
CPI	2	—	1	1	—
BJP	1	1		—	—
LSP	1	—		—	—
AIMIM	—	—	—	—	7
Others	1	2			—
Total	159	57	49	18	11

Source: Surya. (2009, June 3). Telugu Daily.

factions within the Congress party. When the factional feud was settled, he had to give up the post. Traditionally, the Reddy, Kamma and Kapu castes, which constituted the rich peasantry, were the main beneficiaries of the agrarian reforms, thus constituted the core support base of the Congress party in the countryside (Srinivasulu, 2002). This trend is empirically clear if one looks at the winning candidates for 2009 Lok Sabha and assembly elections in the state (Table 9.6)

The domination of agrarian castes at the district level as base for the state-level politics can be inferred from the available data (Tables 9.7 and 9.8). Their representation as members of legislative bodies and various ministries has been overwhelmed. The representation of BCs has been way below their percentage in the total population. The situation of SCs and STs representation is somewhat better because of constitutional mandate in the form of reservations.

Table 9.8 shows that between 1956 and 2008, 12 assembly elections were held in Andhra Pradesh and 27 times chief ministers have taken oath and constituted 38 ministries during the same time. Barring one chief minister from SC community, who served for two years, there were no chief ministers from the lower castes of the state. At the same time, as many as 396 people have served as the

ministers in the state, among them majority were the dominant caste people 275 (70%), especially Reddys and kammas are the dominant social group in the competition, which included 180, constituting 46 per cent.

Coming to the representation of lower castes in the ministries, so far 121 people have become ministers, which included 45 OBCs (11%), 42 SCs (10%), 10 STs (2.5%) and 24 minorities (6%) and thereby, indicating their under-representation. If one looks at the representation in the central ministry from the state, the available statistics indicate the same trend. In the past 52 years, 52 MP from the state were inducted in the central cabinet. Among them 37 (67%) are from dominant castes. In 2004 elections, 48 per cent BCs were supposed to get 152 seats in the assembly but they have only 49 members of legislative assembly (MLAs). Out of 93 castes among BCs, only 16 castes got the representation in the Assembly. As per the proportion of population, Brahmins supposed to get four MLA seats, but got three and Vaisyas got three as they were supposed to get six MLAs. Muslims supposed to get 27 seats but 11 were elected to the Assembly. The 2004 Assembly did not have even one BC MLA from Nellor, Chittoor, Kadapa, Karnool and Medak. There was not even nomination from Nellor in 2004 elections. These statistics show that half of the districts do not have

Table 9.6 Caste-wise Winning Candidates for 2009 Lok Sabha and Assembly in Andhra Pradesh

Caste	Lok Sabha				Assembly				
	Congress	TDP	Others	Total	Congress	TDP	PRP	Others	Total
01: Brahmin	1	-	-	1	3	1	-	-	4
05: Vaisya, Komati		-	-	-	3	2	2	-	7
Upper *Castes*	1	-	-	1	6	3	2	-	11
11: Reddy	9	1	-	10	54	20	4	7	85
12: Kamma	4	1	-	5	4	21	1	1 (LSP)	27
16: Raju	1	-	-	1	4	3	-	-	7
17: Velama	-	-	1 (TRS)	1	2	5	-	4	7
18: Kapu, Balija, Telaga, Ontari	2	-	-	2	7	2	10	-	19
Peasant communities	16	2	1	19	71	51	15	12	149
21: Yadava, Golla, Kuruma	1	-	-	1	4	3	-	-	7
22: Gowda, Setti Balija, Ediga	2	1	-	3	6	3	-	1 (Ind)	10
23: Munnuru Kapu	-	-	-	-	3	3	-	3	9
24: Mudiraj, Mutraju	-	-	-	-	1	1	-	1 (TRS)	3
25: Kalinga	1	-	-	1	2	1	-	-	3
26: Thurpu Kapu	1	-	-	1	5	-	-	-	5
27: Koppulu/Polinati Velama	1	-	-	1	4	2	-	-	6
30: Padmasali	-	1	-	1	1	3	1	-	5
34: Bondili	-	-	1 (TRS)	1	-	-	-	-	-
40: Pallekari, Besta, Gangaputra	-	-	-		3	-	-	-	3
41: Rajaka, Chakali	-	-	-	-	1	-	-	-	1
44: Dudekula, Noor Basha	-	-	-	-	1	-	-	-	1
Other OBCs	1	-		1	1	2	-	-	3
Total OBCs	7	2	1	10	32	18	1	5	56
50: Madiga,	3	-	-	3	16	6	-	2	24
53: Mala,	4	-	-	4	16	6	-	1 (TRS)	23
59: Other SCs		-	-			1	-	-	-
Total Scheduled Castes (SC):	8	-	-	7	32	13	-	3	48
60: Lambadi, Sugali	1	1	-	2	2	2	-	1 (CPI)	5
62: Gond, Gadaba, Koya	-	-	-	-	6	4	-	-	10
63: Konda Dora, Konda Reddi	1	-	-	1	2	-	-	-	2
67: Jatapu	-	-	-	-	2	-	-	-	2
Total Scheduled Tribes (ST)	2	1	-	3	12	6	-	1	19
Muslims	-	-	1 (MIM)	1	2	1	-	7 (MIM)	10
Christians	-	-	-	-	1	-	-		1
Total	33	6	3	42	156	92	18	28	294

Source: Surya. (2009, May 17). Telugu Daily.

AIMIM, All India Majlis-e-Ittehad-ul-Muslimmen; CPI, Communist Party of India; INC, Indian National Congress; LSP, Lok Satta Party; PRP, Praja Rajyam Party; TDP, Telugu Desham Party; TRS, Telangana Rashtra Samiti.

representation from BCs. The TDP contested in 173 seats and gave 43 tickets to BCs and Congress contested in 185 seats and allocated 33 seats to BCs. Even in 1999 election, there was no BC representation from five districts. In 1994 election, no MLA from eight districts

Table 9.7   Seats Won by Different Castes in Andhra Pradesh Assembly Elections, 1983–2004 (District-wise)

Name of District	Upper Castes	BCs	SCs/STs	Others	Total
Srikakulam	17	37	18	0	72
Vijayanagaram	14	39	19	0	72
Vishakhapatnam	29	31	18	0	78
East Godavari	79	18	24	5	126
West Godavari	77	1	18	0	102
Krishna	82	5	12	3	102
Guntur	91	11	6	6	114
Prakasham	69	3	6	0	78
Nellore	54	0	12	0	66
Chittore	71	1	18	0	90
Kadapa	59	1	6	0	66
Anantapur	52	17	12	3	84
Kurnool	47	4	12	15	84
Mahbubnagar	49	14	12	4	78
Ranagareddy	16	7	12	1	36
Hyderabad	26	20	6	26	78
Medak	42	3	12	2	59
Nizamabad	30	13	6	50	54
Adilabad	28	2	24	0	54
Karimnagar	54	2	12	0	78
Warangal	40	16	22	0	78
Khammam	24	2	24	4	54
Nalgonda	50	4	18	0	72
Total	1100	262	330	73	1764

Source: Eenadu. (2007, October). *Telugu Daily*.

and in 1989 nobody from eight districts and in 1985, six districts even did not have representation from BCs. In last six Assembly elections, no BC represented from Nellore district.

STS IN ELECTORAL POLITICS: THE LEGISLATIVE ASSEMBLY

In Andhra Pradesh, after emerging as a separate state from Madras state, the first legislative assembly election was held in 1955. In this election, there were no SC- and ST-reserved constituencies. Hence, one would observe that there was no representation of these communities in the assembly. However, after formation Andhra Pradesh state with merger of Telugu speaking region of Hyderabad state, that is, Telangana region with Andhra state in 1956, the first legislative assembly election took place in 1957 in Telangana region only. In the election, two seats were reserved for STs, these were Asifabad and Yellandu. The SC/ST constituencies were double-member constituencies.[3] Mr. Kashi Ram and Dodda Narsaiah were elected from the Asifabad Yellandu constituencies, respectively. In 1962,

---

[3] Double-member constituencies are those constituencies where two members would bet elected from a constituency one from SC-ST category and another one from general category. It was abolished through an act of

Table 9.8 Caste-wise Representation in the Ministries of Andhra Pradesh Governments (1956–2008)

Caste	Ministers	Twice in Office	Once in Office	3–8 Times in Office
Dominant Castes				
Reddy	102	31	27	44
Kamma	78	11	29	38
Brahmin	29	9	8	12
Kaapu	23	4	9	10
Velama	20	4	6	10
Kshatriya	19	6	4	9
Vysya	4	4	-	-
Total	275	69	83	123
Minorities				
Christians	3	-	1	2
Muslims	21	3	6	12
OBCs	45	6	7	32
SCs	42	9	12	21
STs	10	2	4	4
Total	121	20	30	71
Grand total	396	89	113	194

Source: Eenadu. (2008, March 26). *Telugu Daily.*

unlike earlier elections, election to the legislative assembly took place in united Andhra Pradesh as a single unit. There were 300 seats in the assembly, out of which 11 seats, that is, 3.66 per cent seats were reserved for STs (Table 9.9).

Table 9.9 indicates that between 1955 and 2009 there were 13 general elections that took place to the Andhra Pradesh legislative assembly and a total 3,478 MLAs were elected during this time. Out of these many seats, a total 160 MLAs were elected from tribal communities. It amounts to 4.39 per cent, which is way behind the total ST population of 6.59 per cent. This includes reserved seats and ST candidates who have been elected from the unreserved constituencies. For instance, Mr D. Redya Naik was elected from Dornakal general constituency in Warangal district in 1999 and 2004 elections. However, this constituency was reserved for STs from 2009

general election. This under representation of STs in legislative assembly could be due to the limited number of STs that were included in the list until 1976. In 1976, this position of STs was rationalized with the enforcement of the Constitution Order Scheduled Castes and Scheduled Tribes (Amendment) Act, 1976 and the Removal of Area Restrictions (Amendment) Act, 1976. These acts removed area restrictions on the recognition of STs, making ST list applicable to entire state rather than blocks and districts within states, as was the case earlier. This led to a substantial increase in the ST population as recorded in the census.

The electoral politics in the state is an upper caste and male dominated domain. From 1955 to 2009, only 172 times or 4.94 per cent women from all the categories have been elected to the Legislative Assembly. It is commonly known fact that women constitute

Parliament known as the Two-Member Constituencies (Abolition) Act 1961. This act created single member-member constituency in the place of double-member constituencies.

Table 9.9   Position of ST Members of Legislative Assembly in Andhra Pradesh (1955–2009)

Sl. No	Year	No of Seats in the Assembly	Seats Breakup			ST Candidates				Party of the Elected ST Candidates	Total Women (All Categories)		Elected Party	
			General	SCs	STs	Contested		Elected			Contested	Elected	Seats	Percentage
						Male	Female	Male	Female					
1	1955ª	167	167	0	0	0	0	0	0	0	-	-	INC-119	39.35%
2	1957ᵇ	85	65	18	2	4	0	2	0	INC-2	17	7	INC-68	47.38%
3	1962ᶜ	300	246	43	11	49	0	11	0	INC-10 CPI-1	24	10	INC-177	47.25%
4	1967	287	236	40	11	40	0	11	0	INC-9 SWA-1 IND-1	21	11	INC-165	45.42%
5	1972	287	236	40	11	32	1	11	0	INC-9 IND-2	49	0	INC-219	52.29%
6	1978	294	240	39	15	62	1	15	0	INC(I)-6 INC-3 JNP-3 CPI-1 CPM-1 IND-1	54	10	INC(I)-175	39.25%
7	1983%	294	240	39	15	77	4	15	0	IND (TDP)-8 INC-5 CPI-1 CPM-1	66	11	IND (TDP)-220	56.21%
8	1985	294	240	39	15	60	4	15	0	TDP-8 INC-3 IND-2 CPI-1 CPM-1	66	10	TDP-202	46.21%
9	1989	294	240	39	15	60	4	15	0	TDP-4 INC-7 CPM-1 CPI-2 IND-1	70	17	INC-181	47.09%
10	1994	294	240	39	15	101	9	15	0	TDP-10 INC-0 CPM-1 CPI-4	127	8	TDP-216	44.14%
11	1999	294	240	39	15	66	9	14	2	TDP-10 INC-4 CPM-1 IND-1	157	28	TDP-180	43.87%
12	2004	294	240	39	15	64	8	15	1	TDP-2 INC-4 CPM-2 CPI-2 BSP-1 TRS-2 IND-1	161	26	INC-185	38.56%
13	2009	294	226	48	20	186	30	14	6	INC-13 TDP-6 CPI-1	300	34	INC-156	36.55%

Sl. No	Year	No of Seats in the Assembly	Seats Breakup			ST Candidates				Party of the Elected ST Candidates	Total Women (All Categories)		Elected Party Seats	Percentage
			General	SCs	STs	Contested		Elected			Contested	Elected		
						Male	Female	Male	Female					
Total		3478	2856	462	160	801	70	153	9	--	1112	172	--	--

Source: Compiled from statistical report on general election of various years to the legislative assembly of Andhra Pradesh, Election Commission of India, New Delhi.

BSP, Bahujan Samaj Party; CPI, Communist Party of India; CPM-Communist Party Of India (Marxist); INC, Indian National Congress; INC(I), Indian National Congress (I); IND, Independent; JNP, Janata Party; JS, Jan Sangh; PDF, Peoples Democratic Front; PP, Praja Party; PSP, Praja Socialist Party; REP, Republican: SCF, All India Scheduled Caste Federation; SWA, Swatantra, SOC, Socialist; TDP, Telugu Desham Party; TRS, Telangana Rashra Samiti.

[a]This Election was held in Andhra state prior to formation of Andhra Pradesh.

[b]1957 Election was held in Telangana region after merger with Andhra state in 1956 detaching the Kannada and Marathi speaking districts in the erstwhile Hyderabad. The SC/ST constituencies were double-member constituencies.

[c]This was the first election that was held in the unified Andhra Pradesh state.

% in this election, matinee idol, NT Ramarao established the Telugu Desham party, and in the election data, it has been indicated as independent candidates.

half of the population, but their representation in decision-making bodies is minimal. The position of ST women in total women legislators in these years is negligible. They have been elected from only reserved constituencies for nine times. It makes their representation to 0.25 per cent of the total women legislature. If their position is compared with the male MLAs from the tribal communities, their share is only 5.62 per cent or nine seats. Whereas, male ST legislators have represented 153 times, which constitutes to 95 per cent. For the first time, in 1971, one woman candidate contested, but until 1999, they could not succeed. In 1999 general election, Hymavathi Devi Sobha from Srungavarapukota and Manikumari Matyarasa from Paderu constituency were elected on TDP tickets.

Welcoming development that is taking place is that, gradually there is an increased participation of women in electoral politics. STs have been elected from the tickets of mainstream political parties like INC, Communist Parties, TDP and quite a few times as independent candidates. If one looks at the parties they represented, INC stands as the pioneer, where 39 per cent of ST MLSs have been elected from the Congress. The Congress

dominated the state of Andhra Pradesh under leadership of Reddys until 1983, then the cine-start NT Rama Rao established TDP and came to power in no time by bringing the Kamma, an agriculturally rich and entrepreneur community, into political lime light. Since then the politics in the state was alternating between these political parties. It was broken down only in 2014 after formation of Telangana, when Velama community through Telangana Rashtra Samiti (TRS) under the leadership of K. Chandrasekhar Rao assumed power as Chief Minister of separate Telangana state.

The legislative assembly elections were held concurrently with parliamentary election in May 2014 in the united Andhra Pradesh. After the emergence of Telangana as a separate state in 2014, the political scenario was dominated by the TRS. In 2014 election, the TRS had won the majority seats and formed the government in newly created state (see table 9.10). Thus, a new political party and a new dominant caste captured the power in the state. The first tenure of the TRS government had a distinction of having a cabinet without women ministers. There was a demand from STs to enhance the reservation from 6 per cent to 9.08 per cent in proportion to their

Table 9.10 Position of ST Members of Legislative Assembly after Formation of Telangana

Sl. No	Year	No of Seats in the Assembly	Seats breakup			ST Candidates					Total Women (All Categories)		Elected Party	
			General	SC	ST	Contested		Elected		Party of the Elected ST Candidates	Contested	Elected	Seats	Percentage
						Male	Female	Male	Female					
1	2014*	294	226	48	20	160	31	TS-10+ AP-3 Total-14	TS-2 + AP-4 Total -6	TS- TRS-5 INC-2 CPI-1 CPM-1 YSRCP-3 AP YSRCP-6 TDP-1	317	27	TRS- 63	13.68% (Vote % In Seats % Contested- 34.15)
2	2018	119	88	19	12	125	15	9	3	TRS-5 INC-5 TDP-1 IND-1	140	6	TRS-88	46.87%
Total		413	314	67	32	285	46	23	9	----	457	33	----	----

Source: Compiled from statistical reports on general election of various years to the Legislative Assembly of Andhra Pradesh, Election Commission of India, New Delhi.

Note: Elections took place on 30 April and 7 May 2014. This was the last elections that took place in united Andhra Pradesh.

Table 9.11 Position of ST Members of Legislative Assembly in Andhra Pradesh after Bifurcation

Sl. No	Year	Seats Breakup				ST Candidates					Total Women (All Categories)		Elected Party	
		No of Seats in the Assembly	General	SC	ST	Contested		Elected		Party of the Elected ST Candidates	Contested	Elected	Seats	Percentage
						Male	Female	Male	Female					
1	2014	294	227	48	19	160	31	TS-10+ AP-3 Total-14	TS-2 + AP-4 Total -6	TS- TRS-5 INC-2 CPI-1 CPM-1 YSRCP-3 AP YSRCP-6 TDP-1	317	27	TDP-117	32.53%
2	2019	175	139	29	7	53	19	3	4	YSRCP--7	175	14	YSRCP-151	49.95%
Total		469	366	77	26	213	50	17	10	----	492	41	-----	-----

Source: Compiled from statistical reports on general election of various years to the legislative assembly of Andhra Pradesh, Election Commission of India, New Delhi.

population. However, that demand is yet to be conceded. The TRS government went for election six months prior to completing its tenure, thus necessitated elections in December 2018. The incumbent TRS retained the power. In this election, 12 seats (10%) were reserved for STs, out of which 3 women MLAs (25%) within the ST-reserved constituencies were elected. However, their per cent in total legislatures is just 2 per cent.

The 2019 Assembly Election was held concurrently along with parliamentary election. TDP lost the election to Jaganmohan Reddy's Yuvajana Sramika Rythu Congress party (YSRCP). Out of 175 seats, 7 (4%) seats are reserved for STs, where 4 women candidates contested successfully. It amounts to 2.28 per cent and within the successful ST candidates to 57 per cent (Table 9.11). It seems, for the first time, there are more than half women MLAs within ST category. Whereas total 14 women candidates were elected from across the categories, which constitutes 8 per cent of the total elected MLAs in the state. The state politics in both the Telugu states are under the control of three principle dominant castes, namely, Reddys, Kammas and Velamas. There is hardly any alternate successful politics visible in the state.

STS AND ELECTORAL POLITICS: THE LOK SABHA

The Lok Sabha election in 1951 was held in Hyderabad state, since Andhra was part of Madras state until 1953. In the 1951 election, no seat was reserved for STs; therefore, there was no representation of the community in Lok Sabha from Hyderabad state. After formation of Andhra Pradesh also, in 1957, there was no seat reserved for STs. For the first time, three seats were reserved for STs in 1962 Lok Sabha election. In the election, Matcharasa Matcharaju from Narsipatnam, Datla Satyanarayana Raju from Rajahmundry and

Biddika Satyanarayana from Parvathipuram were elected on INC tickets. All the candidates were from north coastal districts of Andhra Pradesh. There was not even a single seat reserved for STs in Telangana region. By the 1967 election, ST-reserved seats were reduced to two from earlier three seats (Table 9.12). One seat each was distributed between coastal Andhra and Telangana region. V. N. Rao was elected from Parvathipuram constituency on Swatantra Party ticket and B. K Radhabai Anand Rao was elected from Bhadrachalam constituency on INC ticket.

As of 2009, a total 609 members of Parliament (MPs) have been elected to Lok Sabha from erstwhile Andhra Pradesh. Out of which 502 members, that is, 82 per cent, have been elected from the general category. STs have been represented through the reserved constituencies for 28 times, that is, only 4.59 per cent. Out of which men have represented 24 times, that is, 3.94 per cent and women seven times, that is, mere 1.1 per cent. Women in general from all categories have represented 40 times, that is, 6.56 per cent within all women category ST women have represented a respectable seven times, that is, 17.5 per cent. Within the male dominated electoral politics one ST women politician stands exceptional, her name is B. K Radhabai Anand Rao. She was elected for four consecutive terms from Bhadrachalam-reserved constituency during 1967, 1971, 1977 and 1980 elections. Very little is known about her personal life and contribution to the public life. It is interesting to note here is that, until 1999, no ST women could become MLA, in that year for the first time two ST women legislators were elected. However, the case of Radhabai stands exceptional; as she became MP, 32 years prior to these two women were elected. Given the conservative and patriarchal spaces of electoral politics, Radhabai's presence in politics as MP for four times itself was a great achievement. There is a need to do research and bring out her biographical story to the larger population at large.

Table 9.12 Position of ST Members of Parliament in Andhra Pradesh (1951–2009)

SL. No	Year	No of Parliament Seats in the State	Seats Breakup			ST Candidates				Party of the Elected ST Candidates	Total Women (All Categories in Andhra Pradesh)		Elected Party in the Lok Sabha	
			General	SC	ST	Contested		Elected			Contested	Elected	Seats	Percentage
						Male	Female	Male	Female					
1	1951	21	21	4ª	0	0	0	0	0	0	0	0	INC-364	44.99%
2	1957	43	43	0	0	3	0	3	0	INC-3	4	3	INC-371	47.78%
3	1962	43	34	6	3	9	0	3	0	INC-3	7	4	INC-361	44.72%
4	1967	41	33	6	2	6	1	1	1	INC-1 SWA-1	4	3	INC-283	40.78%
5	1971	41	33	6	2	8	1	1	1	INC-2	1	1	INC- 352	43.68%
6	1977	42	34	6	2	6	2	1	1	INC-2	4	1	BLD- 295	41.32%
7	1980	42	34	6	2	7	2	1	1	INC(U)-1 INC(I)-1	12	3	INC(I)-353	42.69%
8	1984	42	34	6	2	7	1	2	0	ICS-1 CPI-1	7	2	INC-404	49.10%
9	1989	42	34	6	2	7	1	1	1	INC-2	6	4	National Front (Coalition) JD-143 BJP-85 CPM-33 CPI-12 TDP-2	17.79% 11.36% 6.55% 2.57% 3.29%
10	1991	42	34	6	2	10	3	1	1	INC-2	26	2	INC-232 CPM-35 CPI-14	36.26% 6.16% 2.49%
11	1996	42	34	6	2	13	3	2	0	INC-1 CPI-1	90	3	United Front a Non-Congress and Non-BJP Govt	

(Continued)

Table 9.12 (Continued)

Sl. No	Year	No of Parliament Seats in the State	Seats Breakup			ST Candidates				Party of the Elected ST Candidates	Total Women (All Categories in Andhra Pradesh)		Elected Party in the Lok Sabha	
			General	SC	ST	Contested		Elected			Contested	Elected	Seats	Percentage
						Male	Female	Male	Female					
12	1998	42	34	6	2	10	1	2	0	TDP-1 CPI-1	16	2	BJP-182 (coalition govt)	25.59%
12	1999	42	34	6	2	8	2	1	1	TDP-2	18	4	National Democratic Alliance BJP-182 TDP-29	23.75% 3.65%
13	2004	42	34	6	2	8	1	2	0	INC-1 CPM-1	21	3	United Progressive Alliance-I (UPA-I) INC-145 CPI-10 CPM-43	26.53% 1.41% 5.66%
14	2009	42	32	7	3	31	1	3	0	INC-2 TDP-1	39	5	United Progressive Alliance-II (UPA-II)	---
Total		609	502	83	28	133	19	24	7	---	255	40	---	---

Source: Compiled from statistical reports on general elections to the Lok Sabha, various years, Election Commission of India, New Delhi.

[a]Double-member constituencies

Table 9.13 Position of ST Members of Parliament in Telangana (2014–2019)

Sl. No	Year	No. of Parliament Seats in the State	Seats Breakup			ST Candidates				Party of the Elected ST Candidates	Total Women (All Categories)		Elected Party in the Lok Sabha	
			General	SC	ST	Contested		Elected			Contested	Elected	Seats	Percentage
						Male	Female	Male	Female					
1	2014	TS-17 AP-25	32	7	3	29	7	2	1	TRS-2 YSRCP-1	43	3	BJP-282	31.34
2	2019	TS-17	12	3	2	20	6	1	1	BJP-1 TRS-1	25	1	BJP-303	37.76
Total		59	44	10	5	49	13	3	2	--------	68	4	------	-------

Source: Compiled from statistical reports on general elections to the Lok Sabha, various years, Election Commission of India, New Delhi.

TRS, Teangana Rashtra Samiti; YSRCP, Yuvajana Shramika Raithu Congress Party.

Note: Elections took place on 30 April and 7 May 2014. This was the last elections that took place in united Andhra Pradesh.

Elections to both Legislative Assembly and Parliament were conducted in May 2014 concurrently before bifurcation of Andhra Pradesh in June 2014. As mentioned earlier, 28 times ST candidates could become MP in undivided Andhra Pradesh. After formation of Telangana, the state was left with 17 MP seats along with two ST-reserved seats amounting to 11 per cent (Table 9.13). In 2019 election, Maloth Kavitha was elected from Mahabubabad constituency on TRS ticket. Soyam Bapu Rao was elected from Adilabad constituency on Bharatiya Janata Party ticket.

The residual Andhra Pradesh has 25 Lok Sabha seats out of which only one seat is reserved for STs, it is 4 per cent of the total

MP seats (Table 9.14). In 2019, elections were held for both Legislative Assembly and Parliament concurrently. Total four women candidates, that is, 16 per cent were elected to the Lok Sabha. From the only ST-reserved constituency Araku, Goddeti Madhavi was elected to the Parliament on YSRCP ticket. It is to be noted that no ST person has ever elected from general constituency in the state since 1950s. It indicates that without reservation for the marginalized communities like STs, it is impossible for them to become people's representatives. The Constitution of India provides reservations for STs. The STs have been representing in legislative bodies almost proportion to their population. However, they

Table 9.14 Position of ST Members of Parliament in Andhra Pradesh (2014–2019)

Sl. No	Year	No of Parliament Seats in the State	Seats Breakup			ST Candidates				Party of the Elected ST Candidates	Total Women (All Categories in Andhra Pradesh)		Elected Party in the Lok Sabha	
			General	SC	ST	Contested		Elected			Contested	Elected	Seats	Percentage
						Male	Female	Male	Female					
1	2014	AP-25 TS-17	32	7	3	29	9	2	1	TRS-2 YSRCP-1	43	3	BJP-282	31.34
2	2019	25	20	4	1	0	3	0	1	YSRCP-1	27	4	BJP-303	37.76
Total		67	52	11	4	29	12	2	2	-------	70	7	-----	-----

Source: Compiled from statistical report on general elections to the Lok Sabha, various years, Election Commission of India, New Delhi.

are not independent to articulate the issues of the community that they represent due to structural reasons of Indian political system. The electoral politics in India are party centric in the sense the representatives from reserved categories are not allowed to articulate the interests of the community that they represent in the name of discipline in the party. It is also individual leader-centric—it means loyalty to the leader in the party plays an important role in securing a seat from the party. Politics at the national level is dominated by the upper varnas of the society, whereas the parties at the state level are in the hands of the local dominant castes. This situation hardly enables tribals to articulate within the system of electoral politics. It is to be noted that tribal communities have historically a robust articulation of their issues outside of the electoral politics through various protest movements. However, electoral politics as a part of formal democratic process at the best remains as a co-optive strategy to accommodate the tribal leaders into the mainstream political system. Another basic problem with Indian electoral system is that it is a first past the post system that allows certain dominant groups to capture excessive political space leaving little or no space for marginalized communities. One of the solutions for providing just and autonomous political space for the marginalized communities is to converting Indian electoral system in to proportional representative system. Otherwise, current system preserves the status quo.

CONCLUSION

The history of electoral politics in erstwhile Andhra Pradesh is the story of domination of two dominant castes ruling the state most of the times alternatively. Even though Telangana and Andhra Pradesh states have witnessed vibrant tribal movements from colonial times to until recent period, and since then they have

questioned the intervention of modern state's expansionist logic through governmentality and influx of non-tribals in their areas, which alienated them from their resources. However, when it comes to the electoral politics, the tribals are not articulative enough and they have failed to raise their autonomous voices. While being elected to State Assemblies and Parliament, they have always become dependent on the patronage of dominant political parties in the state. The tribal electoral politics in Telangana and Andhra Pradesh is not beyond the logic of client and patron relationship. This situation prevents tribal leaders to raise their autonomous voices on behalf of their own community. The electoral politics operates in the case of tribals in assimilation mode only.

REFERENCES

Ambedkar, B. R. (1986). *Writings and speeches: Thoughts on linguistic states* (part-III, Vol-1). Bombay: Education Department, Government of Maharashtra.

Booker, K. (2018). *Rajyadhikaram* (Political Power). Hyderabad: Manavata Prachuranalu.

Deogaonkar, S. G. (1994). *Tribal administration and development*. New Delhi: Concept Publishing Company.

Government of Andhra Pradesh. (2008). *Basic statistics on scheduled tribes in Andhra Pradesh*. Hyderabad: Tribal Cultural Research and Training Institute.

Government of India. (1951, 1957, 1962, 1967, 1971, 1977, 1980, 1984, 1989, 1991, 1996, 1998, 1999, 2004, 2009, 2014, 2019). *Statistical report on general Elections to the Lok Sabha*. New Delhi: Election Commission of India.

Government of India. (1955, 1957, 1962, 1967, 1972, 1978, 1983, 1985, 1989, 1994, 1999, 2004, 2009, 2014, 2018, 2019). *Statistical report on general elections to the legislative assembly of Andhra Pradesh and Telangana*. New Delhi: Election Commission of India.

Government of India. (2010). *Report of the committee for consultations on the situation in Andhra Pradesh* (Chairperson: Justice B. N. Srikrishna). New Delhi: Ministry of Home Affairs.

Government of India. (2013). *Statistical profile of sched-uled tribes in India*. New Delhi: Ministry of Tribal Affairs Statistics Division.

Government of India. (2014). *Report of the high level committee on socio-economic, health and educational status of tribal communities of India*. New Delhi: Ministry of Tribal Affairs.

Government of India. (2018). *Annual report 2017–18*. New Delhi: Ministry of Tribal Affairs.

Government of Telangana. (2017). *Statistical year Book 2017*. Hyderabad: Directorate of Economics and Statistics.

Government of Telangana. (2018). *Outcome of budget-2018–19*. Hyderabad: Department of Tribal Welfare.

Government of Telangana (a). Primitive tribal groups. Tribal Welfare Department. Retrieved from http://twd.telangana.gov.in/tribal-profile/.

Government of Telangana (b). Tribal profile of Telangana. Tribal Welfare Department. Retrieved from http://twd.telangana.gov.in/tribal-profile/.

Ilaiah, K. (1997). Vishalandhra: A Brahmanical (communist) conspiracy. In S. Simhadri, & P. L. Vishweshwara Rao (Eds.), *Telangana: Dimensions of Underdevelopment*. Hyderabad: Centre for Telangana Studies.

Oommen, T. K. (1977). Sociological issues in the analysis of social movements in independent India. *Sociological Bulletin*, *26*(1), 14–37.

Rai, R. (2006). *Globalisation of human rights*. New Delhi: Authors Press.

Rao, K. R. (1984). Peasant movement in Telangana. In M. S. A. Rao (Eds.), *Social Movements in India* (pp. 149–168). New Delhi: Manohar Publications.

Rao, P. T., Reddy, M. G., & Chathukulam, J. (2012). *Implementation of tribal sub-plan (TSP) strategy: Impact on livelihoods of tribals in Andhra Pradesh*. Hyderabad: Research Unit for Livelihoods and Natural Resources.

Reddy, M. G., & Kumar, K. A. (2010) *Political economy of tribal development: A case study of Andhra Pradesh*. Hyderabad: Centre for Economic and Social Studies.

Srinivasulu, K. (2002). *Caste, class and social articulation in Andhra Pradesh: Mapping differential regional trajectories* (Working Paper-179). London: Overseas Development Institute.

Suri, K. C. (2002). *Democratic process and electoral politics in Andhra Pradesh, India*. London: Overseas Development Institute.

Tadakamalla, V., Venugopal, N., Raghavachari, M., Deshpande, S., & Srinivas, S. (2008). *Andhra Pradesh yerpatu vidroha charitra* (in Telugu). Hyderabad: Telangana History Society.

Vaditya, V. (2017). Cultural changes and marginalisation of Lambada community in Telangana, India. *Indian Journal of Dalit and Tribal Social Action*, *2*(3), 55–80.

Xaxa, V. (2014). *State, society and tribes: Issues in post-colonial India*. New Delhi: Pearson.

Democracy with a Difference: Tribal Politics in Arunachal Pradesh

Nani Bath

INTRODUCTION

Arunachal Pradesh, the 24th State of India, is situated at the north-east extremity of the country. It stretches over 83,743 Sq Km with a population of 13.84 lakhs. It attained the fullest political personality, consequent upon the passing of the constitution 55th Amendment Act in 1987.

The present Arunachal Pradesh acquired its independent identity when, in 1914, the North East Frontier Tract was created by separating some tribal areas from the then Darrang and Lakhimpur districts of the province of Assam (Luthra, 1993, p. 9). The Tract was designated to be administered directly and differently by the provincial governor, through the Commissioner or Deputy British Commissioner, with the help of plain

codes and without any help of normal regulations of British Indian government. The Tract was classified as Excluded Area by the Government of India (Excluded and Partially Excluded Areas) Order, 1936.

Prior to the creation of North East Frontier Tract, the region was considered as a 'non-regulated area', the area which was to be ruled by summary legislation in the discretion of the Governor. The powers under summary legislation authorized the then Lt Governor of Bengal to prescribe a line called Inner Line in each or any of the districts beyond which no British subjects can pass without an Inner Line Permit. The Bengal Eastern Frontier Regulation, 1873[1] thus came into existence that laid down such lines in the districts of Kamrup, Goalpara, Darrang, Lakhimpur and Sibsagar. The Inner Line for the first time separated some tracts inhabited by tribal people

---

[1] 'Regulation for the peace and good government of certain districts on the Eastern Frontier', popularly known as Inner Line Regulation or Bengal Eastern Frontier Regulation of 1873, intended to regulate the commercial and economic intercourse between the natives and the non-natives during British period.

from the districts of Assam and British authority. The area was kept outside the purview of regular laws of the country and administered in different way by passing regulations and framing procedures from time to time (Luthra, 1993, p. 9).

Along with Nagaland and Mizoram, Arunachal Pradesh remains an 'Inner Line State', under Bengal Eastern Frontier Regulation, 1873. The Regulation prohibits any outsider, other than natives, from crossing the line, called 'inner line', without obtaining a permit from the state administration. It also prohibits buying of land and exploitation of natural resources by the outsiders.

The sixth schedule to the constitution of India, a well-crafted constitutional mechanism to balance the political aspirations of the tribal communities and Assam's desire to integrate its hill areas, provides special provisions for administration of the tribal areas in Assam. The tribal areas of Assam were divided into two parts: Part A and Part B. The North East Frontier Tract was specified in Part B of the table appended to Paragraph 20 (1) of the Schedule and extension of the Central rule was made possible in the area.[2] However, no attempt was made to introduce Autonomous District Councils or Autonomous Regional Councils in Arunachal Pradesh.

The Government of India administratively controlled the territory through the Governor of Assam, who acted as an agent of the President of India under the provisions of the sixth schedule of the constitution since 1950. For a brief period of time, 1947–1950, the administration of NEFA was handed over to the Government of Assam.

In 1954, a full-scale administration of the area was inaugurated, with the promulgation of North-East Frontier Areas (Administration) Regulation of 1954. The President of India promulgated the North East Frontier Agency Panchayati Raj Regulation, 1967 framed on

the basis of the Dying Ering Committee recommendations in exercise of the powers conferred by Article 240 of the constitution, read with sub-paragraph (2) of para 18 of the sixth schedule to the constitution. The Panchayati Raj Institutions ensured participation of village folks in the developmental initiatives besides providing uniform political structure for otherwise diverse ethnic communities with different socio-political set-up. North East Frontier Tracts came to be known as North-East Frontier Agency (NEFA). In the year 1971, North-East Areas (Reorganization) Act, modifying Article 240 of the constitution was passed by the parliament. The Act provided a new name and new political status to NEFA. NEFA was rechristened as Arunachal Pradesh, and in 1972 it became the union territory of the Republic of India. The union territory of Arunachal Pradesh was placed under the control of a chief commissioner.

The administration of the territory was run by the President of India acting through the chief commissioner of Arunachal Pradesh till 15 August 1975. In this year, the Pradesh council (till 1972, Pradesh council) was known as agency council. Agency/Pradesh council was the fourth tier of the Panchayati Raj system introduced in 1969) was converted into a provisional legislative assembly and a council of ministers was appointed for Arunachal Pradesh (Government of Arunachal Pradesh, 1982, pp. 2–3). The administrator of union territory of Arunachal Pradesh until then designated as Chief Commissioner was upgraded to the Lieutenant Governor.

TRADITIONAL DEMOCRATIC CULTURE

Notwithstanding the late entry of electoral politics, the democratic culture was in practice since time immemorial through the existence

---

[2] The North East Frontier Tract included the Balipara Frontier Tract, Tirap Frontier Tract, the Abor Hills District and the Mishmi Hills District.

and working of traditional village councils in different forms among different tribal groups. The traditional self-governing institution such as *Kebang* of the Adis is essentially democratic in its functions and structure. Elements of electoral system too were not entirely unknown to the tribal people here. It is on record that the Monpa tribe of Tawang and Kameng districts traditionally employed modern methods of election in their process of selection of *tsorgens*, the village head (Elwin, 1988, p. 59–60). Verrier Elwin describes the system as

> the election of *tsorgens* is traditionally initiated at the *Kharchung* level, on the initiative of the various *tsoblas*. The panel of names of person suitable for election as *tsorgens* is drawn up by the *tsobla* concerned after consultation with the entire village population. In practice there is nearly an occasion when a panel has to be prepared and the deliberations normally result in the choice of one person as the most suitable candidate. All the *tsoblas* concerned then approach the person selected and after obtaining his agreement to the nomination, put it up to the *tsotsang zom* or the General Assembly. Three days are normally given for the distribution of the ballot papers and for their collection from the voters. In rare cases where there is a tie, the *tsorgen* is chosen by drawing lots from among the candidates. Participation in the voting is compulsory and the household, whose head does not attend the General Assembly when it meets, or fails to take part in the voting, is fined.

P. N. Luthra, then Adviser to the Governor of Assam, in a 'Foreword' to *Democracy in NEFA* by Verrier Elwin (Elwin, 1988, p. ix), writes that 'there is a wide measure of indigenous democracy in the prevailing patterns of social customs and laws of the people'. He adds, 'the daily humdrum of life in NEFA is by and large, managed by its own people who over the past centuries have come to evolve their own codes and customary laws to adjudicate over disputes and the sharing of nature's

resources available to them'. According to him,

> In India's recent history which is crowded with centuries of alien rule exercised from the centre, there has been gradual decay of the age-old village authority which in ancient times used to managed the affairs at the village and community level. Happily in the North East Frontier Agency the inherent urge of its people to take stock of their problems and deal with them has remained intact...there is a wide measure of indigenous democracy in the prevailing patterns of social customs and laws of the people.

There were certain essential democratic elements inherent in the indigenous self-governing institutions, such as, what Elwin himself pointed out that 'Decisions are not taken by a formal vote but discussions continue until general unanimity is achieved' (Elwin, 1988, p. 18). This is an indication of a democratic tradition where opinion of the minority is respected. In other words, the majority opinion is not imposed, and the decisions are taken on the basis of consensus.

Kebang, the council of elders an Adi[3] village, responsible for day-to-day administrative conduct of the people in accordance with age-old tradition of the tribe, has the authority over the affairs of the village.

Raghuvir Sinha considers that the democratic values have a special value in Adi society. 'The political organization of a tribal community', says Sinha,

> is the traditional way in which the society recognizes the exercise of the authority. This authority may be vested in a single individual acting as the head of the village, or it may entrusted to a few chosen representative of the village forming the council of elders-as among the Adi groups-and acting on behalf of the village community whose confidence they may command, or in the third alternative the village community may keep the authority with it (Sinha, 1988, p. 100).

---

[3] Adis are the second largest tribal community of Arunachal Pradesh with a total population of 1, 46, 244 as per 2001 census.

Expressing similar view with Raghuvir Sinha, P. D. Gogoi classifies tribal councils of the tribes of Arunachal Pradesh, on theoretical plane, into four types: (a) Chieftaincy; (b) Gerentocracy; (c) Arbiter system and (d) Democratic type. He includes Adi Kebang in democratic type of village council. K. A. A. Raja categorizes the socio-political organizations of the tribes of the states into five distinct types: (a) Adi Republican type; (b) the autocratic Nocte and Wanchoo type; (c) the individualistic Mishmi type; (d) the theocratic Monpa type and (e) the Apatani type. The Adi type is considered republican in the sense that all activities of the community were corporate in character which involves joint decisions and communal actions (Gogoi, 1971, p. 12).

Sachin Roy describes Kebang of Siang in the following words,

> The administrative structure of the Adis is essentially democratic; Autocracy in any form has not been known to them and in the absence of a distinct class of nobility, oligarchy has remained equally unknown. This is in a true sense, a Government by the people and for the people. The structure is very simple and effective (Roy, 1977, p. 218).

In 1863, an agreement was concluded between the british government and eight communities of Abors at Lalle Mukh. Alexander Mackenzie's comment on this agreement reads:

> "The democratic nature of the Abor system of government made this course advisable, and the plan has the advantage of giving each leading member of the clan a personal interest in keeping the peace. Numerous other societies of Abors have given their assent to similar engagements (Mackenzie, 2001, p. 44).

This statement reflects the democratic tamper and aspiration of the Adis. It is also evident that some sorts of democratic system of governance did exist in Adi society in olden days.

TRIBAL POLITICS: THE BACKGROUND

The Government of India did not intend to include the then North East frontier Agency under the administrative jurisdiction of the Government of Assam, keeping in view geo-political significance of the Agency. Since the administration had not penetrated deep into this sensitive area and the McMohan Line remained undefined, New Delhi always framed its policy towards the frontier on strategic and 'nationalist' considerations. The claims and counter claims between India and China, on the question of legality of McMahon Line, has placed state's politics and economic development as 'hostage' to geo-politics and 'military strategy'. Sanjib Baruah, thus, argues: 'The goal of nationalizing a frontier space has been the major trust of Indian policy vis-à-vis Arunachal Pradesh' (Baruah, 2005, p. 35).

With the independence of India, an specially designed administrative system[4] was introduced with an aim to bring them quickly at par with other advanced communities of India (Mahanta, 1983, p. 100). Chaube writes that, 'It was shortly after the transfer of power in India that China went Communist (1949) and Tibet was recognized by India as an autonomous region in China (1950). The spade work for real administration actually started in this period' (Chaube, 2012, p. 183). The Government of India, however, was careful enough not to over-administer the territory and hence a policy of 'non-interference' and 'go slow' was followed vis-à-vis the tribal people of NEFA. Alternatively, this policy was known as "Nehru-Elwin Policy" for tribal

---

[4] The Deputy Commissioner (Political Officer before 1965) was vested with the chief administrative authority within the district. He acts as the executive head of the District looking after development, Panchayats, local bodies and civil administration. He also remains the District Magistrate, who is responsible for the maintenance of law and order. This administrative system was known as 'Single Line Administration', introduced in NEFA in 1954.

development. The official position was not to bring out any change to disturb the cultural and social life of the tribals. Administration designed its administrative policies based on Pt. Nehru's famous *Panchsheel*, the five principles for tribal development.[5]

One of the key elements of the policy of 'non-interference' was not to disturb the tribal way of life[6]. Customary laws and traditional self-governing institutions were allowed to be functioned with minimum administrative interference. Customary laws of the tribal communities are protected by the Assam Frontier (Administration of Justice) Regulation, 1945. According to this Regulation, both civil and criminal cases[7] of certain nature are adjudicated in accordance with the tribal code of conduct by the village authorities, appointed by the deputy commissioner of a district. Therefore, judiciary at the lower level still remains accountable to executive, although traditional justice delivery system is being discarded in favour of more sophisticated way of dispensation of justice through regular courts.

A special provision was provided in the Representation of People Act, 1951 because of which the franchise rights were not extended to the people of Arunachal Pradesh till 1977. The Constitution (Removal of Difficulties) Orders VII and VIII withheld from NEFA the right of representation in Assam and central Legislatures. This is, probably, due to the fact that 'Administrative policies of Arunachal Pradesh was long been determined by the anthropological view that election are alien to tribal culture' (Chaube, 2012, p. 191). The North-East Frontier (Assam) Tribal and Excluded Areas Sub-Committee recommended that 'until it is declared that an area (Frontier Tracts) is or can be brought under regular administration, representation cannot be extended.'[8]

The political situation vis-à-vis NEFA during the period has been described by V. Venkata Rao in the following words:

> There was no Legislative Assembly to make laws for the good government of NEFA. NEFA was represented by one member in the Lok Sabha, nominated by the President. Laws made by the Assam Legislative Assembly were not applicable to NEFA. Laws made by Parliament were automatically applied to NEFA unless there was a specific order against the application. Thus, except

---

[5] Jawaharlal Nehru envisaged *Panchshell* (five principles) for tribal development. Please see 'Foreword' by Jawaharlal Nehru, to *'A Philosophy for NEFA'* by Verrier Elwin, Shillong, 1969. The principles are as follows:

i.   'People should develop along the lines of their own genius".
ii. "Tribal rights in land and forests should be respected".
iii. "The Govt. of India should try to train and build up a team of their own people to do the work of administration and development".
iv. "The Govt. should not over-administer these areas or overwhelm them with a multiplicity of schemes".
v.   "The Govt. should judge results, not by statistics or the amount of money spent, but by the quality of human character that is evolved.'

[6] Ostensibly to avoid outside interference, the state administration, then under the Government of India, did not permit the operation of institutions managed by the Christian missionaries of any denominations. However, Hindu missionaries, such as Ramakrishna Mission Vivekananda Kendras were allowed inside the territory with active support from the administration. The administrative machineries were geared up to promote the essence of cultural practices and social ethos of the different tribal communities. Cultural aspects of various tribal groups were highlighted in school textbooks. Some of the textbooks at primary and secondary standard contained chapters on customs, traditions and other cultural traits. This may be a reason that most of the indigenous people of Arunachal Pradesh remain highly 'nationalist').

[7] The village authorities, till today, try any cases involving the following offences within their jurisdiction: Theft, Mischief, Simple hurt, Criminal trespass/house trespass and Assault or using criminal force.

[8] The North-East Frontier (Assam) Tribal and Excluded Areas Sub-Committee, a Sub-Committee under Advisory Committee on Fundamental Rights, Minorities, Tribal Areas, and so on, of the Constituent Assembly, was appointed to recommend appropriate and special administrative framework for the tribal areas of Assam and other un-represented people).

village councils which existed from time immemorial, there were no representative institutions
in Arunachal (Rao, 1995, p. 325–326).

The bonhomie between India and China with
the slogan of *Chini-Hindi-Bhai-Bhai* did not
last long. On 20 October 1962 Mao's China
attacked India with an aim to 'teach Nehru
a lesson'. Almost immediately after the war,
the policy envisaged by J. Nehru, often called
as Nehru-Elwin 'Go-slow' policy, was given
a second look amidst popular resentment
against the policy considering it to be primarily responsible for India's shameful defeat at
the hands of Chinese army. It was realized that
India's defeat in the war was due to lack of
road communication and other facilities in the
State.

After occupying certain strategic parts of
NEFA (Bomdila and Walong) it was feared
that the Chinese troops would descend on
the Assam Valley. The people of Assam were
enraged over this possibility and strongly
criticized the tribal policy followed in the
Administration of NEFA. The NEFA people
had to abandon their native homes and become
refugees in Assam. They too joined the agitation against the 'go slow' policy in NEFA
(Government of Arunachal Pradesh, 1998).
Even J. Nehru seemed to have appreciated that
the book, *A Philosophy for NEFA,* authored by
Verrier Elwin that contains the policy framework for future development of Arunachal
Pradesh, required a second look.

Recognizing the political and geo-strategic
significance of the territory, special and urgent
attention was paid towards its development.
It was during this period that the NEFA
Administration designed its administrative
machinery to achieve twin objectives of bringing the areas to the national mainstream; and
to organize the people to take lively interest in

developmental activities. Modern governmental institutions were sought to be introduced
so that the territory could come closer to the
mainstream of political life in the country. The
first step towards realizing these objectives
was to appoint a four-member committee,
popularly known as D. Ering Committee[9].

The Ering Committee submitted its Report
in January 1965 with certain politically and
administratively significant recommendations. The Committee, apart from suggesting
a four-tier organically linked popular bodies,
had made some miscellaneous recommendations keeping in view the future development
of North East Frontier Agency. At the village
level, there should be a village council, to be
elected or selected as per their customary laws.
Above the village council, there should be
Anchal Samiti at the circle level. At the district
level, over the *Anchal Samities*, there should
be *Zilla Parishads*. The Committee finally
suggested the creation of Agency Council at
the state level. The functioning of the Agency
Council would be to advise the Governor in
the administration and development of NEFA.

Based on the recommendation of the Ering
Committee, North East Frontier Agency
Panchayati Raj Regulation, 1967 was passed.
Elections to the Panchayati Raj bodies, as
per this Regulation, followed tribal customs.
Thus, the introduction of Panchayati Raj, in
Arunachal Pradesh, preceded the universal
adult franchise. The Panchayati Raj institution, which was introduced in 1969, introduced certain elements of modern elections in
the State but a proper electoral politics started
working in Arunachal Pradesh only with the
elections of 1977, the first general election to
the Lok Sabha in the state.

Till 1977–1978, Arunachal Pradesh was
represented by one member in the Lok Sabha,

[9] The committee was constituted by the Government of India. J N Choudhury writes in *Arunachal Through the Ages,* 1982 that though the original suggestion in this regard had struck a sympathetic chord in Nehru, the announcement of the appointment of the committee was made in parliament by Late Lal Bahadur Shastri on 11 April 1964.

to be nominated[10] by the President of India from among the 'Schedule Tribes' of the area by the Section 3 read with Section 4 of the Representation of People Act, 1950.

The North-East Areas (Re-organization) Act, 1971 provides the state with one seat in Rajya Sabha which was to be filled by the nomination by the President.[11] Though the candidates were to be nominated by the President of India, they however, were not exactly nominated. The candidates to be nominated were indirectly elected by the people. With regards to Rajya Sabha seat, the candidate was selected by the Pradesh Council through an election process. An electoral college consisting of all the Zila Parishads elects a candidate to be nominated for Lok Sabha seat. Each Zila Parishad consists of all the Vice-Presidents of all Anchal Samitis within its jurisdiction, one representative from each *Anchal Samiti* in the District, and not more than six persons to be nominated by the Administrator to secure representation in the *Zila Parishad*.

TRIBAL POLITICS: DEMOCRATIC ARTICULATION THROUGH ELECTORAL PARTICIPATION

The first general election to the legislative assembly of erstwhile union territory Arunachal Pradesh, which was held in 1978, consisted of 33 members out of which 30 were elected directly by the people and 3 were nominated. A year earlier, in 1977, the first general election to the Lok Sabha was conducted.

There has been increasing participation of people in every election in Arunachal Pradesh. Significantly, in all the assembly elections held so far the strength of voting electorate outnumbered the strength of the non-voting electorate: 67–84 per cent. On an average, 72 per cent of the voters did exercise their franchise. Apparently, this is an indicator of political consciousness of the people and, may be, reflection of their political maturity. Table 10.1 presents the details.

As seen in the Table 10.2, voting percentage in the parliamentary elections is down by almost ten per cent as compared to the legislative assembly elections. In an average 63.63 per cent voters turn-out is recorded in the parliamentary elections.

In the first legislative assembly, held on 1978, three recognized political parties-Janata Party, People's Party of Arunachal and Congress (I) along with independent candidates participated. The details are presented in the Table 10.3.

The INC played a nominal role in the first Assembly Election by contesting unsuccessfully in only one seat. The State unit of Congress (I) joined the Janata Party, then in power in New Delhi. The Janata Party contested in 30 seats, PPA in 23 seats and there were 32 Independent candidates.

The tenure of the first assembly was cut short because of imposition of President's Rule in the state in 1979. It was held in 1980, simultaneously with the General Election to 7th Lok Sabha. The INC made an impressive comeback in the electoral politics of the state by securing 13 seats out of total 30 seats in the legislative assembly. Apart from INC and

[10] The first nominated member of parliament was Chowkhamoon Gohain, who served as the representative of Assam Tribal Areas (Autonomous District of Assam) for two consecutive terms: 17 April 1952 to 4 April 1957 and 5 April 1957 to 21 March 1962. He was succeeded by D. Ering, who also served for two consecutive terms as the reprehensive of North Eastern Frontier Tracts: 2 April 1962 to 3 March 1967 and 4 April 1967 to 27 December 1970. The last nominated member was Chow Chanderjit Gohain, who represented North Eastern Frontier Agency from 15 March 1971 to 18 January 1977.
[11] (In 1972, Todak Basar became the first member of the Rajya Sabha, to be followed by Ratan Tama (1978–1984), Omem Moyong Deori (1984–1990), Nyodek Yonggam (1990–1996), Nabam Rebia (1996–2002 and 2002–2008) and Mukut Mithi (2008–2014 and 2014–till date).

Table 10.1 Percentage of Polling and Non-Voters in Arunachal Pradesh Assembly Elections (1978–2019)

Legislative Assembly	Year	Total Electorate	% of Polling	% of Non-Voters
1st	1978	2,39,945	68.59	31.41
2nd	1980	2,66,726	67.50	32.50
3rd	1984	3,19,045	74.46	25.54
4th	1990	5,11,305	69.68	30.32
5th	1995	5,34,001	81.20	18.80
6th	1999	6,11,481	69.39	30.61
7th	2004	6,83,542	67.37	32.63
8th	2009	7,25,208	79.50	20.5
9th	2014	7,53,170	67.4	32.6
10th	2019	7,94,162	84.00	16.00

Source: Statistical Report on General Elections to Legislative Assemblies, Issued by Chief Electoral Officer, Arunachal Pradesh, Itanagar.

Table 10.2 Percentage of Polling and Non-Voters in Lok Sabha Elections, Arunachal Pradesh (1977–2019)

Year	Total Electorate	% of Polling	% of Non-Voters
1977	93,770	56.27	43.73
1980	2,66,726	68.58	31.42
1984	3,19,049	75.46	24.54
1989	4,76,057	59.13	40.87
1991	5,19,315	51.28	48.72
1996	5,44,440	55.04	44.96
1998	5,65,626	59.29	40.71
1999	6,11,481	72.15	27.85
2004	68,40,34	56.06	43.94
2009	7,32,956	68.16	31.84
2014	7,59,389	78.61	21.39
2019	7,94,162	78.89	21.11

Source: Statistical Report on General Elections to Legislative Assemblies, Issued by Chief Electoral Officer, Arunachal Pradesh, Itanagar.

Table 10.3 Details of Assembly Election of Arunachal Pradesh, 1978

Sl. No.	Name of Party	No. of Contestants	Seats Won	% of Seats Won
1.	Janata Party	30	17	56.66
2.	PPA	23	08	26.66
3.	INC	01	00	00.00
4.	Independents	32	05	16.66
	Total	86	30	100

Source: Basic Statistical Data and Election Results, (1978–1990). Issued by Chief Electoral Officer, Itanagar, Arunachal Pradesh.

PPA, Congress (U), a new political dispensation had made its entry in the electoral politics of the state. A surprising element was that
Janata Party, which secured majority in the
last assembly election, did not take part. Table
10.4 shows the details.

The general election to the third legislative
assembly was held on 24 December 1984.
PPA suffered a severe defeat and secured only
4 seats. The BJP made its first entry in the
electoral arena in the state by securing a seat.
The details are shown in Table 10.5.

It was in 1990 that the General Election
to constitute the 4 legislative assembly was

held, after Arunachal Pradesh achieved a new
political status. It became the 24th state of
the Union of India and the number of seats in
legislative assembly increased from 30 to 60.
Political Parties like PPA, Congress (U) and
BJP did not put up any candidates. The details
are shown in Table 10.6.

The fifth General Election to the legislative assembly of Arunachal Pradesh was held
on March, 1995. The 1995 assembly election
shows the complete dominance of INC, as the
party secure 43 seats out of 60 seats it contested. Four political parties, namely INC,
Janata Dal, BJP and Janata Party contested the

Table 10.4   Details of Assembly Election of Arunachal Pradesh, 1980

Sl. No.	Name of Party	No. of Contestants	Seats Won	% of Seats Won
1.	INC (I)	29	13	43.33
2.	PPA	27	13	43.33
3.	INC (U)	11	—	00.00
4.	Independents	28	04	13.33
	Total	95	30	100

Source: Basic Statistical Data and Election Results, (1978–1990). Issued by Chief Electoral Officer, Itanagar,
Arunachal Pradesh.

Table 10.5   Details of Assembly Election of Arunachal Pradesh, 1984

Sl. No.	Name of Party	No. of Contestants	Seats Won	% of Seats Won
1.	INC	30	21	70
2.	BJP	06	01	3.33
3.	PPA	13	04	13.33
4.	Janata party	03	00	00
5.	Independents	63	04	13.33
	Total	115	30	100

Source: Basic Statistical Data and Election Results, (1978–1990). Issued by Chief Electoral Officer, Itanagar,
Arunachal Pradesh.

Table 10.6   Details of Assembly Election of Arunachal Pradesh, 1990

Sl No.	Name of Party	No. of Contestants	Seats Won	% of Seats Won
1.	Congress (I)	59	37	61.66
2.	Janata Dal	52	11	18.33
3.	Janata Party	07	01	1.66
4.	Independents	52	11	18.33
	Total	170	60	100

Source: Basic Statistical Data and Election Results, (1978–1990). Issued by Chief Electoral Officer, Itanagar,
Arunachal Pradesh.

election along with Independent candidates. The details are shown in Table 10.7.

This 6th Assembly General Election to the legislative assembly, which was held in 1999, saw the entry of political parties like Arunachal Congress, Nationalist Congress Party (NCP), and Ajaya Bharati Party (ABP). The details are shown in Table 10.8.

The 7th General Elections to the legislative assembly was held in 2004. Besides INC, three other political parties were in the fray-BJP, AC and NCP along with some Independent candidates. The details are shown in Table 10.9.

The 8th General Elections to the legislative assembly of Arunachal Pradesh, held in 2009, was marked by the entry of All India Trinamool Congress (AITC) and the re-entry of the PPA, after its revival. The details are shown in Table 10.10.

In the 9th General Elections to the legislative assembly, held in 2014, Aam Aadmi Party and Naga Peoples Front entered for the first time. The INC almost repeated its performance in the last elections by securing 42 seats (70% of the total seats). The details are shown in Table 10.11.

In the initial years of electoral politics, the tribal voters in Arunachal Pradesh behaved politically in response to the dictate of the society or group. In fact, members of a clan or lineage group functioned as an extended family. They used to vote for a candidate as he is related to the voters either through blood or marriage. In modern time the nature of electoral politics in the state has undergone certain changes, which are the concomitant outcome of restructuring of social and political structures and economic development of the state. Clan or group solidarity is very often diluted because of political compulsions. The competitive party politics has introduced 'politics' among the clan brothers. However, primordial group considerations, to some extent, still influence voters' choice of candidates and

Table 10.7 Details of Assembly Election of Arunachal Pradesh, 1995

Sl. No.	Name of Party	No. of Contestants	Seats Won	% of Seats Won
1.	INC	60	43	71.67
2.	Janata Dal	34	03	05.00
3.	BJP	15	0	00.00
4.	Janata Party	05	02	03.33
5.	Independents	59	12	20.00
	Total	173	60	100

Source: Statistical report on general election to 6th Legislative Assembly, 1995. Issued by Chief Electoral Officer, Itanagar, Arunachal Pradesh.

Table 10.8 Details of Arunachal Pradesh Assembly Elections, 1999

Sl. No.	Name of Party	No. of Contestants	Seats Won	% of Seats Won
1.	INC	56	54	90.00
2.	AC	38	01	01.66
3.	BJP	23	00	00.00
4.	NCP	21	04	06.66
5.	ABP	01	00	00.00
6.	Independents	29	01	01.66
	Total	168	60	100

Source: Statistical report on general election to 7th Legislative Assembly, 1999. Issued by Chief Electoral Officer, Itanagar, Arunachal Pradesh.

Table 10.9   Details of Arunachal Pradesh Assembly Election, 2004

Sl. No.	Name of Party	No. of Contestants	Seats Won	% of Seats Won
1.	Congress (I)	60	34	56.66
2.	A.C	11	02	03.33
3.	BJP	39	09	15.00
4.	NCP	10	02	03.33
5.	Independents	48	13	21.66
	Total	168	60	100

Source: Statistical report on general election to 8th Legislative Assembly, 2004. Issued by Chief Electoral Officer, Itanagar, Arunachal Pradesh.

Table 10.10   Details of the Arunachal Pradesh Assembly Election 2009

Sl. No.	Name of Party	No. of Contestants	Seats Won	% of Seats Won
1.	INC	60	41	68.33
2.	BJP	18	03	05.00
3.	NCP	36	05	08.33
4.	AITC	26	06	10.00
5.	JD (U)	03	00	00.00
6.	PPA	11	04	06.66
7.	Independent	03	01	01.66
	Total	157	60	100

Source: Statistical report on general election to 9th Legislative Assembly, 2009. Issued by Chief Electoral Officer, Itanagar, Arunachal Pradesh.

Table 10.11   Details of the Arunachal Pradesh Assembly Election, 2014

Sl. No.	Name of Party	No. of Contestants	Seats Won	% of Seats Won
1.	INC	60	42	70
2.	BJP	42	11	18.33
3.	NCP	09	00	00
4.	PPA	16	05	8.33
5.	AAP	01	00	00
6.	NPF	11	00	00
7.	Independents	16	02	3.33
	Total	155	60	100

Source: Statistical report on general election to 9th Legislative Assembly, 2014. Issued by Chief Electoral Officer, Itanagar, Arunachal Pradesh.

parties, particularly at local level politics. The general features of electoral politics of the state can be summarized as follows:

First, unlike rest of the states in India, there is a peculiar and unique aspect of politics 'flowing with the ruling party', what a journalist would call, a 'ruling syndrome edge'. Rather than anti-incumbency factor, there is pro-incumbency factor that remains at play, which is evident from the fact that no ruling government is voted out of power nor is any ruling party candidate defeated in Lok Sabha elections except in 1977, 1996 and 2014 elections.

The state has a distinction of electing ruling party candidates in all but three Lok Sabha elections. In the 1996 Lok Sabha elections, Arunachal Pradesh reversed the tradition of electing Congress candidates by voting for the victory of independent candidates Tomo Riba and Wancha Rajkumar, from the western and eastern parliamentary constituencies, respectively. They defeated the official Congress candidates P K Thungon and Laeta Umbrey. The independent winners had the backing of the then Congress Chief Minister Gegong Apang, who at that point of time was not on the best of terms with the Congress high command. Kiren Rijiju, a BJP candidate was elected from western parliamentary constituency in 2014. Earlier, in the first ever parliamentary elections held in Arunachal Pradesh in 1977, regional sentiments seemed to hold sway in the eastern parliamentary constituency. An independent candidate, Bakin Pertin proclaimed himself to be the 'peoples' MP'. It was only in the 1977 elections that an independent candidate was elected without support of the ruling government.

Secondly, another unique feature in the electoral politics of Arunachal Pradesh is that the voters orientation towards party has nothing to do with the policies and programmes of the concerned party. In fact, majority of the party oriented voters were ignorant of the ideological basis of the parties they voted for. Party ticket, therefore, rather than party itself is the prime consideration of the voters.[12] Therefore, the voters are not ideologically committed to a particular political party. Their orientation towards party has little to do with the policies and programmes of that party. Simply put, the tribal voters do not belong to any party but they are committed to their leaders at the local level. Their votes swing with their leaders, especially the local representatives. As a result, no all-Arunachal leadership with wider acceptance has ever evolved. Even

the political leaders in the state do not play politics on any ideological plank. Ideology of the leaders swing with time and it has direct relation with formation of government in New Delhi. One hardly finds any leader who has not changed his political colour more than once in the State.

Thirdly, the issues to which the voters pay attention are basically localized in nature with parochial appeal. The voters have indicated their inclination to vote for such parties with whose programmes they can identify themselves with. Here in Arunachal Pradesh, every candidate issues local manifesto detailing the problems being confronted by the voters of that constituency with promises to be fulfilled in next five years.

Fourth, electoral politics is not actively influenced by regional sentiments. Regional tendency that had developed in the late seventies with the formation of Peoples' Party of Arunachal is no more at play. Evidently the regional parties—Arunachal Congress and Peoples' party of Arunachal—do not receive required support even from the indigenous people of Arunachal.

Fifthly, it may be argued that any study of electoral politics in Arunachal Pradesh cannot risk ignoring ethnicity and clan politics as one of the determining factors in any election. Its degree of influence appears to vary depending on which level of election one is discussing.

In a tribal society 'in group' solidarity is religiously maintained. A tribal voter in Arunachal Pradesh behaves politically in response to the group pressures or community welfare. The voters are bound by a network of social relationships, which often get transformed into political relationships at the time of election. Ethnic considerations are most intense at the time of local body elections as contests are considered between clans and not contests between individual candidates. During assembly elections voters tend to vote

---

[12] Some millions of rupees are believed to have been spent by some of the candidates in their effort to secure party (party in power) nomination.

by and large on ethnic lines, though the fact of party label seems to also exert some influence. The ethnic factor gets a bit diluted in parliamentary elections simply because of the geographical area that constituency covers and the different ethnic groups that may be present in a constituency.

The situation reflects what an American Anthropologist, Oscar Lewis, in his work on village life in Northern India (Lewis, 1965, p. 149), remarks,

> the theoretical assumption behind a democratic system based on voting is that the individual is an independent, thinking being capable and ready to make his own decision. However, in a kinship organized societies it is largely extended family which is the basic unit for most decision making. At best, voting becomes an extended family process, which violates the spirit of individuality inherent in the western electoral system.

Sixth, till recently religion did not get manifest in the electoral politics of Arunachal Pradesh. S. K. Chaube notes that voters in Arunachal Pradesh voted without religious consideration, though the election result reflects a regionalistic thinking, which is very similar to that found in the neighbouring hill states. (Chaube, 2012, p. 194). However, there are reported cases of use of religious oaths and ordeals to influence the voters in favour of a particular candidate. Special prayers are conducted in churches either in support of a candidate or party to which the church or pastor (priest) considers 'anti-believers' (Christians).[13]

In the 2019 general elections, the Arunachal Pradesh Catholic Association, through a 'Prayer letter', appealed and requested all the parishes and catholic churches in the state to 'pray for Mr Nabam Tuki who is contesting ensuing Lok Sabha election 2019 from western parliamentary constituency. He is the pillar of catholic church in Arunachal Pradesh'. The letter added that 'Pray for the peace and prosperity, protection and success of their election. APCA requests all the voters of the catholic community who are going to cast their valuable vote on April 11 to exercise their adult franchise with prayerful clear conscience and vote in favour of him'[14]. Nabam Tuki was an Indian National Congress nominee for both Arunachal West parliamentary constituency and 15-Sagalee assembly constituency.

In a similar instance, an organization in the name of Legal Rights Organization had lodged a complaint to the election commission against the Arunachal Pradesh Christian Revival Church for appealing to voters to support Khyoda Apik, the candidature of National Peoples' Party for the Arunachal West parliamentary constituency (https://www.thehindu.com).

Entry of Buddhist *lamas* (priest) and *Rimpoches* (Buddhist religious head) in the electoral politics in Buddhist-majority Tawang district can be seen as an indirect appeal in the name of religion. In the last assembly election, Thupten Kunphen fought against the incumbent Chief Minister as INC candidate. Two *Rimpoches* were in the electoral fray in the 1995 legislative assembly elections from Lumla and Tawang assembly constituencies.

Seventhly, given the high percentage of voting every general election, there seems to be no issue with the level of participation of

---

[13] The author was told of an incident where believers of a particular church had gone on fasting for some days to wash off their sins for having voted for a BJP candidate in 2009 assembly elections). Again in 1999 elections an instance of intra-religious rivalry was reported from Borduri-Bogapani assembly constituency in which a catholic candidate was fitted against the candidate belonging to Baptist denomination. There was not a single recorded Christian in Arunachal Pradesh in 1951, their number rose to 1,438 in 1961 and 2,593 in 1971. As per the Census Report of 2001, the Christian population constitutes 18.70 per cent of the total population. It increased to 30 per cent in 2011. The percentage of Christian population stands at around 50 per cent of the total tribal population.

[14] The letter was issued and signed in the name of Pekhi Nabam, General Secretary, APCA, dated 28th March, 2019. It was withdrawn with an apology after show-cause notice was issued by the Chief Electoral Officer, Arunachal Pradesh.

the citizens in the elections. What is of our concern is the lack of ethical participation of the citizens in electoral processes. Role of money in election is one of the serious unethical practices in electoral processes. A study has found that not even single voter is ready to identify himself as one who receives payment for votes (Bath, 2009), but a known fact is that one cannot think of entering into electoral fray in Arunachal Pradesh without sound financial background.[15] By any conservative estimates, in an average, there would be expenditure of more than 10 crores in an assembly constituency. An amount of ₹1.8 crore was seized from an MLA contesting candidate by election officials some days before the assembly elections polls 2019 (The Dawnlit Post, 2019).

Some studies have found that money alone does not determine winning chance of a candidate. To quote Kothari and Weiner, 'money by itself did not produce the desire results; it only succeeded only when used as a timely instrument of election strategy' (Kothari, 1965, p. 33). This may not be true in the case of most of the constituencies in Arunachal Pradesh.

To our understanding, huge involvement of money in elections in a small state like Arunachal Pradesh may be attributed to three reasons: one, it is because of prevalence of corrupt practices at different levels. It is unfortunate that in a supposedly egalitarian tribal society, corruption is accepted as a social fact. Two, it is becoming possible because of less numbers of voters in assembly constituencies. One of the assembly constituencies in the state has slightly more than 5,000 listed voters. Three, as provided in Section 10(26) of the Income Tax Act, 1961, members of Scheduled Tribes of Northeast India are exempted from payment of income tax. As such, politicians

or officials do not have to reveal their source of income, which, in turn, provides them more scope to involve in corrupt practices.[16]

Eight, no democracy could claim itself to be a successful one if equal participation and representation of women in politics is ensured. Except voting, political participation of women in the state is extremely low, which reflects the patricidal nature of different tribal communities. When it comes to representation of women in assembly elections, irrespective of regions and communities, it has not crossed more than five per cent in any assembly elections. This is in spite of the fact that, in Arunachal Pradesh, women outnumber male voters[17].

Sibo Kai was the first woman legislator after she was nominated to the assembly in 1978. In the second legislative assembly (1980), Nyari Welly became the first elected woman MLA, representing Peoples' Party of Arunachal. She was re-elected in 1984 as a Congress candidate. No women represented the fourth legislative assembly (2004–2009). The sixth (1999–2004) and ninth legislative assemblies (2014–2019), with three members each, recorded the highest representation of women. It amounted to five per cent of the total members. With the election of Gum Tayeng as a Congress nominee in a by-election in 2013, the numbers of elected women representatives got increased to three in the eight legislative assembly (2009–2014). Similarly, the representation of women in the ninth legislative assembly (2014–2019) was increased by one more member after Dasanglu Pul was elected in 2016 in a bye-election. The details are shown in Table 10.12.

---

[15] An analysis of affidavits file by the candidates of 2019 elections has revealed that are 131 'crorepatis', which accounts to 71 per cent of the total candidates (184, and all 12 ministers in Pema Khandu ministry have property worth more than 100 lakhs. For details, see www.adrindia.org.

[16] Young tribal leaders and intellectuals have started to demand that members of scheduled tribes of Northeast India must also be made to pay income and property tax. It is considered as one of the easy ways of checking corruption.

[17] The state has a total electorate of 7, 94,162 with 4, 01,601 women voters and 3, 92,561 men.

Table 10.12   Representation of Women in Arunachal Pradesh Assembly (1978–2019)

| Legislative Assembly | Total Members | Elected Women | | Percentage (In Relation to Total Seats) |
		Numbers	Names	
1st (1978)	33	01	Sibo Kai	3%
2nd (1980)	33	01	Nyari Welly	3%
3rd (1985)	33	02	Komoli Mossang Nyari Welly.	6%
4th (1990)	60	02	Omem Deori, Komoli Mossang.	3.3%
5th (1995)	60	01	Yadap Apang.	1.6%
6th (1999)	60	03	Mekup Dolo, Nyani Natung Yari Dulom.	5%
7th (2004)	60	—	—	—
8th (2009)	60	02	Karya Bagang, Nang Sati Mein.	3.3%
9th (2014)	60	02	Gum Tayeng Karya Bagang	3.3%
10th (2019)	60	03	Gum tayeng Dasanglu Pul Jummum Ete Deori	5%

Source: Statistical report on general elections to the Legislative Assembly (1978–2009). Issued by Chief Electoral Officer, Itanagar, Arunachal Pradesh.

POLITICS OF IDENTITY: THE ISSUE OF MIGRATION AND INDIGENOUS COMMUNITY

From the years 1964–69, as part of the refugee settlement programme, a total of 2,748 families of Chakma and Hajong refugees consisting of 14,888 (750 Hajongs) persons were rehabilitated in Chowkham in Lohit district, Miao, Bordumsa and Diyun in Tirap (now Changlang) district and Balijan in Subansiri (now Papum Pare) district.[18] Another group of refugee- the Tibetan refugees have been settled in Arunachal Pradesh since early sixties. They had migrated out of their homeland with the 14th Dalai Lama when Peoples Liberation Army of China moved inside Tibet. They are spread in four refugee settlement areas in the state, Tenzingang (West Kameng District),

Miao (Changlang District) and Tezu (Lohit District) and Tuting. In addition, there are the scattered communities of Bomdila, Dirang, Rupa and Tenga. As per the reports of the respective district administrations, there are 4,418 Tibetan refugees in Arunachal Pradesh. However, The Ministry of Home Affairs, Government of India, records a total of 7,530 Tibetan refugees in the state.[19]

The Chakmas, who hail originally from Chittagong Hill Tracts (CHT), Bangladesh are actually displaced indigenous people. The word Chakma or Chukma is a generic term given to a predominant hill tribe of CHT, Bangladesh (Talukdar, 1988, p. 5). They are Buddhist by religion. The Hajongs are Hindus from Mymenshing district of the erstwhile East Pakistan, now Bangladesh.

There are contradictory reports on the numbers of Chakmas in Arunachal Pradesh.

---

[18] *White Paper On Chakma and Hajong Refugee Issue*, issued by Government of Arunachal Pradesh, Itanagar, March, 12, 1996.
[19] Government of India, Ministry of Home Affairs, Rajya Sabha Starred Question No. 69, 29 April, 2015.

The records of the Government of Arunachal Pradesh suggest that there were 48,494 Chakmas and 2415 Hajongs refugees during 2010–2011.[20] An undated pamphlet *Why Arunachalees are Opposed to Permanent Settlement of Chakma and Hajong Refugees*, issued by All Arunachal Pradesh Students Union, has estimated the population of Chakma and Hajong refugees to be 60,000. As per the Census Report of 2011 their population stands at 47, 4713 persons (http://censusindia.gov.in/).

The presence of refugees in thousands in Arunachal Pradesh, a protected area, has not only heightened the 'community consciousness', it has also created a 'space' for the political leaders of diverse ideologies to play their political games. The Chakma-Hajong refugee issue has resulted into a formation of a regional political party, the Arunachal Congress.[21] Arunachal Congress is an outcome of Peoples Referendum Rally held on 20 September 1995 attended by representatives from various political parties, panchayat leaders, representatives of the NGOs, village elders and so on. In an All Party Legislators Meeting held on 6 September 1995, it was decided to hold Peoples Referendum Rally to be spearheaded by All Arunachal Pradesh Students' Union, the apex students' body of the state. The meeting was convened to discuss the problems of refugees and evolve action plan to deport them.

The supreme court ruling of 2015 directed the Government and India and State of Arunachal Pradesh to 'finalise the conferment of citizenship rights on eligible Chakmas and Hajongs..... at the earliest preferably within three months from today (17 September 2015).' The court reaffirmed that they (refugees) cannot be required to obtain any Inner Line permit as they are settled in the State of Arunachal Pradesh.

Yet another institutional intervention that ignited the minds of indigenous people of the state was the decision of the Election Commission of India to include 1,497 eligible Chakma and Hajong voters in the electoral rolls. The Order[22] says that the Chakmas have 'acquired citizenship by birth....and are ordinarily resident in Arunachal Pradesh'. The Order adds, 'Under the provisions of the Constitution read with section 19 of the Representation of the People Act, 1950, these Chakmas are constitutionally entitled to be registered as electors.'

What is of our academic interest is that the Chakmas have been ordered to be enrolled as electors even before citizenship is granted to them. The indigenous voices have questioned the rationality of the action of the Election Commission of India. The All Arunachal Pradesh Students' Union, filing a Public Interest Litigation against the guidelines issued by the ECI for revision of Electoral Rolls, had argued that the impugned Order of the Commission contradicts Article 326 of Indian Constitution and Section 16 of Representation of the People Act, 1950. Article 326 reads: 'The election to the House of the People and to the Legislative Assembly of every State shall be on the basis of adult franchise; that it to say, every person who is a citizen of India......., shall be entitled to be registered as a voter at such election'. Section 16 of the RPA, 1950 says, 'a person shall be disqualified for registration in an electoral roll if he- (a) is not a citizen of India...'

The 2019 Electoral Roll has recorded a total of 4,719 Chakma voters, almost four-fold increase since 2004. As seen for Table 10.13, it might look statistically insignificant but the statistics makes huge electoral sense when the

[20] Government of Arunachal Pradesh, *Special Survey of Chakma-Hajong, 2010–2011*.
[21] After 2009 general election to Lok Sabha (it managed to secure 9.30 per cent of valid vote polled, the party was derecognized by the election commission of India as a state party. Thereafter, it did not put up any candidates in the subsequent elections.
[22] No. 23/ARUN/2003, dated 3 March, 2004.

Table 10.13   Percentage of Chakma Voters in Arunachal Pradesh Assembly Constituencies

Sl. No.	Assembly Constituencies	Total Voters	Total Chakma Population	Total Chakma Voters	Voters Percentage (%)
1.	14-Doimukh (ST)	21,961	2,077	619	2.8
2.	46-Chowkham (ST)	14,058	4,963	511	3.6
3.	49-Bordumsa-Diyun(Gen)	18,188	34,876[a]	3,020	16.6
4.	50-Miao (ST)	19,594	12,295	569	2.9
	Total	73,801	54,211	4,719	25.9

Source: http://ceoarunachal.nic.in/onlineelectorsearch.html

[a]There are 2,415 Hajongs in 49-Bordumsa-Diyun (Gen) Assembly Constituency

Chakmas vote en block for one candidate or party. More than 70 per cent of those respondents, interviewed by the present author, have favoured a candidate 'who is "strong" enough to protect the refugee interests'.[23] This makes the indigenous population more apprehensive—what if they are granted citizenship or all eligible Chakmas are enrolled as voters? For example, 49-Bordumsa-Dayum (unreserved) A.C. has total voters of 18,188. The population of Chakmas and Hajongs stands at 34,876 persons, out of which eligible voters would be more than the present total voters. The indigenous communities have become apprehensive about their political future, hence, urging for protection of their political interests.

A letter from P. M Sayeed, then Minister of State (Home Affairs), Government of India, to Nyodek Yonggam, then MP (RS-Arunachal) sparked a 'critical phase' in AAPSU's movement against the refugees[24]. The AAPSU served a 'Quit Arunachal Notice' to 'all foreigners including Chakmas, Hajongs, Tibetans, Bangladeshis, and Nepalis of Foreign origin to leave the state latest by 30th September 1994'. The State legislative assembly of Arunachal Pradesh has passed four

assembly resolutions so far on the issue for deportation of Chakma and Hajong refugees from Arunachal Pradesh.

It has been argued that 'throughout the course of administrative and political events Arunachal Pradesh has been enjoying a special status under which no person or persons other than the indigenous people have the right to settle in Arunachal Pradesh permanently.'[25] The 'Protected status' was granted to the state even during the British rule in India. Section 7 of the *Bengal Eastern Frontier Regulation*, 1873 reads: 'it shall not be lawful for any person not being the native…to acquire any interest in the land or product of land beyond the said "Inner Line" without the sanction of the Local Government'. By the Foreigners Protected Area Order, 1958, the territory of Arunachal Pradesh was declared as protected area. The civilian authority may, by an Order, may prohibit any foreigner or any class of foreigners from entering or remaining in the area, and impose restrictions on the acquisition of land or any interest in the land within the area.

On more than one occasions, leaders of All Arunachal Pradesh Students Union, the apex students' body of the state, had exhibited

---

[23] ICSSR sponsored project entitled, *Refugee Problems in Arunachal Pradesh: A Study of Contesting Rights, Claims and Discourses.*

[24] The D.O. letter No.13/12/94-MZ, dated 7 July, 1994 reads: 'under the Indira-Mujib Agreement of 1972, it was decided that the Chakma/Hajong refugees who came to India from the erstwhile East Pakistan before 25, 3, 1971 will be considered for grant of Indian Citizenship.'

[25] *Why Arunachalees are Opposed to Permanent Settlement of Chakma and Hajong Refugee*, an undated pamphlet issued by All Arunachal Pradesh Students' Union, p. 3.

what can be termed as 'anti-India tendency' by seeking to look beyond 'McMahon Line' in search of 'lost brothers'. Use of the words like 'McMahon Line' and 'lost brothers' is an implicit expression of seeking assistance from China to help solve refugee problem in Arunachal Pradesh, a territory constantly claimed by Communist China as an extension of mainland China. Countering the 2015 ruling of the supreme court to grant citizenship to the Chakmas and Hajongs, the AAPSU has indicated that 'Arunachal Pradesh may take China's help if the recent Supreme Court judgment granting citizenship to refugees in the state is not overturned'. (https://www.telegraphindia.com) It may also be noted that AAPSU had on many past occasions boycotted Republic and Independence Day celebrations.

The issue of Chakma-Hajong has lingered on for more than half a century with no tangible solution at sight. For national parties, the state of Arunachal Pradesh being a part of India should also share the national responsibility in resettling the refugees. The BJP (forerunner of Jan Sangh) considers Buddhism as a part of the extended family of Hinduism. As such, the party's support for the Chakmas, who are Buddhist by religion and the Hajongs, who are Hindus, may exactly fit into their ideology. The proposal to pass Citizenship Amendment Bill, 2016[26] by the NDA government is an expression in this line. The successive Congress governments' position remained unchanged. After all, it was the same party which brought refugees in the state.

Many believe that the Report of the *Cabinet Committee on Chakma-Hajong Refugee Problem,* submitted to the state government in 2007, has a potential to resolve the vexed issue. The Report says,

..no apparent objection on granting of Indian Citizenship to CHR in conformity with the Rules/

Acts; issue of Inner Line Permits to the CHakmas and Hajongs; conduct a special survey on CH inhabited areas to find out the exact number as on date and also settled during 1964–69 and illegal migrants thereafter; the lone general (unreserved) assembly constituency is not to be earmarked in the CH inhabited area; evict the unauthorized CH from the reserved forests; the CH to be confined to original settlement areas; the original settlement areas to be demarcated.

CONCLUSION

Even after the introduction of statutory Panchayati Raj Institution, tribal society and politics remained intertwined. The NEFA Administration, because of its policy of 'minimum interference', retained the democratic elements in traditional institutions of tribal communities. These elements were incorporated in formal institution, such as, NEFA Panchayati Raj Regulation, 1967. As per the provisions of 1967 Regulation, elections to the panchayati bodies were to be conducted in accordance with the prevailing tribal customs, and the village authorities (councils) recognized under the Assam Frontier (Administration of Justice) Regulation, 1945 were accorded the status of *Gram Panchayats.*

In the absence of 'eligible' panchayat members, village council members and *Gaon Buras* (village elders) were persuaded by the administrative officers to for representation in Panchayati Raj Institution. The scheme, probably, worked well till party politics made its inroads into the workings of grassroots democracy. With an amendment, elections are now fought on party lines that bring clan politics, divisions within the community, and high degree of monetary involvement.

Arunachal Pradesh remained a special category state since 1990 because of which funds were released liberally without any accountability. The unaccounted amounts

---

[26] The Bill amends the Citizenship Act, 1955 to make illegal migrants who are Hindus, Sikhs, Buddhists, Jains, Parsis and Christians from Afghanistan, Bangladesh and Pakistan, eligible for citizenship.

were 'liberally' utilized for managing elections within the state and elsewhere, adding to corrupt practices in elections. By any conservative estimates, in an average, there would be expenditure of more than 100 million in an assembly constituency.

As the tribes of Arunachal Pradesh are exempted from payment of income tax and are not required to reveal their sources of income, it becomes difficult to identify the legitimacy (or illegitimacy) of their income. Hence, to check corrupt practices during elections and eradicate corruption in tribal areas, there is an urgent need to have a relook at Section 10(26) of the Income Tax Act, 1961.

There is an increasing trend of erosion of clan solidarity because of electoral/political compulsions. However, of late, it has been observed that 'neo-rich' social leaders, intending to enter into political arena, exploit kinship connections to their political advantage. For example, new or extended clans are formed by organizing get-together of clan members and other social relatives.

There has been increasing participation of people in every election in Arunachal Pradesh. Significantly, in all the Assembly Elections held so far the strength of voting electorate outnumbered the strength of the non-voting electorate: 67–84 per cent. On an average, 72 per cent of the voters did exercise their franchise. Apparently, this is an indicator of political consciousness of the people and, may be, reflection of their political maturity.

Hence, there seems to be no issue with the level of participation of the citizens in the elections. What is of our concern is the lack of ethical participation of the citizens in electoral processes.

Disproportionate representation of women in both parliamentary and assembly elections is a reflection and continuation of a traditional thinking that 'politics is not a domain for women'. Representation of women has not crossed more than five per cent in any assembly elections, although the state has witnessed huge improvement in literacy rate of women

and their representation in government services in higher educational institutions.

The issue of illegal migrants, particularly of Chakma-Hajongs, remains a force that unites political parties of various ideologies (within the state) and diverse ethnic groups. It also has a potential to become a political tool to be used by politicians of various colours. When democratic processes are not initiated to find an amicable solution, undemocratic forces may take advantage of the situation. The natives are already angered by the supreme court order, directing conferment of citizenship to the eligible Chakmas and Hajongs. The Order is seen as disregarding protective principles designed for the protection of indigenous communities.

The state of Arunachal Pradesh still remains guided by the Government of India because of its geo-strategic location. Article 371 (H) of the constitution of India provides special power to the Governor of the state with regards to maintenance of law and order. A situation has, therefore, been created in which Arunachalees have been psychologically made to believe that the state is not in a position to remain in isolation: economically and politically. This may be one of the reasons that every political leaders rush to join the party that runs the government in New Delhi.

REFERENCES

Baruah, S. (2005). *Durable disorder: Understanding the politics of Northeast India.* New Delhi: Oxford University Press.
Bath, N. (2009). *Electoral politics in Arunachal Pradesh.* Varanasi: Pilgrims Publications.
Chaube, S. K. (2012). *Hill politics in northeast India.* New Delhi: Orient Blackswan.
Elwin, V. (1988). *Democracy in NEFA,* Directorate of Research. Jorhat: Government of Arunachal Pradesh.
Gogoi, P. D. (1971). *NEFA local polity* (unpublished Ph.D. Thesis). Dibrugarh: Dibrugarh University.

Government of Arunachal Pradesh. (1982). *The Arunachal Pradesh code*, Volume-I. Itanagar: Judicial Department.

Government of Arunachal Pradesh. (1998). *Arunachal review*. Naharlagun: Directorate of Information and Public Relations.

Kothari, R., & Weiner, M. (Eds.) (1965). *Indian voting behaviour: Studies of 1962 general election*. Calcutta: Firma K. L. Mukhopadhaya.

Lewis, O. (1965). *Village life in Northern India*. New York, NY: Vintage Books.

Luthra, P. N. (1993). *Constitutional and administrative growth of the Arunachal Pradesh*, Directorate of Research. Itanagar: Government of Arunachal Pradesh.

Mackenzie, A. (2001). *The North East frontier of India*. New Delhi: Mittal Publication.

Mahanta, B. (1983). *Administrative development of Arunachal Pradesh, 1875–1975*. Delhi: Uppal Publishing House.

Rao, V. (1995). *A century of tribal politics in North-East India 1874–1974*. New Delhi: S. Chand and Company.

Roy, S. (1997). *Aspects of Padam Minyong culture*. Guwahati: Government of Arunachal Pradesh.

Sinha, R. (1988). *The Akas*. Itanagar: Government of Arunachal Pradesh.

Talukdar, S. P. (1988). *The Chakmas: Life and struggles*. Delhi: Gian Publishing House.

The Dawnlit Post, Itanagar, 2019.

Tribal Politics in Assam:
1933–1947*

Suryasikha Pathak

The emergence of the Tribal League in 1933 made the provincial politics and its trajectory very dynamic. The Indian National Congress and the Muslim League which were debating on nationalism and identities, this new political body brought into those debates the question of 'tribes' hitherto ignored largely. History writing follows a similar trajectory largely ignoring the other contending ideologies which rephrased regional identities differently. Ideologies like that of the Tribal League were situated outside the primary contradiction of the Nationalist Movement, that is, between the colonized and the colonizers. This essay traverses a different path in the politics of the first few decades of the 20th century, embarking on the journey of the formation of the Tribal League, its leaders and the core ideas and demands raised in delineating a 'tribal' identity for themselves.

Interestingly, these tribes initially united into a political group to struggle for socio-political empowerment as well as fight the hegemony of caste Hindus. The focus of their politics was around issues of defining and constructing a tribal[1] identity, refusal to be absorbed into the Hindu caste society, temple entry, access to land, displacement from traditional habitational areas and general backwardness.

ASSOCIATIVE POLITICS PRIOR TO 1933

'Plains Tribes' is a term used in the contemporary political and administrative discourse from the 1930s when it was introduced by the British[2] as a generic term clubbing the valley tribes like the Bodos (Kacharis), Karbis (Mikirs), Mishings (Miris), Lalung (Tiwa) and

* This chapter was previously published in *Economic and Political Weekly, 45*(10), 2010, 61–69.

[1] The word tribe is used with the understanding that its definition is contested and it does not necessarily denote a fixed social identity.

[2] The British encountered two categories of tribes in north-east India: those who lived in hills and those in plains. The concept of plain tribe was coined to sharpen the differentiation. The earliest possible reference was by Ethnographer Endle (1911). The phrase continued to be used in the post-colonial period.

Rabhas together. Its continued usage by the tribal leaders is indicative of the appropriation of the term in an attempt to unify these varied communities on a single platform for political purposes.

Parallel to the efforts of the colonial state and ethnographers to define and locate tribe in the Brahmaputra valley, there were efforts by various tribal communities to locate themselves in the socio-political milieu of the colonial state. The early 20th century saw the emergence of various associations within these communities, which culminated in the emergence of the Tribal League in 1933 (Barman, 1995; Barua, 2001; Deuri, 2001). A direct cause and effect relation cannot be established between those early quasi-political organizations and the Tribal League, but their importance in shaping the nascent political and socio-cultural consciousness of the people is undeniable. The *Mels*,[3] inspired tribal conventions (like the Kachari convention, Miri convention, etc), matured the nascent 'tribal' consciousness, which resulted in the formation of the Tribal League as a mode of organized tribal politics.

From the 1920s onwards, growing political consciousness with Congress mobilizations and emergence of caste associations (like Ahom Sabha, Kaivartta Sanmilan) gave an impetus to the emergence of associations of tribal communities like Chutiya, Moran, and the Kacharis. Early in the 20th century, through the initiative of an educated middle class, the Kacharis, Mikirs, Miris and Rabhas made certain progress in comprehending the politics of rights, representation and emancipation. In their effort to develop, uplift or improve the conditions of the tribes, various attempts were made by this emerging leadership to locate the reasons for their backwardness and to introduce reforms in social practices. Kalicharan Brahma and Sitanath Brahma Choudhary among the Bodos and Samsonsing Ingti[4] among the Karbis were the real pioneers. Their attempts to redefine tradition and adjusting to colonial modernity were also the first steps towards the construction of the tribal identity.

The arrival of the Simon Commission in Assam in 1929 provided them the scope to put forward their grievances and aspirations to a Royal Commission for the first time. The memoranda and petitions presented to the Simon Commission show the presence of a strong political consciousness, centering on the notion of the tribal identity. Various associations, especially of the Bodo community, submitted a number of memoranda[5] to this Commission. The Commission took into consideration the memorandum by the Bodo community of Goalpara and few representatives from the primitive and backward tribes[6] were interviewed. The petition by the Bodo community observed that the benefits of reforms were enjoyed by the upper castes, thereby depriving the backward communities (Basumatari; also, *Memorandum by the*

---

[3] For details of Mels as an institution, see Barman (2005).

[4] Debendra Nath Sarma, *Gurudev Kalicharan Brahma* (Jorhat 1983); Chitra Mahanta, *Sinhapurush Sitanath Brahma Choudhury* (Jorhat 1983); Samsing Hanse, *Jananayak Samsonsing Ingti* (Jorhat, 1st Published 1983, 2nd 1990).

[5] *Memorandum by the Bodo Community of Goalpara district* (by Mr Ghyassudin Ahmad, B. L. Dhubri). *Assam Kachari Jubok Sammilan* (by Jadav Chandra Khakhlari, Secretary) on behalf of the entire Kachari community; *Proceedings of the Conference held by the representatives of the Kachari community* from different parts of Assam held at Titabar, Jorhat, August 1928; Memorial of the Bodos, Garos and Rabhas of the Goalpara Sub-division, *Boro Jubok Sammilan* (by Shyama Charan Brahma, Secretary).

[6] The deputation of the primitive and backward tribes called and interviewed which consisted of Sonadhar Das (representative- Bania Samaj); Raj Saheb Pyari Mohan Das (representative- Mahisyas); Nila-Kanta Hazarika (representative- Kaivartas); Jogesh Chandra Nath (representative- Yogis); Mahi Chandra Miri (representative- Miri); Jadav Chandra Khakhlari (representative- Bodo); Mahendra Lal Das (representative- Lalungs and Mikirs) and Ramesh Chandra Das.

Bodo Community of Goalpara). In order to safeguard their interests, 'the community demanded separate representative in the local council and one reserved seat for the Bodos in the Central Legislature' (Memorandum by the Bodo Community of Goalpara). They deplored their backwardness and recognized education as a means of development and fight against exploitation. They complained that they were illiterate because 'our people are always misled, they cannot understand the value of reforms, they cannot save themselves from the hands of the foreign moneylenders' (Memorandum by the Bodo Community of Goalpara). The leaders, as representatives of respective tribes, used the colonial imagery of the tribe as backward, semi-savage and ignorant to put forward their political claims and for seeking colonial protection (Memorandum by the Bodo Community of Goalpara). The 10th convention of the Assam Bodo Chattra Sammilon in 1929, under the supervision of Rupnath Brahma, reiterated the necessity of education for progress and better utilization of the opportunities offered by the colonial state. Therefore they urged the setting up of schools to struggle against illiteracy, rather than depending on the government.[7] Likewise, delivering the presidential address to the Assam Kachari Jubok Sammilan in 1929, Benduhar Rajkhowa stressed on establishing schools in every village through the people's own initiative, and by pressurizing the local boards to fund them.[8]

The leadership also contested the classification of these tribal communities as low caste Hindus in the census reports. The memorandum submitted by the Assam Kachari Jubok Sammilan, suggested that to regard the tribal as Hindu was misleading, 'for the latter do not receive them into their society, do not dine with them and are mostly unsympathetic with their ideas and aspiration' (Basumatari, n.d., p. 9). They asserted that the Kacharis

were never a part of the caste-divided Hindu society, and were independent by virtue of not being bound to the 'chariot wheels of the Hindu community' (Basumatari, n.d., p. 10). So, by the late 1920s, ideas about the distinctiveness of tribal culture became an important part of what was defined as tribal identity. The notion of a tribal unity was initially conceived during this period, though the attempt was made on a small scale in imagining a unified great Bodo/Kachari tribe whose past was traced through the invention of a common history. Interestingly, they also refused to totally severe this identity from the Assamese one. On the question of territorial transfer of Goalpara to Bengal, members of the various Kachari organizations claimed themselves to be Assamese on the basis of cultural affinity (Basumatari, n.d., p. 6). As mentioned earlier, Kalicharan Brahma's efforts to introduce Assamese as the medium of instruction also point to a parallel political and cultural identification to an Assamese identity.

The formation and emergence of the Tribal League in 1933 as a common platform of all the Plains Tribes also involved a parallel process in self-representation. The numerically small educated tribal elite attempted to define their tribal identity as a community of the plains tribes. The Tribal League envisioned the unity of the various tribal communities. Thus, there emerged the single, monolithic notion of the plains tribes. Though essentially it was a geographical term delineating the tribes of the Brahmaputra valley as distinct from the tribes who lived in the hills, the tribal elite, and later tribal representatives in the assembly, asserted this community's interests in opposition to the interests of other communities (like the Muslims, caste Hindus, hill tribes and tea garden labourers). The plains tribes category was invented by the colonial authorities to ethnographically classify the tribal section of the population in the plains, which was later,

---

[7] Proceedings of the 10th Convention of the *Assam Bodo Chattra Sammilon*, 1929, pp. 11–12.
[8] Presidential Address to the *Assam Kachari Jubok Sammilani* by Benudhar Rajkhowa, 1929, p. 11.

after the 1935 Act, given the status of a separate constituency. The tribal elite appropriated this construction to articulate their political aspirations.

TRIBAL POLITICS AND LAND QUESTIONS

Tribal land alienation was intensely debated in the legislative assembly in relation to the issues of immigration and occupancy of agricultural land by the immigrants. Immigration from East Bengal had assumed significant proportion in the 1930s. Though the colonial government encouraged the immigration as a means of settling cultivable waste in the hope of raising more revenue, under growing pressure from Assamese middle class and to mitigate impending rural conflicts colonial officers implemented the line system by 1920.[9] The line system envisaged the drawing of an imaginary line demarcating two distinct areas and no occupation of land by the immigrants was allowed beyond this line. It was introduced in Nowgong and, by 1930, it was operating in most districts of upper Assam.[10] The Tribal League saw it as a colonial intervention to safeguard tribal lands (speech by Bhimbar Deuri (Guha, 2006, p. 213). But the system did not work in reality in the same manner as it existed on paper. It was never strictly implemented, nor was it very effective in the absence of a strong government authority at the local level. Despite its existence, there was a land alienation, which led to numerous sessions of questioning, adjournment motions and heated debates in the assembly.[11]

In 1937, the Muslim League moved a resolution for the abolition of the line system (Budget Session. Assam Legislative Assembly Proceedings (ALAP). April, 1937). Members of the Tribal League, Rabi Chandra Kachari and Rupnath Brahma opposed the resolution and it was eventually withdrawn. The necessity of the system as a protective measure was reiterated by Rabi Chandra Kachari in the following words, 'There should be a Line system to protect the weak and backward people. Without a Line of demarcation it is not possible to look into the interests of the poor people who require special protection' (speech by Rabi Chandra Kachari. ALAP. 5 August 1937). The tribal representatives in the assembly, thus, defended the continuation of the line system and expressed their fear that if it was abolished 'rores and crores of immigrants will come in and the original ruling people of Assam will have to leave the place for the jungles and hills' (speech by Rabi Chandra Kachari. ALAP. 5 August 1937). This argument of endangering the tribal by letting them face the immigrants, displacement from their areas, and the crucial question of their existence in peril, was repeated throughout the period of 1937–1947 with growing intensity. Rupnath Brahma demanded enforcement of the line system in Goalpara because 'many tribal people in Goalpara have been compelled to leave their homes and settle elsewhere' (speech by Rupnath Brahma. ALAP. 5 August 1937). Even some non-tribal members of the assembly like Naba Kumar Dutta and Mahi Chandra Bora also condemned the efforts to abolish the line system and criticized the government's lack of concern for the ousted indigenous people including the backward classes like the Bodos and the Mishings (speech by Naba Kumar Dutta. ALAP. 5 August 1937),

---

[9] The idea of Line system was mooted in 1916 and formally introduced in 1920 as a measure to segregate areas specified for indigenous people and immigrants. For further discussion, see Guha (1977); Nag (1990).
[10] *Report of the Line System Enquiry Committee* Vols 1 and 2 (Hockenhull Committee), Shillong 1938.
[11] Adjournment motion on account of recent vast raids by immigrants in certain villages of Howly Mouza in Barpeta subdivision. ALAP. 29 February 1940; Resolution disapproving the land settlement policy of the present government. ALAP. 6 December 1941.

who were driven out from their villages and had "taken shelter in the forests" (speech by Mahi Chandra Bora. ALAP. 5 August 1937).

Under the colonization schemes, the government opened up reserve lands, de-reserved forests and professional grazing reserves, displacing the indigenous people (speech by Haladhar Bhuyan. ALAP. 24 February 1938). The colonization scheme also entailed paying a premium for occupying the land, which, the Congress and Tribal League representatives claimed, the indigenous people could not afford to pay (speech by Rabi Chandra Kachari, Purna Chandra Sarma. ALAP. 24 February 1938). However, as Maulvi Sayidur Rahman said in support of the colonization scheme, legally there was no bar for the indigenous people occupying land (speech by Sayidur Rahman. ALAP. 24 February 1938). Members like F. W. Hockenhull insisted that the indigenous people did not occupy land because of the ample availability of free cultivable lands to them, and not because of want of capital. But, as claimed by others, there was 'practically no suitable arable land outside the colonization areas and almost all cultivable lands have been occupied by the immigrants' and urged the government to stop the process of settlement of lands (speech by Mahi Chandra Bora. ALAP. 24 February 1938). Karka Dalay Miri, the representative of the Mishing tribe in the assembly, opposed colonization because of the growing scarcity of land, which would restrict further expansion for the indigenous people (speech by Karka Dalay Miri. ALAP. 24 February 1938).

In view of the escalating pressure, colonial administrators like Hockenhull asserted that there was "no real issue at all between the indigenous and immigrant population" (speech by Hockenhall. ALAP. 24 February 1938). The logic was that the type of land (char-riverine land) favoured by the immigrants was not being cultivated by the indigenous people (speech by Hockenhall. ALAP. 24 February 1938). Even Purna Chandra Sarma, the Congressman, illustrated the examples

from Nowgong district indicating the defective and biased functioning of the scheme. He complained that the tribals of Nowgong were without land 'and there has been no consideration to those people because they are not immigrants and cannot afford to pay any premium' (speech by Purna Chandra Sarma. ALAP. 24 February 1938). It was also pointed out that these lands originally belonged to the tribal communities like the Tiwas and Bodos which were opened for colonization in Nowgong (speech by Purna Chandra Sarma. ALAP. 24 February 1938). Protest against such violation of rules and regulations evoked, according to the leaders, only mild responses and often biased enquiries. For the officials, the system was working satisfactorily despite reports of violation of rules and regulations. Addressing the 1940 Budget session, Beliram Das, representative of the backward castes, attacked the Sayid Muhammad Saadulla ministry for its policy on the immigrants. The flow of immigrants was compared to an invasion into the lines and reserved areas causing great panic (speech by Beliram Das. ALAP. 24 February, 1938).

The deliberation of the legislative assembly, the subsequent land settlement policy and conflicts over land made it amply clear that available arable land was becoming scarce (Guha, 1977, p. 281). It was further aggravated by occupation of vast wastelands by tea gardens (Behal, 1983) and the opening up of professional grazing reserves for occupation (Bordoloi, 1991, pp. 73–77). As the anti-displacement voice grew stronger, various enquiries were set up by the government to look into tribal land alienation. These discovered that, in many cases, the tribal sold off their lands to the immigrants (speech by Rupnath Brahma. *ALAP*. 25 February, 1938; speech by Khan Saheb Maulavi Muhammad Amiruddin. *ALAP*. 6 March 1944). The Deputy Commissioner's report stated that there were other instances where the tribals sold their land to the immigrants and themselves migrated to central and upper Assam in the hope of getting rehabilitated by the government under some developmental schemes (speech by Lakeshwar Barooah. *ALAP*. 6 December 1941). The absence of cash to pay taxes also forced the tribals to sell their lands. The tribal representatives emphasized the cultural differences between the Muslim immigrants and themselves (speech by Dhirising Deuri. ALAP. 23 March 1944, adjournment motion by Beliram Das, 13 March 1944) and opposed creation of immigrant settlements near tribal villages (speech by Beliram Das. ALAP. 13 March, 1944; speech by Karka Dalay Miri. ALAP. 15 March 1943). Karka Dalay Miri, representative of the Mishing tribe, drew the assembly's attention to the displacement of the Mishing people of Gorumara in Sissi Mauza, Dibrugarh, and also to the cancellation of *pattas* (land records) to Mishings and Deuris, who had settled in Bahgara and Dhunagiri in Bihpuria Mauza, North Lakhimpur (speech by Karka Dalay Miri. ALAP. 5 December 1941).

The Assamese middle class and the Congress also articulated fears that land hungry immigrants were a threat to the existence of the indigenous peasantry. This was evident in Lakheswar Barooah's resolution,

The aggressive attitude of the immigrants which manifests itself in wanton trespass on the land of the indigenous population, offences against women, mischief upon the crops of the indigenous population and various other crimes disturbed the peaceful atmosphere of the local rural people (speech by Lakheswar Barooah. ALAP. 6 December 1941).

The 1931 census aggravated the tension on the question of demographic balance. The superintendent of census operation, M Mullan termed the coming of the immigrants an invasion. J. H. Hutton, the Census Commissioner of India in his report wrote,

These immigrants, who are prolific breeders and industrious cultivators, are unruly and uncomfortable neighbours. These immigrants threaten to swamp entirely the indigenous inhabitants and in the course of two or three decades to

change the whole nature, language and religion of the Brahmaputra valley (Hutton, 1931, p. 12).

The sense of vulnerability increased because of reported cases of forcible occupation of tribal villages and lands (speech by Dhirsingh Deuri. ALAP. 14 March 1944; speech by Karka Dalay Miri. ALAP. 18 March 1941; Rabi Chandra Kachari. ALAP. 6 March 1944; Dhir Singh Deuri. ALAP. 26 February 1940; Kameshwar Das. *ALAP*. 29 February 1940). But such cases were often exaggerated. For example, the Hindu Mahasabha claimed that it was 'getting alarming reports of forcible occupation of lands in mass scale by Muslims in Meteka Borbeal, and many other villages in Namati Mauza in Mikir Hills, Nowgong. Mikirs (were) becoming panic-stricken at this lawless-ness'. Another telegram mentioned that 'innumerable Muslim immigrants, Surma Valley Muslims occupying lands in Meteka Borbeal, Hatipara, Jamunagaon, Maudonga, Howraghat, Dighaepani, Dakmaka, Chulani, Parakhowa, Sorgathi villages within Mikir Hills area, Namati Mauza, Nowgong against all previous restrictive prohibitive order. Great consternations amongst Mikirs prevails. Pray Excellency's immediate intervention' (Adjournment Motion, ALAP. 13 May 1944). The tribal representatives and the Congress leaders attributed the land-grabbing to the connivance of Muslim government officers and the immigrants. Thus, they protested, even genuine complaints and eviction orders were left without any action being taken (Karka Dalay Miri. ALAP. 15 March 1943).

Gradually from 1937 to 1947, such demands became more persistent against increasing violations of rules and regulations. A committee was constituted to inquire into the working of the Line system. The report submitted by F. Hockenhall of the European Party emphasized that the '... indigenous people alone would be unable, without the aid of immigrant settlers, to develop...' (Guha, 1977, p. 261). But it was also in favour of the line system and strong measures to protect tribal lands. The Bordoloi Ministry, after much deliberation, agreed to evict all immigrant squatters from areas declared protected tribal blocks in the submontane regions. Following the Committee's report, the Congress coalition adopted a land settlement policy, which was published in a gazette extraordinary of 4 November 1939. The points it emphasized were (a) the importance of maintaining grazing and forest reserves meant for public use and ordered immediate eviction of encroachers—immigrants or non-immigrants; (b) the interests of the tribal and backward people were to be jealously guarded and large blocks in sub-montane areas inhabited by tribals were ordered to be made prohibited areas; and (c) due provision was to be made for the reservation of large areas for the natural expansion of indigenous populations. Besides these, there was a proposal for planned settlement of the tribals (Guha, 1977, p. 261).

The resignation of the Bordoloi Ministry left such decisions largely unimplemented. During the Saadulla Ministry the Muslim League again demanded the abolition of the line system. Regarding the issue of the protection of the tribals and for that purpose allowing the system to continue, Maulavi Syed Abdur Rauf said, '...the Line system question has been harped upon by the opposition to win over tribal friends ... But if they require protection, they require it against all non-tribals' (speech by Maulavi Syed Abdur Rauf. ALAP. 26 February 1940). Most of the tribal representatives felt that the protective measures that were adopted were inadequate so far as the interests of the tribal people were concerned. The Congress criticized the Saadulla Ministry for failing to provide protection to the tribal. They feared that these 'indigenous people of the province—the tribal and the scheduled castes are soon to be driven away to the hills to make room for the invading hordes

of immigrants' (speech by Chandra Sarma. ALAP. 26 February 1940).

In the 1940s, on the issue of amending the conditions of the line system, the tribal representatives demanded legislative changes and laws to evict all illegal settlers, whether they had settled before or after April 1937.[12] In June 1940, a government resolution put a ban on settlement of wastelands by any immigrants entering Assam after 1 January 1938. The Saadulla Ministry was continuously pressurized by the tribal representatives and Congress members inside and outside the assembly to prohibit the settlement of wastelands by immigrants coming after 1 January 1938. The Muslim League members opposed this for there was no way to distinguish a pre-1938 immigrant and a later intruder. The Saadulla coalition ministry was throughout criticized for its anti-Assamese, anti-tribal and pro-immigrant stand, through its minister Abdul Matin Choudhury declared officially that protection of the backward tribals was the bedrock of their policy (speech by Abdul Matin Choudhury. ALAP. 6 March 1944).

In this period, the debate was around the question of land alienation. As the question of the line system and protection of the backward classes became a contentious issue, the Congress used this as a political instrument against the Muslim League, though its own concerns remained suspect with the Tribal League. Due to the absence of funds, the tribals could not avail various developmental schemes (speech by Rabi Chandra Kachari. ALAP. 14 March 1944). Blocks continued to be opened as also the professional grazing reserves. The Congress continued to stress on the necessity of maintaining the professional grazing reserves and also demanded that wastelands should be measured and areas reserved for the indigenous population before settling the immigrants.[13] However,

---

[12] Adjournment motion on account of recent vast raids by immigrants in certain villages of Howly Mouza in Barpeta subdivision (ALAP. 29 February 1940; Budget Discussion. ALAP. 6 March 1944).

[13] ALAP. 6 December 1941, resolution disapproving the land settlement policy of the Saadualla Government.

the Congress' national level leaders like Jawaharlal Nehru felt that immigration was an economic necessity and, though not supporting its abolition, wanted a relaxation of the line system (Guha, 1977, p. 258). The conflict around the land question acquired new dimensions when the tribal people began occupying areas where the immigrants were settled. According to Md Amiruddin, 'some 350 Mikirs, Lalungs and Kacharis headed by the *gaonburas* (village headman) came ... not only broke down the houses ... set fire to most of them and turned the colonists out of their homesteads and holdings as well' (speech by Md Amiruddin. ALAP. 6 March 1944). He tried to convey that the allegations against the immigrants were baseless and condemned the tribal as rioters and trespassers. The Congress successfully won over the tribal representatives, by focusing on Saadulla and his 'pro-Muslim politics'. Saadulla was caught between the two groups—the tribal representatives demanding protection and the Muslim League calling for the abolition of the line system. From 1937 onwards, the tribal representatives in the assembly demanded more stringent legislation to stop land alienation and blocked efforts of the members of Muslim League to abolish the line system.[14]

1941 CENSUS AS THE SITE OF CONTESTATION

The 1941 Census refrained from providing religious classification in Assam. Compilation for communities was done with reference to race, tribe and caste and not religion, as it was in the case of the 1931 Census. It evoked strong criticism from various sections of Assamese society and led to a debate in newspapers as well as in the assembly. The Congress criticized the government for manipulating the census operations so as to conceal the correct figures of the followers of different religions. An adjournment motion was called to discuss the census operations.[15] It was under the Assam provincial government's insistence that K. W. P. Marar, the census superintendent, issued a special circular to the Deputy Commissioners and census officers in Assam to compile data on the basis of community. He wrote,

> The basis for community is the answer to questions 3, but generally the communities are unavoidably mixed up and where community cannot be ascertained in answer to question 3, to question 4 will be the basis; e g, if a Kachari has not in answer to question 3 mentioned that he is a Kachari, and is returned under question 4 as Hindu, Muslim or Christian, he will be shown as Hindu, Muslim or Christian as the case may be, but if he is returned as a Kachari against question 3 he will be entered such irrespective of his religion (*ALAP*. 4 December 1941: Adjournment motion by Siddhi Nath Sarma).

The government stated that the purpose of clubbing communities professing different religions was to create a 'separate entity under the constitution for the purpose of franchise' (ALAP. 4 December 1941).[16] Siddhi Nath Sarma, for instance, clarified that as the tabulation would be done on the basis of community, and not on religious lines, it would simplify the problem of treatment or classification of the primitive tribes. He added that in this way their total number regardless of their religion could be recorded (speech by Siddhi Nath Sharma. *ALAP*. 4 December 1941). The efforts on the part of the colonial government to seek out community identity corresponded to the Tribal League's own efforts to project

---

[14] The Line system was introduced for the first time in 1920 in Nowgong.

[15] *ALAP*. 4 December 1941: Adjournment motion in connection with the conducting of the last census operations in Assam brought by Siddhi Nath Sarma.

[16] Classification of communities according to Appendix II, prepared by the Assam government, was as follows: (a) Assam valley Hindus; (b) Assam valley Muslims; (c) Surma valley Hindus; (d) Surma valley Muslims; (e) Scheduled castes; (f) Tribal people, hills; (g) Tribal people, plains; (h) European and Anglo-Indian.

the community identity as one, unified, tribal people. And for this purpose, the Tribal League carried out propaganda. A bulletin of the League was taken out with the main objective of instructing the tribal people about enumerating themselves in the census (*The Assam Tribal League [Bulletin 2]*, Deuri, 1940, p. 1). The Tribal League's definition of tribal was broad-based and included those who were otherwise classified as Hinduized. Religion was a secondary aspect of the identity. The essence of *tribalness* was the existence of distinctive rituals and customs, rules and regulations, which were retained, therefore, aiding the preservation of a distinctive lifestyle often in totality and some cases partially (Deuri, 1940, p. 1).

Further, the Tribal League also emphasized the separateness and *differentness* of the social structure of the tribals and caste Hindu Assamese. The focus was on two polarized societies where no intermingling ever existed. The independence of the tribal from the Hindu society was claimed. By rejecting placement in the caste hierarchy, which was perceived as degrading in the Tribal League's discourse, it sought to acquire equality on their own plane, within the restricting political space provided by the colonial state. By not subscribing to the worldview of the caste Hindus, the tribes had already taken a step towards redefining their identity. The discourse contested the efforts of certain groups to classify the tribals as Harijan Hindus, which was perceived as a ploy to club them together with the low castes (Deuri, 1940, p. 1). The Tribal League persistently opposed various moves by more conservative circles and the Congress, to categorize them as a part of the Hindu society.

According to the Congress and some others, the enumeration should have taken into consideration the important factor of religion while classifying the communities. The colonial state claimed that it wanted to simplify complex categorization in tabulation and

wanted to 'avoid in their argument provoking terms such as Hinduised' (speech by Siddhi Nath Sarma. ALAP. 4 December 1941).[17] The superintendents, though, could discuss complexities and it was noted that some discussions on the religious affiliations of the tribals and the degree of their Hinduization would be both of interest and value (speech by Siddhi Nath Sarma. ALAP. 4 December 1941). Hinduization was not the sole concern but conversion to Christianity also drew official attention, and it was suggested, '... it is important to know to what degree they have entered the Christian or other fold' (speech by Rev J. J. M. Nichols Roy. ALAP. 4 December 1941). The Guwahati Rajhowa (Public) Census Committee along with others published a public notice stressing that, despite the instructions of census officers and the Tribal League, the tribal population need not necessarily state their religion, as instructed, according to their *jati* (caste), that is, Kachari religion or Lalung religion. They could enumerate as they were, that is, accordingly stating their religion—Hindu, Muslim, Christian and animist. Such an appeal was made to save and serve the interests of the 'Assamese' (*Teendiniya Assamiya*, 21 January 1941). It was also emphasized that the definition of a Hindu was not narrowly confined to the people in the caste hierarchy but was wide enough to incorporate people who could be termed as Hinduized. It was observed, 'A lot of tribals who have been converted to Vaishnavism, Saraniyas, still stick to certain food habits like eating pork and fowls, but on that basis they should not be classed as otherwise, i.e, according to their tribal name, but be classified as Hindus' (*Teendiniya Assamiya*, 21 January 1941).

Ambikagiri Rai Chaudhuri of the Assam Siksha Prachar Samiti appealed to the tribals to think twice before enumerating themselves. He stressed on their being a part of a greater Assamese society calling them its backbone

---

[17] Siddhi Nath Sarma quoted Mr Marar's instructions to Census Officers.

and asked them to desist from supporting the community-based enumeration to preserve that identity. He referred to the colonial situation and suggested that such divisive tendencies would prolong colonial domination (*Teendiniya Assamiya*, 10 January 1941). More or less similar sentiments were echoed through the articles and editorials of the newspapers (*Teendiniya Assamiya* and *The Assam Tribune*).

The Saadulla government came under increasing attacks from the Congress. The Congress accused the then provincial government of using the census as an instrument to encourage fissiparous tendencies (The Assam Tribune, 19 September 1941). The Tribal League was also criticized for being a pawn in the hands of the colonial government (The Assam Tribune, 21 November 1941). The Saadulla government and the Muslim League were accused of attempting to alter the demographic structure of society in a bid to join Pakistan (The Assam Tribune, 19 September 1941). The overarching concern was the decrease in the population of the Hindus. The concern towards the tribals arose from the fear of growing immigration from East Bengal and census data showing alarming increases in the population of Muslims (The Assam Tribune, 19 September 1941). The only way visible to the middle class leadership to maintain a demographic balance was to conflate the figures of Hindus by adding to it the numbers for the plains tribe's populations.

The 1941 census was perceived as an attempt of the government to fragment the unified Hindu community by stressing on community identity than on religion. This propaganda urged the Lalungs, Rabhas, Kacharis, Mikirs and other communities to demand classification as Hindus as opposed to tribals. Editorials in newspapers also addressed the same issue. It was conceded that there was nothing novel or wrong in calculating the tribal population but doing so solely on the basis of community, not qualified by religion, gave a distorted impression of reality, like showing a huge

increase in the tribal population (The Assam Tribune, 31 October 1941, Editorial).

Protests against such calculation also came from the tribes as well. Many protested against their classification as animist or according to their tribes. The Sonowal Kacharis were, for example, stated to be Hinduized for a long time and followers of rules and regulations of Hinduism, and had priests officiating the rituals (The Assam Tribune, 21 January 1941). Various associations of the tribal communities like the Assam Bodo Sammilan, Assam Kachari Sammilan, Assam Miri Sammilan were not consulted by the Tribal League to discuss the issue of enumeration (The Assam Tribune, 21 January 1941) and therefore the latter could not be said to represent all the tribes. Some sections of the Kacharis refused to be classified as tribal along with Mishings, Deuris and Karbis. The tribal representatives were criticized for attempting to distort reality by categorizing all tribes en masse together under one head. The Rabha tribe asserted that they be recognized as a separate community and not be treated as a branch of the Kachari tribe. It was argued that religion-wise they have to be classified either as Hindus, Christians or animists (The Assam Tribune, 10 January 1941 and 17 January 1941). Other than the Congress, the Christian representatives in the assembly opposed such a classification on the ground that, 'Figures given in the last census are defective and incomplete inasmuch as that Christians have been shown at such a low figure. The word 'community' itself could not be explained, it is a misnomer, when we mean a community, whether religion is to be taken into account or the race that is a question which very few people will be able to explain' (The Assam Tribune, 17 January 1941, Speech by Mr C. Goldsmith. ALAP). In the face of such evident protest from various sections, Rupnath Brahma, member of the Tribal League and then a minister in the United Party government, claimed that he would present before the House 'the exact feelings of the tribal people on the matter' (*The Assam*

Tribune, 17 January 1941, speech by Rupnath Brahma. ALAP). The Tribal League's position was reiterated in the Assembly.

> As regard the tribal people of the plains they have their own Tribal League and there is a feeling, and indeed there had been a solemn resolution of that League to the effect these tribal people should be shown together irrespective of any religion and they feel that unless and until that is done their future is doomed and they will stand nowhere (The Assam Tribune, 17 January 1941).

He also denied the reports that tribal people in some places had protested against classification on community basis and emphasized the fact that 'the existing Tribal League is the only provincial organization under which all the plains tribal people of the province function' (*The Assam Tribune*, 17 January 1941). According to Rev L. Gatphoh, classification on the basis of community brought out the strength of the tribal people and contradicted the impression given by censuses till 1941 'that tribal people in Assam were a dying race or races' (The Assam Tribune, 17 January 1941, speech by Rev L. Gatphoh. ALAP).

Protest, against the manner in which the census was conducted, was registered by people like A. V. Thakkar, a Gandhian. He also called the enumeration on the basis of community a strange phenomenon and questioned the classification which clubbed various tribes under one head, the plains tribes.

> But under the new classification, now adopted in 1941, they are all classed as aborigines or one community of tribals (unless they declined to fill in column 3 for race or tribe) though there is nothing like one community but a number of (more than 20) communities, each tribe being a community by itself (Thakkar, 1941, p. 244).

He also criticized the colonial state's communal award, facilitated by the 1935 Act, which granted separate representation to the tribes for the first time.

> They have since 1935 got separate representation to the tribal for the first time...we have since 1935 got *certain political rights and importance,* a tribal gentleman and a tribal lady MLAs are included in the Cabinet, (by the Congress coalition government only the former and by the present non-Congress government both) and *a wave of awakening* has come over them (Thakkar, 1941, p. 246).

The great increase in the population returned as tribal is, thus, explained not in the positive aspect of identity consciousness but as politically motivated. 'Thus religious faith and cultural affinity have proved to be nothing before political power' (Thakkar, 1941, p. 246). This is because of the colonial state's policies and the tribal elite's manipulation, the tribes who sought to assimilate and were 'slowly absorbed amongst Hindus on one side and among the Christians for the last 50 years on the other, must have en masse swung to the "Tribal Community"' (Thakkar, 1941, p. 246).[18] As a rejoinder to the comment, the editor published a note, which defined tribal in the context of community, and noted that,

> As the word 'tribal' in the present census is not used to indicate religion but only community or tribe, I think, the Assam Census Superintendent would appear to have been quite correct in classifying as aborigines such aboriginal. In fact it is advantageous to the aborigines to be classified as such and injurious to them to get themselves returned as Hindus. For by becoming Hindus they sink into the degraded class of 'Harijan', or depressed classes. Moreover, by recording themselves as 'aboriginal' or '*tribals*' they stand a chance of political advancement. For in the next Indian Government Act, an increase in the recorded number of aboriginals is expected to ensure them a larger number of seats in the Legislatures. We think that lovers of aborigines should rejoice rather than grieve over the

---

[18] The communities he specifically mentioned are Brahmas of Goalpara, Sarnuyas of Kamrup and Darrang, Lalungs of Nowgong and the Miris of Sibsagar and Lakhimpur.

recorded increase of 'Tribals' or 'aborigines' in any province.[19]

ENTRY TO THE TEMPLE

The Tribal League's efforts to distance itself from caste Hindu Assamese society in carving out a tribal identity was also evident when the Assam Temple Entry Bill was introduced in the assembly in 1940. Ghanashyam Das, the mover, regretted the fact that most temples were not open for some sections of the society, especially the so-called depressed and backward classes. According to him, temple entry was not restricted in the past and came into existence only recently. He illustrated how the Vaishnava preacher Sankardeva believed in equality and that is why 'even a *Javan* like Jayahari Ata, a Miri like Bolai Ata, a Bhot like Damudar Ata and a Kachari like Ram Ata were given equal status in his religious society' (speech by Ghanashyam Das. ALAP. 29 February 1940). His treatment of the tribes was reflective of a dominant trend, placing them in the hierarchy of the caste structure and the discourse of upliftment which defines them as low-caste Hindus. The preconceived assumption bracketed the tribal with the low-caste Hindus, who were denied entry into most temples. The dominant Assamese caste Hindu society did not perceive the plains tribals as a separate entity. Such an attitude is evident in Ghanashyam Das' speech:

> ... in the Doul festival in Barpeta a man having sympathy for his fellow brothers cannot bear to see the sight when the tribal and depressed classes are refused, with harsh words, entry to the *Kirtonghar*. You cannot look at their eyes when they return with tears running down their sad faces (speech by Ghanashyam Das. ALAP. 29 February 1940).

He compared the equality shared by tribal and non-tribal representatives in the assembly house where he saw no apparent distinction between Rupnath Brahma, Rabi Chandra Kachari, Rohini Choudhuri and himself. The presence of discrimination in the social structure would not allow the above-mentioned tribal representatives' access into any temple. He pointed out,

> if my friend M. Rabi Chandra Kachari wants to enter the Barpeta temple, he will also get no access there. Is it not painful, sir, and is it not humiliating? Should this distinction remain? No matter, sir, their sympathy with me for their depressed and tribal classes will surface.... I have a duty. I should perform that duty (speech by Ghanashyam Das. ALAP. 29 February 1940).

Doubts were raised by the government about the extent that the Temple Entry Bill would benefit the tribals. Rohini Kumar Chaudhuri questioned whether the Bill would help the Kacharis and other animists (speech by Rohini Kumar Chaudhuri. ALAP. 29 February 1940). He also stated the Bill's definition of a Hindu, which was defined as 'one who is such by birth and religion and one who is a convert into it' (speech by Rohini Kumar Chaudhuri. *ALAP*. 29 February 1940) excluded the tribes. By that logic 'the animists will be clearly excluded by this definition of the term 'Hindu'. So, this Bill will not at all give them any right' (speech by Rohini Kumar Chaudhuri. *ALAP*. 29 February 1940). Rupnath Brahma, then a Minister in the provincial government and representative of the Tribal League, clarified his organization's position whether tribes can be termed Hindus and whether the Bill would benefit them:

> I have been asked by the honourable mover whether I myself and my people are Hindus or not. On this point I do not like to enter into any open discussion in this house, but this much I can tell the house that amongst the tribal people there are Christians and there are some who have adopted the Hindu religion and the rest of them

---

[19] Editorial note as a rejoinder to A. V. Thakkar's comment on the Assam Census in *Man in India*, 21, (1941, p. 247).

have been treated as animists. I may say that *they are quite independent of the Hindu society – they are certainly not so-called low caste Hindus, they have got a distinct form of religion of their own, and they do not care if they are allowed to have entrance in the temples.* I think these people are not so much anxious to have access to public temples, or any temples (speech by Rupnath Brahma on the Assam Temple Entry Bill. ALAP. 29 February 1940, [emphasis mine]).

Another member, Gauri Kanta Talukdar, rejected the necessity of classifying the tribal separately as animists, such categories being largely colonial constructs:

It is a matter of great regret that following blindly the Christian missionaries and their friends, the European writers and some of our own countrymen are calling the tribal peoples 'animists'. Sir, I vehemently protest against the use of the expression 'animists' in the case of our brethren of the tribal communities. It is a misnomer, it is an insult levelled against these people to call them animists. Who has been using this expression? Has it not been done by the missionaries with the object of exploiting these peoples? Is this not a surreptitious attempt to alienate a portion of our brethren from the Hindu fold? (speech by Gauri Kanta Talukdar. ALAP. 29 February 1940).

He used a broad definition of Hinduism, as given by the Hindu Mahasabha, which was inclusive of all religions which had originated in India. According to him the simple act of calling oneself Hindu (irrespective of practices and rituals), made one Hindu because of its all-inclusive paternalistic nature. Rupnath Brahma's denial of the positive effects of the Temple Entry Bill for the tribals people was criticized by the Congress, with its populist claims for social upliftment. According to Ghanashyam Das, Rupnath Brahma represented only the tribal elite and was modern in his views and, therefore, did not attach importance to entry into a temple. Brahma's opinion was called a personal viewpoint and not representative of the voice of the tribal people. The tribal society being a part of the wider Hindu society there were, asserted Talukdar, 'people who are religious minded and who like to worship God inside a temple', and they should

not be deprived of that right (speech by Gauri Kanta Talukdar. *ALAP*. 29 February 1940).

EDUCATION AS A MEANS TO EMPOWERMENT

In the legislative assembly, through the articulation of the Tribal League members, the construction of another image of the plains tribes took shape: the image is of a 'backward' community. In the speeches of the tribal members, we find a sense of self-depreciation, which drew heavily from the internalization of colonial, official and ethnographic images of the tribes.

The sense of cultural inferiority integral with the term 'tribal society' enunciated by the colonial ethnology was too embedded in the psychology of the educated tribals to inspire them... not surprisingly, the tribal leaders consciously presented themselves as 'backward' people before the statutory commission amounting to negation of their own culture (Bara, 1997, p. 789).

By virtue of not being a part of the dominant mainstream culture, the appellation of backwardness in various aspects, subsequently, entitled protection and special provisions so that such conditions disappear. It was stressed that the tribes not only inhabited backward tracts but were backward in every aspect, be it in education or other social conditions. The reasons of backwardness, according to Rabi Chandra Kachari, could be partly attributed to internal inability or handicaps to progress and partly (probably most importantly) 'due to indifference of our more fortunate brethren and want of proper encouragement at the hands of the government' (speech by Rabi Chandra Kachari. ALAP. 7 August 1937). The necessity of 'protection and special treatment—real and substantial' (speech by Rabi Chandra Kachari. *ALAP*. 14 March 1944) for large tribal populations, which were 'poor, weak and ignorant', was the dominant mode of articulation.

Therefore, the tribal leaders perceived education and employment as modern means of empowerment and social emancipation. The emerging tribal elite, who constituted the Tribal League perceived modern education as empowerment. There was the realization that in order to create and preserve, an identity one needed instruments like education. As one tribal member of the assembly observed, At present, education is the most vital problem for the tribal, backward and scheduled castes people. They now feel what is education and they are now realising that without education they are nobody and nowhere in the civilised world (speech by Karka Dalay Miri. ALAP. 2 March 1938).

So within the scope of provincial politics, another aspect of assertion by the representatives of the Tribal League was for securing the right to education. The level of education in colonial Assam was quite low (Guha, 1977, pp. 56-64),[20] and the plains tribes were lagging behind in this aspect more than other communities. So, with the communal award of 1935, and their own representatives in the assembly, demands for better educational facilities and opportunities were put forward. These demands were mostly for setting up more schools in tribal areas, increase in funds, reservation, scholarship and free studentship for tribal students. Bhimbar Deuri, one of the founding member of the Tribal League and also member in the Legislative Council, while discussing the various problems of the tribals, also focused on the question of education:

Amongst these problems—the amelioration of the condition of the masses, the eradication of the opium habit and the spread of education among all classes, particularly among the backward classes, are the most urgent needs... (speech by Bhimbar Deuri. *ALCP.* 11 March 1933).

But cognition of the problem and acting upon it were two separate processes. The initial jubilation among the tribal elite for the communal representation in the assembly and over provincial autonomy soon evaporated. It was evident that development under the colonial government would not be easy. Rupnath Brahma's speech during a budget session reflects this attitude,

> Nowadays we hear a great cry in the country for the upliftment of these backward people, we have been given to understand that the government also have taken up special responsibility for safeguarding of the interests of the minority people... but it is surprising that nowhere in the budget we find any specific provision for the upliftment for the backward tribals of the plains (speech by Rupnath Brahma. ALAP. 9 August 1937).

In fact, inadequate budget allocation for education and grants to fund schools were perennial problems. Rupnath Brahma, another tribal representative in the assembly, expressed his disappointment and dissatisfaction in such a situation:

> We expected this time our popular and responsible government would come forward with definite scheme for education of the backward tribal people of the plains, but unfortunately to our utter disappointment no specific earmarked provision has been made for the plains tribals in the present year's budget also... it is a known fact that the tribal people of the plains are the most backward people in the whole province and I think government has greater responsibility for the education of these people. If there is no definite move from the government for education of these people, then I think all nation-building projects will be left far behind in Assam (speech by Rupnath Brahma. ALAP. 18 February 1938).

Not much was done to address those grievances and conditions did not improve radically as evident in Rabi Chandra Kachari's speech.

> ...the tribal people of the plains are very backward in the point of education. But we find a small amount of rupees, 8000, has been earmarked for the expansion of primary education among the tribal people of the plains. This money is quite insufficient because on average

---

[20] In these pages, he discusses the growth of the middle class.

only 4 schools from each of the 12 subdivisions will be benefited from this grant. But in each subdivision we have got more than 50 lower primary schools. We are also neglected by the local boards, as we cannot be properly represented in the boards. So I request government to earmark a sufficient amount for the expansion of education in the tribal areas of the plains, so that we may have a special impetus in education (speech by Rabi Chandra Kachari. *ALAP.* 22 March 1941).

The reliance on liberal policies of the colonial state to improve their conditions and civilize them soon disappeared and most of the tribal representatives lamented that after more than a century of British rule in Assam, there was a lot to be done yet. Karka Dalay Miri, representative of the Miri tribe, complained that though hill tribes and the Muslim students were conferred free studentship and scholarship, no such special provisions had been accorded to the backward tribals of the plains (speech by Karka Dalay Miri. ALAP. 17 August 1937). The backwardness was due to the absence of supportive provisions. According to him, groups like the Miri, Kachari, Deuri, Lalung, Khampti, Mikri, and so on, were backward in education due to the lack of adequate schools (speech by Karka Dalay Miri. ALAP. 17 August 1937). Khorsing Terang, representative of the Mikir Hills, stressed that education was necessary to transform the 'inhibited, animal like Mikir', into a 'proper civilised human being' (speech by Khorsing Terang. ALAP. 10 August 1937).

The tribal representatives came up with various solutions to the problem of providing education. It was suggested that such problems could only be solved if the government established one lower primary school in every five to six villages. In many areas the local people (the tribals) took the initiative to open schools in the hope that such venture-schools would be taken over by the local board. But not many schools were actually taken over by the local boards and very few scholarships were

provided. Another demand was that a special officer for education of these people should be appointed, as it was done for the Muslims. Under such pressure the Congress Ministry, when in power, increased funding of tribal education.[21] It was also decided that eight tribal students will receive free studentship. The earlier norm was that out of 13 free studentship, eight would be for the Muslims and rest to others (ALAP. 26 February 1940). Lack of adequate funding and disinterest on the part of the colonial authorities was observed by the tribal representatives and the Congress members who criticized their motives, 'Instead of giving us better facilities for education they have given us facilities for opium pills and some doses of liquor only' (ALAP. 2 March 1938). Haladhar Bhuyan, Congressman, pointed to the self-interest of the colonial government in their policy towards the tribes, for whom nothing was done till the declaration of provincial autonomy. The awareness of the tribals regarding the necessity of education was also attributed to the spread of Congress' message since 1921 (speech by Haladhar Bhuyan. ALAP. 5 December 1935).

By the 1940s, the Tribal League had reified the idea of a distinctive tribal identity, mostly for political and social reasons. The tribal elite, in envisioning an identity constructed a discourse of backwardness and differentness in opposition to other communities. Though there was consensus on the idea of 'backwardness', it came into conflict with other political organizations like the Congress on the question of identity. Issues of land alienation, displacement and deprivation also the tribal leadership received the support of the Congress. The controversy around the census gave rise to sharply defined notions about religion and identity. The Tribal League's support for the community-based enumeration bereft of any religious content, illustrated the strength of the idea of unified plain tribes as a political

---

[21] Out of ₹50,000.00, ₹29,000.00 was kept for the tribals.

category. Likewise, in the temple entry issue the clear position maintained by tribal leaders, of not being part of the Hindu society, also points towards efforts of engendering identity in opposition to the caste Hindu society. In this, it came into conflict with that section of the Assamese society which believed that the Assamese community was endangered from the immigrants and was trying to build a greater Assamese nationality. This Assamese middle class wanted the tribes to remain an integral part of the Assamese nationality.

Scholars like Sujit Choudhury and Amalendu Guha writing about the period of 1930s and 1940s have commented on the complex and sometimes complicit relationship between the political parties – the Congress, the Muslim League, United Party and the Tribal League. It has been a long held opinion that the Congress, more specifically Gopinath Bordoloi raised 'the bogey of tribal people in the plains losing their lands to immigrants.' (Guha quoted by Choudhury, 2007, p. 71). Tribal League leaders were suspect to colluding with the 'power nexus' (Choudhury, 2007, p. 70) as they participated in all governments that were formed since 1937. In these formative years of provincial politics, Tribal League leadership had the option of either recognizing the ties with the Assamese and accept a position in a caste society, or move away from it and claim separate identity. The tribal leadership constructed a discourse which hinged on difference as it is evident from controversies, which pointed towards engendering identity in opposition to caste Hindu society and politics. It revolved around the question of rights, modern rights of education, employment and equality, not merely traditional and customary notion of identity. It is the negotiation of this relationship that has defined politics in colonial and post-colonial Assam.

REFERENCES

Bara, J. (1997). Western education and rise of new identity: Mundas and Oraons of Chhotanagpur, 1839–1939. *Economic and Political Weekly, 32*(15), 785–790.

Barman, S. (1995). *Asamer janajati samasya: Aitihashik utsa sandhan.* Guwahati.

Barman, S. (2005). *The Raijmel: A study of the mel system in Assam.* Guwahati: Spectrum.

Barua, K. (2001). *Jananeta Bhimbar Deuri.* Guwahati.

Basumatari, B. K. (Ed.) (n.d.). *Plains tribes before the Simon commission.* Darrang: BEACON Publication.

Behal, R. P. (1983). *Some aspects of the growth of plantation labour force and labour movement, 1900–1947* (Unpublished PhD Thesis). New Delhi: Jawaharlal Nehru University.

Bordoloi, B. N. (1991). *Transfer and alienation of tribal land of Assam: With special references to the Karbis of Karbi Anglong district.* Guwahati: B. N. Bordoloi.

Choudhury, Sujit (2007). *The Bodos: Emergence and assertion of an ethnic minority.* Shimla: Indian Institute of Advanced Studies.

Deuri, I. (2001). *Janagosthiya samasya: Ateet, bartaman, bhabishyat.* Nalbari.

Endle, S. (1911). *The Kacharis,* London: Macmillan and Co.

Guha, A. (1977). *Planter raj to swaraj: Freedom struggle and electoral politics in Assam 1826–1947.* New Delhi: Indian Council of Historical Research.

Guha, A (2006). Planter Raj to Swaraj: Freedom Struggle and Electoral Politics in Assam 1826–1947. New Delhi: Tulika Books.

Hutton, J. H. (1933). *Census of India 1931, volume I: India. Part I: Report.* Delhi: Government of India Publications Department.

Mahanta, C. (1983). *Sinhapurush Sitanath Brahma Choudhury.* Jorhat.

Nag, S. (1990). *Roots of ethnic conflict: Nationality questions in Assam.* New Delhi. Manohar.

Samsing, H. (1983). *Jananayak Samsonsing Ingti.* Jorhat.

Sarma, D. N. (1983). *Gurudev Kalicharan Brahma.* Jorhat.

Teendiniya Assamiya. 21 January 1941 (Guwahati).

Thakkar, A. V. (1941). Census of Assam tribals. *Man in India,* 21.

The Assam Tribal League (Bulletin 2), Bhimbar Deuri 1940 (In Assamese).

12

Transitional Political Environment: Bodos and Tribal Politics in Assam

Himani Ramchiary

It is pertinent for any minority-linguistic community within a majority-linguistic state to find expressions in their political institutions and organizations. Assam is one such linguistic state which is home to many minor communities wherein some are tribal communities and some are just non-tribal communities. The Bodos of Assam are one of the tribal communities of Assam accounting to possess the highest number of tribal population as per the census of 2011. Of late, the Bodos are seen to take part actively in politics. The social mobility of the Bodos in terms of political institution is seen to be very recently emerging as one of the strong fields where the Bodos have started to express their dissent or favour. The emergence of the Bodos into the political realm is, however, not a recent process, though active participation and emergence of new ruling Bodo political parties is. Looking at the political aspects of the Bodos, the emergence of new ruling

parties is, in general, a normal adverse result of the absence of any rigid political system within the Bodos. The general Bodo narrative is that regional Bodo parties emerged as a fallout of the administrative grievance of Assam towards the Bodos. This is indicative of the pride the Bodos take in the administration of their own territories. The formation of regional parties as of such is also indicative of the presence of divisiveness in a state's political unity.

The chapter dwells around the political system of the Bodos. The chapter begins with a brief discussion on the Bodos and then focuses on the entry of the Bodos into the realm of Indian politics before Independence. Then it discusses the nature of Bodo politics till the formation of the Bodoland Territorial Council (BTC), followed by the dynamics of Bodo politics after the formation of the BTC.

HISTORICAL ACCOUNTS OF THE BODOS

The Bodos are considered as the first Tibeto-Burman speakers entering the northeast region (Kundu, 2010; Pulloppillil and Aluckal, 1997). The Bodos were also known as Kacharis and were the aboriginal and the first settlers of modern Assam, North-Bengal and parts of Bangladesh (Baruah, 1972; Gait, 1926; Kundu, 2010; Sarma and Devi, 1993). Pulloppillil and Aluklal (1997) argue that the Bodos ruled Assam unto the 20th century AD and moved to western part of the Brahmaputra valley, North Cachar Hills and the plains of Cachar in 16th century AD to stay away from the Ahom onslaught.

Hodgson used the term Bodo for the first time in his work on the Koch, Bodo and Dhimal tribes in 1880. To him, Bodo means man. According to him, 'A Kachari or Mech will call himself *Bara f'se*[1] to distinguish himself from Sim-Sa (Bhutia) or Chin-fsa' (Gait, 1926, p. 26). In the contemporary times, Bodos those living in the west of the Kamrup districts are called the Mechs and those in the eastern side as Kacharis. Even though Kachari is considered to be the original word to describe the Bodos, at present, the Constitution of India has recognized this group of tribe as the Bodos. Kos-ari is derived from *Kos-arui*, meaning, the sons of the *Kos. Ari* or *arui* is a patronymic, commonly used by the Bodo people in naming their clans. The word Kachari is, thus, a generic term, which is used to denote a number of tribal groups speaking more or less a common dialect or language and claiming a common mythical ancestry (Pulloppillil and Aluckal, 1997, p. 1).

The 2011 Census indicates that Assam is one of the largest multi-ethnic states in Northeast India with 68 languages and local parlance. Based on the place of inhabitance and ecological standpoint, the tribes of Assam are basically categorized into hill and plain tribes. According to the 2011 Census, the total population of Assam is 31,205,576. Out of which, 3,884,371 are tribal, constituting 12.44 per cent of the total population. There are 2.90 and 97.10 per cent Scheduled Tribes (ST; hills) and ST (plains), respectively. The plain tribes include Burmans of Cachar, Bod-Kachari, Deori, Hojai, Sonowal, Lalung, Mech, Mishing and Rabha. The hill tribes are Hajong, Dimasa, Miri (Mishings), Mech, Lalung, Syntheng, Pawi, any Naga tribe, Mikir (Karbis), any Mizo (Lushai) tribe, Man (Tai speaking), Lakher, Any Kuki tribe, Khasi, Jaintia, Synteng, Pnar, War, Khoi, Lyngngam, Hmar, Garo, Dimasa-Kachari and the Chakmas. The plain tribes are dispersed over different districts of Assam on the north and the south banks of the river Brahmaputra. On the other hand, the hill tribes are mostly confined to the two hill districts of Karbi-Anglong and North Cachar Hills.

Among the ST, the Boro or Boro-Kachari has the highest proportion of population in comparison to other tribes in Assam (Table 12.1). Along with the Bodos (35.05%), Miri (Mishings, 17.51%), Mikir (Karbis, 11.08%), Rabha (7.62%), Sonowal Kacharis (6.52%) and Lalung (5.17%) are the other major ST having more than 5 per cent of the total ST population and they constitute more than 87 per cent of the total tribal population along with Dimasa Kacharis (3.15%) and Deoris (1.12%). The other tribal population constitutes a very small portion in their population demography (Table 12.1).

Table 12.2 indicates that the Bodos have chequered history in terms of their demographic composition. The Bodos are concentrated most populously in the districts of

---

[1] *Bara F'sa* is actually pronounced as Boro Fisa. *Fisa* here means a child and by saying *Bara Fisa* the writer meant as the child of a Boro.

Table 12.1   Population of Some Major ST Communities of Assam, 2011 Census

Sl No.	Name of the Scheduled Tribe	Total Tribal Population	Proportion to the Total Tribal Population (in %)
1	All ST	3,884,371	100
2	Bodo, Bodo-Kachari	1,361,735	35.05
3	Miri (Mishings)	680,424	17.51
4	Mikir (Karbis)	430,452	11.08
5	Rabha	296,189	7.62
6	Sonowal Kacharis	253,344	6.52
7	Lalung	200,915	5.17
8	Dimasa	122,663	3.15
9	Deori	43,750	1.12

Source: Government of India (2011).

Table 12.2   Bodo Population of Assam (1951–2011)

Year	Total Population of Assam (in Lakhs)	Bodo Population (in Lakhs)	Percentage of Bodo Population
1951	80.29	3.64	4.53
1961	108.37	3.46	3.19
1971	146.25	6.10	4.17
1981	180.41	7.41	4.10
1991	224.14	11.84	5.28
2001	266.38	14.72	5.52
2011	312.05	14.16	4.53

Source: Government of India (1951–2011).

Kokrajhar, Udalguri and newly formed Baksa and Chirang of the Bodoland Territorial Autonomous District (BTAD)[2] region. In addition, they can also be found in the districts of Dhubri, Goalpara, Barpeta, Nalbari, Kamrup (both rural and metro), Darrang, Sonitpur, Lakhimpur, Karbi Anglong, etc. The Bodos can also be found in the adjoining states of Nagaland, Meghalaya and West Bengal, and adjoining countries of Nepal and Mynmar. In Assam, the Bodos are generally notified as the scheduled plain tribes except in the autonomous hill districts where they are noticed as scheduled hill tribes.

ENTRY OF THE BODOS INTO THE REALM OF POLITICS (PRE-INDEPENDENCE)

The north-eastern part of India has experienced the problems of separatist in-group[3] political activities within the federal state from colonial

---

[2] BTC is the territorial council and the area which falls under the jurisdiction of the BTC government is called the BTAD. BTC was formed after Memorandum of Settlement (MoS) was signed between the All Bodo Students Union (ABSU) and the Bodo Liberation Tigers (BLT) leaders with the central and the state government. This MoS as described by the Bodoland movement actors was signed to sabotage the Bodo movement for a separate state. The Government of Assam also accepted and approved the aforesaid MoS on 31 October 2003 by vide notification number TAD/BTC/161/2003/6. The Government of Assam thus resolved to extend executive powers to 40 subjects according to the BTC agreement in the said MoS.

[3] By the term 'in-group' the scholar meant to denote the social group to which a person psychologically identifies himself/herself as a member.

rulers. The in-group political activism has inti-mated the very idea of federal structure and in spite of developing a unitary governance, this often leads to many separatist demands in the region. As a result, the region has witnessed the restructuring of the federal states during the last four decades. The creation of the state of Meghalaya, Mizoram and Nagaland are the fallouts of such federal restructuring.

The divide and rule policy of the British administration has led to the declining of the socio-economic conditions of the tribal com-munities in Northeast India. The divide and rule policy was successful in bringing out a division between the hill and plain tribes. This division thereby created a space for suspicion among the two tribal counterparts (plain and hill). In this context, it would not be wrong to articulate that tribal politics in the region started with the introduction of such appre-hending policies of the British administration and the Bodos are one of those tribes who were part of the same. The Bodos are the majority plain tribal group in Assam[4] and have been playing a consequential role in the tribal pol-itics of Assam since the colonial days. There were also other factors that added to the upris-ing of the Bodo politics. One such factor was the fear of the Bodos to be completely domi-nated by the Assamese middle-class elites in the state politics. Such fears had supplemented the need of a separate political identity for the Bodo tribes. However, initially the Bodos did not have a separate political identity.

Gradually, the Bodos became con-scious about their political identity since the British rule. The birth of the Kachari Youth Association (Kachari Jubok Sanmilan) of the 1920s is an example of Bodo conscious-ness. The formation of this youth association took place owing to their impressive efforts to re-assert traditional culture and litera-ture and also to secure their collective rights and for correcting perceived injustices, dis-criminations and alienation from the main-stream political and economic development (Chaudhuri, 1992). The youth organiza-tion placed their demand before the Indian statutory commission, that is, the Simon Commission in 1929.[5] The demand included seeking permission for the entry of this group into public sphere by bringing forth the eco-nomic and political rights of the Bodos. Datta (1993, p. 175) states that this same group had also submitted a memorandum to the commis-sion demanding a separate electorate for the Bodos so that the Bodo group too may have ample representation in the provincial assem-bly. This was the first time that the Bodos expressed their political aspirations and sen-timents formally. Following the submission of the memorandum, the Simon Commission allowed the reservation of four seats in the provincial assembly for all the plain tribes, which accommodated the Bodos as well.

In view of the above submission, the British government introduced the new liberal intel-lectual conditions, which initiated the process

---

[4] As per the census reports of 1971, 1991 and 2001, there are about 23 ST (Hills and Plains) in Assam. The Bodo-Kacharis shared 33.36 per cent of the total tribal population in 1971, 44.07 per cent in 1991 and 44.08 per cent in 2001. The Miris (Mishings) shared 13.52 per cent of the total tribal population in 1971, 13.52 per cent in 1991 and 16.27 per cent in the 2001 Census report. The Mikirs (Karbis) percentage to the total ST population in Assam was 9.23 in 1971, 9.94 per cent in 1991 and 9.94 per cent in 2001 Census as well. The other ST major group Deoris' percentage to the total tribal population was 1.20 per cent in 1971 Census and 1.25 per cent and 1.34 per cent in 1991 and 2001 Census, respectively. The details of 2011 Census tribal population is given in Table 12.1.

[5] The British government appointed an Indian statutory commission on 8 November 1927 under the chairman-ship of S. Simon, what was accompanied by six other members. All the members were British members of the Parliament and had no Indian members in it. Therefore, Indians had derogatorily termed this commission as 'all white commission'. This Commission arrived in Shillong (erstwhile capital of Assam) on 2 January 1929 and left on 11 January 1929. For detailed account, see Deka (2014, p. 102).

of constitutional changes.[6] These constitutional changes brought forward by the British government provoked the Bodos to assert their community identity. This also instigated the need for a platform to express the same. Again, the identity consciousness made the Bodos feel that there is a need to review and restructure their culture, tradition, custom and language in order to assert their community identity. Owing to all these conditions, the Bodos underlined the need of a platform created by a regional political party to fulfil their aspirations. The complexities within the elite communities of Assam had also marginalized the Bodos and considered them as a backward community by excluding them from various mainstream activities of the society. The dominant Bodo narrative is that after the annexation of the Bodo kingdom by the British, the Bodos have lost their political independence in their own territory. This has left the Bodos to become victims of exploitation, subjugation and marginalization and hence they were compelled to be assimilated with the upper-caste Assamese and face the consequences of being a marginalized community.

The probable cause of such exploitations and subjugations virtually points that the Bodo problem was essentially linked to the processes of assimilation and absorption with the then Assamese culture. However, it was not possible for the Bodos alone at that time to form a political party of their own. Owing to such circumstances, the Bodos joined the section of plain tribal groups of Assam and advocated an independent political expression

that would enable all the tribal to protect their tribal identity. Subsequently, the All Assam Plain Tribal League (AAPTL) was formed as a tribal political party in 1933 and this was the first political party exclusively comprising the leaders of the plain tribes of Assam. The Bodo-Kacharis, Rabhas, Mishings, Deuris and the Mutaks were the main tribal-community members of this political party. Pegu (2004) indicates that the AAPTL first participated in the Assam provincial assembly in 1937, which was held under the GOI Act of 1935. The Indian National Congress (INC) emerged victorious in the election, which formed the coalition government with the support of AAPTL. Rupnath Brahma of the AAPTL was the first eminent Bodo leader to be elected to the Assam provincial assembly (Deka, 2014). Hence, the formal entry of the tribal politics in Assam can be accounted to the formation of the AAPTL.

On 16 March 1940, AAPTL signed an agreement with the Saadullah Ministry in Assam.[7] The agreement between the state government and AAPTL proposed for the inclusion of all the tribal people, irrespective of religion, under the category of tribal in the census of 1941, which the government conceded. Subsequently, there was a substantial increase in the numerical strength of the tribal population in the state. Owing to such political intuitions, the tribal league hereafter became an elite organization of all the plain tribes of Assam. This league became a platform where all the plain tribal could articulate

---

[6] The new liberal intellectual conditions set-up by the British rule consisted of activities like issuing of the white paper in March 1933, setting up of new electorates on the basis of recommendations of the Simon Commission, selection of joint selection committee to consider government schemes of constitutional reforms in India, etc. In short, such initiatives resulted in the formation of the Government of India (GOI) Act, 1935 (Deka, 2014: 103).
[7] The INC emerged as the single largest party in the 1937 Indian provincial elections in Assam. The INC, however, refused to form the constitutional government under the British Raj and the party joined the boycott of the pan-India policy to refrain from being under the British further. They instead became the main opposition party then. At this backdrop, the Governor approached the Assam Provincial Muslim League (APML) led by Sir Syed Muhammad Saadulla, with the proposal to form the Assam government in April 1937. This was the first Saadullah Ministry whose tenure lasted only till September 1938. The Saadullah Ministry was formed again on 17 November 1939 and 24 August 1942. The periods were intervened with the Governor's rule in between the gaps (Deka, 2014).

their political aspirations along with the other tribal groups of Assam.

However, like other parts of India, the colonial rule was continuing in Assam. Subsequently, after the formation of the first tribal political party in Assam, the constitution-making body was being formed in central India around 1946. This constitution-forming body received the powers passed down by the British colonial rulers directly to the INC. Baruah (1999) argues that the Bodo politics received major applause when one of the Bodo leaders of AAPTL, Mr Dharani Dhar Basumatary, was selected as a member of the constitution-making body from Assam. His selection was made to represent the interest of the Bodo society in the making of the Indian Constitution. However, the selection of a Bodo leader created further division among the other tribal communities of the AAPTL and has paved the way for further suspicion within the group. Meanwhile, other tribal groups raised eyebrows concerning the credibility of AAPTL in creating a political space for tribes and moved away from the tribal league. As a result, the AAPTL lost its political credibility and relegated itself to merely a sociocultural organization in the post-Independence period.

BODO POLITICS IN THE POST-INDEPENDENCE PERIOD

The post-Independence political environment was the result of amalgamation and dissolution of tribal parties in the initial stage. This marks the other phase of political mobilization among the Bodos. While the initial phase focused on land, the next phase focused on culture. Mochahary (2014 p. 77) narrates this phase as the vicious cycle of constantly deteriorating situation of the people, which opened up scope for a section of the educated Bodo people to come together in order to form a multiple community-centric organization. At this backdrop, different platforms were created by the Bodos under different ideologies which includes organizations such as the Bodo Sahitya Sabha (BSS), The Plains Tribals' Council of Assam (PTCA), ABSU, Boro Security Force (BrSF) and National Democratic Front of Boroland (NDFB). In the post-independence period, the earlier political party made its presence in the form of literary organization, militant outfit, some student organization, social and political organization. Mochahry argues that these organizations were formed with a view to work for the welfare of the community and negotiate with the powers concerning sociocultural, economic, linguistics and political rights. Thus, we can find the presence of fragmented tribal political party in different forms in the post-colonial India.

The formation of the BSS in 1952 was a significant step used by the Bodos to articulate their distinct identity and this enabled the Bodos in ascertaining their political aspirations as well. As mentioned earlier, on the political front, the AAPTL transformed itself into a sociocultural organization as All Assam Tribal Sangha (AATS) in 1954. From this transformation of AAPTL, a new political front known as Plain Tribal Council of Assam (PTCA) was formed in 1966 under the leadership of Samar Brahma Choudhury and Charan Narzary. The political environment of the Bodos took a new direction with the formation of the PTCA. The contestants from the PTCA initially contested as independent candidates till it gained full momentum as a regional Bodo political party. Henceforth, since its inception, the PTCA participated in the Assam assembly elections and won seats till the ABSU was formed.

After its formation, the PTCA focused on the political identity of the Bodos. The PTCA submitted a memorandum to the then President of India, Zakir Hussain, on 20 May 1967, demanding full autonomy for the plain tribal areas that spread over the northern tract of Goalpara, Kamrup, Darrang, Lakhimpur and Sibsagar districts. Such move of the PTCA indicated the motive of protecting the tribal lands and saving the tribal from economic exploitation by the non-tribals. This was the first instance where the question of autonomy surfaced among the ethnic groups (Bodos) of Assam. The Bodos considered that autonomy would end the political domination of non-tribals over tribals. Deka (2014, p. 110) argues that such an arrangement would also give tribals the opportunity to grow according to their genius and conserve their traditional culture and language.

The PTCA henceforth launched the Udayachal movement for a greater tribal land by keeping in mind the object of a separate autonomy. This demand resorted the central government to propose for an autonomous council in 1968. However, this proposal was not acceptable to all the Bodos. The refusal of the council then by some prominent Bodo leaders resulted in the fragmentation of the PTCA into two parts—PTCA (inclusive of any tribal communities of Assam) and PTCA (Bodo student union faction, wherein members were only from the Bodo community). The division was created due to various ideological differences among the Bodo leaders, wherein some of them were in favour of the council and others were not. Some members of the PTCA proposed armed struggle while some others were engaged in the formation of a new group by now. As a result of this political turbulence, new student politics, the ABSU emerged among the Bodos. Henceforth, ABSU became the prominent group which shaped the direction of Bodo identity politics.

In 1987, the ABSU redefined political movement of the Bodos by demanding the division of Assam on a 50-50 formula, rejecting the earlier PTCA's demand for Udayachal or greater tribal statehood. Along with the student organization, other armed groups also reinforced the identity issue of the Bodos. The demand of the student organization changed when, in a press release on 7 October 1988, the ABSU declared the demand for union territory with full-fledged statehood and more autonomy and political power, which Deka (2014) terms as the demand for Bodoland.

As seen in Table 12.3, the breakdown of the PTCA was an end to another tribal political party that had lasted for more than a decade. However, PTCA was successful in winning at least some political power in favour of the Bodos and sustaining their presence in the Assam assembly elections. The PTCA had contested for four consecutive assembly elections and won three to four seats on average in all the contested years, except the 1972 election (Table 12.3). The realm of the Bodos in the political sphere of Assam went down after the breakdown of the PTCA. Again, there was another rumour of the PTCA reflecting aspirations of the Bodos only, and thus, sidelining the other non-Bodo tribal leaders to move out of the group before the mass breakdown of PTCA. Even after the break down, the Bodos still contested the assembly elections but as independent candidates or on other political parties' tickets. Hence, there was an absence

Table 12.3 The Bodo Political Parties of Assam at a Glance (1972–2016)

Political Parties	Assembly Election Year	Seats Won	Total Seats in Assam	Percentage of Seats
PTCA	1972	1	114	0.91
PTCA	1978	4	126	3.17
PTCA	1983	3	109	2.31
PTCA	1985	3	126	2.75
BPF	2006	11	126	8.73
BPF	2011	12	126	9.52
BPF	2016	12	126	9.52

Source: Government of India (1972, 1978, 1983, 1985, 2006, 2011, 2016).

of Bodo political party(ies) between 1985 and 2006.

The dominant Bodo narratives capture the reasons for the absence of any Bodo political party between 1985 and 2003. One prominent factor that emerged during my fieldwork pointed towards the process of assimilation of the tribal with the upper-caste Assamese. The Bodos were also involved rampantly in the process of getting converted or assimilated to the Assamese fold generally. The other factor that mattered at that time was the introduction of the Assam Accord of 1985. The Assam Accord significantly affected the political environment of the Bodos. After the breakdown of PTCA, the educated Bodos were also involved in another project, precisely the creation of a separate homeland for the Bodos— the Bodoland, which had diverted them away from the political sphere in Assam. The newly formed ABSU leaders moved from village to village as an act of mobilizing the people for creation of a separate state. Moreover, the continuing dissent among the leaders themselves had left the Bodos ambiguous and they could not stand unitedly to form a tribal or say, another Bodo political party.

However, after lots of drifts and trials, the BTC was formed in 2003, which was the result of the agreement between the central government, the state government and some influential Bodo leaders. The formation of the BTC was a boost to the political environment among the Bodos. As a consequence of various peace process in Assam, after more than a decade, a new political party of the Bodos, Bodoland People's Progressive Front (BPPF), was formed on 20 April 2005. The creation of the BTAD has succeeded to create a rigorous political consciousness among the larger section of the Bodo people. The BTAD has also provided a significant political autonomy to at least some sections of the Bodo leaders like the Bodoland's Progressive Front (BPF), the Ex-BLT cadres and their supporters in particular. The creation of the BTAD has also brought forward new political dimension in the

Bodoland movement. The Bodoland movement started afresh via a conference held in Mazbath in 2010 by reviewing the ideologies associated with the movement. The Bodoland movement was by now taken up to the national capital. The ABSU declared to continue the movement for a separate state even after separate territorial council was carved out of Assam for the Bodos by considering issues faced by the Bodo people such as identity crisis, cultural distinctiveness, growing erosion of community rights over resources, dispossession, marginalization and deprivation of tribal communities, sociopolitical and economic marginalization, and land alienation and massive migrants from outside.

TRIBAL POLITICAL PARTIES IN BTAD

In a democratic state, political parties play significant role in smooth functioning of the democracy. The articulation of people's interest in the election process and the clustering of interest for the same among the masses become the prime activity of the political parties. The political parties enable the people to take part in the activities of the government directly or indirectly. The political parties establish relations with their supporters and sympathizers which, in the long run, play a very vital role in the election process. By establishing such direct and intimate contacts, the aspirations regarding various developmental programmes of social reconstruction and welfare of the people are incorporated in the election manifestos to prove that their relations with people are not vague. Different political parties put up a competition among each other even in their manifestos so that they can capture more sympathy and support of the masses and win the elections.

Multiparty system exists in the Indian political system and there are number of parties competing for seats. In India, it is possible even for one person to float a party very easily and the supporters can be attracted at a later period. Barker (1953) argues that there is a necessity of political party to be existent and also the operation of modern political system. Both of these entities provide indispensable link between people and the working representatives of the government. It is also necessary for a political party to exist because people cannot govern themselves in a free manner unless they are given the freedom to choose between different candidates whom they consider as their leaders. The choice of the people may, however, differ due to different factors like the manifestos, policies, sympathizing aspect, local influence, support or other factors. The citizens are, thus, given the alternative choices before them by different political parties where they exercise their right of freedom of choice in choosing their preferable candidates. In this regard, Barker argues that the choice of a citizen is the root of democracy. He substantiates his argument by saying,

> The 'citizens', as it may be called, is the tap-root of democracy. I must be free to choose if I am to have a free government, and if I am to free to choose I must have an alternative before me—the alternative offered to me by different political parties. (Barker, 1953, p. 8)

Political party is, however, an association organized in support of some principles or policies by constitutional means. The political parties strive to make the contributing factor for government. (MacIver, 1955, p. 396). He further argues that without party organizations, there can be no unified statement of principles, no orderly evolution policy and no regular resort to the constitutional devices of parliamentary elections, nor, of course, any recognized institution by means of which a party can seek to gain or to maintain power (MacIver, 1955, p. 398). Fights for important position in the autonomy and dissent among the party and association members have led to the origin of some regional political as well as other associations in the BTAD region of Assam as well. Pertaining to the same, the history of electoral politics among the Bodos

witnessed the birth of different political parties, which are described in the following paragraph.

BPPF

The state election commission declared the council election for BTC on 13 May 2005, after the provisional functioning of the council for a period of one year. On declaration of the election in BTC, the leaders of the ABSU and the Ex-BLT Welfare Association decided to form a political party to contest in the election. On 12 April 2005, 16 membered convenor's committee gathered at the Ganga cinema hall in Kokrajhar, Assam, before forming the government. This meeting was held with a view to form a political party. As a result, BPPF was to be formed on 20 April 2005. But BPPF could not be formed on the specified date because as per the announcement of the state election commission, nominations had to be filed by 19th April 2005. Hence, owing to such factors, the first election of the council was contested by the Bodo politicians as independent candidates.

Finally, the BPPF was considered to be informally formed on 20 April 2005. The formation of BPPF gave birth to a new political party of the Bodos. When the party was formed, the new party had two main working committees: the executive committee and the policy-making committee. The executive committee had 11 members with Rabiram Narzary as the president and Chandan Brahma and Baktar Ali Ahmed as the vice-presidents. Emmanuel Mushahary became the secretary of the committee and Hemendra Nath Brahma the general secretary of the executive committee. Other leaders such as Sobharam Brahma, Jagadish Sarkar, Lwmsrao Daimary, Niren Roy, Badan Hasda and Ripon Daimary remained as members of committee. On the other hand, the policy-making committee of BPPF had mainly four members in total with Hagrama Mohilary and Pramila Rani Brahma as the convenors. Bodo political leaders like

Sansuma Khungur Bwiswmutiary and Urkhao Gwra Brahma remained as members of the committee along with other 10 member representatives from each of the four districts.

This division of the party members brought about radical thinking in the minds of the newly elected Bodo political leaders. Different scholars studying the electoral process in BTAD debate upon this issue in different ways. According to Daimary (2015, p. 8), 'The student union, particularly the ABSU, being overground, had advantage to play much more role in the new dimension of new politics.' While some others like Karjie (2017) opine that the architect of BTC, Mr Hagrama Mohilary was sidelined by the BPPF on the pretext of being new to politics and the party hesitated to elect Mohilary as the chief of BTC. In general, the student body considered the Ex-BLT members to be relatively new to politics in comparison to them. The ABSU claims to have been in the politics since the inception of the student body in 1967. Also, the student leaders being more learned and experienced did not consider equalizing the representation of the interests of the underground group (Ex-BLT) with other intellectuals. It was this thinking that formed the main cause of split within the newly born regional party. Thus, the negligence of some Bodo leaders in the party structure of the BPPF led to the fragmentation of the party into two factions: BPPF (Hagrama faction)—BPPF(H), led by Ex-BLT chief Hagrama Mohilary and his cadres—and BPPF (Rabiram faction)—BPPF(R), led by former ABSU leader Rabiram Narzary. On account of this split in the regional party, a condition of political disorganization prevailed in the BTAD region for a significant period of time.

The first council election in BTC took place on 13 May 2005. This was a significant event in the political discourse of the BTAD. BPPF was an amalgamation of leaders from both ABSU and Ex-BLT leaders. In the first election of the BTC, although the BPPF(H) candidates contested independently, out of 40 seats, the party won 39 seats losing just 1 seat to the Asom Gana Parishad (AGP). Interestingly, only the candidates who earlier belonged to the BLT or BPPF(H) won the election. On the other hand, BPPF(R) could not even win a single seat. This political development resulted in the shifting of support base from the BPPF(R) to the other faction under Mohilary. The new BTC government was thus formed after rigorous choice of making the architect of BTC, Mr Hagrama Mohilary as the chief of the BTC. This significant turn in the political history of the Bodos also brought the erstwhile new amalgamated regional party to an end and witnessed the new dimension of power politics in BTAD for the first time.

BPF

The signatory faction of the Ex-BLT cadres was mostly dissatisfied since the formation of the BPPF. As a result, Mr Hagrama Mohilary along with the support of other Members of Council of Legislative Assembly (MCLAs) members decided to form a new party. Thus, a new party, the BPF, was formed under the leadership of Mr Hagrama Mohilary with the mission and vision to bring uniform political sovereignty. Accordingly, a big political convention took place in Debargaon on 4–5 December 2005 to formally declare the formation of the new party. Mr Hagram Mohilary, Mr Emmanuel Moshahary and Mr Khampa Borgoyary became the president, general secretary and spokesperson of the party, respectively.

The BPF was formed with certain mission and vision associated not only with the Bodos but also with other communities living within BTAD. The main ideology of BPF includes:

1. Administering the BTAD and Assam as a whole through the principles of democracy
2. Working for the elimination of poverty and the upliftment of the subjugated people living in BTAD and Assam as well

3. Working for the strengthening of Indian nationalism by providing due respect to the identities of all
the sections of people
4. Striving for the all-round development of the
people of BTAD as well as Assam.

Hence, keeping at par with the ideology of the
party, the BPF started off its work in full swing
with certain aims and objectives. The aims
and objectives of the party were—working for
sovereignty and integrity of the country; political rights, economic development and social
justice to all irrespective of any community;
making BTC a model and self-sufficient by
influencing the government both at the central and the state level to explore the abundant
natural resources like water, forest, minerals
and human resources; etc. The party also had
the objective of working for free nationalism
detaching the community from the prejudices
of castes, religions and languages to stand by
the principles of cooperation, trust, tolerance,
fraternity and coexistence. The party also
aimed to bring about reforms in the field of
education, to implement the Bodo Accord of
2003 and seek cooperation of both the central
and state government in the fair running of
the territorial council. Hence, there was support from all communities to the BPF party
(Daimary, 2015).

United People's Party (UPP)

In 2015, the UPP was formed. This party
was formed to contest against the BPF in the
MCLA election. The former Rajya Sabha MP
and ex-President of ABSU, Mr Urkhao Gwra
Brahma became the president and Mr Pradip
Daimary, an ex-member of BPF, the general
secretary. In other words, it can be said that
this party is the political wing of the ABSU
and it comprises of many former ABSU leaders and activists. Karjie (2017, p. 774) terms
the UPP as the offset of the earlier BPPF.
The party emerged with a promise to provide
good governance. The announcement of the

formation of the UPP was made on 6 August
2015 at a special convention held by the
People's Coordination for Democratic Rights
(PCDR) in Dotoma. However, during the
formative stage, the party could not be fully
active as it was not able to gather support. The
UPP stood as a feeble opponent in comparison
to the political negotiation of the ruling party
of BPF with the people of BTC.

The 2019 Lok Sabha election of Assam
saw the emergence of UPP with some broader
and new manifestos. The party modified its
name to United People's Party-Liberal (UPP-
L) before the Lok Sabha election of 2019. The
UPP-L emerged with some new agendas like
revamping existing scheduled caste cell of the
party and forming of other backward classes
(OBC) cell and many others as such (NE Now,
May 2019). Here again, Urkhao Gwra Brahma
had contested as the candidate for UPP from
the ST constituency of Kokrajhar.

PCDR

The PCDR is a conglomeration of various
political and non-political parties present
in BTAD. The formation of the PCDR was
announced ahead of the 2016 Assam assembly
election. The party had far reaching impact on
the politics in the Bodo belt which was till
then dominated by the BPF. It was found out
from the narratives of some of the senior party
members that the PCDR party was formed
by uniting the regional political parties such
as the BPPF and United Democratic People's
Front. According to one of the ABSU activists, the PCDR is not a political body, rather it
is a non-political body formed by the Bodos to
bridge various committees present in BTAD.
However, the UPP stands as a newly formed
regional political party and was structured to
act and work as the voice of the Bodo people.
As per the report of a journalist, UPP President
U. G. Brahma mentions that the UPP party is
a product of the people's voice and it has clear
ideology which would work for the welfare

of the people irrespective of caste, creed and religion (Daimary, 2015, p. 7). The PCDR was backed by ABSU and it contested in the BTC election of 2015. The PCDR gave a tough contest to the ruling BPF. It won seven seats in the election and the PCDR was a close competitor in other seats.

ELECTORAL POLITICS IN BTAD

The formation of the BTC became a new breeding ground for many aspiring politicians. There was also the emergence of some new and local political parties such as BPF, PCDR and UPP erupting among the Bodos in the BTAD region. The area which comes under the jurisdiction of the BTC government is called the BTAD region. The BTAD comprises four districts of Assam namely, Kokrajhar, Chirang, Baksa and Udalguri. However, in the recent elections, the national parties were also seen participating remarkably in the council and assembly elections. The national parties such as the Bharatiya Janata Party (BJP) and INC contested the council and assembly elections fully or partially within the territorial extent. This nature signifies the nation's urge to set a foothold in the electoral domain of the BTAD, thus, inviting perpetual haul to the course of electoral politics in BTAD.

The BTC is entitled with 40 constituencies under its purview. Out of 40 seats, 30 seats are reserved for contesting among the ST (P) candidates, 5 seats are reserved for non-tribal candidates and 5 are reserved for General category candidates. In the recent decades, the BTC has undergone three subsequent elections. Initially when BTC was formed in 2003, there was no election immediately, rather it was administered in ad hoc basis by BPPF party formed by former BLT cadets and the ABSU leaders. An interim government had, thus, administered the council for around one and half year till the elections were finally conducted in 2005.

The first council election was a significant one in the political history of the Bodos. The newly emerged political governance faced various turfs and trials owing to the selection of the council chief of the BTAD. This tussle amongst the members of erstwhile BPPF resulted in splitting the newly formed political party into two factions even before election could take place. Hence, 2005 council election was contested without formal registration of any regional political party and the former BPPF was split into BPPF(H) and BPPF(R). BPPF(H) was led by Ex-BLT chief Hagrama Mohilary and BPPF(R) was led by former ABSU leader Rabiram Narzary. The main reason for the split was resultant of the attempt to sideline the chief architect of BTAD, Mr Hagrama Mohilary himself.

The BTC's first election was conducted on 3 May 2005 abiding by the law and order of the election commission of India. The election result paved the way for the victory of the BPPF(H), which won 39 out of 40 contested seats. All these 39 MCLA were contested successfully by the Ex-BLT cadets. The BPPF(R), however, failed to win any seats in the first election with its leader also losing himself. Surprisingly, however, the AGP could win one seat from Mudwibari constituency and thereby representing one MCLA to the new assembly. Even though AGP did not perform well in the later years, yet it had marked its presence in the very first council election unlike the BPPF(R). On 5 December 2005, a new political party, the BPF, was formed under the guidance and leadership of the council chief Hagrama Mohilary. With the formation of BPF, the BPPF(H) was formally dissolved.

The second council election took place on 19 May 2010. Unlike the first council election, the 2010 election witnessed a neck to neck competition under the aegis of independent candidates and several political parties registering for the same. The election also witnessed several national and regional political parties taking part in the electoral battle of

2010 in BTAD (Table 12.4). There was moderate violence erupting in some places due to the rivalry between regional parties. The BPF party contested in all the 40 constituencies and won 31 seats and formed the government. However, BPF could not bring much prominence unlike the first election. National parties such as the INC and BJP, and other state political parties such as the AGP, All India United Democratic Front (AIUDF), Sanmilita Janagosthiya Aikya Mancha (SJAM) and many others also contested the election. The INC contested in 23 constituencies of the 40 and won only three seats. Four seats were successfully contested by the independent and one seat by an AIUDF candidate.

The exit polls had, however, predicted a 100 per cent win to the BPF party but the result showed only 77.50 per cent. But the BPF was still in majority and they managed to form the government for the second time consecutively. Of late, the environment of electoral politics in BTAD has witnessed an undeniable and marked changes. This has been the fallout of ABSU's rigorous mobilizations and influential sympathy towards the demand for a separate state of Bodoland. Owing to such mobilization and growing influence of the ABSU, the PCDR emerged as a strong political opponent to the BPF in the BTC election of 2015.

The council election of 2015 created havoc among the ruling BPF leaders. As Table 12.4 indicates that when we compare the contested and victorious seats, the BPF could cater only 20 seats in this election. It suffered a major setback as their number reduced from 39 in 2005

Table 12.4   Members of the BTC and Their Portfolios between 2005–2010, Assam

Sl No.	Designation	Name of Member	Department and Portfolio Allocated
1	Chief of BTC	Mr Hagrama Mohilary	Public work department, panchayat and rural raj development, welfare of plain tribal and backward class and departments not allowed to other executive members
2	Deputy chief of BTC	Mr Kampha Borgoyari	Planning and development, forest, tourism, sericulture, land and land revenue
3	Executive member	Mr Derhasat Basumatary	Flood control, public health engineering
4	Executive member	Mr Hitesh Basumatary	Irrigation, handloom and textile, sports and youth welfare
5	Executive member	Mr Sobharam Basumatary	Social welfare, animal husbandry and veterinary
6	Executive member	Mr Emanuel Muchahary	Education, health and family welfare
7	Executive member	Mr Mitharam Basumatary	Agriculture, weights and measures
8	Executive member	Mr Lwmsrao Daimary	Printing and stationary, food and civil supplies, publicity and public relations
9	Executive member	Mr Shyam Sundi	Relief and rehabilitation, labour and employment, soil conservation
10	Executive member	Mr Lakhiram Tudu	Fishery, market and fairs
11	Executive member	Mr Maheshwar Basumatary	Urban development, town and country planning, municipal corporation, improvement of trust, district boards and local authorities, cultural affairs
12	Executive member	Mr Mono Kr. Brahma	Welfare of plain tribal and backward class (state plan), transport, excise
13	Executive member	Mr Singha Ram Boro	Cooperation, library services, museum and archaeology
14	Executive member	Mr Buddha Narzary	Industry, lottery, cinema and dramatic performance

Source: Executive Council of BTC, 2010.

election to 31 in 2011 election and then to 20 seats in the 2015 council election. Regardless of the lesser council assembly seats, the BPF again managed to form the government for the third year consecutively in 2015 with the support of the independent candidates. The main competitors for the ruling BPF were PCDR, SJAM and AIUDF. The 2015 election marked the opening success for the ABSU-backed political party, PCDR, which won seven seats. The SJAM, AIUDF, Anaboro Suraksha Samiti and BJP won three, four, two and one seats, respectively. Thus, 2015 election witnessed the dispersion, in other words, the rattling down of the otherwise strong Bodo regional party and stiff competition among the political parties.

ASSAM ASSEMBLY ELECTIONS IN BTAD AREA

Out of 126 assembly constituencies in Assam, largely, a total of 28 constituencies fall within the territorial boundary of BTC. All these assembly constituencies, however, do not solely comprise BTAD region, rather some constituencies also have some villages, which do not fall under the territorial ambit of BTC. Out of 28 assembly constituencies, 8 constituencies are solely spread over the villages that exclusively come under the BTAD region. On the other hand, the rest 20 constituencies cover the villages from both BTAD and non-BTAD region. The eight constituencies which strictly fall under the purview of the BTC government are Chapagurii, East Kokrajhar, Mazbat, Sidli, Panery, Tamulpur, Udalguri and West Kokrajhar. Out of these eight constituencies, four constituencies—Chapagurii, East Kokrajhar, Sidli, and West Kokrajhar—are reserved for the tribal communities. The other 20 constituencies that partly encompasses BTAD region are Barama, Barchalaa, Bhabinipur, Bijni, Bongaigaon, Dolgaon, East Bilasipara, Gauripur, Golokganj, Gossaigaon,

Kalaigaon, Kamalpur, Mongoldoi, Nalbari, North Abhayapuri, Patacharkuchi, Rangia, Sipajhar, Sorbhog and West Bilasipara.

The regional party, BPF, debuted during the 2006 assembly election right after its major victory in the council election of 2005. The campaigning of BPF's first entry into the Assam election had been carried out without any conflicts. This was the first time a purely Bodo political party participated in the assembly election of Assam. Even though PTCA had taken part earlier, it was, however, considered to be a party of all the plain tribes of Assam. BPF, in its inception, was a purely Bodo political party. However, later on, the BPF had members from other communities as well who were from tribal as well as non-tribal communities. The BPF won 11 seats in its debut to the Assam assembly election in 2006. As the INC was 53 short of majority to form the government in 2006, the BPF extended its support to the INC. As a result, the BPF managed to bargain for cabinet ministerial seat in the Tarun Gogoi-led INC government in the state. The 2006 election also witnessed the victory of the BJP in 10 assembly constituencies. The offshoot party of Assam movement, the AGP, emerged victorious in 24 seats in 2006 election.

The AIUDF also won 10 seats in its debut election of 2006. It has been alleged that the AIUDF gathered communal sentiments and played the game of minority politics. This was the main factor that helped the AIUDF to win such a huge number of votes in its debut election. The formation of a minority party led to the fragmentation of the otherwise compounded society of Assam. The alarming win of the AIUDF led many intellectuals and political analysts to rethink the various political tides that could play cards in winning or changing the game of election. However, the growing of new parties in Assam led to the declining of old parties, such as the Communist Party of India, Communist Party of India—Marxist, Nationalist Congress Party, etc., in the state politics of Assam.

The assembly election of 2011 continued the victory trend of 2006. The INC had an overwhelming landslide victory with a total of 78 seats. The BPF, former ally of the INC, managed to add one more seat, which took it to the final tally of 12 seats. The BPF with its 12 MLAs joined hands with the INC again for the second time to form the government. The INC could have formed the government on its own as the party secured the magic number this time on its own. However, the party continued its ally with the BPF and, in this term, the INC offered only one cabinet ministerial berth to the BPF.

The tenure of 2011 election, however, witnessed many rifts between political parties. The INC in the state experienced internal fraction between the two significant leaders of INC—the chief minister, Tarun Gogoi and Himanta Biswas Sharma. The INC ally BPF also had some differences with the ruling party and eventually by the end of the tenure, the BPF began to withdraw its support to the ruling party. During this time, the BTAD region also witnessed growing scams, corruption and conflicts. The ruling party seemed to have mishandled this issue, which indicated

the early sign of potential electoral outcome of the 2016 state assembly election.

By 2014, India was already filled with the magic forecasted by Narendra Modi in the history of Indian politics. This magic also had its implications in the northeastern states and Assam was the first state to witness the same. The BJP had an alarming rise in the number of seats it won. There was a significant rise in the final tally of the BJP from merely 5 seats in 2011 to 60 in 2016 assembly election. By now, the BPF had changed its ally from the INC to the BJP and it secured equal term of 12 seats in 2016 assembly election as well. The AGP too had entered into the pre-poll alliance with the BJP and secured 14 assembly seats. Notably, the BPF maintained its consistency in terms of winning the seats since its debut to the state election. No doubt they had shifted their ally from the INC to the BJP; this could be one of the calculated moves to sustain and retain the party's significance in the state.

Table 12.6 depicts the seat sharing of various political parties that contested the 2011 and 2016 assembly elections. The result of the 2016 assembly election indicates the gradual declining of the INC from 78 seats in 2011

Table 12.5   Political Parties in BTAD Elections, Assam

Political Parties	2010 Election		2015 Election	
	Contested	Won	Contested	Won
BPF	40	31	40	20
BPPF	26	1	–	–
PCDR	–	–	40	7
IND	40	4	40	3
INC	23	3	40	–
AIUDF	–	–	8	4
UDPF	24	1	–	–
AGP	9	0	6	0
CPI (M)	6	0	7	0
AITC	3	0	–	–
SJAM	–	–	9	3
Anaboro Suraksha Samiti	–	–	9	3

Source: Government of Assam (2010, 2015).

Table 12.6   Assam State Assembly Election Result, 2016

Political Parties	2011		2016		Votes share (in %)	
	Contested	Won	Contested	Won	2011	2016
INC	126	78	122	26	78.81	20.63
BJP	120	5	89	60	23.56	71.42
AGP	104	10	14	8	36.01	58.33
BPF	29	12	13	12	31.29	75
AIUDF	78	18	74	13	32.44	17.56
CPI	17	0	19	0	0	0
CPM	17	0	19	0	0	0
RJD	–	–	12	0	–	0
JD	–	–	12	1	–	0
UPP	–	–	4	0	–	0
RJAM	–	–	1	0	–	0
IND	263	2	126	1	21.69	1

Source: Government of India (2011, 2016).

to 26 in 2016, with a vote share of 20.63 per cent in 2016 (Table 12.6). The decline of INC has also been witnessed at the centre during the 2014 Lok Sabha election. In BTAD, the INC had formed a new ally with the UPP, the major rival of BPF in the region. As already discussed in the earlier part of the chapter, the UPP emerged as the masterpiece of Mr Urkhao Gwra Brahma, former MP of the Rajya Sabha. The pre-poll alliance between the INC and the UPP in BTAD was, however, not welcomed warmly by the people of the region. Despite that, this ally was looked upon as some evil foreplay of politics by some political analysts and intellectuals (Basumatary, 2018, p. 221). This ally rather faced criticism at many grounds by the public and was overlooked as another cheap game of politics. On the other hand, people were already motivated to bring down the governance of INC in Assam, like the centre, owing to the rising Modi wave. Owing to such circumstances, the UPP could not win even one seat in the state assembly election of 2016. The INC, however, managed to retain 26 seats, but this was not a sufficient number to form the government. The Modi magic had by then already engulfed the people of Assam and it helped the BJP to have a record victory

with 60 seats for the first time in the political history of Assam. In addition, the pre-poll alliance of the BJP with the AGP and other tribal parties such as the BPF, Rabha Jatiya Aikya Manch (RJAM) and Tiwa Jatiya Aikya Manch (TJAM) helped the BJP to secure assembly seats. The BJP formed the coalition government with its pre-poll alliance partners, the AGP and the BPF, for the first time in the political history of Assam. Needless to mention that other pre-poll alliance partners of the BJP, RJAM and TJAM that had contested one seat each, did not record any victory in 2016 assembly election.

CONCLUSION

Over the period, Bodo politics has been revolving around various issues related to their backwardness, political instability or insecurity, unchecked illegal influx, land rights, identity crisis, etc. These political issues were essentially addressed in terms of the movement for a separate state of Bodoland and this movement was noteworthy in the regions for the last five decades.

The political environment in the BTAD region has become more visible after the creation of the BTC. The creation of the council, however, has brought about a change in the political history of Assam by creating new political opportunities for the Bodo tribal leaders. With the entry of BPF in the Assam politics, the entry of a tribal Bodo party can at least be recognized by the people of Assam now. However, the regional parties are still in its dormant form and so they have to think and rethink and develop well designed strategies to sustain themselves first and make the people feel the importance of the party in the state. This potpourri act of the party has caught the eyes of the people from other states as well. The BTC, since its inception, has been ruled by the BPF, no doubt owing to the captivating efforts of its leader Hagrama Basumatary. The BPF has been able to sustain its domain in BTAD due to the absence of any practicable substitute political party. However, the party has also met at least some of the expectations of the people, and thereby it has been able to sustain its stronghold in the territorial council, which also has greater implications over state politics in Assam.

REFERENCES

Assam legislative assembly election in 2016 party wise. (2020, 3 May). *Elections.in*. Retrieved from http://www.elections.in/assam/assembly-constituencies/2016-election-results.html

Barker, E. (1953). *The party system*. Bombay: Casement Publishers.

Baruah, B. K. (1972). *A cultural history of Assam*. New Delhi: National Book Trust.

Baruah, S. (1999). *India against itself: Assam and the politics of nationality*. New Delhi: Oxford University Press.

Baruah, S. (2005). *Durable disorder: Understanding the politics of northeast India*. New Delhi: Oxford University Press.

Basumatary, S. (2018). BTAD, electoral politics and ruling BPF. *International Journal of Research in Economics and Social Sciences*, 8(1), 215–226.

Retrieved from http://euroasiapub.org/wp-content/uploads/2018/02/20ESSJan-18-5966ESS-1.pdf

Chaudhuri, B. (1992). *Tribal transformation in India* (Vol. 3). New Delhi: Inter India Publications.

Daimary, R. (2015). Trace back to the formation of BPPF. *Journal of North East Region*, (3), 1–9. Retrieved from http://www.joner.co.in/pdf/ISSUE_III/Rahul.pdf

Datta, P. S. (1993). *Autonomy movements in Assam*. New Delhi: Omsons Publications.

Deka, H. (2014). *Politics of identity and Bodoland movement in Assam*. Delhi: Scholars World.

Executive Council of BTC. (2010). Retrieved from http://www.bodoland.gov.in/executive.html

Gait, E. (1926). *A history of Assam*. Guwahati: Lawyers Book Stall (Reprint).

Government of Assam. (2010). *Bodoland territorial council election-2010: A report*. Guwahati: Assam State Election Commission.

Government of Assam. (2015). *Bodoland territorial council election-2015: A report*. Guwahati: Assam State Election Commission.

Government of India (1951–2011). Census reports 1951–2011. New Delhi: Registrar General & Census Commissioner.

Government of India. (1972). *Statistical report on general election, 1972 to the legislative assembly of Assam*. New Delhi: Election Commission of India.

Government of India. (1978). *Statistical report on general election, 1978 to the legislative assembly of Assam*. New Delhi: Election Commission of India.

Government of India. (1983). *Statistical report on general election, 1983 to the legislative assembly of Assam*. New Delhi: Election Commission of India.

Government of India. (1985). *Statistical report on general election, 1985 to the legislative assembly of Assam*. New Delhi: Election Commission of India.

Government of India. (2006). *Statistical report on general election, 2006 to the legislative assembly of Assam*. New Delhi: Election Commission of India.

Government of India. (2011). *Statistical report on general election, 2011 to the legislative assembly of Assam*. New Delhi: Election Commission of India.

Government of India. (2016). *State election, 2016 to the legislative assembly of Assam*. New Delhi: Election Commission of India. Retrieved from https://eci.gov.in/files/file/4017-assam-general-legislative-election-2016/

Karjie, K. B. (2017). Voting behaviour in BTAD elections. *International Journal of Creative Research Thoughts*, 5, 771–776. Retrieved from http://www.ijcrt.org/papers/IJCRT1704101.pdf

Kundu, D. K. (2010). *The state and the Bodo movement in Assam*. New Delhi: APH Publications.

Maciver, R. M. (1955). *The modern state*. Oxford, England: Oxford University Press.

Mochahary, M. (2014). State hegemony, identity politics and resistance in Bodoland. *Daltri Journals, 2*(4), 77–80.

NE Now. (2019). https://nenow.in/north-east-news/upp-l-gears-2019-

lok-sabha-polls-assams-kokrajhar.html

Pegu, J. (2004). *Reclaiming identity: A discourse on Bodo history*. Kokrajhar: Jwngshar.

Pulloppillil, T., & Aluckal, J. (1997). *The Bodos: Children of bhullumbutter*. Delhi: Spectrum Publications.

Sarma, S., & Devi, P. (1993). *A brief account of the Bodo-Kacharis of Assam* (pp. 96–100). Proceedings of Northeast India History Associations, 13th Session, Shillong.

Tribes and Electoral Politics in Chhattisgarh: Alternative Sites of Assertion

Bipin Jojo and H. Beck

Electoral politics all over the country, especially in tribal areas, has rarely focused on dignity and survival issues of common people. The socio-cultural context of the tribal ecology distinguishes it from the rest of the society and so are the issues faced by the tribal people. Electoral politics deemed common man, especially the tribal people, to be incapable of and unworthy for a serious political dialogue (Wolff, 2007) and induced populist demands are brought to the central stage with the nefarious design to let the inconvenient basic issues remain buried or camouflaged. This chapter analyses the situation of the tribes in the state of Chhattisgarh and their assertion through the electoral politics in the village panchayat election in Sarguja district in the year 2005, following an experiment in Jharkhand legislative assembly election with the premise of participation, transparency and accountability of the people's representatives in governance and fulfilling the aspirations of the electorate.

The Indian constitution is enshrined with the ideals of justice, equality, liberty and fraternity with adequate safeguards for the vulnerable groups particularly the tribal communities. The villages have been given the provision to function as a republic with the purpose of decentralization for not merely to help development, but to create an integrated structure of self-governing institutions from the village and small town onwards to the national level in order to enable the people to manage their own affairs.

The 8.6 per cent tribal population of India is considered to be socially and economically backward due to their relatively isolated inhabitation and primitive life. Since independence, the Indian state initiated several programmes and schemes for the protection and development of tribes such as Multi-Purpose Tribal Block (which was later called as Tribal Development Block), Tribal Sub-Plan and special central assistance in different five year plans in consonance with the constitutional provisions. However, these programmes have been mostly techno-bureaucratic, which ignored the socio-cultural and political foundations of tribal society, that is, like the collective ownership of resources, land, forest, water, governance systems and so on. With the objective of fast economic growth to tackle the poverty and unemployment, modernization and industrialization was the path of development adopted by India ever since the independence. Following the fifth and sixth schedules of the constitution, some of the tribal areas got the provisions of self-governance through Tribal Area Development Councils and especially in the sixth schedule areas. But the fifth schedule areas continued with the techno-bureaucratic approach to tribal development. With the 73rd Constitutional Amendment Act, 1993, the provisions of the Panchayats (Extension to Scheduled Areas) Act, 1996, the tribal communities are given power to plan, administer and manage development of their villages as per their customs and traditions.

Despite several development programmes by the state, a large percentage of tribal population is lagging behind the general population in terms of various development indicators. All the rhetoric of development achieved by India in past few decades fades when the situation of tribals is exposed. Going by any indicator of development, the tribals still feature as the most deprived and marginalized community (Government of India, 2014).

The tribal areas are the richest zones of minerals in the world. The states of Jharkhand, Odisha and Chhattisgarh are widely acclaimed as the regions of the future, having immense potential for industrialization with a large deposit of minerals of the country, which provides a firm launching pad for various industries. The geological exploration and exploitation of gold, silver, base metals, decorative stones, precious stones and so on, are the potential areas of future. These mineral deposits have witnessed a number of large steels plants, sponge iron factories, thermal plants, cement factories, aluminium smelter plants,

water reservoirs, expansion of highways and railways. With the onset of globalization, the states are determined to accelerate this industrialization process by providing incentives and concessions for large private investments. With the open invitation and concessions for mining and industries in the region, a number of large national and transnational companies and many other small and medium industrialists have been setting up sponge and cement industries along with the mining. This will certainly increase the number of displaced tribals from their home and resources. Such scenario invites migration of people from other parts of the countries to take the benefit of employment and economic opportunities in tribal areas and leads to further alienation of existing resources like land and forest.

It is, however, a pity that the people who are facing the brunt are not considered to be fit enough for informed political dialogue about the issues of transition in the face of dramatic economic development. The confrontation between the tribal communities and the state which began after the adoption of Indian constitution and non-recognition of traditional system of governance of the tribes has been accentuated because of non-implementation of reasonable policies. The tribal communities are facing challenges unprecedented in history because of the simultaneous presence of diverse forces which are not accountable to the people as should be in the democracy.

ELECTORAL POLITICS

In a parliamentary democracy, people participate in the governance system through their elected representatives who get elected to the legislatures through different political parties. Whatever be the origins of various political parties, they are the instruments to acquire power, control the state apparatus and govern. Most of the issues facing tribal groups have been solved by local social and political movements which were not active in party politics. Therefore the advocates like Jayaprakash Narayan for party-less democracy where democratic society is based on free will of individual citizens without the intermediation of political parties. However, such unalloyed idealism could not withstand the power of organized political parties, and ultimately failed to take off.

Several castes and tribes still feel that they are not getting their share of power as compared to other upper caste privileged groups. Accountability to the local masses especially tribes in a democracy has been substituted by accountability to the party reducing democracy to a mere ritual. Manipulation of votes in this ritual with appeal to caste, religion, ethnicity and such like, through inducement of pecuniary gains, feasts and drinks or capture/denial through force have come to be accepted as common place to an extent that the voter himself may volunteer to barter the same. In a milieu of accepting 'perversion' of democratic process as a norm, the political dialogue within the ruling elite is superficial as no one is prepared to take the risk of adopting the 'right path'. Even the intervention by the constitutional bodies like the election commission and the courts are to keep up the forms and appearances. Often, even these interventions get trivialized. The common man is reduced to an amused passive spectator. The above manipulative practices have given rise to a political regime in which people with money and mafia are capturing power and are not amenable to even the discipline of the party. The tribal communities have been rendered most vulnerable in this milieu. The confrontations between the state and the people have been accentuating especially in command over resources. The distorted politics of vote is weakening the natural defence of the community. The state is assiduously refusing to go by the constitutional mandate taking advantage of the fact that the people's representation are either beholden to the party or are becoming law unto themselves or subservient to vested interests.

ALTERNATIVE SITES OF ASSERTION

Failures of statist projects of social transformation have led to many thinkers of the political left to come up with new transformative democratic strategies with a focus on participative governance. According to Fung and Wright (2003), the challenge today is to 'develop transformative democratic strategies that can advance our traditional values— egalitarian social justice, individual liberty combined with popular control over collective decisions and the flourishing of individuals in ways which enable them to realize their potentials'. These strategies varying from participative planning as seen in Kerala (Tharakan, 2004) to participatory budgeting in Porto Alegro (Schonleitner, 2004) have many characteristics in common. They all invariably involve action at the local level. They have a practical orientation, focussing on specific, tangible problems; they involve a deliberative approach to finding solutions to the problems. Analysing the nature of these movements, Harriss, Stokke and Tornquisi (2004) note, '(these local political actions) ... represent attempts to realize the idea of deliberative democracy, in which, it is held, by coming together, and discussing the ideas and interests which they bring to public decision making'. It seems quite clear that the 'transformative democratic strategies' as innovative as they may be, focus that innovations to strengthen and democratize further the existing democratic institutions.

New social movements, which are collective actions by people to address 'new grievances' based on identity and social location that are not necessarily class based have become another prominent form of people's protest against state failure (Melucci & Lyrra, 1998). In contrast to the transformative democratic strategies, these movements are more about mobilising people through the informal channels and are invariably outside the formal political structure and processes. However, one cannot see them as clear dichotomies as political mobilization of groups and democratization of society as a whole are both processes that span across the formal and informal spaces of political articulation in democracy. And in the recent past, in response to the increasingly skewed pattern of development, a series of initiatives have come up in India that seek to either simultaneously mobilize people along collective identities or bring about transformative change in governance structures, or better, attempt both simultaneously. And elections have been major sites of activities for many of these people's movements.

Appreciation of the damage, which the ordinary people's life has undergone by their neglect, a regime of active and informed political dialogue is essential preconditions for any 'salvage operation of true democracy'. The rejection of 'supremo'/'high command' premises being legitimized in the democratic polity and assertion of accountability to the people through the community, that is the general assembly of people in the village/mohalla are necessary first steps in the 'operation salvage' of democracy. Some of the people's organizations have attempted to push the people in the centre of electoral politics at various levels as paradigm shift (Jojo, 2014).

BHARAT JAN ANDOLAN

Bharat Jan Andolan (BJA), a peoples' organization initiated by Dr B. D. Sharma, former Commissioner for Scheduled Castes (SCs) and Scheduled Tribes (STs), facilitated to revive the consciousness of the tribal people towards active involvement and representation in electoral politics. It is an initiation of people's movements towards electoral politics that would lead to participative, transparent and accountable governance at the grassroots level. Accordingly, the BJA experimented for *the rule of village republic* known as *Gaon Ganraj* (in Hindi) [rule of village republic] by contesting and supporting those who believed in their premises in the assembly election of Jharkhand in 2005.

BASIC PREMISES OF INTERVENTION

The politics of vote in the present form was essentially viewed as a raw struggle for capturing the power with hardly any place of ideological refinements. This scramble had led to breaking of community life in the village and the exploited, each faction hoping for some share in the booty, should the party of their affiliation come to power. The scenario at the other end, that is, of the urban-organized, that largely comprises of the ruling elite was different. In their case, the issue was perceived as enhancing the share in the loot, which could be a 'friendly' form of competition or even 'war', the common interest of all being adequately taken care of.

According to Log Tantra Mahotsav 2005 document of BJA, the worst trickery with the people in the hills and forests of Jharkhand had been committed through distortion of its history itself (Bharat Jan Andolan, 2005). Their valiant forefathers through countless encounters and battles, recorded as Santhal revolt of Tilka Majhi, Siddhu-Kanu, Bhumij (sardar) revolt, Vir Buddhu Bhagat revolt, Tana Bhagat movement, the revolt of Birsa Bhagawan and so on, did not allow the British to set their feet on the sacred land. But the crafty British recorded these territories as 'excluded' to mislead the world. Accordingly, their territories remained outside the purview of the general law. Their traditional system remained in vogue undisturbed. But what an irony of fate, there was no place for this system in our constitution after independence. The result was an automatic extension of the general laws to these areas. Accordingly, the state acquired control over the resources. The entire community became an 'offender' in the eyes of law. There were movements for separate identity of Jharkhand. But the spirit of self-governance, a natural right of the community was forgotten. The issues raised in Jharkhandi Ulgulans (revolts) remained unattended. The valiant challenge of Tana Bhagats 'land was created by god, we are god's children, pray, from where has the government appeared in between!'; their resolve not to pay 'revenue', the promises of restoration of their auctioned lands on that count have all been shelved quietly.

Therefore, the basic objective of an intervention aimed at strengthening the community and addressing the basic issues of expropriation cannot be fulfilled if the intervention leads to formation of yet another political party, notwithstanding the ideal it may set for itself. According to the movement, all political formations in the beginning were idealistic, the degeneration started when compromises had to be made in the vote bank politics and sharing of power. This intervention was not to float a new political party at any of time. In operational terms, it was envisaged that 'membership of a political party shall not be a disqualification provided that the concerned person is not an office bearer of a political party and agrees to abide by the code of conduct adopted by the people collectively'.

This experiment was facilitated by BJA to contest in three constituencies of the state assembly election, that is, Kolebira, Torpa, and Borio (core areas), while it supported candidates in three constituencies, that is, Sisai, Khunti, and Litipara (support areas). The areas were largely populated by Santhals, Mundas, and Hos, where the 'village community' had been incorporated in the legal frame of Panchayat (Extension to Scheduled Areas) Act in 1996 as the competent body to govern the village as per their tradition. Thus, the tribes had been actively asserting their natural and constitutional rights. Hence, the unanimous decision in the deliberations was that the first step towards meeting the grave challenges of reversing the selection of candidates in the election would be that all 'village republics' collectively decide that this time the candidate shall be 'Ours, Not Theirs'. The issues raised by Gaon Ganraj during the election campaign were: rights over land, water, and forest, honouring the Tenancy Acts and the traditional governance system, powers of Gram Sabha and so on. Though none of the candidates won the election, they left an impression that

election could be contested 'differently' like in the selection of the candidates, methods of campaign, role of village communities, without extravagant expenditure, etc.

TRIBES IN SARGUJA, CHHATTISGARH

Chhattisgarh came into being on 1 November 2000 after getting separated from Madhya Pradesh. Since then there have been many socio-political developments which have attracted the attention of political sphere, media and people across India. With the formation of Chhattisgarh as a separate state, it was envisaged that the process of socioeconomic development of hitherto neglected tribal people will be spearheaded by the government.

As per the 2011 census, over 76 per cent of the population continues to live in rural areas. In the development of Chhattisgarh, a state predominantly (32%) inhabited by tribal communities, a majority of whom are still dependent upon primitive farming and forest produce for their livelihood, the role of Gram Panchayats becomes quite significant. Chhattisgarh state has rich natural resources, which not only provides sustainable and sufficient livelihood sources to its tribal population but also supplies various ores and coal which are essential for industrial activities. With the continuous expansion of industrialization and ever growing demand for these raw resources, one can witness the plundering and excessive exploitation of natural resources across the country. In such scenario, it becomes the responsibility of state to safeguard the rights of tribal communities over these natural resources which have been part of their life, culture and tradition for centuries. Since independence, there have been innumerable incidents of forced displacements, alienation from land, violation of forest rights and so on, in the name of development and growth and these activities have ultimately put the local tribes at receiving end, alienating them from their livelihood resources and putting them on the verge of destitution and acute poverty.

Table 13.1 indicates that a look at the profile of districts by select social, economic and political indicators shows that most parts of the Chhattisgarh continue to leave in a state of abject standard of living. Districts such as Koriya, Surguja, Jashpur, Korba, Kanker and Bastar where the rural low standard of living (SLI) ranges between 44 and 66 per cent. Over 60–55 per cent households possess below poverty line (BPL) cards. It is important to note that most of the economically backward districts are also regions with high proportion of SC and ST population.

The state of Chhattisgargh has 90 assembly seats, out of which 29 seats are reserved for the tribes. As the Sarguja district is tribal populated, two out of three legislative assembly seats are reserved for tribes, namely Sitapur and Lundra. Table 13.2 shows the number of tribal candidates contested either as independents or under the banner of political party. In all these elections, the candidate of the Congress party have got elected except for Lundra in the 2003 assembly election. It is important to note that Ambikapur was ST seat during the 2003 assembly election, there after it has become unreserved seat. However, the tribes have contested even if the seat is not reserved for them. This trend has been observed in rest of the state as well. There are 61 unreserved constituencies but the tribes contested even in the unreserved constituencies. So, 66, 58 and 58 tribal candidates contested the unreserved constituencies during 2008, 2013 and 2018 assembly elections, respectively.

Table 13.1   Profile of Districts by Social, Economic and Political Indicators, Chhattisgarh

District	Have a BIL card (%)		Standard of Living Index				Female literacy rate 2011		% SC-ST population 2001	Schedule V Areas
			Low (%)		High (%)					
	Total	Rural	Total	Rural	Total	Rural	Total	Rural		
Koriya	46.9	58.8	43.1	60.3	16.1	1.5	61.01	55.11	52.57	Fully
Surguja	65.6	68.7	56.3	59.5	5.6	3.1	50.88	47.57	59.40	Fully
Jashpur	52.2	53	62.8	65.3	2.5	1.1	59.05	57.15	68.14	Fully
Raigarh	63.7	68.8	26.3	29.6	8.1	3	63.25	60.31	49.58	Partially
Korba	56.1	77	28.6	42.7	12.1	0.8	62.26	54.06	51.48	Fully
Janjgir-champa	58.6	59.6	13.5	14.9	8.1	5.1	61.72	59.86	34.10	Partially
Bilaspur	60.2	69.5	23.9	30.6	12.5	1.9	60.12	53.86	38.34	Partially
Kawardha	64.9	66.7	34.7	37.6	3.8	1.1	48.94	46.51	33.58	Partially
Rajnandgaon	50.3	54.3	22.2	25.6	7.9	1.1	66.98	64.19	36.56	Partially
Durg	40.9	50.2	11.8	17.2	18.9	2.1	70.51	64.92	25.20	Partially
Raipur	45.5	55.3	20.3	28.3	18.7	3.2	66.21	59.22	28.27	Partially
Mahasamund	53.5	55.9	30.2	32.8	5.8	2.2	60.37	58.53	39.16	Partially
Dhamatri	53.8	58.8	17.9	20.9	11.6	4.5	69.24	67.32	33.25	Partially
Kanker	61.6]	62.9	42.8	44.3	3.8	1.5	61.08	58.67	60.33	Fully
Bastar	69.6	73.4	61	66.7	5	1.4	44.49	39.52	Na	Fully
Dantewada	64.9	69.3	67	74	7.2	2.4	32.88	24.89	81.88	Fully
Narayanpur							40.22	39.52	na	Fully
bijapur							31.56	27.18	na	Fully
Chhattisgarh	56.8	62.7	34.8	41.1	9.3	2.5	60.59	55.4		

Source: Government of Chhattisgarh (2013); Government of India (2001, 2011); International Institute for Population Studies (2010).

Table 13.2   Number of ST Candidates Contested in Assembly Elections, Chhattisgarh

Year of Election	Sitapur Assembly (ST)	Lundra Assembly (ST)	Ambikapur (Open)	Total Candidates for the State
2003	8	7	9	246
2008	15	13	16	270
2013	10	11	13	225
2018	12	10	3	262

Source: Government of India (2003, 2008, 2013, 2018).

Despite the seats are reserved for the ST candidates, they have been the representatives of the political party though elected by the electorate of Indian democracy. However, whether they are able to fulfil the aspirations of the electorate remains a question.

The tribal population in the area had always felt sidelined by the so-called domination of the mainstream thought of governance. Within this stream of governance, there had always been a tendency of domination, subjugation and objectification of the local populace, that is, tribals. This was exerted in varied forms, for example, the way dominant caste groups perceived the tribal social life inferior to their own, illiterate, ignorant and prone to easy victimizations of diverse incentives.

Most of the hamlets and villages have homogenous communities with Gond tribe population predominantly constituting it, yet they did not have unity among themselves. The community which was thought once as one of the strong unifying factors of people was rapidly losing its grip over the community.

SPREAD OF THE IDEA OF GAON GANRAJ (RULE OF VILLAGE REPUBLIC)

There were communities who got inspired by the idea on the supremacy of the village republic in some parts of Chhattisgarh where BJA had not intervened in those areas. As an effect, communities had put candidates in 18 gram panchayats during the 2005 gram panchayat

election in Sarguja district of Chhattisgarh. Thus, the basic premise of this initiative was to alter the party driven electoral politics to the community driven politics. These villages were mainly belonging to two major communities of Gond and Oraon with agriculture as the main occupation.

B.D. Sharma was the brain child for the spread of Gaon Ganraj in the region as a whole. He delivered a few public addresses in the region/neighbouring state that caused sparks of Gaon Ganraj and through some most devoted village leaders, the concept and ideology was carried over on to their different villages. Some of the mechanisms most popularly used in dissemination of the ideology pertained to dialogue and talking to people individually, in groups and communities wherever it was possible. Dialogue was the most frequent mechanism used for attending and facilitating others to join in the public meetings at all levels (village, taluka and district headquarters). However, they were farmers primarily and, hence, it was difficult to avail time for attending meetings outside the village.

Dr. Sharma was the catalyst who sowed the seed of Gaon Ganraj without any financial backing to the groups interested to adopt it and made it as their integral part of panchayat governance. The newly emerging local leaders visited several villages for dissemination of the concept of Gaon Ganraj and mobilized people to strengthen it as a movement. Organizing meetings and delivering public addresses implied financial needs but Dr Sharma had a firm conviction that the movement should survive without any external financial support and should be carried by people who are interested to promote its objectives. The locals inspired by Dr Sharma's stance on their own, requested their fellowmen to contribute @ ₹10/- or any amount as they wished to the common cause. Whenever a meeting was organized, many individuals came forward voluntarily with some resources such as rice, dal, vegetable, cash and so on, to meet the expenses of the gathering. During the initial days of inception and propaganda, there was a collective pooling of funds by the people and they were extremely enthusiastic. But later on, it could be sudden fall out of the spirit of people towards collective pooling of funds and support for the initiative could be witnessed. However, it was not a deliberate act and gesture of withdrawal, but got discontinued owing to reasons of inconveniences in making collection at a central place. Nevertheless, some of them still continued giving their share to the common fund/pool.

In the initial phase of the spread of Gaon Ganraj, it created a terror in the area especially the intruders who were being perceived as exploiters. Every village and area resounded by the movement of Gaon Ganraj. It implied and called on people of villages of the area to unite and fight against injustices meted to them by the exploiters. They sensed it as an excellent opportunity to rise up and retrieve their lost property from the dominant intruders. People came in big number, marched from village to village mobilizing to join them. Every meeting and public address had great tempo and zeal, inspiring the people to opt for Gaon Ganraj as a system of their swaraj and governance. Every village and public address by the local leaders had some elements of speech (words like 'now we had got our own Gaon Ganraj, please come together, be together, let us protect our interest, we were bound to retrieve our lost property (land), regain our past glory and drive the intruders away from our area. There was nothing to fear, we will definitely secure victory, say all of you

jai Gaon Ganraj' and so on). Thus, it was a direct challenge of the poor against the rich and the intruders.

EMERGENCE OF A LOCAL LEADERSHIP

The advent of Gaon Ganraj witnessed several leaders from the local soil. There were many active leaders acting as volunteers in the primary dissemination of the concept of Gaon Ganraj and mobilization of the people for the same. These leaders were neither known for their excellent educational qualification nor any better social, economic and political stature. Many of the people had not even seen Dr B.D. Sharma nor heard any of his public address anywhere but were fascinated with the concept of Gaon Ganraj. These leaders were self-motivated though some of them had a chance of attending some public address of Dr Sharma in their region, which enhanced their inspiration working for the spread of Gaon Ganraj. Some could access accidentally certain literature by Sharma on the subject and were greatly influenced by the message and teaching it contained.

The literature immensely boosted and inspired the leaders who in turn disseminated it to their fellowmen in their villages. Spread of the concept and ideology took varied forms like distribution of literatures on the subject, dialogues at an individual as well as group level, and village meets and so on, the concept was so appealing that it spread to various neighbouring villages like wild fire. There was a trickling and ball rolling effect in the spread of the concept as it was passed on to others in the process of household, street, friend circle, neighbouring talks and village meeting and so on.

Gaon Ganraj knew no specific categories of people but touched every person irrespective of his/her age, caste, creed, class, gender, rich and the poor. Everybody was influenced by the forethought of Gaon Ganraj. However, the most volatile group was the village youth which was energetic and sharp in recognizing the authenticity of the system of governance which was people friendly and people centred.

GRAM PANCHAYAT ELECTION

There were two dates for the village panchayat election, one was in on 15 January and second was 20 January 2005. Entire village did not know the date of election declared right from the very first day and date of its declaration but some of the village leaders especially those who were aspiring to contest for election did come to know about it from the very first day of its declaration.

ISSUES RAISED DURING ELECTIONS

Gaon Ganraj primarily emphasized land dispute issues, village development schemes, creation of employment avenues, protection of natural resources and development of village infrastructure. It was also trying to mobilize people towards wiping out corruption at every level of panchayat and bureaucracy. The reasons mainly stated by the respondents for their dissatisfaction with the functioning of panchayat comprised of corruption, misappropriation of the panchayat fund for vested interests of the leaders who never take public into their confidence while taking major decision for the development of the village, etc. Besides, the panchayat body was also accused of non-committal and non-accountable to the people whom they represent.

If anyone was desirous of contesting village panchayat election, he/she had to meet one's own electoral expenses. Persons with a better financial status election expenses especially in relation to preparing posters, formal and in-formal contact with officials, people, coordination, networking, offering

treats to their near and dear ones consisting of food and liquor in order to please and win their vote banks and so on. It was a delicate subject, therefore, many of the respondents did not disclose directly but made vague statements which had elements of truth in it. Nevertheless, it was true that none of the Gaon Ganraj candidates made such expenses for the campaign and contested the panchayat election. They primarily contested election and won their votes on the basis of their good leadership qualities based on the service of people. Such electoral expenses were not even favoured by the villagers who were influenced by Gaon Ganraj concept. They appreciated for incurring expenses most judiciously for better public meeting, printing and distribution of posters and other noble campaign methods and not in distribution of incentives and offering liquor and so on, with a motive to influence the voters.

Prior to the election of village panchayat, the supporters of Gaon Ganraj expressed their opinions and reached consensus on the choice of their favourable candidate to make him/her stand and contest the panchayat election. The choice of the candidates was primarily governed by leadership qualities and the level of commitment to the service of common mass. This process of selection took place through series of meetings. The manifestoes of the Gaon Ganraj candidates comprised of generate employment schemes and avenues at their panchayat jurisdiction, improve infrastructure facilities of their villages, promote welfare programme to the people, fight against the prevalence of corruption, manipulation, misappropriation of common resources of cash and kind and so on.

Many of the supporters of Gaon Ganraj in fact had taken an oath of good governance as a mark of selfless service to people. The oath chiefly entailed abstaining from bribing and even receiving a bribe, committal and accountable to people, simplicity of life, surrendering of salary to the cause of Gaon Ganraj, refraining from personal and vested interest and not showing any undue favouritism to the people for awarding any kinds of benefits. Large extent of respondents were aware about such oaths being taken by people actively involved in the spread of Gaon Ganraj especially the Gaon Ganraj panchayat body members in the area.

FACTORS DETERMINING THE ELECTIONS

The Gaon Ganraj did not witness a hay day for its spread but faced many hurdles created by the different stakeholders comprising of the political parties who anticipated a severe jolt in pursuit of their vested interest. Gaon Ganraj was perceived as a tool of eroding the power and monopoly of party leaders on the village governance and administration. As a matter of fact, the political party leaders opposed the introduction and spread of Gaon Ganraj in the area. The bureaucrats especially the lower and middle cadres also did not have a favourable opinion about the Gaon Ganraj. But the traditional village leaders seemed to be quite open about the coming of Gaon Ganraj and did not perceive any threat to their functioning. It was true that these traditional leaders were pro-people service oriented. However, the tribal community was very enthusiastic with the advent of Gaon Ganraj as it widened up the scope of their involvement in their own governance with transparency. Most striking about the implanting of Gaon Ganraj in the area was the younger generation. It had shown immense enthusiasm about the spread and dissemination of Gaon Ganraj in the area. The youth and women members played a big role in the spread of the Gaon Ganraj.

IMPACT OF GAON GANRAJ

When Gaon Ganraj spread in the area, the poor people who had been almost bonded for

work with their masters of land owners were the worst hit. They did find Gaon Ganraj with an immense potential for their empowerment and showed enthusiasm to join it but at the same time found them at a precarious situation as they were caught between want of liberty and sustenance. Gaon Ganraj, if strengthened, could emancipate the poor and marginalized from the clutches of rich land owners. At the same time, fear and isolation and deprivation of the little scope of livelihood avenues that were available with the land owners (intruders) was a reaction from those who sensed a threat to their own existence by the fast spread of Gaon Ganraj.

Gaon Ganraj was perceived as a direct attack on the interest of the rich lots especially the intruders and non-tribal section of population for obvious reasons of their exploitative role against the poor and marginalized section of the local population. The message of Gaon Ganraj was all embracing disregards of caste, creed, rich and poor and so on, but the local tribal population assumed it as their own explicitly. In the process of embracing Gaon Ganraj and taking on the role and advocacy to its spread, they made the non-tribals feel amply clear that their weapon to fight against exploitative forces targeted to them. Obviously, they targeted the intruders whom they perceived as their exploiters. Gaon Ganraj was pro-poor and marginalized friendly but anti-non tribals was made loud and clear through the mode of its advocacy carried out in the form of individual dialogue, family talk, neighbourhood chats, group, community, village meeting as well as the public addresses.

It was an issue of perception where people differed in their adoption of strategies of intervention. Some people from amongst the tribal population regarded Gaon Ganraj as a means of governance to bring upon change and transformation of the people by securing social, economic and political justice while other set of people took it not only as an anti-intruder movement, but also implied their own community fellowmen who were considered as exploiters with certain issues in question with them such as internal conflicts, group dynamics and the land disputes in particular.

Subsequently, there were two fractions of groups: the exploiter and the exploited. The exploited was trying to target the exploiters group and perceived Gaon Ganraj as the ultimate end to get them justice in the form of collective strength under the broad umbrella of Gaon Ganraj. It was quite unfortunate that the people of the same community/tribe were fighting with each other and trying to use Gaon Ganraj as their weapons against each other. Besides, there was another tussle between the sub-tribes as well as inter-religious groups, for example, Gond versus Christians and these two sub-tribes taken together against the Muslim groups. Gaon Ganraj was precisely perceived as a force to subdue the exploiters by the exploited rightly coming under the shield of Gaon Ganraj.

The other set of people in the village, averted to the ideology of Gaon Ganraj, were those who derived huge benefits from the existing village panchayat system. Their financial status was relatively better than others in the village. Moreover, most of these people were some public figure as they were political leaders, present Panchayati Raj functionaries and other stake holders in varied aspects of their indigenous customary and traditional life. The acceptance of the Gaon Ganraj ideology was a direct denial of their age old hegemony, exertion of power and functions in the public affairs often oriented with vested interest. Once the Gaon Ganraj substituted the prevalent system of Panchayati Raj, the scope of popular participation by common mass would increase and thereby decrease the scope of malpractices of people with selfish ends.

Farsagudi panchayat was one of the 18 panchayats where the Sarpanch had contested panchayat election making Gaon Ganraj as the base of election. It has a tiny hamlet of an odd 30 families though mixed population but Christians comprised predominantly. These Christian women had very strong bond amongst themselves. Their strength may have been strengthened due to their frequent collective meet every Sunday for their regular prayer service. They also regularly met as a community on numerous occasions. It was this small group of women got highly inspired by the ideology of Gaon Ganraj and its potentiality for resolving issues of common concern as collective body. They had been witnessing atrocities committed by police and forest officials in the area. It was undue harassments especially from the forest guards and officials. Access to forest resources by the villagers was strongly dealt with by the forest authorities.

Villagers used to access the forest to gather minor forest produce, for example, sal fruits, leaves, dry branches as firewood. They also acquired some useful wood to their minimum for either repairing of old houses or construction of new houses. The police personnel along with the forest authorities would come to village inspection, look for new construction of houses and approach the same with a demand of fine rating from ₹5,000 to ₹15,000/- depending upon the use of wood materials and financial status of the family concerned. Refusal to comply with the bribe demand of the authorities usually were recorded to be met in the form of damage and demolition of the houses including confiscation of all the construction materials used in the house. The actions of the kind were not to prevent people from the use of construction materials from the forest that belong to the people themselves, but to seek bribe, commission to satisfy their greed, failing of which was met with severe consequences, for example, damage of houses, beating, further terrorise for greater amount of bribes, and even confiscation of construction of materials with a view to teach a lesson to people who dared not to comply with the whims and loot of the authorities. Police inspection of the village and their harassment of the people were a regular affair. Such harassment meted to the villagers was tolerated silently and no one dared to take up a challenge against. On the other hand, the police and the forest authorities themselves would permit private contractors to take trucks of loaded wood from the forest.

In this context, a group of women who had been witnessing the loot of forest resources by none other than the very forest officials in the form of contractors were highly inspired and motivated by the idea of Gaon Ganraj. They had been witnessing such an indiscriminate felling and draining the forest woods by the contractors for the last several years. However, they did not dare to stop them except making a formal complaint to forest officials concerned who were also an integral part of the loot. They paid least heed to their complaints. This time the group was firm and determined to take action against the incident on their own without fearing any action. These women sparked in the form of Gaon Ganraj in challenging the situation without fear of consequences of any kind whatsoever. They got in action when they spotted a truck of a contractor loaded with fresh wood dashing down the forest through the village. They stopped it and asked them to produce legal documents for draining of the wood.

Sensing the situation, tensed and furious truck driver abandoned the truck and ran away. The group did not permit the truck to be driven off without a legal proof of the same, failing of which, the group unloaded the truck on the spot (the wood was still available at the spot, even during the field work in May–June 2005). It was believed that the government machinery in the area was on a constant look out for any mistake by any of the individuals or groups of Gaon Ganraj so that it could book them under some legal clauses for further suppressing and harassment. Hence, it went without saying the entire episode of the action taken by the group of women, was given a different twist by the truck owners and the contractors. They implied and associated the group of women with Naxalites and charged them for engaging in unlawful activities. Further, they stated that this group of Naxalites tried to hijack and snatch the truck engaged in transporting wood. It was informed that the

police virtually believed them and instead of taking action against the culprits (contractors) and other people in nexus with, the women's group itself was booked under some clause and there was a case against them.

It flared up some other problems in the community. Men folk did not expect the women getting entangled with legal hurdles especially with the police and forest departments. According to men folk, any woman getting caught up in any activities with legal implications, disregarding the noble values of such actions, drew public attention and defamation with an inherent attachment of ill image to the village community. This was precisely what happened with the group of women. One of the women members who was very active and took all the initiatives and lead to mobilize other women and the ultimate action mentioned above had to face some unpleasant reaction from her own husband, who was greatly disturbed by the initiative and action taken against the forest and police authorities. The husband was in complete confirmative with the cause and action taken by his wife but he feared stringent action and harassment to the family by the police and forest officials.

Under stress and anxiety, the husband refused his wife even entry to his house. This painful drama went on in the family of the person concerned for a week or so and was normalized by series of dialogues and counselling by other village leaders and women members of the group. The hamlet had come to its normalcy but at the same time it also witnessed a sudden cool down of the enthusiasm of the women for reasons of not gathering positive appreciation and support from their men folk in the hamlet. Secondly, this particular group of women constituted Christians only and did not have any kind of support from other section of non-Christian communities in the village. It was obvious to expect such reaction from the group while others in the village were silent spectators. However, while talking to this group of women, one could sense a strong feeling of enthusiasm and commitment to stand for their social and political justice which was just dormant temporarily initially and was ready to burst out at any point of time along with the ripening of the idea of Gaon Ganraj in the village and area.

Whatever may be the reaction of the people against the action taken by the women's group, it had achieved a lasting effect on the people as well as the government officials in particular. The very action of halting a running truck with load of wood sent a message of intolerance against the atrocities and harassment meted to tribal communities in that area. Hearing this incident many people in and around neighbouring villages got inspired and courage and revolted against such undue pressure tactics and exploitation. The government authorities did not dare to enter the villages, sensing the situation to be volatile. After the incident, the police as well as the forest officials had stopped going to the villages to carry out inspection of house construction and other forest material use. The action of the tribal communities had in fact terrorised the government officials. During instances of any violence within the village, the police started going there only after seeking the consent of the village panchayat or after they had been informed. But rarely did such issues went to the police, as people in the village like Farsagudi preferred settling their disputes, if any, in the village itself with the help of the panchayat rather than letting the issue go to the government machinery. Thus, the women's group through its one time action could set up a noteworthy precedent.

ISSUES AND CHALLENGES

There were several difficulties faced by the respondents especially those who played prominent role in the spread of Gaon Ganraj in the area. One of the biggest hindrances was embracing the concept and ideology of Gaon Ganraj itself. The village environment was quite volatile as many of the villagers instigated one against the other. There was a deliberate effort of misguidance, discouragement and instigation of common men by persons who did not favour Gaon Ganraj model of governance. People who favoured Gaon Ganraj were threatened of dire consequences by the opponents of such model. Such threatening was possible because many of the people in the area were landless agricultural labourers and quite a few of them were also with minimum quantity of land ownership. These individuals were very vulnerable and extensively depended upon the big landholders for their sustenance. Consequently, it was more than natural for them to get frightened of such threats.

The Gaon Ganraj candidate elected as the Sarpanch of the panchayat at that time faced lack of support from other panchayat members of different villages. Though they carried one ideology of Gaon Ganraj, due to inherent complexities in the existing panchayat system, they faced fear of isolation and non-support. They also ran the risk of deprivation of government support in terms of schemes for village/rural development and general good will from the government departments. In this case, the panchayat treasurer who enjoyed years of service had established very good nexus with the politicians and bureaucrats, he also controlled most of the finances of the panchayat. The Sarpanch being a new comer did not have any adequate experience of the financial transactions and this in turn gave additional strength to the treasurer for influencing the newly elected panchayat body.

There were almost 18 village panchayats that had contested election on the basis of Gaon Ganraj concept and ideology and secured majority support. The Sarpanches of these village panchayats actually did not command sound economic power/influence in their villages. It was true even for the active village leaders of Gaon Ganraj. Under such juncture, it became difficult for the leaders to exert command over people especially on the traditional and non-Going ganraj influential leaders. They suffered from social and psychological inferiority complexes. However, they were sincere, hardworking, people friendly, pro–people service oriented, transparent, less susceptible to corruption, humane, broad minded and desire to promote welfare and justice to every member of the villages. They also enjoyed greater support and appreciation from the BJA.

CONCLUSION

In fact, there was an inherent complexity in the existing panchayat functionaries comprising of the Sarpanch, Deputy Sarpanch and other elected representatives including the treasurer. While all the other representatives of the panchayat body were elected, the treasurer was not and continues his/her post even with the newly elected body of panchayat. He was basically an appointee of the government. Being an appointee of the government, capable of reaping the support from his higher authorities, he need not bank on the support of the voters to remain in his post. Due to his well-established position, he enjoys a neutral position and continues to be independent without having moral obligation and accountability to the voters. This had resulted the treasurer to be a very important stakeholder in the panchayat body. In practicality, he enjoys much greater power than even the elected Sarpanch and often becomes the main culprit for the misappropriation of the panchayat finance. Control of panchayat finance largely depends upon them which was very vital organ of the panchayat. The newly elected Sarpanch did not have adequate knowledge on how the financial transaction in the panchayat operates. As a consequence, they substantially depend upon the experienced and expertise of the treasurer.

There was an emergence of a new and complex phenomenon in the overall functioning of the newly elected Gaon Ganraj panchayats in the area. Instead of gaining mutual support from each other, the Gaon Ganraj Sarpanches largely remained fragmented and scattered. They were caught between deep sea and devil whether to go astray of the principles of Gaon Ganraj by following the whims and wishes of the treasurer or to stand firm with the ideology of the Gaon Ganraj and challenge the loot system in the governance. Supporting and standing by the concept and ideology of Gaon Ganraj would give a new outlook, positive and people friendly system of governance but going against the tide of age old corrupt system of governance implied huge repercussion. Entire government machinery from top to the bottom in the hierarchy was against the establishment of Gaon Ganraj in the area/region. Panchayat being the grassroots organization entirely depended upon the financial and administrative support of the government machinery. Going against the established government machinery implies running a risk of losing its support and distancing themselves from the favours of various government departments, bureaucrats and the politicians as a whole and further face the denial of all the development schemes channelized through Panchayati Raj for their own development. It implies losing of the faith, trust and confidence of the voters in the years to come. This has become a huge dilemma for the Sarpanches to choose for an option.

According to the people, some of the Sarpanches of Gaon Ganraj had fallen into the trap of loot system of governance because they did not want to lose the confidence of the voters and their position. Subsequently, they had been already blessed with many development schemes for the villages. Their contribution as Sarpanches for the villagers has become tangible and visible that will enable them to retain the confidence of the voters. Siding with the loot system precisely was perceived as sustaining and perpetuating their vote banks. The Sarpanches, who denied to comply with the whims and fancies of bureaucrats, had to sacrifice the support of the bureaucracy and thereby lose the opportunity of gaining any development schemes to the villages they represented. The voters were interested in development schemes to enhance infrastructures and other essential services to their villages, in the absence of which they were bound to lose their confidence on the Sarpanch as a worthy representative. This was precisely what had happened with one of the Sarpanches of village Farsagudi in Rajpur development block.

Since he denied to be an integral part of the loot system of governance, he lost not only the support of his Gaon Ganraj fellow Sarpanches in the area but also the government machinery as well. He had been categorically communicated that unless and until he abandoned the system of Gaon Ganraj model of governance and become part of their own age old system of gram panchayat, he would never be able to secure any scheme for his village. He was the sole Sarpanch daring to stand by the principle and values cherished by Gaon Ganraj, but at the same time facing frustration of his voters as he was not able to secure any development activities from the government. This internal politics and dynamics were subtle and unknown to the voters.

These newly emerging leaders of Gaon Ganraj were in fact perceived as naxalites by the government machinery. First of all, the emergence of Gaon Ganraj itself was a stumbling block to the existing corrupt government. Thus, there was a need for more reasons to crash such initiatives, leadership and movement as a whole. Even the voluntary contribution/collection of the people in Gaon Ganraj was misinterpreted as extortion. It was the attempt of some miscreants who did not wish Gaon Ganraj to emerge as system of governance. Police was more than alert to look for such allegations in order to book the village leaders and jeopardise the spread of Gaon Ganraj movement.

There was no support by the top cadre leaders to the local village leadership in the crisis situation. In fact, there was no one to fall back on in such a situation. In the absence of right guidance and direction of the youth in diverse legal matters, irrational approach to

the resolution of issues, jailing of youth and general repression of the people by politicians, bureaucracy and government machineries and so on, the local leaders/people were often left to their own fate/strength without any support even from their own communities. Under such circumstances, the village leaders became very vulnerable to suppression of the government machineries.

Lack of rigorous approach to mobilization of people/community by Gaon Ganraj leadership was a weakness. Their approach had to be door-to-door, cluster of villages, caste, class, region and so on, and leaders needed to be open, broad minded, accommodative, tolerant, etc. in order to attract many people in the movement. Along with grass roots support, an intervention at higher level (Taluka, district bureaucracy) was necessary for strengthening the movement.

However, the BJA facilitated to revive the consciousness of the tribal communities towards active involvement and representation in electoral politics in the context where there is an absence of party politics dictated by party high command. It is an initiation of people's movements towards electoral politics which would lead to participative, transparent and accountable governance at the grassroots level.

REFERENCES

Bharat Jan Andolon. (2005, January 30). *Rajavasa panchasheel resolve.* (unpublished).

Fung, A., & Wright, E. (2003). *Deepening democracy: Institutional innovations in empowered participatory governance.* London: Verso.

Government of Chhattisgarh. (2013). *Administrative report (2012–2013).* Raipur: Panchayati Raj and Rural Development Department.

Government of India. (2001). *Census India 2001- Chhattisgarh.* New Delhi: Ministry of Home Affairs.

Government of India. (2003). *Statistical report on general election 2003 to the Legislative Assembly of Chhattisgarh.* New Delhi: Election Commission of India.

Government of India. (2008). *Statistical report on general election 2008 to the Legislative Assembly of Chhattisgarh*. New Delhi: Election Commission of India.

Government of India. (2011). *Census India 2011-Chhattisgarh*. New Delhi: Ministry of Home Affairs.

Government of India. (2013). *Statistical report on general election 2013 to the Legislative Assembly of Chhattisgarh*. New Delhi: Election Commission of India.

Government of India. (2014). *Report of the high level committee on socio-economic, health and educational status of tribal communities of India* (chairman: Prof. Virginius Xaxa). New Delhi: Ministry of Tribal Affairs.

Government of India. (2018). *Statistical report on general election 2018 to the Legislative Assembly of Chhattisgarh*. New Delhi: Election Commission of India.

Harriss, J., Stoke, K., & Tornquist, O. (2004) (Eds.), *Politicising democracy: The new local politics of democratisation*. Houndmills: Palgrave-Macmillan.

International Institute for Population Studies. (2010). *District level household and facility survey (DLHS-III) 2007–08*. Mumbai: International Institute for Population Studies.

Jojo, B. (2014). People's movement for accountable electoral politics and empowerment of tribals. In

C. S. Ramanathan, & S. Dutta (Eds.), *Governance, Development and Human Service Professionals* (pp. 29–45). London & New York: Rutledge.

Melucci, A., & Lyyra, T. (1998). Collective action, change and democracy. In M. Giugni, D. M., & C. Tilly (Eds.), *Contention and Democracy*. Lanham: Rowman and Littlefield Publishers Inc.

Schonleitner, G. (2004). Can public deliberation democratise state action?: Municipal health councils and local democracy in Brazil. In J. Harriss, K. Stokke, & O. Tornquist (Eds.), *Politicising Democracy: The New Local Politics of Democratisation*. Houndmills: Palgrave Macmillan.

Tharakan, P. (2004). Historical hurdles in the course of people's planning campaign in Kerala. In

Thomas, M. M., & Taylor, R. W. (1965) (Eds.) *Tribal awakening*. Bangalore: Christian Institute of Religion and Society.

Wolff, J. (2007). (De-)Mobilising the marginalised: A comparison of the Argentine Piqueteros and Ecuador's indigenous movement. *Journal of Latin American Studies, 39*, 1–29.

14

Tribal Politics in Gujarat

N. Rajaram and Ashvin Vasava

The feature of post-Independence tribal politics of Gujarat is that it has been a continuous attempt and effort to overcome marginality in social, economic, cultural and political spheres. The analysis of tribal politics in Gujarat over the last seven decades (1947–2019) is seen through three phases—the Nehruvian era (from 1947 to 1964), when the present areas of Gujarat were part of multilingual Bombay state; post-Nehruvian Congress rule (from about 1964 to 1990) as Nehru passed away in May 1964; and the rule of the Bharatiya Janata Party (BJP; from 1998 onwards). The period between 1990 and 1998 was a phase of transition to BJP rule, which witnessed coalition governments in Gujarat where the BJP was also a part for short periods.

In retrospect, the phases of the Congress and the BJP broadly overlapped two phases of economic development in the country. The Congress era was the pre-liberalization phase, which was an era marked by the role of the state and its interventions in development policies for tribes and in the economy. During this phase, socialist ideals prevailed in different parts of the world including India. The post-liberalization phase, the era

of neoliberalism, began under Rajiv Gandhi government in the mid-1980s, but more markedly in 1991. This was the era when Soviet Union collapsed and left ideologies got a setback worldwide. The decades since the 1990s have seen market penetration into more and more areas of society and economy. This was also the phase when the BJP gained ascendancy in Gujarat. The tribes of Gujarat have been caught up in these changes. This chapter analyses these developments within the broader framework of tribal politics in India and concludes with the challenges they face in the contemporary period.

BACKGROUND

According to 2011 census, Gujarat has about 14.8 per cent of Scheduled Tribe (ST) population, residing predominantly on the eastern fringes of the state in the areas bordering Rajasthan, Madhya Pradesh and Maharashtra. The tribal population is mainly found in 14 eastern districts and 48 talukas, in about 5,884 villages.[1] The state government's Tribal

---

[1] The figures are from the Government of Gujarat's tribal department web portal (Government of Gujarat, 2019).

Table 14.1 Major Tribes in Gujarat (2011 Census)

Tribes	Population in Lakhs	% to State's ST Population	District of Concentration
Bhil	42.70	47.89	Dang, Panchmahal, Bharuch, Sabarkantha, Banaskantha
Halpati	6.43	7.21	Surat, Valsad, Navsari, Bharuch
Dhodia	6.36	7.13	Valsad, Surat
Rathawa	6.42	7.20	Chhota Udepur
Naikda	4.60	5.16	Panchmahal, Valsad
Gamit	3.78	4.25	Surat
Kokna	3.62	4.06	Navsari, Valsad, Dang
Chaudhri	3.03	3.40	Surat, Tapi, Bharuch
Varli	3.28	3.68	Valsad, Navsari
Dhanka	2.81	3.15	Vadodara, Bharuch, Panchmahal
Patelia	1.14	1.28	Panchmahal
Others	2.89	3.23	Surat, Tapi, Narmada
Total	**89.17**	**100**	

Source: Government of Gujarat, Tribal Development Department. Retrieved from https://tribal.gujarat.gov.in/demographic-fact

Development Department quotes 2011 census to show that there are an estimated 89.17 lakh tribals in the state, and they have a literacy rate of 62.5 per cent as against the state average of 78 per cent.[2] The existing documents provide conflicting date in terms of number of tribal communities. For instance, census documents listed 29 communities as STs (Government of India, 2000, p. 16), however, the Tribal Development Department, Government of Gujarat, has mentioned that there are 25 ST communities in the state.[3] Further, it has classified them into 14 major categories based on their population (Table 14.1). Table 14.1 also indicates the district-wise concentration of tribal population. The state has also categorized five tribal communities as particularly vulnerable tribal groups (PVTGs), namely Kathodi, Kolgha, Kotwalia, Padhar and Siddi.

They are numerically small, being less than one lakh each.

Gujarat is also a state where the tribal population is nearly twice that of the Scheduled Caste (SC) population, in contrast to the national scenario. Gujarat's tribal population strength is similar to that of neighbouring states of Madhya Pradesh and Rajasthan.[4] Right from the time the state came into existence on 1 May 1960, the proportion of ST and SC population to the total population has been more or less the same.[5]

THE ISSUES

The issues that will be analysed are: politics of development and its effect on tribals of

[2] The figures are from the Government of Gujarat's tribal department web portal (Government of Gujarat, 2019).
[3] From the Government of Gujarat's tribal department web portal. Retrieved from https://tribal.gujarat.gov.in/
[4] Planning Commission data quoting Census 2011 figures mention that in Rajasthan, the ST population is 13.47 per cent of the state's population; in Madhya Pradesh, the STs constitute 21.09 per cent (GOI, 2011).
[5] A scrutiny of census documents of 1961, 1981, 2001 and 2011 indicates that the proportion of SC population to the state was 6.62 per cent (1961), 7.15 per cent (1981), 7.09 per cent (2001) and 6.74 per cent (2011). The percentage of ST population was 13.34, 14.22, 14.76 and 14.75 in 1961, 1981, 2001 and 2011, respectively (GOI, 1962b, p. lxvi; GOI, 1984, pp. 14–15; GOI, 2004, p. 7; GOI, 2011).

Gujarat, and sociological features of tribal politics of Gujarat. Both these issues will be analysed cutting across the phases of Nehruvian
Congress, post-Nehruvian Congress and the
current phase of BJP rule.

As per the provisions of the Indian
Constitution, the constituencies which have
been demarcated as reserved for STs have
been in regions where tribes have been pre-
ponderant. At present, there are 4 and 27 parliamentary and assembly seats, respectively,
reserved for ST. The constituencies reserved
for tribes have also non-tribals residing in
them. So as Xaxa (2019, p. 10) pointed out,
'districts and reserved constituencies are not
coterminous, though there may be an overlap'.
This is also true for Gujarat. So there are ST
constituencies which have non-tribals voting
in them; and there are a few general constituencies which have a large proportion of tribal
voters. So not surprisingly, political parties
have put up tribal candidates in these 'general'
constituencies. The Constitution of India has
provided reserved constituencies for STs and

SCs under Articles 330 and 332 in Lok Sabha
and Vidhan Sabha (lower house of the assembly). The seats reserved for STs and SCs in
the Gujarat state assembly are shown in Table
14.2.

POLITICS OF DEVELOPMENT AND ITS EFFECT ON TRIBES OF GUJARAT

This section analyses the issue of displacement of tribes owing to development, especially dams, next, the changing nature of
education among tribal youth is examined and
finally, how discrimination continues in areas
like health has been pointed out.

Development

Jawaharlal Nehru's ideas about tribal development have been based on the foreword he
wrote for Elwin's *A Philosophy for NEFA*

Table 14.2 Seats Reserved for STs and SCs in the Vidhan Sabha of Gujarat and Population Proportion of SCs and STs to State Total

Year	General[a]	SC[a]	% SC Population to State Total[b]	ST[a]	% ST Population to State Total[b]	Total[a]	State Population[b]
1	2	3	4	5	6	7	8
1962	122	11	6.62 (1961)	21	13.34 (1961)	154	20,633,350
1967	136	12		20		168	
1972	135	11	6.84 (1971)	22	13.99 (1971)	168	26,697,475
1975	145	12		24		181	
1980	143	13		26		182	
1985	143	13	7.15 (1981)	26	14.22 (1981)	182	34,085,799
1990	143	13		26		182	
1995	143	13	–	26	14.92 (1991)	182	41,309,581
1998	143	13		26		182	
2002	143	13	7.09 (2001)	26	14.76 (2001)	182	50,671,017
2007	143	13		26		182	
2012	142	13	6.74 (2011)	27	14.75 (2011)	182	60,439,692
2017	142	13		27		182	

Sources: [a] GOI (1962, p. 3); GOI (1967, p. 3); GOI (1972, p. 3); GOI (1975, p. 3); GOI (1980, p. 3); GOI (1985, p. 3); GOI (1990, p. 3); GOI (1995, p. 3); GOI (1998, p. 3); GOI (2002, p. 3); GOI (2007, p. 3); GOI (2012, p. 4); GOI (2017, file 3).
[b] GOI (1962b, p. lxvi); GOI (1971, pp. 34–35); GOI (1982, p. 14–15); GOI (2013, p. 121).

(Patel, 2013, p. 34; Xaxa, 2014, pp. 6–7). There are five principles Nehru mentioned in his foreword, but the first two are worthy of reproduction. Nehru states, 'People should develop along the lines of their own genius and we should avoid imposing anything on them. We should try to encourage in every way their traditional arts and culture'. The second is, 'Tribal rights in land and forest should be respected'. But Nehru, in his initial years as prime minister, was influenced by socialist ideas and planning. He considered science and technology, public sector undertakings, heavy industries and big dams as 'temples of modern India', a term which he first used at the inauguration of Bhakra Nangal Dam.[6]

On 5 April 1961,[7] Nehru laid the foundation stone of a dam to be constructed on the Narmada River, which came to be known as Sardar Sarovar Dam (SSD). However, the actual construction of SSD started nearly 27 years later in 1987[8] at a new location and the main dam has been recently completed. SSD and other dams that came up in tribal areas of Gujarat in post-Nehruvian years have had profound effect on the tribes living there.

Shivani Patel (2011, p. 17), an environmental activist, states that in Gujarat, 'independence marked the beginning of accumulation of wealth and power for Patels, Rajputs, and other upper-castes who became the actual beneficiaries of land reforms; Gujarat's Adivasis steadily lost their rights over their traditional resource base ever since'. She goes on to state, 'Gujarat laws and policy have been systematically eliminating the safeguards for the land resources of the marginalised' (Patel, 2011, p. 17).

The Government of India Committee 'Report of the High Level Committee on Socio-economic, Health and Educational Status of Tribal Communities of India', also known as the Xaxa Committee, GOI (2014, p. 259, Table 8.1) estimates that in Gujarat, over the years, 44.43 per cent of the people have been displaced by developmental activities. However, Lobo (2014, p. 287, Table 10.1) puts forward a higher figure. He states, 'sixty one percent of the land acquired, which lies in the tribal dominated eastern forest region of Gujarat, is for water resources; subsequently, fifty nine percent of the total families displaced or affected are tribals' (Lobo, 2014, p. 287).

There are 13 large and medium dams constructed in tribal-dominated areas which have displaced large number of families (including non-tribals) being displaced (Patel, 2011, Table 21). 'STs form 42 percent of the project affected population but 76 percent of those displaced. Much of this displacement directly results from the construction of dams' (Patel, 2011, p. 97). The tribal activist, Gemjibhai Vasava (2006, p. 141–147) lists 12 big, medium and small dams which have displaced tribes. Another issue that angers the tribal communities is the compensation they have received. Thus, Manani (2017) makes a poignant statement. He says,

> Hitendra Desai government in Gujarat compensated by paying ₹11,000/- per acre to landholders of Gandhinagar where only 'bajri' (millet) and 'makki' (corn) was grown; whereas the landholders of Ukai dam area which has black soil up to 20 feet depth, were compensated at the rate of ₹120/- per acre by the Government of Gujarat. (Manani, 2017, p. 97).

Needless to say, Gandhinagar, the present capital of Gujarat, was constructed around the same time as Ukai Dam.

---

[6] Retrieved from https://www.dnaindia.com/special-features/report-psus-modern-industrial-temples-of-india-1296571
[7] Retrieved from https://www.indiatoday.in/india/story/narendra-modi-sardar-sarovar-dam-gujarat-narmada-jawaharlal-nehru-1046511-2017-09-17
[8] Retrieved from https://www.indiatoday.in/india/story/narendra-modi-sardar-sarovar-dam-gujarat-narmada-jawaharlal-nehru-1046511-2017-09-17

Now in the BJP era, in the 21st century, development-induced displacement continues. Tribes continue to protest, and the most visible recent protest has been at the inauguration of the Statue of Unity on the Narmada on 31 October 2018. Local activists claim '75,000 tribals have been adversely affected'.[9] The report goes on to state 'Out of the 72 villages affected by the statue project, the most affected are 32, where 19 villages are where rehabilitation has not been allegedly completed'. Another report states that on the day of inauguration, 300 protesters were arrested.[10] A protester, according to the same news report, states, 'this project has no benefit whatsoever for people living here' and he goes on to say, 'little employment they are promising to give locals will be on a contract basis. The government is concerned with tourism profit, but shouldn't tourism project involve participation of local people?' Further, he alleged, 'if this was Patidar land, instead of Adivasi land, they would not dare do this' (Manani, 2017, p. 97).

The neoliberal approach to development and ignoring the needs of marginal people got a big boost when 'In 2005 the State government resolved to give away wastelands at throwaway rates for corporate farming, while the government resolution to allot leases for wasteland to the poor and marginalised communities was hardly implemented despite the passage of two decades' (Patel, 2011, p. 17).

Furthermore, tribal areas are rich in mineral resources, and there is now an open and explicit desire to exploit them. So *Indian Express* of 30 August 2013 has a headline 'Rich in Mineral Resources, Chhota Udepur Set to Become Highest Revenue-earning District'.[11] If there is protest by tribals, the state finds legal ways to cow down the protesters. This is what happened to Rathwas in Chhota Udepur, where some of them were de-notified as tribes[12] (Rathwa, Rai, & Rajaram, 2014). It was our conclusion that 'The Indian state and particularly the Gujarat government is now creating legal ways to intervene in the scheduled areas to exploit natural resources'.

Reservation and Education

The constitutional provisions of reservation in legislature, education and government jobs aim to benefit the tribes. These reservations have resulted in some tribes coming into political institutions such as Parliament and Vidhan Sabha (Desai, 2006, p. 258; Joshi, 2017).

Xaxa Committee (GOI, 2014, pp. 54–190) has analysed the all-India picture regarding education advancement of STs. Although the state-wise disaggregation data has not been given, the grim picture of the state of education among tribes pointed out in the report holds true for Gujarat as well. GOI (2014, p. 169–170, Table 6.9) shows the gross enrolment ratio (GER) at various levels of education. Perhaps what the table shows that there has been an improvement in GER of tribes from 1986–1987 to 2010–2011. But still much needs to be done at school and higher education levels.

Focusing on higher education, Desai (2006, p. 252) in his study of south Gujarat in the 1960s points out that there existed a perception of discrimination among educated tribes. He quotes a legislator of that time to state 'an MA degree gets (a job paying) 100 or 150

---

[9] Retrieved from https://www.ndtv.com/india-news/sardar-patel-statue-why-75-000-tribals-are-planning-a-mass-protest-against-statue-of-unity-1934779

[10] Retrieved from https://scroll.in/article/900473/drowned-dreams-why-nearly-300-adivasis-were-detained-before-modi-could-unveil-the-statue-of-unity

[11] Retrieved from http://archive.indianexpress.com/news/rich-in-mineral-resources-chhota-udepur-set-to-become-highest-revenueearning-district/1162154/

[12] The notification was issued by the state government's tribal department. Whether it was challenged in a court of law for its legality is not clear. However, this publication brought the matter into public domain.

rupees. How will he (Adivasi) be satisfied? On the other hand he sees that the man who was studying with him becomes a Collector or Mamlatdar. Why this inequality?' This legislator goes on to state, 'you might say that 5 percent seats are reserved for Adivasis. But is the Adivasi taken? Suitability is made a big qualification'. This was the story of pre-liberalization era under the Congress rule in the 1960s.

The transition to BJP rule occurred in a period when neo-liberalism was taking roots. The last 30 years since 1990, especially in the sphere of higher education, have witnessed the emergence of a large number of private universities all over India, and Gujarat is no exception. Further, the state has been finding ways to reduce financial support to traditional public-funded universities and encouraging them to raise fees and start self-financed courses. This trend has affected the marginal sections of the society more than other sections and strata. As a consequence, tribal-dominated districts lag behind other districts in levels of education and literacy rates.

To perhaps woo, especially the tribal youth, to the BJP (who seem to be moving away to rivals), the state government recently started two universities named after two tribal icons. Both are located in two district headquarters of two tribal-dominated districts: Shri Govind Guru University in Godhra and Birsa Munda Tribal University in Rajpipla. Shri Govind Guru University is named after a tribal spiritual leader of Bhils, Govindgiri. He tried to spread Hinduism and social reforms by asking his followers to give up liquor in the early decades of the 20th century among the Bhils in the region bordering present-day Gujarat and Rajasthan (Vashista, 1991). His name became etched in tribal folklore owing to the bloody confrontation that took place on 17 November 1913, at Mangarh Hill, near

Sarwai village at the border of present-day Panchmahal district of Gujarat and Dungarpur district of Rajasthan.

Scholars belonging to tribal community, like Pandar (2017, pp. 34–37), say, '1500 people were martyred; and in modern Indian history, the Mangarh massacre of Adivasis even though being bigger than that Jallianwalabagh, continues to be ignored by historians. But this incident resonates in the songs of Adivasis'. Interestingly, the historian Vashista (1991) does not mention about the number killed although his paper was on that confrontation. To commemorate this icon, Gujarat government formed a new university in 2015 and named it as Shri Govind Guru University at Godhra.[13] This university is open to students of all communities. It is an affiliating university catering to five districts of central Gujarat, which has a sizeable tribal population. The second university is Birsa Munda Tribal University and is situated at Rajpipla, headquarters of Narmada district.[14] This university aims to provide avenues of higher education and research facilities primarily for tribal population of the state of Gujarat. The act of the university also spells out in various ways to link the tribal students to the agenda and needs of the market economy. Narmada district, as the analysis in the sections shows, is the epicentre of politics for a separate state led now by Chhotu Vasava.

One of the consequences of the spread of education, especially higher education among tribal youth, has been the documentation of their culture and history. Young academics, who are tribals, are in the forefront of documenting atrocities which tribals continue to face. Pandar (2017) captures recent incidents of confrontation between tribals and the police in north Gujarat during 2013–2014 over the death of a tribal leader in suspicious circumstances. Vasava (2006) narrates about

[13] Retrieved from https://sggu.ac.in/wp-content/uploads/2016/06/GUJARAT_ACT_NO24OF2015SHRIGOVIND GURUUNI.pdf
[14] See Act 5(1) of Birsa Munda Tribal University Act, 2017.

such incidents in Narmada district. However, sociologist Joshi (2017) points out an interesting contrast in relation to the educated tribal youth before the 1990s and those who were educated after 1991. In the pre-liberalization phase, the (few) educated tribals perhaps owing to the influence of Gandhian ashrams were enticed into politics by the then leaders of the Congress. But after liberalization, many of the educated tribals became doctors, engineers, professors and senior officers in bureaucracy. These educated tribals have now started focusing on tribal identity and preservation of their culture.

Health

The structure of development in the state, having been uneven and unequal, continues to reflect the marginalization of tribes. There was a time in the past when tribal areas were considered not accessible as they lacked roads and bus services. Thus, social isolation was reflected in geographical isolation. During the Congress era, there were attempts by the state to build roads and make available bus services to remote tribal villages. In addition, access to electricity and piped potable water were provided to many villages. Government initiatives resulted in availability of primary schools. Although the geographical isolation has gradually been overcome, the social exclusion continues. This is best reflected in the area of health infrastructure.

On 22 July 2019, the health minister while replying to a question raised by a member of legislative assembly (MLA) stated in the assembly that there is a dearth of doctors in tribal areas. So the state government is considering to incentivize the posting by offering additional salary.[15] The same newspaper report goes on to say,

> the Gujarat government makes medical students sign a bond of ₹5 lakh to work in rural areas for three years after passing MBBS and completing internship in government medical colleges. The government would recover the amount if the bond is violated. In the past two years, the government has recovered ₹21.85 crore from doctors for violation of the bond.[16]

This works out that 437 doctors have been willing to pay the bond (between 2017–2018 and 2018–2019) rather than working in rural areas, reflecting the attitudes and priorities that exist in the society.

SOCIOLOGICAL FEATURES OF TRIBAL POLITICS

The areas of present-day Gujarat in the pre-Independence era were either under the control of the British Bombay presidency or under the rule of princely states. This was also true of tribal areas, many of which were under Rajput feudatories,[17] although some areas were having their own chieftains who were rebellious and resisting attempts to control them by the colonial powers. At the time of Independence, the princely states were coaxed into merging with the then Bombay state. Bombay state was multilingual and had Marathi, Gujarati and Kannada speaking areas. The reorganization of states on linguistic lines resulted in Bombay state being bifurcated on 1 May 1960, into Maharashtra

---

[15] Retrieved from https://indianexpress.com/article/cities/ahmedabad/gujarat-govt-plans-30-extra-pay-for-doctors-in-tribal-areas-5843012/
[16] Retrieved from https://indianexpress.com/article/cities/ahmedabad/gujarat-govt-plans-30-extra-pay-for-doctors-in-tribal-areas-5843012/
[17] Right from the north to the south of the eastern tribal belt of present-day Gujarat, there were numerous princely states and feudatories. Some of them were Danta, Vijaynagar, Sant, Banswara (in Rajasthan), Sanjeli, Devgarh Baria, Chhota Udepur, Naswadi, Rajpipla and Bansda. Patel (2011, pp. 31–32, Table 4) lists out the present blocks in tribal areas and the controlling authority in the pre-Independence period.

(predominantly comprising Marathi-speaking areas) and Gujarat (comprising Gujarati-speaking areas) of erstwhile Bombay state.

So for 13 years, 1947–1960, the areas of present Gujarat state were either under Bombay state or Saurashtra state or Kutch state (until Kutch and Saurashtra states merged with Bombay state, on 1 November 1956). In this period, the Congress party was in power both at the centre and in Bombay state. It was also the era when Jawaharlal Nehru was the prime minister of the country and, as mentioned before, he left an imprint on the country's politics, governance structure and development policies and programmes including those meant for tribals. Rajni Kothari (1961) called this era of one-party domination of Congress 'party system', and later in another publication, he called it 'Congress system' (Kothari, 1964).

Factionalism and Marginalization of STs in Politics

In the first two elections of independent India, 1951 and 1957, there were double-member constituencies, where two candidates were elected. The thinking of the upper-caste political elites of that time was that these double-member constituencies would enable the political parties to give representation, as per the Constitutional provisions, to SCs and STs in the assemblies.

So in 1951 assembly elections, of the total 268 constituencies in the Bombay assembly, there were 47 double-member general constituencies and even one three-member constituency (Nasik–Igatpuri) in 1951. There were also eight constituencies reserved for STs, and none for SCs in the 1951 elections (GOI, 1951, p. 13). Owing to the fact

that 47 double-member constituencies, one even being three-member, the strength of MLAs in the assembly having 268 constituencies became 315. The Congress party at that time gave tickets to ST candidates in the double-member constituencies (for instance, Lunawada–Santrampur, Ankleshwar–Hansot–Jhagadia–Valia and Bardoli–Valod–Palsana–Mahuva constituencies)[18] or to SC candidates (like in Matar–Cambay). Interestingly, the eight reserved ST constituencies were single-member constituencies, and they were all in Gujarat region and not in the Marathi-speaking regions of Bombay state.

In the 1957 assembly election, the reservation scenario changed. This was based on the recommendations of the Delimitation Commission notification of 1955 (GOI, 1955). The number of constituencies was 339, out of which 42, 31 and 226 constituencies were SC, ST and general constituencies, respectively. However, this time, of 266 general constituencies, the number of double-member 'general' constituencies was only 3. But in the case of SC constituencies, out of 42, 39 were double-member constituencies and only 3 were single-member SC constituencies. For STs, of 31 reserved seats, 15 were double-member constituencies, of which 5[19] were in Gujarat region (GOI, 1957, p. 15). Owing to this provision of double-member constituencies, the strength of MLAs in the assembly (having 339 constituencies) became 396 (GOI, 1957, p. 14). The interesting aspect of the recommendation of the Delimitation Commission of 1955 was that in each of the double-member reserved constituency, whether for SC or ST, only one seat was reserved, and for the second seat, an upper-caste person could contest. However, the double constituency provision was abolished in the next elections. An act was passed in the Parliament in 1961 ending this provision of double-member constituencies.[20]

---

[18] In the 1951 elections, constituencies tended to have conjoint names. A scrutiny of records indicates the effort to give tickets to ST candidates.
[19] The Delimitation Commission of 1955 mentions four (GOI, 1955, pp. 162–177).
[20] Retrieved from http://theindianlawyer.in/statutesnbareacts/acts/t33.html

In that era, the upper-caste-dominated Congress party's efforts at being 'inclusive' appeared as tokenism. The attempts of the upper-caste political elites seemed to thwart the STs and SCs from getting substantive power. Kothari (1961), who has analysed the Congress party of that time, states that the Congress party was divided into 'factions' and these factions had competing interests. To quote, 'Factions at the local level are based on caste, kinship and personal loyalties, the last being the most important' (Kothari, 1961, p. 849). He further adds, 'political adjustments are confined to the dominant caste.... The depressed communities are denied any real access to power' (Kothari, 1961, p. 851). But it is the 'dynamics of the faction system itself obliging local leaders to cast their net wider than their own community and extend their patronage system beyond their own kin'. This holds true for Gujarat. It was the competitive nature of faction-driven politics, and reservation provisions, which resulted in tribal people getting representation in the assembly or Parliament, although without getting access to substantive power in that era.

Manani (2017) narrates the marginalization and exclusion of the tribes from power structure owing to the factional fights in the upper-caste-dominated Congress party of Bharuch in the 1950s and the 1960s. Mention has been made earlier of a double-seat general constituency in the 1951 Bombay state assembly elections, Ankleshwar–Hansot–Jhagadia–Valia in Bharuch district. Two persons won from this seat in that election: one was the Adivasi Congress leader, Mulji Narsibhai Vasava, and the other a Rajput leader, Harisinh Mahida. In the politics of the then Bharuch district, Mulji Narsibhai Vasava and Harisinh Mahida were in constant tussle in the party. So in the 1957 election, Mahida got the ticket, to the exclusion of Mulji Vasava, for the Ankleshwar general seat, which was now converted to a single-member seat, and Mahida won. This tussle within the Congress party continued in the subsequent decades. Manani

(2017, p. 100) writes about the situation in that era, 'in Jhagadia taluka (of Bharuch district), the situation of Adivasis was that of a bonded labourer; and the situation of Adivasi MLAs to the ruling Gujarat Congress party was also like that of bonded labourer'. According to Manani, this was done so that tribals do not get into positions of leadership to voice their grievances. Manani goes on to state that the then upper-caste Congress leaders cherished in the tribal leadership the following qualities:

[F]irstly, keeping quiet when they hear about atrocities on Adivasis; secondly, when people come to them to narrate their grievances then to listen from one ear and to out it from the other; and thirdly, to close their eyes to the incidents of atrocities on Adivasis. (Manani, 2017, p. 101)

However, Mulji Narsibhai Vasava, although not much educated, could speak in English and was not cowed down, and in that era, where English was a cultural sign of being part of elite power structure, he would constantly raise issues of exploitation of tribals. This process of attrition ultimately resulted in him being killed on 21 September 1971 (Manani, 2017, p. 100).

The Post-Nehruvian Era: A Period of Turbulence and Emergence of KHAM

The decade of the 1960s also marks the disillusionment of politics of the Nehruvian era. One consequence was the end of the 'Congress system'. This happened with the 1967 elections (Kothari, 1970). While many states of India voted for opposition parties which had middle-caste leadership or were left-leaning parties, in Gujarat the preference was towards the right-leaning Swatantra Party. Swatantra Party's entry in the state was with the 1962 elections itself, just after the state was formed, winning 23 seats (and 24.4% of votes), the Congress party won 113 seats (50.8% of votes) in a house of 154 (GOI, 1962a, p. 8). The Praja Socialist Party (PSP) won 7 seats and Jan Sangh which contested 26 seats did not win even a single seat. In the subsequent election of 1967, Swatantra party improved its tally and won 66 seats in a house of 163 (GOI, 1967, p. 8). However, the Congress party formed the government having won 93 seats. In this election, the Jan Sangh made its entry into the state assembly winning one seat, and three seats were won by PSP.

The 1960s was also a decade of turmoil in the ruling Congress party. In 1969, it split into Congress (O) (the nickname of Indian National Congress [Organisation]) and Congress (I) (the name of Indian National Congress [Indira]) factions at the time when Indira Gandhi was the prime minister. In the immediate years after the split, the Congress in Gujarat was affiliated to Congress (O), owing to its links to Morarji Desai. Unlike the earlier Nehruvian era, the Congress in this period under Indira Gandhi centralized decision-making in the Congress party and in the polity (Hankla, 2006). It was in this period of political turmoil, as Desai (2006) points out, that some tribal MLAs made a demand for a separate state for tribal communities.

Compared to the 1960s Gujarat, the 1970s was a more turbulent period politically. The state had six chief ministers in the 1970s, interspersed with periods of president's rule. The early 1970s saw the state rocked by Navnirman agitations, which had echo effects elsewhere in the country resulting in the Bihar agitation under leadership of Jaya Prakash Narayan. This decade also saw the infamous Emergency (1975–1977) and the emergence of a coalition of non-Congress parties merging to form the Janata Dal, which emerged victorious in 1977 parliamentary election.

At the state level, in the 1970s, the dominant Patidars, once the backbone of the Congress party, now moved away from it. So the Congress embarked on strategy of KHAM—Kshatriya, Harijan, Adivasi and Muslim—vote banks to win the assembly elections in 1980 and 1985. This strategy worked well in the decade of the 1980s and

the Congress even made the tribal Amarsingh Chaudhari the chief minister. Amarsingh Chaudhari remained in office from July 1985 to December 1989.

The decision of V. P. Singh government at the centre to give reservation to Other Backward Classes (OBCs) in 1990 had its repercussions on the polity. The assassination of Rajiv Gandhi in May 1991 helped the Congress to come back to power at the centre in the 1991 election. This was also the era when the economy was liberalized. This was also the period when Soviet Union collapsed (in December 1991) and left ideologies took a beating. This was also the period when Ram Janmabhoomi movement began (in October 1990) and the demolition of Babri Masjid in December 1992. All these developments polarized the society leading to the emergence of the BJP as a pivotal political force. Within a few years, it became the major fulcrum around which a coalition was formed at the centre and in states like Gujarat. By March 1998, the BJP came into power on its own strength in Gujarat.

Tribes and Communalism

Shah (1996) says that the emergence of the BJP in Gujarat has been based on its effort at building a base among OBCs, tribals and Dalits. However, the rise of the BJP also saw the tribal areas of the state being rocked by communal incidents (Lobo, 2002; Lobo & Macwan, 2002; Rajaram, 2005). In the decades before, at the time of infamous 1969 communal riots and the intermittent riots of the 1980s, tribal areas were not affected as these incidents usually occurred in big cities such as Ahmedabad, Vadodara and Surat. Sometimes, smaller towns were also engulfed. But the tribal areas were far from the madness of communal riots. However, between 1997 and 2000, a large number of attacks on Adivasi Christians in south Gujarat took place (Lobo, 2002; Lobo & Macwan, 2002), even though as Chaube (1999) points out that Christian population in Gujarat has been more or less stagnant between 1951 and 1991. According to Lobo and Macwan, there was a conscious attempt by the Sangh Parivar in tribal areas to integrate the tribals into Hinduism and strategies were formulated by them to spread communal hatred against Christian tribals.

Then, in the infamous post-Godhra riots of 2002, the tribal areas of central Gujarat such as Jabugam, Tejgadh, Kwant, Naswadi, Panwad, Rajpardi, Valia, Netrang and Chhota Udepur were affected (Lobo, 2002; Lobo & Macwan, 2002, pp. 2–5). What have been the

electoral consequences of communal riots? Table 14.3 indicates the number of seats won by the two dominant parties of Gujarat, the Congress and the BJP, at each of the assembly elections between 1962 and 2017.

During the first 30 years of Gujarat (1960–1990), the Congress party won most of the ST reserved seats in the state. In 1985, the year when KHAM became the poll plank, the Congress won all 26 reserved seats, and which no other party, nor even the Congress itself, has ever been able to repeat. In the 1990 election, the Congress lost to a coalition formed by the Janata Dal led by Chimanbhai Patel

Table 14.3   ST Seat Sharing of the Congress and the BJP in Gujarat Assembly, 1962–2017

Year of Assembly Elections	Total Assembly Seats	Total Reserved Seats for STs	Total Seats in Assembly Won by INC	ST Seats Won by INC	Total Assembly Seats Won by the BJP	ST Seats Won by the BJP/Jan Sangh	Others Who Won ST Seats	Remarks
1	2	3	4	5	6	7	8	9
1962	154	21	113	17	None	None	4	2 seats each won by the Swatantra Party and the PSP
1967	168	20	93	15	1	None	5	Swatantra won 4 and PSP 1
1972	168	22	140	19	3	None	3	3 seats won by Congress (O)
1975	181	24	75	14	18	1	9	8 were won by Congress (O) and 1 by Kisan Mazdoor Lok Paksha of Chimanbhai Patel; Bharatiya Jana Sangh won for the first time a ST seat (Pardi)
1980	182	26	141	25	9	1	–	BJP won 1 ST seat (Chikli)
1985	182	26	149	26	11	None	–	Congress won all ST seats
1990	182	26	33	7	67	6	13	11 seats were won by Janata Dal (led by Chimanbhai Patel) and 2 were won by Independents
1995	182	26	45	8	121	14	4	4 were won by Independents
1998	182	26	53	15	117	8	3	3 were won by Janata Dal of Chhotu Vasava
2002	182	26	51	11	127	13	2	2 were won by Janata Dal (United) (Chhotu Vasava)
2007	182	26	59	14	117	11	1	1 by Janata Dal (United) (Chhotu Vasava)
2012	182	27	61	16	115	10	1	1 by Janata Dal (United) (Chhotu Vasava)
2017	182	27	77	15	99	9	3	2 by Bharatiya Tribal Party of Chhotu Vasava, 1 by Independent

Sources: GOI (1962a, pp. 3–8); GOI (1967, 3–8); GOI (1972, pp. 3–8); GOI (1975, pp. 3–9); GOI (1980, pp. 3–9); GOI (1985, pp. 3–9); GOI (1990, 3–9); GOI (1995, 3–9); GOI (1998); GOI (2002, pp. 3–9); GOI (2007); GOI (2012, pp. 4–9); GOI (2017, files 3, 4, 5).

in the state with the BJP as a junior partner. With the passing away of Chimanbhai Patel in February 1994, the influence of Janata Dal waned and that of the BJP grew still further. So in 1995 assembly election, the BJP did extremely well, winning 14 of the 26 reserved ST seats. However, the BJP in subsequent elections has not replicated that performance in ST reserved seats, even while it has done well in the rest of the state as shown in Table 14.3. Indeed, the data presented in Table 14.3 may make one to infer that the infamous post-Godhra communal riots of February–March 2002 have not brought dividends to the BJP in the ST reserved seats as seen in seats won in elections of December 2002. This argument at the macro level may be correct. But if we disaggregate the results in terms of regions, then a different pattern emerges. In Table 14.4, the election results of 1998, 2002, 2007, 2012 and 2017 elections are disaggregated and displayed through region-wise data, showing the party performance in each of these elections.

Godhra is located in the central Gujarat region, and when the infamous riots that followed the train burning on 27 February 2002, the entire region of central Gujarat was affected. The tribal regions were also engulfed at that time as pointed out by Lobo (2002), Lobo and Macwan (2002) and Rajaram (2005). Some scholars, like Shah (2003), have tried to explain this as owing to the process of Sanskritization going on in the tribal areas and how Hindutva forces used this opportunity to consolidate its base in tribal areas.

At the electoral level, the BJP won 9 of the 11 constituencies of central Gujarat, while 2 were won by JDU in 2002 assembly election. This was in contrast to the 1998 election, where the Congress had won 8 seats in central Gujarat, which it lost in 2002 assembly election. But in the 2007 assembly election, the

Congress regained and the BJP was reduced to 4 seats in contrast to the 9 it won in 2002. However, scholars like Shah, Patel, and Lobo (2008) interpret the 2007 election victory as owing to a mix of 'Gujarati *asmita* (identity) and Hindu pride'. They attribute the success of the BJP in Gujarat as owing to (Hindu) 'cultural uniformity' overriding caste and tribal identities. Unfortunately, this analysis is partial at best, for it has not analysed the performance of the Congress in ST seats of 2007 elections. If cultural uniformity was overriding tribal identities, then the BJP performance in ST seats should have improved and not declined. In the subsequent elections of 2012 and 2017, the seats won by the BJP has further declined as shown in Table 14.4.

By the 2012 assembly election, a revision in the delimitation of constituencies took place. This resulted in the ST-reserved seats being increased to 27, and further, there was a region-wise redistribution of these seats. In spite of the increase in number of ST-reserved constituencies, the performance of the BJP in subsequent elections of 2012 and 2017 has declined. The tribal-reserved constituencies still continue to favour the Congress. This does not mean that communalism has declined in the tribal-dominated regions. Even now, brazen communal threat is used as a weapon as seen in the campaign for Lok Sabha election of 2019 in ST constituencies. One communal threat issued was that 'tribal converts would lose benefits'.[21] Another threat made was more bizarre. The MLA claimed that cameras had been installed inside each polling booth so as to see to whom people have voted, and if the tribal voters do not vote for the ruling BJP, they would not get work[22] (perhaps referring to NREGA work).

So why has the performance of the BJP declined in ST-reserved seats? One reason

---

[21] This was issued by a state minister for forest and tribal development. Retrieved from https://timesofindia.india-times.com/city/ahmedabad/tribal-converts-will-forfeit-benefits/articleshowprint/67032651.cms
[22] Retrieved from https://www.newsnation.in/election/lok-sabha-election-2019/gujarat-bjp-mla-claims-pm-modi-installed-cameras-at-polling-booths-threatens-voters-article-220783.html

Table 14.4   Region-wise Performance of the Congress and the BJP in Gujarat Assembly Elections (1998–2017)

S. No.	Region	Constituency	1998	2002	2007	2012	2017
1	North	Danta	–	–	–	INC	INC
2		Bhiloda	–	–	–	INC	INC
3		Khedbrahma	INC	INC	INC	INC	INC
4	North Gujarat total		INC 1	INC 1	INC 1	INC 3	INC 3
5	Central	Santrampur	–	–	–	INC	BJP
6		Morva Hadaf	–	–	–	INC	IND
7		Fatepura	–	–	–	BJP	BJP
8		Jhalod	INC	BJP	INC	INC	INC
9		Limdi	INC	BJP	INC	–	–
10		Dohad	INC	BJP	INC	INC	INC
11		Limkheda	INC	BJP	INC	BJP	BJP
12		Randikpur	BJP	BJP	BJP	–	–
13		Garbada	–	–	–	INC	INC
14		Chhota Udepur	INC	BJP	BJP	INC	INC
15		Jetpur	–	–	–	BJP	INC
16		Naswadi	INC	BJP	INC	–	–
17		Sankheda	INC	BJP	BJP	INC	BJP
18		Nandod (Taluka name; headquarter is Rajpipla)	–	–	–	BJP	INC
19		Jhagadia	JD	JD(U)	JDU	JDU	BTP
20		Dediapada	JD	JD(U)	INC	BJP	BTP
21		Rajpipla	INC	BJP	BJP	–	–
22	Central Gujarat total		T 11 INC 8 BJP 1 JD 2	T 11 INC NIL BJP 9 JDU 2	T 11 INC 6 BJP 4 JDU 1	T 13 INC 7 BJP 5 JDU 1	T 13 INC 6 BJP 4 BTP 2 IND 1
23	South	Nijhar	INC	INC	INC	BJP	INC
24		Mangrol	JD	BJP	BJP	BJP	BJP
25		Mandvi	–	–	–	INC	INC
26		Songadh	INC	INC	INC	–	–
27		Vyara	INC	INC	INC	INC	INC
28		Mahuva	BJP	BJP	INC	BJP	BJP
29		Bardoli	BJP	INC	INC	Now SC	Now SC
30		Kamrej	INC	BJP	BJP	Now GEN	Now GEN
31		Navsari	BJP	BJP	BJP	Now GEN	Now GEN
32		Chikli	BJP	INC	BJP	–	–
33		Dangs-Bansda	INC	INC	BJP	INC (now Dangs)	INC

S. No.	Region	Constituency	1998	2002	2007	2012	2017
34		Vansda	–	–	–	INC	INC
35		Gandevi	GEN seat	GEN seat	GEN seat	BJP	BJP
36		Dharampur	BJP	INC	INC	INC	BJP
37		Mota Pondha	INC	INC	INC	–	–
38		Pardi	BJP	INC	BJP	Now GEN	Now GEN
39		Kaprada	–	–	–	INC	INC
40		Umbergaon	BJP	INC	BJP	BJP	BJP
41	South Gujarat total		T 14 INC 6 BJP 7 JD 1	T 14 INC 10 BJP 4	T 14 INC 7 BJP 7	T 11 INC 6 BJP 5	T 11 INC 6 BJP 5
42	Gujarat total for state		GT 26 INC 15 BJP 8 JD 3	GT 26 INC 11 BJP 13 JDU 2	GT 26 INC 14 BJP 11 JDU 1	GT 27 INC 16 BJP 10 JDU 1	GT 27 INC 15 BJP 9 BTP 2 IND 1

Source: GOI (1998, pp. 4–8); GOI (2002a, pp. 4–8); GOI (2007); GOI (2012, pp. 5–9); GOI (2017, file 4).

Note: 1. T: Total, 2. SC: Scheduled Caste, 3. GEN: General, 4. INC: Indian National Congress, 5. BJP: Bharatiya Janata Party.

for this is to do with the policies of the state government regarding development, which has perhaps upset the tribes, and second, in the last two decades, the emerging tribal academic intellectual writings have started expressing their concerns by focusing on matters of identity and culture of tribals as being distinct from that of caste-laden Hinduism. Let us elaborate.

As mentioned earlier, in May 2005, about two years after the infamous Godhra incidents, the state government took a decision to allot wasteland to industrial houses for corporate farming, agro-processing, herbal and food parks to seven companies in pursuance of decisions taken at the Vibrant Gujarat Investment Summit.[23] This was in contrast to the neglect of long-standing demands of landless tribals and Dalits for land, so there was a political fallout. These tribals and Dalits

started getting organized and protests began, and gradually over the years, their protests have been increasing. The most recent protest took place in 2018. 'Despite repeated petitions and judicial orders, the government has not implemented that Act (Land Ceiling Act of 1961) properly, giving out token amount of land here and there', said Jayanti Makadiya, president of the Gujarat Dalit Sangathan (Kukreti, 2018). As for the tribals, they demand the proper implementation of the Forest Rights Act of 2006.

According to the… Monthly Progress Report, August 2018 on the implementation of FRA of the Ministry of Tribal Affairs, only around 46 percent of the claims filed between 2008 and 2018 were approved and moreover, titles deeds for only 45 percent of all the FRA claims approved have been disbursed by the state till August 31. (Kukreti, 2018)

[23] Retrieved from https://www.financialexpress.com/archive/gujarat-set-to-provide-wasteland-to-industries/138113/

The pro-corporate neoliberal developments on matters of land, forest and mineral resources in Adivasi areas have made the tribal organizations wary of the motives of the BJP government. These developments along with the attempts to Hinduize tribals have had their cultural repercussions as well. Academics and scholars from the tribal communities are now writing and expressing their concerns about the cultural identity of tribals and how it is under threat with the developmental policies of the state. Gamit and Patel (2013) reflect these changing concerns of scholars of tribal issues and tribal academics. Besides this, there are other journals which reflect this trend. Rathwa (2018) writing in the first issue of the journal of Adivasi Sahitya Akademi, *Adivasi Bharat*, states, 'Adivasis are the only communities who have been continuously losing their ideological space and as well as the physical hold of resources', underlying the link of their identity and development. The formation of Adivasi Sahitya Akademi with its headquarters at Sagbara, Narmada district, is a reflection of this changing concern to preserve tribal identity and culture.

Emergence of the 'Electable' Leader

As stated earlier, the nature of politics got changed in the post-Nehruvian era. Owing to the period of turbulence of the 1960s, the 1970s and the 1980s, tribal political issues of Gujarat were overshadowed by these larger developments both within the country and in the state. But in these decades, a new kind of leader began to emerge. It was also the period when the nature of contesting and winning elections was getting transformed. Constituencies which were small in the 1950s and the 1960s were now becoming big and large numerically, and by the 1990s, each constituency had become big demographically. So the first consequence of this was that tribes which were numerically small in number, especially the PVTG tribes (Kathodi, Kolga, Kotwalia, Padhar and Siddi)

lost out in the leadership race. Not only were they numerically small and thus at a disadvantage in electoral politics, but they were also economically weak. Those who had the advantage of numbers continued to dominate and grow in clout and increase their influence. Second, the changing demographic increase in the electors per constituency over this period also brought about a change in the nature of leaders getting elected. This affected all constituencies, tribal and non-tribal. But its effect was more remarkable in tribal areas, as persons aspiring to leadership positions being socio-economically not strong enough are and were at a disadvantageous position vis-à-vis those who had already established themselves as 'leaders'. Let us illustrate with the example of a tribal constituency Chhota Udepur in central Gujarat. Some of its important features are shown in Table 14.5.

Not only has the number of electors increased, but from the 1972 elections, only Rathwas have won in this constituency. Furthermore, the contest since 1972 has been confined to a few persons, as seen from who the winner is and the runner-up. This data reflects the changes in the nature of politics in relation to the emergence of the 'electable' person.

To win elections to political positions be it in the assembly or in Parliament, now require a different set of capabilities and skills in the candidates. A person now has to have, besides caste and kin and personal loyalties, an organization comprising persons who could raise resources, use technology and have other skills to mobilize votes and voters. In the 1970s and the 1980s, it was often dubbed as 'money, muscle, and manpower': money to conduct the campaign, muscle to protect and use against opponents and manpower to reach out to people and conduct campaigns. But by the end of the 1990s, new technologies of communication got added to the other skill sets that were required. This organization and skill set which a person brings with him or her makes the person be considered 'electable'.

Table 14.5 Changing Electoral Strength in Chhota Udepur Assembly Constituency (Central Gujarat)

S. No.	Year	Polling Stations	Total Number of Electors	Votes Polled	Vote Percentage	Status of Constituency	Winner	Party	Remarks
1	2	3	4	5	6	7	8	9	10
1	1951	–	55,187	–	–	Reserved for ST	Bhaijibhai Tadvi	INC	Uncontested
2	1957	–	117,916	114,920ᵃ	48.73ᵃ	Double-seat constituency: one reserved for ST	Bhagwan Patel Bhaiji Garbad (ST)	INC INC	Only winners name given
3	1962	-	57,506	29,853	51.44	General seat	Bipin Bhatt	Swatantra	INC: Siva Amin runner-up
4	1967	–	55,413	31,766	57.73	Reserved for ST	B. G. Tadvi	INC	Swatantra Party: K. B. Koli was runner-up
5	1972	–	63,480	31,844	49.60	Reserved for ST	Karsan Rathwa	INC	NCO: Raman Rathwa runner-up
6	1975	101	73,256	38,971	53.20	Reserved for ST	Raman Rathwa	NCO	INC: Karsan Rathwa runner-up
7	1980	107	84,557	37,704	44.59	Reserved for ST	Karsan Rathwa	INC(I)	JNP(JP): Raman Rathwa runner-up
8	1985	114	98,814	32,098	32.48	Reserved for ST	Sukhram Rathwa	INC	JNP: Raman Rathwa runner-up
9	1990	152	125,629	59,365	47.25	Reserved for ST	Sukhram Rathwa	INC	JD: Gulabbhai Rathwa runner-up
10	1995	185	151,634	95,035	62.67	Reserved for ST	Sukhram Rathwa	INC	BJP: Tarjun Rathwa runner-up
11	1998	183	150,080	79,973	53.29	Reserved for ST	Sukhram Rathwa	INC	BJP: Gulab Rathwa runner-up
12	2002	200	172,425	104,126	60.39	Reserved for ST	Shankarbhai Rathwa	BJP	Sukhram Rathwa of INC runner-up
13	2007	248	192,304	98,300	51.10	Reserved for ST	Gulsingbhai Rathwa	BJP	Sukhram Rathwa of INC runner-up
14	2012	286	213,248	147,911	69.36	Reserved for ST	Mohan Chotu Rathwa	INC	Gulsingh Rathwa of BJP second
15	2017	323	241,916	163,582	67.62	Reserved for ST	Mohan Chotu Rathwa	INC	Jashu Bhilu Rathwa of BJP second

Sources: GOI (1951, p. 79); GOI (1957, p. 112); GOI (1962a, p. 129); GOI (1967, p. 139); GOI (1972, p. 138); GOI (1975, p. 153); GOI (1980, p. 155); GOI (1985, p. 155); GOI (1990, p. 156); GOI (1995, p. 160); GOI (1998, p. 156); GOI (2002, p. 156); GOI (2007); GOI (2012, p. 156); GOI (2017, file 9).

Notes: ᵃFrom Election Commission of India reports, INC: Indian National Congress, INC(I): Indian National Congress (Indira), NCO: Indian National Congress (Organisation), BJP: Bharatiya Janata Party, JD: Janata Dal, JNP(JP): Janata Party, JNP: Janata Party.

In areas where the party organization is weak, these qualities in candidates become a feature sought by parties. So in this culture, it is not surprising to see candidates party hopping and furthermore, parties admitting leaders who till a few days back were with the opposition and were critical of them. This has happened in Gujarat and in tribal constituencies as well. So over time, some candidates become indispensable for the party, and as they become powerful, they sometimes become larger than the party in that constituency. These leaders tend to be self-centred and concerned with own interests and benefits in every task. This culture also has created a divide within the tribal communities and has brought a new culture in the politics of contesting elections in these areas.

Here are a few case studies of some tribal constituencies.

Dahod

In Dahod (ST) constituency of central Gujarat, in the first three elections of 1962, 1967 and 1972, the Congress Party put up three different candidates and won each time. Then in the 1975 elections, Lalit B. Patel (a Pateliya Bhil) of the Congress Party won and continued to win the subsequent two elections of 1980 and 1985. He was again nominated in the 1990 elections but lost to the BJP candidate Tersingh Damor (Bhil tribe). When the Congress Party changed its nominee for the seat, Lalit B. Patel contested as an independent candidate in the 1995 assembly election. He lost by a narrow margin of 588 votes to the BJP candidate Tersingh Damor (GOI, 1998, p. 133). The official Congress candidate came third. In 1998 election, Lalit B. Patel (now back in the Congress) won and Tersingh Damor of the BJP lost the election. This got reversed in 2002 election when Lalit B. Patel of the Congress lost to Tersingh Damor of the BJP. The era of Lalit B. Patel ended, and in the elections of 2007, 2012 and 2017, a new

leader of the Congress, Vijay Panada, has been winning.

Jetpur

The story of another constituency of Jetpur in central Gujarat is interesting. This constituency came into existence in 1972 assembly election as reserved for ST. The candidate who won belonged to Congress (O). But in 1975 election, the constituency was converted into unreserved constituency and Chimanbhai Patel who lost his post owing to the Navnirman agitation contested from this constituency after floating his own party. In this election, a young tribal leader, Mohan Rathwa (Rathwa tribal), who was given ticket by the Congress (O) party, defeated him and he became a 'giant' killer. So Mohan Rathwa won in the subsequent elections of 1980, 1985 and 1990 on Janata Party and Janata Dal tickets. In 1980 election, he defeated the BJP candidate, and in 1985 and 1990 elections, he defeated the Congress candidates. But by the next election, Mohan Rathwa joined the Congress party and won the elections of 1995 and 1998. It is only in 2002 election that he lost to the BJP candidate. However, he won the 2007 election on Congress ticket. During 2012 election, he contested from the neighbouring ST-reserved constituency and emerged victorious and in the subsequent election of 2017.

Umbergaon

The third case is of Umbergaon constituency and of Ramanlal Patkar (Warli tribal). He contested his first election from Umbergaon ST constituency in 1980 election on a Janata Party ticket and lost. He contested the subsequent two elections of 1985 and 1990 on a Janata Dal ticket and again lost. So in 1995 election, he joined the BJP and won by defeating the Congress candidate Chotu Vestabhai

Patel (Dhodia tribal), who had won the previous four assembly elections. Patkar won the 1998 election but lost the 2002 election. Again, he contested the subsequent elections of 2007, 2012 and 2017 on a BJP ticket and emerged victorious.

Demand for a Separate State and the formation of the Bharatiya Tribal Party

Some of the tribals think that one of the ways to overcome the marginalization is to have a separate state of their own. This demand for a separate state for tribes of Gujarat has been in existence for some decades now. Nowadays, this demand is put up by the Bhils, who have been spread over three states such as Gujarat, Rajasthan and Madhya Pradesh. The Bhils comprise about 47 per cent of the Gujarat's ST population. Their demand has been given a boost with the formation of the Bharatiya Tribal Party (BTP) in late 2017 and the electoral success of two Bhil candidates each in the assembly elections of Gujarat in 2017 and Rajasthan in 2018. The BTP was formed by Chhotu Vasava, an iconic Bhil tribal leader of Narmada district.

However, the demand for a separate tribal state was first raised in 1969 in the Gujarat state assembly during the budget session by an Adivasi PSP MLA from Dangs, Ratan Singh Gamit. Gamits are separate from Bhils. Ratan Singh Gamit stated in the budget session, 'he would raise a "Dangi Sena" and ask for a separate state because the present state could not solve the problem of Dangis. Subsequently a conference was held at Ahwa in Dang in May 1969 which demanded the creation of an autonomous state' (Desai, 2006, p. 246). Desai (2006, p. 255), who conducted a study on this movement for a separate tribal state, states that this call had resonance in some areas more than others. Bharuch district had communist-leaning activists in the late 1960s, who took this idea forward. But this call did not find much support in other districts, says Desai.

Desai notes that Adivasis got a chance to participate in the new 'opportunity structure' only after Independence, but as they got educated, their desire for a share in the power and authority increased. However, the jobs the educated tribals got were low-paying ones, while those who studied with them became officers. Whenever the tribal case came up for consideration, the factor of 'suitability' was raised to eliminate them. In the 1960s, the educated tribals along with the landowning sections among the tribals were articulate in expressing their grievances and feeling of being discriminated. It is this section which has been supporting the demand for a separate state. One consequence of this political articulation was the attempt of the state government to stem it by setting up in 1970 a separate board for Harijan and Adivasi welfare, largely with Harijans (former untouchables/SCs) and tribals (Desai, 2006, p. 259). This empowered board was to formulate and sanction schemes for the welfare of SCs and STs.

However, this demand for a separate state has been echoing in the Bharuch district for a long time. Bharuch and Narmada districts have a high presence of Vasava Bhils. When Narmada district was formed by carving out talukas from Bharuch and Vadodara district, it became the epicentre of agitations for this demand. The person who most articulates today for this has been Chhotu Vasava.

Chhotu Vasava is fiercely independent. He belongs to Jhagadia taluka of Narmada district. When he was getting educated, his abilities and qualities were noticed by a former MLA of the district, Mulji Narsi Vasava, who had successfully contested the first elections held in independent India in 1951 for the Bombay state assembly. Muljibhai Vasava had one of his daughters marry Chhotubhai Vasava (Manani, 2017, p. 97). Chhotu Vasava accompanied his father-in-law when he went to meet the political leaders of the district Congress at that time. At the age of 18, he became a *talati* (village accountant), but within three years gave it up and decided to plunge into raising the voices of tribals against exploitation, while supporting himself by cultivating his own land. At that time, he came under the influence of Communist leaders of Bharuch district (Manani, 2017, p. 99). Whenever he would come to know about incidents of atrocity on tribals, he, along with his supporters, would go to the place and try to raise 'awareness'. On 21 September 1971, his father-in-law, Muljibhai Vasava was murdered at the behest of landed feudal interests of the district, which dominated the ruling party at that time.

During the Emergency, he was arrested but was released in 1976. Soon thereafter, he contested an election of a village sarpanch and won (Manani, 2017, p. 105). He went on to be president of Gujarat Kisan Sangh, which had Communist leaders of Bharuch district as members. He was associated with various agitations, including that for minimum wages. The agitations continued throughout the 1980s. It was in the election of 1985 that he got a Janata Dal ticket and contested the elections of the state assembly from Jhagadia ST constituency; he came second. But in the 1990 election, he again contested on a Janata Dal ticket and won. But when the Janata Dal collapsed in Gujarat, he contested as an independent candidate in 1995 election and emerged victorious. Then he again won on a Janata Dal ticket in 1998 and continued to win in 2002, 2007 and 2012 elections. When Janata Dal (U) split owing to differences in its national leadership in 2017, he, along with his supporters, formed BTP and, in the elections, reiterated their long-standing demand for a separate state of 'Bhilistan'.[24] To further

this cause, Chhotu Vasava has floated a 'Bhilistan Tiger Sena', comprising youth and other supporters, which makes its presence felt around election time. His continuous victory of seven elections has, in spite of waves in favour of other leaders, earned him a reputation as an iconic political leader. But owing to the nature of competitive democratic politics in the state, as his strength increased, other Bhil leaders and of other tribal ethnic groups have become suspicious of him in the state. So his support base has not yet expanded and he is yet to establish himself as a trans-ethnic tribal leader. However, in Rajasthan, where he is not a threat to the local Bhil leaders, his party's message has got resonance and support. In the state assembly election held in December 2018, the BTP put up 11 candidates in the Bhil-dominated districts of southern Rajasthan, and even won two seats.[25] This success made headlines in the Delhi media and has created a buzz about its demands.

During the Lok Sabha election of 2019, BTP put up candidates in Gujarat and Rajasthan, but they lost. Their slogan, as noticed by the *Economic Times*,[26] was *na Lok Sabha na Vidhan Sabha, sabse oonchi gram sabha* (neither Lok Sabha nor Vidhan Sabha, but gram sabha is supreme). This is in consonance with their current demands of BTP to implement Forest Rights Act. BTP is part of the all-India struggle to ensure that tribals are not evicted from their lands on a case being fought in the courts now. BTP is tech savvy and uses social media. It has a Facebook account through which anyone can follow their posts and statements.

[24] Retrieved from https://www.ibtimes.co.in/what-bhartiya-tribal-party-all-you-need-know-about-new-political-outfit-gujarat-elections-2017-753593; https://scroll.in/article/856382/in-gujarats-adivasi-belt-bjp-has-to-contend-with-bhilistan-separatists-boycotts-and-big-people
[25] Retrieved from https://scroll.in/latest/905310/rajasthan-poll-results-in-debut-elections-bharatiya-tribal-party-wins-two-seats
[26] Retrieved from https://economictimes.indiatimes.com/news/elections/lok-sabha/india/bharatiya-tribal-party-queers-pitch-in-rajasthan/articleshow/69018456.cms

Table 14.6 Voting in General, SC and ST Constituencies in Gujarat Assembly Elections

Year	General (in %)	SC (in %)	ST (in %)	Total (in %)
1	2	3	4	5
1962	58.99	49.14	56.81	57.97
1967	64.56	62.70	58.70	63.70
1972	59.88	51.46	49.94	58.10
1975	62.00	54.75	50.95	60.09
1980	50.57	42.00	38.95	48.37
1985	51.59	42.33	35.80	48.82
1990	53.63	46.94	46.32	52.20
1995	63.81	60.43	69.77	64.39
1998	59.63	56.64	58.68	59.30
2002	61.52	60.60	62.13	61.54
2007	59.87	56.79	60.72	59.77
2012	71.68	69.91	74.98	72.02
2017	68.53	66.52	73.03	69.01

Sources: GOI (1962a, p. 9); GOI (1967, p. 9); GOI (1972, p. 9); GOI (1975, p. 10); GOI (1980, p. 11); GOI (1985, p. 11); GOI (1990, p. 11); GOI (1995, p. 12); GOI (1998, p. 11); GOI (2002, p. 12); GOI (2007); GOI (2012, p. 13): GOI (2017, file 7).

Beside BTP, there are other organizations like Adivasi Ekta Parishad which has been working for nearly 25 years. Although this organization has brought various tribal groups on a common platform and has raised issues of tribal development, it has not supported the demand for a separate state. Many of its leaders are Gandhian in their approach (Rathwa, 2018). Compared to it, BTP appears more militant. Further, there are other leaders from BJP who belong to Vasava community of Bhils, and who occupy prominent positions in the state government. They are an alternative magnet. Some of the recent initiatives like starting universities in name of tribal icons are an attempt to stem Chhotu Vasava's appeal among the tribal youth. The Congress also has its tribal leaders from other tribal groups who are equally ambitious and have their own agendas. So the future of a separate state is caught in the ambitions and politics of a three-way tug of war, and at present, is heard only at election time in Narmada district.

Electoral Participation in ST Constituencies in Gujarat

Table 14.6 points out the changes in voting pattern over the last 60 years in assembly elections in ST-reserved constituencies of Gujarat. In Table 14.6, the voting/polling percentage of general constituencies and reserved constituencies is shown for all the general assembly elections held since 1962. It is interesting to note that between 1967 and 1990, the polling percentage in ST-reserved constituencies was consistently below the polling percentage in general and SC-reserved constituencies. In 1962 assembly election, the SC constituencies had a lower polling percentage. But from 1998 election, a change is seen, there is a perceptible increase in polling in ST constituencies. This is seen in the elections of 2002, 2007, 2012 and 2017. This increase could be a result of better mobilization at election time by rival parties contesting now, as compared to the past. This can also be inferred that STs have started participating in electoral process more than before. It could also be a sign that electoral process is gaining more legitimacy amongst the STs.

the legitimacy of the electoral process has increased in these constituencies.

CONCLUSION

The above narration has highlighted the changing dimensions of tribal politics in Gujarat over the last 70 odd years. The analysis has been in three phases: the Nehruvian era of the Congress rule, the post-Nehruvian phase and the current BJP phase of rule in the state. The first feature of tribal politics is the attempt to overcome development-induced displacement, which started in the Nehruvian era and continues even now. Tribes are being displaced and their lands continue to be taken for development activities from which they do not seem to be benefitted. Second, tribals are getting educated but they are not getting commensurate benefits. It appears that the state is opening institutions in tribal areas and/or in the name of tribal icons to socialize the tribals into the world of market economy.

In the world of politics, they continue to be marginalized without wielding any substantive power. With the emergence of the BJP era, this has resulted in them facing additional challenges: the threat of being absorbed into Hinduism and the BJP government's support to forces of neoliberalism. Both of these have aroused the fear in tribals of losing their cultural resources. Owing to changing nature of electoral politics over the last six decades, a new kind of political leadership has emerged. This is the 'electable leadership', a person who is self-centred and promotes own interests. Some tribals think that the formation of a separate state is a solution to overcome marginalization, but this demand becomes visible in media at periodic intervals, especially around election time. Finally, in spite of the exclusionary processes faced by tribals, there is also an increase in voting in ST constituencies (since 2002), perhaps reflecting that

REFERENCES

Chaube, S. K. (1999). The scheduled tribes and Christianity in India. *Economic & Political Weekly, 34*(9), 524–526.

Desai, I. P. (2006). The tribal autonomy movements in south Gujarat. In K. S. Singh (Ed.), *Tribal movements in India* (Vol. II, pp. 243–269). New Delhi: Manohar Publisher.

Gamit, M., & Patel, J. C. (Eds.). (2013). *Tribal development: Perspectives and issues.* Jaipur: Vista Publishers.

GOI (Government of India). (1951). *Statistical report on general election 1951 to the legislative assembly of Bombay.* New Delhi: Election Commission of India. Retrieved from https://eci.nic.in/eci_main/Statistical-Reports/SE_1951/StatReport_51_BOMBAY.pdf

GOI. (1955). *Gazette notification number 156 of 23 May 1955. Delimitation commission of India. Final order no. 27.* New Delhi: Election Commission of India. Retrieved from https://eci.gov.in/files/file/3962-final-order-dc-1953-1955/

GOI. (1957). *Statistical report on general election 1957 to the legislative assembly of Bombay.* New Delhi: Election Commission of India. Retrieved from https://eci.nic.in/eci_main/StatisticalReports/SE_1957/StatRep_Bombay_1957.pdf

GOI. (1962a). *Statistical report on general election 1962 to the legislative assembly of Gujarat.* New Delhi: Election Commission of India. Retrieved from https://eci.nic.in/eci_main/StatisticalReports/SE_1962/StatRep_Gujarat_1962.pdf

GOI. (1962b). *Census of India, 1961 Paper I of 1962.* New Delhi. Retrieved from http://censusindia.gov.in/DigitalLibrary/data/Census_1961/Publication/India/43176_1961_FPT.pdf

GOI. (1967). *Statistical report on general election 1967 to the legislative assembly of Gujarat.* New Delhi: Election Commission of India. Retrieved from https://eci.nic.in/eci_main/StatisticalReports/SE_1967/Statistical%20Report%20Gujarat%201967.pdf

GOI. (1971). *Census of India, 1971. Series 1–India Part V-A (ii) special tables for scheduled tribes.* New Delhi: Registrar General and Census Commissioner. Retrieved from http://www.censusindia.gov.

in/DigitalLibrary/data/Census_1971/Publication/
India/50760_1971_SPE.pdf

GOI. (1972). *Statistical report on general election 1972
to the legislative assembly of Gujarat*. New Delhi:
Election Commission of India. Retrieved from *https://
eci.nic.in/eci_main/StatisticalReports/SE_1972/Sta-
tisticalRep_GJ_72.pdf*

GOI. (1975). *Statistical report on general election 1975
to the legislative assembly of Gujarat*. New Delhi:
Election Commission of India. Retrieved from *https://
eci.nic.in/eci_main/StatisticalReports/SE_1975/Sta-
tistical%20Report%20Gujarat%201975.pdf*

GOI. (1980). *Statistical report on general election 1980
to the legislative assembly of Gujarat*. New Delhi:
Election Commission of India. Retrieved from https://
eci.nic.in/eci_main/StatisticalReports/SE_1980/Sta-
tistical%20Report%201980%20Gujarat.pdf

GOI. (1984). *Census of India, 1981. Series-I India Paper 2
of 1984 general population and population of scheduled castes and scheduled tribes*. New Delhi: Registrar
General and Census Commissioner. Retrieved from
*http://www.censusindia.gov.in/DigitalLibrary/data/
Census_1981/Publication/India/29426_1981_GEN.
pdf*

GOI. (1985). *Statistical report on general election 1985
to the legislative assembly of Gujarat*. New Delhi:
Election Commission of India. Retrieved from https://
eci.nic.in/eci_main/StatisticalReports/SE_1985/Sta-
tistical%20Report%20Gujarat%201985.pdf

GOI. (1990). *Statistical report on general election 1990
to the legislative assembly of Gujarat*. New Delhi:
Election Commission of India. Retrieved from https://
eci.nic.in/eci_main/StatisticalReports/SE_1990/Sta-
tRep_GJ_90.pdf

GOI. (1995). *Statistical report on general election 1995
to the legislative assembly of Gujarat*. New Delhi:
Election Commission of India. Retrieved from https://
eci.nic.in/eci_main/StatisticalReports/SE_1995/Sta-
tisticalReport-GUJ95.pdf

GOI. (1998). *Statistical report on general election 1998
to the legislative assembly of Gujarat*. New Delhi:
Election Commission of India. Retrieved from https://
eci.nic.in/eci_main/StatisticalReports/SE_1998/Sta-
tisticalReport-GUJ98.pdf

GOI. (2000). *Census of India-2001: List of scheduled
castes and scheduled tribes*. New Delhi: Office of Registrar General and Census Commissioner. Retrieved
from *http://censusindia.gov.in/DigitalLibrary/data/
Census_2001/Publication/India/40932_2001_LIS.
pdf*

GOI. (2002). *Statistical report on general election 2002
to the legislative assembly of Gujarat*. New Delhi:
Election Commission of India. Retrieved from https://
eci.nic.in/eci_main/StatisticalReports/SE_2002/Sta-
tReport_GUJ2002.pdf

GOI. (2004). *Census of India, 2001, Series 1: Final
population totals*. New Delhi: Registrar General and
Census Commissioner. Retrieved from*http://censusin-
dia.gov.in/DigitalLibrary/data/Census_2001/Publica-
tion/India/36922_2001_FPT.pdf*

GOI. (2007). *Statistical report on general election 2007
to the legislative assembly of Gujarat*. New Delhi:
Election Commission of India. Retrieved from https://
eci.nic.in/eci_main/StatisticalReports/SE_2007/Sta-
tReport_DEC_2007_GUJARAT_after_IC.pdf

GOI. (2011). *Census of India, 2011: Final population
data*. Retrieved from http://planningcommission.
nic.in/data/datatable/data_2312/Databook-
Dec2014%20307.pdf

GOI. (2012). *Statistical report on general election 2012
to the legislative assembly of Gujarat*. New Delhi:
Election Commission of India. Retrieved from *https://
eci.nic.in/eci_main/StatisticalReports/SE_2012/
Reports_Index%20Card_ECIApplication_Gujarat-
State_CEO.pdf*

GOI. (2013). *Statistical profile of scheduled tribes in
India*. New Delhi: Ministry of Tribal Affairs, Statistics
Division. Retrieved from https://tribal.nic.in/ST/Statis-
ticalProfileofSTs2013.pdf

GOI. (2014). *Report of the high level committee on
socio-economic, health and educational status of
tribal communities of India*. New Delhi: Ministry of
Tribal Affairs.

GOI. (2017). *Gujarat general legislative election, 2017*.
New Delhi: Election Commission of India. Retrieved
from *https://eci.gov.in/files/file/3841-gujarat-gener-
al-legislative-election-2017/*

Government of Gujarat. (2019). *Tribal demography*.
Ahmedabad: Tribal Research Training Institute.
Retrieved from *https://tribal.gujarat.gov.in/demo-
graphic-fact*

Hankla, C. R. (2006). Parties and patronage: A comparative analysis of the Indian case. *Political Science Faculty Publications*. Paper 1. Georgia State University.
Retrieved from http://scholarworks.gsu.edu/politi-
cal_science_facpub/1

Joshi, V. (2017). Chootnioma adivasi pratinidhtva [in
Gujarati Adivasi representation in elections]. *Adhilok*,
9(6).

Kothari, R. (1961, June 3). Party system. *The Economic
Weekly*, 847–854.

Kothari, R. (1964). The Congress 'system' in India. *Asian Survey*, *4*(2), 1161–1173.

Kothari, R. (1970). Towards a political perspective for the seventies. *Economic & Political Weekly*, *5*(3–5), 101–116.

Kukreti, I. (2018). Dalits, adivasis to protest in Gandhinagar for land rights. *Down to Earth*. Retrieved from https://www.downtoearth.org.in/news/governance/dalits-adivasis-to-protest-in-gandhinagar-for-land-rights-62127

Lobo, L. (2002). Adivasis, Hindutva and post-Godhra riots in Gujarat. *Economic & Political Weekly*, *37*(48), 4844–4849.

Lobo, L. (2014). Land acquisition and displacement among tribals, 1947–2004. In A. Shah & J. Pathak (Eds.), *Tribal development in western India* (pp. 285–309). New Delhi: Routledge.

Lobo, L., & Macwan, J. (2002). *Shoshan and antak ni aag ma adivasiyon* (in Gujarati) [Adivasis in the grip of exploitation and terror]. Vadodara: Centre for Culture and Development.

Manani, J. (2017). *Jharkhand se Gujarat: Moolnivasi adivasi andolan* (in Hindi) (*Jharkhand to Gujarat: Indigenous adivasi movement*). Udaipur: M. M. Printers.

Pandar, S. (2017). *Adivasi andolan* (in Gujarati) [Adivasi agitations]. Ahmedabad: Anuraj Graphics.

Patel, J. C. (2013). The status of tribals in India. In M. Gamit, & J. C. Patel (Eds.), *Tribal development: Perspectives and issues* (pp. 30–39). Jaipur: Vista Publishers.

Patel, S. (2011). *Gujarat. Status of indigenous/adivasi people's land series 1*. New Delhi: Aakar Books and the Other Media.

Rajaram, N. (2005). *Social processes and communal tension*. New Delhi: National Foundation for Communal Harmony.

Rathwa, A. (2018). Identity: Reflection of adivasi movements on rights in Gujarat. *Adivasi Bharat*, *1*(1), 18–21.

Rathwa, A., Rai, D., & Rajaram, N. (2014). Denotification of Rathwas as adivasis in Gujarat. *Economic & Political Weekly*, *49*(6), 22–24.

Shah, A. M. (2003). The tribes—'so called'—of Gujarat. *Economic & Political Weekly*, *38*(2), 95–97.

Shah, A. M., Patel, P., & Lobo, L. (2008). A heady mix: Gujarati and Hindu pride. *Economic & Political Weekly*, *43*(8), 19–22.

Shah, G. (1996). BJP's rise to power. *Economic & Political Weekly*, *31*(2–3), 165–170.

Vasava, G. (2006). *Adivasi asmita ane astitva vinash ni oar* (in Gujarati) [Adivasi identity and status: Towards destruction]. Surat: Mahesh Vasava.

Vashista, V. K. (1991). The Bhil revolt of 1913 under Guru Govindgiri among the Bhils of southern Rajasthan and its impact. *Proceedings of Indian History Congress, 1991–92, 51*, 522–527. Retrieved from https://archive.org/stream/in.ernet.dli.2015.170000/2015.170000.Proceedings-Of-The-Indian-History-Congress_djvu.txt

Xaxa, V. (2014). *State, society and tribes: Issues in post-colonial India*. New Delhi: Pearson.

Xaxa, V. (2019). Tribal politics in Jharkhand. *Economic & Political Weekly*, *54*(28), 10–11.

Tribal Politics in Himachal Pradesh: Issues and Concerns

Mini Pathak Dogra

The concept of 'tribe' is defined vividly and changes its dimension from place to place and time to time and is true in academic discourses as well. A sociological definition of tribes as who are culturally different and socially backward, that is, they have less communication with other communities of the region they reside, in terms of maintaining relations. Whereas, for an anthropologist, tribals are racially different and historically are believed to be descended from common ancestor centuries ago. It is difficult to arrive at commonly accepted definition of tribe which is all encompassing and acceptable to all. In India, in pre-independence period, terms like adim jati, vanavasi and so on, were used to denote tribes but in post-independence period, the word scheduled has been attached to word tribe instead of using the primitive terminology but nowhere it has been defined properly what is meant by term 'tribe'. However, to overcome this unsettled issue of defining tribe, some common features are taken into consideration while notifying any community as tribe.[1] In India, the tribes are notified by the Presidential Orders.

Tribes once were the communities living in the far flung areas having a kind of primitiveness and least communication with the outside world but with the passage of time, mobility has increased to many fold due to access to modes of communication and means of transportation. Due to the present day technology and the speedy transformation of the world into a place called 'global village', every nook and corner is now well connected. The processes of modernization and development are transforming every section of society and tribals are no exception to it. In other words, it appears that the primitiveness associated with the word 'tribe' is now not completely true and tribes are not so detached from mainstream society as they were in the past.

---

[1] The common features of tribes that gradually were taken into consideration while notifying tribes were like Autochthony, primitive way of living, social or economic backwardness etc. although they are nowhere included formally in the constitution (Negi, 1976, p. 6).

India is a land to numerous tribes for which constitution has adopted word scheduled tribes (STs) and power has been given to President to notify any community as ST keeping in view various dimensions which justify the claim of any community. This is a kind of protective discrimination which helps the backward communities to move upward through the ladder of progress. This has not only helped in uplifting the tribal people but also in generating awareness about their rights. In reference to tribes, it will not be out of place to categorize Indian tribes into two, that is, one which reside in notified tribal areas and the other who are dispersed, that is, they are tribal communities but are not residing in any particularly demarcated geographical area. This is something important to be noted when it comes to tribes of Himachal Pradesh.

The chapter focuses on the tribes of Himachal Pradesh and their participation as well as involvement in politics. This chapter deals with the major issues that revolve around the tribes and what factors have influenced tribal politics in the state. The objectives of the chapter are to find out the issues that have shaped the tribal politics and how far tribes have been able to exert their influence in the state politics of Himachal Pradesh. It also explores the challenges that tribes have been facing in general and if these issues impact their participation in the politics of the state or not.

INTRODUCING HIMACHAL PRADESH

Himachal Pradesh as a full fledge state came into being in 1971 but its foundation was laid down as early as in 1948. Its political journey has witnessed many ups and downs since then, moving from Part C state to status of union territory and then its reorganization

in 1966 and merger of areas of Punjab with it specially Shimla hill areas. This actually is important to mention because it had changed both the geographical as well as demographical dimensions of the state from time to time. Since 1971, Himachal Pradesh actually started moving to a goal-oriented direction of development. Despite having limitations in geographical front that puts check on the pace of development, the state has still shown high progress in various sectors like health and education when it comes to a comparison with other states of India. The visionary political leadership and the effective administrative implementation have made Himachal Pradesh achieve high standards of growth with the given limitations. Probably this is the reason that Himachal Pradesh is considered as one of the peaceful state.

DEMOGRAPHY

According to 2011 census, Himachal Pradesh has a total population of about 686,4602, of which 3,481,873 are males and 3,382,729 are females. Of this total population, 392,126 are notified as ST population which constitutes 5.71 per cent of the total population.[2] At present, Bhot or Bodh, Gaddis, Gujjars, Jad, Lamba, Khampa, Kanaura or Kinnara, Lahaul, Pangwala, Swangala, Beta, Beda, Demba, Gara, Zoba are the communities that have been notified as STs of Himachal Pradesh. These STs have been notified from time to time by the government of India and have entered the ST list through various Presidential Orders after independence. This also has increased the population of STs from time to time.

Table 15.1 demonstrates the decadal growth of tribal population in Himachal Pradesh. Table 15.1 shows that when the state

---

[2] Statistical Profile of Himachal Pradesh. Retrieved from himachalservices.nic.in/tribal/pdf/statistical profile 1415_ A1b.pdf.

Table 15.1   Decadal Growth Rate of ST Population of Himachal Pradesh, 1971–2011

Year	Total Population of the State	Total ST Population	% of ST Population
1971	3,460,434	141610	4.09
1981	4,280,818	197263	4.60
1991	5,170,877	218349	4.22
2001	6,077,900	244587	4.02
2011	6,864,602	392126	5.71

Source: Census of India Reports (1971–2011)

attained full-fledged statehood in 1971, it had 141,610 tribal population. It is worth mentioning here that prior to year 1971, in the year 1956, when the state was Part C state, six entries were made in the Scheduled Tribes Orders (Amendment) Act, 1956 which were further amended in the year 1976 to add two new entries making a total of eight. However, the Gaddis and Gujjars of merged areas which were added after the reorganization of Punjab in 1966 were excluded from the list.

Table 15.1 shows that in 1971, the tribal population of Himachal Pradesh was 4.09 per cent, which increased by 0.59 per cent to constitute 4.60 per cent in 1981. However, during 1991 census, the tribal population was increased to 4.22 per cent, and further decreased to 4.02 per cent in 2001. However,

there is a 1.69 per cent increased in the tribal population of Himachal Pradesh during the 2011 census. This is due to the inclusion of communities of merged areas being given status of ST under the Scheduled Castes and Scheduled Tribes Orders (Amendment) Act, 2002 which came into force in 2003.

Table 15.2 clearly shows that Kinnaur and Lahual and Spiti districts of the state are having 57.95 per cent and 81.44 per cent of tribal population in proportion to the total population of the districts, respectively. Chamba district has the third largest concentration of tribal population with 26.10 per cent. Other districts of the state have very less presence of tribal population ranging from 5.60 per cent in Kangra to as low as 0.67 per cent in Hamirpur. Thus, out of 12 districts, only 3 are having

Table 15.2   District-wise Tribal Population of Himachal Pradesh, 2011

Sr. No	Name of the District	No. of Census Villages	Total Population	ST Population	Percentage to Total Population	Percentage of ST Population of the Total Population of the District
1.	Bilaspur	953	381,956	10,693	0.155	2.80
2.	Chamba	1,110	519,080	135,500	1.974	26.10
3.	Hamirpur	1,671	454,768	3,044	0.044	0.67
4.	Kangra	3,617	1510,075	84,564	1.231	5.60
5.	Kinnaur	241	84,121	48,746	0.710	57.95
6.	Kullu	314	437,903	16,822	0.245	3.84
7.	Lahaul-Spiti	280	31,564	25,707	0.374	81.44
8.	Mandi	2,850	999,777	12,787	0.186	1.28
9.	Shimla	2,705	814,010	8,755	0.127	1.08
10.	Sirmour	968	529,855	11,262	0.164	2.13
11.	Solan	2,383	580,320	25,645	0.373	4.42
12.	Una	790	521,173	8,601	0.125	1.65
	Total	17,882	6,864,202	392,126	5.709(5.71)	---------

Source: Tribal Sub-Plan 2018–2019, Tribal Development Department, Government of Himachal Pradesh.

substantial presence of tribes and the rest are accommodating very less tribal people.

It is worthwhile to mention that none of the district is totally inhabited by the tribal population. Hence, it can also be stated that the tribal population of Himachal Pradesh is both heterogeneous or fragmented as well as dispersed. Kinnaur and Lahaul and Spiti districts and Pangi-Bharmour area of Chamba district are declared as scheduled areas due to high concentration of tribal population.

Table 15.3 shows the areas which have been declared as the scheduled areas of the state. Kinnaur and Lahaul-Spiti districts are declared as totally scheduled areas and Chamba district is declared as partially scheduled area. They are amongst the remotest and most inaccessible areas of the state. They cover around 23,655 Sq. Km area of the state out of 55,673, that is, about 42.49 per cent of the total area but the total concentration of population in these areas is very low.

Table 15.3 indicates that Kinnaur district has 57.95 per cent tribal population, constituting 12.43 per cent of the total tribal population of the state. Similarly, Lahaul has 79.36 per cent tribal population, which accounts 3.87 per cent of the total tribal population of the state. The concentration of tribal population in Spite stands at 84.64 per cent, which contributes 2.69 per cent of tribal population to the total tribal population of the state. Similarly, Pangi and Bharmour areas of Chamber district record 90.18 and 82.17 per cent of tribal

population, which houses 4.34 and 8.19 per cent of tribal population of the state, respectively. Table 15.3 shows that the tribal population of the scheduled areas of the state stand at 71.16 per cent, which contributes 31.52 per cent to the total tribal population of the state. In other words, large chunk of tribal population of Himachal Pradesh continue to live in non-scheduled areas of the state.

Kinnaur and Lahaul-Spiti districts, in their entirety, and Pangi and Bharmour (now tehsil Bharmour and sub-tehsil Holi) subdivisions of Chamba district constitute the scheduled areas in the state, fulfilling the minimum criterion of 50 per cent ST population concentration in a Community Development Block (Government of Himachal Pradesh, 2019, p. 1). Although there are vast differences in area and population, having a population density of 7 per square Km in scheduled areas, it was essential to constitute them into separate districts not only because of cultural reasons but also because of administrative reasons as they are on the border of India and Tibet region forming sensitive zones. Negi (1972, pp. 144–145) points out that, 'it was a very wise step by the Government of India to organize Kinnaur and Spiti-Lahaul in separate districts in 1960 for administrative and developmental purposes. The close and special attention so focused has paid rich dividends.' These areas are also declared as scheduled areas under the fifth schedule of the constitution by the President of India as per the Scheduled Areas (Himachal

Table 15.3   Tribal Population in Scheduled Areas of Himachal Pradesh (2014–2015)

Sr. No	Scheduled Areas	Total population of the Area	ST population of the Area	Percentage of ST Population to Total Population of the Area	Percentage of ST Population to the Total Tribal Population
1.	Kinnaur	84,121	48,746	57.95%	12.43%
2.	Lahaul	19,107	15,163	79.36%	3.87%
3.	Spiti	12,457	10,544	84.64%	2.69%
4.	Pangi (Chamba)	18,868	17,016	90.18%	4.34%
5.	Bharmour (Chamba)	39,108	32,116	82.17%	8.19%
	Total	173,661	123,585	71.16%	31.52%

Source: Statistical Profile of Tribal Areas.

Pradesh) Order, 1975 (Constitutional Order 102) dated the 21 November, 1975. The five ITDP's are Kinnaur; Lahaul; Spiti; Pangi and Bharmour. Except Kinnaur which is spread over three Community Development Blocks, rest of the ITDP's comprise one Community Development Block each (Government of Himachal Pradesh, 2019, p. 1).

Table 15.4 Shows the concentration of STs in Himachal Pradesh other than scheduled areas which further clarifies that even among the dispersed tribes of about 68.48 per cent the tribal people who are living in the villages where tribal concentration is more than 40 per cent of the total population is also very less.

Table 15.4 shows that out of 17,361 inhabited villages only 519 (other than the scheduled areas) are having ST population with more than 40 per cent concentration. Large number of villages with more than 40 per cent of tribal population are located in Chanma and Kangra districts. Out of these 519 villages with more than 40 per cent of tribal population, only 151 villages are in other eight districts which means that the presence of ST population in these areas is negligible. Out of total of 17,361 villages in all, the presence of STs can be found in 924 villages in total The STs of the

state are also divided into too many categories due to their adherence to different culture, language as well as religion. This further contributes to the complexity to come under one ambit and create a common group for achieving common purpose. The unorganized nature and too much fragmentation among STs lead to the absence of any strong pressure group for having a say in decision making as such. The tribes do have formed certain groups like Khampa Welfare Board, Gaddi Welfare Board, and so on, which aimed to protect their culture and identity, albeit little influential to represent whole tribal population.

Table 15.4 further shows the segregation of tribal population. It is worth mentioning that other than Chamba district no other district is having sizeable concentration of tribal people. This affects not only the cultural identity but also the level of political participation and consciousness. These dispersed tribes usually face threats to their culture from other communities as well as dilution of their interest in the interest of the majority when it comes to participation and representation. This can also be cited as one of the reasons that no parliamentary constituency is reserved for them. Not only the less population is one of

Table 15.4   District-wise Number of Villages with ST Population Excluding Scheduled Areas, Himachal Pradesh

Sr. No (1)	Name of the District (2)	Total no. of Villages (3)	Out of total villages No. of Villages Having more than 40% Tribal Population (4)	%age Col.3 & Col.4 (5)	No. of Villages Having ST Population More than 100 Persons but Concentration Less than 40% of Total Population (6)	%age Col. 3 & Col.6 (7)
1.	Bilaspur	953	30	3.14	18	1.88
2.	Chamba	1,110	192	17.29	110	9.90
3.	Hamirpur	1,671	10	0.59	2	0.11
4.	Kangra	3,617	176	4.86	132	3.64
5.	Kullu	314	5	1.59	37	11.78
6.	Mandi	2,850	26	0.91	25	0.87
7.	Shimla	2,705	14	0.51	8	0.29
8.	Sirmour	968	12	1.23	17	1.75
9.	Solan	2,383	43	1.80	45	1.88
10.	Una	790	11	1.39	11	1.39
	Total	17,361	519	2.98	405	2.33

Source: Tribal Development Department (census 2011).

the major causes but also the dispersed nature of the tribes that no significant mobilization could take place or could not establish any platform so far to raise their voices in relation to the need for demanding ST reserved parliamentary constituency for the tribal communities of Himachal Pradesh. This may be somehow because of the less presence of tribal population in Himachal Pradesh. Tribal area is geographically much wider but the population density is very less, indicating less contact with the people of other areas. However, this must not be understood as isolation. But lesser contact somehow impact the political solidarity.

POLITICAL SCENARIO

Due to policy of reservation, the scheduled areas are getting due representation in the state legislative assembly. Kinnaur and Lahaul-Spiti have been given one seat each in the state assembly since their formation as separate districts. Whereas Pangi and Bharmour the two sub areas of District Chamba are also scheduled area of the District and their constituency has been clubbed under one assembly seat, namely, Bharmour constituency. However, interestingly, in scheduled areas, the demographic disadvantage has led leadership to come from the more populous regions mainly from Lahaul in case of Lahaul and Spiti and Bharmour from Pangi-Bharmour constituency. Deeper analysis of Kinnaur region also shows that Pooh region which is uppermost region of the area and is also demographically least populous has been at the disadvantaged end. In case of Pooh, predominance of Buddhism instead of Hinduism has also affected the emergence of leadership because other two blocs, that is, Nichar and Kalpa are

largely Hindu-dominated areas. This aspect also leaves room for further investigation and research in the aforesaid areas.

On the other hand, if we see the dispersed tribes of the state, the dominance of the Congress and the BJP is visible. The presence of two national political parties viz. the Congress and the BJP has made tribals probably (especially dispersed ones) to follow one or the other. The state has witnessed the failure of formation of Third Front many times,[3] leaving greater scope for national political parties to dominate the state politics since the attainment of statehood. The leadership of these parties gets support from the common masses and the participation of ST population and their support to either of the party is not an exception. In the case of dispersed tribes, candidates of the party get support from the ST population due to the minority status of tribes in most of the villages (Table 15.4). The demographic disadvantage along with the geographical locations and the scattered nature makes it difficult for tribal population to demand representation especially in terms of leadership from the major political parties. The scheduled areas also get the candidates from their communities supported by major political parties and give full support to them only. Table 15.5 shows the strong hold of bi-party system in scheduled areas of the Himachal Pradesh.

Tables 15.5 and 15.6 clearly show that more often there is a competition between the Congress and the BJP, and thereby not yet let any other force to enter the competitive political space. The 'others' category in Tables 15.5 and 15.6 indicates parties like Bahujan Samaj Party, Himachal Vikas Congress, Himachal Lokhit Party and so on, along with other independent candidates but almost every time the stiff competition has been between the BJP and the Congress. The close observation of

[3] In Himachal Pradesh, there has been a several attempts for making of third front like Himachal Vikas Congress, Himachal Lokhit Party, and so on. The Third Front most of the time emerges from the major political parties due to the factionalism prevalent within the parties but so far has not emerged so strong to damage the bi-polar party system. Even the parties like Bahujan Samaj Party are trying to mobilize people but they have not succeeded.

Table 15.5   Vote Share of Major Political Parties in Parliamentary Elections in Scheduled Areas, Himachal Pradesh

Name of the Constituency	Year of Election	Vote Share in %		
		Congress	Bhartiya Janata Party (BJP)	Others
Lahaul and Spiti	2014	49.96	46.24	3.81
	2009	47.04	46.55	6.41
	2004	55.45	42.46	2.09
Kinnaur	2014	49.06	42.21	8.73
	2009	50.75	42.86	6.40
	2004	57.90	38.94	3.16
Bharmour	2014	57.81	37.94	4.25
	2009	44.05	52.17	3.78
	2004	54.33	41.43	4.24

Source: Data compiled from Reports of Election Commission of India.

state politics in Himachal Pradesh suggests that Himachal Vikas Congress, which has been under the 'Other' category, secured a large chunk of vote share during 1998 assembly election. Considering the overall impact on the state and national politics, the voters have not shown too much of positive response to the election campaigning of the 'Others'.

Tables 15.5 and 15.6 also suggest that not only in parliamentary elections but also in state assembly elections, the national parties have played a major role and no tribal political party has emerged so far.

However, even if the strong presence of two dominant party is still evident in the state politics of Himachal Pradesh, tribals

Table 15.6   Vote Share of Major Political Parties in Assembly Elections in Scheduled Areas, Himachal Pradesh

Name of the Constituency	Year of Election	Vote Share in %		
		Congress	Bhartiya Janata Party (BJP)	Others
Lahaul and Spiti	2017	36.93	45.63	17.44
	2012	51.35	44.16	4.49
	2007	48.10	48.14	3.77
	2003	50.70	11.76	28.11
	1998	30.54	4.33	34.95 (Himachal Vikas Congress)
Kinnaur	2017	47.89	47.60	4.51
	2012	54.09	37.67	8.24
	2007	44.29	51.46	4.24
	2003	54.33	33.21	12.46
	1998	39.70	49.58	10.72
Bharmour	2017	35.45	49.62	14.93
	2012	60.33	38.44	1.23
	2007	41.39	54.29	4.32
	2003	61.58	34.29	4.13
	1998	40.12	52.65	7.23

Source: Data compiled from reports of Election Commission of India.

are trying to register their presence. This was visible in the 2019 by-elections that were held for two assembly constituencies, such as Dharamshala of district Kangra and Pacchad of district Sirmour. In Dharamshala, major contest was between the Congress and the BJP but it was for the first time Congress has given its ticket to Vijay Inder Karan who is from Gaddi community. However, this happened due to withdrawal of Sudhir Sharma from the elections but the Gaddi community has made it possible to register their presence in this constituency. The BJP also gave its ticket to Vishal Naheriya, a youth belonging to Gaddi community (Divya Himachal, 2019, p. 2). Gaddi voters are the second largest group in this area with about 22,000 voters but are much less than the first vote bank of OBC's including Gorkhas having about 36,000 voters (Divya Himachal, 2019, p. 2). This shows that tribes are making their presence felt in the electoral politics of certain areas where demographic advantage is with them and they cannot be neglected by the political parties. The election results of by-elections 2019 of Dharamshala also reflected the strong hold of parties instead of community affiliations because by nominating candidates from the same community by the Congress and the BJP, the parties divided the community votes otherwise that might have not been divided.

By and large, although tribal communities of scheduled areas are experiencing proportionate representation because of the presence of reserved constituencies, but dispersed tribes do remain unrepresented most of the time. However, the under representation of dispersed tribes has not led to any strife

resistance or any violent movement in state politics of Himachal Pradesh. The available statistics appear to suggest that tribal communities of scheduled areas and the dispersed tribes are politically conscious, leading to high voter-turnout in reserved constituencies. This shows that tribal people are aware about their rights, among others, political rights and the level of awareness among tribals is also high which can be proved by stating a simple example of the highest polling station Tashigang in Spiti valley situated at 12,256 feet recorded 142.85 per cent [4] voter turnout in state assembly elections in 2017. In another unique feature the smallest polling booth *Ka* had poll percentage of 81.25 per cent. [5]

Himachal Pradesh has remained largely a peaceful state. Hence, there is no history of any significant violent movements for the demand of tribal status as such may be due to the timely inclusion of the communities in the list of STs and granting them tribal status. This has also affected the political mobilization of the tribal population. The subsequent Himachal Pradesh governments have worked effectively to deal with the tribal issue like recommending communities to the central government for granting ST status to those belonging to merged areas.

However, the scheduling and de-scheduling of communities are on-going process. Within this backdrop, it is worth mentioning that there is an ongoing movement of Hatti community living in Trans-Giri area of Sirmour district of Himachal Pradesh demanding ST status.[6] The Kendriya Hatti Samiti is justifying the demand on the ground that their counterparts living in the Jaunsar Bawar area of Uttarakhand state (which was earlier part of

---

[4] *Tashigang* registered 74 per cent turnout but the hike up to 142.85 per cent was due to the desire of many poll officials, deployed at *Tashigang* and other neighboring polling booths to cast their votes at the world's highest polling station.
[5] Retrieved from http://www.ndtv.com/india-news/himachal-pradesh-polls at 12,256 feet-worlds-highest-polling-station-records-132-voting in tashigana-2039855).
[6] The kendriya Hatti Samiti is leading the movement demanding ST status to the Hatti community in Himachal Pradesh. It appears that the Samiti launched the movement in response to the false promises made by the politicians in facilitating the process of granting ST status.

Uttar Pradesh) have been granted this status much earlier in 1967. Hatti community states that it shares common cultural traits, traditions and life styles with the people living in Jaunsar Bawar. The Hatti community is persistently pursuing this matter through peaceful means and wants government to solve this issue at the earliest.[7] The present state government has also raised this issue with the present Home Minister.[8]Although this may seem to be a petty issue right now in context of tribal politics but may culminate into larger one with passage of time if not addressed well on time as people are now aware and well connected as well as well informed.

The increased connectivity and the level of awareness help communities to raise their demands and act as a powerful lobby especially at the time of elections. This has already been proven from time to time by inclusion of tribes in the list of ST not only in Himachal Pradesh but nation-wide. Writing about Gaddi tribe of Himachal Pradesh particularly, Kapila (2008) notes that there has been on-going politics of reclassification of tribes in North India. She has summed up the tussle between the various communities of who should be getting the benefit of protective discrimination in the form of reservations. The emphasizes that the Gaddi tribe has been succeeded in demanding the constitutional reclassification to include them in the ST list (Kapila, 2008).

However, as far as Himachal Pradesh is concerned, the government initiatives have convinced the tribals not to adhere to any violent means. The tribal development department of government of Himachal Pradesh has also been catering to the needs of the tribals whether they are from scheduled area or the dispersed tribes. The allocation of funds through Tribal Sub-Plans and the welfare policies of the state government had reduced the risk of generation of any conflict between the authorities or administration and the tribals.

The initiatives of successive governments have resulted in the peaceful integration of the tribals with the mainstream communities. They have been forced to neither assimilate completely nor live in isolation but to integrate in such a manner that they have their own identity protected in terms of culture, customs and traditions. The level of political awareness among the tribes is relatively high viz-a viz their living standards because of their changed outlook and their transformation especially from traditional occupations like agriculture to areas like horticulture in which government has played a significant role and has uplifted the tribal people despite the hard topography and has made them comparatively better than most of the tribes of other states. These efforts of the successive governments can also be a role model that can be followed by other states.

However, this should not be considered as there are no challenges in front of tribes. The participation of tribal population in politics no doubt reveals that they have proportionate awareness level and they are also aware about other rights. The front on which the state has failed or is in confrontation with the tribal population is the installation of hydro-power projects which is one of the major source of earning for the state government. These projects have been severely criticized by the residents of the tribal areas. The installation of these projects have made people to form numerous organizations to save their interests especially in Kinnaur and Lahaul-Spiti districts of Himachal Pradesh. Various organizations have come up in these districts to protect environment and community rights as well. People even dared to go against the dictates of union government in some cases as in Lippa village of Kinnaur district. Paryavaran Sanrakshan Sangharsh Samiti (PSSS), an environment protection group of villagers, moved to National Green Tribunal (NGT)

---

[7] Retrieved from https://timesofindia.indiatimes.com/city/shimla/hatti-community-demand-st-
[8] Retrieved from http://www.tribune.com/news/himachal/cm-seeks-tribal-status-for-hatti-community/785107.html

against the construction of hydro-electricity project for which water of Kareng stream was to be diverted. The Tribunal then directed the Union Ministry and state government to get a No Objection Certificate (NOC) from Gram Sabha of four villages including Lippa where the project was proposed to be constructed. However, gram sabha denied to provide NOC to project developer. Gyan Negi, an activist of PSSS, stated, 'we can't take such arm twisting lying down. It's our forest and our future that's at stake'.[9]

Similarly, Himalaya Niti Abhiyan, another organization which is working for protection of people's right over resources, is also against the construction of these projects. An activist, Bhagat Singh Kinner, who represented Rarang village at NGT stated, 'We, the Kinnauris living along Satluj are simple people. But the Government and project developers should not mistake that simplicity for frailty'. People of Jangi village fought against Army's plan to acquire 5,500 bigha for its depot in the village. The villagers have also filed a community rights claim under the Forest Right Act, 2006, over the forest area.[10] Tribal people of the respective areas have a major concern for environment protection as well as concerns over water scarcity for irrigation and drinking. This also impacts their economy in the long run.

Satluj Bachao Jan Sangharsh Samiti welcomed the decision of World Bank for not funding Luhri project even when its capacity was reduced from 775 MW to 612 MW. This people's front kept on protesting the project even after the Union Ministry of Environment and Forests also reduced the capacity of the project from 775 MW to 612 MW. 'Reduction in capacity is not a solution. The project must be scrapped', said the representatives of the

front.[11] In Lahaul also in 2012 people knocked doors of Union Environment and Forest Ministry for protesting the then upcoming hydropower projects on Chenab river basin.[12]

Another current issue that made tribal people of scheduled areas resent was the demand that emerged from the Leh and Ladakh (which earlier was part of the state of Jammu and Kashmir, but after abrogation of article 370 and change in the status of the state as union territory comprised of two separate UT areas of Leh and Ladakh and Jammu and Kashmir) that is of merger of the scheduled area of Lahual and Spiti into Leh and Ladakh due to cultural affinity. Not only the state government but the people also took great interest in denouncing that demand. This also shows that they feel may be more protected and privileged in Himachal Pradesh then in any other state. In other words, there is almost no trust deficit among tribals of Himachal Pradesh.

CONCLUSION

By and large, tribal politics of Himachal Pradesh can be one of the examples which can be put forward as having integrationist approach rather than forceful assimilation or the approach based on isolationism. No severe conflict has ever emerged so far among the tribes themselves neither with the authorities as such and the tribes have also not faced any threat to their identity as such from the other communities so far. Tribal communities are relatively okay within the competition between the Congress and the BJP and also are living harmoniously with the other communities of the state maintaining trade and business relations. It can also be stated that

[9] Retrieved from http://Indiawaterportal.org/articles/power-play-kinnaur.
[10] Retrieved from Indiawaterportal.org/articles/power-play-kinnaur.
[11] Retrieved from https://www.downtoearth.org.in>news>world bank-wont-fund-luhri-hydropower-project-in-himachal-44004
[12] Retrieved from https://Economictimes.indiatimes.com/industry/energy/power/37-hydropower-projects-in-eco-logically-sensitive-lahaul-spiti-/articleshow/30235957.cms?from=mdrs

although the tribes in the state are numerically small but they have not faced any kind of discrimination or exploitation which is visible through their peaceful integration. This has a positive impact on their political participation as well as the level of awareness.

Tribal politics in Himachal Pradesh indicates that voting percentages and the level of general awareness of ST's is relatively high and the representation given to them has made it possible to avoid confrontationist tendencies. The nature of tribal politics is governed by twin principles of heterogeneity that exists within tribal population and the dispersed settlement of the majority of tribal population outside the scheduled areas of the state. The dispersed nature and fragmentation within can also be seen as a disadvantage for the formation of any political identity in terms of homogenous tribal organization. Probably this can also be considered as one of the factors which has made tribal people to satisfy themselves within the larger groups. So far no common platform has emerged representing demands or interests of tribal people in the state, however, this has not affected the participation as well as the development of the tribal people. But the isolation must not be taken for granted as the encroachments being done in the tribal land in the name of development especially by the construction of hydro-power projects and illegal mining is making tribals to raise their voice and protest to protect their interests. To avoid any future confrontation these issues have to be addressed. So far as politics is concerned, tribal communities are not showing any sign of resentment and dissatisfaction but have started making their presence felt in at least at the state level politics. Tribal communities of Himachal Pradesh are vigilant and are aware about their rights as is indicated by the participation level. Thus, so far as tribal politics of Himachal is concerned, it is showing signs of mature political settings.

REFERENCES

Government of Himachal Pradesh. (2019). *Draft annual sub-plan: 2018–2019*. Shimla: Tribal Development Department.

Kapila, K. (2008). The measure of a tribe: the cultural politics of constitutional reclassification in North India. *Journal of the Royal Anthropological Institute, 4*(1), 117–134.

Negi, T. S. (1972). The tribal situation in Himachal Pradesh: Some socio-economic considerations. In K. S. Singh (Ed.), *The Tribal Situation in India* (pp. 141–157). Shimla: Indian Institute of Advanced Study.

Negi, T. S. (1976). *Scheduled tribes of Himachal Pradesh: A profile*. Meerut: Raj Printers.

Gujjars and Tribal Politics in Jammu and Kashmir

Subeno Kithan

INTRODUCTION

In the state of Jammu and Kashmir, the Gujjars find themselves in an interesting juxtaposition of unique history and tradition; their sociopolitical interests and their participation in the state.[1] Gujjars are recognized as the Scheduled Tribes (STs) in Jammu and Kashmir since 1991.[2] This enables them to have a social and political identity for availing state's benefits. They have not been indifferent to the political affairs of the state, even though most of them still abide by their traditional practices of cattle rearing and seasonal migration along high-altitude ranges. As much as the various issues of pastoral lifestyle and sedentarization matter to them, they are equally concerned about the conflict happening in the state border areas or matters related to elections, political

parties and also the government that comes to power. They are vocal about their role in state politics and also about their participation as a community to bring a collective voice for their socio-economic upliftment.

The abrogation of Article 370,[3] which entitles special status to the state of Jammu and Kashmir, came with a surprise for the residents of the state and evoked mixed responses from all sections of society. Particularly in the Kashmir Valley, the recent move by the central government has been seen as draconian and evoked fear and feeling of violation of the rights of the residents of the state. What is at stake for the Gujjars in Jammu and Kashmir who form the third highest population in the state? Various media reports inform that the reactions of Gujjars by and large have been positive in welcoming the

---

[1] The data presented in this chapter come from ethnographic fieldwork that was carried out between 2009 and 2011 in Jammu and Kashmir as part of the PhD dissertation work, as well as subsequent interaction with the community through telephonic conversation till 2018.

[2] The Constitution (Scheduled Tribes) Order (Amendment) Ordinance, 1991. Retrieved from https://tribal.nic.in/DivisionsFiles/clm/17.pdf

[3] Article 370 confers maximum autonomy to Kashmir, which assured the state all benefits of independent Kashmir without sacrificing the advantages of being part of the larger Indian federation (Sathe, 1990, p. 932).

government's decision to remove the special status of Jammu and Kashmir under Article 370A (Sahli, 2019). However, the question is how such a step is going to engage the most vulnerable within the community, especially those who are still engaged in the pastoral nomadic traditions.

Gujjars have been able to woo political parties as an important vote bank because of their large population; however, there is discontent among them with regard to their political representation in state politics. It is also their unique history as an ethnic group with a pastoral nomadic tradition whose origin is traced beyond the subcontinent, which makes them distinct from other communities in the state.[4] In this chapter, I argue that the ST status allows Gujjars in Jammu and Kashmir to occupy a strategic political position that is at odds with their social and demographic position within the state. Many other smaller communities in the state are perturbed when it comes to Gujjars' participation and opportunities when compared to theirs. For the Gujjars, their ST status provided economic privileges but had limitations, as many are not able to access privileges due to illiteracy, poverty, internal divisions based on sociocultural and economic differences. The aspirations of individual strata within the community are different. These individual strata and groups are hardly the concern for the state that sees the community as a homogeneous entity. The other important problem emanating from outside their community is the growing animosity from the dominant local population with regard to the sharing of resources in the form of grazing lands and the migratory routes they undertake during their seasonal migration. The apathy by government officials, forest departments and forest policy has posed numerous challenges for the community (Rao, 2002, p. 77; Rawat, 1993, p. 640). The chapter will

also help in understanding the nexus between poor policy and governance around pastoralism, the nexus between cultural practices and economic aspects of group unity and the nexus between elite men and politics of the common Gujjars.

SOCIAL HISTORY OF THE GUJJARS IN JAMMU AND KASHMIR

The region administered by India is made up of three parts: Jammu in the south consists of plains and hills, which include the Pir Panjal range, the Kashmir Valley in the north with an average altitude of 2,000 m between the Pir Panjal and the great Himalayas and the high mountain area of Ladakh situated in the east and north of the Kashmir Valley (Sōkefeld, 2013, p. 90). The Jammu region has been divided into 10 districts: Kathua, Jammu, Samba, Udhampur, Reasi, Rajouri, Poonch, Doda, Ramban and Kishtwar, and the Kashmir Valley has another 10 districts, namely Anantnag, Kulgam, Pulwama, Shopian, Budgam, Srinagar, Ganderbal, Bandipora, Baramulla and Kupwara. In Ladakh region, there are only two districts, namely Kargil and Leh. Kashmiris, Dards, Hanjis, Gujjars, Dogras, Chibalis, Paharis, Rhotas, Gaddis and Sikhs constitute the major communities in Jammu and Kashmir. These groups are found in different parts. For example, Kashmiris are mainly concentrated in the Valley bottom; Dards occupy the valley of Gurez; Hanjis are confined to the water bodies of Kashmir; Gujjars and Bakarwals live and oscillate in the Kandi areas of Jammu; Dogras occupy the outskirts of the Punjab plain, while Chibalis and Paharis live between Chenab and Jhelum rivers. Moreover, there are numerous small ethnic groups, such as Rhotas, Gaddis and

---

[4] Gujjars are an ethnic group found scattered across southern Asia, ranging from the far west as central Afghanistan and across large areas of Pakistan to almost the whole of northern India (Casimir & Rao, 1982; Marsden, 2005; Rose & Howell, 1968; Sharma, 2019; Turner, 1992; Tyagi, 2009).

Sikhs, which have a significant concentration in isolated pockets of the state (Husain, 1998; Kaul, 1963; Warikoo, 2000). Thus, Jammu and Kashmir is extremely diverse regarding culture, language, religion, ethnicity and similar other factors. It is characterized more by differences than by unity as a region. Muslims predominate in the valley and there is a significant number of Hindus and Sikhs who have traditionally lived in Jammu region and the valley, while, in addition, a small number of Buddhists live in Ladakh (Schofield, 1997). Jammu region has the majority of the population consisting of Dogras and Punjabis.

Although Gujjars are the third largest in population, they are among the least educated and most neglected communities in Jammu and Kashmir. It was only in 1991 that the president of India issued an ordinance whereby the Gujjars and Bakarwals were included in the list of STs with respect to Jammu and Kashmir. They were notified as the ST vide the Constitution (Scheduled Tribes) Order (Amendment) Act, 1991, while the Gujjars in Rajasthan, Haryana and Madhya Pradesh are still under the Other Backward Classes (OBCs).[5] The Gujjars in Rajasthan are still demanding ST status from their current higher OBC status. Most of the Muslim Gujjars are listed as one of India's STs that inhabit Himachal Pradesh and Jammu and Kashmir (Singh, 1991). However, even after having ST status, the reality of the Gujjar Bakarwals of Jammu and Kashmir is grim with a lack of employment opportunities and a better lifestyle (Shoukat, 1999). The move by other communities in the region for the demand for ST status, like the Paharis, is seen as a threat to their already marginalized position in the political, administrative and other institutional structures of the state (Warikoo, 2000).

According to Census 2011, the ST population of Jammu and Kashmir is 11.9 per cent, which is 1,493,299.[6] It consists of Baltis, Beda, Bot/Boto, Brokpa/Drokpa, Dard, Shin, Changpa, Gaddi, Garra, Gujjar, Mon, Purigpa and Sippi. In the census, Gujjar and Bakarwal are separately enumerated with a total population of 980,654 and 113,198, respectively. Gujjars constitute 7.81 per cent of the total population of the state of Jammu and Kashmir and 65.67 per cent of the total tribal population of the state. Bakarwals constitute 7.58 per cent of the total tribal population of the state. In India, they are mostly found in parts of Jammu and Kashmir, Gujarat, Rajasthan, Himachal Pradesh, Haryana and Uttar Pradesh. In Jammu and Kashmir, they are scattered in different parts of the state, such as Samba, Rajouri, Udhampur, Poonch, Uri, Ganderbal, Anantnag, Daksum, Naranag and the Kandi areas. Gujjars internally may be divided into three subcategories on the basis of the animal they rear and the livelihood they engage in (Bisht & Bankoti, 2004; Kithan, 2015; Sofi, 2013). They are the Dodhi Gujjar, also known as Banihara Gujjar (those who rear buffaloes); the Bakarwal (those who rear sheep and goats) and the Desi/Muquami Gujjars (those who have become sedentary and engage in agriculture or other jobs). Due to various factors, such as pasture scarcity, children's education and availing health services, they are slowly taking up sedentary lifestyle. Also, the border conflict and restrictions imposed by security forces and threats by militants are impacting their mobile tradition (Sofi, 2013, p. 65). Many Dodhi Gujjars and Bakarwals still undertake seasonal migration and are known as *khana-badosh*.[7] Thus, the term 'Gujjar' is inclusive of all these subcategories. Also, they are divided

---

[5] Before that, the Gujjars and Bakarwals, who constitute a major portion of the STs in Jammu and Kashmir, were already getting reservation in services as well as professional institutions under notification no. 37-GR of 1970, dated 28 April 1970, under the caption 'Weak and Under Privileged Classes' (Bhushan, 1999).

[6] Retrieved from http://tribalaffairs.jk.gov.in/StPopu.pdf

[7] The term 'Khanabadosh', which is used as the prefix to Gujjar or Bakarwal, originally refers to nomads or people on the move. According to Khatana (1992, p. 23), even the Nomadic Tribes Report has highlighted the distinct features of the Indian Khanabadosh (wandering tribes). Raghaviah (1968, p. 154) also refers to Indian nomads as

on the basis of region: Jammu, Poonch-Rajouri, Kashmir Valley or by *zat* or clan name. They would often say, 'we are Poonchi Gujjars' or 'we are Baderwahi Gujjars.'

Semi-nomadic Gujjars and Bakarwals may be further divided by historical regional links. Altogether, there may be a matrix of these and other factors both linking and disassociating them one from another. Originally, the Gujjars and Bakarwals of Central Asian origin were one tribe. With the passage of time, the division of labour resulted in the Bakarwals taking up the rearing of sheep and goats, and becoming nomads in search of fodder for their herds, while the rest, like the Gujjars, slowly became sedentary, took up cultivation of land wherever they could find it vacant (Qaisar, 1995, p. 8).[8] The difference between the Gujjars and the Bakarwals is the vocational pursuits that happened due to a different turn of events in the course of history. Otherwise, their language and the *gotras-zat* classification are the same.[9] They often say, *Hum Gujjar zat hein* (we belong to Gujjar jat) or *Hum Bakarwal zat hein* (we belong to Bakarwal jat). Here, the word *zat/jat* is used to describe a coherent social group—the Gujjars as opposed to the Dogras or any other Hindu caste. The term *jat* itself is a complicated one derived from the word *jati*, an endogamous unit that has a much more broader meaning.[10] The main function of the *zat* distinction is in the regulation

of marriage as well as other economic and migratory transactions. They also tend to use the term *zat* interchangeably with *gotra*. But for clarity, it may be said that the *zat* is divided into several *gotras*.

There are more than 30 *gotras* among the Gujjars and Bakarwals, and they share similar *gotra* names. Some of them which are commonly found among the Gujjars and Bakarwals in Jammu and Kashmir are Poswal, Char, Bajran, Chechi, Khatana, Kasana, Baniya, Thikriya, Lodha, etc. Generally, *gotra* refers to people belonging to the same ancestor, household or related by blood. Each *gotra* is a main kinship group among the Gujjars. The principal function of a *gotra* is a corporate body with reference to herding and is formed when a group of *deras* come together, which helps in efficiently grazing and caring of cattle (Sashi, 1994, p. 32). The *deras* are also referred to as household (Warikoo, 2000, p. 181). Four to five *deras* moving together form a *kafila* (Kithan, 2015, p. 304). The term *kumba* is also used to denote a collection of numerous clear or extended families descended from one living man (Rao, 1995, p. 152).

Gujjars and Bakarwals speak Gojri and also value Arabic education for their children. Among the Dodhi Gujjars, most of the children read and write Arabic.[11] They also understand Urdu and Hindi to some extent,

---

khanabadosh which, according to him, is a common term used in north-western India, referring to a group of people who are generally shy and not ambitious, have a mobile lifestyle and travel on familiar paths with their kin groups. There are some who hunt and collect food, while some others graze their cattle or sell petty artefacts, etc.

[8] Information on the origin of the Gujjars is debated, as some consider them to be of foreign origin, with possible connection with the Huns (Smith, 1914, p. 32), while some others view them as Aboriginals having close association with the Ahirs and the Jats of northern India (Ibbetson, 1882, pp. 6–7). Indian historians such as Bhandarkar (1989) and Munshi (1955) have been critical of such postulations.

[9] The classification of Gujjars is also done on the basis of their social organization, like *zat* (jat) division. These are Desi, Dodhi and Bakarwal. It refers to a unit of social organization between the Gujjars and the Bakarwals (Rao, 1988, pp. 195–227).

[10] According to Ghurye (1969, p. 176), the word *jati* is a specialized one to denote caste, which is a group the membership of which is acquired by birth, etymologically meaning 'something into which one is born'. It is occasionally used by good ancient authorities as equivalent to *varna*.

[11] It is a part of their religious training which begins early. Also, for the Gujjars and the Bakarwals, Arabic is considered as the heavenly language since the Quran was revealed in Arabic to the Prophet Muhammad.

and they can converse with outsiders using it. They somehow manage to speak Urdu, as it is the official language of the state of Jammu and Kashmir. In terms of the Urdu literacy tradition, they are unable to educate themselves with the Urdu language medium. Yet, in fact, it may be observed that Gujjars tend to excel far above the Kashmiris in terms of functional capacity in the Urdu language. Gujjars tend to be conversant in Urdu and Kashmiri, as well as in other languages, where they undertake seasonal migration, but sedentary Kashmiris in remote villages tend to struggle more with Urdu unless they have managed to attain higher levels of education. Also, schools in Gujjar areas do not generally function as faithfully or skilfully as those in the more affluent Kashmiri areas. English is still considered to be a language of the *angrez* (English foreigners). Most of the Gujjar children in the towns in Jammu attend English medium schools, but they tend to do well more in Urdu than the former subject.

Their pastoral semi-nomadic tradition, adherence to Islam, *zat* classification, distinct language, that is, Gojri and a sense of shared history make them all 'Gujjar' compared to 'Kashmiri', 'Dogra' or any other Indian. In this regard, the total population of Gujjars, which is inclusive of entire subgroups stands at 1,093,852.

TRADITIONAL FORM OF POLITICAL AUTHORITY

Traditionally, in tribal societies, political systems involve an acute struggle for power and prestige that was fought along the lines of territorial and genealogical cleavages. It was not between differently endowed economic groups (Gluckman, 2012, p. 82). The majority of pastoral groups in the world are patrilineal and organized around descent groups (Bhasin, 2011, p. 161). Gujjars are divided into several *gotra* which are equivalent to the clan. Traditionally, each clan has its own *mukkadam* (chief/leader) and a council known as *zirga* (also referred to as panchayat). Generally, disputes over stealing cattle or encroachment over grazing lands are taken care of by *zirga*. While the *mukkadam* controls the clan and looks after its needs, the *zirga* adjudicates and administers justice in civil and criminal cases to which the members of the clan are parties.[12] Gujjars are also part of *birādari*, which is a 'corporate group' and generally refers to a larger group of people who are consanguinally and affinally related (Rao, 2011, p. 64). We find social solidarity being expressed when the members of *birādari* come together on different life cycle rituals. The *birādari* are generally relatives related by the male line or the same caste names and are scattered in different parts of the state. When it comes to the influential men politically, the lumberdar[13] has an important influence. He plays a significant role in keeping the community together (Rao, 1995, p. 152). Such traditional form of authority still plays an important part in the decision-making process in the community, which needs to be consulted even for larger decisions relating to their participation and representation in state politics.

A lot of things have changed in traditional political systems that were least interested in gaining power or having any economic interest.

[12] There are approximately 500 sub-castes or *gotras* within the Gujjars (Tyagi, 2009, p. 241). The earliest reference of the *gotra* of the Gujjar was mentioned in the Sanskrit-literary endeavours, Samskarakaustubha (18th century), which is said to be 1,178 in number, most of which are territorial in origin (Ghurye, 1969, p. 232). The word *gotra* is actually connected to the Hindu social system of social classification on the basis of some mythical ancestor or names of the early places where they have settled or the names of their founders.
[13] Influential men in the community who have charisma were appointed traditionally as lumberdars. In North India, under the colonial regime, lumberdar is referred to a man who is a representative of smaller landholders, selected to hold responsibility for law and order within their respective groupings (Rao, 1995, p. 152).

Contemporary political authority consists of economically wealthy and powerful men who exert their influence over the community. Although *birādari* exists, political decisions are also made under the influence of men who have good economic and political influence. There is a lack of one voice and stable leadership to represent the entire community. Gujjar leaders who are elected achieve a political mileage for themselves as the representative of the community at large; however, they have not been able to successfully unite the community or adopt a common approach for the welfare of the people. Despite the fact that they represent the third largest community in Jammu and Kashmir after the Kashmiris and the Dogras, they still lack 'co-ordinated, constructive and objective-oriented political organization' (Chowdhary, 2001, pp. 21–22). This is a big hurdle for the community that makes their participation in the larger political arena of the state challenging.

POLITICAL MILIEU AND PARTICIPATION

Ever since India achieved independence, Jammu and Kashmir has been in a state of political turmoil and uneasiness owing to conflicts and violence experienced by civilians as well as terrorists and armed security forces. The different communities living in the state have experienced conflict in one way or another, while trying to keep intact their distinct identities and political participation. Since the election of 1983, the contemporary political situation in Jammu and Kashmir is revealed by the politics of the state. Electoral politics in Jammu and Kashmir functions differently in their geographical locations. While in Jammu, separatists have been a nuisance

creating disturbances for the proper conduct of elections leading to less voter turnouts, in the latter case, politics is quite vibrant and competitive. The Jammu region is heavily divided on the lines of class, ethnicity and religious background, that is, between the urban Hindu-dominated districts of Jammu and Kathua (and partially Udhampur) and the backward Muslim-dominated districts of Poonch, Rajouri and Doda. Further, it is divided on the lines of caste and tribe (Gujjars and Paharis) ethnic divisions (Chowdhary & Rao, 2003, 2004). Islam is practised by about 68.31 per cent of the population of the state and is the majority religion in 17 out of 22 districts of Jammu and Kashmir. Hindus form about 28.44 per cent of the population (followed majorly in 4 out of 22 districts), Buddhist about 0.90 per cent, Sikhs about 1.87 per cent, a few Christians about 0.29 per cent, Jain about 0.02 per cent and other religions about 0.01 per cent.[14] Around 99.32 per cent of the population of Gujjar and 98.66 per cent of Bakarwal in Jammu and Kashmir follow Islam.[15]

Religion is generally regarded as the binding force for adherents of the same faith and could influence gaining political solidarity; however, in Jammu and Kashmir, ethnicity plays a very important role in politics. Muslim communities are divided on both sectarian and cultural lines, Sunnis and Shias; Gujjars who, though are Sunni, have their own cultural and linguistic identity, but whose aspirations are different from those of mainstream Kashmiri Muslims (Engineer, 2000, p. 2360). In the case of Gujjars, their ethnic identity comes first, rather than their religious identity. The Muslim Gujjars are facing two simultaneous identities: Muslim consciousness and Gujjar consciousness (Rao, 1995, p. 163). Also, the Pahari Muslims[16] are asking for a separate identity and recognition, like

---

[14] Retrieved from https://www.census2011.co.in/data/religion/state/1-jammu-and-kashmir.html

[15] Retrieved from https://www.cpsindia.org/dl/Blogs/Blog%2033-ST-JK-HP.pdf

[16] They are regarded as an ethnic community speaking Pahari language. They are mostly found in the Pir Panjal region (Rajouri and Poonch districts) of Jammu province and some areas in Baramulla, Kupwara, Bandipora,

that of the Gujjars, whom they feel have got more attention than them, despite being recommended, along with other communities by the government of Jammu and Kashmir vide cabinet decision 159 of 1989 (Chowdhary & Rao, 2004, p. 5455; Shah & Bukhari, 2016, p. 2). The Kashmiri Muslim population are regarded as the privileged group when it comes to access to better socio-economic opportunities by the Gujjars and Bakarwals.

Gujjars' political stand as a community has been strong right from the very beginning of the formation of the state (Shabaz, 2015, p. 588). Gujjars and Bakarwals show a very strong hint of patriotism. They often boast of their involvement in helping the Indian Army during militancy operations and the Indo-Pakistan wars. They were troubled and harmed by militants in the Kashmir Valley. They often reiterate that being a Muslim does not make them a supporter of Pakistan in any way, and that they are devoted to India. When the Indian cricket team played cricket with the Pakistan team, an elderly Gujjar from Rakh Baroti, a Gujjar settlement in Samba district, remarked, 'I am an Indian first than a Muslim...I live and eat in Indian soil and so I will support India unquestionably.' An elderly Bakarwal from Kashmir valley remarks:

> From the beginning, we know that it is God above who provides and no one else. In this world today, people respect those who have power. We are poor and illiterate, but we are not dishonest. We just eat dry bread. Our lifestyle is simple. We may be backward due to our illiteracy, but we are good at our religion and our tribe. Our religion is right, and we are faithful to our tribe.

We find that the Gujjars stress on their *quom* (group/tribe), their *mazhab* (religion) and their condition of simple and hard life, and they value it and are proud of it. They are sensitive about several issues pertaining to their daily struggles, dignity of labour, lifestyle and religion.

One of the demands of the Gujjars has been the proper representation in the state politics along with improving their standard of living and other socio-economic privileges. The lack of adequate representation in the Lok Sabha or the state assembly for the STs in Jammu and Kashmir is also responsible for the lack of development of the communities, including the Gujjar Bakarwals too (Shabaz, 2015, p. 588). Gujjars are considered to be backward even after having ST status since 1991, and their political representation has been miniscule, and they have not received their share of the assembly seats. They, however, constitute an important vote bank for political parties in the state of Jammu and Kashmir. Javaid Rahi, a prominent Gujjar scholar, claimed that there are around 5 lakh votes of the Gujjar Bakarwal communities in Jammu-Poonch seat, while in Udhampur-Doda seat the estimated votes are about 3 lakhs (Sharma, 2019). They often complain that politicians come with big promises during election time, which remain unfulfilled. They feel betrayed as the promises are not fulfilled. Somewhere in this historical depth in the alienation of the region (Dole, 1990, p. 972) is also the alienation of many smaller communities. Their issues and political participation are sidelined, especially by Kashmiri Muslims, who constitute the majority population in the Kashmir region, receiving the maximum attention, while other non-Kashmiri-speaking populations have often been sidelined (Puri, 2001, p. 72). Smaller communities like the Paharis claim that they have been neglected and that Gujjars have been getting more attention.

Electoral politics in Jammu and Kashmir on the lines of communal polarization cannot be sustained for long time due to its mosaic of religious, caste, tribal and linguistic groups and identities (Chowdhary & Rao, 2004, p. 5455). The fact is that, within each category, there are layers of identities and aspirations that make the entire issue complicated.

---

some parts of Shopian and Budgam, which are in Kashmir province (Shah & Bukhari, 2016, p. 5).

Gujjars are labelled under the ST category for claiming state benefits and that does solve the problem of their political representation and participation. Even in the case of their political participation, though political parties try to reach out to them with unifying slogans, the fact is that they are internally segmented. The Gujjars, though referred to as a homogeneous group, are deeply entrenched in divisions within, with multiple voices and aspirations. The *khanabadosh* Dodhi Gujjars who follow a distinct lifestyle, depending on the buffaloes for their subsistence, would always like to represent themselves as distinct from the Bakarwal and the Desi Gujjars. Bakarwal refers to those who rear sheep and goats, and are also mobile pastoralists generally moving at higher altitudes along the Himalayan slopes in search of better pastures for their sheep and goats. They trace their origin from the Kaghan Valley which is in Pakistan (Casimir & Rao, 1985, p. 222). They are also the Bakarwals who are *khanabadosh*, where many are continuing with the tradition of *radari* or the seasonal movement. According to Rao (2011), official documents presented them as an ethnic group in 1912, which may be local—those who have migrated from the border and stayed in the country for a generation or a foreigner—those considered to be undesirable new migrants (Rao, 2011, p. 59). They are internally economically stratified in terms of possession of herds belonging to a family on the basis of which they are classified as 'very poor (*lachar*), poor (*miskin*), medium (*guzarwalo*), rich (*maldar*) and very rich (*moto*)' (Rao, 1995, p. 150). In these internal divisions and distinctions within the Gujjars, who follow the same faith and also tradition, political mobilization becomes challenging.

There are challenges in regard to their proper representation and participation in the general election programmes with the hurdles of seasonal migration. Classification and enumeration of nomadic communities has been problematic, as their names could not be properly enumerated in the list of voters. The government blames it to their seasonal migration to various parts of the state, which makes it impossible to enumerate properly and so they are not able to adequately look into their grievances. The 2011 census has been rejected by most of the Gujjars, stating that they were not adequately covered within the census. As a result, there has been a displeasure over the entire issue and a few organizations, like the Tribal Research and Cultural Foundation, Jammu, have suggested for conducting a 'special census' on them (*Business Standard*, 2013).

Also, there are a few elite or dominant men who represent the voice of the community; they are part of a wider network that monopolizes the scarce economic resources with their involvement beyond the state (Rao, 1995, p. 13). In transhumant societies, the basis of local-level leadership or prestige depends on 'the charismatic personality, mediation ability and social work attitude' (Bhasin, 2011, p. 151). This is what we see among the Gujjars, too, where prominent Gujjar political and spiritual leaders take the lead role in representing the community during the elections. They are among the wealthy and affluent segments, and they actively take part in state politics. They have a certain charisma, religiously inclined and vocal, as a result of which they have been able to attract the participation and support of the larger community. The mobilization of the voters during the election is done through the religious heads as well as the elders of the community, while the common Gujjars seem to be voiceless. Tribal politics among the Gujjars is dominated by a few powerful men whose influence has been far-reaching and the entire community follows them.[17] Also, since

---

[17] It is a known fact that prominent Gujjar political leaders are Mian Bashir Ahmed and his son Mian Altaf Ahmed, who have represented the Gujjars in the state legislative assembly. Other upcoming Gujjar leaders are also playing an important role in representing the community. Many of them are from a wealthy and well-connected family and are likely to have probable influence to powerful politicians (IANS, 2014).

the 1970s, various political parties have tried to woo this community with pasture lands during migration, because with their help they can win elections. However, the favour did not continue for long as there were bureaucratic and political tussles in which pastoral nomads were caught in between (Rao, 2002, p. 84). They do not have any direct say in any affair of the state and become the puppet in the political game.

INTERNAL CONSTRAINTS AND RESOURCE STRUGGLES

Most of the nomadic Gujjars in due course of time have adapted to settled life. With scarcity of land and resources, high expenses of transportation during their seasonal migration, and also the need to avail themselves with other opportunities such as education, security, health and family welfare, they have joined the mainstream population living a settled life. They no longer undertake seasonal migration. They are the Desi Gujjars, meaning those who own lands. They also attribute their sedentary lifestyle because of the efforts of the state government. They are employed most often in white- and blue-collar jobs, such as in government offices and also in private institutions, as workers in shops, hotels and other private establishments. They still keep few buffaloes for their use as well as for generating additional income. Some of their family members or relatives, however, still undertake seasonal migration. Most Desi Gujjars have no recollection of their ancestral heritage of nomadic life and are contented in their present state. But they have their own subtle prejudices against the semi-nomadic Gujjars. They dislike their hard tedious life, their poor economic condition, also for being unclean and illiterate. This shows the socio-economic stratification of the community.

Internally, Gujjars and Bakarwals also have bias towards each other, especially in terms of their social and cultural practices. Bakarwals consider themselves as genuine adherents of Islam, and they also handle their daily affairs and family life well. They admit being highly protective of their children, especially their daughters, whom they do not send out of their homes without properly covering their heads and with a female companion. They are also strict adherents to the pir (saint) reverence and visit the shrines (*dargah*) of prominent Muslim pirs and offer them prayers. The Dodhi Gujjars are perceived as liberal in their accountability towards their family and religion by the Bakarwals. For instance, they dislike the latter for being lenient towards women, as there are a lot of Dodhi Gujjar women who smoke bidis (locally made cigars) and mingle with men more often. They often allege that their daughters are allowed to sell milk alone in the market and without proper veiling, which they feel is not in accordance with the Quranic law. On the other side, a lot of Dodhi Gujjars see distinction in terms of the reverence of saint worship by the Bakarwals. Many Dodhi Gujjars who claim themselves to be Wahhabi[18] do not like the idea of a mediator to reach out to God, which is highly contested among them. Most Gujjars are more or less influenced by the superstitions about spirits and myths related to the spiritual world. They believe in the power of *tawiz* (amulets), *mantras* (mystical chants) and they believe that *phook marna* (blowing of breath) by a living pir can heal a sick person or an animal. All these perceptions, based on cultural practices and religious views, can be a threat to the unity of the group. Variations in religious schools of thought and sociocultural practices create conflicts and tensions within the group.

---

[18] Wahhabi is referred as a sect or branch of Islam, whose origin is in Saudi Arabia and it adheres to strict interpretation of the Quran and the Hadith and discourages cult of saints and shrines in Muslim world.

There are organizations in which they have taken the lead to give a common platform and represent a collective voice for the Gujjars, such as the Gujjar United Front and the Bhartiya Gurjar Mahasabha. They started due to the pressure that Gujjars had been facing with their participation in a larger society.[19] Such organizations act as mouthpieces for the community though, on the other hand, many common Gujjars are not aware about such organizations. They engage in the social, political and economic issues of the community and are often critical about the development activities of the government with regard to the community. Other than that, institutions like the Gurjar Desh Charitable Trust (GDCT) and the establishment of school for Gujjar children in the Jammu Tawi area also benefit the community. The GDCT is a nongovernmental organization established in 1992 with a vision to promote the socio-economic, cultural as well as educational interests of the community by a group of intellectuals from the community (Lal, 2008, p. 5). The initiative was taken to emancipate the community from the morass of poverty, illiteracy and exploitation. The trust has also set up a school named K. B. Public School, which also provides free education to students from economically poor communities. Besides this, a library on Gujjars is also set up by the trust. Apart from this, the trust conducts various cultural programmes, conducts orientation for various employment schemes that can help Gujjars, or other economic assistance to the needy, especially from the community. However, such platforms are also not accessible for many, as those who have settled down in the city can avail the benefits than those who are still in their transhumance tradition. Schools are accessible for Desi Gujjar children and children from nearby towns, while most of the Dodhi and Bakarwal Gujjars who undertake seasonal migration hardly have access to such benefits

and opportunities. Even though a few powerful individuals or leaders of the community can give a general opinion about the group, however, experiences and aspirations of each family or *dera* can be different. Also, the aspirations are also mixed, though the commonality can be in terms of wanting a decent life and security for themselves and their families. The obvious segmentation of their communities into Dodhi, Bakarwal and Desi Gujjars is already part of the social organization of the community. So when it comes to politically addressing the aspirations of the Gujjars, it is a big challenge.

The other important problem emanating from outside their communities is about the growing animosity from the dominant local population with regard to the sharing of resources in the form of grazing lands and migratory routes they undertake during their seasonal migration. The apathy by government officials, forest departments and forest policy has been posing numerous challenges for the community (Rao, 2002, p. 77; Rawat, 1993, p. 640). Degradation of pasture lands due to heavy grazing and soil erosion is becoming common in alpine areas where the Gujjars move during their seasonal migration (Casimir & Rao, 1985, p. 228). However, attributing the depletion of grazing lands only to mobile herds is also questionable, as it has little scientific evidence. Pastoralism is a rational and sustainable livelihood strategy (Morton, 2010, p. 7). Scholz and Salzman reveal that many nomadic cultures and societies have been able to successfully manage pasture lands using their own strategies and are highly focused on achieving specific production rules (cited in Bhasin, 2011, p. 153). Forest and grazing lands have been encroached by rural and semi-urban sedentary communities for the purpose of agriculture and habitation, along with government departments built for various facilities (Rao, 2002, p. 76). Their traditional

---

[19] Salzman (1967, p. 129) notes that 'indigenous organisation of politics is significantly influenced by the pressure which participation in a larger society puts upon a nomadic group.'

routes for migration (*rasto*) as well as their temporary camps they set up as shelters by the *kafila* during their seasonal migration are not accessible to them today due to encroachment of the areas. They often narrate that such problems were not there so much during their forefathers' time, but have become frequent in recent years. Conflicts over traditional grazing spaces and routes happen frequently between them and local people, which often lead to quarrels, theft of cattle and verbal abuse by the latter (Kithan, 2015, p. 307). The recent horrific incident of rape and murder of a young Gujjar girl in Rasana village reveals the harsh reality of their environment, the insecurity and also the vulnerability as they go about with their daily routines of life. The community desires a more secure future for itself and hope from the political leaders. From the periphery, it looks as though their semi-nomadic lifestyle is the reason for their lack of integration with the local community, which leads to their seclusion and thereby making them victims of hatred. However, it is not completely true, as they have also been interacting with the local population for decades with their milk selling activities, as well as with the sharing of other resources, such as providing grazing lands and migratory routes. There is a sense of accountability they have with the local resources, with their neighbours in their seasonal homes, with whom they can relate and stand up for if need arises. An elderly Gujjar from Samba district comments:

> If you go to a Hindu village regarding your research work, the Hindus will help you to the fullest, but Musalmans will not. They show more pity in the hearts of the Hindus than Musalmans whom they consider unsympathetic. A Hindu will never do such things. Maybe one in a hundred could do it, but in general the Hindus are better than the Musalmans.

PRESENT SOCIOPOLITICAL DILEMMAS

The abrogation of Article 370,[20] which entitles special status to the state of Jammu and Kashmir, evoked mixed responses among the Gujjars, as it will threaten not only the relationship of the state with the rest of the country but also the age-old migratory traditions of pastoral nomads in the region with regard to their land use (*PTI*, 2019). While for others within the community, such as the Gujjar United Front and the Bhartiya Gurjar Mahasabha, the step taken by the central government is a welcomed step as it has given a ray of hope to all for direct access to many benefits of the various welfare schemes provided to the STs in the state that they were denied of earlier (Om, 2014). Such claims give some hope to the community and new possibilities that can be generated for their overall welfare. However, few things need to be taken into consideration. First one is whether the entitlement to a special status with the new legislation will create threats to their existing strategies in terms of the issues of accessibility and sustainability of their livelihoods and grazing lands. Second is on the issue of being able to get adequate attention to their issues, which are to be done in accordance with the sensitivity to their cultural tradition and present aspirations. For the state, the tradition of pastoralism is the cause of their lack of development. However, scholars are of the view that poverty and vulnerability that pastoralists face are problems that originate outside the pastoral system (Morton, 2010, p. 7). For the Gujjars, their mobile lifestyle is their identity and gives them dignity and economic stability, besides recognition as a social group with a unique tradition (Kithan, 2015, p. 311). The move by the state to sedentarize pastoral nomads would be a reality, and alternative arrangements, like providing them with other modes of livelihood, will be on the cards. But in reality, how it would affect

---

[20] Article 370 confers maximum autonomy to Kashmir, which assured the state all the benefits of independent Kashmir without sacrificing the advantages of being part of the larger Indian federation (Sathe, 1990, p. 932).

the community is altogether a very important question. Kavoori (2007) in the case study of Gujjars in Rajasthan found that many Gujjars had little choice but to de-pastoralize. This is because of the lack of local resources and supportive institutions to keep buffaloes. When they shifted to buffalo keeping and small-scale agriculture, many of them lost the competitive advantages that go with a specialized niche. The Gujjars then are facing ecological and economic handicap. According to Kavoori, the collapse of cattle pastoralism lies at the heart of the Gujjar problem. This situation can be a warning for the possibility of such impairment, even among the Gujjars of Jammu and Kashmir.

A very important question is also regarding whether the availability of more political opportunities alone provides them scope for their holistic development. Many scholars on pastoral communities in Jammu and Kashmir reiterated the fact that they are backward, illiterate and also economically disadvantaged despite the ST status they had been accorded over the last decade (Shabaz, 2015, p. 592). What went wrong, and where did the policy interventions fail? Studies have revealed that Gujjar children are enrolled in primary schools more and only a few complete high school studies and a handful become graduates (Tufail, 2014, p. 29). This means that even if the reservation under ST status is in place, hardly few could take advantage of the benefit. Another hurdle which the community has to overcome is gender inclusivity in political participation. Even among men, disparity exists; however, when it comes to women's participation in political processes, which is not just about casting votes but also in decision-making in the traditional political milieu, they are highly marginalized. There is not a single woman member in a *zirga* and not a single woman candidate to represent the community in the state elections so far. They also do not show much interest due to the influence of a patriarchal mindset and the religious teachings that dictate their conduct and way of life. Women are generally confined mostly to household chores and child rearing and looking after the cattle, thus limiting their mobility and freedom of expression. Most Gujjar women express their desire to travel and learn about other places, people and things. It is men who take control of decision-making at various levels of their lives and rarely give them the opportunity to pursue their desires. Even in terms of educating their girl children, they are laid back and most of them hardly go beyond their high school level. Thus, there are not many educated girls in the community, especially those who are still undertaking seasonal migration. All of these aspects limit the participation of women in public space and in political participation.

CONCLUSION

Gujjars's distinct identity as part of the nomadic pastoral tradition and unique history set them apart from the rest of the tribal communities in the state of Jammu and Kashmir. Their ST status allows them to occupy a strategic political position that is at odds with their social and demographic position within the state. Although they are referred to as Gujjars, internally they are highly stratified in terms of their lifestyle (nomadic/semi-nomadic or settled), cultural practices and economic differences. This has created a huge challenge in raising a unified voice in addressing the community's aspiration for state's political participation and socio-economic engagements. Such differences are barely noticed by the state that sees the community as homogeneous in terms of their perspective on their socio-economic development. Semi-nomadic Gujjar issues are different from sedentary ones. For the former, it is more about the challenges with regard to resources, traditional grazing spaces, the conflict with the local population and their uncertainty of a good future. For the latter, it is about getting benefits in local jobs, looking up at the dominant communities and trying to be on par with them. There is an economic difference within them, as well as growing psychological and social alienation, a lack of apathy among them. The semi-nomadic Gujjars feel alienated in the social, economic and political engagements by the sedentary Gujjars and those who represent them on the political platforms. Their internal segmentation and lack of a collective voice are detrimental to their solidarity, which is essential for a proper political aspiration. Also, recognition of the aspirations of Gujjars—sedentary or semi-nomadic; wealthy or poor; men and women—is highly important.

It has also been observed that few elites monopolize the identity of the community for their own gain, and they do not really represent the aspirations of the common Gujjars from within, which is not going to be of any help. Common Gujjars hardly have a say in the decision-making process and their aspirations for their families, the *dera* and their pastoral tradition rarely get noticed. The different stakeholders within the community need to be involved to be able to understand how best they want themselves to be represented politically. More new participants from marginalized Gujjars/semi-nomadic ones, as well as women's representation, need to come forward for strengthening the community. Within the same community, there may be differences and inequalities; however, there can be collective aspirations as well (Moodie, 2015, p. 5). Collective aspirations become more prominent during elections and other instances such as social tensions over issues of grazing. For the Gujjars, collective aspirations get reflected mostly on the line of socio-economic development and community empowerment.

Since pastoral life is closely linked to their livelihoods, the ST label has certainly given them the opportunity to obtain certain economic and political benefits. However, it has created tension outside and inside the community. The problem outside the community

is the growing animosity that the community at large faces with the other non-ST communities that are also state minorities and feel neglected. Within the community, the benefits of ST status only benefit those who have access to it and more so those who are sedentary. This creates further socio-economic disparity among them. There is a need for equitable and efficient implementation if the existing policies need to be made for all-round inclusivity. Awareness about their rights in general should be generated from within. The engagement of pastoralists in providing specific knowledge about their own environments and livelihoods must be incorporated in policymaking (Morton, 2010, p. 8).

Various activities of pastoral nomadic communities are vanishing in the post-colonial state of modern times. The state insists on the loyalty of all persons dwelling within its territory, while for the tribe, its allegiance towards primary ties of kinship and patrilineal descent is important (Tapper, 2009, p. 37). The loyalty that the state demands of its citizens is to abide by the rules, the mandate and political participation in state electorate, which, however, overlooks other inherently vital characteristics of tribal life. For the former, expectations are impersonal, contractual and for achieving goals, while for the latter, aspirations are personal, natural and a way of life. If the ideals of the latter are compromised, it will surely impact the functioning of the state. The state looks at the issues of the community from a top-down approach, not realizing how inherently complex any community is with regard to its sociocultural dispositions. Assimilating with the local population and adapting with the rules of the state seems to be the only option left for them to survive as a group. Gujjars too fall under the pressure of adjusting with whatever is given by the state without much choice. Who cares about the aspirations of the individual or subgroup? Among nomads or semi-nomads, social and economic differentiation has increased with ownership of properties and an intensive interaction with multicultural communities outside their fold (Khazanov, 1984, p. 198). This is what has been happening since the Gujjars, who were traditionally nomadic, started to own property and lead sedentary lives, etc.

The abrogation of Article 370 has certainly generated a new hope for the community; however, the perspective about its prospects are also coming from the representatives of the Gujjar organizations that speak for the community. What about the view of the ordinary Gujjars on it and whether they will be consulted for various inputs into the new legislation for their welfare? The real impact of the new legislation is still a guesswork for many, and it is not clear as to how it is going to benefit or not benefit the community. For now, many Gujjars see this step as a liberation from the dominant Kashmiri hegemony over the different services in the state. Tribal politics in the state cannot be separated from its economic implications. Livelihood and social identity influence political participation. For now, this is what the Gujjars are looking forward to. They want better representation in the regional political scenario, security of livelihoods and a better lifestyle, without compromising their tradition of mobile pastoralism, their beliefs and practices that sustain who they are.

ACKNOWLEDGEMENTS

I am deeply indebted to Gujjar and Bakarwal informants of Sanasar, Jammu (Vijaypur), Udhampur, Reasi, Jindrah and Srinagar for their hospitality and their participation in making this research possible. I would also like to thank Professor N. Sudhakar Rao, Dr Jagannath Ambagudia and Dr Sanjay Barbora for their valuable comments and suggestions on this chapter.

REFERENCES

Bhandarkar, D. R. (1989). *Some aspects of ancient Indian culture*. New Delhi: Asian Educational Services.

Bhasin, V. (2011). Pastoralists of Himalayas. *Journal of Human Ecology, 33*(3), 147–177.

Bhushan, S. (1999). S.T status and adoption. *Awaz-E-Gurjar, 5*, 31.

Bisht, N. S, & Bankoti, T. S. (2004). *Encyclopaedic ethnography of Himalayan tribes* (vol. I). New Delhi: Global Vision Publishing House.

Business Standard. (2013). Gujjars file petition before tribal commission. Retrieved from https://www.business-standard.com/article/pti-stories/gujjars-file-petition-before-tribal-commission–113050500548_1.html

Casimir, M., & Rao, A. (1982). Mobile pastoralists of Jammu and Kashmir: A preliminary report. *Nomadic Peoples, 10*, 40–50.

Casimir, M., & Rao, A. (1985). Vertical control in the western Himalaya: Some notes on the pastoral ecology of the nomadic Bakarwal of Jammu and Kashmir. *Mountain Research and Development, 5*(3), 221–232.

Chowdhary, A. A. N. (2001). Gujjar leadership at the crossroads. *Awaz-e-Gurjar, 7*, 21–24.

Chowdhary, R., & Rao, V. N. (2003). Jammu and Kashmir: Political alienation, regional divergence and communal polarisation. *Journal of Indian School of Political Economy, 15*, 189–219.

Chowdhary, R. & Rao, V. N. (2004). Jammu and Kashmir: Electoral politics in a separatist context. *Economic & Political Weekly, 39*(51), 5449–5455.

Dole, N. Y. (1990). Kashmir: A deep-rooted alienation. *Economic & Political Weekly, 25*(18/19), 978–979.

Engineer, A. A. (2000). Kashmir: Can autonomy be a solution? *Economic & Political Weekly, 35*, 2359–2360.

Ghurye, G. S. (1969). *Caste and race in India*. Bombay: Popular Prakashan.

Gluckman, M. (2012). *Politics, law and ritual in tribal society*. Piscataway, NJ: Transaction Publishers.

Husain, M. (1998). *Geography of Jammu and Kashmir*. New Delhi: Rajesh Publication.

IANS. (2014). Will history repeat itself in J&K's Kangan? The Hindu, 9 November. Retrieved from https://www.thehindu.com/news/national/will-history-repeat-itself-in-jks-kangan/article6580477.ece

Ibbetson, D. (1882). *A glossary of the tribes and castes of North West Frontier province*. New Delhi: Nirmal Publishers and Distributers.

Kavoori, P. (2007). Reservation for Gujars: A pastoral perspective. *Economic & Political Weekly*, *42*(38), 3833–3835.

Khatana, R. P. (1992). *Tribal migration in Himalayan frontiers: Study of Gujar Bakarwal transhumance economy*. Haryana: Vintage Books.

Khazanov, A. M. (1984). *Nomads and the outside world (Julia Crookenden with Foreword from Ernest Geller, Trans)*. Cambridge: Cambridge University Press.

Kithan, S. (2015). Those pleasant green mountains: Memories of migration, place and the environment of a pastoral nomadic Gujjars of Jammu and Kashmir. *The Eastern Anthropologist*, *68*, 299–312.

Lal, B. (2008). Gurjar Desh Charitable Trust: 15 years of existence. *Awaz-e-Gurjar*, *14*, 5–7.

Marsden, M. (2005). *Living Islam-Muslim religious experience in Pakistan's north-west frontier*. New York, NY: Cambridge University Press.

Moodie, M. (2015). *We were adivasis: Aspiration in an Indian scheduled tribe*. Chicago, IL: University of Chicago Press.

Morton, J. (2010). Why should governmentality matter for the study of pastoral development? *Nomadic Peoples*, *14*(1), 6–30.

Munshi, K. M. (1955). *The glory that was Gurjar desa* (part 1). Bombay: Bharatiya Vidya Bhavan.

Om, H. (2014). Article 370 has shackled STs. *The Pioneer*, 6 January. Retrieved from https://www.dailypioneer.com/2014/columnists/article–370-has-shackled-sts.html

PTI. (2019). Gujjar leader bats for Article 370 and Article 35A. The Week, 24 February. Retrieved from https://www.theweek.in/wire-updates/national/2019/02/24/des25-jk-gujjar–35a.html

Puri. B. (2001). Major Identities of Jammu and Kashmir state. *India International Centre Quarterly*, *28*(3), 69–79.

Qaisar. (1995). Gujars in historical perspective. *Awaz-e-Gurjar*, *1*, 7–12.

Raghaviah, V. (1968). *Nomads*. New Delhi: Bharatiya Adimajai Sevak Sangh.

Rao, A. (1988). Levels and boundaries in native models: Social groupings among the Bakarwal of the western Himalayas. *Contributions to Indian Sociology*, *22*(1), 195–227.

Rao, A. (1995). From bondsman to middlemen: Hired Shepherds and pastoral politics. *Anthropos*, *90*(1–3), 149–167.

Rao, A. (2002). Pastoral nomads: The state and a national park: The case of Dachigam. *Nomadic Peoples*, *6*(2), 72–98.

Rao, A. (2011). The many sources of identity: An example of changing affiliations in rural Jammu and Kashmir. *Ethnic and Racial Studies*, *22*(1), 56–91.

Rawat, A. S. (1993). Deforestation and its impact on the Jammu Gujjars of sub-Himalayan tarai: A historical perspective. *Proceedings of the Indian History Congress*, 54, 631–640.

Rose, H. A., & Howell. E. B. (1968). *North-west frontier province*. Oxford: Horace Hart.

Sahli, P. (2019). Muslims in Jammu stand by govt in scrapping of Article 370, Gujjar Bakarwals celebrate move. *India Today*, 12 August. Retrieved from https://www.indiatoday.in/india/story/muslims-in-jammu-stand-by-govt-in-scrapping-of-article–370-gujjar-bakarwals-celebrate-move–1580171–2019–08–12

Salzman, P. C. (1967). Political organization among nomadic peoples. *American Philosophical Society*, *III*(2), 115–131.

Sashi, S. S. (1994). *Encyclopaedia of Indian tribes: Himachal Pradesh and northern highlands* (vol. 6). New Delhi: Anmol Publication.

Sathe, S. P. (1990). Article 370: Constitutional obligations and compulsions. *Economic & Political Weekly*, *25*(17), 932–933.

Schofield, V. (1997). *Kashmir in the crossfire*. London: I. B. Tauris.

Shabaz. (2015). Participation of Gujjar and Bakerwal in state politics: Problems and prospects. *Journal of Business Management and Social Sciences Research*, *4*(9), 587–594

Shah, M., & Bukhari, O. (2016). Pahari speaking community: Ethnic and linguistic identity in the state of Jammu and Kashmir and Pahari-Gujjar faultline. *Remarking*, *2*(12), 45–50.

Sharma, A. (2019). PDP eyes Gujjar Bakarwal votes in Jammu. *Tribune News Service*, 21 March. Retrieved from https://www.tribuneindia.com/news/jammu-kashmir/pdp-eyes-gujjar-bakerwal-votes-in-jammu/746376.html

Shoukat, J. (1999). Scheduled tribe: Deprived of its share in mass employment. *Awaz-E-Gurjar*, *5*, 4–5.

Singh, K. S. (1991). *The anthropological survey of India*. New Delhi: Government of India Publications.

Smith, V. A. (1914). *Early history of India*. Oxford: Clarendon Press.

Sofi, U. J. (2013). The sedentarization process of the transhumant Bakarwal tribals of Jammu and Kashmir. *IOSR Journal of Humanities and Social Sciences*, *11*(6), 63–67.

Sōkefeld, M. (2013). Jammu and Kashmir: Dispute and diversity. In P. Berger & F. Heidemann (Eds.), *The modern anthropology of India: Ethnography, themes and theory* (pp. 90–105). London: Routledge.

Tapper, R. (2009). *Tribe and state in Iran and Afghanistan: An update. Etudes Rurales, 184*(2), 33–46.

Tufail, M. (2014). Demography, social and cultural characteristics of the Gujjars and Bakarwals: A case study of Jammu and Kashmir. *IOSR Journal of Humanities and Social Sciences, 19*(1), 24–36.

Turner, D. H. (1992). We will always be Gujar: The politics of nomadism in northern Himachal Pradesh. *India International Center Quarterly, 19*, 251–263.

Tyagi, V. P. (2009). *Martial races of undivided India.* New Delhi: Gyan Publishing House.

Warikoo, K. (2000). Tribal Gujjars of Jammu and Kashmir. In K. Warikoo & Sujit Som (Eds.), *Gujjars of Jammu and Kashmir* (pp. 176–196). Bhopal: Indira Gandhi Rashtriya Manav Sangrahalaya.

17

Tribal Identity and Governance in State Politics of Jharkhand

Sujit Kumar

FRAMING THE PROBLEM

When faced with the question of analysing the nature of tribal politics, it is important to keep in mind certain distinct features that characterize the community. For example, the tribal population is mostly concentrated in the peninsular belt and north-eastern India, with a sparse and scattered population in other parts. The other proposition that is essential to remember is that tribal communities have not undergone a uniform process of political socialization, and the nature of their political structures, in general, has remained different across various regions. Accordingly, areas predominantly comprising tribal population are earmarked as the Fifth Schedule (peninsular India) and Sixth Schedule (north-eastern India), with provisions for recognizing their distinctiveness.

Guha (2007) argues that the tribal population, unlike the Scheduled Caste (SC) population, is concentrated in certain regions and hence does not enjoy the same political clout in national politics. Difference between the case of Dalits and Adivasis in explaining

their political advantage does not really serve any significant purpose. One can understand the equal marginalization, in some ways more Dalits than Adivasis, of both communities in Indian politics by simply asking how many Dalits and Adivasis are elected to the Lok Sabha from unreserved constituencies? One does not find any difference. Moreover, Guha's (2007) assertion may be true when one looks at national politics and general elections, but in states with a significant tribal population, such as Chhattisgarh (32%), Jharkhand (26%), Odisha (22%) and Madhya Pradesh (18%), the community can play a major role in state politics. Their significance, however, shall be contingent upon the nature of their political socialization and their ability to comprehend elections as a tool to access power. Jharkhand is one such state where the tribal community has shown better political inclusion with robust tribal politics. Broadly speaking, tribal politics depends on the presence of local political parties like Jharkhand Mukti Morcha (JMM) as well as resistance struggle revolving around their identity of whatsoever hybrid nature.

This chapter analyses the 'fault lines' in the project of discovering and asserting the common use of Adivasi *identity* as a tool of politics. It also explicates the myriad ways in which the Adivasi community expresses its political choice and the reasons behind it. In Jharkhand, it has been observed that the manner in which the political socialization of the Adivasi community has taken place is quite diverse. One can sense the influence of factors such as missionary education, rebellion against the British authorities, state jobs, resistance movements against neoliberal capitalism and interaction with religions determining their voting behaviour to a large extent. At present, the community stands at a crossroads where the well-wishers are searching for a reasonable approach of 'integration' in the mainstream as well as 'autonomy' in their political self-determination. Scholars like Shah (2007) have argued that even state elections are an opportunity for the community to claim their autonomy. But Kumar (2018) argues that the community's approach to state accommodation has remained selective and depends on factors such as education and class in determining their political behaviour. Moreover, a systematic 'detribalization of government'[1] is underway in Jharkhand. In continuation with this thesis, the chapter proposes that an attempt to organize Adivasi politics around the axis of Adivasi *identity* is enigmatic in nature and has to deal with 'fault lines' within the discourse. In addition, the Bharatiya Janata Party (BJP) government aims at creating a juridical discourse through anti-conversion law that seeks to divide the community along religious lines. However, a more proactive design of the government to delegitimize popular resistance movements can be associated with the rise of the 'police state'.[2]

The chapter is arranged into four sections. The first section analyses the identity politics as a dialectical process engaging the colonial and post-colonial state and its evolving consciousness and accommodation in an Adivasi society. The second section problematizes the understanding of Adivasi society by considering it on the parameters of civil and political society. The purpose is to assess the political movements and see whether they are part of post-civil society! The third section explains the phenomenon of 'detribalization of government' and its impending influence on the Adivasi people. The fourth section provides a view of the state response to popular resistance movements and the rise of the 'police state'. The chapter concludes by examining the prospects for a robust tribal politics in the state of Jharkhand.

ADIVASI AND THE 'IMAGINED STATE'

Systems approach, as articulated by scholars such as Talcott Parsons and Edward Shils in sociology, claimed that societies are not only bound through material and instrumental relations, thus blurring the locus of authority (Migdal, 2001, pp. 6–7). This assertion goes against the statist approach, which considers the power and autonomy of the state as central in defining the patterns of behaviour and stratification. Identifying a more robust approach to understand the state–society interface, Migdal (2001, p. 11) proposes the 'state-in-society' model that emphasizes upon 'the ongoing struggles among shifting coalitions over the rules for daily behaviour'. Migdal (2001, p. 11) states that

---

[1] Kumar (2018) argues that there is a systematic assault by the BJP government led by Raghubar Das against the protective legislations such as the Chotanagpur Tenancy Act (CNTA), 1908, and the Santhal Pargana Tenancy Act (SPTA), 1949, as well as the growing underrepresentation of tribals in the government.

[2] A police state largely employs intelligence agencies instead of the police for continued surveillance, interception and occasional burglary against people who challenge their views.

...no single, integrated set of rules, whether encoded in state law or sanctified as religious scriptures or enshrined as the rules of etiquette for daily behaviour, exists anywhere...the state-in-society model uses the conflict-laden interactions of multiple sets of formal and informal guideposts for how to behave that are promoted by different groupings in society.

Migdal (2001, p. 16) further argues that 'actual states are shaped by two elements, image and practice, and the two can be overlapping and reinforcing, or contradictory and mutually destructive.' While the state induces people to perceive its agencies as an integrated system that tends to act together to reinforce its image, practices such as *routinized performative acts* can actually deconstruct and batter the image of a coherent, controlling state (Migdal, 2001, p. 19). My attempt to capture the imagination of the state as held by the Adivasi community is informed by Migdal's 'state-in-society' approach and relies upon historical facts, cultural values and social myths that the community relies on to foment this image through contestation and adaptation.

The Adivasi community has a long history of interaction with the political authority today regarded as state. For our purpose, we explore the formulation of the image of the state during the colonial and post-colonial times. The process of image formation itself is complicated and can be regarded mostly as a dialectical process of synthesizing the alien concept of centralized and overarching political authority with the decentralized and lucid institutions of the Adivasis. The colonial state made its first mark as a revenue government in Adivasi society. This was met with resistance by the community and was put down militarily by the British. But the community continued to resist the British administration and intermittently broke into rebellion.

However, the administrative and missionary accounts of Adivasi society and culture led to new breakthroughs. The British administration now took several steps not only to recognize the customary political institutions of the Adivasis but also to redefine their role in the administration (Dasgupta, 2011; Sen, 2012).[3] This strategy, while fulfilling the purposes of revenue administration, still could not make a legitimate space for the colonial state in Adivasi life and was resisted continuously. If we look at the nature of the demands made by the *Sardari or Mulki Larai*,[4] the Kol rebellion and the Birsa Munda rebellion, it becomes clear that the Adivasis were reluctant to accept any mediating agency between them and their resources with which they shared not only material but also cultural relationship. As a result, special laws recognizing their land rights were introduced in the form of the CNTA, 1908. Another major bone of contention that remained largely unresolved until the enactment of the Forest Rights Act (FRA) of 2006 was community rights over forest resources. As a matter of final assessment, it can be said that the colonial government was imagined to be an alien institution to be met with hostility.

Even though politics of self-determination through the demand for Jharkhand became part of the struggle in the colonial era itself, it remained confined to mission-educated youth while remaining elusive for the community in general. Not surprisingly, the Adivasi community was still not able to come to terms with the notion of a modern state and preferred its autonomy. As a result, in post-independence India, the demand for statehood remained tumultuous and restricted to tribal elites who were already able to make inroads in mainstream politics by joining hands with national political parties like the Congress. The

[3] It is argued that the role of village headmen during the colonial times was revised to also include the collection of agricultural revenue to be paid to the state.
[4] *Sardari* or *Mulki Larai* basically refers to the resistance struggle organized by the customary Munda leaders of Chota Nagpur against the British collaborators (missionaries as well as officials) of the landlords during 1858–1895.

post-colonial developmental regime, however, enthused a new sense of resistance against the state, and the community responded through wide-ranging options, from striving to become vociferous in mainstream politics to joining the Naxalite movement to protect their livelihoods. Participation in state politics was mostly driven by the intention to reclaim their legal rights. Deprivation at the hands of the state was articulated under terms such as 'internal colonialism' and 'adverse inclusion'. The wider perception within the community was that the development of other regions was fuelled by their continued pauperization. The opportunities for their integration were also marked by their absorption in low-paid jobs provoking a sense of relative deprivation. While the factions seeking more political representation remained proactive in organizing popular movements against the exploitation of the community by outsiders,[5] the statist institutions were still suspected. This era can be defined as the 'reluctant and selective' adoption of the state.

The state in modern times is considered to be a means of political self-determination for the people and is believed to be constituted by them mutually through consensus as they agree upon some common objectives to be achieved and rights to be preserved. Individual privileges must be surrendered for collective benefit, and individual and group rights must be adjudged against the interests of the majority. A liberal state carries an additional burden of protecting even the group rights of minority communities, particularly their culture and language. In the post-liberalization phase, the battle lines have been redrawn as the community resistance is now targeted against market forces rather than the state. The creation of the Jharkhand state in 2000 is itself a post-liberalization phenomenon, and the state has been largely governed by pro-market forces. Recently, more aggressive privatization of resources has been pursued through state policy like 'momentum Jharkhand', inviting corporate investments in sectors such as mining and industry. It would not be an exaggeration to say that the state and market forces are perceived to be coterminous by the community. To some extent, the resistance against dispossession has lost its connection with regional political parties and is primarily organized by urban-educated Adivasi youth to reclaim community rights over resources. The vocabulary used in the grassroots movements has significantly shifted as they question the neoliberal developmental regime. However, a closer look at the anti-dispossession resistance movements reveals that some of the generic notions used for movements are contested. For example, Adivasi identity is a contested terrain and holds a different meaning for different Adivasi communities. Communities prefer to subscribe to their particular history and culture in the construction of identity as against their generic notion (Kumar, 2016).

Moreover, as against the perceived severity of the slogan, like *jan denge par jameen nahi denge* (we will lay down our lives but would not give up land), the movements engage in a more locally rationalized bargaining process serving the utility of the protesters (Kumar, 2016). Hence, it can be argued that the Adivasi community adopts multiple strategies to deal with the state as well as changing social dynamics rather than staying in a hyphenated space. Modern vocabulary of legal rights to vague oral histories defines the range of options available to them for engaging the state that is still considered to be an alien institution. Given the fact that traditional weapons become an essential component of the Adivasi movements even today as against the constitutional proscription of 'assembling

---

[5] Outsiders are popularly regarded as *diku* and exploitation mainly takes place through moneylending, illegal sale and purchase of Adivasi land, etc. The Special Area Regulation Act, 1969, was passed to deal with cases of illegal transfer of Adivasi land, but it largely remained unsuccessful in addressing the grievances (Sharan, 2009).

peacefully without arms', there is testimony to the contestation implicit in the mode of protest. This, however, does not mean that the community forthrightly rejects the state for a transition from rebellion to non-violent and peaceful means of resistance, which fits completely within the accepted vocabulary of the state. Nevertheless, both the community and the state find themselves in the grey zone of politics, which simultaneously serves as a site of contestation and reconfiguration. For the community, it is the image of the state that is vaguely reinforced and, for the state, it is the autonomy of the community which is recognized and respected.

UNDERSTANDING THE ADIVASI SOCIETY

This section describes the nature of Adivasi society for a meaningful interpretation of the course of political action that emerges from the community. It, hence, becomes pertinent to engage with questions such as follows: can we call Adivasi society a 'civil society'? If not, what theoretical term is best suited to explain society? And how do we make sense of the political movements organized by the community? Providing a broad definition of 'civil society', Sunil Khilnani says:

> Civil society presupposes a concept of 'politics': a conception which both specifies the territorial and constitutional scope of politics, and recognises an arena or set of practices which is subject to regular and punctual publicity, which provides a terrain upon which competing claims may be advanced and justified.... In this respect, even in situations of great social heterogeneity, politics can function not simply to entrench social division, but it can act as a cohesive practice. (Khilnani, 2001, p. 26)

Gudavarthy (2013b, p. 48) considers that this very site of civil society is comprised of social and economic hierarchies and argues that the political movements that had previously resisted these hierarchies have now begun to

consider themselves as the embodiment of civil society and that the oppressions in civil society are simply regarded as 'dysfunctions in civil society'. He further states that

> The human rights movements in moving from the 'rights-based' version of civil society to the notion of civil society as a pure 'realm of freedom' was replicating or instantiating the logic of circularity, where power relations by remaining shrouded consolidate themselves. (Gudavarthy, 2013b, p. 49)

As opposed to this civic and legalized sphere of civil society, there exists a 'political society' which represents 'the politics emerging out of the developmental policies of government', and the politics of democratization has to be understood as a transaction between the state and this legally ambiguous and strategically demarcated terrain of political society (Chatterjee, 2005). Political society, however, also suffers from many discrepancies (Gudavarthy, 2013b, p. 187). First, they are not spaces for 'resistance', but for 'managing' social and political conflicts through negotiations with both the state and civil society that make it palatable for the state. Second, acting on behalf of the subaltern agency on the basis of organic political acts, 'the valorised idea of autonomy and self-constituted subjectivity not only results in "simple-minded voluntarism" but also effectively obscures the social hierarchies within "communities" that represent and constitute an "autonomous domain."' Hence, according to Gudavarthy (2013b, p. 225), the *logic of circularity* that has brought complacency in political movements can be overcome only through a transition to politics of 'post-civil society'; a policy that moves beyond identity and recognition to combine the imperatives of recognition with the demands for redistribution and justice 'for all'. This politics is premised upon the awareness that oppression forms a 'part of everyone's identity' and connects itself 'to justice' as it 'alone can become the durable basis for the post-civil society practices, of allowing for solidarity to coexist with resistance and conflict' (Gudavarthy, 2013b, p. 225). It is against this theoretical backdrop that we have to adjudge whether the political movements organized by the Adivasi intelligentsia and their disenfranchised counterparts form a part of post-civil society.

The long process of haphazard mainstreaming of the Adivasi community has resulted in their gradual integration. This process, however, has been lopsided in the sense that it has given rise to marked inequality within the community. One section benefitted because of state's affirmative policies and the modern education imparted by missionaries as well as public and private educational institutions giving rise to tribal elitism. This section forms a civil society among the Adivasis and is aware of the modern vocabulary required to negotiate with the state. They hold a consciousness about Adivasi rights, embedded in legal notions, and consider the state as inevitable. This educated and well-to-do Adivasi section uses the notion of 'civic republicanism' and stands for entitlements as citizens.

Civic republicanism projects an image of an active republican citizen, guided by common virtues and a commitment to the common good, whose active engagement in the life of the *polis* and in the affairs of the community would revitalize civil society (Rose, 1999, p. 169). In solidarity with their underprivileged counterparts, they demand accountability from the state according to the values enshrined in the Indian Constitution. Uprooted from their traditions and worldview, this section paints a rather romantic picture of Adivasi society. This essentialized notion of Adivasi society also serves the purpose of framing an *Adivasi identity*, which in turn draws a lot from the constitutional imagining of the community. Moreover, the section of civil society advocates the retention and recognition of cultural specificity while sounding confused about redefining political

autonomy. Their vision of political autonomy comprises the revival of customary institutions according to the Panchayats (Extension to Scheduled Areas [PESA]) Act of 1996. This demand seems to be in complete disregard of the rise of traditional elites[6] in Adivasi society (Majumdar, 1937). Even today, there are instances of corruption by several customary leaders, and the demand for restoring customary institutions has proved to be a last-ditch effort at reinstating their own position within the community (Kumar, 2017).

Another section among the Adivasi community subscribes to the idea of 'Adivasi republicanism' in articulation of their political resistance against dispossession and disenfranchisement. It can be regarded as a post-civil society phenomenon due to its reliance upon tradition and culture as existing in its transformed nature. The vocabulary of political movements is not confined to legally permissible spaces, and their engagement with the state is not through negotiation. These movements do not shy away from owning and making sense of the coarse and stark realities pervading their social milieu (Kumar, 2019). Unlike the usage of generic notion like Adivasi identity, political movements are based upon more local identities like that of *being Ho, being Munda* or *being Santhal* (Kumar, 2016). The movements hold a quotidian understanding of the everyday functioning of society engaged with the state seeking justice for all. Their participation in even a purely class-based movement like that of Maoists is informed by the suffocating realities of social change. As stated by Shah (2018, pp. 142–145), the Naxalite movements become their preferred destination to seek temporary relief from social restrictions and to actualize their wishes as mundane to avoid scolding at home to realize their love life. This section is the custodian of Adivasi culture and tradition, and is completely immersed in social customs

---

[6] Majumdar (1937) argues that corruption prevailing among customary leaders after coming into contact with outsiders resulted into the rise of inequality among the community.

that others might consider to be promiscuous. Community feast and drinking, as well as the mingling of the sexes, might appear to an outsider as complete lawlessness and immorality, but for the community such occasions are guided by strict community rules (Engels, 1972, p. 46).

ELECTORAL POLITICS AND GOVERNANCE

Adivasis in Jharkhand have been part of the political movement for statehood on ethnic lines and have been through the process of political socialization for several decades. Even though their idea about the state remained problematic, they participated in state-run elections to 'keep the state away' (Shah, 2007). The community has admired the constitutional ideals showing due diligence to their culture and often partake in the democratic process of electing their representatives. However, one can notice heterogeneity in their political behaviour according to their closeness to different religious persuasions, class and linkages with the local state (Kumar, 2018). This diversity is clearly reflected in the voting behaviour of the community (Table 17.1). A good number of Adivasi populations which have adopted Hinduism have shown their political inclination towards Hindu nationalist

parties, like the BJP, while those following the *Sarna* mostly vote for regional parties like the JMM. Even the Adivasi population, converted to Christianity, has shown its preference for secular parties like the Congress or the JMM. Overall, one can notice a very diverse political affiliation and changing preferences among the community.

This pattern becomes more interesting to study if one looks at the social classes voting for one party or the other. The fact that almost 45 per cent of the Adivasis return as Hindus has given sufficient traction to the Hindu-Right wing of the BJP, giving the party almost 50 per cent of the seats reserved for the Scheduled Tribes (STs) in the Jharkhand assembly election conducted in 2014 (Table 17.2). Most of the people belonging to this category have a long history of socialization through a dense network of educational institutions run by Rashtriya Swayamsevak Sangh and its affiliates. This class among the Adivasi population receives state benefits due to its close association with the BJP, which has ruled the state for most of the years[7] since its creation. Benefits accrue in the form of local contracts for state-run projects to build village roads, schools, etc. BJP's aggressive stance at corporatization and privatization of natural resources also gives this section an opportunity to get hired in supervisory and other positions, even though it causes acute dispossession of its own Adivasi brethren. Millenarian movements

Table 17.1 Community-wise Voting Pattern in Jharkhand Assembly Election, 2014

Community	BJP	JMM	Congress	JVM	Others
Hindu Upper Castes	50	15	10	10	15
OBCs	40	19	15	10	16
SCs	29	24	11	15	21
STs	30	29	10	9	22
Muslims	14	18	34	7	27

Source: CSDS post-poll survey (Kumar & Sardesai, 2015).

[7] The BJP governed the state under the leadership of Babulal Marandi (2000–2003), Arjun Munda (2003–2006 and 2010–2013) and Raghubar Das (2014–till date). Intermittently, the state was governed by Shibu Soren, Madhu Koda and Hemant Soren, while the president's rule was imposed thrice for short intervals.

Table 17.2   Jharkhand Assembly Constituencies Reserved for STs, Percentage of ST Population and the Winning Political Parties in 2014 Election

Serial No.	Assembly Constituencies Reserved for STs	ST Population (%; 2001 Census)	Political Parties Winning in 2014[*]
1	Khijri	44.51	BJP
2	Ghatshila	48.29	BJP
3	Khunti	71.16	BJP
4	Jagannathpur	69.72	Others
5	Chaibasa	67.66	JMM
6	Manoharpur	67.32	JMM
7	Simdega	66.17	BJP
8	Barhait	60.36	JMM
9	Gumla	60.28	BJP
10	Maheshpur	59.30	JMM
11	Shikaripara	57.60	JMM
12	Tamar	57.40	AJSUP
13	Chakradharpur	56.95	JMM
14	Sisai	74.37	BJP
15	Bishunpur	72.90	JMM
16	Lohardaga	55.70	INC
17	Potka	51.80	BJP
18	Dumka	45.99	BJP
19	Torpa	73	JMM
20	Saraikela	34	JMM
21	Mandar	59.65	BJP
22	Kolebira	71.20	Others
23	Majhgaon	69.30	JMM
24	Litipara	45.40	JMM
25	Borrio	55.84	BJP
26	Jama	48.57	JMM
27	Manika	58.70	BJP
28	Kharsawan	53.6	JMM

Source: Election Commission of India (2014).

Note: [*]Election Commission of India.

like Tana Bhagat, which led to the imitation of Hindu practices among the Oraon Adivasis, were also crucial. Culturally, they endorse the festivals and religious functions of the Hindus but are still located at their margins without any derogatory incorporation (Kumar, 2018, p. 108).

The usage of Jharkhandi identity for electoral purposes is also a robust phenomenon and is mostly used by regional parties like the JMM to garner votes in appreciation of the community's vision for alternative development resting upon their worldview in congruence with their culture and customs. After the creation of Jharkhand, identity politics is used to assert Adivasi versus non-Adivasis, isolation versus integration and tribal way of life versus exploitative outsider (Hebbar, 2003, p. 49). Jharkhand-based parties have shown their solidarity with organizations protesting against resource grab. Local parties have a reliable support base among the Adivasi middle class who have been a beneficiary of state's affirmative policy (Corbridge, 2000). There has also been evidence of JMM leaders collaborating with corporate forces on some occasions as it ensures the monetary supply that is crucial for contesting elections. Moreover, the track record of even the Jharkhand-based parties in implementing the welfare schemes for the community is poor. This reluctance can be explained by the fact that appeal for votes is made on the basis of kinship, ethnic and community.

Of the three main ethno-religious groups, that is, tribal Hindus, Sarna tribals and tribal Christians, the last two groups largely prefer to vote for the regional parties. But it is also evident that even Sarna Adivasis voted for the BJP and that this mostly happened in areas where the communal polarization between Sarnas and Christian Adivasis was visible. Voter bribing is another popular option of garnering votes and is used widely by political parties. However, anti-dispossession movements rarely influence the voting pattern, except in areas of ongoing state–community face-off. In terms of priority, the factors influencing the voting pattern can be listed as an ethnicity and kinship factor followed by religious persuasion. The programmatic and non-programmatic benefits accruing to the voters, in addition to voter bribing, take the third place, while the least effective is the mobilization around the issues of dispossession.

In Jharkhand, the multiple electoral strategies adopted by the parties and the nature of governance are mutually reinforcing. The creation of a truncated tribal state was possible due to the ups and downs witnessed in the Jharkhand statehood movement, bringing the BJP to power instead of the JMM, at the time considered to be the custodian of the Jharkhand movement. Even though it is true that the movement and its popularity

spread to the Adivasi and *moolvasi* (domicile of Jharkhand as per the land records of 1935) population, the political leadership spearheading the movement looked confused on the blueprint of governance once the state was created. A group of Adivasi intelligentsia, however, prepared a people's agenda[8] that is commensurate with the Fifth Schedule, PESA and FRA in defining community rights. The first demand states that the chief minister and their deputy, as well as the administrators who come in direct contact with the people, should be local and belong to a tribal group of the area. The second demand is that 'tribal land should be restored and the leases of mines in the area should be taken away from non-tribals and given to local tribal groups.' The third demand is related to the cost of development and argues against the displacement due to developmental projects. Finally, the organization demanded a committee comprising leaders of the Jharkhand movement, intellectuals, representatives from minority communities and weaker sections, such as women, STs and SCs, to oversee that their interests are not compromised.

However, the idea of a non-interventionist, welfare state with autonomous governance of resources does not seem to have found sufficient traction with the ordinary Adivasi population. In fact, their long exposure and interaction with outsiders has developed among them an ambivalent attitude towards arbitrary social change. This ambivalence can be very well regarded as an indifference towards governance and government. Absence of any vibrant pro-Adivasi programme in society has further emboldened the BJP to aggressively pursue a neoliberal agenda of corporate-led development. Building upon their support base among the Adivasis, they have also been able to attack protective legislations such as the CNTA and the SPTA that

---

[8] A manifesto for governing the scheduled areas of Jharkhand, giving due consideration to Adivasi culture and society, was prepared by BIRSA (2000, p. ii), a prominent human rights organization.

grant protection to tribal land and resources. Furthermore, the discourse of governance is also used to change the political landscape by passing laws with social and cultural implications, for example, the Anti-Conversion Act, 2017.

RISE OF A 'POLICE STATE'

The radical Adivasi politics, mostly visible in the form of popular resistance in post-independence India, has continued in the same form but with changed targets; first, the state and, after the liberalization of the economy, the corporate. Again, to consider this as a 'crisis of governability' is a mistaken notion. In his seminal work, Kohli (1991, p. 19) considers that India's growing crisis of governability depends upon 'the changing role of the political elite, weak political organisations, the mobilisation of new groups for electoral reasons, and growing social unrest, including class conflict'. He considers the erosion of previously existing political structures to be the reason behind this. However, we see a different scenario since the 1990s as market forces have come to replace the state in the domain of production and partial distribution. Thus, most of what is regarded as a failure of governance in the Adivasi areas is rather a series of unbroken conflicts.

Community demand veers around less governance and a credible grant of autonomy to govern their resources. In this matrix of conflict between the state, the market and the society, the Maoist movement has made its mark in most of the Adivasi areas. But due to their ideological leanings on a class war, the Maoists have not been able to garner enough support within the community. Their mundane intervention comes mostly in the form of wage improvement and democratized control over systems of production that are crucial for the reproduction of the community. Scholars have, however, highlighted the dark side of Maoist presence in the Adivasi areas by arguing that 'they have also perhaps inadvertently acted as an arm of the postcolonial state and enhanced the processes of class differentiation it generated' (Shah, 2013a, p. 447). Another argument made by Gudavarthy (2013a) considers the Maoist movement as eating upon the space created—due to its presence—for democratic movements. But is the Maoist movement only constraint on the popular expression of dissent against the corporate developmental model? To answer this question, I would like to analyse the role that the state has increasingly acquired in the post-liberalization era.

In a commentary written around the mid-1980s, Jacobs (1986, p. 67) traces the emergence of the police state to the free-market conservatism model adopted by Margaret Thatcher. Jacobs argues that the two narratives serving the neoliberal state are interlinked and legitimizing, that is, the protection of national security and the maintenance of law and order. He further argues that 'liberal economic policy has been accompanied by a simultaneous political authoritarianism which has been a substantial enlargement of State power' (Jacobs, 1986). The regime largely employs intelligence agencies instead of police for continued surveillance, interception and occasional burglary against people who challenge their views. Certainly, the genocide that started under the previous government in the name of operation green hunt is not simply out of the government's concern to restore law and order by wiping out the Maoists through military action. It is equally about terrorizing ethnic communities that are perceived by the state as the biggest impediment in the way of neoliberal growth. While the forces causing threats of this conflict have been largely the notorious 'red corridor' of India recently, the war has spread to urban areas as well. Following a broader strategy, the government cracked down upon the so-called 'urban Naxals' with a clear aim to attack the ideological premises upon which most of the grassroots protests are organized.

In a developing country like India, where mass poverty prevails, the twin narratives of national security, and law and order have been complemented by yet another vocabulary of 'anti-developmentalism'. Protesting farmers and Adivasis who face eviction and dispossession in the wake of land acquisition are projected as anti-developmental. This is the method of delegitimizing popular resistance by the communities in the eyes of the same 'public' that emerged as the beneficiary of the statist model of development relying upon *modern temples*, such as dams and industries, justified through the phrase 'public purpose'. The federal government is still perceived as the pursuant of development with the rationalized participation of corporate forces. State aid in this model mostly comes in the form of resolving economic issues and suppressing the political resistance related to the desired projects. As far as Jharkhand is concerned, the domination of the political scene by a national political party like the BJP has the tendency to move aggressively in the direction of a 'police state'. Entries 54 and 23 of the Seventh Schedule of the Indian Constitution give power to the union and the states, respectively, to regulate mines and mineral development. Due to the majority government of the same party, that is, the BJP, both at the centre and the state, the deliberative forces have been weakened.

Post-1990s, the cooperative federal structure has been replaced by competing regions and a union whose role is confined to the issuing of broader guidelines. In its industrial policy, the centre has hardly recognized the differences existing in the scheduled areas, largely inhabited by the Adivasis. State governments have taken such policies as an excuse for disregarding the special nature of such areas and the people therein. In the name of 'ease of doing business', they attempt to streamline policies on mining and mineral exploration vis-à-vis other states. Such attempts are usually corporate-friendly. Very often, the reprieve from state policies and actions has come from the judiciary, as several projects have been denied on the ground that they are illegal. But this happens only after a viable protest against the projects is organized and the protestors are able to approach the court. As *jury politics*[9] has become part and parcel of a broader lexicon of people's protest against corporate grab of resources, the state has grown cautious and uses its coercive apparatus to frame protestors as Left-wing extremists. As both the United Progressive Alliance (UPA) and National Democratic Alliance (NDA) governments at the centre have uniformly disregarded local realities existing in resource-rich areas, it can be argued that the rise of a police state is contingent upon the existence of state governments led by these parties. This situation is quite visible in Jharkhand, where the absence of a regional party, the JMM, from the ruling coalition has reduced the space for more democratic deliberation and increased the use of coercive state measures typical of the police state.

RUN-UP TO THE 2019 ASSEMBLY ELECTIONS

This section is included as a post-scriptum to the already presented analysis and provides a glimpse of the political equations developing between the different political parties operational in Jharkhand and their possible fallout. The ruling BJP–AJSUP alliance is under threat as the BJP is eager to ascertain that in post-election scenario it should be capable to form a government on its own. Even though the AJSUP looks like a small party, stitching

---

[9] Jury politics refers to the strategy applied by protestors under which they challenge the legality of the proposed project in a court of law. It was observed on several occasions, such as Niyamgiri and Posco.

the alliance is crucial for the BJP if it does not want to take a chance on non-Adivasi votes, particularly the *Kurmi Mahato* caste. Even the Lok Janshakti Party, a constituent of the NDA, which commands *Paswan* caste votes, has fielded candidates from almost six constituencies. The hard bargaining that the AJSUP has shown is due to a rising concern among the smaller parties in the NDA that the BJP is not treating them fairly despite drawing crucial support from their social base during the elections. If left unaddressed, this development can have serious consequences for the BJP, as the *Kurmi Mahatos* and the *Paswans* constitute a good part of the electorate. Driven by their enthusiasm of the 2019 electoral victory and their ambition to govern on the basis of their Hindutva ideology, the BJP is slowly trying to encroach upon the space of the regional political parties, including its own allies. These events seem to lead to a 'centrifugal' tendency in the nature of the NDA coalition, where smaller partners are forcing themselves away from the BJP in a bid to safeguard their political existence.

Moreover, jealous bargaining can also be observed in the UPA coalition between the JMM, the Congress and the Rashtriya Janata Dal (RJD). Each party seems to be asking for seats that could possibly ensure them a better bargaining position during the government formation. Nevertheless, these coalition partners have the experience of working together earlier under the leadership of Hemant Soren and are united on this issue. Other than this, for the Mahagathbandhan success in Jharkhand, elections will determine their political fortunes in Bihar as the RJD and the Congress are also coalition partners there. Babulal Marandi-led Jharkhand Vikas Morcha has decided to contest the elections alone as it could not agree with Hemant Soren as a leader of the UPA coalition. Multi-cornered contests are expected to give the assembly election a very different colour in comparison to the earlier elections. The BJP will be facing gross hostility from the Adivasi community due to several unpopular moves, such as installing a non-tribal as chief minister, attempts to amend the CNTA and the SPTA as well as the high-handed approach in dealing with the Pathalgadi movement. It seems highly unlikely to observe any significant change in the voting behaviour of the groups, as the issues of governance and development still take a back seat. But the change in the fortunes of the political parties will certainly depend upon the working equations among the coalition partners during the voting.

As far as tribal votes are concerned, there can be a 'loose polarization' of their votes, but it can certainly provide an edge to the JMM coalition due to the particularly unpopular image of Chief Minister Raghubar Das among the community. In a nutshell, tribal politics is bifurcated between Hindutva sympathizers on the one hand and ethnic identity politics on the other. However, it is the nature of the polarization itself that determines the voting pattern among the community. The issues affecting tribal voting behaviour do not seem to be leading to their fragmentation and there is a high possibility of the polarization of tribal votes. Even though there are several tribal leaders in the state, the acceptance of Hemant Soren as the JMM leader seems to have addressed the issue of reliable Adivasi leadership for tribal voters.

CONCLUSION

The 'state-in-society' approach used to analyse politics in Jharkhand helps us to understand the 'fault lines' within Adivasi society and to analyse state–community interactions. While a broader Adivasi identity is used as a political construct by urban-educated Adivasi activists to articulate their resistance against the onslaught of the neoliberal state, its reverberation among the ordinary Adivasi population

is mostly missing. A silent and gradual transformation has taken place in Adivasi society,
affecting their voting behaviour and their
association with the state. The preference for
the BJP among the Adivasi population has not
only expedited the 'detribalization of government' but has also emboldened the party to
pursue socially divisive steps.

Many issues and concerns that were central to the demand for Jharkhand were not
only systematically ignored but also violated under the Raghubar Das-led NDA government. However, the reducing space for
regional political parties, like the JMM, indicates a dangerous turn of events. Reduced
political space for authentic Adivasi concerns might prove to be fatal for democracy
itself as disgruntlement with the state has
the potential to push Adivasis for opting
extra-constitutional measures to address their
grievances. To a certain extent, the strengthening of the Maoist stronghold in Jharkhand
is a testimony to this concern. Surprisingly,
the state's response to this issue is a military
solution that makes Jharkhand a police state.
Only a popular representation of tribal aspirations and efforts of governance granting
more autonomy to the community within the
constitutional framework can shield tribals
from further political alienation. The upcoming elections will be crucial for Adivasis as
a last recourse to revival through political
means.

REFERENCES

BIRSA. (2000). *Jharkhand ko Jharkhandi banaye* (Peo-
ple's Agenda). Chaibasa: BIRSA.
Chatterjee, P. (2005). *The politics of the governed:
Reflections on popular politics in most of the world.*
New Delhi: Orient Blackswan.
Corbridge, S. (2000). Competing inequalities: The sched-
uled tribes and the reservations system in India's
Jharkhand. *The Journal of Asian Studies, 59*(1),
62–85.
Dasgupta, S. (2011). *Adivasis and the raj: Socio-economic
transition of the Hos, 1820–1932.* New Delhi: Orient
Blackswan.
Election Commission of India. (2014). Statistical report
on general election, 2014 to the Legislative Assembly
of Jharkhand. Retrieved from https://eci.gov.in/files/
file/3787-jharkhand-2014/
Engels, F. (1972). *The origin of the family, private prop-
erty and the state.* Moscow: Progress Publishers.
Gudavarthy, A. (2013a). Democracy against Maoism,
Maoism against Itself. *Economic & Political Weekly,
48*(7), 69–77.
Gudavarthy, A. (2013b). *Politics of post-civil society:
Contemporary history of political movements in India.*
New Delhi: SAGE Publications.
Guha, R. (2007). Adivasis, Naxalites, and the Indian
democracy. *Economic & Political Weekly, 42*(32),
3305–3312.
Hebbar, R. (2003). From resistance to governance. *Sem-
inar, 524*, 45–50.
Jacobs, M. (1986). United Kingdom: Towards a 'police
state'. *Economic & Political Weekly, 21*(2), 67–68.
Khilnani, S. (2001). The development of civil society. In
S. Kaviraj & S. Khilnani (Eds.), *Civil society: History and
possibilities* (pp. 11–32). Cambridge: Cambridge Uni-
versity Press.
Kohli, A. (1991). *Democracy and discontent: India's
growing crisis of governability.* Cambridge: Cam-
bridge University Press.
Kumar, S. (2016). Revisiting anti-dispossession resistance
movements. *Seminar, 682*, 43–47.
Kumar, S. (2017). The face and mask of 'autonomy':
Reinvigorating customs among the Ho adivasis of
Jharkhand. *Studies in Humanities and Social Sciences,
24*(1), 95–116.
Kumar, S. (2018). Adivasis and the state politics of
Jharkhand. *Studies in Indian Politics, 6*(1), 103–116.
Kumar, S. (2019). Muzzling artistic liberty and protesting
anti-conversion bill in Jharkhand. *Economic & Political
Weekly, 54*(2), 16–18.
Kumar, S. & Sardesai, S. (2015). BJP wins with some help
from the opponents: Jharkhand Assembly elections.
Economic & Political Weekly, 50(19), 62–65.
Majumdar, D. N. (1937). *A tribe in transition: A study in
culture pattern.* Calcutta: Longmans, Green & Co. Ltd.
Migdal, J. S. (2001). *State in society: Studying how states
and societies transform and constitute one another.*
Cambridge: Cambridge University Press.
Rose, N. (1999). *Powers of freedom: Reframing political
thought.* Cambridge: Cambridge University Press.

Sen, A. K. (2012). *From village elder to British judge: Custom, customary law and tribal society.* New Delhi: Orient Blackswan.

Shah, A. (2007). Keeping the state away: Democracy, politics, and the state in India's Jharkhand. *Journal of Royal Anthropological Institute, 13*(1), 129–145.

Shah, A. (2013). The agrarian question in a Maoist guerrilla zone: Land, labour and capital in the forests and hills of Jharkhand, India. *Journal of Agrarian Change, 13*(3), 424–450.

Shah, A. (2018). *Nightmarch: A journey into India's Naxal heartlands.* Noida: HarperCollins.

Sharan, R. (2009). Alienation and restoration of tribal land in Jharkhand. In N. Sundar (Ed.), *Legal grounds: Natural resources, identity, and the law in Jharkhand* (pp. 82–112). New Delhi: Oxford University Press.

18

Political Intersectionality and Tribal Politics in Karnataka

Pradeep Ramvath J.

INTRODUCTION

Understanding tribal communities through an intersectionality approach provides better insights into their intra- and inter-group political behaviours. Tribal communities become more vulnerable and prone to political extinction if we apply multiple intersectional markers of identification, such as region, religion, language and gender in respect of their horizontal positioning. This chapter deals with the political intersectionality of tribal communities in Karnataka.

Political intersectionality is a form of structural intersectionality that addresses casteism, regionalism, linguistic exploitation, ethnicity, religious identities, sexism, racism, class exploitation, etc., in policymaking processes and policies. It indicates how inequalities and their intersections are relevant to political strategies (Verloo, 2006). The application of this framework to particularly vulnerable tribal groups (PVTGs) such as Soligas and

Jenu Kurubas would lead to a matrix of domination that operates from multiple dimensions and suppresses developmental capabilities. Similarly, understanding some of the dominant tribes such as Beda within the political intersectionality perspective would require an effort to zoom out the magnification of the framework as it moves out from a population range of 10,000 (mesoscopic) to 33 lakh (macroscopic) population.

Thus, within the dominant tribal political network of Bedas (Nayakas, Valmiki), we come across high-stake claims pertaining to inseparable links of Nayaka Bedas with mythology and the history of the kingdoms that ruled important regions of Karnataka. This further warrants one to look at the grounded understanding of this type of 'tribal groups', which worked very closely with dynasties, princely states and the feudatory kingdoms for capture of political power (Nayaka, 2010–2011). An interesting corollary will be the counter-mapping[1] of the Karnataka state through the

---

[1] Counter-mapping refers to efforts to map against dominant power structures to further seemingly progressive goals.

Table 18.1   Population Size and Annual Growth Rate, Karnataka

	Social Group	Population in Million				Annual Growth Rate (in %)			
		1981	1991	2001	2011	1981–2011	1981–1991	1991–2001	2001–2011
Total	SC	5.6	7.4	8.6	10.5	2.1	2.8	1.5	2.1
	ST	1.8	1.9	3.5	4.2	2.9	0.5	6.2	1.9
	Non-SC/ST	29.7	35.7	40.8	46.4	1.5	1.9	1.3	1.3

Source: Census of India, 1981, 1991, 2001 and 2011.

history of tribal communities, which can possibly provide a concrete understanding of the political configurations spread across time and space. Within this backdrop, the chapter discusses the political scenarios offered to different categories of tribal communities through an act of political reservation by policy elites after the reorganization of the state.

POLITICAL DEMOGRAPHY OF TRIBES IN KARNATAKA

Demographically Scheduled Tribes (STs) in Karnataka are a unified category of around 51 heterogeneous and divided tribal groups, often referred to as castes by state authorities with around 106 synonyms. This unified category of STs in its current format[2] is a product of the consolidation of the various inclusion and exclusion processes. In accordance with the provision of Article 342 of the Constitution, the first list of STs in respect of the state of Karnataka (the then state of Mysore) was notified vide the Constitution (Scheduled Tribes) Order, 1950. List of STs of Karnataka has been modified through the Scheduled Castes and Scheduled Tribes Orders (Amendment) Act, 1956; the Scheduled Castes and Scheduled Tribes Orders (Amendment) Act, 1976; the Constitution (Scheduled Tribes) Order (Second Amendment) Act, 1991; the Scheduled Castes and Scheduled Tribes Orders (Amendment) Act, 2002; the Constitution

(Scheduled Tribes) Order (Amendment) Act, 2012; and the Constitution (Scheduled Tribes) Order (Second Amendment) Bill, 2019.

In 2011, Karnataka had 4.2 million ST and 46.4 million non-SC/ST populations, and according to Census estimates, 3.4 million ST populations were found to be residing in rural areas. In spite of the high growth of the urban population, a large number of ST populations are still found to be living in rural areas. The annual growth rate of the ST population is higher than that of the non-SC/ST population (Table 18.1). STs recorded more than 2 per cent annual growth rate between 1981 and 2011, whereas the non-SC/ST population recorded slightly higher than 1 per cent. During 1998–2001, the annual growth rate for ST was 2.9 per cent and for non-SC/ST 1.5 per cent. During 1991–2001, the ST population recorded the highest growth (both in rural and urban areas) due to the nomenclature change and the removal of the area restriction for the dominant tribal group Beda Valmikis. At present, the 1981 ST figures appear to include high returns relating to certain communities with nomenclatures similar to those included in the list of STs consequent on the removal of area restrictions.

Out of the total population, the percentage of the ST population has significantly increased. It was 4.9 per cent in 1981 which reached 7 per cent in 2011 (Table 18.2). The percentage of non-SC/ST population has, on the other hand, declined from 80 per cent to 75.9 per cent in 2011. Both SC and ST communities recorded a steady increase in the percentage

---

[2] The Constitution (Scheduled Tribes) Order (Second Amendment) Bill, 2019.

share, but the percentage of non-SC/ST communities was found to fall below 80 per cent in 2011. As per 2011 census, 98 per cent of the tribes reported being Hindus, 1 per cent Muslims and 1 per cent belonging to other religions including no religious affiliation. The *Hinduization* of the tribes was linked to their affiliation to the Hindu dynasties and kingdoms that ruled Karnataka, including the Vijayanagara dynasty. Their allegiance to the Hindu religion is deeply rooted through the tribal epic of Ramayana, associating Valmiki and *Bedara Kannayya* as their ancestors.

Tribal communities of Karnataka are not homogenous communities, but rather reflect the complex heterogeneity of sub-ethnic identities. There seems to be an unending exercise carried out by the political parties to consolidate the vote bank of segregated tribal communities across Karnataka, as the population of the ST category showed a steep increase from 0.84 per cent in 1956 to 6.79 per cent in 2011. On a general note, the consolidated demography of tribals, such as 875,742 households with a population of 4,248,987 having a sex ratio of 990, a literacy rate of 62.08 per cent and a population of children (0–6 years) as 13.19 per cent, will not help much in understanding the nature of 51 tribal groups.

POLITICAL RESERVATION FOR TRIBALS: A FOCUS ON LEGISLATIVE CONSTITUENCIES

The practice of reservation in the political sphere is one of the features of the affirmative action policy in Karnataka to achieve a larger goal of democracy, that participation of every section of society is an embodied principle. The rooted caste system and inequality hinder the equal participation of SCs and STs in the social, political, civic and economic spheres. Reservation in the Parliament and state assemblies is a step towards addressing the existing contradictions in society. Reservation for STs in state legislative assemblies follows a single policy rule that applies to all states in India. According to Article 332 of the Indian Constitution, the number of seats reserved for the STs is such that the share of the total seats reserved for each group in the state assembly equals to that group's share of the total state population in the last preceding census. ST figures of 1981 would appear to include high returns relating to certain communities with nomenclatures similar to those included in the ST list consequent on the removal of area restrictions.

In Karnataka, the number of MLA seats increased from 208 in 1962 to 224 in 1978, and continuing ever since, more than 180 seats have been won by people belonging to non-SC/ST communities. ST representation has been very less mostly limiting to two seats in a 224-member assembly from 1972 to 2004. It is only after the implementation of the Delimitation of Parliamentary and Assembly Constituencies Order 2008 that there has been a considerable rise in the number of ST candidates to 15. Thus, prior to the implementation of the Delimitation of Parliamentary and Assembly Constituencies Order 2008, the share of elected candidates from SCs and STs has been 14.73 and 0.89 per cent, respectively.

Table 18.2   Population Size across Social Groups, Karnataka (in %)

	Social Group	1981	1991	2001	2011
Total	SC	15.1	16.4	16.2	17.1
	ST	4.9	4.3	6.6	7.0
	Non-SC/ST	80.0	79.4	80.5	75.9
	Total	100.0	100.0	100.0	100.0

Source: Census of India, 1981, 1991, 2001 and 2011.

Table 18.3   Share of MLAs Population in Preceding Census among STs, Karnataka

| Year of Election | Census Year | ST | | |
		Share of MLAs	Share of Population in Preceding Census	Difference
1983	1981	0.9	4.9	−4.0
1985	1981	0.9	4.9	−4.0
1989	1981	0.9	4.9	−4.0
1994	1991	0.9	4.3	−3.4
1999	1991	0.9	4.3	−3.4
2004	2001	0.9	6.6	−5.7
2008	2001	6.7	6.6	0.1
2013	2011	6.7	7	−0.3
2018	2011	6.9	7	−0.1

Source: Retrieved from http://www.elections.in/karnataka/assembly-constituencies and Census of India (various years).

Table 18.3 shows how the representation of the STs has not taken place in Karnataka according to the constitutional provision of Article 332. In proportion to the census estimation of the tribal population, the representation of the STs has been very low, except in the last three assembly elections of Karnataka.

POLITICAL PARTIES AND REPRESENTATION OF STS

In Karnataka, the major political parties have been Indian National Congress (hereafter the Congress), the Janata Party (JNP), the Bharatiya Janata Party (BJP), the Janata Dal, the Janata Dal (Secular), the Communist Party of India (CPI), the Communist Party of India (Marxist; CPI[M]), etc. These parties have shown their considerable relevance in the political landscape of Karnataka. Existing data indicate that the Congress has largely dominated the state assembly elections since 1957, and has won the assembly elections repeatedly till 1972. In the 1978 election, the Congress-I (Indira) won. During the 1972 election, when Mr Devaraj Urs became chief minister of Karnataka, the state remained under the regime of the Congress till 1978, finding immense recognition at the national level. This recognition

was majorly attributed to the setting up of the of L. G. Havanur Commission, which masterminded the development of backward communities, including the STs in the state. L. G. Havanur (1975) was a genius from the Beda Nayaka community who spearheaded the backward classes commission during 1975 to bring victory to Mr Devaraj Urs.

During 1983 and 1985 elections, the JP emerged as the dominant political party. However, the Congress did revert to its original position with the largest mandate of 179 seats in the following elections held in 1989. Since then, there have been shifts in power among three major parties, namely the Congress, the BJP and the Janata Dal. During the 2004 and 2008 elections, the BJP emerged as a reckoning force in the political scenario of the state. However, the Congress did come back with a majority in the assembly elections held in 2013.

There have been some other political parties that became quite relevant in the political history of the state. The CPI and the CPI(M) have been two major Left parties, but had a very limited impact on the politics of the state. However, the CPI won a few seats till 1985. The rise of the CPI had taken place in Karnataka from the support it achieved from coffee-growing areas in the state, and the subsequent decline of the party was also due to the weakening of the support base from the same region (Assadi, 1998). Karnataka did witness the rise of socialist parties in the form of the Socialist Party (SP) and the Praja Socialist Party but at a very marginal scale. The struggle of landless tenants, including important tribal communities in the region, against landlords over terms of tenancy, especially in the Shimoga district of Karnataka, was the main reason for the rise of the SP in Karnataka and Gopala Gowda won thrice (1952, 1962 and 1967) from the SP from different constituencies in the Shimoga district. The SP's main demand for security of tenure for tenant farmers was crucial, which was later taken up by the Congress party in its 1974 land reform legislation.

Table 18.4 on the distribution of ST MLAs among the various political parties shows that all ST MLAs were from the Congress party till 1978. During the 1983 and 1985 elections, the majority of the ST representatives came from the JNP. Since 1994, the representation of the ST MLAs has rotated between the Congress, the Janata Dal and the BJP (Tables 18.4 & 18.8). The higher distribution of victorious ST candidates has always corresponded with the political party(ies) that secured majority in the respective election(s). According to Rodrigues (2014), the time period conforming with the leadership of Devaraj Urs from 1972 to 1983 witnessed major changes in the representation of the upper castes in public services

and higher education. Women representatives from different caste groups showed that non-SC/ST candidates performed better than the STs during the elections. However, the ST women were also elected thrice (1985, 1989 and 1999) to the assembly, and all were from the Congress party only (Table 18.5).

Exploring the caste dimension, Karnataka is a state that has witnessed the dominance of two important communities, namely the Lingayats and the Vokkaligas. Political power has been defined by the stronghold of both groups. The unification of the state in 1961 enabled the Lingayats to become a dominant caste group. It is said that between 1952 and 1967, the three caste groups, Lingayats, Vokkaligas and Brahmins, which constituted one-third of the state's population, occupied two-thirds share of the assembly seats. However, this caste dynamic experienced transformation in the 1972 election, when the Devaraj Urs government accommodated many Muslims and backward castes, and the trend continued till 1978 (Rodrigues, 2014). With the coming of the JNP to power in 1983, the Lingayats reinstated their dominance. As a dominant caste group, Lingayats have been able to retain the power of decision-making by being leaders, MPs, MLAs and ministers both from the Congress and the JNP, while the other caste groups, including the STs, remained marginalized (S. S., 1990).

Table 18.4 Distribution of ST MLAs across Major Political Parties, Karnataka, 1962–2018 (in %)

Political Party	1962	1967	1972	1978	1983	1985	1989	1994	1999	2004	2008	2013	2018
INC	100	100	100	100	50.0	50.0	100.0	0.0	100.0	50.0	40.0	60.0	53
JNP	0	0	0	0	50.0	50.0	0.0	0.0	0.0	0.0	0.0	0.0	0
BJP	0	0	0	0	0.0	0.0	0.0	50.0	0.0	50.0	46.7	6.7	37
JD	0	0	0	0	0.0	0.0	0.0	50.0	0.0	0.0	0.0	0.0	0
JD(S)	0	0	0	0	0.0	0.0	0.0	0.0	0.0	0.0	6.7	6.7	6
CPI	0	0	0	0	0.0	0.0	0.0	0.0	0.0	0.0	0.0	0.0	0
Others	0	0	0	0	0.0	0.0	0.0	0.0	0.0	0.0	6.7	26.7	0

Source: Retrieved from http://www.elections.in/karnataka/assembly-constituencies

Table 18.5   Representation of ST Female Candidates in Political Parties in Karnataka Assembly

Social Groups	1962	1967	1972	1978	1983	1985	1989	1994	1999	2004	2008	2013
ST	0	0	0		0	1 INC	1 INC		1 INC	0	0	0
Non-SC/ST	14 INC, 1 PSP	3 INC, 1 PSP	0	2 INC(I), 2 JNP	1 INC, 1 JNP	3 INC, 1 JNP	5 INC	1 INC, 4 JD, 1 BJP, 1 AGP	4 INC	1 INC, 1 JD(U), 2 JD(S), 2 BJP	3 BJP, 1 INC	3 INC, 1 BJP

Source: Retrieved from http://www.elections.in/karnataka/assembly-constituencies

Table 18.6   Distribution of Tribes across Various Regions and Districts of Karnataka

S. No.	Regions	Districts	Cumulative Population	% of Population
1	Coastal Karnataka	Uttara Kannada, Udupi, Dakshina Kannada	169,404	3.98
2	Mumbai Karnataka	Bijapur, Gadag, Dharwad, Bagalkot, Haveri, Belgaum	724,297	17
3	Malnad Region	Chikmagalur, Kodagu, Shimoga, Hassan	200,765	4.7
4	North-eastern Karnataka	Gulbarga, Yadgir, Koppal, Bidar, Raichur, Bellary	1,430,678	33
5	Old Mysore Region	Mandya, Ramanagara, Bangalore Rural, Kolar, Chamarajanagar, Chikkaballapur, Bangalore, Tumkur, Davanagere, Chitradurga, Mysore	1,723,843	40

Total population = 4,248,987

Source: Census of India 2011.

TRIBAL REGIONS AND ZONES OF POLITICAL MANOEUVRING

Considering the significance of tribal politics in Karnataka, tribal areas of the state can be divided into different regions zones (Tables 18.6 & 18.7). Demographically, districts in Zone 1 are the weakest regions for tribal politics. However, we have also noticed Naxalite adventurism in this region after 2000 in the backdrop of the eviction of tribal communities, particularly Malekudiyas, from Kudremukh National Park. Assadi (2004) observes that Left adventurism provided visibility to basic issues affecting tribal communities, including land and livelihoods. On the other hand, it also provided space for the confrontation between the Naxalites and the Hindutva forces at the expense of the tribes. In essence, this has resulted in an increasing marginalization of social movements in the state and has helped Hindutva lobby to consolidate and expand its base at the cost of popular social movements emerging from this zone.

Zone 2 has a very interesting spread of tribal groups such as Maratis, Bhils and Bedas along with other mesoscopic tribes such as Hakki Pikki, Kadu Kuruba, Koraga, Hasalaru, Yerava, Soligaru and Jenu Kuruba, which are key to determine the developmental politics relating to the tribes in this region. Further, population-wise Zones 3, 4, 5 and 6 are territories where Valmiki Bedas have a large influence as far as tribal politics is concerned. Three districts, namely Mysore, Raichur and Bellary, in Zone 6 have around 27 per cent of the total tribal population in the state (Table 18.7), thereby offering a fertile terrain for political processes involving Bedas as the dominant tribe in the region. In the Mysore region, Vokkaligas and Lingayats control the political fate, and in the Raichur and Bellary regions, Bedas themselves have sufficient political capital, which helps them

Table 18.7   Distribution of Tribes across Various Districts of Karnataka

Zone	Population Range (in Millions)	Number of Districts	Names of the Districts	Total Population	% of Tribal Population
1	0.02–0.08	13	Mandya, Ramanagara, Hassan, Uttara Kannada, Bijapur, Chikmagalur, Udupi, Bangalore Rural, Kodagu, Gadag, Gulbarga, Shimoga, Kolar	631,254	14.85
2	0.08–0.14	4	Dakshina Kannada, Dharwad, Bagalkot, Chamarajanagar	387,238	9.11
3	0.14–0.20	5	Haveri, Yadgir, Chikkaballapur, Koppal, Bangalore	799,226	18.80
4	0.20–0.26	3	Tumkur, Davanagere, Bidar	678,493	15.96
5	0.26–0.32	2	Belgaum, Chitradurga	599,752	14.11
6	0.32–0.38	3	Mysore, Raichur, Bellary	1,153,024	27.13

Source: Census of India 2011.

Table 18.8   ST MLAs from Different Political Parties during 2018, Karnataka

S. No.	District	Number of ST-MLA Constituency	Won by INC	Won by BJP	Won by JD(S)
1	Bellary	6	3	3	0
2	Raichur	4	2	1	1
3	Chamarajanagar	1	1	0	0
4	Chitradurga	1	1	0	0
5	Davanagere	1	0	1	0
6	Yadgir	1	0	1	0
7	Belgaum	1	1	0	0

Source: Compiled from Election Commission of India report on 2018 Karnataka Assembly election.

to exert their political influence. But in both scenarios, the upper castes, particularly Vokkaligas and Lingayats, who control and manage political negotiations concerning whether to get access to party high commands or influence the general category of voters, have the ultimate say in political manoeuvring. However, in Zone 6, particularly in the Raichur and Bellary districts, Bedas sometimes behave as a dominant caste in the region. Table 18.9 indicates that there are three broad typologies and classification. They are microscopic minority tribes, mesoscopic significant tribes and macroscopic politically dominant tribes.

MICROSCOPIC MINORITY TRIBES: ZONE OF 'SILENT EXCLUSION'

The typology of microscopic minority tribes connotes to voiceless communities in the political and policymaking spaces. Most often, there is ambiguity about this group, as many argue about the extinction or assimilation of groups with low population presence during census operations. Apart from enumerative and methodological faults in reaching out to these inaccessible communities, there are faulty bureaucratic and political assumptions about the disappearance of these groups. Since they are numerically very small and

Table 18.9   Political Typologies of Tribal Communities in Karnataka

S. No.	Population Range (in Number)	Name of the Community	Number of Communities	Cumulative Population	% Within Total ST Population	Typology
1	Less than 100	Vitolia (synonyms Kotwalia, Barodia), Kokna (synonyms Kokni, Kukna), Maha Malasar, Rathwa, Sholaga, Patelia, Varli, Malasar	8	385	0.009	Microscopic minority tribes (Politically voiceless) Zone of Silent exclusion
2	Between 100 and 500	Malayekandi, Chodhara, Kota, Toda, Kattunayakan, Palliyan, Dubla (synonyms Talavia, Halpati), Barda, Kathodi (synonyms Katkari, Dhor Kathodi, Dhor Katkari, Son Kathodi, Son Katkari), Kurumans, Koya (synonyms Bhine Koya, Rajkoy), Kaniyan (Kanyan in Kollegal taluk of Mysore district), Maleru, Paniyan	14	3,759	0.088	
3	Between 500 and 5,000	Gamit (synonyms Gamta, Gavit, Mavchi, Padvi, Valvi), Irular, Adiyan, Kammara (in South Kanara district and Kollegal taluk of Mysore district), Chenchu (Chenchwar), Bavacha (Bamcha), Kudiya (Melakudi), Kuruba (in Coorg district), Maratha (in Coorg district)	9	13,516	0.318	
4	Between 5,000 and 10,000	Bhil (synonyms Bhil Garasia, Dholi Bhil, Dungri Bhil, Dungri Garasia, Mewasi Bhil, Rawal Bhil, Tadvi Bhil, Bhagalia, Bhilala, Pawra, Vasava, Vasave), Konda Kapus, Gowdalu, Malaikudi	4	31,495	0.741	
5	Between 10,000 and 1 lakh	Iruliga, Siddi (in Uttar Kannada district). Pardhi (synonyms Advichincher, Phase Pardhi, Haran Shikari), Hakki Pikki, Kadu Kuruba, Koraga, Hasalaru, Yerava, Soligaru, Jenu Kuruba, Meda (Medari, Gauriga, Burud), Marati (in South Kanara district)	12	321,448	7.565	Mesoscopic significant tribes Zone of negotiation
6	Between 1 lakh and 2 lakhs	Koli Dhor (Tokre Koli, Kolcha, Kolgha), Gond (Naikpod, Rajgond), generic tribes, etc.	3	582,030	13.69	
7	More than 30 lakhs	Naikda (synonyms Nayaka, Cholivala Nayaka, Kapadia Nayaka, Mota Nayaka, Nana Nayaka, Naik, Nayak, Beda, Bedar and Valmiki)	1	3,296,354	77.57	Macroscopic Politically dominant tribe Zone of domination

Source: Compiled from Census of India.

dispersed in different parts of the state, it is easy to manipulate their existence. This typology is a 'zone of silent exclusion', where communities are present in their hamlets but are missing from the census and population registers. New discourses on citizens proposed by the Indian state could be a possible threat to these communities, as most of them neither possess legal entitlements to land and shelter nor they are enrolled in the election registers. However, they are in a constant state of nomadism.

Historically, there were honest efforts to show an increasing population projection to a tune of 20–28 per cent by the L. G. Havanur Commission of enquiry during 1975. This could be seen as a counterpoint to the previously constituted advisory committee report on the revision of the lists of SCs and STs lists under the chairmanship of B. N. Lokur (Government of India, 1965) which advised for the exclusion of communities such as Chodhara, Bavcha, Dubla, Kammara, Gamit, Konda Kapu, Maha Malasar, Patelia, Varli and Vitolia from the ST list. The reasons provided seem to be very absurd. In most cases, the Lokur Committee indicated that the population and the extinct communities were insignificant, thus providing a claim to eliminate microscopic communities from the list of STs. This historical blunder was later addressed by L. G. Havanur, who was proactively mobilizing these microscopic communities and trying to provide more space for these communities by reaching out to them. He championed the cause of mobilization of small tribal groups from 1956 onwards, looking at the drawbacks of Kaka Kalelkar (1955) Commission report.

MESOSCOPIC SIGNIFICANT TRIBES: 'ZONE OF NEGOTIATION'

Mesoscopic tribal communities are negotiators at the level of policy implementation. Due to their number at the district level, they are able to bargain for few facilities through government schemes and programmes. These groups mostly have a very close linguistic affinity to Kannada and most often it is a dialect within the Kannada language. Few tribes such as Hakki Pikki and Phardi, even though their dialect is closely associated with the Marwari language, have mastered the art of negotiations with the state. For example, Hakki Pikkis are nomadic groups and, due to their livelihoods related to micro-trading of herbs, cosmetics, jewelleries, etc., they are able to settle down in notified villages with all the amenities. Hakki Pikki habitation, such as Bharathipura in Channagiri taluk in the Davanagere district, is able to negotiate for village amenities directly with the local MLA Mr Madaalu Virupakshappa and get the required facilities for the development. One can also notice similar trends among Iruliga, Pardhi (synonyms Advichincher, Phase Pardhi, Haran Shikari), Kadu Kuruba, etc., who have a linguistic mix of Kannada language and mostly forest dwelling communities.

The Koraga community suffers from the practice of untouchability. Few upper caste groups in coastal Karnataka still perform an inhuman act of untouchability commonly referred to as *Ajalu practice*—a practice performed to differentiate between Koragas and persons belonging to other communities, to treat Koragas as inferior human beings, to mix hair, nails or any other inedible or obnoxious substance in food and to ask them to eat that food and to make them to run like buffaloes before the beginning of traditional buffalo running game called Kambala. Presently, there are efforts to provide better educational facilities by the state due to a higher level of visibility of the community on the practice of *Ajalu*. We also hear few instances of Koraga youth enrolling in higher educational institutions and passing UGC-NET exams. Due to the efforts of Koraga Abhivridhi Sanghagala Okkoota (Federation of Koraga Development Associations), Koragas are able to overcome their hardships and try their emancipation along with a strong feeling to be part of the Hindu religion.

Hasalaru, Soligaru, Jenu Kuruba communities are forest dependent and have good exposure to development sector organizations compared to other groups. They have been exposed to nutrition, health and education programmes by civil society organizations and non-governmental organizations (NGOs). There is a growing realization of the need to develop a healthy partnership between the government and the NGOs. Yerava is a forest dwelling nomadic group and has been the victim of bonded labour practice within coffee estates. Marati (in South Kanara district) has emerged as a strong political negotiator at the local levels due to their concentrations in the Marati camps and their negotiating abilities due to their affiliation to the martial race and their strong belief in the identity of the Hindu.

Recently, during 2017–2018, Talasamudaayagala Adhyayana Kendra (Centre for the Study of Marginalized Communities) of the National Law School of India University undertook participatory policy action research involving four tribal groups, namely Malekudiya, Yeravas, Hasalaru and Jenu Kurubas—which fall in this zone. Now, after one year of intensive field research by community researchers and leadership development programmes, these selected tribal groups developed their capabilities required for bargaining with the state authorities for facilities and entitlements, including land.

MACROSCOPIC DOMINANT TRIBE: 'ZONE OF DOMINATION'

It is the only tribe visible at the state level, as it consolidates 77 per cent of the total ST vote share in the state, 15 ST MLAs, 2 MPs and more than 95 per cent of panchayat members belong to this single large tribal community. As stated earlier, the present-day Karnataka state is the embodiment of consolidated cartographies defined through the primary marker of the Kannada language. Thus, the affiliation and primacy of the tribal group, such as 'Bedas' to the Kannada language, gives strength to their primordial identity and feeling of 'sons of the soil', 'original inhabitants', 'natives', 'moolniwasis', etc. Also, as Bedas are historically a community that has affiliation and proximity to rulers as hunters, soldiers get both historical pride and contemporary political mileage due to their numbers. It has been noticed that the sharp rise in the demographic dividend among Bedas has been a watershed for all political parties, particularly the Right-wing BJP, as this tallies in to their larger political vision of the Hindu *rashtra* (nation). As Devi (1939, p. 94) lamented,

As long as the hill-tribes of India (the so-called 'animists', etc.) do not feel that their primitive forms of worship are one of the innumerable aspects of manifold Hinduism, and that they are a part and parcel of manifold Hindudom, their strength is lost to the cause of Hindudom. And it is a pity, for they are sturdy fighters. But they will never feel themselves Hindus unless the Hindus make them feel so, through their behavior towards them; unless they are treated as Hindus.

Thus, all political parties are deeply engaged in strategically extracting the muscle and money power offered by political elites within the dominant tribal group like Bedas.

On 27 December 2019, Shree Prasannanandapuri Swamij, Seer of Valmiki Gurupeeta, Rajanahalli, Harihara, stated that '…we will decide whether Mr B. S. Yediyurappa will sit in third floor of Vidhan Soudha as chief minister of Karnataka or rest in his house.'[3] This statement from the chief seer, who heads the Beda Valmiki mutt, is a clear warning that if the state government is

---

[3] Retrieved from https://www.prajavani.net/stories/stateregional/shri-valmiki-prasannananda-swamiji-criticized-bs-yediyurappa-693706.html

not going to increase the current reservation of the *Valmiki Beda Nayaka* community from 3 per cent to 7.5 per cent, they will take suitable action to destabilize the government through the support of their 15 MLAs, 2 MPs and thousands of panchayat members at different levels.

Now, recently, the state government constituted Mr Nagamohan Das Commission (2019) to look into the matter of increasing the reservation basket to SCs and STs. The chief seer demanded from the state to spell out its decision before 9 February 2019 on its stand of providing more ministerial berths to the Beda community, or else it had to face the difficulty. He further demanded for making Beda ST leader as one of the deputy chief ministers of Karnataka, to establish a separate ministry for the development of the Beda tribe and to rename Hampi Kannada University to Maharshi Valmiki University. Further, there are recent efforts to change the name of Indira food canteens to Maharshi Valmiki Anna Kuteera (food centres). Earlier, Indira food canteens were established during the Siddaramaiah regime for providing subsidized food to poor people in city areas. These

canteens were named after the former prime minister, Mrs Indira Gandhi. The renaming policy of the Indira food canteens by the ruling regime clearly shows the propaganda of diverting tribal attention from the core development issues of reservation, employment and providing educational access to rhetorical community emotions.

DEVELOPMENT POLITICS

In Karnataka, the Human Development Index for the general population is at 0.60 and for STs is at 0.378. Further, if one looks at the ST-reserved assembly constituencies and the Gram Panchayat Human Development Index (GPHDI), there are direct connections between both. The GPHDI is below the state average in the ST-reserved assembly constituencies and the areas with high tribal concentration (Table 18.10). For example, Devadurga and Shorapur are the most backward taluk in the state with the highest tribal population, indicating a low level of educational and health achievements.

Table 18.10   ST-reserved Assembly Constituencies and GPHDI Performance, Karnataka

S. No.	Constituency Name	% of Tribal Population (2011)	MLAs 2018	Party	Votes	GPHDI below State Average (2005)
1	Heggadadevankote	20	Anil Kumar C	INC	76,652	5.65
2	Jagalur	21	S. V. Ramachandra	BJP	78,948	22
3	Sandur	25	E. Tukaram	INC	78,106	53
4	Bellary	18	B. Nagendra	INC	79,186	57
5	Molakalmuru	37	B. Sriramulu	BJP	84,018	80
6	Siruguppa	18	M. S. Somalingappa	BJP	82,546	92
7	Challakere	23	T. Raghumurthy	INC	72,874	94
8	Kudligi	31	N. Y. Gopalakrishna	BJP	50,085	94
9	Raichur Rural	20	Basanagouda Daddal	INC	66,656	97
10	Shorapur	19	Narasimha Nayak	BJP	104,426	100
11	Manvi	22	Raja Venkatappa Nayak	JD(S)	53,548	100
12	Devadurga	33	Shivanagouda Nayak	BJP	67,003	100
13	Maski	18	Pratap Gouda Patil	INC	60,387	NA
14	Kampli	18	J. N. Ganesh	INC	80,592	NA
15	Yemkanmardi	25	Satish L. Jarkiholi	INC	73,512	NA

Source: Election Commission of India report; Census of India; Shivashankar & Ganesh Prasad (2005).

Further, the STs in Karnataka are also the socially and economically most backward social group. However, the government made efforts to formulate and implement a special development programme for upgrading their socio-economic status. As a part of the programme of advancing tribal communities, the government launched the Tribal Sub-Plan (TSP) in 1976–1977. The analysis of the budgetary allocation in respect of the TSP for various years brings out the following points:

1. Funds under this scheme were modest in the beginning, but there was a sharp increase in the budgetary allocation subsequently with the decision of upgrading the amount in proportion to the population of the tribes.
2. Sub-plan funds are treated as additional and allocated to different sectors, which will impact the livelihoods of the tribal population. These sectors are more than 30 in number and cover sectors such as agriculture and related sectors, the cottage and village industries, rural development, healthcare and housing sectors, among others.
3. Although the allocation of the plan allocation was quite encouraging, the release of the funds did not keep pace with the allocation. As a result, the proportion of expenditure was less than 90 per cent and, during some years, it went down to even 70 per cent of the allotted budget.
4. The reason for the gap between allocation and expenditure is, of course, due to the release of funds not being commensurate with the allocation. Since we have also observed that there is a gap between release and expenditure, it may be reasonable to argue that the department perhaps does not have an adequate absorption capacity.
5. Analysis of the TSP fund allocation across various sectors over a period of time brings out the point that the priorities given by the department are rural development and panchayat raj tribal welfare, major irrigation, primary and secondary education, public works, housing and so on. There appears to be some degree of overlooking on the part of the authorities in sectors such as agriculture and related activities, women and child development, minor irrigation, health and family welfare and higher education, since these are the sectors that directly affect the tribal population's development.

6. Ideally, the share of TSP should be equivalent to the proportion of the ST population in the state. In this case, the TSP should be around 7 per cent of the total financial outlay in the annual plans of Karnataka.
7. TSP was streamlined with a regular allocation starting from the 2007–2008 with an allocation of 112,911.89 lakhs having a share of 6.3 per cent, then it shrunk to around 4.3 per cent till 2013. Then later on, it was strengthened by bringing the Karnataka Scheduled Castes Sub-Allocation and Tribal Sub-Allocation (Planning, Allocation and Utilization of Financial Resources) Act, 2013, during Mr Siddaramaiah's regime. It was thought to be a model legislation for the development of the ST population in the state. Later, the allocation increased in proportion to the tribal population of the state. Recently, efforts have been made to weaken the TSP mechanism for the allocation of the state sector and divert funds for non-ST construction activities, including the disaster relief programme.

CONCLUSION

One can easily sense deep-rooted group inequalities through the examination of available demographic data with respect to tribal representation. Differences in capabilities, along with type of livelihood, make it difficult for hill and forest dwelling, wild and hunting communities to take part in political processes of the state. Even though some isolated efforts were carried out to include them at the local-level politics, especially in panchayat committees, they have been silently excluded from political processes. In Chamarajanagar, Mysore, Kodagu and Coastal districts, we hear about electing these vulnerable groups to panchayats in order to exclude them from decision-making processes. Mr Ashok, Tribal leader from Udupi lamented that

> Most of the times, our issues are related to basic survival questions such as food, shelter, educational access to our children…but the Gram Sabhas discuss majorly on the building of village temples and the construction of roads. Those issues do not have any relevance to us.

One can easily understand the systematic political exclusion and its impacts on the lives of tribal communities by analysing the enacted public policies to growth and development processes. Further, caste/tribe-based census and participatory policy action research methods are important strategies for inclusive India and are tools to address deep-rooted group inequalities perpetuated in tribal communities through the identities of caste, religion, gender, ethnicity and race. As demonstrated in this chapter, the political intersectionality of tribal communities plays a key role in understanding the impact of development interventions. Further, the macroscopic and dominant majority community among the STs in Karnataka, like Bedas, clearly dominates the political negotiations. Microscopic communities among tribals do not get opportunities in political participation, since most of our democratic institutions and structures impacting the lives of tribals are designed on the basis of majority participation in electoral processes. Thus, it is high time for us to graduate from the idea of social citizenship to the idea of social inclusion of left-out microscopic tribal communities through appropriate corrective strategies, including exploring the possibility of special representation.

REFERENCES

Assadi, M. (1998). Saffronisation with upper caste support. *Economic & Political Weekly, 33*(12), 626–628.

Assadi, M. (2004). Forest encroachments, left adventurism and Hindutva. *Economic & Political Weekly, 39*(9), 882–885.

Devi, S., (1939). *A warning to the Hindus.* Calcutta: Hindu Mission.

Government of India. (1965). *The advisory committee on the revision of the lists of Scheduled Castes and Scheduled Tribes* (Lokur Committee). New Delhi: Government of India.

Havanur, L. G. (1975). *Karnataka backward classes commission report* (vol. I, part I). Bangalore: Government of Karnataka. Retrieved from http://censusindia.gov.in/Tables_Published/SCST/dh_st_karnataka.pdf

Kalelkar, K. (1955). *Report of the backward classes commission.* New Delhi. Manager of Publications.

Nayaka, H. (2010–2011). Situating tribals in the early history of Karnataka. In *Proceedings of the Indian history Congress* (vol. 71; pp. 97–109). New Delhi: Indian History Congress.

Rodrigues, V. (2014). Political power and democratic enablement: Devraj Urs and lower caste mobilisation in Karnataka. *Economic & Political Weekly, 49*(25), 62–70.

S. S. (1990). Caste and power game in Karnataka. *Economic & Political Weekly, 25*(42–43), 2359–2360.

Shivashankar, P. & Ganesh Prasad, G. S. (2005). *Human development performance of gram panchayats in Karnataka-2005.* Abdul Nazir Sab State Institute of Rural Development and Panchayat Raj, Mysuru & Planning, Programme Monitoring and Statistics Department, Government of Karnataka.

Verloo, M. (2006). Multiple inequalities, intersectionality and the European Union. *European Journal of Women's Studies, 13*(3), 211–228.

Political Articulations of Adivasis in Kerala

Abhilash T.

INTRODUCTION

The death of Madhu, a 27-year-old Adivasi man who belonged to the Kurumba tribe in Attappadi—a region known for the destitution of tribal communities and high infant mortality rates—in Kerala on 22 February 2018 triggered the discussion about the prejudices that are still prevalent against oppressed sections in the progressive and socially developed state in India. Madhu's death, the medical report confirms the signs of lynching,[1] was significant in the atrocities committed against Adivasis in the state, because this time the attackers were courageous enough to click a selfie with Madhu and circulate it through social media before he died, which went viral on social media. The killing of a 'mentally ill' tribal man, Madhu, in Attappadi in Palakkad by tying him up and circulating images of this on social media has been the most recent incident of violence, highlighting the Kerala paradox (Kottai, 2018). On the other hand,

the story of Madhu can be seen as the microcosm of the political economy of six decades of tribal development in Kerala, which has prompted researchers to look into the trajectories of inclusionary measures taken by the state for Adivasis over the years.

ADIVASIS AND KERALA MODEL DEVELOPMENT

The Kerala Model of Development (KMD) has been characterized by high levels of social development with minimum economic infrastructural input. In the available literature, KMD has generally been evaluated as doing comparatively well in terms of an acquired quality in social life and human development indicators. The state has the highest literacy rate (93.9%) in India, while all India literacy rate is 74 per cent and also has the highest life expectancy rate–nearly 74 years—and

---

[1] The post-mortem report revealed that the deceased had sustained serious injuries on the head and bruises all over the body, and there was internal bleeding and he had broken ribs.

highest sex ratio (1,084 females per 1,000 males) (Census of India, 2011). After the reorganization of the states in 1957, the political leadership undertook three measures for the development of the people. The first was a land reform programme that was legalized by the state government in the 1960s, triggering social change, especially in the mainland. The second was the implementation of the minimum wage for manual labour, both in the agrarian and industrial sectors of the economy. The third was the abolition of landlordism and land distribution to former tenants. Kerala's success on the social front is commonly attributed to the effectiveness of public action and popular mobilization (Dreze & Sen, 1996) which ultimately culminated in more responsible governance. Nevertheless, concerns have been expressed regarding the relative exclusion of social sections such as Dalits, Adivasis and fisherfolks from the model. In short, the peculiar geographical features and settlement patterns of the region and its possible implications for social development were ignored (Rammohan, 2000). Government investments in the social domain of the state are visible in the plains. Here, a major chunk of the people who belong to the lower strata of the society received the benefits of land reforms as well as state-initiated developmental measures.

Compared to the political and social empowerment of Kerala's mainland, the traditional Adivasi[2] areas on the geo-cultural fringes were largely left out. Although the communities have a literacy rate of 75.8 per cent, among rural females it is only 69 per cent (Census of India, 2011). The poverty among the tribal population of Kerala is 44.3 per cent, which is higher than Andhra Pradesh, Assam, Gujarat, Rajasthan, Tamil Nadu, Karnataka, Uttar Pradesh and West Bengal. This reflects their inadequate access to resources considering their spatial settlement in the forests, their sociocultural specificities and their historical deprivation. Interestingly, all of them have no land rights over the land where they live. Earlier, land reforms were thought of as an initial entitlement to social development and progress. Social entitlement to land in the mainland eventually leads to unprecedented growth in the service-based tertiary sector. But unfortunately, the traditional Adivasi habitats in the highlands were excluded from it. As a result, the Adivasis were marginalized from the development process.

Moving beyond the popular perception of the KMD as a single developmental attainment, the creation of the Left movement and the action of a single political organization, it is essential to address the issues that evolved during the implementation of the project. Relative exclusion of the outlying population, like that of Adivasis, substantially proved the unpleasant side of the KMD. A vast array of literature on it has initiated a chastisement in terms of post-colonial tribal development (Ajith, 2002; Rammohan, 2000). There are three sets of literature available on Adivasi marginality in Kerala. The first elucidates the socio-economic and ethnographic aspects of tribal life. The second set deals with the relationship between the tribals and the state in the post-colonial period. The final set addresses the Adivasi movements, including those initiated by subsidiaries of mainstream political parties, with a view to the Adivasis regaining their sources of livelihood and alienated land through various means. Existing literature, however, often fails to comprehend the substance of indigenous life and economy *vis-a-vis* the pre- and post-colonial policies towards Adivasis. Moreover, a lack of knowledge about home-grown Adivasi movements from indigenous groups often prevented scholars from formulating a feasible answer to the Adivasi question.

Therefore, this chapter looks into the crystallization of land rights movement led by the Adivasi Gotra Maha Sabha (AGMS). It argues

---

[2] This chapter interchangeably uses the terms 'tribe' and 'Adivasi'.

that this movement has put forth a critique of the national project of modernization in the post-colonial context, and has also challenged the derived wisdom of modernity in Kerala. The land rights movement of the AGMS represented a process of collective identity articulation or assertion, along with a systematized effort for democratic bargaining. It further focuses on its efforts to build political consciousness among the highly heterogeneous and geographically disbursed Adivasi communities in Kerala with a brief evaluation of the political party, Janadhipathya Rashtriya Sabha (JRS), established by AGMS's leadership and contested in 2016 state assembly elections.

UNDERSTANDING PRE- AND POST-COLONIAL ADIVASI SITUATION IN KERALA

The pre- and post-colonial Adivasi situation is not uniformly dismal in the eastern mountainous belt, where Adivasis mostly live. Thurston says, 'There are evidently certain spatial variations in the levels of socio-economic development of the different tribal groups. The tribal economy of Kerala has not been subject however, to a systematic investigation and analysis, though several scholars have studied the tribal economy within the state' (Thurston, 1909). Many studies focus on the sociocultural and linguistic aspects of the Scheduled Tribes (STs).[3] The intra-regional variations of the socio-economic life of Adivasis across the Western Ghats were visible since the colonial period. The Adivasis in Kerala live largely on the fringes of the western side of the Western Ghats which demarcate the eastern boundary

of the state (Kunhaman, 1982). Therefore, the socio-economic landscape and settlement pattern of different heterogeneous Adivasi groups vary for each region. Wayanad is home for 31 per cent of Adivasis in the state (Census of India, 2011).

COLONIAL ROOTS OF ADIVASI MARGINALITY

British forest policy in the Madras presidency was an extension of the imperial strategy to extract maximum profit, which adversely affected the livelihoods of the Adivasis. The British put the forest range in the presidency under a conservator, excepting the cardamom plantations in Thodupulay (Thodupuzha) taluk in southern Travancore (Maclean, 1877). They were aimed at bringing cardamom under regular cultivation, as in the cardamom hills. The latter were under the supervision of the conservator of the forests till 1944, when they were transferred to a special superintendent. However, the hill tribes were excluded from cardamom cultivation. Ironically, the administrative reports of both Madras presidency and Travancore–Cochin barely mention the existence of indigenous people since 1877. The state initiative to address landlessness among the depressed classes came only in 1925–1926 when it assigned 394 acres of *Puthuval*[4] and the wastelands to them. Moreover, the British granted concession in regard to the assignment of lands in the names of ex-soldiers who served abroad in the First World War only in 1918 and which were extended for a further period of three years from 21 November 1925. An area of 3,799.12 acres was reserved

---

[3] Thurston largely focuses on the ethnographic roots of the southern Indian tribes. He encompasses information about the changing pattern of the life of the hill tribes in Kerala. He also discusses the original way of life, customs, manners, religious beliefs, superstitions, etc., of tribal communities. L. A. Krishna Iyer's study is a general description of the castes and tribes of Travancore–Cochin, with emphasis on their sociocultural milieu (Iyer, 1941). However, it concentrates on the economic aspects of the hill tribes.

[4] Puthuval land includes (a) *Puramboke* (surveyed and unassessed) transferred to assessed waste, (b) assessed waste (surveyed) and (c) unassessed waste (unsurveyed).

for this purpose and another 4.25 acres were registered (Government of Travancore, [1925–1926]1927). As mentioned earlier, these reports, while reiterating the necessity to protect forest tracts, were silent about the Adivasi livelihood in the forest, but emphasized the need for strengthening forest laws to protect the forests from 'trespassers'.

In this period, the government began to notify reserve forests to effectively control and exploit forests and their resources. A special forest settlement officer was appointed in every forest stations near to all tribal habitats in 1926 and continued during the next year. He was responsible for settling down the nomadic slash and burn agricultural system[5] of the hill tribes in Travancore–Cochin. That prevented the free movement of Adivasis in the forests for hunting and gathering. This situation became much more dysfunctional in 1928. During this year, proposals for 23 reserves were pending and two more reserves were notified since then and, there were, therefore, finally 25 reserves for settlement. Settlement of 16 reserves was completed during the year, leaving 9 pending settlements at the end of the year. The total number of claim cases for disposal was 189 of which 144 were dismissed by the forest settlement officer (Government of Travancore, 1929). The deprivation of the major chunk of their claim over the forest land adversely affected their livelihoods and forced them to settle down in the colonies proposed by the government. Finally, by strengthening the land use pattern and effectively controlling forest resources, the government removed the territorial rights enjoyed by the Adivasis in the forests.

Studies carried out by British anthropologists have disregarded Adivasi marginality in princely states. For example, L. A. Krishna Iyer emphasized the geographical conditions of Travancore as a significant reason for the backwardness of the hill tribes (Iyer, 1941). In northern Kerala, the geographical concentration of hill tribes is related to the vast stretches of paddy fields in Wayanad valley, where the scarcity of agricultural slaves (Adivasis) during the 18th century prompted non-tribal landlords to bring in a large number of Adivasis, mostly Paniyans and Adiyans, who constitute 27 per cent of the Adivasi population in the state from the neighbouring forests of Karnataka and Tamil Nadu (Kunhaman, 1982). Adivasis in Wayanad were in a primitive state till the middle of the 18th century when they were enslaved by the immigrants from the plains (Logan, 1887). History of entrusting rights for collecting and removing minor forest produce (MFP) by the colonial administration reveals that there is not even a passing remark about the Adivasis *vis-a-vis* MFP in Travancore–Cochin. Meanwhile, it was leased out for the years 1947–1948 for a yearly rental of ₹25,575 (Government of Travancore and Cochin, 1950).

Post-colonial Predicaments

From 36 tribal communities, Kerala has a tribal population of 4.84 lakhs, which is 1.4 per cent of the state's population (Census of India, 2011).[6] It was 3.64 lakh (1.1%) in 2001. It also shows 3.31 per cent annual growth. Their population is largely concentrated in Wayanad, Idukki, Kottayam and Pathanamthitta districts. Among them, Paniyan is the most populous group with a population of 88,450, forming

---

[5] This agricultural technique involves cutting and burning small trees and plants in forest and woodlands to create agricultural fields. Subsistence agriculture typically uses little technology. It is part of the shifting cultivation practised by Adivasis.

[6] Although the present list consists of 43 communities serially numbered from 1 to 43, as per the Scheduled Caste and Tribe Orders (Amendment) Act, 2002 (Act 10 of 2003), five communities (serial numbers 7, 11, 12, 14 and 28) have been excluded and two communities (serial numbers 31 and 32) have been clubbed with the existing community (serial no. 30). As much there are only 36 communities on the list (Kotta, Kamara, Konda Reddies, Konda Kapus and Maratti were excluded. Palliyar included with Palliyan).

18.2 per cent of the total Adivasi population in the state, which was 22.5 per cent in the 2001 census. Kurichchan is the second largest tribe with a population of 35,171, constituting 7.2 per cent, which was 32,746 (9%) in the 2001 census. Six groups, namely Kanikar, Irular, Muthuvan Kurumans, Mavilan and Malai Arayan, with populations ranging from 21,000 to 33,000. Seven tribes, namely Malayan, Malai Vedan, Adiyan, Mannan, Urali, Ulladan and Karimbalan, with a population of 5,000–20,000, account for another 15.8 per cent and the communities with a population of less than 500 population are 5 in number, which was 11 in the 2001 census. Out of them, Kochuvelan, 10 Kurumban are the smallest groups with a population of less than 50.

On the social front, Adivasis in the state are subjected to various levels of livelihood inequalities. From the total of 103,268 households, around 37,685 are landless and derive a major part of their income from manual casual labour, and also around 63,692 households are facing deprivation. At district level, Wayanad has the highest number of landless Adivasi households. Approximately, 8.4 per cent of Adivasi households are landless in Wayanad. Adivasis in Kerala have an impressive record in literacy, approximately 75.8 per cent, whereas the national rate is 68.5 per cent. Interestingly, 74 per cent of the rural tribal population is literate in the state. It was 64.4 per cent in 2001. However, 2010–2011 data shows that the dropout rate between primary and high schools is 29.1 per cent (Census of India, 2011).

The idea of Adivasi development and empowerment, initiated by the unified Left government, advocated the formation of the 'linguistic state of Kerala' on the ground that linguistic homogeneity facilitated the unification of oppressed classes against landlordism. It also followed the policy of providing opportunities to Adivasis not only by way of access to land but also complimentary facilities for

their socio-economic advancement. Thus, the Left was in favour of introducing modern agricultural technologies in the Adivasi areas, as it believed that it was the only option for the socio-economic advancement of these marginalized communities (Prasad, 2004).

Damodaran says, 'This was virtually the approach suggested by the Dhebar Commission as well. This policy fitted well in the tendency of successive state governments in permitting settlers to occupy forests and traditional tribal habitats for cultivation purposes' (Damodaran, 2006). Men from the plains of the Travancore state resorted to moneylending to usurp Adivasi land through unfair deals (Mathur, 1977). In this way, state-sponsored plantation and migration drives from the plains dispossessed Adivasis from their land. The Adivasi concept of land and space was almost against the idea of land encroachment that was invented and implemented by governments both before and after 1947. With the development of plantations in Wayanad from the latter half of the 19th century, the process of 'proletarianization' of the hill Adivasis started, which continued through the early decades of the 20th century. However, feudal vestiges such as bonded labour are still prevalent to some extent and the Adivasis are subject to exploitation (Kunhaman, 1982).

The story of Attappadi hills[7] is different from the story of Wayanad. Due to the high incidence of malaria, the area remained inaccessible to outsiders. The Adivasi communities, such as Irulas, Mudugas and Kurumbas, were its inhabitants. From the mid-1950s onwards, a large-scale influx of immigrants from Travancore–Cochin and also the *Gouwndars* (landlords) from Karnataka and Tamil Nadu took place that dispossessed Adivasis from their land, pushing them down to inferior land. The history of Cochin is dissimilar to that of Attappadi and Wayanad. Here, the tribal population was very small and engaged as labourers in the commercial

---

[7] The second largest area of the Adivasi concentration of Malabar region, situated in the Palakkad district.

extraction of forest products. After the establishment of the state monopoly of the forests towards the end of the 18th century, the hill Adivasis came under the government's control, which maintained a paternalistic relation with them. Therefore, some Adivasis began to take to settled agriculture towards the end of the 19th century (Iyer, 1941).

Events took a different course in Travancore. The general policy of conferment of peasant ownership rights, which gained momentum from the middle of the 19th century, encompassed the hill Adivasis. The rulers had a specific protective policy for them, which included a ban on the entry of outsiders into tribal hamlets. Traders were required to obtain licenses from divisional forest officers (DFOs) (Kunhaman, 1982). Iyer argues:

> Apart from other hill-tribes, there is a small-scale economy which existed among the Mala Arayar, the hill-tribe who live in Idukkki and Kottayam districts of Travancore state. They practised shifting cultivation in which clearing jungles, cultivation of food crops and selection of fresh sites for cultivation when the soil became toxic. If a man is unable to do any work in the field, the headman and others help him in clearing jungle and in other works. In some hamlets, people meet once in a month, discuss village affairs, and depart after a feast. A fund is raised and which is in possession of the Kanikaran—the headman. Loans are given to the needy and the amount recovered in instalments. The influence of village government is weakening under the control of the forest department. After the establishment of state monopoly over forests towards the end of 18th century, the hill-tribes came under the control of the government. (Iyer, 1941)

But compared with other princely states, towards the end of the 19th century, most tribes in Travancore were permanently settled as independent cultivators with minimum landownership. However, the government did not implement legally binding policies to prevent the alienation of Adivasi land until the enactment of the Kerala Scheduled Tribes (Restriction on Transfer of Lands and Restoration of Alienated Lands) Act, 1975, which is considered a landmark for recovering Adivasi land from the encroachers.

Traditionally, land is the pivot of the economy and livelihood of Adivasis in Kerala. However, the question of the ownership of land did not arise among the Adivasis as long as the land was commonly owned. After they reached the stage of *puthuvayal krishi* or slash-and-burn agriculture, each family within the Adivasi community was allocated an area by the headman according to its needs and ability to cultivate. As long as a family remained within the Adivasi organization and cultivated the plot, its occupancy and operational rights over the plot remained undisturbed. Thus, the Adivasi as a whole retained the 'ownership' rights, the individual Adivasi family enjoying the operational rights. This type of institutional arrangement was possible because land was not a limiting factor of production, and labour alone was scarce. It made Adivasis a homogeneous community of primary producers. Meanwhile, the state-sponsored migration from the plains to the Adivasi hills began to take place. The interaction that developed between the Adivasis and the emigrants gradually transformed the structure of the Adivasi economy and society. Policies followed by successive governments debilitated the Adivasi space and the concept of landownership rights. Alien forces pushed the Adivasis to the ambit of market economy that sowed the seeds of a differentiated Adivasi economic structure (Kunhaman, 1982). When the state-sponsored market economy was established, settled agricultural groups among the Adivasis began to participate in the economy.

Theoretically, a free market enables a producer to decide on the price of a commodity, the time and place of marketing and to realize the full value of the marketed surpluses. In an imperfect market, with the active operation of intermediaries, the choice of a producer gets restricted and, consequently, they are handicapped in realizing the full value of their marketed surplus. This situation will be more acute if the producers are poor and depend on the credit from the intermediaries. In the case of Adivasis, non-Adivasi intermediaries manage to mobilize the marketed surplus of the Adivasis through the advancement of loans during the off-season agricultural period. As these loans are often secured for crops, Adivasis are obliged to sell the produce immediately after harvesting at predetermined prices. Once indebted, a vicious circle develops from which Adivasi households seldom escape (Kunhaman, 1982). The Adivasis of Kozhikodu and Kannur are subject to exploitation in this product market.

Due to the penetration of modernity-induced market forces in the Adivasi habitats, the traditional monoculture has given way to a diversified agriculture with commercial crops claiming a high weightage in the overall crop mix. The role of the Left was pertinent in this regard. Damodaran says:

> overall, the tribal development programmes in the post-colonial Kerala, in accordance with the thinking of the Dhebar Commission and the Communist parties also suffered serious limitations. Adivasis, barring few exemptions, found it difficult to adjust to changes brought by schemes of 'intensive development' introduced by the Government of Kerala. Furthermore, notable case in point was the Wayanad colonisation scheme, whereby tribals were made to stay with non-tribal settlers from plains and encouraged to take settled agriculture. Thus, the colonisation scheme, which was based on the principle of 'one size for all', created social tensions in the tribal district of Wayanad. (Damodaran, 2006).

Evidence and after-effects of state-sponsored migration drive show the marginalization of Adivasi communities of South India in general and Kerala in particular.

LAND ALIENATION

Land alienation and landlessness are two major causes of Adivasi marginality in Kerala. Modernity-led state-sponsored plantation and migration drives had a major role in it. As

has already been discussed, the Adivasi concept of land is different from that of migrants. Although the princely states in southern Kerala had done pretty good against the encroachment of land, the post-colonial governments were unable or reluctant to enact legislation to prevent Adivasi land encroachment by outsiders. With the gradual destruction of Adivasi sources of livelihoods, Adivasis became dependent on government assistance. The opening up of plantations by the British in the mountains set the stage for permanent migration and eventual encroachment of forest land for settlements. The first major migration of peasants to the highlands took place in the 1940s. Most migrants were from the crowded southern part of the state. Although by 1954 the government had stopped granting land titles, illegal encroachment continued. The settlers emerged as a powerful group demanding regularization of encroachment through political support and legal deeds (Sreekumar & Parayil, 2002).

Compared with southern Kerala, the proportion of landless Adivasi households in Wayanad and Malabar is high. Extensive tracts of Adivasi land were usurped by cultivators who immigrated from the plains, and the Adivasis were reduced to landless labourers. Great suffering was inflicted on Paniya and Adiya Adivasis (Raman & Bijoy, 2003). Grow more food campaign of the government contributed to migration in Malabar. There appear to be commonalities between the patterns of Adivasi land alienation in Wayanad and Travancore regions. Encroachers from mainland, largely supported by political parties and government, played a major role. Meanwhile, the politically divided civil society did not heed the Adivasi marginality.

The State as Perpetrator

Even after 1947, both central and state governments followed British forest policies. This is shown in Table 19.1.

Table 19.1   Colonial and Post-colonial Forest Laws in India

Year	Law	Results
1878	Indian Forest Act	State became the custodian and proprietor of classified forest land.
1890	Forest Department Resolution	Previous rights of access and use redefined as 'privilege' for specific tribes, caste, villages and organizations.
1927	Indian Forest Act	Refurbished the 1878 Act and it remains the legislative basis for the state forest management today. The government adopted the 1927 Act after Indian independence.
1952	National Forest Policy	Set out guidelines which were, for the most part, directed towards the supply of cheap timber and non-timber forest products for state-sponsored industrialization and modernization.
1976	Indian Forest Act added to the concurrent list of the Constitution of India	Both central and state governments obtained shared control over the forests.
1980	Forest Conservation Act	The central government reasserted some of its control over the forest-based resources. The Act restricts its power to de-reserve the forest and restricts the use of forest land for non-forestry purposes without its prior approval.
1988	National Forest Policy	Envisaged people's involvement in the development and protection of forest for the first time. It was never implemented.

Source: Various year's forest laws, acts and policies.

Table 19.1 gives a clear picture about the forest laws. Interestingly, they are less sympathetic to Adivasi livelihoods and rights. The perceived logic behind the formulation of forest policies and state's ultimate control over forests has many facets. As Das Gupta argues, 'The close affinity between human and nature as seen among the Adivasis should not lead to the assumption that they were in anyway ecologically conscious conservators of the forest' (Das Gupta, 2009). Such an argument indicates a negative notion that Adivasi societies had no recognizable means of knowing if going beyond a certain limit could damage the locality's ecosystem in the long run.

The state used various methods to encroach upon the Adivasi land. Its policies supported outsiders to encroach on forest land. Meanwhile, the forest department advocated imposing of more restrictions on Adivasis as they were responsible for declining forest coverage. Therefore, it imposed restrictions on them for entering forests. P. K. Prakash writes:

The total area of wild-life sanctuaries in Kerala is 2315.44 square kilometers. This will come under the 25 percent to total forests in state and six percent of the total land area of the state. The state has encroached the Adivasi land in two ways. One is to construct the dams in Adivasi habitats and adjacent areas which fall under the projects and to declare wildlife sanctuaries. Secondly, the Adivasis who are evicted from the project area will migrate to the other/peripheral areas of the forest, and then the government will declare the newly built Adivasis habitats as wildlife sanctuaries. Such a covert attempt of the state had eventually alienated Adivasis from the forest. Hydroelectric projects and dams such as those in Idukki, Chimmini and Karappuzha have resulted in a swelling of the numbers of the landless Adivasis. Wildlife sanctuaries and national parks like the Periyar and Wayanad sanctuaries have all driven thousands of Adivasis from their hearths in a colonisation of the last few rich patches of forests which have been thrown open to tourism operators, both within and outside of the state. (Prakash, 2002)

Mannan Adivasi groups who live in the peripheral areas of Idukki hydroelectric projects are among the worst sufferers of such projects. After the commissioning of the project, their hunting and gathering activities are strictly prohibited in the forests.[8]

---
[8] Interview with the late Kozhimala Ariyan Raja Mannan (tribal king) on 22 February 2010.

Unimplemented Legislations

The state's response towards Adivasi land alienation was almost negative until the radical Left resurfaced across the Indian villages in the late 1960s and the early 1970s. This resurgence was spearheaded by the Communist Party of India (Marxist–Leninist) which had a strong base in the Adivasi belts. It was a major reason for renewed interest in tribal land question (Sreekumar & Parayil, 2002). The Government of India appointed the Dhebar Commission in 1960 to look into this matter. It recommended that alienated tribal lands be restored to their original owners and that 26 January 1950 be taken as the cut-off date for this purpose (Dhebar, 1961). In April 1975, the central government advised the state governments to enact necessary legislations for the restoration of alienated tribal lands in line with these recommendations. As a consequence, the Kerala Legislative Assembly unanimously passed the Kerala Scheduled Tribes (Restriction on Transfer of Lands and Restoration of Alienated Lands) Act, 1975. It did not lead to a solution of the Adivasi land question. It was included in the Ninth Schedule of the Constitution.[9] It was not implemented till 1986 when the necessary regulatory framework was finalized. However, this did not result in any positive action.

Responding to a public interest litigation on 15 October 1993, Kerala high court ordered the government to implement the Act within six weeks. But the government sought extension of time for its implementation repeatedly after six months. In 1996, it proposed to promulgate an ordinance to unilaterally amend the pro-Adivasi clauses, but the governor rejected it. Thereupon, the government submitted an affidavit to the court that the implementation of the Act was no longer possible due to the organized resistance by the settlers and other encroachers. The court rejected it and directed the government to implement the Act within six weeks. The political elite resorted to scuttle its implementation by introducing into the assembly Kerala Scheduled Tribes (Restriction of Transfer of Land and Restoration of Alienated Lands) Amendment Bill, 1996, which made legal all transactions of Adivasi land between 1960 and 24 January 1986. It was passed by the assembly in September 1996, but it failed to secure presidential assent for the assembly cannot amend an act included in the Ninth Schedule of the Constitution. Therefore, the government passed Kerala Restriction on Transfer by the Restoration of Lands to Scheduled Tribes Bill, 1999, under the state subject 'agricultural lands' to avoid the presidential assent. It provided that lands of up to 2 hectares held by encroachers would be validated. But the high court stayed it because it violated the act of 1975 (Sreekumar & Parayil, 2002). Therefore, the government went to the Supreme Court, which on 25 July 2009 judged in its favour. This was against the spirit of the act of 1975.[10]

ASSEMBLY CONSTITUENCIES FOR ADIVASIS

The state has two assembly constituencies reserved for Adivasis. Historically, out of 140 assembly constituencies, only one seat was reserved for the STs until 2008, and the second after the implementation of delimitation order of 2008. Presently, Sultan Bathery and Mananthavady assembly seats in the Wayanad district are reserved for Adivasis. Generally, candidates for assembly elections in these reserved constituencies are decided and fielded upon their political affiliations not in line with the Adivasi political consciousness emerged in response to the repressive and hegemonic state. Therefore, the candidates

---

[9] An act included in the Ninth Schedule cannot be challenged in the court, as implementation is a constitutional obligation.
[10] Interview with the AGMS leader M. Geethanandan after the court verdict on 6 May 2010.

are generally drawn from the cadres of the Communist Party of India (Marxist; CPI[M]) and the Indian National Congress (INC). As a result, apart from the promise of implementing few welfare schemes, it never focused upon Adivasis rights over productive resources. Their larger project of Adivasi emancipation sided with the exploitation of powerful settlers whose interests were closely linked to forest machinery and the political class. Landmark legislations like the Panchayats (Extension to Scheduled Areas [PESA]) Act, 1996, never reflected in any political party's electoral manifesto. A field survey was conducted in Kattunayakan—which comes under particularly vulnerable tribal groups—settlements in Noolpuzha Panchayat in Sultan Bathery assembly in 2017. Out of 44 houses surveyed, only 15 had Forest Right Act (FRA) titles. The remaining 27 households (61%) did not have any documents to prove their right over the land they have been living on since time immemorial. From the seven settlements surveyed, approximately 84 per cent households were involved in non-timber forest produce (NTFP) collection for livelihoods. However, there is no proper price mechanism available for NTFP at settlement level. The mechanism that is run by the forest department for procuring NTFP seems less concerned with providing Adivasis a fair price for the products, which is against the spirit of FRA (Thadathil, 2017). Around 22 per cent of the households depend on Mahatma Gandhi National Rural Employment Guarantee Act for their livelihoods. Around 13 households have a stable source of income because they are salaried. Many of them work with the forest department as forest watchers and elephant trainers. It confirms the fact that the structural changes in Adivasi livelihoods, through the implementation of progressive legislations, does not seem to be the agenda of the political class, even in reserved constituencies.

It is also essential to discuss the performance of different political parties in these constituencies in different elections. After declaring it a reserved constituency, Sultan Bathery stood with the INC. I. C. Balakrishnan, from the Kurichiya Adivasi community, holds a seat for two consecutive assemblies. However, his vote share was reduced by 5.1 per cent in the 2016 election, largely because of the fact that National Democratic Alliance (NDA) fielded C. K. Janu as his opponent. Miss Janu scored 16.23 per cent of the vote and came in third, while CPI(M) candidate Rugmini Subramanian secured second position with 37.53 per cent vote share. Interestingly, Bahujan Samaj Party candidate C. Mukundan scored 791 votes in this constituency. In Mananthavady, the fight was between the INC and the CPI(M) and the latter secured the seat with a narrow margin. CPI(M) candidate O. R. Kelu secured 42.88 per cent vote from a total poll of 145,596 votes, while INC's P. K. Jalaja scored 41.99 per cent votes.[11] The voting behaviours show the fact that it was not Adivasi consciousness that played a major role in the electoral process, rather mobilization largely based on the traditional class-based organization of the Left parties and the Nehruvian programmes that invested heavily in the social welfare mechanisms followed by the INC, and it hardly addressed the community's far cry for structural changes that were aimed to address their vulnerabilities in accessing political power and natural recourses.

It is pertinent to note in this context that Adivasis are not yet disillusioned with the political parties in the state. Rather, their political orientation has changed over time and seems to be aligned with the Left or the INC. These are constituencies where the mainstream parties have their cadres functions in a very systematic fashion. As a result, for many Adivasis, shifting their loyalty and aligning with a community-based Adivasis consciousness in the electoral process would

---

[11] Details are collected from the official website of the Election Commission of India.

be a difficult task. Therefore, though this reserved constituencies have ensured Adivasi representation in the state assembly, they have hardly made any significant impact on their community consciousness on constitutional rights. Moreover, the political class in the state has guardedly implanted the logic: 'your emancipation is our responsibility and we are always magnanimous to your cause' into the conscience of the Adivasi electorate.

Towards Adivasi Mobilization

As a result of their marginality, Adivasis began to mobilize themselves to bargain collectively with the government to regain their land and livelihood. Adivasi mobilization against the encroachers has three phases. First, the anti-colonial Pazhassi Revolt in Wayanad during the British period. They played a major role in the first armed struggle against British rule in Kerala. Adivasis have shown their militant nature since ancient times. Freeman says:

> Groups of militant tribals were recruited in the war-service of the mountain kings in southern India. For instance, when a lineage of former Tulu chiefs fled to Muslim incursions (reportedly from Malik Kafur) into the highlands to the east of Neeleswaram, they set up a small kingdom based on swiddening, and recruited tribals called *Malamkudiyans* as their *Padanayar* or warriors. The latter are said to be the group related to the famous *Kurichyas* who fought against the British in the rebellion of Pazhasi Raja. (Freeman, 1999)

The second period falls between the 1960s and the early 1970s. It witnessed the establishment of Adivasi interest groups within the political parties. This concluded with the Naxalite movement, which struck a chord among the Adivasis, especially in the Wayanad district. The Karshaka Sangam of the Naxalites was soon disbanded, with its leader Varghese killed in a fake police encounter in February 1970 (Raman & Bijoy, 2003). The third phase, beginning from the late 1980s, witnessed the emergence of Adivasi welfare organizations both inside and outside the Adivasi spheres. They are Adivasi Sangam, Kerala Girivarga Sangam (Kerala Tribal Collective) and Kerala Adivasi Samajam (Kerala Adivasi Association). New Adivasi organizations, namely Girivaga Sevak Samithy (Tribal Servant Committee) in Attappadi, Akhila Thiruvithamkoor Mala Araya Maha Sabha (All Travancore Mala Araya Maha Sabha) (ATMAMS), Idukki and Kottayam, All-Kerala Workers' Union, Pathanamthitta, Adivasi Vimochana Munnani (Adivasi Emancipation Front) in Kannur, Adivasi Kshema Samithi (Adivasi Welfare Committee) by the CPI(M) and finally the Adivasi Dalit Samara Samithi (Adivasi Dalit Strike Committee) (ADSS) were established at the state level. The ADSS was a conglomeration of Adivasi and Dalit organizations that became AGMS in 2002.

Many of these groups are subsidiaries of mainstream political parties as well as settled agricultural Adivasi groups, such as Mala Arayan and Mannan. However, the AGMS is entirely an Adivasi organization[12] that specifically focuses on issues related to Adivasi marginality and land question and the cadre mostly drawn from landless Adivasi communities from northern and central Kerala. Interestingly, settled agriculturists communities seem to be less active in the AGMS. It was the first home-grown movement that brought out issues of indigenous people in highland Kerala. Compared with other organizations, it was capable of (re)claiming their identity and their land rights.

Sumit Guha argues, 'In case of Kerala, the discourse of tribals as indigenous only became explicitly politicised in the nineties, partly under the influence of the international indigenous movement' (Guha, 1999). The global upsurge of the indigenous cause may have

---

[12] After C. K. Janu left the organization to form the political party, M. Geethanandan took over the responsibility of the leadership. At present, M. Geethanadan is the leader of the AGMS.

played a role at the local level. But the afore-mentioned facts indicate that the politicization of Adivasis in the state had taken place much before the emergence of AGMS in 2002. The lack of leadership within the group was often manipulated by mainstream political parties in line with the predatory instincts of the set-tlers. The credit of politicizing Adivasis goes to the mainstream Left parties, particularly the CPI(M) and the Naxalite movement in the 1970s. For example, Luisa Steur says:

> Though C. K. Janu[13] was dissatisfied with the CPI(M) for rounding up the Adivasis by the Party leaders to participate in strikes and shouting slo-gans they hardly understood and the party did not implement but she acknowledged that the CPI(M) had in fact laid the basis for her political experience and awareness. (Steur, 2009)

EMERGENCE OF A HOME-GROWN ADIVASI MOVEMENT: AGMS

At the beginning of the liberalization period in Kerala, tensions inherent in an alterna-tive model of development, which forsakes capitalist accumulation and global competi-tiveness in favour of redistribution of wealth through land reforms and the provision of general social security through social pro-grammes and labour regulations, have become ever more pronounced. The lack of industriali-zation and mechanization, the high unemploy-ment rate and the fiscal deficit that the state faced in an increasingly liberalized market strengthened the hands of those calling for investment-friendly reforms (Tharamangalam, 2006). That gradual market-oriented reforms in this 'epitome of the welfare model of

economy' would actually lead to starvation deaths by the turn of the century was startling (Singh, 2001). Such a finding has exposed the vulnerability of the Kerala model. Therefore, the Adivasis—traditionally marginal—began to rearticulate their identity to reclaim their alienated space and memory in the political landscape by launching their own indigenous home-grown movements. Such Adivasi ide-ological articulation culminated in the estab-lishment of ADDS and later of AGMS.

Since 1994, the ADSS has actively partic-ipated in tribal issues under the leadership of C. K. Janu. In mid-July 2001, 32 starvation deaths were reported in Palakkad, Kannur and Wayanad districts. This was followed by an intense struggle launched by Janu and Geethanadan, another senior leader. The ADSS came into the limelight in Kerala as it set up refugee camps and conducted a 48-day dharna before the residence of the chief min-ister and secretariat at Thiruvananthapuram on 30 August 2001. During the agitation, ADSS became AGMS, which was the first state-wide social movement explicitly aiming at Adivasi rights. It successfully negotiated an agreement with the government in 2001. This agreement had the following provisions:

1. Five acres of land to be provided to all Adivasi fam-ilies having less than 1 acre of land. To begin with, 42,000 acres of land of between 1 acre and 5 acres would be distributed and work would begin from 1 January to 31 December 2002.
2. A master plan would be made before December 2001 to be included in the Tenth Five-Year Plan beginning from 2002.
3. A cabinet decision to be taken to include Adivasi areas in the Fifth Schedule of the Constitution and a proposal made to the centre for notification by the president.

---

[13] C. K. Janu belongs to the Adiya (slave) community in Wayanad district. She began her political career as an activist of the CPI(M) when she became a wage labourer in her early teens. Around that time, she was also attending the literary classes for Adivasis conducted by the Solidarity, a church funded non-government organ-ization, since she could not receive formal education earlier. She worked as a domestic helper in the houses of landlords in her neighbourhood in Thirunelly at the age of 5. She became disillusioned with the CPI(M) when she found that it did not safeguard the interest of Adivasis. She became the leader of Adivasi movement.

4. The state government would abide by the Supreme Court's judgement related to the case pending on the act of 1975.
5. A tribal mission would be constituted to carry out these provisions.

The government and AGMS signed another agreement on 14 September 2001 to withdraw the fund (₹4,000 lakhs) earmarked for local bodies as grants-in-aid under the Tribal Sub-Plan (TSP). The amount was to be reallotted to the director, scheduled tribe development, under TSP-pooled funds.[14]

The tribal mission is actively engaged in finding lands and dealing with procedures for obtaining the central government's permission to distribute forest lands to the Adivasis. The Master Plan Committee (MPC) was also formed, which proposed the constitution of Gothra Sabha (Adivasi assembly) and Ooru Koottangal (village assemblies; Sivanandan, 2003). However, the government halted all of these processes without giving any explanation and reduced the tribal mission to an advisory body and redeployed the employees who were engaged in the work. The principal secretary responsible for the implementation of the master plan was replaced by the forest secretary, who was antagonistic to the plan. The MPC was thus sabotaged by the government and the draft plan was suspended (Sivanandan, 2003). Although the tribal mission estimated the area of land for distribution (Thadathil, 2004), the government failed to implement the agreement even after one year.

To protest the government's reluctance to implement the agreement as well as to demand Adivasi self-rule as stipulated by the Constitution, the AGMS entered the deforested areas of the Muthanga Wildlife Sanctuary in Wayanad district. But after 46 days, the government evicted them with an iron hand. It has been reported that in the police action, one policeman and an Adivasi were killed.

The selection of the Muthanga forest was not accidental. It is a protected area that falls under the Nilgiri Biosphere Reserve under state laws and entry without permission in it is punishable. Therefore, the AGMS gave an advance notice to the government that they would be occupying these lands. The selection of degraded eucalyptus plantations as *samar bhoomi* (struggle-land) demonstrated the ecological concerns of the AGMS as well as their attempt to avoid direct confrontation with the state forest department, which would have arisen had they occupied a natural forest.

What survived the ravages of time in Muthanga were the temples of Adivasis. These symbols of belief in the power of nature stood firmly rooted. Two decades ago, Muthanga was a place of rich biodiversity. Swampy lands, running streams, wild trees, diverse wildlife and Adivasi symbiotically related to nature. There was no better place to reassert the Adivasi rights over the forests. According to Janu:

> There is no other way but to return to the locale and the roots of the primordial conflict with the rulers of the land who had usurped our forest rights and turned us into the wretched of the earth, bereft of rights over even our own life. (Janu & Geethanandan, 2004)

As an act of protest against the state to recover land and customary rights, the Muthanga struggle failed to achieve its goals. However, the AGMS presented a model of self-rule to the Adivasis to regain their collective past. Since the constitution has provisions for self-rule in the Adivasi areas, the AGMS has fantasized the establishment of tribal self-rule under the state. Leadership also played a major role in the rearticulation of the Adivasi identity. Gujala says:

> instead of incorporating pre-national meanings and practices into the multicultural present, Janu showed present conflicts to be 'primordial'

---

[14] Government Order (P) No.43/01/Scheduled Caste and Scheduled Tribe Development Department, dated, 20 September 2001.

and ongoing. Rather than acknowledge the olive branch of cooperative governance, she demanded exclusive indigenous rights to rule forest and selves. She turned 'the cunning of recognition' upside-down. (Gajula, 2007)

Memorials of the participants underscore the importance of the struggle more clearly. Conversation with the participants provides a clear picture about the short span of life in the forest. M. B. Manoj, who participated in the Muthanga struggle, said to the author in 2003:

> every Adivasi, who participated in the struggle, has a nostalgic feeling about the Muthanga struggle. The 46-day life in the sanctuary fully satisfied their needs. All the families who participated in the strike/struggle had a clear determination and they erected big houses with grass, bamboo and agricultural works in the land (*Bhoomi*). They cultivated yam, plantains, peas, tomatoes, lettuce, bitter guards, tapioca, brinjals, etc. The households were divided into 24 *Oorukoottangal* (village collectives), and members were elected from each *oorukoottam* to form an *Oorusabha* (village assembly). It was responsible for supervising the day-to-day affairs of the community, including the purchase of foodstuffs using money pooled from the households, and solving any problem which might arise. The *Oorusabhas* were arranged and linked to the '*Gothras*'. Plots were issued in a mingling way between various *Gothras*. It was an evidence of Adivasi solidarity.

Although differences among heterogeneous Adivasi groups are prevalent, the struggle of the AGMS has produced positive insights among the new generation of Adivasi youth in the state. Purushan, a leader of the Mala Araya Maha Sabha (an organization of Malayaraya Adivasi community at Kombukuthy village in south Kerala), told the author:

> though we have differences on many issues we support AGMS in their land struggles. They have successfully brought together many belligerent tribal communities and more importantly implanted the idea of 'one for all and all for one' among the Adivasi communities, which was not possible earlier.

Purushan's perception of the AGMS is an endorsement of the newly found leadership of the Adivasis in the state for their collective articulation and bargaining within the deeply fragmented political landscape. Later, the AGMS was split into two factions, one led by M. Geethandan and another by C. K. Janu. However, Janu later formed a political party JRS in 2016 and contested the 2016 Kerala assembly election in alliance with the NDA from Sultan Bathery unsuccessfully. Given the demographic dynamics in the Adivasi areas, it seems to be difficult for a communitarian candidate to make inroads. Years of activism at community level made her realize the significance of political power because, ultimately, only a share in power could make a positive change for the community and also reiterated JRS never endorse the ideological positions of the BJP (Janu, 2018). However, the JRS left the NDA in 2018 because many of the promises given to them were not fulfilled, including the demand to pass the scheduled area law in Kerala, and the JRS was not considered to hold positions in any board or corporation. Earlier, in 2014, the AGMS launched another struggle called *nilpu samaram* (a standing protest) at the government secretariat in Thiruvananthapuram against the government's failure to keep its promises on rehabilitation of landless tribal households and rehabilitation package for tribal families who had taken part in the Muthanga agitation; compensation to tribal children and other victims who were arrested in connection with the agitation; steps to eradicate neonatal deaths among the tribal people in Attappadi and handing over of 19,600 acres of forest land allotted by the central government against the government's failure to keep its promises on rehabilitation and providing compensation. Surprisingly, the *nilpu samaram* was well received by Kerala's civil society. Students and other groups stood hand in hand with the Adivasis. As Roopesh Kumar points out, 'they reject the small scale relief programs as inadequate remedies for the poverty deaths or any other backward conditions of this society. It was the historical mistake of the ruling parties to avoid the representations of these sections in the decision making bodies' (Kumar, 2014). However, the promises made by the government in response to the struggle never materialized.

NEW COMMUNITY-BASED POLITICAL CONSCIOUSNESS

It is pertinent to note the impact of the Muthanga struggle awakened the community-based political consciousness among Adivasis in the state. The state witnessed the mushrooming of Adivasi land struggles across Kerala ranging from the Aralam farm in north (Sreerekha, 2010) to Chengara (Sreerekha, 2012) and Arippa (Kumar, 2013) in south Kerala. Latest among these struggles was the Thovarimala land struggle in Sultan Bathery taluk of Wayanad district. This land issue is more convoluted. Following the implementation of the Kerala Land Reforms (Amendment) Act in 1969, the then government leased 104 hectares of this land to Harrisons Malayalam Limited in Thovarimala deemed as excess land. Its custodianship was given to the forest department, and under the Kerala Private Forests (Vesting and Assignment) Act, 1971, the land was deemed as a vested forest. As per this Act, the government can convert this into agricultural land in the wake of the welfare of agriculturists, primarily Adivasis, who are willing to take up agriculture as a means of their livelihood. Adivasis can live on this land and cultivate it. However, as Adivasis have accused, the company has encroached many acres of land here with the tacit support of the forest department (Joseph, 2019). However, the protesters were dispersed by the police on 24 April 2019 allegedly by force.

As mentioned earlier, Adivasi experience in southern Kerala was somewhat different from Wayanad, largely due to the protective policies of the Travancore state. Although they were subjected to land alienation and exploitation by outsiders, it was not at extent of their northern counterparts. This resulted in the emergence of a few settled agriculturist Adivasi community organizations among

Mala Araya, Mannan and Kanikar in Idukki, Kottayam and Thiruvananthapuram districts, respectively, in the late 1950s. The ATMAMS and the Aikya Mala Araya Maha Sabha (AMAMS) were prominent among them. Access to education in the late 1950s made the Mala Araya community capable of attaining a relative amount of social and economic mobility among the Adivasi community in the state. Over a period of time, these communities had earned substantial organizational strength in order to garner the attention of government and political parties.

The claim raised by the Mala Araya community, especially the AMAMS, over the Sabarimala Temple and its ritual in the context of the Supreme Court's verdict on the entry of women in Sabarimala, turned the entire dimension of the issue. The verdict provided momentum to the Adivasi community's articulation of their rights in the public sphere, especially about their tarnished history, the stolen gods and the socio-economic alienation inflicted upon them by the state and its agencies in collusion with caste forces (Thadathil, 2019). Political parties are using this verdict to convince believers that the ruling government is less concerned with their (believers) sentiments. The sudden entry of the Adivasi communities reclaiming the temple's rituals and custodianship has given a new dimension to the issue. On a theoretical level, their claim has the potential to develop a structured counter-narrative against the arguments of those who are supported by religious fundamentalist organizations against the implementation of the Supreme Court verdict. For the Mala Arayas, the deity Ayyappan is their ancestral god, and it was Brahminism that, with the help of state institutions, forcefully appropriated their god and the rights over the temple in the beginning of the 19th century (Kannadu, 2012).

'The appropriation of Adivasi god Ayyappan by the king and Brahmins happened through the mystification of history,' says P. K. Sajeev, the secretary of the AMAMS (*Madhyamam Weekly*, 2018). The Travancore

Devaswom Board and the forest officials displaced Mala Arayans from their lands through violence and intimidation. The community has a list of priests who had association with the Sabarimala Temple to substantiate this claim. They were Karimala Arayan, Talanani, Korman and Kochuraman. They lost their rights over the temple around 1800. As P. K. Sajeev says:

> The forest officials harassed our community members living in the forests in various ways. They used to go back to practice the ritual even after that. But when threats and harassment increased, it became impossible. Aruvikkal Appooppan was a priest and an oracle in Karimala. He had to move to Kalaketty village due to the threats. He still walked all the way back to light the lamp and had to trek several hills to make it. Forest officials and people from the Devaswom board threatened him and drove him away. (Konikkara, 2018)

The oral history of this Adivasi community established that the temple was gender neutral before falling into the hold of Brahminism. The exclusion of women on the basis of age and physical conditions was never imposed. It was only after the 1950s that Ayyappan was turned into a hyper-masculine deity. It brought a sense of transcendence specific to men with a hyper-masculine heroic overtone (F. Osella & C. Osella, 2003).

Surprisingly, the claim of the Mala Arayas shifted the point of discussion in three different dimensions. First, it more or less helped the government to successfully counter the Right-wing narrative that vehemently opposed the court verdict. It is no wonder that some members of the Right-wing intelligentsia became co-petitioners with the Mala Arayas in the high court to reclaim their rights to light the Makaravilakku, and sometimes tried to use them as cannon fodders in protests against the court verdict. Second, it is the first time, the progressive intelligentsia in Kerala's public sphere passionately listened and became more sympathetic towards Adivasis' concerns and stood by them. Finally, it gave a momentum to the Adivasi community to successfully

articulate their rights in the public sphere, especially their history, the stolen gods and the socio-economic alienation inflicted on them by the state and its agencies in collusion with Brahminism.

The caste organizations and the Right-wing political parties were against the court verdict. Many of them blamed the government for the order of the Supreme Court. In fact, many parts of Kerala were on the verge of experiencing communal tension. The timely intervention of the state prevented an escalation of violence. The message given by the indigenous community on this issue seems to be significant. It also has the potential to rupture this violent celebration of masculinity that not only deems womanhood inferior but also tries to destroy the much cherished secular fabric of Kerala.

CONCLUSION

In spite of its roots within the plain normative of modernity, both in its colonial and post-independence varieties, KMD was dysfunctional to the Adivasis of Kerala. Adivasi marginality was always at loggerheads with the super-local/instrumental and rational idioms of modernity. Development programmes which were imbibed from the very notions of politico-economic modernity, as they circulated in Kerala, had a decisive role in the marginalization of Adivasis in the post-colonial democratic framework. Government-sponsored migration and plantation drives, successive reform legislations regarding landed property and, above all, the operational logic of a competitive multi-party system were incompatible with the social and material realities of the Adivasi ecology as well as economy. Although there were few offshoots by mainstream political parties that were supposed to address the concerns of Adivasis, they prevented them to develop an Adivasi consciousness among the Adivasis. Therefore, the crystallization of an agitational mode with the initiation of the AGMS can be articulated in different ways. On the one hand, the AGMS was a direct response to the hard realities of an Adivasi background, with 40 per cent of its households tied to perennial landlessness. And it was the AGMS that gave an ideological foundation for C. K. Janu to create her own political party JRS. On the other hand, the AGMS was conscious of its extra-foundational nature *vis-à-vis* the received wisdom of modernity. It is easy, as many observers of post-modernist persuasion do, to bracket the AGMS and its agitation as an 'anti-modern' or 'event'. Even after 10 years of Muthanga struggle, the AGMS seems to be fraught down in materializing an idea of a 'common Adivasi space in Kerala'. It worked in a situation where intra-cultural differences among different indigenous groups and the infiltration of mainstream political parties into each group posed a serious threat to a common Adivasi space.

Before the arrival of the AGMS, the popular notion was that Adivasis were a group of poor and landless people who lived in the fringes of civil society that required rehabilitation/inclusion within the mainstream by political and social movements. Meanwhile, the electoral system, along with the reserved constituencies, did not provide them with a space for the articulation of the political consciousness of the community-based Adivasis, but the AGMS does so. This perhaps was the genesis of 'Adivasi politics' in the state. It has transformed the image of a 'helpless', 'illiterate' and 'uncivilized' Adivasi into one engaged in a militant struggle for their rights. Later, the claim raised by the settled agriculturist Adivasi groups over Sabarimala on the threshold of the verdict of the Supreme Court could be evaluated in this fashion. Adivasi leadership used communitarian politics to counter or demystify the state politics of Adivasi welfare. Here, unlike before, specific communities (Adiya and Paniaya in Wayanad, Irurla and Kurumba in Attappadi, Mala Araya in Kottayam and Idukki) presented themselves as the first inhabitants of their regions with natural rights over their historical homelands.

This perhaps is the genesis of Adivasi politics in the state, especially in the wake of the movements of the AGMS and the claim raised by the AMAMS over Sabarimala. Such assertions need to be seen in a context where a highly heterogeneous Adivasis group used communitarian politics to counter and demystify the state politics of Adivasi welfare. The electoral victory of an independent Adivasi candidate even in reserved constituency seems to be a distant dream, because it would be difficult to break away the vice-like grip of mainstream political parties over the vulnerabilities of each Adivasi communities in a highly politically charged state. Nevertheless, the ideals invoked by the AGMS would give ebullience for the future political articulations of Adivasis in Kerala.

REFERENCES

Ajith. (2002). *Bhoomi, jati, bandhanam: Keralathile karshikapPrasnam* (Land, caste and bonding) (Malayalam). Kozhikode: Kanal Publications.

Census of India, 2011. Retrieved from https://censusindia.gov.in/2011-common/censusdata2011.html

Damodaran, A. (2006). Tribals, forests and resource conflicts in Kerala, India: The status quo of policy change. *Oxford Development Studies, 34*(3), 357–371.

Das Gupta, S. (2009). Accessing nature: Agrarian change, forest laws and their impact on an Adivasi economy in colonial India. *Conservation and Society, 7*(4), 227–238.

Dhebar, U. N. (1961). *Reports of scheduled areas and scheduled tribe commission.* New Delhi: Government of India.

Dreze, J., & Sen, A. (1996). *India: Economic development and social opportunity.* New Delhi: Oxford University Press.

Freeman, J. R. (1999). Gods, groves and the culture of nature in Kerala. *Modern Asian Studies, 33*(2), 257–302.

Gajula, G. (2007). Sacred grove lore and laws: On the beliefs of ecologists, environmentalist-historians and others. *Indian Folklore.* Retrieved from http://indianfolklore.org/journals/index.php/IFL/article/view/250

Government of Travancore and Cochin. (1950). *Report on the administration of Travancore and Cochin—*

1124 ME (17 August 1948 to 16 August 1949). Thiru-vananthapuram: Government Press.

Government of Travancore. ([1925–1926]1927). *Report on the administration of Travancore.* Thiruvananthapuram: Government Press.

Government of Travancore. (1929). *Report on the administration of Travancore–1103 ME, 1927–1928* (Seventy-second Annual Report). Thiruvananthapuram: Government Press.

Guha, S. (1999). *Environment and ethnicity in India, 1200–1991.* Cambridge: Cambridge University Press.

Iyer, L. A. K. (1941). *Travancore tribes and castes: The Aborigines of Travancore.* Thiruvananthapuram: Government Press.

Janu, C. K. (2018). CK Janu leaves NDA. *Mathrubhumi News,* 24 October. Retrieved from https://www.youtube.com/watch?v=MlbQl7aD_YA

Janu, C. K., & Geethanandan, M. (2004). The return to Muthanga. *PUCL Bulletin.* Translated from the original Malayalam Muthangayilekkulla Thirichhupokku-Oru Sathyavangmoolam (Malayalam), 11 June. Retrieved from http://www.pucl.org/Topics/Dalit-tribal/2003/muthanga.htm

Joseph, N. (2019). Why hundreds of Adivasis are protesting over 104 hectares of land in Kerala's Wayanad. *The News Minute,* 24 April. Retrieved from https://www.thenewsminute.com/article/why-hundreds-adivasis-are-protesting-over–104-hectares-land-keralas-wayanad–100649

Kannadu. (2012). *Samboorna Ayyappa charithram* (Complete history of lord Ayyappan) (Malayalam). Kottayam: Aranyadeepam Publications.

Konikkara, A. (2018). History is being deliberately neglected: Sabarimala and the Brahminisation of an Adivasi deity. *Caravan,* 28 October. Retrieved from https://caravanmagazine.in/religion/pk-sajeev-sabarimala-mala-araya-brahminisation-Adivasi-deity

Kottai, S. R. (2018). How Kerala's poor tribals are being branded as 'mentally ill'. *Economic & Political Weekly, 53*(24), 1149–1154.

Kumar, A. A. S. (2013). Arippa land struggle: The geography of caste in India. Retrieved from https://roundtableindia.co.in/index.php?option=com_content&view=article&id=7127:arippa-land-struggle-the-geography-of-caste-in-kerala&catid=119&Itemid=132

Kumar, R. (2014). Nilpu samaram (standing protest): Redefining political struggle in a democracy. Retrieved from https://roundtableindia.co.in/index.php?option=com_content&view=article&id=7948:why-should-the-international-media-discuss-the-standing-strike-in-kerala&catid=119&Itemid=132

Kunhaman, M. (1982). *The tribal economy of Kerala: An intra-regional analysis* (MPhil dissertation submitted to the Jawaharlal Nehru University). New Delhi: JNU.

Logan, W. (1887). *Malabar manual* (vol. 1). Madras: Government Press.

Maclean, C. D. (1877). *Official administration report of the Madras presidency in each department.* Madras: Government Press.

Madhyamam Weekly. (2018). *Njangalude mala bhumikal njangalkku Thirichu Nalkanam* (Return our hills and land). Interview with P. K. Sajeev, 19 November. Kozhikode: The author.

Mathur, R. P. G. (1977). *Bonded labour system in Wayanad and tribal situation in Kerala.* Thiruvananthapuram: University of Kerala.

Osella, F., & Osella, C. (2003). Ayyappan saranam: Masculinity and the Sabarimala pilgrimage in Kerala. *The Journal of the Royal Anthropological Institute, 9*(4), 729–754.

Prakash, P. K. (2002). *Adivasi bhumi prasnathinte charithravum rashtreeyavum* (History and politics of Adivasi land issue) (Malayalam). Kozhikode: Pappiyon.

Prasad, A. (2004). *Environmentalism and the left: Contemporary debates and future agendas in tribal areas.* New Delhi: Left Word Books.

Raman, R., & Bijoy, C. R. (2003). Muthanga: The real story, Adivasi movement to recover land. *Economic & Political Weekly, 38*(20), 1975–1982.

Rammohan, K. T. (2000). Assessing reassessment of Kerala model. *Economic & Political Weekly, 35*(15), 1234–1236.

Singh, K. S. (2001). *The dark clouds and silver lining: Adivasi struggle in Kerala.* New Delhi: Kalpana Printing House.

Sivanandan, P. (2003). Master plan committee sarkar attimarichu (Government undermined the master plan committee). In D. Raj (Ed.), *Tanddangal: Kerala samoohapadam Muthanga samarathinushesham* (Bravery: A study of Kerala society after Muthanga struggle). Kottayam: D. C. Books.

Sreekumar, T. T., & Parayil, G. (2002). Democracy, development and new forms of social movements: A case study of indigenous peoples' struggle in Kerala. *Indian Journal of Labour Economics, 45*(2), 287–310.

Sreerekha, M. S. (2010). Challenges before Kerala's landless: The story of Aralam farm. *Economic & Political Weekly, 45*(21), 55–66.

Sreerekha, M. S. (2012). Illegal land, illegal people: The Chengara land struggle in Kerala. *Economic & Political Weekly, 47*(30), 21–24.

Steur, L. (2009). Adivasi mobilisation: 'Identity' versus 'class' after the Kerala model development? *Journal of South Asian Development, 4*(1), 33–38.

Thadathil, A. (2004). *Constitutional rights of tribals and land issue in Kerala* (MA dissertation submitted to the School of International Relations). Kottayam: Mahatma Gandhi University.

Thadathil, A. (2017). Socio-economic inclusion of particularly vulnerable tribal groups (PVTGs) in Kerala: A case study of Kattunayakan, Cholanaikan, Kurumbas, Kadar and Koraga Communities (Unpublished Monograph).

Thadathil, A. (2019). Adivasi claims over Sabarimala highlight the importance of counter-narratives of tradition. *Economic & Political Weekly, 54*(1). Retrieved from https://www.epw.in/engage/article/adivasi-claims-over-sabarimala-highlight-the-importance-of-counter-narratives-of-tradition

Tharamangalam, J. (Ed). (2006). *Kerala: The paradoxes of public action and development.* New Delhi: Orient Longman.

Thurston, E. (1909). *Castes and tribes in southern India* (vol. VII). Madras: Government Press.

Emerging Pattern of Tribal Politics in Madhya Pradesh

Sudha Pai

Tribes constitute poorest and most marginalized sections of Indian society. Until recently, the tribal population was studied largely by sociologists and particularly by anthropologists. The study of tribes can be traced to the 19th century, when British scholars with the rise of anthropology as a discipline began to study their culture, religion, economy and lifestyles. At that time, most scholars viewed them as people living outside the mainstream society, describing them as 'aboriginals' (Guha, 1996; Sherring, 1872–1881); 'primitive or wild tribes' (Risley, 1891; Rowney, 1882); 'hill tribes' (Grigson, [1938]1991) or as 'animists' (Crooke, 1896). In the immediate post-independence period, eminent Indian anthropologist G. S. Ghurye described the tribals as 'backward Hindu' (Ghurye, 1963). In recent years, the term 'Adivasi' (*Adi* literally meaning the original, and *vasi* meaning the inhabitants) has become the current term to designate this group, and the term *Anusuchit Janjati* or the Scheduled Tribe (ST) is the constitutional name covering all of them.

A key debate in the colonial and immediate post-colonial period centred on whether or not tribes constitute a 'special category' and the appropriate policy to be adopted towards tribal communities in independent India. This was because, historically, tribal communities were characterized by a lifestyle distinct from the agrarian communities, subsisting on different combinations of shifting cultivation, hunting and gathering of forest products. Their cultures fostered a close bond with nature, while emphasizing communal ownership and consumption, closely knit kinship structures and minimal hierarchies. This debate is best exemplified in the controversy over 'protection versus assimilation' with Verrier Elwin arguing for special provisions to safeguard their rights based on the distinctive political economy of tribal communities and their history of disempowerment (Guha, 1996). Ghurye (1963), on the other hand, asserted that the question of 'aborigines' and 'Adivasis' was a mischievous one, aimed at fragmenting the fragile national identity that was emerging; the cultural difference between the tribes and the Hindu mainstream was too insignificant to accord any special status. The position of the intelligentsia and the Indian state was one of integrating them into the larger Indian society to enable the tribes, in the phraseology of citizenship rights, to share in the social heritage and life of a civilized society. Others argue that this 'integration' has, however, done as much damage as earlier 'invasions' of outsiders into tribal territory, and identity definition for the tribals after independence has been largely 'a process from outside' (Xaxa, 2008).

With the waning of this debate, the focus shifted to the analysis of changing tribal culture, identity, religion and Hinduization. Writing in the 1970s, the Rudolphs held that it is questionable whether 30 million out of 38 million tribals classified as Hindus in the 1971 census share a 'Hindu' identity and, in fact, many were actively engaged 'in asserting a variety of cultural or sub-national identities and defending their interests against "Hindu" encroachment and appropriation' (S. H. Rudolph & L. I. Rudolph, 1980, pp. 575–594). Most recently, some scholars have argued that communities such as Santhals and Bhils are, in fact, proto-nations or nationalities in the same sense in which Tamils, Bengalis, Gujratis, etc., can be called 'nationalities' (Omvedt, 2005, p. 4883). Virginius Xaxa, supporting the argument, writes:

> ...tribes besides being a type of society, also constitute a society as such. This means that the terms of references or description in tribal studies should not be caste, peasant, or social heterogeneity, but rather groups or communities, such as regional communities.... A tribe are a whole society like any other society, with their own language, territory, culture, customs, and so on. (Xaxa, 2008)

Attention has also been paid to attempts to safeguard tribal culture and values from 'outsiders', including demands for a separate tribal state among the Gonds of Madhya Pradesh (MP; Poyam, 2016).

In more recent years, many studies of movements against exploitation, preservation of culture and way of life during the colonial period and the socio-economic condition of tribals in MP after independence have been undertaken. Human development reports from states with a large tribal population have also devoted attention to their lack of education, poor health and a deteriorating environment and unemployment. A recent report jointly by the Ministry of Health and the Ministry of Tribal Affairs shows that the tribal population suffers greatly from health problems that require urgent attention (Government of India [GOI], 2018). Also, problems disrupting the lives of the tribal population have attracted scholarly analysis. Movements against displacement and lack of rehabilitation by large dams in MP, such as the Sardar Sarovar Dam in the 1980s, have been extensively studied (Baviskar, 1997). Attention has also been paid to new civil society movements since the late 1970s in central India, beginning with the Chhattisgarh Mines Shramik Sangh in Dalli Rajhara, followed by various tribal mobilizations against the Bhopal gas tragedy (Pai, 2010, p. 175). By the 1990s, the region witnessed the formation of a large number of civil society organizations such as Eklavya, PRIA, Samarthan, Narmada Bachao Andolan, Action Aid, DANIDA, Gramin Khetikar Majdoor Sangathan and the Ekta Parishad that have taken up issues of land, water, forests, which they believe are better solutions for tribal poverty than government welfare programmes (Pai, 2010, p. 174).

The present chapter is limited to the state of MP, which has a large tribal population. The tribal population in India is divided into three zones with the help of geography and distribution of tribal population: (a) the north and north-eastern zone, (b) the central or middle zone and (c) the south zone (Guha, 1951). Over half of the tribal population is concentrated in five states in the central zone, with MP being the state with the largest tribal population.[1] This makes MP an important site to understand the large tribal population in the

---

[1] MP (15.4 million), Bihar (6.6 million), Odisha (7.0 million), Andhra Pradesh (4.2 million) and West Bengal (3.8 million) as per the Census 2011.

central part of the country where most of them reside. Moreover, MP is home to a large section of the Gonds, who constitute the biggest and most important tribe in central India, which has been the vanguard of social movements against exploitation since the colonial period, for the preservation of their culture and values and, more recently, have entered into mainstream politics.

Much less scholarly attention has been paid to rising political consciousness among tribals in MP since at least the 1990s, which has brought a section into the political mainstream. This chapter, which focuses on this significant development, argues that in the 2000s, politics has become an important avenue through which tribal aspirations, unhappiness and, at times, anger have been stridently expressed against the state for lack of attention to tribal problems. As our study shows, in a bi-party situation, both the Congress and the Bharatiya Janata Party (BJP) are making considerable efforts to gain electoral support, and tribal groups have contributed substantially to their victories and losses. However, despite heightened competition between the two national parties for the support of tribals and the formation of their own political organizations, the tribal voice and position in politics remain weak in MP at present.

TRIBAL POPULATION OF MP

India has more than 700 tribal communities, speaking over 100 different languages, with each tribe having its own ethnic and cultural identity. The ST population as per the 2011 census is 10.43 crores, constituting 8.6 per cent of the total population; 89.97 per cent of them live in rural areas and only 10.03 per cent live in urban areas. MP, a large state with 52 districts and an area of 308,252 sq. km (119,017 sq. miles), has a ST population

of 73.34 million, constituting as much as 21.1 per cent of the total population (Census, 2011). There are 46 recognized STs and MP holds 1st rank among all states/union territories in terms of 'particularly vulnerable tribal groups' of which there are three, and 12th rank in respect of the proportion of the ST population to the total population.[2] The Saharias, the largest particularly vulnerable tribe, are found in north-western MP regions such as Gwalior, Shivpuri, Morena, Bhind and Guna.

The main tribal groups are the Bhil, Gond, Baiga, Korku, Bhadia or Bhariya Halba, Kaul, Mariya, Malto and Sahariya. Dhar, Jhabua and Mandla districts have more than 50 per cent of tribal population. In Khargone, Chhindwara, Seoni, Sidhi, Singrauli and Shahdol districts, tribes constitute between 30 per cent and 50 per cent of the population. Tribal areas in MP extend over 63,798 square miles and are divided into four zones—western, central, eastern and southern—on the basis of physical features, social structure and economic needs. Dhar, Jhabua, Khargone and Ratlam districts form the western zone and are largely populated by Bhils and Bhilalas; Betul, Chhindwara, Shahdol, Balaghat, Mandla and Seoni are populated mainly by Gonds, Baigas, Kols, Korkus and Pardhans and constitute the central zone, which is very rich in mineral deposits. Sarguja, Raigarh and Bilaspur are inhabited mostly by Oraons, Korwas, Gonds and Kanwars form the eastern zone, whereas Bastar, Durg and Raipur districts having large populations of Halbas, Maria and Murias and other subtribes of Gonds are included in the southern zone (Singh, 1994, p. 179). Census 2011 shows that Hinduism is the predominant religion (91.1%) in the state and as many as 96.1 per cent of the STs are Hindus. Tribes following other religions and persuasions account for 3.2 per cent, Christians 0.5 per cent and Muslims 0.1 per cent; 17 per cent of the population in Jhabua is Christian; the

---

[2] Retrieved from www.tribal.mp.gov.in/CMS

tribal regions are experiencing violent conversion drives (Singh, 1982).

According to the 2011 census, Bhil is the most populous tribe with a total population of 4,618,068, constituting 37.7 per cent of the total ST population. Bhils have the highest population in Jhabua, followed by Dhar, Barwani and Khargone districts. Gond is the second largest tribe, with a population of 4,357,918 constituting 35.6 per cent with major concentrations in Dindori, Chhindwara, Mandla, Betul, Seoni and Shahdol districts. The next four populous tribes are Kol, Korku, Sahariya and Baiga, and they constitute 92.2 per cent of the total ST population of the state. Pardhan, Saur and Bharia Bhumia form 3.2 per cent of the state population. Four tribes, namely Majhi, Khairwar, Mawasi and Panika, account for another 2.2 per cent of the ST population. The remaining 33 tribes (out of the total of 46 tribes) along with the generic tribes constitute the residual 2.5 per cent of the total ST population. Tribes with a population of less than 1,000 are 12 in number (MP, Data Highlights the Scheduled Tribes, Census 2011).

The Gonds, though constitute the second largest tribal group and are viewed as aborigines, are a significant group as they have historically formed the vanguard in tribal movements, and today there is a high level of social and political consciousness and participation in politics among them. Originally inhabiting an area called Gondwana, they are spread over a vast region, speak several languages/dialects and display cultural differences. The Gonds constitute 13.45 per cent of the total ST population of India, with MP (including Chhattisgarh) having the highest percentage (43.69%). According to the Scheduled Castes and Scheduled Tribes Orders (Amendment) Act, 1976, the Gonds have more than 50 subgroups inhabiting MP (Singh, 1994, p. 294). Historically, they founded a number of states, graphically described in the mediaeval chronicles, and their political authority survived in a number of the Gond zamindaries until recently, which gave them a measure of social

dominance over other communities (Poyam, 2016; Singh, 1982, p. 177).

Historically, the foray of the Britishers during the colonial period into tribal regions like MP was delayed because of the absence of developed productive forces and the presence of many princely states. But once in control, they resorted to massive exploitation of large forest and mineral resources and imposed a system of revenue collection leading to exploitative non-tribal moneylenders and traders entering tribal areas. The commercialization of agriculture entailed further alienation of the tribals from the land on which Kunbi Patidars and Jat farmers from Gujarat and Rajasthan, respectively, were settled (Gupta, 2009, pp. 5093–5100). In 1874, the promulgation of the Scheduled District Act delineated tribal areas as 'scheduled areas'. The first serious attempt to list the 'primitive tribes' in the country was made during the Census of 1931. The GOI Act of 1935 classified tribal areas into the north-eastern tribal region, which was totally excluded from Indian laws, and other backward tribal regions, which were partially excluded. The Thirteenth Schedule to the GOI (Provincial Legislative Assemblies) Order, 1936, specified certain tribes as 'backward'. More importantly, as categories were created and consolidated by colonial administrators, over time, these categories came to have a life of their own.

After independence, the tribals were accorded special rights and protection under Article 342 of the Constitution with the GOI's tribal development policy aiming to bring them the benefits of economic development without eroding their traditional culture and identity. Tribal areas outside the north-eastern region come under the Fifth Schedule of the Constitution and special provisions were made for promoting their educational and economic interests and to protect them from social injustice and exploitation. Article 366(25) of the Constitution describes the STs as those communities which are scheduled in accordance with Article 342 of the Constitution or which are subsequently added due to an amending act of the Parliament. The essential character-istics, first laid down by the Lokur Committee, for a community to be identified as STs are (a) indications of primitive traits; (b) distinctive culture; (c) shyness of contact with the com-munity at large; (d) geographical isolation and (e) backwardness.

Socio-economic Condition of Tribes

MP is a backward state, and tribal majority areas which overlap with the country's major forest areas are also areas with the highest concentrations of poverty. Among the social groups, STs have the highest proportion of the poor (54%), followed by Scheduled Castes (50%). Of the total rural poor population, STs account for about 15 per cent, though their share in the entire population is only 11 per cent. A study examining changes in poverty and related poverty factors among tribals in south-west MP found that while there is evi-dence of some positive changes in tribal pop-ulation as a result of economic development and anti-poverty strategies implemented, the overall effect is fairly limited, especially among the poorer sections. Some of the less favoured rural areas have faced deterioration due to a shrinking land base and restricted access to forest resources. The slow pace of economic growth only partly explains the exclusion of certain categories of households, indicating that parts of the rural community, particularly landless and small marginal farm-ers, remain unaffected by even a moderately faster growth rate. The study points to the need for establishing basic infrastructures, especially for health and education, and that crop productivity and market support do not develop at a sufficient rate to have an impact on the reduction of chronic poverty (Shah & Sah, 2004, pp. 249–263).

While the total literacy rate in MP is 69.3 per cent, among the tribal population, it is 50.55 per cent lower in rural areas, females and smaller tribes. The literacy rate among the tribal population in MP is lower than the national tribal average which is 58.95 per cent and is the lowest among states (Census, 2011). Due to the different linguistic, cultural and geographical environment and its peculiar complications, the diverse tribal world of MP has been largely cut off from the mainstream of development. The state ranks very low on the human development index (HDI) value of 0.375 (2011), which is below the national average and ranks 20th among 23 states (United Nations Development Programme [UNDP], 2011). Human development reports show that a large majority of them live in mud, stone and thatch homes with no toilets, relying on handpumps for drinking water. A major problem is also lack of employment, the only employment being collecting wild honey, forest produce or working in the fields of affluent landowners (UNDP, 2011).

Tribals in MP face the problem of lack of arable land as they did not receive land under the Land Reform Act. The Verrier Elwin Committee of 1952 recommended that all tribal cultivators should be given ownership rights in land and that the size of the landhold-ings should be at least 2.5 acres. Although land ceiling laws were enacted and surplus land was distributed, the total beneficiaries were only a fraction of the total tribal popula-tion (Prasad, 2002, p. 268). In many cases, the beneficiaries did not know where the allocated land was located; some villages even lacked a map; as a result, without acquiring land from the big landowners, it was allotted to the beneficiaries who could not gain possession. The Patwaris, the lower bureaucrats and the police sided with the landlords. The records of the Commissioner of Land Records and Settlement, Gwalior, showed that by 1988, 10,896 tribal persons had been dispossessed of 15,811.97 hectares of land after allotment to them (Prasad, 2002, p. 268). A study by the Tribal Research Institute of MP showed that many tribals were forced to sell their bull-ocks and other equipment in lieu of debts; or land that was in the name of the tribals was cultivated by non-tribals to whom they were in debt; or non-tribals got whatever harvest the tribals received from their lands in return for money lent. Thus, the informal moneylending system took a heavy toll on tribal access to land and the resources necessary for producing enough for a decent livelihood (Prasad, 2002, p. 268).

Another difficult problem tribals have faced is the displacement due to large dams— the Sardar Sarovar being the best example—as their relationship with the environment renders them especially vulnerable to the dislocation caused. The accelerated pace of resource consumption due to industrialization has directly cut into the livelihoods and way of life of groups which include forest-dwelling tribal communities, traditional fisherfolk, peasants and artisans. This process of restricting their access to and control over natural resources started during colonial times, but has gained momentum since independence (Baviskar, 1997, pp. 195–223). The state has exercised its prerogative of 'eminent domain' to acquire land, forests and water for the 'national purpose' of constructing projects for irrigation, power generation, defence and mineral extraction. Not only have the displaced communities been deprived of the fruits of this development, they have not even been compensated for the hardships they have had to endure for the sake of 'the nation'. Their economic and political impoverishment has prevented most tribal communities from negotiating a better deal for themselves vis-a-vis displacement and development.

Already disadvantaged by the processes of state-led industrialization, many tribal groups have scarce material and symbolic capital; the little that they have is also destroyed by displacement. Given the utter inadequacy of the rehabilitation programmes, the ability of these groups to cope with changed circumstances is cause for serious concern. While no precise government figures are available on the total number of people likely to be adversely affected by this project, anti-dam activists

claim that about 1,000,000 people were displaced and affected by direct submergence, building of canals, weirs, dykes and the project colony, by catchment area treatment and compensatory afforestation, and due to secondary displacement and downstream effects (Baviskar, 1997, pp. 195–223).

Social Reform and Autonomy Movements among the Gonds

A number of movements have taken place after independence in MP for the preservation of tribal culture, exploitation by outsiders, against the state for not fulfilling their needs and for a separate tribal state. The Gonds provide the best example, as they have historically been the most conscious and active in preserving tribal culture and autonomy, and have been at the forefront of movements in central India. Two types of movements can be identified: the first phase, beginning in 1916, described as a 'renaissance' centring around sociocultural movements to prevent the rapid degeneration of Gondi *punem* (values) and the formation of the Gond Mahasabha, and the promotion of Gondi literature (Mollick & Mukherjee, 1999, pp. 279–282; Poyam; 2016). A second phase in the early post-colonial period witnessed movements for a separate state, beginning in Nagpur and Bilaspur districts, they slowly spread over the Gondwana region (Singh, 1982). Akash Poyam argues that the Gondwana movement does not imply a single mass movement, on the basis of 'ethnicity' and 'shared history, it incorporates many small regional struggles as well as larger struggles towards Gonds' sociopolitical objectives (Poyam, 2016). These varied movements have led anthropologists to raise a significant question whether Gondwana is a political or sociocultural reality (Mollick & Mukherjee, 1999, pp. 279–282).

The Gond movements of the colonial period underwent a number of transformations and became disintegrated and marginalized into the forests after their incorporation into the Indian state (Mollick & Mukherjee, 1999). However, movements demanding a separate tribal state in central India continued after independence. On 9 May 1963, Gond leader Raja Naresh Singh submitted a memorandum to the government demanding the formation of a separate state carved out of the tribal areas of Chhattisgarh, Rewa and Vidarbh districts (Singh, 1982, p. 181). Narain Singh Uikey, President of the Gondwana Adivasi Seva Mandal, demanded the formation of a Gondwana State, consisting of the Gond regions of Chhattisgarh and the contiguous districts of Vidarbha. Hira Singh founded Bharatiya Gondwana Sangh in August 1959 and later declared the formation of Gondwana Raj, which would solve the problems of the 40 lakh tribals in India (Mollick & Mukherjee, 1999, p. 279).

The demand for a separate Gondwana state has not received enough attention or importance to befit even a discussion in the state assembly, probably because it is viewed as a social movement. Virginius Xaxa, writing on tribal movements, pointed to the 'Jharkhand movement' as the only tribal autonomy movement worth its name in India (Xaxa, 2008). In 2000, the BJP and the Congress divided MP and created Chhattisgarh for their own political ends. The result has been that post-2000, unlike the earlier demand for a Gondwana state that was politically consolidated and socially homogenous, at least in terms of its objectives and territories imagined, the contemporary struggle is fragmented and there is an absence of consensus on territory and territorial claims. Following the formation of the Gondwana Gantantra Party (GGP), its Vice-President, Gulzaar Singh Markam, argued that 'Rejection of Gondwana state demand was nothing but Centers apathy and a deliberate act of dividing Gonds into state boundaries'. He recalls that 'even before the formation of GGP, independent MLAs from the Gond community had captured political spaces but were either controlled by ruling parties or, were

indifferent to their Gond identity' (Poyam, 2016). The apathy shown by central and state governments towards the demands for a separate Gondwana state has contributed to the reassertion of their historical rights over land and territory. It has provided the Gonds with a political identity and underlies their rising political consciousness, their desire to participate in politics and, as discussed further, the formation of a political party the GGP (Poyam, 2016).

RISING POLITICAL CONSCIOUSNESS AND ELECTORAL POLITICS AMONG TRIBALS

In recent years, key features of tribal politics in MP have been rising political consciousness, particularly among the bigger tribes, heightened competition between the Congress and the BJP for the tribal vote, and the emergence of small independent tribal parties among the Gonds and Bhils. Political consciousness and voting by tribals was low in the immediate post-independence period. From the mid-1960s, participation of the tribal population began to rise, but initially was higher in Gujarat and Rajasthan than MP (Krishna, 1967, pp. 179–190). Today, voter participation among tribals is high in MP. In the 2018 assembly election, the tribal-dominated Jhabua district topped the state, with the voting percentage going up to 76.39 per cent from 69.04 per cent earlier; in Harda and Dewas, it was more than 80 per cent (Shukla, 2018a).

While tribals are unevenly distributed across MP, about one-fifth of the assembly constituencies in the state (48 out of 230) are reserved for them. Till 1998, an undivided MP had 320 assembly seats, 75 of which were reserved for tribals. After the creation of Chhattisgarh in 2000, the number of reserved seats dropped to 41, but the delimitation of the assembly and parliamentary seats before the

2008 assembly election pushed the number up to 48. Among the tribal communities in MP, the Gond community has a major influence in the Mahakoshal region and can impact results in Balaghat, Mandla and Shahdol, while Bhils have a sizeable presence in the Malwa-Nimar region. Tribals in recent years also had an impact on parliamentary elections. Out of a total 29 parliamentary seats in MP, tribal groups hold significant influence in at least six reserved seats—Shahdol, Mandla, Dhar, Ratlam, Khargone and Betul; and in some others such as Balaghat, Chhindwara and Khandwa.

Till almost the late 1990s, the tribals supported the Congress party. A study shows that in the 1967 election of 17 districts with a heavy concentration of STs, only one district Bastar gave the Congress less than 20 per cent. Nowhere else was Congress' share of popular votes less than 39 per cent; in fact, in 8 districts, it improved its position compared to earlier elections. Even in Madhya Bharat, where it got a jolt, it got 8 out of 14 seats; in VP, it obtained all 6. But even then, in Mahakoshal, the Jan Sangh emerged as a competitor bagging 14 out of 61 (Chandidas, 1967, pp. 1503–1514).

Table 20.1 shows the overwhelming support that the Congress received on tribal seats till the late 1990s, after which its support has gradually decreased. Despite this, the Congress did not throw up many tribal leaders, nor have these leaders attempted to mobilize the tribals in various parts of the state. A major problem is that until recently the tribals had lacked leadership and an educated middle class and therefore could be easily co-opted by the Congress party. As the share of tribal votes in the victory of Congress was high, demands were constantly made for making even a chief minister from the tribal community, time and again. But it was only after the formation of the GGP in the 1990s that Congress accommodated these aspirations by making Jamuna Devi, Urmila Singh as deputy chief minister, party chief and leader of

opposition, respectively, but never gave away the chief ministership. Shift to an alternative political party was tried. Dileep Singh Bhuria switched to the BJP, but lost the election in 1998 as the Congress support base in tribal areas was strong. Bhuria then tried to form his own party, also a third front with the help of Lok Janshakti Party, GGP, etc., but could not succeed.

In the 1990s, the Gondwana movement transformed from a social-reformist to an organized political movement with the formation of the GGP and the Gondwana Mukti Sena in 1991 by Sri Hira Singh Markam and Kausalya Porte, respectively (Mollick & Mukherjee, 1999, p. 279). It was the first instance of an attempt at independent tribal political mobilization after many decades of supporting the Congress. Initially, there were reports that it was encouraged by dissident members of the Congress unhappy with the programmes of the Digvijay Singh government, particularly land distribution. But in the 1996 election, Hira Singh Markam was elected from the Janjgir parliamentary constituency and the party fared well in other constituencies.

The 2003 assembly election was a turning point that witnessed the success of the BJP in penetrating tribal areas, leading to a considerable disintegration of the Congress tribal base (Murg, 2004, pp. 16–19). Jai Murg's study argues that, prior to the 2003 election, the Congress was slowly losing its mass base in the backward and tribal regions of the state. It faced severe setbacks in the backward regions of Bundelkhand, Baghelkhand and the tribal pockets of Gondwana and Bhilistan (western MP). In both the 1993 and 1998 elections, the Congress had a 4–5 per cent lead over the BJP in the ST seats. But in 2003, the BJP gained 42.5 per cent of the vote, leading to a positive swing of 3.5 per cent in its favour, while the Congress lost 9 percentage points as compared to 1998, polling 31.6 per cent of the votes. The BJP established a staggering 12 per cent lead over the Congress in the ST seats, with

Table 20.1   Party Position on Reserved Seats for STs in Various Assembly Elections in MP, 1952–2003

Party	1952	1962	1967	1972	1977	1980	1985	1990	1993	1998	2003
Congress	22	13	28	30	11	36	37	09	35	28	02
BJS/BJP	01	10	06	05	29*	05	04	29	05	12	37
Socialists	–	11	04	01	–	–	–	03	01	–	–
Independents	02	01	–	02	01	–	–	–	–	01	02**
Total	26	35	38	38	41	41	41	41	41	41	41

Source: Compiled from reports of the Election Commission of India.

Notes: *Socialist and Jan Sangh were part of Janata Party In 1977 election.

** Gondwana Gantantra Party (GGP).

its highest positive (+12%) swing in Bhilistan, while the former had its most negative swing (–12%) in Gondwana. In Bhilistan, the BJP polled 52 per cent of the votes winning 19 out of the 23 seats at stake.

While the BJP was the principal beneficiary of the erosion in the Congress vote, smaller parties, such as the Bahujan Samaj Party (BSP) and Samajwadi Party (SP), but most particularly the GGP, contributed to the latter's defeat. There was also increased participation by a number of smaller tribal groups. In Gondwana, the Congress vote share was reduced to 28 per cent. The GGP polled 2 seats and close to 11 per cent of the votes; its vote share in the ST seats was 7 per cent, way above its state-wide average vote share of 2 per cent. About 10 members of the Kol tribe contested election on tickets of various non-Congress, non-BJP parties such as the Rashtriya Samanta Dal, BSP, SP, Janata Dal (United), Lok Janshakti Party and a few independents (Murg, 2004, pp. 16–19). In the 2004 Lok Sabha election, the GGP contested from MP, Chhattisgarh, Bihar, Uttar Pradesh and Maharashtra. But despite its victories in 2003, its influence remained largely limited to the Mahakoshal region (Murg, 2004, pp. 16–19).

The success of the BJP in the 2000s was due to the sustained grassroots mobilization of the tribals by the Vanvasi Kalyan Parishad, an affiliate of the Rashtriya Swayamsevak Sangh (RSS), and the Hindu Mahasabha since the 1950s and the 1990s, by the RSS, Vishva

Hindu Parishad, Vidya Bharati, Seva Bharati, etc., *in the fields of health, education and livelihoods. In the process, they reshaped cultural, religious and political consciousness.* Hanuman idols and *trishuls* (three-edged spear carried by the Hindu god Shiva) were distributed as symbols of faith, and their conversion drive led to an amendment in the anti-conversion law in the state (MP Freedom of Religion Act, 1968). Consequently, polarization on the lines of Hindus versus Christians has taken deep roots in tribal society and politics (Gupta, 2009, p. 3139). Others have argued that it is not only the work of these organizations, but the inability of the Congress to give space to tribals and create tribal leaders in the party, and its inability to gauge its losing grip on both the eastern tribal belt of Mandla and the western Jhabua belt till they lost considerable ground. Still others *point to a wave in 2003 in favour of the BJP in MP and argue that tribals, like any other section of society, supported it* (Shukla, 2018b).

However, in the 2008 assembly election, the Congress made inroads among the Bhils and Gonds gaining more tribal votes than the BJP compared to the 2003 election (Pai, 2010, p. 489). The GGP could not sustain itself. Following the differences among its three MLAs and the party's top leadership, in the 2008 assembly election, it could not gain a single seat and finished second in only one constituency. Similarly, in the 2009 parliamentary election, the Congress led in a big way among the Bhils and, to a lesser degree, among the Gonds, but the BJP led among the rest of the tribal communities. The GGP could not win a single seat, a study shows that only 6 per cent of the Gonds voted for it. The Congress got more votes from the bottom of the social pyramid, while the BJP got more votes from the upper castes and the OBCs, except for tribes such as the Minas, Marias and Bhatras (Ram & Sisodia, 2009, pp. 35–38). In recent years, the political strength of the GGP has waned and they do not have a single MLA or MP.

As Table 20.2 shows, in the 2013 assembly election, out of 48 tribal seats in MP, the BJP obtained 34 and the Congress 14. But in 2018, this pattern was reversed with the Congress obtaining 32 and the BJP 16.

The 2018 assembly election witnessed a tough fight in which the tribal factor played an important role. In the Malwa region, where the Gonds do not have strength, the Bhil tribal leadership began to assert itself. Amita Baviskar's study of the Bhils of Jhabua district in the late 1990s points to the 'emerging differentiation of the tribal community into two distinct classes, a process accelerated by the intervention of the state and market forces' (Baviskar, 1997). A tiny section of the Bhils, who were economically and politically more powerful, whose ancestors were village headmen, were able to seize the opportunities offered by tribal development programmes and

gain access to jobs on the lower rungs of the government bureaucracy. Baviskar points out that over time, with the spread of education, this section grew and gained economic security and respectability of the lower middle-class, moved away from land and into a class dominated by non-tribals, engendered a strong desire to shed the stigmas of tribal identity and adopt Hindu practices (Baviskar, 1997).

A section of this tiny educated class among the Bhils took to politics and formed a political party, Jai Adivasi Yuva Shakti (JAYS) prior to the 2008 assembly election, together with a demand for a separate Bheelistan region. In the 2018 election, the JAYS, following negotiations, contested on Congress tickets and their leader, Hiralal Alawa, a former All India Institute of Medical Sciences doctor, won from the Manawar constituency of Dhar district, and their en masse and tactical voting influenced the results in Barwani, Jhabua, Alirazpur and Dhar districts (Kumar, 2018). The JAYS slogan has been *ek teer ek kaman, saare adivasi ek saman* (one bow, one arrow, all tribals are equal) under which they want to unite and fulfil the basic needs of the entire tribal population. They allege that the 15-year rule of the BJP has divided tribals through the work of their subsidiary organizations.

In the 2018 assembly election, the Congress gained 114 seats as against 109 by the BJP, but in terms of the vote percentage it was a close

Table 20.2 Tribal-reserved Seats Won by the BJP and the Congress in 2013 and 2018 MP Assembly Elections

48 Reserved Tribal Seats	Total Tribal Assembly Seats	Assembly Results 2013 BJP	Assembly Results 2013 INC	Assembly Results 2018 BJP	Assembly Results 2018 INC
Shahdol	8	6	2	4	4
Mandla	8	4	4	2	6
Dhar	8	6	2	2	6
Ratlam	8	7	1	3	5
Betul	8	7	1	4	4
Khargone	8	4	1	1	7
Total	48	34	14	16	32

Source: Compiled from the reports of the Election Commission of India.

fight, with the former gaining 40.9 per cent and the latter 41 per cent. The smaller parties obtained much less, the BSP 2 seats and 5 per cent the GGP 1.8 per cent and the others 11.3 per cent of the votes. Among the constituencies where Congress gained over the BJP in 2018 are Morena, Bhind, Gwalior, Tikamgarh, Dewas Rajgarh Shahdol, Mandla Ratlam Dhar and Betul. Tribal anger translated into support for the Congress, particularly in Khandwa, Betul, Mandla, Dindori and Shahdol districts (Tiwari, 2019).

The reasons lie in unhappiness against the 15-year old BJP government led by Shivraj Singh Chouhan, witnessed in a number of demands put forward by tribal leaders in rallies prior to the 2018 election: implementation of the Fifth Schedule which gives autonomy to tribal areas, creation of jobs in home districts to stop tribal migration, conservation of forest lands and addition of the Gondi and Bheeli tribal languages in the Eighth Schedule of the constitution. Across the state's tribal-dominated Mahakaushal region, it is reported that tribals are unhappy over poor educational facilities, absentee teachers, lack of healthcare and being uprooted for developmental projects (Sharma, 2018).

However, a key grievance was the demand to uphold the Forest Rights Act (FRA), 2006, and the withdrawal of the proposed amendment in the Indian Forests Act, 1927, by the government. It led to many agitations prior to the elections, a major one being the massive *Adivasi Adhikar Chetavni* Rally in Burhanpur district on 1 April 2018 organized by the Jagrit Adivasi Dalit Sangathan (JADS) in which over 5,000 tribals participated. Tribal leaders addressing the rally criticized Narendra Modi's government for its disinterest in presenting the tribals' side in the Supreme Court, which ultimately led to the verdict of the eviction of tribals from the forests.[3] Also, they

alleged that the government had proposed the amendment to the Indian Forests Act, 1927, just three days before the model code of conduct was imposed with the intention to benefit industrialists and businessmen. Further, a report tabled before the Parliamentary Standing Committee showed that in the last five years, around 2.15 lakh acres (868,909 hectares) of forest lands have been given for industries; that in recent months the union government had handed over 4 lakh acres of forest land to the Adani group in Chhattisgarh (Tewari, 2018).

A second important reason for anger among tribals is difficulty in accessing government welfare schemes due to the trouble in obtaining an Aadhaar card. Tribals across Khandwa, Betul, Chhindwara, Umaria, Mandla, Jabalpur, Shahdol and Dindori districts, many of whom are located in inaccessible, remote areas with poor connectivity, argue that they find it difficult to fill in numerous forms with correct data and get little help from officials. Additionally, when they make the journey to centres to get their details updated, spending time and money, fingerprint authentication at banks often fails, hindering access to their own money. They need middlemen who charge 10 per cent of the loan amount as processing fee, while they are supposed to get 0 per cent loan (Tewari, 2018).

Another major demand by the Barela tribals since 2012 led by the JADS has been compensation and rehabilitation following land acquisition for the Kharak Dam, which has submerged over 300 villages. Tribal protests in Khargone were met with severe repression in which tribals—including women and children—were brutally lathi-charged and 27 people were arrested. The high court endorsed their claim to rehabilitation in July 2016 and, in January 2017, the Supreme Court also categorically ordered that they be rehabilitated

---

[3] On 13 February 2019, the apex court directed state governments to ensure the eviction of around 2 million tribals from forest areas spread across 17 states. The verdict could render 2.26 lakh tribal families of MP homeless. However, the Supreme Court stayed its own order till July 2019, following massive backlash from tribal rights groups across the country.

under the most beneficial provisions of the MP Rehabilitation Policy of 2002 and the Narmada Valley Development Authority policy of 2008. However, prior to the election, the issue of compensation and rehabilitation of tribal population remained unsolved (Pal, 2018). Thus, tribal anger against the BJP government contributed to it getting fewer seats in the tribal belt and its defeat in 2018.

CONCLUSION

The chapter illustrated that even after more than 70 years of independence, the large majority of the tribal population of MP remains backward, poor and marginalized. The colonial period witnessed massive exploitation of forest areas, affected livelihoods, brought in 'outsiders' who posed a threat to their culture and values, leading to autonomous movements against the British colonial authorities. In independent India, while the Constitution granted special protection to tribes, it remains questionable whether these measures have provided protection to their culture and economic interests. In MP, the condition of tribals, except among sections of the larger groups, has not improved. Major problems faced by them have been the lack of arable land and the felling of forests, large-scale displacement due to the construction of large dams, accompanied by the lack of adequate compensation and rehabilitation by the state. High poverty levels, poor health and lack of jobs are witnessed among the tribal population. The question of whether to preserve their distinct identity and lifestyle, or to enter the mainstream, remains a troubling and unresolved issue, particularly among the smaller and more backward tribal groups. Until recently, it was only a few groups, such as the Gonds, Bhils and Baigas, who had taken up issues of water, forest and land with the government. The large majority were silent, unable to voice their demands. However, in more recent years, rising social

and political consciousness among the larger tribal groups has led to numerous protests in the 2000s, the latest example being massive agitations demanding the FRA to be upheld prior to the 2018 assembly election. While the state has not taken adequate steps to help the tribals preserve the forests and the livelihoods and culture associated with them, in MP, civil society organizations are trying to help the tribal population.

The idea of a separate tribal state, despite numerous demands, was not considered in post-independence India, and the tribal population became divided among a number of states in central and eastern India. The formation of Jharkhand and later of Chhattisgarh in 2000 both portrayed as tribal states, has not satisfied tribal leaders who feel that it was the narrow political interests of the national parties, the Congress and the BJP, which drove the formation of these states. The formation of Chhattisgarh out of MP once again divided the tribal population between two states in central India. Arguably, from the tribal point of view, the movement for a separate state for tribals has become even more relevant from the 1990s onwards, with the introduction of privatization and liberalization of the Indian economy. In the present political and economic situation, with the rise of a strong corporate sector, the conscious invisibilization of Gondwana, or any tribal state demand, is also because of an enormous struggle for control over natural resources. The tribal regions of MP have a large amount of natural resources that could provide raw materials to industries. Any autonomy to tribals would hinder state and capitalist powers to exploit these resources. Despite all the welfare and development projects by the government in tribal regions, tribal groups have not benefited, rather they have lost their livelihoods.

These seminal issues, discussed earlier, underlie the rising participation by some tribal groups in politics in recent years, which have been the focus of this chapter. It is only since the late 1990s that a section of the tribals in MP with a rising social and political awareness has begun to participate in politics. In the immediate post-independence period, a few participated and voting percentages were low. The tribals supported the dominant Congress party, and it was only in the early 2000s that there was a shift towards the BJP. Recent years have also witnessed the independent mobilization and formation of parties and organizations by the Gonds, Bhils and Barelas—the GGP, JAYS and JAD, respectively. This has contributed to a greater mobilization of the tribal population, increased political activity, agitations against the ruling party, particularly prior to the elections, on specific problems faced by tribals.

However, these developments have not provided an independent space to these tribal groups to negotiate their demands, rather they have become enmeshed in the highly competitive politics between the Congress and the BJP, with the BJP contributing to the defeat/victory of either in assembly elections. They remain small players unable to gain a substantial number of seats. The GGP remains limited to Mahakoshal and the JAYS to Malwa, where the Gond and Bhil population, respectively, is considerable. The binary arrangement of political competition has continued elsewhere in MP with a high entry-level barrier for small, new parties such as the GGP, JAYS or even the BSP. As small, narrow and identity-based parties that cannot gain support beyond their own core constituency, they remain spoilers grabbing from one or other of the national parties. JAYS required the support of the Congress to participate in the 2018 assembly election. Hence, they have not been able to play a determining role in MP politics. Moreover, even these changes are witnessed among the few tribal groups such as the Gonds and Bhils, the large majority of the tribal population remains somewhat untouched by these changes. The tribal voice remains limited and weak in MP, and it will take considerable social and political change for them to make an impact on politics.

REFERENCES

Baviskar, A. (1997). Tribal politics and discourses of environmentalism. *Contributions to Indian Sociology, 31*(2), 195–223.

Chandidas, R. (1967). The fourth general elections: Madhya Pradesh: A case study. *Economic & Political Weekly, 2*(33/35), 1503–1514.

Census of India, 2011.

Crooke, W. (1896). *Tribes and castes of the north western provinces and Oudh.* Calcutta: Cambridge University Press.

Ghurye, G. S. (1963). *The scheduled tribes.* Bombay: Popular Prakashan.

Government of India. (2018). *Report of the committee on tribal health bridging the gap and a roadmap for the future.* New Delhi: Ministry of Health and Ministry of Tribal Affairs.

Grigson, S. W. ([1938]1991). *Maria Gonds of Bastar.* Delhi: Oxford University Press.

Guha, B. S. (Ed). (1951). *The tribes of India* (vol. 2). New Delhi: Bharatiya Adimjati Sevaksangh.

Guha, R. (1996). Savaging the civilised: Verrier Elwin and the tribal question in late colonial India. *Economic & Political Weekly,* 31(35/37), 2375–2389.

Gupta, D. (2009). Social bases of politics in Madhya Pradesh. *The Indian Journal of Political Science, 70*(1), 31–39.

Krishna, G. (1967). Electoral participation and political integration. *Economic & Political Weekly, 2*(3/5), 179–190.

Kumar, A. (2018). MP tribal leader gives Congress an ultimatum: Decide by 2 Oct or there's no alliance. *The Print,* 24 September. Retrieved from https://theprint.in/politics/mp-tribal-leader-gives-congress-an-ultimatum-decide-by-2-oct-or-theres-no-alliance/123843/

Mollick, F., & Mukherjee, B. M. (1999). Gondwana whether political reality or Socio-cultural reality. *Anthropologist, 1*(4), 279–282.

Murg, J. (2004). Changing patterns of support. *Economic & Political Weekly, 39*(1), 16–19.

Omvedt, G. (2015). Capitalism and Globalisation, dalits and adivasis. *Economic & Political Weekly, 40*(47), 4881–4885.

Pai, S. (2010). *Developmental state and the Dalit question in Madhya Pradesh: Congress response.* New Delhi: Routledge.

Pal, S. (2018). Four years on, tribals in MP still await compensation for Kharak dam construction: The protest by tribals in Madhya Pradesh's Khargone has entered the 10th day amidst the silence of the authorities. Retrieved from https://www.newsclick.in/four-years-tribals-mp-still-await-compensation-kharak-dam-construction

Poyam, A. (2016). Gondwana movement in post-colonial India: Exploring paradigms of assertion, self-determination and statehood. In S. R. Bodhi (Ed.), *Tribal and Adivasi studies: Perspectives from within* (pp. 131–166). Kolkata: Adivani publications.

Prasad, A. (2002). Tribal survival and the land question. In P. Jha (Ed.), *Land reforms in India: Issues of equity in rural Madhya Pradesh* (vol. 7; pp. 258–276). New Delhi: SAGE Publications.

Ram, S., & Sisodia, Y. S. (2009). Madhya Pradesh: Overriding the contours of anti-incumbency. *Economic & Political Weekly, 44*(6), 35–38.

Risley, H. H. (1891). The study of ethnology in India. *The Journal of the Anthropological Institute of Great Britain and Ireland, 20*, 235–263.

Rowney, H. B. (1882). *The wild tribes of India*. London: Thomas De La Rue & Co.

Rudolph, S. H. & Rudolph, L. I. (1980). The centrist future of Indian politics. *Asian Survey, 20*(6), 575–594.

Shah, A., & Sah, D. C. (2004). Poverty among tribals in South West Madhya Pradesh: Has anything changed over time? *Journal of Human Development, 5*(2), 249–263.

Sharma, N. (2018). Tribals in Mahakaushal unaware of central schemes, bemoan lack of development. Retrieved from https://economictimes.indiatimes.com/news/elections/assembly-elections/madhya-pradesh-assembly-elections/tribals-in-mahakaushal-unaware-of-central-schemes-bemoan-lack-of-development/articleshow/66723355.cms

Sherring, M. A. (1872–1881). Hindu tribes and castes (3 vols.). Calcutta: Thacker, Spink & Co.

Shukla, A. (2018a). Madhya Pradesh assembly election 2018: In voter turnout, tribal Jhabua district tops state. Retrieved from https://timesofindia.indiatimes.com/city/bhopal/madhya-pradesh-assembly-election–2018-in-voter-turnout-tribal-jhabua-district-topsstate/articleshow/66915652.cms

Shukla, A. (2018b). Will Congress manage to win back tribals in MP. Retrieved from https://timesofindia.indiatimes.com/india/will-congess-manage-to-win-back-tribals-in-madhya-pradesh/articleshow/66232202.cms

Singh, K. S. (Ed.). (1982). *Tribal movements in India* (vol. 2). New Delhi: Manohar Publications.

Singh, K. S. (1994). *The schedule tribes: People of India project* (National Series vol. 3). New Delhi: Oxford University Press.

Tewari, R. (2018). The tribals of MP have the power to swing elections, not much else. *The Print*, 19 November. Retrieved from https://theprint.in/politics/the-tribals-of-mp-have-the-power-to-swing-elections-not-much-else/151130/

Tiwari, R. (2019). In tribal Madhya Pradesh, BJP grapples with anger over Aadhaar glitches, delay in welfare schemes. *The Indian Express*, 7 April. Retrieved from https://indianexpress.com/article/india/madhya-pradesh-election-bjp-congress-shivraj-singh-chouhan-tribals5405399/

United Nations Development Programme (UNDP). (2011). *Madhya Pradesh: Economic and human development indicators*. New York, NY: United Nations.

Virginius Xaxa, V. (2008). *State, society and tribes: Issues in post-colonial India*. New Delhi: Pearson Longman.

Tribal Politics in Maharashtra

Pandurang Bhoye

I

Tribes are one of the most marginalized communities in India. They are neglected by the state for decades and living in poverty, deprivation and impoverishment. Although the Constitution of India has provided reservation in jobs and education to raise and bring them at par with other communities, their conditions have remained miserable. They have faced tremendous problems when the state pushed its development agendas in tribal areas. Development processes have led to many social spaces of inequalities and have alienated these marginalized groups not only from development processes but also from their own dwellings. Against this backdrop, the chapter briefly highlights various social and political movements among the tribal communities of Maharashtra while critically engaging with numerous organizations that have been working among them for a very long time and elaborates and analyses tribal politics in Maharashtra.

Maharashtra has a long history of tribal movements. These movements are concerned with social, cultural and political issues. While some of these organizations are concerned with their development, others are concerned with the issues of their exploitation and oppression. Before I do this, I would like to outline the geographical spread of the tribal population in Maharashtra along with their ethnic and demographic profile.

II

TRIBAL REGION IN MAHARASHTRA

In Maharashtra, tribal communities are mainly concentrated in three regions, namely Sahyadri, Satpura and Gondwana. The Sahyadri region includes Pune, Nashik, Thane, Raigad, Mumbai, Palghar and Ahmednagar districts. The Varli, Katkari, Mahadev Koli, Kokna, Thakar and Malhar Koli are the major tribal communities inhabited in these districts. Dhule, Jalgaon, Aurangabad, Amravati and Nandurbar districts are part of the Satpura region. This region is mainly inhabited by tribal communities such as Bhil, Kokna, Dhanka, Gavit, Dubala, Korku, Tadavi and Pavara. The Gondwana region includes Chandrapur, Gadchiroli, Bhandara, Nagpur and Yavatmal

Table 21.1   Total and Tribal Population of Maharashtra (1961–2011)

Particulars	1961	1971	1981	1991	2001	2011
Total population	39,554,900	50,412,240	62,782,820	78,937,190	96,752,500	112,372,927
Tribal population	23,97,159	29,54,249	5,772,038	7,318,281	8,577,276	10,510,213
% of Tribal population	6.06	5.86	9.19	9.3	8.9	9.35

Source: Census of India.

districts. The major tribal communities inhabiting this region are Madia, Gond, Korku, Kolam, Andh and Pardhan (Mugade, 2014, pp. 51–52). The changing demographic profile of the tribes in Maharashtra is presented in Table 21.1.

According to 2011 census, the population of Maharashtra was 112,372,927 out of which 10,510,213 were tribes, constituting 9.35 per cent of the total population. Table 21.1 indicates that the tribal population has a chequered history in terms of growth. For instance, the tribal population has increased during 1981 and 2011 census in relation to the previous census years. However, it also experienced a decline during 1971, 1991 and 2001 in comparison to the preceding census years. There are 45 tribal communities in Maharashtra, out of which Bhil, Mahadev Koli, Gond, Kokna, Thakar and Andh are major tribes. They are situated in Nandurbar, Gadchiroli, Dhule, Nashik, Palghar, Pune, Ahmednagar, Jalgaon, Nanded, Amravati, Yavatmal, Nagpur, Bhandara and Chandrapur district of Maharashtra.

III

Many social and political movements and organizations are working among the tribal communities of Maharashtra. These movements address health, education, identity, rights, lifestyle, culture, social and political issues that are critical to the tribal communities of Maharashtra. Before engaging with the discussion on Tribal politics in Maharashtra, I would like to focus on movements and

organizations working in the tribal areas of Maharashtra. These movements have drawn leadership from tribal and non-tribal communities. As the organizations and individuals behind the movements vary in respect of issues addressed and ideology, the movements took different forms. This was evident in the organizational structure and mobilization. The following have been the important social and political movements that can be seen in Maharashtra.

COMMUNIST MOVEMENTS AND TRIBAL MOBILIZATION

Communist movement had started its work in Thane district before independence. Godavari, Shamrao Parulekar and Dalvi started work among the Adivasis at Talasari and Dahanu area. They focused their attention on the exploitations of tribal communities. According to Godavari Parulekar, it was only when they began organizing and mobilizing them. Tribal communities realized and became aware of their rights. They got the courage to stand up heroically against exploitation, forceful slavery, loss of land rights, land alienation, cruel behaviour of outsiders, landlords, moneylenders, government officers, police and others (Parulekar, 1970, p. 9). Godavari Parulekar and other activists not only organized their movements against such cruel activities but also led them to fight against acquisition of their lands, higher wages, the abolition of forced labour and the slavery of marriage (*Lagin Gadi*) tradition (Parulekar, 1970, pp. 71–72).

GANDHIAN ACTIVIST AND LEADER'S EXPERIMENT AMONG TRIBALS

Thakkar Bappa had started experimenting with Gandhian thoughts with the establishment of the Panchmahal Bhil Seva Mandal. In 1947–1948, he set up the forest worker's service organization, including Whig cooperative society related to forest and educational development. He structured cooperative institutions and organized tribals (Bhoye, 2016, p. 385). During the same period, Tarabai Modak worked for the educational development of Adivasis. Later, Anutai Wagh made successful experiments in educational fields for Adivasis of Boardi, Dabhon and Kosbad villages (Wagh, 1980, 1990). These organizations also did their work among the tribes affected by the Narmada Valley project, which affected the Adivasis of Gujarat, and parts of Maharashtra and Madhya Pradesh, especially those living along the Narmada river. These activists worked under the guidance of Medha Patkar and highlighted the positive and negative sides of the projects (Sangvai, 2000, 2004)

KASHTAKARI SANGHATANA (LABOURER ORGANIZATION)

Adivasis of the Dahanu and Talasari regions were facing a number of problems, such as the acquisition of forest land, violation of human rights, forced labour from the hands of merchants, shopkeepers and landlords (Kashtakari Sanghatana, 2005, pp. 2–3). In 1978, Pradip Prabhu organized a three-month political study camp for tribal youth. All activists and participants then decided to have an organization in the meeting of 2 October 1978. Finally, on 23 December 1978, Pradip Prabhu and other activists formed an organization named Kashtakari Sanghatana (Kashtakari Sanghatana, 2005, pp. 4–5).

SHRAMJIVI SANGHATANA (WORKING-CLASS ORGANIZATION)

Vivek Pandit and Vidyulata Pandit established this organization in 1982 by organizing Adivasi people of the Vasai, Wada, Bhiwandi and Shahapur regions with a view to address their development, rights and issues of their exploitation. Shramjivi Sanghatana started agitation by organizing and mobilizing tribals against rich farmers, merchants and government officers who were involved in exploitations of tribals (Pandit, 2014, p. 24).

SHOSHIT JAN ANDOLAN

This organization was a committee of Dalit–Adivasi–Kashtakari (hard-working) people. This organization worked for land rights of Adivasis (Shoshit Jan Andolan, 2004, pp. 1–2). From 1975 to 1976, a number of organizations came together to ensure the rights of Adivasi of the Thane district over land for regularizing of the forest land cultivation (Shoshit Jan Andolan, 2004, p. 1).

HINDUTVAVADI ORGANIZATIONS AND VANAVASI KALYAN ASHRAM

Hindutvavadi organizations claim that tribals are part of the Hindu religion. They consider them *vanvasis* (the people living in forest). According to them, *vanvasis* are the people who live in *van* (forest) (Vaid, 2011, pp. 13–16). These organizations are centred on the spread of Hindu cultures and traditions among tribals, as they consider tribals as originally Hindus. The organizations working among them are the Vishva Hindu Parishad, the Rashtriya Swayamsevak Sangh and the Vanavasi Kalyan Ashram. They organize tribals around issues of education, health and

Hindu tradition and culture (Vanavasi Kalyan Ashram, 2004, p. 3).

IV

PARTICIPATION OF TRIBAL ACTIVISTS AND LEADERS IN MOVEMENTS

Bhil Resistance in Dhule

The Bhils, Thakkars, Varlis and Katkaris Adivasis mainly live in the Dhule district. Government officers, forest officials and police, on the one side, and moneylenders, landlords and rich people of Gujarat, on the other, were exploiting tribals by dispossessing them from land and denying access to forest resources (Bhoye, 2016, p. 4). Against such exploitations and physical and mental torture of Adivasis, many social activists such as Gulabrao Maharaj, Babubhai Mehta and, after 1956, Damodar Das Mundada and others (Gare, 1998, p. 48) got actively involved with Adivasis and organized them for resistance. They also introduced education among them with a view to raise consciousness to fight against injustice and exploitation. Around 1956–1957, while surveying Bhil Adivasi area and life, Ambarsing Suratvanti came into contact with Mr Mundada and became an active worker and engaged with their development (Gare, 1998, p. 48). Another event that strongly affected Ambarsing and forced her to work with Adivasis was the incident that occurred in May 1971. Vishram Patil, a rich landlord, first refused and then distributed grains (20 kg each) to the Adivasi people in the time of drought. But immediately thereafter, he contacted the police and registered it as a robbery.

The Adivasis were suddenly surrounded at Mhasavad village by the police from one side and the landlords of nearer villages on the other side. The landlords ordered the police to fire at Adivasis, but they refused. Suddenly, the landlords themselves started firing on Adivasis. One Bhil Adivasi was sentenced to death as the post-mortem report declared the death caused by the arrow. But after Bhil Adivasis' complain for his reinvestigation, the dead body was reinvestigated by another doctor, and it was found that the Adivasi had died due to bullets in the body. This resulted in the imprisonment of seven landlords and the suspension of the investigating officer. Later, they were released on bail. The Bhil Adivasis who had been arrested before, including Ambarsing, were badly tortured and beaten in prison. Their hamlets were burned and their family members beaten. There was a false complaint against Ambarsing, who was emerging as a leader for Adivasis (Kulkarni, 1982, p. 267).

BHOOMI SENA (LAND ARMY)

The Bhoomi Sena owed its emergence to the efforts of a single person, born around 1943, named Kaluram Dhodade, also known as Kalu Kaka in the Palghar region. He originally came from the Kondhan village and belonged to the Malhar Koli tribe (Deshpande, 1984, p. 22). During the period, landlords, moneylenders, mediators and forest contractors were controlling the Adivasi areas of the Thane district. The de Symington's report highlighted the feudal system prevailing there and described it as 'terrible system, which entailed conditions of life hardly distinguishable from slavery on the bulk of the aboriginal population' (De, 1978, pp. 9–16). Such prevailing feudal system led to the emergence of the Bhoomi Sena in 1970, where the feudal system was marked by dominance, exploitation, forceful slavery and landlessness of the Adivasis. The youth group led by Kaluram rose in protest against this and organized the Adivasi people and gave them the courage to stand collectively against exploitation, injustice and all types of oppression (later collaborated from 15 May 1972) with the support of Aba Karmarkar of Bhoomiputra Pratishthan. They visited different places and made Adivasis aware about land grabbing, securing minimum wages, bureaucracy and social customs (Bhoye, 2016, p. 4).

and continues to organize the *sammelan* on the same date every year. For this *sammelan*, 14 and 15 January have been fixed as date on which the earth changed its direction (Adivasi Ekta Parishad, 2014, p. 5).

V

ADIVASI EKTA PARISHAD (ADIVASI UNITY CONGRESS)

The Ekta Parishad emphasized and made visible the value of being Adivasi, their life, history, culture, forest and nature-based equality. They mobilized Adivasis in a sustained manner raising Adivasi-related issues in the Adivasi areas of Maharashtra, Madhya Pradesh, Gujarat and Rajasthan (Adivasi Ekta Parishad, 2014, pp. 4–5). Later, after interaction and visit to Adivasi areas all over Maharashtra, Ekta Parishad activists decided to establish the 'Adivasi Ekta Parishad', which was formally formed in 1992. Presently, the work is continued under the guidance of Vaharu Sonawane, Kaluram Dhodade (Maharashtra), Gajanan Brahmane, Shankar Tadavala, Fatesingh Solanki (Madhya Pradesh), Sadhanaben Meena, Mogijbhai Bhagora, Jivram Damor (Rajashthan), Sanglyabhai Valvi and Ashokbhai Chaudhari (Gujarat) (Adivasi Ekta Parishad, 2014, p. 4).

This Parishad organized the first *sammelan* (convention) on 14–15 January 1994 at Ankushvihar, Akkalkua (Dhulia district)

POLITICS IN TRIBAL-RESERVED CONSTITUENCIES OF MAHARASHTRA

The Indian Constitution makes provision for the representation of tribal communities in the Parliament and the state legislature. The share of the representation has been worked out on the principle of the size of the population in the state. Accordingly, the system of reserved constituency has been evolved for states and union territories in the country. The Delimitation of Parliamentary and Assembly Constituencies Order, 2008, indicates that, at present, four parliamentary seats are reserved for the tribal communities of Maharashtra.

According to the 2001 Census, the Delimitation Commission in 2008 reserved four parliamentary constituencies for the Scheduled Tribes (STs) in Maharashtra. These constituencies as obvious from Table 21.2 are based on the size of the tribal population spread over the state. On the same principle, the assembly-reserved constituencies were evolved. Table 21.3 provides the number of ST-reserved assembly constituencies and the way they were operationalized.

Table 21.2   ST Population in ST-reserved Parliamentary Constituencies, Maharashtra

Sl. No.	Parliamentary Constituencies	Total Population	ST Population	% of ST Population
1	Nandurbar	1,976,290	1,164,897	58.94
2	Gadchiroli-Chimur	1,925,588	589,142	30.60
3	Dindori	2,024,688	677,239	33.45
4	Palghar	2,035,075	829,725	40.77

Source: Government of India (2008, pp. 934–935, 891–899).

Table 21.3   ST Population in ST-reserved Assembly Constituencies, Maharashtra

Sl. No.	Assembly Constituency	Total	STs	% of STs
1	Akkalkuwa (ST)	314,241	280,275	89.19
2	Vikramgad (ST)	331,531	285,180	86.02
3	Nawapur (ST)	314,637	267,498	85.02
4	Kalwan (ST)	310,744	246,557	79.34
5	Dahanu (ST)	348,482	256,150	73.50
6	Dindori (ST)	361,501	228,959	63.34
7	Shahada (ST)	349,869	211,105	60.34
8	Melghat (ST)	334,972	199,882	59.67
9	Igatpuri (ST)	319,095	165,964	52.01
10	Sakri (ST)	327,028	168,437	51.51
11	Aheri (ST)	315,449	160,504	50.88
12	Akole (ST)	315,745	134,559	42.62
13	Boisar (ST)	337,089	141,172	41.88
14	Shirpur (ST)	337,553	136,886	40.55
15	Armori (ST)	308,241	119,313	38.71
16	Shahapur (ST)	312,775	116,620	37.29
17	Baglan (ST)	311,395	107,288	34.45
18	Palghar (ST)	349,546	108,214	30.96
19	Nandurbar (ST)	332,962	100,696	30.24
20	Ralegaon (ST)	336,202	98,546	29.31
21	Chopda (ST)	351,739	96,653	27.48
22	Bhiwandi Rural (ST)	346,291	93,492	27.00
23	Amgaon (ST)	305,391	82,184	26.91
24	Arni (ST)	359,595	96,430	26.82
25	Gadchiroli (ST)	346,604	91,879	26.51

Source: Government of India (2008, p. 891).

Table 21.3 indicates that, as per the Parliamentary and Assembly Constituencies Order, 2008, the Delimitation Commission reserved 25 assembly constituencies for the STs. The number of reserved constituencies for STs in the state assembly increased from 22 in 1976 to 25 in 2008. These constituencies are Akkalkuwa, Shahada, Nandurbar, Nawapur, Sakri, Shirpur, Chopda, Melghat, Amgaon, Armori, Gadchiroli, Aheri, Ralegaon, Arni, Baglan, Kalwan, Dindori, Igatpuri, Dahanu, Vikramgad, Palghar, Boisar, Bhiwandi Rural, Shahpur and Akole. Among the constituencies reserved for the STs, 11 have more than 50 per cent of ST population in proportion to the total population of the constituency. The proportion of STs is found to be the highest in Akkalkuwa assembly constituency (89.19%), while Gadchiroli has the lowest share of STs (26.51%).

VI

After having outlined the reserved constituencies, I would like to now discuss the electoral politics of the tribes in Maharashtra. Tables 21.4 and 21.5 explain the status of electoral politics both at the level of the Parliament and the state legislature between 1951 and 2019.

Table 21.4   Seat Sharing of Political Parties in Maharashtra Assembly (1951–2019)

Years	Total Constituencies	ST Constituencies	Congress	NCP	BJP	Shiv Sena	CPI	Other Political Parties	Independent Candidates
1951	268	8	8	–	–	–	–	–	–
1957	339	31	19	–	–	–	2	PSP=4 PWP=2	4
1962	264	14	11	–	–	–	1	PWP=1	1
1967	270	16	10	–	–	–	1	RPI=1 PWP=1	3
1972	270	16	13	–	BJS–1	–	–	BKD=1	1
1978	288	22	3+9*	–	–	–	3	PWP=1 JP=4	2
1980	288	22	18	–	–	–	2	Congress (S)=1 JP=1	–
1985	288	22	11	–	1	–	2	JP=2 Congress (S)=5	1
1990	288	22	10	–	5	2	2	JD=03	–
1995	288	22	7	–	5	3	1	NVBS=1	5
1999	288	22	5	5	4	4	2	BBM=1 GGP=1	–
2004	288	22	6	7	4	2	2	–	1
2009	288	25	12	4	3	2	1	BVA=1 SP=1	1
2014	288	25	5	4	11	3	1	BVA=1	–
2019	288	25	4	6	9	2	1	PJP=1 BVA=1	1

Source: Compiled from Government of India (1951–2019).

Note: *Congress (I) won 9 seats in 1978 election.

NCP=Nationalist Congress Party, BJP=Bharatiya Janata Party, CPI=Communist Party of India, PSP=Peoples' Socialist Party, PWP=Peasants and Workers Party of India, RPI=Republican Party of India, BKD=Bharatiya Kranti Dal, JP=Janata Party, JD=Janata Dal, NVAS=Nag Vidarbha Andolan Samiti, BBM=Bharipa Bahujan Mahasangh, GGP=Gondwana Gantantra Party, BVA=Bahujan Vikas Aaghadi, SP=Socialist Party, BJS=Bharatiya Jan Sangh, PJP=Prahar Janshakti Party.

VII

FEATURES OF TRIBAL ELECTORAL POLITICS IN MAHARASHTRA STATE LEGISLATIVE ASSEMBLY

Indian National Congress

The Congress was a dominant party in the state politics of Maharashtra till 1977. In the electoral politics of Maharashtra, the Congress party was a leading political player. In tribal-reserved constituencies, the

Congress party had a major share of representation in the Parliament and the assembly. Before the creation of Maharashtra as a separate state, the Congress party had won all 8 seats in the 1951 election. In the bilingual Mumbai State Legislative Assembly election, the Congress won 19 out of 31 seats. After the formation of the Maharashtra state, the Congress won 11 out of 14 seats in the 1962 assembly election and 10 out of 16 seats in the 1967 assembly election. In the election held in 1972, the Congress party won 13 out of 16 seats.

Table 21.5 Seat Sharing of the Congress and Other Political Parties in Lok Sabha (1951–2019)

Years	Total Consistency	ST Consistency	Congress	Other Political Parties
1951	45	–	–	–
1957	66	04	03	Peoples' Socialist Party=1
1962	44	02	02	–
1967	45	03	03	–
1971	45	03	03	–
1977	48	03	01	Indian Communist Party=1 Bharatiya Lok Dal=1
1980	48	04	04	–
1984	48	04	04	–
1989	48	04	03	Janata Dal=1
1991	48	04	04	–
1996	48	04	01	BJP=1
1998	48	04	01	BJP=2 Janata Dal (Secular)=1
1999	48	04	01	BJP=1
2004	48	04	03	BJP=1
2009	48	04	02	BJP=1 Bahujan Vikas Aaghadi=1
2014	48	04	–	BJP=4
2019	48	04	–	BJP=3 Shiv Sena=1

Source: Compiled from Government of India (1951–2019).

In 1969, the Congress party was split into two groups. The first group, the National Congress (O) won 3 seats and the other fraction, the Congress (Indira) won 9 seats in the election. In Maharashtra after 1977, the Congress began to lose its domination. However, in the 1980 assembly election, the Congress won 18 out of 22 seats in tribal-reserved constituencies. The number was 11 and 10, respectively, in the 1985 and 1990 legislative assembly elections. After 1977, the Congress party was continuously losing its power base. In reference to the numerical loss–win along party lines, the Congress kept leading in tribal-based areas till 1990. After that, the political scenario in Maharashtra underwent change. The tribal areas also got affected by such changes. The Congress won only 7 out of 22 seats in the 1995 assembly election. In 1999 assembly election, only 5 seats were won by the Congress. In 2004

legislative assembly election, the Congress secured 5 seats. The Congress secured 12, 5 and 4 out of 25 ST-reserved assembly constituencies during 2009, 2014 and 2019 elections, respectively.

In tribal areas, the Congress was led by leaders such as Mahadev Kadu, Surupsingh Naik, Adv. Shivajirao Moghe and Vasant Purke. Most of the political leaders were connected with organizations such as the Forest Cooperative Society, Dang Seva Mandal and other educational institutions that were involved with the Congress party. These leaders were the first generation of political leaders who were involved in democratic politics. The Congress party highlighted the political agenda and issues such as opening ashram schools for tribal children, employment through establishing forest workers societies, restriction of alienation of lands from tribes to non-tribes, construction of dams in tribal areas, abolition of bonded labour system, protection of tribal rights, formation of separate tribal ministry and separate department, prevention of atrocities, implementation of Tribal Sub-Plan, Scheduled Tribes and Other Traditional Forest Dwellers (Recognition of Forest Rights) Act, the introduction and implementation of provisions of the Panchayats (Extension to Scheduled Areas [PESA]) Act, the educational and health needs and reservation in private higher educational institutions (Indian National Congress, 2014, 2019; Indian Oversees Congress, 2014).

Bharatiya Janata Party

Before the establishment of the Bharatiya Janata Party (BJP), there was a Bharatiya Jana Sangh Party; the Bharatiya Jana Sangh Party won 1 seat in the 1972 legislative assembly election. Even in the legislative assembly elections of 1985 and 1990, it had won 1 seat each. In 1995, the government was formed by an alliance in which the BJP was a partner. At that time, the BJP had won 5 seats in tribal-reserved constituency. In 1998, the BJP won 2 seats. In the following legislative assembly election, they won 4 seats each in 1999 and 2004. In 2009, in legislative assembly election, they won 3 seats. In 2014, in legislative assembly election, they had a huge electoral success in tribal areas. In fact, it won 11 seats in the legislative assembly. In this election, the party raised issues connected with the needs of the tribal people. Still the question remained as to whether the powerful and elected parties and leaders had developed the tribal people. The tribal development agenda of the BJP got strong support from the tribal population.

In 2014 and 2019, in the state legislature elections, the BJP expanded considerably in tribal areas and won 9 seats in the tribal-reserved constituency. It was almost 50 per cent seats of tribal-reserved constituencies in the state legislature elections that the BJP

had won. The BJP expanded its base in tribal areas on account of social and religious organizations (on hidden religion politics) that had been working among tribal people.

From the BJP, the main elected tribal leaders were Govindbhai Chaudhari, Vishnu Savara, Dilavar Padvi and Sandip Durve. Most of these political leaders had been connected with Vanavasi Kalyan Ashram and other Right-wing cadre activities. The BJP had entered tribal areas through Rashtriya Swayamsevak Sangh, Vanavasi Kalyan Ashram and Swadhyay Parivar. Through programmes organized by Swadhyay Parivar, such as tribal education, health awareness, the organization had succeeded in instilling the identity of 'tribals as Hindus'.

Shiv Sena

During 1990s, the Shivsena also entered the tribal politics. The Shiv Sena won 2 seats in 1990, 3 in 1995, 4 in 1999, 2 in 2004 and 2 in 2009 legislative assembly elections. In 2014, in the legislative assembly election, the Shiv Sena won 3 seats and, in 2019 election, it won 2 seats from the tribal-reserved constituencies. The success of Shiv Sena in tribal areas was due to poor development status in tribal areas and unhappiness with the Congress party. The Shiv Sena raised issues of protection of tribal rights and development in tribal areas. Avinash Sutar, Hariram Varkhede, Mansi Nimkar, Ramkrishna Madavi and Rajendra Gavit are the main tribal leaders of the Shiv Sena.

Communist Party of India

In tribal area, the Communist Party had succeeded in winning 1–3 seats in Maharashtra. The Communist Party won seats in the various legislative assembly elections. It won 2 seats in 1957, 1 in 1962, 1 in 1967, 3 in 1978, 2 in 1980, 2 in 1985, 2 in 1990, 1 in 1995, 2 in 1999, 2 in

2004 and 1 in 2009 election. In 2014 and 2019 legislative assembly elections, the Communist Party of India won 1 seat each from the reserved constituency. B. K. Deshmukh, Jiva Pandu Gavit, Lahanu Kom and Ramdas Bagul are the main tribal leaders in the Communist Party of India. This party organized tribes on issues of exploitation, tribal rights, land and forest land questions, enforced acquisition of tribal lands, implementation of the Forest Rights Act, implementation of the PESA Act, prevention of harassment by forest officers, etc.

Nationalist Congress Party

With the establishment of the Nationalist Congress Party in 1999, tribal senior leaders, such as A. T. Pawar, Madhukar Pichad and Vijaykumar Gavit, joined the party. The NCP won 5, 7 and 4 seats in the 1999, 2004 and 2009 elections, respectively. Similarly, it won 4 and 6 seats in the 2014 and 2019 legislative assembly elections, respectively. The party organized different developmental plans for tribals, such as implementation of the PESA Act, execution of tribal development schemes and providing travelling facilities and irrigation facilities.

Other Political Parties and Independent Leaders' Politics

Other political parties and independent leaders played important roles in tribal areas. In the 1957 legislative assembly election, the Socialist Party won 4 seats and the Shetkari Kamgar (Peasants and Workers) Party won 2 seats. After the formation of Maharashtra, in the 1962 legislative assembly election, the Shetkari Kamgar Party won 1 seat and the independent leaders won 3 seats.

In 1978 legislative assembly election, the Peasants Workers Party won 1 seat and 4 seats

were captured by the Janata Party and 2 by independent candidates. The Congress (S) and the Janata party won 1 seat each in the 1980 legislative assembly election. In the 1985 legislative assembly election, the Janata Party got 2 seats and 5 seats went to the Congress (A) and 1 to independent candidates. In 1990 legislative assembly election, the Janata Dal secured 3 seats. In 1995 assembly election, Nag Vidarbha Andolan Committee won 1 seat and the independent candidate won 1 seat. In the 1999 legislative assembly election, the Bharipa Bahujan Mahasangh and Gondwana Gantantra Party won 1 seat each. In the 2004 legislative assembly election, independent candidate won 1 seat. In 2009 legislative assembly election, the Bahujan Vikas Alliance, the Socialist Party and independent candidate secured 1 seat each. In 2014 legislative assembly election, the Bahujan Vikas Alliance won 1 seat. In the 2019 legislative assembly election, the Prahar Party and the Bahujan Vikas Aaghadi secured 1 seat each in the 2019 assembly election.

PARLIAMENTARY POLITICS

Congress Domination and Its Decline in the Lok Sabha Election

In the 1957 Lok Sabha election, the Congress party won 3 out of 4 ST-reserved seats. The Lok Sabha election of 1962 benefitted 2 seats to the Congress. In the 1967 Lok Sabha election, the Congress won all 3 seats. In the 1971 Lok Sabha election, the same number of seats won by the Congress. In the 1980 Lok Sabha election, the Congress won all 4 seats. In the 1989 Lok Sabha election, they won 3 out of 4 seats. In the 1991 Lok Sabha election, all 4 seats were won by the Congress party. In the tribal area, Congress dominated in ST constituencies during the 1991 election. The charisma of Pandit Nehru and Indira Gandhi was the key factor for the victory of the Congress. In the 1996 Lok Sabha election, it won 1 seat. In the 2004 and 2009 Lok Sabha elections, the Congress won 3 and 2 seats, respectively. Sitaram Bhoye, Zamru Kahandole, Manikrao Gavit, Reshma Bhoye and Bapu Chaure were the main leaders. In the 2014 and 2019 Lok Sabha elections, the Congress did not win any seat. This was due to the unhappiness with the Congress and the rise in popularity of the Modi leadership, which articulated the issue of development.

BJP Expansion in the Lok Sabha Election among Tribal Communities

In the Lok Sabha elections of 2004 and 2009, the BJP won 1 seat each. In the 2014 election of the Lok Sabha, it won all 4 seats. In the recently concluded 2019 election, it won 3 seats. From the BJP, the elected main tribal leaders were Harishchandra Chavan, Kacrubahu Raut, Chintaman Vanaga, Heena Gavit and Bharati Pawar. Most of these political leaders have the connection with the Vanavasi Kalyan Ashram and with the activities of the other Right-wing organizations.

The BJP announced the political agenda such as the Vanbandhu Kalyan Yojana at the national level to be overseen by a Tribal Development Authority, the protection of the Forest Rights Act, the incorporation of tribal freedom fighters into the history chapter in the school syllabus, the provision of special services for issuing tribe certificates and various government documents, the introduction of tribal development projects, the setting up of an entire education network for tribals, the promotion of the products associated and created on the basis of tribal culture by situating tribal tourist towns and other centres, the establishment of the National Centre for Tribal Research and Culture to preserve tribal culture and languages, and the enhancement of the funds for tribal welfare and development (Bharatiya Janata Party, 2014a, 2014b).

Other Political Parties in the Lok Sabha Election

In the 1957 Lok Sabha election, the Praja Socialist Party got 1 seat. In the 1977 Lok Sabha election, the Bharatiya Lok Dal party got victory in 1 reserved constituency. In the 1977 Lok Sabha election, 1 seat was won by the Communist Party of India. In the 1989 Lok Sabha election, the Janata Dal succeeded in getting 1 seat. In the 1999 Lok Sabha election, the Janata Dal (Secular) won 1 seat. In the Lok Sabha election of 2014, the Bahujan Vikas Alliance won 1 seat. In the Lok Sabha election of 2019, the Shiv Sena won 1 seat. These political parties, from time to time, organized and raised issues such as educational facilities, travelling facilities, job-related support for tribals, the implementation of tribal plans and developmental programmes in tribal areas.

CONCLUSION

To conclude, the Congress party was very influential in tribal areas till 1990. The Congress extended its base through its role in India's freedom struggles. It won more than half of the seats in the Lok Sabha and the legislative assembly election. After 1990, the Congress party continuously declined in Maharashtra politics, which affected tribal areas. The BJP expanded in tribal areas because of the social and political institutional support of the organizations related to the BJP. After 1990, the BJP introduced its agenda among tribal belts through the Vanavasi Kalyan Ashram and other organizations. These organizations have been working among the tribal population on issues of health, education, representation of tribes in the form of Hindu identity and the incorporation of Hindu cultures, ethos and values among tribes. The involvement of tribal women in politics has been very limited. In different assembly elections, only seven women representatives have been elected.

Politics in tribal-reserved constituencies is generally no different from mainstream state politics and party ideology. Tribal politics in Maharashtra does not represent autonomous and self-governing space for tribal politics, governance and development.

ACKNOWLEDGEMENTS

I would like to thank Shankar Bhoir, Babasaheb Mundhe, Rajendra Bhoiwar and Shivaji Motegaonkar for extending their help and cooperation in collecting information and preparing the present chapter. I am indebted to them for their support.

REFERENCES

Adivasi Ekta Parishad. (2014). *Ghoshanapatra* (Marathi). Jalgaon: Adivasi Ekta Parishad.

Bharatiya Janata Party. (2014a). Lok Sabha election 2014 manifesto: Ek Bharat shreshtha Bharat, sabka saath sabka vikas. Retrieved from https://www.bjp.org/images/pdf_2014/full_manifesto_english_07.04.2014.pdf

Bharatiya Janata Party. (2014b). BJP Maharashtra assembly election 2014 manifesto. Retrieved from http://mumbaivotes.com/parties/manifesto/131/

Bhoye, P. (2016). Maharashtatil Adivasintil chalvaliani sanghatna (Marathi). In P. N. Kumbhar (Ed.), *Vicharshalaka samkalin samajik chalvali visheshank* (pp. 383–392). Latur: Aai Shiv Nagar Sutmil Marg.

De, Silva. (1978). *Bhoomi sena: A struggle for people's power*. Bombay: National Institute of Bank Management.

Deshpande, V. (1984). *Tribals of Thane: The struggle of the deprived for development*. Pune: Dastane Ramchandra & Co.

Gare, G. (1998). *Adivasi vikasatil deepstambh* (Marathi). Pune: Shreevidhya Prakashan.

Government of India. (1951–2019). *Statistical reports on general election to the legislative assembly of Maharashtra and general election Lok Sabha*. New Delhi: Election Commission of India.

Government of India. (2008). *Changing face of electoral India: Delimitation 2008, Volume-I*. New Delhi: Delimitation Commission of India.

Indian National Congress. (2014). Lok Sabha election 2014 manifesto: Your voice our pledge. Retrieved from https://www.thehindu.com/multimedia/archive/01813/Congress_Manifesto_1813003a.pdf

Indian National Congress. (2019). Lok Sabha election 2019 manifesto: Congress will deliver. Retrieved from https://manifesto.inc.in/pdf/english.pdf.

Indian Oversees Congress (2014). Suggested policies and programmes for consideration Congress government (2014–2019): Empowering scheduled castes, scheduled tribes and other backward classes. Retrieved from https://www.iocongress.org/uploads/manifesto/1547546632_Sub_Manifesto_2014.pdf

Kashtakari Sanghatana. (2005). *Kashtakari sanghatana: Manav muktichya dishene* (Marathi). Thane: Kashtakari Sanghatana.

Kulkarni, S. (1982). The Bhil movement in the Dhulia district. In K. S. Singh (Ed.), *Tribal movement in India* (vol. 2; pp. 261–272). New Delhi: Manohar Publishers and Distributors.

Mugade, V. (March, 2004). *Mahrashtratil advasinci olakh* (Marathi). *Tribal Research Bulletin, 27*(1), 50–56.

Pandit, V. (2014). *Dusrya swatantryacha ladha* (Marathi). Speech delivered on 15 August. Thane: Shramajivi Sanghatana.

Parulekar, G. (1970). *Jenvha manus jaga hoto* (Marathi). Mumbai: Mauje Publication House.

Sangvai, S. (2000). *The river and life: People's struggle in the Narmada Valley*. Mumbai: Earth care Books.

Sangvai, S. (2004). *Samkalin satyagrahi sangharshache nave roop: Narmada khoryatil jan andolan* (Marathi). Kolhapur: Mahatma Gandhi Abhyas Kendra, Shivaji University.

Shoshit Jan Andolan. (2004). *Jamin hakk parishad* (Marathi). Mumbai: Shoshit Jan Andolan.

Vaid, S. (2011). *Vanavasi Kalyan Ashram: Karya parichay* (Marathi). Chhattisgarh: Akhil Bhartiy Vanavasi Kalyan Ashram.

Vanavasi Kalyan Ashram. (2004). *Olakh Vanavasi Kalyan Ashramachi* (Marathi). Mumbai: Vanavasi Kalyan Ashram.

Wagh, A. (1980). *Kosbadchya tekdivarun* (Marathi). Thane: Rucha Prakashan.

Wagh, A. (1990). *Dabhonachya jangalatun* (Marathi). Aurangabad: Saket Prakashan.

The Politics of Tribal Representation in Manipur*

Joseph Riamei

HISTORICAL BACKGROUND

The hill areas of the present-day Manipur have been inhabited by tribal communities, and have never been part of Manipur ruled by Meitei Raja or Kangleipak until the advent of the British colonizers. It was with the coming of the British colonizers who placed Manipur under their protectorate with a political agent that was changing from time to time. After the British conquest of Manipur in 1891, the hill areas came under the rule of the British political agent. The British introduced the system of indirect rule. Under this system, the British did not rule the hill tribes directly. They did not interfere in the internal affairs of tribal villages. They introduced the Hill House Tax of ₹3 per household per year. They made the chiefs or the headmen of the villages responsible for the administration of the villages. Although the Raja of the valley was handed over the administration of the state of

Manipur, his jurisdiction was confined to the valley and he was not allowed to administer in hill areas (Kamei, 2011).

On the 15th day of October 1949, Manipur merged with the Indian Union. The experiences of the tribal people in Manipur were concerned with this merging, as they were left out to be protected under the Sixth Schedule of the Constitution of India or any other provision for the protection of the hill people. However, when Manipur was alleviated to a full-fledged state, an attempt was made by the Government of India to deal with the critical issues of the tribal people of Manipur. After the introduction of the Union Territory Council Act, 1956, Manipur had 30 members of council and 2 nominated members. This council created a committee known as 'Hill Standing Committee' with a separate chairman. At this time, the movement for statehood in Manipur was gaining momentum, and tribal leaders were demanding for

* Some of the arguments put forward here are based on my PhD thesis entitled 'Asymmetrical Federalism and Peoples' Response in North East India: A Case of Manipur (Hill Areas) District Council' (2015), School of Social Work, Tata Institute of Social Sciences, Mumbai and a publication appeared in www.daltrijournals.org.

constitutional safeguard for tribal people (Kamei, 2011). Thus, the Constitution (27th Amendment) Act, 1971, made a specific provision in relation to the formation of the Manipur Legislative Assembly (Hill Areas Committee [HAC]) by inserting Article 371C to safeguard the rights of the people in the hill areas of Manipur. The North-Eastern Areas (Reorganisation) Act, 1971, was accompanied by the insertion of Article 371C into the Constitution of India. With this insertion of Article 371C, the Legislative Assembly of Manipur renamed the Standing Committee as 'the HAC'.[1] The HAC is a special provision provided by the Constitution of India to monitor the lawmaking and administration of hill areas which are dominated by tribal people.

In the Constitution of India, the Fifth and Sixth schedules provide the mechanism for the administration of the Scheduled Tribes (STs). The Sixth Schedule deals with the administration of tribal areas with the formation of the Autonomous District Council (ADC) in the states of Assam, Meghalaya, Mizoram and Tripura. The tribal areas of Manipur are included in the schedule areas but are not covered by the Sixth Schedule. The tribal area of Manipur is called 'Hill Areas'. The term *Hill Areas* has a historical background. During the colonial period, the term 'Hill Tribes' was used under the Rules for the Management of Hill Tribes, 1935. Kamei (2011) noted that, at the time of India's independence, the term 'Hill Tribe' was substituted by the term 'Hill People' in the Manipur State Hill People (Administration) Regulation, 1947, and the Manipur State Constitution Act, 1947. After the merger of Manipur to the dominion of India as per the order of the president of India in 1950, the term ST was used to mean Naga, Kuki and Lushai tribes.

Table 22.1 highlights the analysis of the Population Census 2011 published by the Government of India for Manipur state, which reveals that the population of Manipur has increased by 24.50 per cent in this decade compared (2001–2011) to the past decade (1991–2001). The density of the Manipur state in the current decade is 331 per sq. miles.[2]

Table 22.1 District-wise Tribal Population of Manipur, 2011

S. No.	District	Population	Increase (in %)	Sex Ratio	Literacy (in %)	Density
1	Imphal West	517,992	16.56	1,031	86.08	998
2	Senapati	479,148	68.94	937	63.60	146
3	Imphal East	456,113	15.51	1,017	81.95	643
4	Thoubal	422,168	15.94	1,002	74.47	821
5	Churachandpur	274,143	20.29	975	82.78	60
6	Bishnupur	237,399	13.93	999	75.85	479
7	Ukhrul	183,998	30.70	943	81.35	40
8	Chandel	144,182	21.85	933	71.11	44
9	Tamenglong	140,651	26.15	943	70.05	32

Source: https://www.census2011.co.in/census/state/districtlist/manipur.html

---

[1] The Hill Areas Committee Order, 1972, states:

There shall be a Hill Areas Committee of the Assembly consisting of all the members of that Assembly who for the time being represents the Assembly constituencies situated wholly or partly in the Hill Areas of the State. Provided that the Chief Minister of the State and the Speaker shall not be members of the Hill Areas Committee.

[2] For details, see https://www.census2011.co.in/census/state/districtlist/manipur.html

POLITICS OF REPRESENTATIONS AND ITS IMBROGLIO

According to the 2011 census, the total percentage of STs in India is 8.6 and Manipur has 37.6 per cent of the ST population.[3] Out of its total geographical area, about 10 per cent is in the valleys, which is home to around 65 per cent of the total population, and the remaining areas are hilly areas inhabited by various tribal communities belonging to the Naga and Zo (Kuki-Chin) tribal people. Manipur has 60 members in assembly and has 2 seats in the Lok Sabha, representing Inner Manipur (the Imphal Valley) and Outer Manipur, representing the hill areas of Manipur. Out of the total of 60 members of the legislative assembly (MLAs), 40 are from the districts of the Imphal Valley. Out of the 40 MLAs, 9, 15, 10 and 6 MLAs represent Imphal East, Imphal West, Thoubal and Bishnupur districts, respectively. The remaining 20 MLAs are from tribal dominant areas representing the districts

of Chandel (2 MLAs), Senapati (6 MLAs), Tamenglong (3 MLAs), Churachandpur (6 MLAs) and Ukhrul (3 MLAs). Out of a total of nine districts in Manipur, five and four are located in hill and valley areas. Needless to mention, districts located in hill and valley areas are dominated by tribal communities and Meiteis, respectively.

As shown in Table 22.2, the districts dominated by tribals, which I termed here as 'Tribal Districts', have the total area of 20,089 sq. km out of the total area of 22,327 sq. km. The non-tribal districts areas which I termed here as 'Valley Districts' occupied only 2,238 sq. km out of the total area of 22,327 sq. km. This shows that the tribals dominate about 90 per cent of the total geographical areas of Manipur.

The contentious issue is regarding peoples' representation in the Legislative Assembly of Manipur. As shown in Table 22.3, the total number of MLAs from the tribal districts is 20 out of the total of 60 MLAs. The remaining 40 MLAs are from the valley districts. Peoples'

Table 22.2 Area in Square Kilometres, Population and Number of Member in State Legislative Assembly in Tribal and Valley Districts, Manipur

Tribal Districts	Area in Sq. Km	Population	MLAs
Chandel	3,313	144,182	2
Senapati	3,271	479,148	6
Tamenglong	4,391	140,651	3
Ukhrul	4,544	183,998	3
Churachandpur	4,570	274,143	6
Total	20,089	1,222,122	20
Valley Districts	Area in Sq. Km	Population	MLAs
Imphal East	709	456,113	9
Imphal West	519	517,992	15
Thoubal	514	422,168	10
Bishnupur	496	237,399	6
Total	2,238	1,633,672	40

Source: Census of India, 2011.[1]

[1] Retrieved from http://www.censusindia.gov.in

[3] Retrieved from http://www.censusindia.gov.in

Table 22.3   Performance of Some Major Political Parties in 2012 and 2017 Assembly Elections, Manipur

Political Parties	2017	2012	Changes
INC	28	42	−14
BJP	21	0	+21
TMC	1	7	−6
Independent	1	0	+1
Others	9	11	−2

Source: *The Times of India*[1] and Election Commission of India.[2]

---

[1] For details, see https://timesofindia.indiatimes.com/elections/assembly-elections/manipur/results
[2] See https://eci.gov.in/files/file/3712-manipur-2012/

representation in the state assembly is based on the premises of population size. According to the 2011 census, the tribal districts have a population of 1,222,122, whereas the total population of the valley districts stood at 1,633,672. Statically, there is only a difference of 411,550 population between the tribal and valley districts. In contrast, the representation in the state assembly is in the ratio of 2:4 between the hill and the valley districts. This allocation of seats in the Legislative Assembly is with effect since 1972.

India is the biggest democratic country in the world and, in that essence of rule by the people, the representation in the Parliament or in the Legislature of the state is based on the logic of population enshrined in the Constitution in Article 4(1){6} and Article 80(2).[4] In this logic, for instance, we have 25 seats from the eight states of the Northeast in the Lok Sabha, whereas Uttar Pradesh alone has 80 seats. In the case of Manipur, there has been a misrepresentation and skewness in peoples' representation in the state legislative. For instance, the total population of the Senapati district in the hill area is 479,148 and the Thoubal district in the valley is 422,168. Statistically, the Senapati district has more population of 56,980 as compared to the Thoubal district. However, in terms of the number of constituencies in the legislative assembly, it is 6 in Senapati and 10 in Thoubal. Examining the ratio of per constituency and per average population coverage, the average population of each assembly constituency is 79,858. In contrast, the Thoubal district represents only 42,216 populations per constituency. A comparison between the hills and the valley district shows that the average peoples' representation in one constituency stands at 61,106 for hills, whereas for the valley districts, it is only 40,841. This clearly shows that the peoples' representation in the Legislative Assembly of Manipur is unconstitutional, undemocratic and is driven by the politics of dominant elites, in spite of the two delimitations process that were carried out in 1976 and 2008.

Considering the average geographical area (in sq. km) per constituency between the hills and the valley districts, it is revealed that hills have 1,004 sq. km. In contrast, the valley

---

[4] The allocation of seats in the Council of States to be filled by the representatives of the states and of the union territories shall be in accordance with the provisions in that behalf contained in the Fourth Schedule. Any law referred to in Article 2 or Article 3 shall contain such provisions for the amendment of the First Schedule and the Fourth Schedule as may be necessary to give effect to the provisions of the law and may also contain such supplemental, incidental and consequential provisions (including provisions on representation in the Parliament and in the legislature or the legislatures of the state or states affected by such law) as the Parliament may deem necessary.

districts have only 55 sq. km per constituency. This is a striking difference in the context of peoples' representation and the geographical domination in Manipur.

The comparison of the Manipur assembly elections of 2012 and 2017 indicates that the people of Manipur are always in favour of the central ruling political party. The comparison table (Table 22.3) is given further. If we take the case of the Bharatiya Janata Party (BJP), there is a sudden jump from none in 2012 to 21 seats in the 2017 election. It is interesting to point out that the BJP was ruling at the centre in 2017 and that, in 2012, the Indian National Congress (INC) was in power at the centre. Even in the case of 2007 assembly election, the INC won 30 seats out of 60 and not even a single seat was won by the BJP. This indicates that, at the state level, the people of Manipur prefer the political party that is in power at the centre, and it appears that the ability of the candidates or their agendas do not matter much to the voters of Manipur.

In the case of the Lok Sabha election in 2014, INC candidates for both Inner and Outer Manipur won the election with a huge margin of about 1 lakh for Inner Manipur and about 15,000 for Outer Manipur. It is important to note that the INC political wave was still strong in the case of Manipur, as the party was in power at the pre-2014 Lok Sabha election in the centre. It is also interesting to note that, even in 2009, INC candidates won both the Inner and Outer Manipur parliamentary constituencies with a vote margin of 1 lakh to 2 lakhs differences.

For the Lok Sabha election of 2019, many candidates were in fray for BJP tickets as compared to other political parties as the BJP was in power at the centre. As Table 22.4 indicates, the BJP won with a huge margin for Inner Manipur. Interestingly, for outer Manipur, the Naga People's Front (NPF) emerged with a landslide win in spite of the fact that the BJP was the ruling political party. This landslide win for the NPF is due to the ongoing Indo-Naga political talks and negotiations with central government, as the majority of voters in Outer Manipur are from the Naga community. It is imperative to point out that, in the case of Outer Manipur parliamentary constituency, there is more to do with the ethnic identity agenda than with the state assembly election in the present context. The two major ethnic groups, Naga and Kuki, with their separate demands, are in favour on the basis of the ethnic line of the candidature. The Naga for Naga sovereignty issue will campaign on the basis of these demands and Kuki for Kuki land or state. Nevertheless, the political party ruling in state and centre factor greatly influenced on the voting for the political party by the people.

Nevertheless, the favouritism of party-in-power trend has strong political influences since the emergence of Manipur as a state. For that matter, if the ruling central government changes, there is a high possibility of changing the government in favour of the ruling party, as had happened in Manipur before.

The 42nd Constitutional Amendment Act 1976 had put a ban on any further delimitation

Table 22.4 Electoral Outcomes of the Lok Sabha Elections, 2004–2019, Manipur

Year	Inner Manipur	Margin	Outer Manipur	Margin
2019	BJP	16,830	NPF	75,649
2014	INC	94,674	INC	15,637
2009	INC	30,960	INC	119,798
2004	INC	4,933	IND	82,193

Source: Office of the Chief Electoral Officer, Manipur.[1]

[1] For details, see https://ceomanipur.nic.in/ResultSheets/LSResult2014.html

of the constituencies till the year 2000. This ban was imposed mostly on account of the fear that a few states to get more seats in the Lok Sabha on the basis of a large population may not take much interest in family planning. Further, the 84th Amendment Act 2002 extended the freeze till the year 2026. This was based upon the calculations of the population planners that by 2026 India will be able to stabilize the population. So the next allocation of seats would be probably carried out on the basis of the census after 2026, and the number of seats will not change by then. So the 84th Amendment Act did two things—freeze the fresh delimitation till 2026 and allowed to readjust the existing seats. The year 1991 was later altered to 2001 by the 87th Amendment Act, 2003. However, in the case of the Northeast, the Guwahati High court stayed the delimitation exercise in respect of Arunachal Pradesh, Assam, Nagaland, Manipur (5 states) on the basis of the disputes in the census figures. In Manipur, the work of delimitation was later resumed after the Supreme Court stayed on the order of the Guwahati High Court.[5] Nevertheless, there was no impact or readjustments in the number of representations in Manipur both on assembly and parliamentary constituencies in spite of the changes in the 2001 census.

After Manipur gained statehood in the year 1972, the number of seats both in the assembly and the parliamentary constituencies has remained the same till date, that is, 60 and 2, respectively. In Manipur, one parliamentary constituency is reserved for the STs (Outer Manipur) and the other is unreserved constituency as per the delimitation orders of 1976 and 2008.[6] It is interesting to note that a population of 238,572 (out of 919,009 voters of Outer Manipur)[7] individuals living in eight assembly constituencies belonging to general category in Thoubal and Imphal east districts are getting their candidature and voting rights in the outer manicured parliamentary constituencies, which are reserved for the STs. The eight assembly constituencies are Heirok, Wangjing Tentha, Khangabok, Wabagai, Kakching, Hiyanglam, Sugnu and Jiribam, which come under the outer parliamentary constituency.[8] With the demand by several rights bodies such as Thoubal district MP Candidature Demand Committee and Thoubal District Demand Committee, it was resolved in the Fifth Session of the 8th Manipur State Assembly to recommend the inclusion of these eight assembly segments in the inner parliamentary constituency and also to forward the resolution of the assembly to the chairperson, Delimitation Commission, Election Commission of India.[9] As discussed, there are many flaws and politics in the nature of representation in the state of Manipur. The delimitations process in the past has not resolved these anomalies and has further weakened the democratic and constitutional principles of representation. The upcoming delimitation process proposed for the post-2026 period, as per the 84th Amendment Act, 2002, should be deliberate on the line of the geopolitics of the state without the influence of the dominant politics. It should relook and readjust representation as per the principle of the Constitution and the democratic framework of the state, and rework the political imbroglio of representation currently plaguing the state.

It must be further noted that there are huge disparities when it comes to the development of infrastructure in the hill and valley areas. All the centrally sponsored institutions such as the Central Institute of Plastics Engineering and Technology, the Manipur Institute of Technology, the Central Agricultural

[5] For details, see https://www.gktoday.in/gk/delimitation-in-india/
[6] For details, see https://eci.gov.in/files/file/5520-scsts-seats-in-lok-sabha-as-per-last-two-delimitation-orders/
[7] See https://www.firstpost.com/lok-sabha-elections-2019/manipur/outer-manipur-election-result-2019-s14p02
[8] See http://e-pao.net/epRelatedNews.asp?heading=8&src=160303
[9] See http://e-pao.net/epRelatedNews.asp?heading=8&src=160303

University, the Government Polytechnic, the Indian Council of Agricultural Research, the Jawaharlal Nehru Institute of Medical Sciences, the Manipur University, the Jawaharlal Nehru Hospital, the Multi Stadia Complex, the National Institute of Technology, Manipur, the Regional Institute of Medical Sciences, the Rice Research Station, the State Soil Testing Laboratory, the Small and Medium Enterprises Development Institute and the State Institute of Rural Development are all located in the valley districts. On the other hand, there is not even a single central institution in the hill districts. This clearly indicates the disparities of development in the hill and valley areas of Manipur. It is clear from the data that the development in Manipur is valley-centric. Therefore, it is ludicrous to call *Ching-tam amatani*[10] by the valley people (Meitei) in Manipur. Ziipao (2019) argued that, apart from the skewed infrastructure development between hills and valley districts, the state has faced political instability, law and order problems, layers of corruption, systemic loopholes in the implementation of various programmes, contradictions between different ethnic communities, the issue of uniform land laws, political manipulation of ethnicity, deeply embedded hostility between hills and valley, increasing securitization and mushrooming insurgencies. All of these have a bearing on the infrastructure development.

POLITICS OF PROTECTION AND TRIBAL RIGHTS IN MANIPUR

Article 371C provides Constitutional safeguards for legislation and administration in the hill areas of Manipur. According to this Article:

The President may...provide for the constitution and functioning of a Committee of the Legislative Assembly of the State consisting of the members of the Assembly elected from the Hill Areas...for any special responsibility of the Governor in order to secure the proper functioning of the Committee.

The subsection no. 2 of this Article further states:

The Governor shall annually or whenever so required by the President, make a report to the President regarding the Hill Areas in the State of Manipur and the execution power of the Union shall extend to the giving of direction to the state as to administration of the said area.

The then President of India, Dr V. V. Giri, promulgated the Manipur Legislative Assembly (Hill Areas Committee) Order, 1972.[11]

The only constitutional protection that the tribal people of Manipur have is provided in the Constitution of India under Article 371C by providing the 'HAC'. However, since the formation of the committee, it was argued by many scholars and social activists that the powers and provisions enshrined in the article have never been implemented. Further, it points out that the HAC members become the puppet of the ruling political party. One of the tribal leaders said that the post of the chairman of the HAC is a 'ceremonial post' and they want to become the chairman or members of the HAC for their own political scores and benefits. There has also been a series of agitation and protests by the tribal organization to sincerely and honestly implement the power of the HAC. However, the constitutional power for the protection of tribal people under Article 371C is incarcerated in the whims of the ruling political party.

There are arbitrary and illegal alterations of two vital words in the Manipur Legislative Assembly Secretariat, Government of

Manipur (GoM) (Eight Editions, 2005) as compared to the HAC Original Order, 1972, which bluntly curtailed the powers of the governor, namely (a) *governor* to *government* and (b) *discretion* to *direction*. This totally dethroned the power of the HAC by curtailing the power of the governor by the GoM. The sole power of the governor under Article 371C of the Constitution of India has been limited to his direction after these amendments. There are other deletions of significant words such as 'legislation' in serial number 1 and 'bill' in serial number 4 from the original order 1972. The official of hill areas and tribal affairs, the GoM, brusquely commented in this regard that it was a printing mistake and did not make any further comments.[12]

The HAC is a statutory body with legislative powers in regard to the hill areas of Manipur. The chairman of the HAC is equal to the rank of cabinet minister and has the power to make the law applicable to the hill areas. There are 20 members in the HAC, including the chairman and vice chairman, and all elected MLAs from the hill areas. It is very interesting to find that even the vice chairman of the HAC agreed that the power of the HAC has been sabotaged by the ruling political party. The vice chairman states:

> Under article 371-C the HAC has constitutional power but it is not been practice in reality and the HAC is not functioning as per the provision under article 371-C. The HAC is influenced by the politics of the ruling party and since the majority rule, and the majority are non-tribal, the Government did not want to sanction the power to HAC which the HAC should have under the Article 371-C. The Government did not even consult on making the budget for District Council or development of Hill. The power and functions of HAC has been controlled by the ruling political party.[13]

This clearly illuminates the realities of the HAC and how the constitutionally sanctioned power has been curtailed by the state government. The responses and realities that are being witnessed in the state of Manipur strongly reflect on how the politics of dominant government has dethroned the constitutionally sanctioned power. Although constitutionally the HAC has legislative and administrative power in the affairs of the hill areas, it is impractical in the rigid political domination in the state of Manipur.

On 31 August 2015, the Manipur Assembly passed three bills, such as the Protection of Manipur People Bill, 2015, the Manipur Land Revenue and Land Reforms (Seventh Amendment) Bill, 2015, and the Manipur Shops and Establishments (Second Amendment) Bill, 2015. These bills were passed in a special session of the Assembly in response to the demand of the people of the valley for the implementation of an inner-line permit system in the state. The fundamental problem of the bills is in their interpretation. While the valley people, who are predominantly Meiteis, view the bills as a mechanism to protect the state and its people from outsiders, the hill people (Kukis and Nagas) view the bills as a threat to their rights over identity and land[14] as the bills intend to extend the land rights of non-tribals in the hill areas with amendments.

The argument of the state government and the valley people is that the bills are largely misunderstood and misinterpreted by the hill people. They claimed that the bills were meant to check the migration of people from outside the state, and would not negatively affect the hill people. Interestingly, the bills were passed without any consent of the HAC, though constitutionally the HAC should be consulted and approve them. The GoM termed it as 'Money Bill' and bypassed the constitutionally sanctioned power of the HAC under Article 371C.

---

[12] Based on interview by the author.
[13] Excerpt from interview by the author.
[14] For details, see http://www.huffingtonpost.com/entry/politics-of-3-bills-and-9_b_9147904.html?section=india

On the floor of the highly charged upper house of the Parliament, a Rajya Sabha member from Uttarakhand, Tarun Vijay, vociferously said that the three bills passed by the Manipur Assembly on 31 August 2015 constitute a gross violation of the constitutional and democratic rights of the tribals in Manipur. He stated:

> They are protesting against the three Bills which had been passed without any discussion; without consulting the stakeholders; without discussing with the tribal organization. So, only few decide the fate of Manipur tribals. Nobody takes them into confidence; No body consults them; Nobody seeks their opinion. This is gross violation of their constitutional rights. This is gross violation of their democratic rights.[15]

The bodies of the nine people killed by the state forces in protest against the bills were kept in the morgue for more than 200 days by the Joint Action Committee against the bills until the bills were withdrawn and termed it as 'the dead bodies waiting for justice'.

THE MANIPUR (HILL AREAS) DISTRICT COUNCIL AND TRIBAL RESISTANCE

The Manipur (Hill Areas) District Council Act was enacted by the Parliament of India on 26 December 1971, when the present-day Manipur was still a Union Territory. The Act, among others, established six ADCs in the hill areas of Manipur, namely (a) Manipur North ADC, now Senapati ADC, (b) Sadar Hills ADC, (c) Manipur East ADC, now Ukhrul ADC, (d) Tengnoupal ADC, now Chandel ADC, (e) Manipur South ADC, now Churachandpur ADC and (f) Manipur West ADC, now Tamenglong ADC.

The Act met with severe opposition from its inception on the grounds that it posed a threat to the rights and autonomy of tribal communities enjoyed under their traditional systems of self-governance. The unified demand of all tribal communities (Kuki and Naga organizations) was that the Act be modified to include the provisions of the Sixth Schedule of the Indian Constitution. The tribals of Manipur had been actively participating in this grassroots democracy till the early 1980s. But as the last elections were held in 1984 and 1987, the process came to an abrupt halt, with the hill people of Manipur working out from the ADCs demanding more autonomy (power). The elections to the ADC were successfully boycotted in the next two decades. The government responded by taking one step forward and two steps backwards: in 1975, the First Amendment Bill was passed with some changes, followed by a more substantial move towards making the district councils 'autonomous' by passing the Manipur Hill Areas Autonomous District Council Bill in July 2000. However, no further progress was made on this and a second amendment bill was passed in March 2006 effectively revoking it. After another two years of silence, the third amendment bill was presented in the Legislative Assembly on 19 March 2008 (Bhatia, 2010). However, there were allegations of irregularities in the processes that followed, and the bill was eventually withdrawn. Two irregularities were primarily pointed out:

> (i) The state assembly constituted an extra constitutional body called the select committee to work on {the principal bill 2008} introduced by the HAC. Three of the five members...are not elected from the hill areas of the state. (ii) Many clauses in the report of the select committee...were found in bad taste. {It} wanted to delete the word 'autonomous' from the title...{replace} 'self government' {with} 'local self governance', 'tribals' {with} 'people of the hill areas'.[16]

---

[15] As per the mandate of Article 371-C, the Government of Manipur have to consult the HAC in all matters relating to Hill Areas legislative and developmental affairs.

[16] See https://shodhganga.inflibnet.ac.in/bitstream/10603/39715/11/11_chapter%203.pdf

Despite the legitimate claim for the Sixth Schedule and the rejection of the Act, it became clear to the tribals in March–April 2010 that the state government was planning to hold the ADC election soon. This led to the revival of the earlier agitation on the issue. The Manipur Tribal Joint Action Committee and the All Manipur Tribal Union declared the day as 'black day' in the history of the tribal people of Manipur, accusing the chief minister of attempting to get the ADCs in place 'manipulatively'. Other tribal organizations such as the United Naga Council and Kuki Inpi Manipur (the apex body of the Kukis) reiterated the objection and demanded that the elections be held under the provisions of the Sixth Schedule to fulfil the aspirations of the tribal people of Manipur and to protect the integrity of the state.

The tribal organizations then met with the governor, the prime minister and the home minister and sought their urgent interventions. The governor told them to cooperate with the election process and said that all necessary amendments would be made after the elections. This was unacceptable to these organizations which maintained that nothing short of the Sixth Schedule would be acceptable.[17] They believed that once the elections were held under the Act, tribal people would be victims of economic and political exploitation and stagnation for another generation to come.

The All Naga Students Association Manipur (ANSAM) called for a 6-day blockade of the two national highways leading to Manipur and all state highways between 11 and 17 April 2010. Despite taking such drastic steps, the GoM failed to respond and instead, on 22 April 2010, announced its decision to go ahead with the ADC election. ANSAM responded to this by calling for a lightning indefinite economic blockade of the two national highways on 24 April 2010. This was quickly followed by the GoM's announcement on 26 April 2010 of a detailed schedule for holding the election.

The Naga Frontal Organisations' sponsored *chakka bandh*[18] on 6 April 2011, the People's Democratic Alliance (PDA), a political party based in Manipur Hill, urged the GoM to amend the Manipur (Hill Areas) District Council Act and stated that the 12-hour Manipur Hill Areas *chakka bandh* on 6 April 2011 called by the United Naga Council, ANSAM, Naga Peoples' Movement for Human Rights, Naga People's Organisation (Senapati), Zeliangrong Interim Body and Tangkhul Naga Long was to protest against the imposition of election on the basis of the status of the Act, 1971, that is, third amendment, 2008.[19] PDA urges the state government to review its decision for holding an election in view of the agitation. The Committee for Protection of Tribal Areas, Manipur, called for a 60-hour strike on 24 June 2011 against the Manipur (Hill Areas) District Council on the fourth amendment stating that it has failed to provide judicial, legislative and financial autonomy to the tribal people of Manipur and is also a threat to the protection of tribal land, culture and traditional institutions.[20]

Resistance from tribal organizations is justifiable as the governance mechanisms to protect and uphold tribal communities turn out to be the exploiters of their rights. The central government and the state GoM are constitutionally responsible for the injustice done to the hill people of Manipur under the Act of 1971. As such, the onus to respect the cultural, social, religious and political rights of the hill people was heavily casted upon the two governments by immediately bringing the

---

[17] The present ADC of Manipur is merely administrative power under the Government of Manipur, whereas the Sixth Schedule is under the Constitution of India, which gives legislative, executive and judiciary power.
[18] Total ban on all moving vehicles.
[19] See http://e-pao.net/epRelatedNews.asp?heading=7&src=040410
[20] For details, see http://e-pao.net/GP.asp?src=9..240611.jun11

hill areas of Manipur within the purview of the Sixth Schedule of the Constitution of India. Tribal communities, since then, have been carrying out different agitations and demands (since the inception of the Act) to include the Act under the Sixth Schedule. Although many amendments to the Act have been made, in reality, nothing 'autonomy' is being made to the Act. After the last election of the District Council (1987), the tribal people formed a committee called the Six Schedule Demand Committee Manipur (SDCM) under the aegis of both the Kuki and Naga tribes. Although the genesis of the movement of the Sixth Schedule can be traced back to 1975, it has been realized of late that even the Sixth Schedule, as it is, is not the proper instrument for hill autonomy. Thus, the SDCM, which was enthusiastically leading the demand for the extension of the Sixth Schedule in the hill areas of Manipur, was of the opinion that there should be certain important modifications to the provisions of the Sixth Schedule. Hence, in 1991, the SDCM prepared a draft on modality on the Sixth Schedule.[21]

The Manipur (Hill Areas) District Council Act of 1971 is such an example where it is witnessed by strong resistance and even boycotting for more than 20 years by tribal communities themselves. It is therefore imperative to determine what and under which conditions these diverse identities can be recognized and thereby accommodated. It is important to find out the aspirations of other smaller tribes in Manipur who are a minority within the ethnic line of Naga and Kuki, such as Zomi, Maring, Kom, Lamkang, Gangte, Hmar, Tarao and Chothe. It is also significant to look at the larger frame in the region and outside to understand the micro Manipur experience in order to connect with the larger theoretical and conceptual frame. The framework should be designed to meet the aspirations of different ethnic communities by ensuring their rights, dignity, identity and respect for their coexistence. If it fails to tackle the issues that are going on right now, the apprehension is that the issue may return to the scene in the near future.

CONCLUSION

The self-governance framework for tribal groups in the case of Manipur is very weak and vague. This has created tensions and contestations against the dominant government by tribal minority groups. Further, it has created division among tribal groups, and the demand for effective governance by tribals has grown more stronger and become more politically organized. This reflects the failure of the framework for ensuring self-governance for minority groups as enshrined in the Constitution.

The government, though dominated by the dominant community, should play a proactive role in resolving the issues. The case of Manipur is totally a stern political issue with serious misgovernance and politics of representation. It is time for the government to practically work on political issues instead of being mere rhetoric and change the pejorative culture towards the voices of the tribal communities. The persistent instability of the present and the chaotic uncertainty of the future is the defining life world of the people inhabiting the state of Manipur. In such a scenario, any future politics therefore demands a great degree of sociohistorical sensitivity and political maturity in tackling such layers of complexities.

The contestations and resistances by tribal minority groups are not constituted by mere figments of imaginary existential threats, they are sublime articulations of real existence. While coexistence should remain the

---

[21] See https://shodhganga.inflibnet.ac.in/bitstream/10603/39715/11/11_chapter%203.pdf

mainstay in any proposed framework of political decentralization, a fine balance must be arrived at to negotiate historical tensions that persist. There is a need to relook into the realities and diversities rather than propagating mere promises and agendas. Until and unless the historical-politico realities of the state are not considered in any frame of governance in its true sense, Manipur as a state will always be a contested state.

REFERENCES

Bhatia, B. (2010). Justice denied to tribals in the hill districts of Manipur. *Economic & Political Weekly, 45*(31), 38–46.

Kamei, G. (2011). Colonial policy and practice in Manipur. *Kanglaonline*, 2 August. Retrieved from http://kanglaonline.com/2011/08/colonial-policy-and-practice-in-manipur/

Ziipao, R. R. (2019). What are the impediments to road infrastructure in Manipur? *Economic & Political Weekly, 54*(14), 45–51.

Khasi Political Reality and the Struggle for Statehood: History, Context and Political Processes

Bodhi S. R.

RUMBLINGS AGAINST THE SIXTH SCHEDULE

In the post-independence period, political leadership in Khasi Jaintia Hills was provided mostly by the elected representatives of various constitutional bodies, such as the Autonomous District Councils (ADCs) and the Legislative Assembly. Traditional heads such as the Syiems, the Lyngdohs and the Dollis became invisible and were treated as subordinate bodies within the Sixth Schedule, and their powers and functions were greatly curtailed.

The United Khasi and Jaintia Hills ADC, which came into being on 27 June 1952, was a realization of the provisions of the Sixth Schedule of the Constitution of India. The Sixth Schedule was intended to integrate tribal people living in the Northeast under one composite state of Assam. This was in recognition of their time-tested autonomous polity, safeguarding their traditional heritage, customs, practices, usages and economic security while

conferring in them executive, legislative and judicial powers, along with developmental and financial powers and functions. The Sixth Schedule contains its own power. Paragraphs 3 to 10 of the Sixth Schedule envisaged powers of the ADCs within the autonomous areas to make laws on land, management of forests, except reserved forests, regulation on trade by persons not being local Scheduled Tribes, appointment or succession of chiefs and headmen, inheritance of property, marriage, divorce, social customs; establishment and maintenance of primary schools, markets, taxation, share from issue of licenses, lease for extraction of minerals, etc. While the powers given to the ADC seemed highly accommodative, yet the ADC subsumed within its juridico-legal structure the system of Syiemship without their consent, and thus put the ADC in direct conflict with the traditional Khasi chiefs. Gassah (2007) notes, 'The constitutional provisions contained in the sixth schedule of the constitution have empowered the Autonomous District Council

(ADC) to place the traditional chiefs at a subordinate position to that of the ADC' (Gassah, 2007, p. 175).

On 27 June 1952, the day the ADC was to be inaugurated by the chief minister of Assam, there was a protest in Shillong. During the inauguration, the Khasis staged a black flag demonstration. There was tear gas and lathi-charge against the demonstrators, and a number of people were arrested. This protest which spelled out a contradiction and unravelled a political asymmetry reverberates to this very day.

Rumblings against the Sixth Schedule continued throughout the period from 1952 to the late 1960s. A number of key events took place during this period. There were some events related to the chief of Hima Mylliem. This was followed by the unrest resulting from the language policy of the Government of Assam, resulting in the emergence of the All Party Hill Leaders Conference (APHLC) and, later, a massive movement demanding for the bifurcation of Assam. The key events during this period are presented in Table 23.1.

RISE OF THE DEMAND FOR A SEPARATE STATE

The context for the rise of the demand for separate statehood had deep roots in the period spanning 1947, but became more pronounced in the 1960s. Lyngdoh (1981) wrote a widely read piece published in a local newspaper on the subject, quoting Gopinath Bardoloi, the then premier of Assam, as declaring, 'The new accepted policy of his Government was Assam for the Assamese.' In the same year, he once again quoted Bardoloi asserting, 'Undoubtedly, Assam is for the Assamese. By Assam it means the entire territory within the geographical limit of the State of Assam and by Assamese is meant only those whose mother tongue is Assamese.' In the floor of the State Assembly, Nilmani Phookan was also quoted as saying

regarding our language, Assamese must be the State Language...there can be no gain-saying of it even if the Government stand or fall by it...all languages of the different communities and their culture will be absorbed in Assamese

Table 23.1 Chronology of Meghalaya, 1949–1952[1]

Year	Description
1949	Governor convened the Khasi States Constitution Making Durbar
1949	(26 November) no more Lakhimpur only Balipura, Tirap, Abor and Mishmi. The Assam Tribal Areas known as Naga Tribal Areas. The NEFA constituted of Balipura, Tirap, Abor and Mishmi, and were under the direct rule of the president. Sends no representative to the Assam Assembly.
1950	From 26 January 1950 up to 26 June 1952—administration of the United Khasi-Jaintia Hills Autonomous District vested in the Governor of Assam as per paragraph 19 of Sixth Schedule.
1951	Two blocks from the Jowai subdivision (notification no. TAD/R/31/50/148 dated 13 April 1951) were excluded and included in the Mikir Hills Districts (notification no. RAD/R/31/50/149 dated 13 April 1951, published *Assam Gazette*, Extraordinary, April 1951, pp. 50–60).
1952	Republic of India's first general elections Inauguration of the Autonomous Khasi-Jaintia District Council by Shri Jairamdas Daulatram on 27 June in Dinam Hall, Jaiaw • Khasi National Durbar assisted in the Black Flag demonstration • Khasi National Durbar President Wilson Reade handed a memorandum to Nehru • Tura meeting in December resolved to form the AHTU

Source: List of events chronologically compiled from the archive of the office of John F. Kharshiing.

---

[1] John F. Kharshiing was the spokesperson for the Federation of Khasi states, Laitumkhrah Shillong.

culture…this State cannot nourish any other language in this province.

These sentiments articulated by the political leaders of Assam were also expressed much earlier in the Constituent Assembly (CA) debates which took place on 5 September 1949. In the CA debates, Kuladhar Chaliha, arguing against the Sixth Schedule stated:

If you see the background of the schedule (6th schedule) you will find that the British mind is still there. There is the old separatist tendency and you want to keep them away from us. You will thus be creating a Tribalstan just as you have created a Pakistan…. There is no need to keep any Tribalstan away from us.

Rohini Kumar Chaudhuri, another leader from Assam, even wanted complete assimilation of the tribal people into the Assamese community, noting, 'We want to assimilate the tribal people. We were not given that opportunity so far.'

Right from the CA debates till the 1960s, when the Assamese language started becoming an issue, the expression of such sentiments perceived as the use of force to assimilate tribal people was seen with disdain by the communities that were by this time framed as 'tribes'. On this count, Lyngdoh (1981, 1996) noted:

They (Assamese) could not see the distinction between integration and assimilation. This is really unfortunate. According to popular conception, assimilation involves a total loss of cultural identity of a group which is being assimilated and its complete absorption into the dominant group on the terms of the latter. It is this type of attitude of the leaders of the dominant group which generates fear in the minds of the minorities. Usually it leads to tension; antagonism and increasing alienation each from the other…one should not lay emphasis on assimilation but must encourage integration. But the leaders of Assam valley closed their eyes to these basic tenets. Hence their attitude of superiority complex combined with imperialist attitude was responsible for the future disintegration of Assam.

The genesis for a separate statehood demand has its roots in the politico-historical conditions of the 1950s. Voices of separation emerged as early as 27 June 1952 in the protest

that erupted in Shillong. It was led by students who were supposedly against the principle of nomination to the district council. There was an open call for a separate Hill State in the public meetings held then. Wilson Reade (President, Khasi National Dorbar [KND]; as I mentioned earlier in this chapter) had submitted a memorandum to Jawaharlal Nehru on his visit in 1952, noting the opposition of the KND to the proposal to make Assamese as the state language of Assam.

Immediately thereafter, Captain Williamson A. Sangma, Chief Executive Member (CEM) of the Garo Hills District Council, sent a telegram to Wilson Reade on 20 October 1952, noting that 'Garos support the stand of the Khasi National Durbar' (Lyngdoh, 1996, p. 307). This communiqué led to a gathering of the hill leaders at Tura in December 1952, where they decided to form the Assam Hills Tribal Union (AHTU). The aim of the AHTU was to realize a separate Hill State. The AHTU, in a short period of time, changed its name to the Eastern Indian Tribal Union (EITU) at its meeting in Aizwal in October 1953 (Lyngdoh, 1981, p. 4).

When the States Reorganisation Commission (SRC) was constituted by the Indian government, the KND was among the first to submit a memorandum on 18 April 1954, demanding for the creation of a separate Hill State. The memorandum was signed by Wilson Reade and Hoover Hynniewta, president and secretary of the KND, respectively. W. A. Sangma followed it up by sending an express wire to the SRC on 19 April 1954, noting 'Garos fully support demand by Khasi National Durbar for formation of separate Hill State. Reasons for support being submitted' (Lyngdoh, 1996, p. 307). This was followed up by a meeting on 16 and 17 June 1954, where members of executive committees of the United Khasi and Jaintia, Garo Hills, Lushai Hills and North Cachar Hills District Councils met in Shillong to deliberate on the matter. The decisions in this meeting laid the groundwork for the struggle. They demanded for the constitution of a separate Hill State for all the hill areas of Assam, inclusive of other areas geographically contiguous to the autonomous district, inhabited by tribal people. The decision of this meeting was conveyed to Jawaharlal Nehru by Bishnuram Medhi (chief minister of Assam). In response to the same, Nehru replied:

> Broadly speaking, I think that our approach (to the tribal areas) should be towards somewhat greater autonomy of these districts within the State of Assam. They have a very definite individuality of their own and they should be allowed to feel that they are looking after themselves. That was the sole object of having these autonomous districts. If we go a little further in that direction, it will help in solving the problems and making them contended members of the State of Assam. (Lyngdoh, 1981, p. 4)

B. R. Medhi, however, conveyed to Nehru that it was his and his colleague's considered view that the time was not opportune enough to think in terms of greater autonomy for the district councils because it might strengthen the 'disintegrating forces'. On the eve of the visit of the SRC to Shillong, the leaders of the Hill Areas met in Tura from 6 to 8 October 1954. Interestingly, J. J. M. Nichols-Roy also attended, even though he was minister of excise, jail, etc., in the Medhi cabinet. The conference drafted a memorandum signed by W. A. Sangma and B. M. Roy, as co-president, asserting the strong urge for the creation of a separate Hill State. It was also argued that there be an amendment to the Sixth Schedule.

Many other organizations submitted a memorandum to the SRC demanding a separate Hill State. These organizations were the Highlanders' Union, the Hill's Union, the Garo National Council (GNC) and the United Mizo Freedom Organisation (UMFO). However, it is important to note that the Mikir Hills District Council and the North Cachar Hills District Council demanded only greater autonomy and increased financial assistance to their district councils and were not at ease with the demand for separate statehood.

The Government of Assam, however, did exactly the opposite. It pleaded that a greater Assam be created which would include the whole of Assam, Manipur, Tripura, Sikkim, the North East Agency and the districts of Darjeeling, Jalpaiguri and Cooch Behar in West Bengal. It also gave a number of reasons why a Hill State should never be created. Later, J. J. M. Nichols-Roy pointed out that this memorandum of the Assam government was never shown to him. He instead submitted his own secret memorandum to the SRC. However, Lyngdoh (1981, p. 4, 1996) noted that

> from the arguments advanced forward by Rev. Nichols Roy in favour of Hill State and the refutations made by him against the reasons given by the Government of Assam clearly indicates that Rev. Nichols Roy might have seen the said Memorandum. Rev. Nichols Roy was in full agreement with the Tura Conference.[1]

The final report of the SRC sided with the position articulated by the Assam government. R. S. Lyngdoh notes:

> The SRC appears to have approached the issue with a prejudiced mind. The language used by the SRC was that of the politician of the plains. The Commission said that the demand for a separate Hill State emanated from the extremists with separatist tendencies, which is not a fact. The demand for Hill State was first made by Wilson Reade, the most non-controversial leader and a respected teacher. The movement for Hill State was carried on under the leadership of Capt. Sangma. These leaders were not extremists. Sangma is a compromiser, conciliator and a moderator; and by temperament, conviction and training, he is a constitutionalist. Even under the most provocative circumstances, the hill State leaders had never demanded secession from India. (Lyngdoh, 1981)

The SRC went to the extent of identifying the inner line policy (Bengal Eastern Frontier Regulation, 1873) followed by the Government of India as being responsible for separatist tendencies while also pointing out

---

[1] Also see the detailed Memorandum submitted by Rev. Nichols-Roy (Lyngdoh, 1996, pp. 315–318).

the economic non-viability of a separate Hill State. It also stated that the security of the frontier would be jeopardized with the creation of such a hill state, thereby rejecting the idea totally.

On 17 November 1955, Lyngdoh noted that 'there was an interesting debate in the Assam legislative assembly. Although several members from the hills areas supported the demand for Hill State, some members did not support the proposal' (Lyngdoh, 1981). Yet under the banner of the EITU, the GNC and the UMFO, the hill state struggle gained momentum. In the 1957 general elections, these three parties captured an absolute majority in their respective three district councils. They won 10 out of 15 seats in the Assam Legislative Assembly and the EITU candidate won by an absolute majority from the Autonomous Districts Parliamentary Constituency.

Two incidents, however, marred this victory and somewhat destabilized the movement. The first is related to J. J. M. Nichols-Roy, who was 'elected in the 1957 elections on the issue of hill state' but changed his mind. In place of a separate Hill State, he instead suggested an alternative to the hill state by proposing a Plan for a Hill Ministry. Second, the EITU leaders under the influence of Nehru and G. B. Pant joined the Chaliha Ministry in 1958. W. A. Sangma was appointed as Minister of Tribal Affairs, Lawmawia as Minister of State and Larsingh Khyriem as Deputy Minister.

The association of the EITU with the Congress Legislature party created resentment among the people. In the upcoming three by-elections, the EITU candidates were defeated. Nonetheless, the relationship between the EITU and the Congress Legislature party was cordial. It seemed that the EITU leaders had given up their demand for a separate state.

While overtly, things looked settled, the sudden and persistent attempt by the Assam Government to enact a state language policy generated tremendous insecurities among the hill leaders. The short-lived cordial relationship between the Congress Legislature party and the EITU ruptured. The demand that Assamese be made the official state language was made in the budget session of the Assam Legislative Assembly in 1960. Hareshwar Goswami, Gaurishankar Bhattacharjee and others were vehement on this issue. In his reply to this demand, the then Chief Minister Chaliha, on 3 March 1960, stated that

> the Government have not taken a decision on the subject. I would however, mention that the Government have not underestimated its importance or the request that has been made by the Assam Sahitya Sabha and other institutions for the declaration of Assamese as the State language.... Perhaps there are two important reasons for an enactment on State language. The first is to make official communications easily understandable to the common man and the second is to break the barrier of language which now separates the diverse population of Assam.... The Government feels that this question should be judged more from the point of view of majority and minority. If the issue is decided only on the basis of majority and minority, Government is afraid that its object would be defeated. Government would prefer to wait till they get the same demand from non-Assamese speaking population for the declaration of Assamese as State Language. (Lyngdoh, 1981, p. 3)

This statement, noted Lyngdoh (1996)

> was welcomed by the moderates. But the militants thought that Chaliha was pro Bengali if not anti-Assamese, because the Bengalis would never demand Assamese to be the official language of the State. Therefore, the Assam Pradesh Congress Committee (APCC) which met on 22 April 1960 directed the Chief Minister to declare Assamese as the State language. (Lyngdoh, 1981, p. 3)

This decision of the Assam Pradesh Congress Committee (APCC) aroused resentment among the Hill leaders and immediately a meeting of the 'All Assam Hill Leaders Conference' was convened at Tura on 28 April 1960, which opposed this bill. However, there was no statement about a separate Hill State demand emerging from this platform, instead only amendments to the Sixth Schedule were mentioned. However, on 3 June 1960, when Chaliha announced that the bill would be introduced in the current session, as suggested by the APCC, the hill leaders and even the leaders from the Cachar district sought clarification. The chief minister argued that it was no longer desirable to postpone the decision on the same, noting that 'Emotions have been roused and sentiments played up and the State has passed through some unfortunate tragic happenings…which brought shame and disgrace to the fair name of the State' (Lyngdoh, 1981, p. 3).

Expressing resentment over the decision, W. A. Sangma decided to convene a meeting of the hill leaders of all political parties, and even those with differing opinions on 6 July 1960, in a place called 'Good Wood'. The first conference of the APHLC of the Autonomous Districts of Assam was held in Shillong on 6 and 7 of July 1960. B. M. Pugh was the chairman of the conference. The main purpose of the conference was not to demand for a separate state for the hill areas of Assam, but to press for the withdrawal of the Assam Official Language Bill. They stated seven arguments against the Bill in the resolutions passed. These resolution concerns

(a) …would place the Assamese in a more dominant position, will lead to the assimilation of all the Hills people into the Assamese community… (b) The imposition of the Assamese language will over-burden the Hills people with too many languages (Hindi, the Vernacular, English and Assamese) different scripts, (c) will adversely affect the opportunities and prospects of the Hills people in the government services and other avocations not withstanding any amount of safeguards which can always be circumvented, (d) no real justification for the declaration of Assamese as the official language even from a population point of view, as less than fifty per cent of the population have Assamese as their mother tongue, (e) …move has already created

discord, disruption and violence among different language groups of the State… (f) imposition of the language by law will create more chaos and insecurity in this frontier state, which will be catastrophic especially in view of the Chinese aggression, (g) proper language should be Hindi. Meanwhile, English should continue as the official language until such time as the people of the State are ready to adopt Hindi as the official language.

The last paragraph of the first APHLC resolution reads as follows:

This conference, therefore urges upon the Government of Assam to drop the proposed bill in fairness to the just claims of the linguistic minorities of Assam, in particular the claims of the people of the Autonomous Districts, and in the interests of the unity and security of India.[2]

On 21 August 1960, a delegation of the APHLC met with a Parliamentary delegation over the Language Bill and, in no less than one sentence, asserted, 'We will not accept the Official Language Bill of the State.' Following this, by 22 August 1960, in the Second Conference of the APHLC, it was resolved that if Assamese was going to be declared as the official language of the state, the Hill people would have no other alternative but to demand the separation from Assam. The Council of Action of the APHLC took two resolutions:

(i) this Conference appreciates and approves the Memorandum submitted by the Council of Action to the President of India on the 21 of August, 1960, and resolves that the Council of Action be authorised to prepare a plan or pattern of separation, to submit the same to all Political Parties and District Councils in the Autonomous Hill Districts of Assam, and finally to present it before the Third All-Party Hill Leader's Conference for final approval (ii) Further, this Conference assures all non-tribal residents in the Autonomous Hill Districts that their legitimate interests will be fully safe-guarded in the proposed new State.

[2] Pamphlet released titled 'Resolution Passed by the All Party Hill Leaders Conference of the Autonomous Districts of Assam Held at Shillong, on 6 and 7 July 1960' released by the All Party Hill Leaders Conference (1976). Also see Lyngdoh (1996, pp. 340–341).

This prompted the president of the APCC and the chief minister of Assam to organize a conference of all political parties in the presence of the Union Home Minister. The Union Home Minister suggested a bilingual formula that was rejected by the people of the plains. On 10 October 1960, the chief minister sought permission of the House to introduce the Assam Official Language Bill, prompting W. A. Sangma to declare on the floor of the House that this declaration of Assamese as a state language would bring the disintegration of the state. Others such as A. Thanglura, Maham Singh, Jormanik Syiem and Biswanath Upadhyaya supported him by noting instead that English be the official language of the state till replaced by Hindi. As a mark of protest against the Bill, most tribal members of the Ministry resigned en bloc. When the Bill was introduced on 18 October 1960, tribal members except those of the Mikir Hills staged a walkout. As a mark of protest, on 24 October 1960, Shillong witnessed a massive public meeting and procession. The day was marked as a 'protest day' (Lyngdoh, 1981, p. 4).

In the third conference of the APHLC from 16 to 18 November 1960 held in Haflong, it was noted (All Party Hill Leaders Conference, 1960):

> ...the declaration of Assamese as the Official Language, despite vehement protests, is a clear proof of the unfair attitude and firm determination of the Assamese community to avail themselves undue advantages and thereby enhance their domination over the Hill people and the rest of the people of the State of Assam. This attitude and motive behind the whole Assamese language movement is the final reason that has convinced the hill tribal people represented by this Conference that the question of compromise cannot arise, even if the Language Bill is modified, and that separation is inevitable.

They demanded the creation of a hill state to be called the Eastern Frontier State.[3] A blueprint was also framed for the constitution of the Eastern Frontier State. Assuring full protection of minority rights in the proposed state, members were selected to represent their cause to Delhi to negotiate with the central government. The Prime Minister, Jawaharlal Nehru, had already consulted the chief minister of Assam on the subject before meeting the APHLC delegation on 24 November 1960.[4] W. A. Sangma began by raising the language issue, and the Prime Minister immediately assured the delegation

> that there was no need to fear that Assamese would be imposed on the hills people; that knowledge of Assamese would not be necessary for work in the secretariat; that English, Hindi and Bengali could be used in the Assembly or for the purpose of letters, petitions and memorials; that Assamese would not be insisted upon for the recruitment of officers for the Assam Civil Service. (Lyngdoh, 1981)

However, 'all officers were required to pass a departmental test in Assamese or Bengali or any tribal language.' At this point, Stanley D. D. Nichols-Roy pointed out that 'recent events in Assam had convinced the hill people that their progress, the preservation of their culture, the development of their area could be achieved only by the creation of a separate State' arguing vehemently that 'the Assamese were making every effort to thrust their culture and their language on the hills people.'

Chaliha later explained that the prime minister had told the delegation that 'Article 210, 350 and Article 348 would give the hills people enough safeguard,' further assuring that English would continue as an associate language. To all these arguments, the APHLC leaders were not very convinced, noting that Chaliha cannot be trusted, since

---

[3] Plan for the creation of the Eastern Frontier State adopted by the 3rd APHLC held at Haflong from 16 to 18 November 1960.
[4] Representation for the creation of the Eastern Frontier State submitted to the prime minister of India by the delegation of the APHLC.

Chaliha himself had to change his mind over the language issue under the pressure from his Assamese colleagues.

On 25 November, the APHLC leaders met with Govind Ballabh Pant, the Home Minister, who told the delegation that there was no need for a Hill State and that the 'resources of the hills and the plains were interrelated and complementary.' Nevertheless, he assured the leaders that 'the centre was keenly interested in the development of the Hill areas and the Government of India would consider the case of granting more powers to the District Councils.' He also pointed out that a small state with slender resources would not be able to make much progress and argued that the Hill Districts were not geographically contiguous from one another. At this point, Pu. Saprawnga intervened and asserted that 'if geographical factor was an obstacle in the formation of a hill State, the Mizo Hills would stay out of the hill State.' Not convinced by the argument put forth by the home minister, the leaders warned the home minister that 'the Hill people were becoming restless and that nothing short of a separate Hill State was absolutely necessary, otherwise the extremist would capture the leadership and develop an ugly situation.'

THE SCOTTISH PLAN OF NEHRU

The following day, the APHLC leaders again met with the prime minister. While the same arguments were articulated by the contesting parties, the prime minister opined that probably the only solution to resolve the problem was to

give the hill areas full authority in internal affairs and complete control over the expenditure and also freedom to use the language they liked...necessary funds would be placed at the disposal of the Tribal Areas Department which would be invariably headed by a hill Minister...the representatives of the hill areas could discuss their development plans with the

Planning Commission and he would welcome them to meetings of the National Development Council...any legislation affecting the hill areas which might be passed by the State Assembly would not be enforced in the hill areas without the consent of the representatives of the hill areas...a Council of Representatives from the autonomous hill districts should consider all bills passed by the State Assembly...he would seriously consider the measures necessary to ensure adequate delegation of powers in order to enable the hill people to undertake development programmes in the hill areas. (Lyngdoh, 1996, pp. 348–349)

This plan, known as the Scottish Pattern Plan, was taken up for deliberations in the Council of Action of the APHLC which met on 7 January 1961. However, the Council rejected this plan and, in its meeting on 9 January 1961, adopted the following resolution.

The Council of Action having rejected the alternative proposal to the creation of a separate State on the pattern approved by the 3rd All-Party Hill Leader's Conference hereby resolves that steps to be taken to persuade the Prime Minister, by further negotiations, to agree to the creation of a separate State...should the creation of a separate State be not achieved by negotiation, the Council further resolves that the movement be intensified and that all the hill leaders and the hill people be called upon to prepare for all eventualities for the achievement of the separate Eastern Frontier State. (Lyngdoh, 1996, p. 350)

The prime minister was invited by the APHLC's general secretary to visit Shillong, but the request was declined. This caused heartburns on both sides. Another meeting of the Council of Action was held on 15 March 1961. From this meeting, recommendations were made to the General Conference to fix a date 'for the resignation of the entire hill MLAs and to boycott the 1962 elections'. This decision was also to be conveyed to the prime minister and a delegation be sent to Delhi to appraise him of the reasons for rejecting his proposal.

Interestingly, the Scottish Plan of Nehru was accepted by the District Congress Committees in the hill areas and, as a political strategy, they suddenly severed all connections with the

APHLC. While some had expected this move, many among the Khasis felt betrayed by this action of the District Congress Committee. There were rumours, however, that went around Shillong that Chaliha, the chief minister of Assam, was in agreement with Nehru's plan, even though there was no documentary evidence to authenticate the same, except for a letter written by Nehru to the governor mentioning the same.

By the fourth congress of the APHLC held on 6 and 7 April 1961, the decisions of the Council of Action were fully endorsed by the conference. Another APHLC delegation went to meet with the prime minister on 17 May 1961 to persist on the issue. This was in the presence of Lal Bahadur Shastri, then home minister. While it is stated that the 'Prime Minister began to spell out the salient features of the plan in which the full details can be further worked out by a special Commission,' the delegation resisted the very idea of a commission after their experience with the earlier SRC 'who spoke more the language of the plains than of the hills'. Further meetings with the prime minister were held on 21 May 1861, this time in Shillong, but no headway was made by either side.

In the fifth conference of the APHLC, scheduled from 29 June to 1 July 1961, the demand for a separate Hill State was reiterated, calling to all 'its members to resign from the membership of all of all elective bodies and the other bodies set up by the Government of Assam'. Unfortunately while many paid heed to the call of the APHLC, Larsingh Khyriem and A. Thanglura refused to resign from the assembly and Kistobin Rymbai refused to resign from the membership of a committee. All three severed their connections with the APHLC.

From the side of the Congress party, a Hill Congress Convention was held in Shillong on 31 July 1961. In this gathering, they affirmed the decision of the District Congress Committees, which openly accepted the Scottish Pattern Plan as an alternative to a separate Hill State. On the side of the APHLC, in a meeting held on 4 September, the Council of Action decided to observe 24 October 1961 as the Demand Day.

Leading to the sixth conference of the APHLC, scheduled from 14 to 16 September 1961 in Aizawl, the Council of Action was authorized to 're-examine the questions of boycotting or contesting the 1962 general elections'. The Council of Action, meeting on 6 October, decided that 'the APHLC should contest the elections because it feared that its opponents might return uncontested and that they might demonstrate to the civilized world that the APHLC had no following in the Hill areas" but noted that 'all the successful candidates should resign their membership of the state assembly.'

Till 1962, the APHLC included the Mizo Union, the Jaintia Durbar, the EITU, the Khasi Jaintia Conference, the Communist Party of India, the GNC, even the District Congress and other political groups. As one can observe, the issue of language was an extremely complex one, as it depended so much on how it was conceived on the basis of ethnic locations. However, for the Khasis, who were at the forefront of the struggle against what was conceived as a short change by the forceful inclusion of the 25 Khasi states into the state of Assam, disregarding the Instrument of Accession (IOA), noted with fear and contempt the language politics of the Assamese leaders.

The elections of 1962 witnessed the APHLC contesting the issue of an independent 'Eastern Frontier State', while the Congress fought on the issue of Nehru's Scottish Pattern Plan. When results poured in, the APHLC won all five seats from Khasi and Jaintia Hills. They also won all three seats from the Mizo Hills and three out of four in the Garo Hills. The Congress won all the three seats in the Mikir Hills and North Cachar Hills, plus one seat in the Garo Hills. For the prized parliamentary seat reserved for the autonomous districts, the APHLC won the seat, thereby establishing its position as the most popular party in the hill districts.

In spite of the spectacular APHLC victory and the increased pressure asserted on the prime minister, the demand for a Hill State remained stagnant. This forced the APHLC to persist with their agitation. As part of their strategy, they moved around the hill areas, educating people about their demands and deepening their organizational base. Immediately after the election victory, the Council of Action directed all the elected MLAs to resign from the state assembly, of which seven heeded, while four refused to resign. Those who did not resign were H. E. Poshna, Emerson Momin, Nalindra Sangma and R. Thanhlira. This was followed by a call for a 'non-violent satyagraha'; however, due to the Chinese aggression, the same was postponed. In the by-elections that followed in 1962, the APHLC won five out of seven seats, two of the remaining being won by the Mizo National Front. The Mizo Union, which was an active member of the APHLC till this moment, decided to sever ties with the APHLC.

In 1963, the leaders of the APHLC met with Lal Bahadur Shastri, the Union Home Minister, in Shillong on 10 February. The talks centred on the demand for a separate Hill State, arguing with the Home Minister about the necessity of such a state. It was argued that there was a plea from one of the leaders to the Minister that he considered such a demand in the light of *Ngi don u Dragon na shatei, u Sein iong na shathie bad marjan u Thlen ha Rithor*, meaning 'we have a dragon from above, a snake from below and close by 'U Thlen' from the valley.' The 'dragon' refers to China, 'snake' refers to East Pakistan and 'U Thlen' refers to the inhabitants of the Assam valley. The Home Minister noted that he would convey this demand to the prime minister.[5]

THE NEHRU PLAN

It is in these circumstances that the APHLC indicated that they wanted to meet with the prime minister. The response of the prime minister was negative, stating that 'no useful purpose would be served to consider "rigid demands."' However, in an interesting meeting between the prime minister and some representatives of the APHLC on 10 June 1963 at Borjhar Airport, Nehru 'made some concrete proposals which were further elaborated in the meetings that he had with the APHLC on the 4 and 5 October 1963'. This somewhat concrete proposal came to be called the 'Nehru Plan', which fundamentally aimed at 'conferring full autonomy to the hill areas subject to the preservation of the unity of Assam'.

However, things took a different turn in the hill districts immediately after the creation of a separate state of Nagaland on 1 December 1963. On this issue, W. A. Sangma, who was still a minister in the Assam government, wrote to Chaliha:

> The recent decision of the Government of India to create a new State for Nagaland is bound to lead to far reaching repercussions in the other hill districts unless the amendment of the Sixth Schedule, as recommended by the Advisory Committee can be taken up at a very early date.

In the midst of the excitement generated by the aforementioned incident, the APHLC placed the Nehru Plan in front of the general public. This plan, however, caused both elation for some and heartburn for others. However, in its conference held on 17 and 18 April 1964, the members decided to give a 'fair trail' to the plan, but with a rider; that should the recommendations of the Commission to be appointed for the purpose fall short of the assurances given by the prime minister, it would immediately revise its decision. Like a breather, the Khasi and Jaintia Hills Districts

---

[5] The leaders who met with the Home Minister were G. G. Swell, R. S. Lyngdoh, Saprawnga, B. B. Lyngdoh, S. J. Duncan, M. N. Swer, J. Swer, T. Cajee and S. D. D. Nichols Roy (*U Nongsain Hima*, 12 tarik Rymphang 1963).

Congress Committee also welcomed the call. However, the Government of Assam opposed the same on the grounds that it would bring about a deadlock in the functioning of the cabinet system of the government. But Nehru either way went ahead or started to think and plan to appoint the proposed commission.

Initially, it was stated that the prime minister wanted a one-man commission headed by C. P. N. Singh. However, Chaliha asserted that the Commission should have three members and it should be headed by H. V. Pataskar as chairman. Unfortunately, Nehru died on 27 May 1964, before he could give any concrete shape and finalize the Commission. Hence, the process was kept in abeyance. Nonetheless, the Commission was finally appointed on 16 March 1965 with G. S. Venkatachar and C. S. Rau as members and H. V. Pataskar as chairman. Interestingly C. S. Venkatachar withdrew from the Commission on health grounds, and Shankar Prasad was appointed in his place.

In the meantime, an interesting event took place in the Assam Legislative Assembly. A Commission, known as the Jarman Commission, which was set up in 1964 by the state to look into the reorganizations of districts in the United Khasi and Jaintia Hills, had just submitted its report and placed it in the assembly. This Commission comprised of M. N. Goswami (member), B. L. Sen (member) and G. P. Jarman (chairman). In the arguments put forth before the Commission, Mr Hoover Hynniewta made a strong case about the oneness of the Khasi community. Gilbert Shullai notes these exchanges as *ka jingiasaid kaba yn sah pyrto pateng la pateng* (a debate that will be remembered for generations to come). The Jarman Commission recommended that a separate subdivision be created for reasons other than the oneness shared among those inhabiting the district. Debates around the proposal of the Commission took place on 7

and 8 October 1964. On 23 November 1964, the Government of Assam declared the creation of the Jowai Autonomous District with effect from 1 December 1964 as per notification no. TAD/R/50/64 dated 23 November 1964. A case was filed in the Guwahati High Court challenging this decision of the government.[6] Later, an appeal was filed in the Supreme Court.[7] In the appeal petition by Mr Edwingson Bareh, arguing for the oneness of the Khasi-Jaintia community, stated that

the people inhabiting the territory comprised within the United Khasi Jaintia Hills District are ethnically, racially, culturally, economically and by tradition are one and the same people. When the British subjugated and annexed the territory they divided it into different units for administrative conveniences, but the people of the said area continued to remain united and maintained the existing closest relationships. (Shullai, [1981]2017, p. 6)

THE PATASKAR COMMISSION

The Pataskar Commission became a hotbed of politicking with accusations and counter-accusations made by the Assam government on the one side and the APHLC on the other. The final report favoured the Government of Assam with a great degree of dilution on the points of assurance given by Nehru to the APHLC. Thus, in the conference of the APHLC held from 19 to 21 of May 1966, a decision was taken to reject the recommendations of the Pataskar Commission and, as a mark of protest, a call for a non-violent direct action was made. The Council of Action was authorized to fix a date for launching the same.

At this point in time, an interesting turn of events began to shape the political process of the local district congress in the Khasi and Jaintia Hills. It first began with A. Alley, a

[6] Civil Rule No. 280 of 1964 and Civil Rule No. 303 of 1964.
[7] Civil Appeal No. 968 of 1965 and decision of the Supreme Court can be found in AIR 1966 Supreme Court 1220 (V) 53 C 237.

popular Congress leader, who put forth a suggestion that the Hill areas should be declared a Union Territory. Many did not agree with him. This was followed by the Khasi and Jaintia Hills District Congress Committee (KJHDCC) calling for the creation of a separate Khasi and Jaintia state on 16 June 1966. It noted the following in its memorandum to the prime minister:

> We have rejected the report of the Pataskar Commission. We cannot accept the demand for creation of the Eastern Frontier State either; and we cannot remain in Assam...we therefore decided to demand the creation of a separate State for Khasi and Jaintia Hills on the pattern of Nagaland State. (Lyngdoh, 1981)

Fortunately, this argument by the KJHDCC was not received positively by the people at large, seeing in the action of a Congress' ploy to break the APHLC's popularity, which by the 1967 general elections was clearly observed. The Congress, which fought on this argument, failed to get any seat in the District Councils, the State Legislature and the Parliament.

GULZARILAL NANDA COMMITTEE

Following the rejection by the APHLC of the report of the Pataskar Commission in its meeting with the subcommittee in August 1966, the Cabinet Subcommittee offered the APHLC a Sub-State Plan which they rejected again. Another Cabinet Subcommittee was constituted by the Government of India, under the headship of Gulzarilal Nanda, to examine the proposals of the Pataskar Commission.

It is noteworthy to recognize the fractured nature of the debate around the demand of a separate Hill State. Various narratives emerged from Shillong, the capital of Assam. As noted earlier, Shillong constituted of two very distinct areas; those falling under the British areas and those outside the British areas, but both within the Hima Mylliem area. The area under the British had a European

ward that included Khyndailad (Police Bazar), Pine Mount, Rildbong, Bishnupur and others. When the hill state demand was being articulated, residence in these areas, which had a mixed population of various ethnicities and religious communities, demanded for themselves a Union Territory (Saitang, 2014, p. 441).

THE POSITION OF VISHNU SAHAY

To break the deadlock, a suggestion was made by Vishnu Sahay (Governor of Assam). He argued that one way of resolving the irreconcilable difference was to create a federal structure. He said, 'federalism is the best solution' in this case. In response to the governor's suggestions, Tarlok Singh proposed that 'certain contiguous Hill areas be converted into a Union Territory' while agreeing with the idea of a federal plan of the governor. On these debates, Lyngdoh (1996) noted the following:

> Governor of Assam was attracted by the idea of Federal Plan propounded by B. N. Rau which had been explained in full details by Dr V. V. Rao in his series of articles published in the *Frontier Times*. The Plan was similar to the Government of Ireland Act, 1920, and to the Ausgleich which existed between Austria and Hungary during the period 1867–1914. Therefore, Vishnu Sahay suggested to the Government of India that federalism is the best solution. (Lyngdoh, 1981)

THE INDIRA GANDHI MODEL

After these very strenuous negotiating but static processes, the APHLC was gearing itself to launch a non-violent direct action fixing 30 December 1966 as the date for 'satyagraha'. This was seen by many as the final battle of the APHLC, which had carried the issue of separate statehood for nearly six long years without making much headway. The satyagraha was publicized in such a way as to seem like the last and grand battle to either get a separate state or a fight till the 'end'. However, to the APHLC's great surprise, Prime Minister Indira Gandhi stated that she would come to Shillong on 27 December 1966 and meet with them. She asked the APHLC to organize a public meeting where she will address the people. Three days before the satyagraha, in a public meeting organized by the APHLC, Indira Gandhi arrived as scheduled and proclaimed in her maiden address that she would work to give the Hills people 'the requested status and dignity'. She invited the APHLC leaders to Delhi for further deliberations on the matter. She also invited the chief minister of Assam and his colleagues to the meeting in order to discuss threadbare the reorganization of Assam. Thunderous applause arose in the hills and celebrations erupted everywhere in the Khasi and Jaintia Hills.

The meeting convened by Indira Gandhi took place on 11 January 1967. By 13 January of the same month, Indira Gandhi announced that Assam would be reorganized on federal lines. 'The proposed Federation would consist of two units, with equal status and each unit should not be subordinate to the other.' By evening, when the APHLC leaders met the with the Home Minister, Yashwantrao Chavan, they were told in clear terms that 'if the people of the plains would not accept the federal structure, the other alternative was clear, which meant the clean cut separation of the hills from the plains.'

THE MEHTA COMMITTEE

The APHLC was jubilant and immediately accepted this plan, but this caused great hurt among the leaders of the plains who opposed the same. This could be the reason why the centre did not constitute a joint committee to work out the details of the plan within the first six months and instead called for further joint discussions. Lyngdoh (1996) noted that

'even Chaliha who did not object to the Plan had to back out in view of the opposition to the plan by the people of the plains.' Initially, the APHLC openly stated that they did not want to participate in any joint discussion, but was later persuaded by the Home Minister to do so, and they relented. The joint discussion scheduled for 1, 7 and 8 July 1967 could not proceed beyond a point. This led the government in Delhi to appoint a committee under the leadership of Ashok Mehta. Strategically, the APHLC, as on 14 July 1967, decided not to participate in meetings with the Mehta Committee.

In the discussions that ensued, the chief minister of Assam proposed that 'each autonomous district should be converted into an autonomous area.' Another leader, Hem Barua, argued for the implementation of the Pataskar Commission with a little more modifications, but another leader, Phani Bora, went against the flow and instead pleaded that the hill areas should be granted a separate Hill State. Nonetheless, the Mehta Committee was still inclined to go on the lines of the ideas suggested by Chaliha. So, while the Government of Assam accepted the proposals of the Mehta Committee, the APHLC rejected the proposals outright putting the whole situation in jeopardy. The contradictions were so sharp that it was a make-or-break situation for both sides. While the plains and the political leadership from there were against the principles of the federal plan and the idea of a separate state for the hills carved out of Assam, the APHLC was simply not willing to compromise with anything less than a separate state. Lyngdoh (1996) notes, 'the Government of India was then like a headless mother sitting between two warring sons' and referred the whole issue to a National Forum without making any comments or decisions on the recommendations of the Mehta Committee report. Intense lobbying was reported to have taken place during this period by both the leaders of the plains and those from the hills.

The APHLC went back to their strategy room and decided that they must keep the protest going. In their meeting on 20 December 1967, they declared that the time had come to prepare for 'real non-violent direct action'. It is reported that, on 24 January 1968, tension was running high and there was news that disorder and violence, plus large-scale destruction of property had taken place in the Assam Valley directed against the hill people. It was even reported that a National Flag was desecrated on 26 January. This gave the APHLC an apt reason to argue that, in the light of this assault, there was no way out but the ultimate separation from Assam, *for now it was not a matter of assimilation, but of physical dominance.*

THE AUTONOMOUS STATE PLAN

The prime minister convened a meeting on 21 March 1968 and requested the participation of the APHLC. Others present in the meeting were the home minister and members of the Internal Affairs Committee. This was followed by another meeting on 29 April 1968. Following these deliberations, the prime minister assured the APHLC delegation that the Government of India would finally make a decision within a fortnight. Exactly on 14 May 1968, the home minister announced that the Government of India intends and plans to create an autonomous state within Assam. Celebrations erupted again in the hill districts. The APHLC publicly appreciated this statement by the prime minister in its conference held from 25 to 30 June 1968, noting 'the sincere attempts made by the prime minister' but did not make any further comment on the matter.

TENSION IN THE APHLC

Things were moving back and forth on separate state demand. There was delay in articulating the autonomous state plan by the Indian government. This prompted the APHLC to declare a non-violent direct action on 10 September 1968. There were reports of a conflict on this matter between members of the APHLC in the Khasi Hills, especially between G. G. Swell and Stanley D. D. Nichols-Roy. While G. G. Swell tried to persuade Stanley D. D. Nichols-Roy to call off the non-violent direct action programme, the majority of the leaders, it was stated, felt that it was an opportune time to do so. The programme was launched, despite opposition from some, but the Government of India responded immediately the very next day, that is, 11 September 1968. The details of the whole plan were shown to Captain W. A. Sangma, who was then camped in Delhi. W. A. Sangma immediately made a telephone call to S. D. D. Nichols-Roy to temporarily call off the non-violent direct action.

The APHLC Conference held on 19 September 1968 was an exciting one. It placed the autonomous state plan before the conference. After detailed deliberations on the subject between the leaders and the general public, the conference concluded on 15 October 1968 that the plan would be given a fair trial. It was noted, however, that their acceptance of this plan was merely a first step towards realizing full separate statehood.

Interestingly, another regional party with a presence among the Khasis; the Hill State People's Democratic Party (HSPDP) opposed this plan but was not able to stop the process of legislation being drafted. The 22nd Constitution (Amendment) Bill was passed in September 1969. Although it was supposed to have been introduced in the budget session earlier in the same year, it could not be done because of a lack of the required quorum. But on 24 December 1969, both Houses of Parliament passed the Assam Reorganisation (Meghalaya) Bill.

The prime minister inaugurated the autonomous state of Meghalaya on 2 April 1970. As per the Act, the autonomous state of Meghalaya within the state of Assam comprised of the

United Khasi-Jaintia Hills District and the Garo Hills District. This Act also inserted paragraph 12(Aa)[8] and 12(Ab)[9] making special provisions with respect to the application of the laws made by the Parliament and the State Legislature to the tribal areas in Meghalaya.

TOWARDS A FULL-FLEDGED STATE

As soon as the Government of India decided to grant full statehood to Manipur and Tripura, the Meghalaya Legislative Assembly passed a resolution on 30 September 1970, by unanimous vote, to convert the autonomous state into a full-fledged state. This was accepted by the prime minister, who informed the Lok Sabha that her government was willing to recognize Meghalaya as a full-fledged state. During this time, there were problems in the light of the troubles in East Pakistan, so the process got delayed.

On 22 December 1971, the two Houses of Parliament passed the North-Eastern Areas (Reorganisation) Bill. A new state of Meghalaya was officially born on 21 January 1972. As per the aforementioned Act, the state of Meghalaya comprised of '(a) the territories which immediately before that day were comprised in the autonomous State of Meghalaya and (b) so much of the territories comprised within the cantonment and municipality of Shillong, as did not form part of that autonomous State.' Part II of the table covered the

tribal areas of the state of Meghalaya, which were the United Khasi-Jaintia Hills District, the Jowai District and the Garo Hills District.

The inauguration of the new state of Meghalaya, however, took place one day prior to the official date of 20 January 1972. The prime minister came down to grace the occasion. It is reported that in a gathering held in Polo ground to commemorate this event, about one-third of the entire population of Meghalaya turned up to listen to Indira Gandhi. By midnight on the same day, Shri B. K. Nehru (Governor) administered the oath of office in the Raj Bhavan to the chief minister and his colleagues and the oath of allegiance to the honourable speaker.

NEW STATE OF MEGHALAYA

The state of Meghalaya encompasses three distinct autonomous areas known as the Garo Hills, the Khasi Hills and the Jaintia Hills, each predominantly inhabited by the three ethnic groups, namely the Garo, the Khasi and the Jaintias, respectively. Today, the Garo Hills have been subdivided into five districts, the Khasi Hills into another four and the Jaintia Hills into two districts.

Meghalaya is the only state in the Northeast where the entire area is governed by the provisions of the Sixth Schedule (with the exception of the historically controversial areas of the Cantonment and Municipality in the

[8] 12A. Application of the Acts of Parliament and of the Legislature of the State of Meghalaya to autonomous districts and autonomous regions in the State of Meghalaya. Notwithstanding anything in this Constitution, {12A(a)}, if any provision of a law made by a district or regional council in the state of Meghalaya with respect to any matter specified in sub-paragraph (10 of paragraph 3 of this Schedule) or if any provision of any regulation made by a district council or a regional council in that state under paragraph 8 or paragraph 10 of this Schedule, is repugnant to any provision of a law made by the Legislature of the state of Meghalaya with respect to that matter, then, the regional council whether made before or after the law made by the Legislature of the state of Meghalaya, shall, to the extent of repugnancy, be void and the law made by the Legislature of the state of Meghalaya shall prevail.
[9] 12A (b). The president may, with respect to any Act of Parliament, by notification, direct that it shall not apply to an autonomous district or any autonomous region in the state of Meghalaya, or shall apply to such districts or regions or any part thereof, subject to such exceptions or modifications as may be specified in this notification, and that any such direction may be given so as to have retrospective effect.

capital of Shillong). The United Khasi-Jaintia Hills District and the Garo Hills District were parts of the tribal area of Assam having been placed at serial nos. 1 and 2 of Part A of the table appended to paragraph 20 of the Sixth Schedule as originally enacted.

The Governor of Meghalaya altered the names of 'the United Khasi-Jaintia Hills District' as 'the Khasi Hills District' and the name of 'the Jowai District' as 'the Jaintia Hills District' by notification dated 14 June 1973 issued under paragraph 1(3)(f) of the Sixth Schedule. Paragraph 12A, after being substituted by the North Eastern Areas (Reorganisation) Act, 1971, provides that if any law or regulation made by the District or Regional Council under paragraphs 3, 8 or 10 is repugnant to the law made by the Meghalaya Legislature, then the law or regulation made by the district or regional council, to the extent of repugnancy, shall be void and the law made by the State Legislature shall prevail. With respect to the Acts of Parliament, the power of the president to issue notification directing that any Act will not apply to Meghalaya was retained.

The current constitutional political structure in the state is constituted by the state government at the helm of all districts, the District Council at the helm of each of the Khasi, Jaintia and Garo-inhabited districts and for the Khasi districts, the traditional institution of the Syiem, Lyngdoh, Wahadadar and Sirdar and for Jaintia Hill district—the Dollis and Sirdar. For the Garo Hills district, there is the institution of the Nokmas.[10]

POST STATEHOOD

As noted, while it was the Language Policy of the Government of Assam that kick-started the movement initially, the demand for the separation of the hill areas from Assam was made vigorously only in the second conference of the APHLC in Shillong held on 22 and 23 August 1960, presided by E. M. Sangma. The first party to dissociate from it was the Congress at the time when the Scottish Pattern plan was offered by the then Prime Minister of India, Mr Jawaharlal Nehru. By 1970, the People's Democratic Party of North Cachar Hills and the Mizo Union also dissociated themselves from the APHLC as the Government of India created an autonomous state for the present area of Meghalaya.

The APHLC, it is important to note, had only a political programme for the initial period of 10 years. It applied its mind to economic and other programmes only in 1969, when it was sure that something very important was coming to it, which it has to shoulder. When the autonomous state was inaugurated on 2 April 1970 and later upgraded into a full-fledged state on 21 January 1972,[11] some kind of thought came before its leaders and supporters that they must return in kind the decision of the prime minister. By 1972, when the Meghalaya Legislative Assembly elections came, the leaders of the party wanted to show their gratitude as a party to Mrs Indira Gandhi for her efforts to push for the new state. Thus, in their general conference, they adopted a resolution to the effect that it will cooperate with the Indian National Congress

---

[10] There are currently three ADCs, namely Garo Hills ADC, Khasi Hills ADC and Jaintia Hills ADC. Each ADC has 30 members, 29 of whom are elected by the people and one member is nominated and holds office at the pleasure of the governor. All elected members and a nominated member shall have to subscribe an oath as provided in the Assam (and Meghalaya) Autonomous Districts (Constitution of District Councils) Rules, 1951. The term of office is 5 years and the session of the ADC shall be summoned by the chairman at least *three–four* times a year and all business transactions shall be conducted by the chairman in accordance with the normal parliamentary practice and procedure envisaged in the Assam (and Meghalaya) Autonomous Districts (Constitution of District Councils) Rules, 1951.

[11] The first Meghalaya Council of Ministers after 21 January 1972 was Captain Williamson A. Sangma as chief minister and Stanley D. D. Nichols-Roy, Brington Buhai Lyngdoh, Edwin Bareh, Standford K. Marak, Darwin Diengdoh Pugh, Shersingh Grohon Marak, Ripple Kyndiah as ministers.

at all levels. So when the elections came, they adjusted few seats in each district with the Congress. This decision was carried out in the Khasi Hills and Garo Hills districts only, where four seats in the former and five seats in the latter were given to the Congress. The APHLC won 32 seats, the Congress won 9, the HSPDP won 9 and 10 were won by independent candidates. When the president of India proclaimed an emergency on 25 June 1975, the leaders of the Congress in the state of Meghalaya took the opportunity to threaten the members of the APHLC, especially those who held office, that if they did not join the Congress, something would happen to them. So 'out of fear' by November 1976 in the now famous Mendipathar Conference of the APHLC, a move led by W. A. Sangma to merge with the Congress was formalized 'in response to the desire of the Prime Minister, Mrs Indira Gandhi', which then led to a split within the party.

INTEGRATION BY DECLARATION

Over the years, that is, from 1946 to 1998, the political processes in the Khasi-inhabited areas were characterized by struggles for keeping the Khasi institutions alive. After the very complex 'integration' process in which the IOA and the Annexed Agreement (AA) were dishonoured, contradictions in Khasi society began setting in. While the Federation of Khasi States (FKS) was active in the initial period, after the 1959 Act, they withdrew. It was during this period that fault line between the FKS and the Khasi Hills Autonomous District Council (KHADC) became more pronounced.

After the 1959 Act, most of the processes were centred on separate state movement,

which were realized in 1972 onwards. While the FKS remained vocal throughout this struggle, it was not at the forefront of the movement. Instead, it was the KND and other leaders who provided leadership to the Hill State movement. However, the struggle on and around indigenous institutions persisted despite structural changes in the state political system. The new state of Meghalaya did bring in some needed change, but the subjugation of the chiefs and the Khasi institutions remained.

REFERENCES

All Party Hill Leaders Conference. (1976). Resolution Passed by the All Party Hill Leaders Conference of the Autonomous Districts of Assam Held at Shillong, on 6 and 7 July 1960 released by the S. D. D. Nichols-Roy, General Secretary, Council of Action. *Implanter*, *8*(55).

All Party Hill Leaders Conference. (1960). *Resolutions Passed by the 3rd All Party Hill Leaders Conference of the Autonomous District of Assam held at Haflong, N. C. Hills on 16, 17 and 18 November 1960*. Meghalaya: The author.

Gassah. L. S. (2007). Prelude to integration: Political consciousness, political organisations and development in Khasi-Jaintia Hills (up to 1952). In S. Nag, T. Gurung, & A. Choudhury (Eds.), *Making of the Indian union: Merger of princely states and excluded areas* (pp. 20–75). New Delhi: Akansha Publishing.

Lyngdoh, R. S. (1981). Evolution of Meghalaya (in a nutshell), Section I, II and III. *Ropeca* (regional newspaper), 22 August–31 October 1981.

Lyngdoh, R. S. (1996). *Government and politics in Meghalaya*. New Delhi: Sanchar Publishing House

Saitang, O. L. (2014). *U Rev. J. J. M. Nichols-Roy Bad ka Sixth Schedule* (vol. 6), *Ka Standstill Arrangement, Ka Instrument of Accession, Ka Annexed Agreement, Ka Sixth Schedule Bad Kiwei*. Shillong: Library of Khasi Christian Literary, Classic Edition.

Shullai. ([1981]2017). Jarman Commission. *U Nongsain Hima* (local Khasi newspaper), 9 October.

Tribal Politics and New Electoral Directions in Meghalaya

Moses Kharbithai

INTRODUCTION

Meghalaya, a small state with the total population of 29.7 lakhs as per 2011 census,[1] is one of the four tribal-dominated states in Northeast India. It is inhabited predominantly by three tribes—Khasi, Jaintia and Garo, who all practise matrilineal social and lineage system. Almost 80 per cent of the population today is Christian, with only about 8.71 per cent professing indigenous faith and 11.53 per cent professing to be Hindus.[2] Carved out of Assam in 1972 after persistent demand for a separate hill state to protect and ameliorate the conditions of tribal communities in the region, the tribes elected their first representatives for the state assembly in 1972. On the 27 February 2018, election for the 10th Meghalaya state assembly was held in the state. Although Meghalaya came into existence as a result of

the tribal apprehensions over Assamese and non-tribal hegemony and domination, yet even after four decades of statehood, public discourse during the electoral processes is still dominated by the issue of politics of identity crisis and insecurity from domination of 'the others'.[3] This has always been the major agenda of all political parties during elections in Meghalaya. This is even truer with the regional parties gaining dividend and wielding significant influence in the state politics through the use of these issues, especially during elections.

The 2018 state assembly election, however, seems to have shifted the focus from the regions that are usually driven by such appeals to putting priorities in issues other than the conventional identity politics. The difference in electoral appeal in the 2018 election can be seen by the electoral agenda of the four major

---

[1] https://www.census2011.co.in/census/state/meghalaya.html
[2] https://www.census2011.co.in/data/religion/state/17-meghalaya.html
[3] 'The others' here mean the non-tribal from mainland India who is always seen by the tribal communities as a threat towards their identity, economy and culture. In the recent past, illegal immigrants from Bangladesh have also been added to this category and there is a constant apprehension in public debates against the rise of illegal immigrants in the state of Meghalaya.

players that gripped the electoral imagination of the people in the state. The Indian National Congress (Congress) facing anti-incumbency had made great emphasis on Hindu cultural nationalism of the Bharatiya Janata Party (BJP) as a major carrying point in the Christian-dominated state. Major campaign against BJP was carried out to dissuade the people from voting in favour of the dominant party in national politics. The BJP was projected by the Congress party as an anti-Christian and anti-minority party. The National People's Party (NPP), on the other hand, presented itself as the fresh political alternative to Congress in the state. Although an ally of the NDA at the centre and North-East Democratic Alliance (NEDA) in the region, it projected itself as a separate identity in the state. The BJP coming out with massive success in Assam and Manipur, while also promising similar performances in Nagaland and Tripura, made its best bid to project itself as a secular party focused on development with its primary agenda of lifting the image of a dependent state into a self-reliant one, given the opportunity. The fourth major player was the regional alliance between the United Democratic Party (UDP) and Hill State People's Democratic Party (HSPDP), which is different from all the three political forces. This alliance concentrated on their being a regional force that understands the actual aspiration of the people. They focused on identity politics and asserted as the custodian of indigenous knowledge of unity, development and peace.[4] They also focused on the role of regional parties, especially with regard to safeguarding and judicious utilization of natural resources for the development of the state based on grassroots dreams. The last factor was Khun Hynniewtrep National Awakening Movement (KHNAM) which has much lesser following in the state, although it considered itself as the only indigenous party

of the Khasi-Jaintia. It also contested only in the Khasi-Jaintia region.

ELECTORAL COMPETITIONS AND UNPRECEDENTED TREND OF 2018 ELECTIONS

In one of its rare moments, the state of Meghalaya had gone for elections in 2018, after it had a government which completed its term unperturbed from 2013 to 2018. Like in the previous occasion, this time too it is Congress government which completed its term of five years. However, unlike in the past, the elections to the 10th Meghalaya assembly was fought with the Congress on one side alongwith only the NCP as its natural ally and the three bloc on the other—the NPP, BJP and 'others'.[5] Although the 'others' seemed insignificant by the way they have been connoted by most of the national media, but the fact remains that this is the bloc that holds the button in the formation of government this time around as it has always been the case in the state which has always had fractured mandates. This conglomerate includes UDP (6), PDF (4), HSPDP (2), KHNAM (1) and Independents (3). The common agenda of all the three mentioned blocs is a desire to form a non-Congress government in the state. The dominant regional parties such as the UDP and HSPDP were left out of government formation in the preceeding term by the Mukul Sangma-led Congress government throughout the period of five years. This was because the government was then formed with the help of the 13 independent MLAs.

PDF, on the other hand, is a party which was formed by its former Congress legislator, P. N. Syiem, after he had been largely targeted and left out by Mukul Sangma government while being the CEM of the KHADC. The state government introduced the Prevention of Disqualification (Members of the Legislative Assembly of Meghalaya) Amendment Bill, 2015, that intends to disqualify a person holding both the post of an elected MLA as well as Member of District Council (MDC). P. N. Syiem saw this as a direct attack on him because of his constant tussle with Mukul Sangma for the interferences in the KHADC. As such, it became natural that this party, which emerged as a result of the internal conflict within the Congress, would have found it odd to ally with the same party. Furthermore, what made it easier for the three blocs to come together, although they fought elections separately, is the fact that, except for the HSPDP and PDF, the NPP, BJP and UDP were already part of the NEDA even before elections, with the same agenda of working towards the goal of Congress-free Northeast India. At the state level, UDP, HSPDP and GNC have also had pre-poll alliance with the aim of getting the requisite number for government formation.

Therefore, considering the circumstances of the political situation in the state of Meghalaya, the development in the state indicated that the struggle for power during election was divided mainly between the Congress party on the one side and all others on the other despite separate approaches, appeals and support base. Although regional parties fought separately on different platforms such as the UDP-HSPDP-GNC alliance, the PDF, KHNAM and BJP, none of the non-Congress parties showed any inclination towards working with the Congress in the post-poll scenario. While UDP did not put up many candidates in Garo Hills, HSPDP expressed support for GNC as both wanted separate Khasi-Jaintia and greater Garo states. PDF did not put up any candidate in Garo Hills citing its focus in regions where it had chances of winning. The Congress by virtue of having won 29 seats of the 60-member house in the 2013 election thought that it was prudent to take only independent MLAs elected during the previous tenure into confidence. This was

a major mistake the party had committed as it had excluded and closed all negotiations with any of the regional parties in the state as it considered itself capable of getting majority in the 2018 elections. In the process throughout the five-years term, it had only made efforts to alienate all other parties to the extent that none of the parties left out found it necessary to even consider any attempt by the Congress to work together.

The natural allies such as UDP and HSPDP found it easier to repose their trust in NPP with its fresh face in the leadership. While the PDF had no other option as it is a party founded by the former Congress leader in protest against the party leadership of Mukul Sangma, KHNAM, on the other hand, focused primarily on the concept of indigenous identity and aspiration of the indigenous population. The party projected itself as a political force with priorities on the preservation of indigenous culture, anti-infiltration and for setting priority of economic development that should focus more on the upliftment of indigenous population. This party appealed on the basis that it wanted a non-Congress and non-BJP government and it is determined to forge a post-poll alliance with like-minded regional parties but not with either of the national parties. True to its election agenda, KHNAM remained outside of both the parties in the assembly after the formation of government by the NPP-led alliance.

With such a scenario before elections, the electoral results also differed significantly from the previous years. This time, the number of independent candidates who won the election were reduced from 13 to 3. What is significant in this is the awareness and apprehension that the people realized during the last assembly when almost all independent MLAs joined the government despite the mandate being against the ruling dispensation of the time. This, in fact, has always been the trend in Meghalaya when the independent MLAs have always been instrumental in the formation and collapse of governments. It must be remembered that Meghalaya is the only state in the country which has had a government led by an independent MLA, Dr F. A. Khonglam, which lasted from 2001 till the end of the term in 2003.

Therefore, the political environment in the state of Meghalaya during the period leading to elections shows that the state was to witness closely fought elections with so much of hope and expectations of change and transformation. However, the multi-cornered contest was supposed to be gradually narrowed down to two major factions. The BJP projected itself as an alternative force to reckon on lost steam as elections got closer. The reason for this is the fact that the party, which initially had made a huge impact, especially in Jaintia Hills, because of its promise to lift the National Green Tribunal ban on cold mining in the area, realized that most of its prospective candidates had defected to either NPP or other parties. The party actually woke up very late in the state and, therefore, by the time they could set up candidates, it could not undo the image created by its principal opponent, the Congress, that it is an anti-Christian and anti-minority party. The efforts made to shed this image and to convince the voters in Meghalaya that BJP is inclusive and focused on development—by appointing a former catholic seminarian, Mr K. Alphons as a minister at the centre and in-charge of Meghalaya along with Mr Nalin Kohli, considered as a liberal face of the party—did not succeed. The party even made efforts to woo the voters in the state by calling on Christian religious leaders and seeking their support in undoing the manufactured image created by the Congress against the party, but they never came to power in the state. The party even tried to convince people that it is not communal by offering financial assistance to Christian churches to develop and modernize their facilities, churches and places of importance through the Union

Tourism Ministry with the aim of attracting tourists to these places but the same was not received well in the heat of the approaching elections. Many saw these efforts as too little and too late. For instance, the two dominant churches, Catholic Church and the Mawkhar Presbyterian Church, rejected the offer.[6] Some of the religious leaders of Christian denominations even considered this as appeasement policy meant only to manoeuvre electoral gain.

Electoral competition during elections is deemed important in a democratic set up. Such competitions among political parties are expected to create awareness among the voters which will add as incentives to them as principal agents to political change. Traditionally, it is argued that increasing competitions among political parties to contest and form government maximizes the welfare of voters as the latter would be informed to ensure efficient use of public resources, and with the help of revealing information, citizens welfare would be enhanced (Dash and Mukherjee, 2015). However, the case of Meghalaya is quite different. The recently held elections made the voters puzzled between the incumbents—the NPP which the electorates were apprehensive of being the team B of the BJP in the state. The Khasi-Jaintia population was also faced with another significant slogan of identity politics and that is that the NPP is a Garo-based party. The other regional parties were busy redefining their priorities and mooting various possible post-poll alliances. The UDP, with its slogan 'unity, development and peace' as the focus of their manifesto, slipped the attention of the public who saw the lack or reproduction of similar manifestos across parties with only little differences in the approach and priorities. Therefore, the only competition among parties was limited between the performances of the incumbent and the campaigning strategies of other parties that can magnetize the attention of the electorates. Under such an atmosphere of apathy, significant efforts were to be made by different parties to evolve campaign strategies which can draw and sustain the imagination of people till the day of voting.

Similarly, from the point of view of accountability, political competitions will make the incumbent politicians accountable for their actions. However, intense political competitions have induced incumbent political parties to resort to populism rather than implement growth-promoting policies (Dash and Mukherjee, 2015). The probability of the incumbent government getting re-elected goes down as the degree of political competition becomes higher. Meghalaya as a state has been a witness to this approach over many years, especially before elections, and this time too is no exception. As mentioned earlier, at least two political parties opted to associate themselves in the opposite platforms—the NEDA—to counter the ruling Congress party in the state, which had kept them at bay for five years.

The natural response of the Congress, as can be seen before the election, was slippery. As expected, they adopted pork-barrel approach in policies to cater to the narrow interests of specific groups instead of implementing the policies that would benefit the majority. This was particularly done by way in which those in the ruling partnership including independent MLAs who were seen as potential party candidates were distributed with schemes and projects that the target of ensuring their re-election through such inducement would help them get re-elected. Strategies were made in order to concentrate even the MLA schemes only on targeted voters to convince them so as not to go against the incumbent MLA. While most of the MLAs favoured by the ruling dispensation got access to schemes and projects from Integrated Basin Development Programme, National Aqua Mission, etc., many of the opposition party

MLAs were deprived of these schemes and projects and as such the people of those constituencies were deprived as to make them understand the cause of electing MLAs who may not make it to the ruling dispensation. Some of the rebel MLAs from within the Congress party also suffered the same fate as elections drew near. Their MLA schemes were rejected and delayed on various grounds such as not fulfilling the necessary criteria, among others. Therefore, many of them left the party and joined NPP. Some of the prominent figures in the party such as Mrs Roshan Warjri and Mr D. D. Lapang even declined from contesting elections. This, somehow, led to the result of election being unusual from all previous elections as regions in the state saw different results in terms of party performances. Table 24.3 explains the changes in terms of results and party performances.

The performances of different political parties are indicated in Table 24.1, which are represented by the number of seats parties won as against the total number of contested candidates. Although BJP vote share is way below their arch-rival in the state—Congress, it must be noted that the party has done exceptionally well this time around winning 2 of the 47 seats it contested. This was possible because of its increasing support base in urban areas. Two seats that BJP won were only from the urban constituencies of Shillong city. The party came second to Congress in Shillong East as well as in Shillong North constituencies where it was defeated by the lone KHNAM candidate by a very small margin of about 400 votes.[7] Although the BJP did quite well in many urban seats in terms of vote share, it could not do the same in rural constituencies where people are still apprehensive of its agenda which is coupled by the lack of party workers. The role of social media plays a very important role, especially in undoing the efforts of party candidates and workers in rural areas where people actually cannot differentiate between fake and

---

[7] https://www.electionsinindia.com/meghalaya/north-shillong-assembly-vidhan-sabha-constituency-elections

Table 24.1   Vote and Seat Share of Political Parties in 2018 Assembly Election, Meghalaya

Political Parties	Party Type	Number of Contestants	Seats Won	Votes of Party	Votes (%)	Vote (%) in Seats Contested
BJP	National Party	47	2	151,292	9.63	12.47
INC	National Party	60	21	447,770	28.50	28.87
NCP	National Party	21	1	25,247	1.61	4.96
AITC	National Party	8	0	5,544	0.35	2.69
HSPDP	State Party	13	2	84,011	5.35	23.98
NPP	State Party	52	19	323,745	20.60	24.11
UDP	State Party	35	6	182,494	11.61	20.43
PDF	Registered (Unrecognized) Party	26	4	128,413	8.17	18.02
KHNAM	Registered (Unrecognized) Party	8	1	14,164	0.90	6.50
GNC	Registered (Unrecognized) Party	6	0	21,682	1.38	14.41
NEINDP	Registered (Unrecognized) Party	1	0	327	0.02	1.83
RPI (A)	Registered (Unrecognized) Party	1	0	169	0.01	0.73
AAP	State Party—Other State	6	0	1,410	0.09	0.83
LJP	State Party—Other State	1	0	104	0.01	0.31
Independents		85	3	170,269	10.84	

Source: Election Commission of India, Meghalaya State Assembly Election, 2018.

true information. As indicated in Table 24.1, the Congress party, although has retained its percentage of vote share from the previous elections, it was not able to convert the same into seats share.

Table 24.2 indicates that the number of seats it had won crumbled from 29 in 2013 to 20 in 2018. The factor that affected the party first of all was defection by many of its legislators and leaders. The party also had to face the vacuum left by leaders who decided not to

contest elections again. Apart from these two factors, there were also instances where senior leaders and grassroots workers were dissatisfied with the performance of their own government, especially the style of functioning of the leaders in the government and as such they were only looking for opportunities beyond the party.

The Congress actually benefitted from the last election with its focused campaign to project the BJP as a communal party. As

Table 24.2   Party-wise Seat Share in 2018 and 2013 Assembly Elections, Meghalaya

Political Parties	Seats Won in 2018	Seats Won in 2013	Gain and Loss
INC	21	29	−8
BJP	2	O	+2
NPP	19	2	+17
UDP	6	8	−2
HSPDP	2	4	−2
PDF	4	NA	+4
KHNAM	1	O	+1
NCP	1	2	−1
GNC	0	1	−1
NESDP	0	1	−1
Independents	3	13	−10

Source: Election Commission of India, Meghalaya State Assembly Election, 2018.

Table 24.3   Change of Party in Different Constituencies between 2013 and 2018 Elections, Meghalaya

Constituency	2013	2018	Constituency	2013	2018
Nartiang	INC	NPP	Rambrai	HSPDP	INC
Jowai	INC	NPP	Mawshynrut	HSPDP	NPP
Raliang	INC	NPP	Ranikor	INC	INC[a]
Mookaiaw	INC	UDP	Mawkyrwat	INC	HSPDP
Sutnga	IND	INC	Kharkutta	INC	NPP
Khliehriat	IND	UDP	Mendipathar	NCP	INC
Amlarem	IND	UDP	Resubelpara	INC	NPP
Mawhati	IND	NPP	Bajendoba	IND	NPP
Nongpoh	INC	INC	Songsak	NPP	INC
Jirang	NESD	NPP	Rongjeng	INC	NPP
Umsning	INC	PDF	Williamnagar	INC	NPP
Umroi	INC	INC	Raksamgre	INC	NPP
Mawryngkneng	IND	INC	Tikritilla	IND	INC
Pynthorumkhrah	INC	BJP	Phulbari	INC	NPP
Mawlai	UDP	INC	Rajabala	IND	INC
East Shillong	INC	INC	Selsella	INC	INC
West Shillong	UDP	INC	Dadengre	NPP	NPP
South Shillong	NCP	BJP	North Tura	INC	NPP
North Shillong	INC	KHNAM	South Tura	IND	NPP
Mylliem	INC	PDF	Rangsakona	INC	INC
Nongthymmai	UDP	INC	Ampati	INC	INC
Nongkrem	HSPDP	IND	Mahendraganj	INC	INC
Sohiong	INC	HSPDP	Salmanpara	INC	INC
Sohra	UDP	PDF	Gambegre	IND	NCP
Mawphlang	INC	IND	Dalu	INC	NPP
Mawsynram	INC	INC	Rongara Siju	IND	NPP
Shella	UDP	UDP	Chokpot	GNC/INC	
Pynursla	INC	NPP	Bagmara	IND	NPP
Mawkynrew	UDP	PDF			
Mairang	UDP	UDP			
Mawthadraishan	UDP	UDP			
Nongstoin	HSPDP	PDF			

Source: Election Commission of India, Meghalaya State Assembly Elections, 2018.

Note: [a]This sat was won by the Congress candidate but he immediately resigned to join NPP after the Congress could not form the government. However, he unsuccessfully contested the by-election, and the UDP candidate won the seat.

mentioned earlier, it succeeded in spreading fear psychosis among the people against the BJP terming it as a party whose ideology is based on Hindutva politics and propelled by the Rashtriya Swayamsevak Sangh (RSS) machineries which is hugely against the interest of minorities like Christian population. The same yardstick was drawn against all other regional parties, especially UDP whom the Congress projected and convinced people that their association with NEDA is actually a deal made that if any party other than the Congress wins this election, then it will be BJP which will take the shots in the affairs of the state. This remained as the major campaign strategy in most of the rural constituencies and as such,

Table 24.4 Vote Share of Political Parties, Meghalaya

Political Parties	Votes (%)	Vote Count
INC	28.50	447,770
NPP	20.60	323,745
UDP	11.61	182,494
BJP	9.63	151,292
PDF	8.17	128,413
HSPDP	5.35	84,011
NCP	1.61	25,247
GNC	1.38	21,682
KHNAM	0.90	14,164
AAP	0.09	1,410
NEINDP	0.02	327
RPI (A)	0.01	169
LJP	0.01	104
Independents	10.84	170,269

Source: Election Commission of India, Meghalaya State Assembly Election, 2018.

Table 24.5 Voter Turnout Trend in Meghalaya, 1972–2018 (in %)

Year	Votes
1972	51.58
1978	67.18
1983	72.58
1988	77.51
1993	79.52
1998	74.52
2003	70.42
2008	88.99
2013	86.82
2018	86.78

Source: Election Commission of India, Meghalaya State Assembly Election, 2018.

they succeeded even in places where chances seemed bleak for the party.

Looking at Table 24.4, it is indicative that the Congress party remains dominant in terms of its vote share which is followed by the NPP which is significantly new in the state. Apart from these, two other regional parties also struggled to retain their vote share, or rather are in the declining trend. The BJP, on the other hand, has also increased in its vote share particularly in the urban constituencies.

Table 24.5 shows that the democratic process is getting more and more entrenched in the state of Meghalaya. There is a consistent rise in the percentage of voters' turnout trend which was 51.58 per cent in the first state assembly elections and 86.78 per cent in 2018, which is consistent with the 2013 turnout.

CHANGING POLITICAL NARRATIVES: CAMPAIGN TRAIL

Election campaign is not an easy term to define. There are two distinct broad ways to conceptualize election campaign. The first one focuses on institutional or quasi-institutional conditions and the other considers the period of uncommon intensity in the political order (Brady, Johnston, & Sides, 2006). As such, this situation can either broaden the period of campaign or narrow it. The institutional or quasi-institutional understanding of campaign delineates the period officially declared for election campaign after the date of election is known. The parties officially announce the names of candidates for constituencies. The candidates then make sure that they spend virtually all their time in the designated constituencies. With the election dates having been announced, certain actions, public behaviour, movement and financial activities during such period are regulated.

Although this institutional definition of campaign may officially set the tone for election fever, yet in many instances, this period may also determine the end of political influences that may have an impact on the decision of voters. The most important condition for election is rather the environment of heightened intensity of political activities. Scenario of festivities and focused attention is paid to attract electorates to certain ideas of governance and ideology. This constitutes the moment when the candidates contesting for elections decide to lure the electorates and the political parties start focusing on strategies and tactics to influence the outcome of elections. An election campaign may begin early as and when the candidates start hustings and attending to the needs and aspirations of the voters. In this way, election campaign may be minimally defined as the period of organized efforts to influence the decision-making process of the citizens for making a real political choice. It is determined by the period when political parties and candidates try to reach out to the electorates and intensify their attention towards politics through public proclamation about the capacity, leadership skill, network of the candidate, designing of manifestos, oratory skills in pursuing agenda and a multiple ways of creatively registering on the voters' mind as the election day draws near.

Election campaigns have always been a big crowd puller in India and Meghalaya is no exception. Although unlike in other parts of India, political campaign may not attract the general public, however, the period before the declaration of election schedule by the Election Commission of India (ECI) is crucial for any political party and its candidates as this is the time that determines the capacity of the party and its candidates to manoeuvre the final electoral decision of the citizens. In the state of Meghalaya, where the population of electorates is very small as compared to the rest of India, there is a general assertion that campaign does not matter as long as the candidates can expand their personal relations with the general public. This is because the constituencies in Meghalaya have electorates ranging only between 18,000 and 36,000. Very often, it is said that monetary inducement is the deciding factor in Meghalaya politics. However, it is important to understand that in the heat of political competitions the parties and their candidates have to be able to capture and sustain the imagination of the people, and

this is why campaign does matter in any elections including Meghalaya.

As mentioned previously, 2018 elections were completely unprecedented and different from any other previously held elections. Much attention has to be given to campaign as the campaign trails indicate that the sheer noise and glamour created, especially by the NPP in almost all constituencies became the game changer. The BJP initially, took most political parties by surprise with its efforts by presenting a huge list of star campaigners.[8] Meghalaya as a state had never, in the past, experienced so much noise and advertising for elections. The strategy of the BJP—to fly as many high-profile leaders as possible to the state—backfired. The party submitted a list of 40 star campaigners, which the people of Meghalaya did not find attractive. Therefore, the party gradually lost steam, especially due to lack of grassroots and booth-level workers in rural areas. The minimal response that the saffron party managed to obtain in rural areas made it difficult for the party to manage any big programme for their show of strength.

MEANS OF ELECTION CAMPAIGN

Music

Meghalaya elections showed a few peculiarly interesting unique characteristics, aesthetics, innovations and strategies. This time, all these were complimented by the rise of usage of social media coupled with the unlimited internet data that almost all mobile service companies provided to the people. With young and old in urban and rural areas having access to smart phones and internet, information and campaign materials were easy to reach for the consumption and spread to electorates in different constituencies.

---

[8] BJP Meghalaya state convener, Election Coordination Committee submitted a list of as many as 40 ministers and important functionaries that would campaign for the party in Meghalaya during the period of campaign.

Meghalaya is known for people's love for music and they associate with music with much pride. What makes Meghalaya elections more interesting and peculiar is primarily the use of music of different kinds to persuade voters. All parties made sure that they have official songs composed as a theme song for the party, where they focus on the basic tenets of the party's stand on various issues ranging from development, security for women, ethos of *jaitbynriew* or race, farmers and other issues central to parties' manifestos. The genre of music ranges from folk to hip-hop to K-pop melodies and rock music. *Phawar* or musical slogan earrings in the form of indigenous musical tune of storytelling are often performed melodiously during the elections in which various topics of everyday life, social and political issues are drawn to the attention of the listeners. As they are considered closely attached to tradition, they have a great recollection value and are mostly composed to cater to rural folks. There are instances when this form of music is also fused with instrumental and singing style linked to rock music. This is often done by regional parties to link traditional music with international flow of popular western culture and bypassing the Indian mainstream culture as a sign of telling that the state has inculcated western culture, including religion.

However, the popularity of Bollywood music also is not ignored by parties and candidates. In some areas, even Bollywood Bhangra music made to the campaign trail of some candidates to attract those who are familiar with such music. Parties and candidates often customized music to specific contexts. Different political parties organized musical concerts where they engage local music bands, who perform rock music, to reach and influence the larger groups that consists of lovers of such music. This is done so as to correspond closely to the contemporary cultural preferences in Meghalaya. Thus, all these actually form as important performative aspects of campaigning in Meghalaya. As such, most of the parties advertise their major rallies in district headquarters, civil sub-division and marketplaces by announcing the rock band that would perform during such functions. The importance of being seen and heard requires that messages are communicated in ways that can be contained in the minds of people for long. Along with official party songs, candidates also compose and produce songs and music meant to attract the imagination of local voters and, as such, they focus on the issues of their constituencies. The reverb of the tune of folk music or even rock music with folk narration is almost common in all campaign music. To capture the general public, sometimes even very popular old, western music of various kinds are used by candidates to present them as iconic figures as the song may convey.

As Cornelia Guenauer, while observing election campaign during the 2014 general election, pointed out that semiotic level of campaigning and of reading the drive of voters was important in Meghalaya and, as such, songs were played from loudspeakers and driven vehicles (Guenauer, 2016). The same ethos and excitement exist in other elections as well in the state. Specific arrangements were made to entertain the waiting voters with songs during hustings. The ban of party flags and posters during campaigning is replaced by musical shreds and echoes of various defining tunes across the street in public transport, households, during picnics and sporting events and sometimes at various family and social gatherings. Such excitements also show the inclinations of various groups towards parties or candidates of their choice. In this context, if attempts are made to understand electioneering in Meghalaya, then music should be understood not merely as entertainment for the voters but instead as one of the most powerful tools of election-campaign communication in the state, where music is in the heart and soul of every member of the society. The connotation of Shillong as the rock capital of India must be understood by music which is the most powerful tool of communication in the state whether political, religious, cultural or otherwise. There have been consistent arguments that money and alcohol play very important role in electioneering process of Meghalaya (Mukhim, 2013). There is certainly no dearth of doubt about these influences on the ground. However, if proper analysis is made about the effects of music, it certainly cannot be equated in the same line as that of money and alcohol because the sound of music affects the thought process of people. It also sustains longer even than the period of electioneering. It is not expensive, and it is redistributed to the extent that it can reach the maximum targets.

Music attaining a category of being a significant tool of communication during campaign in Meghalaya is possible because listeners of music share a collective system of musical meaning. The common stock of musical knowledge helps in attaching specific meanings to generate specific associations and emotions. In this way, therefore, music can become a symbol and a tool for formulating and expressing social identity (Guenauer, 2016). The social identity aesthetically expressed through music has the capacity to mobilize people. As mentioned earlier, it also helps in raising and keeping attention span over a long period of time and addresses the listeners at an emotional, subconscious and effective level. Music may not solve problems of the people but it is a catalyst for change. Candidates may campaign hard-raising pertinent issues like lack of employment, inadequate health care, education, coal mining ban, etc., but not all people are interested in what the loudmouth politicians said from the dais. Hundreds are drawn to the rallies by the foot-tapping music. Even the State Election Commission has been using this art form to get voters registered. It yielded results as voters increased from 18 lakhs in 2013 to 42 lakhs in 2018. All political parties make the best use of this art. The Congress party president, Rahul Gandhi, began his campaign in Meghalaya by attending a rock concert campaign in January 2018.

Similarly, the BJP, which drew a blank in the 2013 elections, had roped in local musical icon, Lou Majaw for their campaign video. The regional parties like the UDP, HSPDP, KHNAM, etc. were no exception. The UDP, although it did not publish new album this time, had used the number of songs published during the last general elections. These songs were fused *phawar* structure with instrumental and singing style linked to rock music (Guenauer, 2016). KHNAM, a regional party formed in 2002, had during the launch of the party itself published an album with as many as 11 songs composed. The number was added during each election with numbers that appeal to the call of identity focusing on concepts like *jaitbynriew* or race, *hynniewtrep* or the seven communities forming the Khasi identity. All the songs strike extreme emotional chords invoking tradition, ethnicity and the aspiration of the youth.

The candidates have their own theme songs for the campaign. They took time to get their songs composed and recorded. For example, sitting Congress legislator from Shillong East constituency Ms M. Ampareen Lyngdoh's campaign song became hugely popular among the people. The song was inspired by Shaggy's popular number 'strength of a woman'. It speaks highly of what a woman can achieve in her struggles and drew notes of inspiration (Indian Express, 2018). The candidate then goes around campaigning, urging people to stand with her because she represents the woman in the song.

If music is understood as a tool of communication, then one of the reasons that pushed down the performance of NPP in Khasi and Jaintia Hills is the music which fails to appeal to the sensitivity of the people in these areas. The official music that the party made did try to appeal both the Garos and the Khasi-Jaintia. The mistake was that in one song both Garo and Khasi languages were used. Although the party had huge prospect in Jaintia Hills and also in some of the Khasi Hills regions, yet the electorate found the fusion of Garo and Khasi music in one song foul. The composition lacking in undercurrent sensitivity of communities across the state through fusion music was something which dented the prospect of the party in Khasi and Jaintia Hills. This was in line with the generated apprehension that the NPP is a Garo dominated party. In West Khasi Hills, this was projected by opposing candidates as a threat to the bordering community's fate. This song was interpreted as a message that the NPP is determined to create a greater Garo-land and in that process, many Khasi villages would form part of that new state of the Garos.

Sports

Another significant campaign tool in Meghalaya that is fascinating is the use of sporting events as platform to which people can easily be drawn to. Usually, before the candidates introduce themselves to the public and to ensure that they can attract people to their gatherings and meetings, they make it a point to sponsor and attend sporting events. In most parts of Meghalaya, like the rest of Northeast India, football is the most convenient sports to attract people. So, very often, the increasing number of football tournaments in villages mark the setting of election fever and campaign. From the beginning, candidates utilize the help of sports lovers and sports clubs to reach out to public. The more the candidate appears during such sporting events, the more the trust factor is developed.

Public Rally

However, like in the rest of the country, the last and the major event that should determine as the culminating point of the parties and candidate's prospect is often the final-day rally. This is often the most important and final campaign strategy in which the show of strength is seen as a sign of victory or defeat. In almost all elections in Meghalaya, the counting is virtually done on this day, which is usually kept apart as a day of public rally. If the gathering is huge, then this has a major impact even on the undecided voters. This day is marked by the confluence of people in a selected location and then followed by motor rally. Usually, on this day, candidates arrange as many vehicles as possible. In 2018 election, in various constituencies, prominent candidates were seen carrying out rallies with number of vehicles crossing even more than 2,000 mark. In many places, such practices caused even major hurdle to the public because of day-long traffic jam. A candidate's capability, his network and the confidence of electorates on his candidature is often determined through this event. Almost all parties save the best for the last and, therefore, they make sure that the last and final day is full of glamour, grandeur and it's a show of strength. Major parties like the Congress, NPP, UDP, HSPDP, PDF, BJP and even independent candidates organized such major events in almost all constituencies.

Much before this, the parties often make the announcement of candidates a major event. During the 2018 election, new parties like the NPP and PDF used this event not only to introduce candidates, but also to outline their party's agenda and priorities. The more people a candidate could draw during this introduction, the more the party can consider their prospects. The NPP, since it is a relatively new party to a larger section of Meghalaya population especially outside of Garo Hills, made it a point to bring people together with all leaders at least present during such introduction programme. Apart from candidates' rallies, the party also organized party rallies in all major urban centres and district headquarters, along with a gala programme in the state capital. Similarly, the PDF, which is a new party, organized such events with the sole purpose of pointing its priorities as a new political outfit.

The UDP and HSPDP organized a joint programme in Shillong and also wherever they had common candidate, they conglomerated as partners. These parties, too, list down their priorities and agenda as an alliance while also infusing confidence in the newly found unity among the two important regional parties in the state.

In the 2018 election, this was not largely done by the Congress party as an incumbent party. In constituencies where sitting MLAs were the undeclared candidates of the party, the distribution of MLA schemes became its major drawing point in which each beneficiary attended along with their near and dear ones. During such events, the party gathered full strength showing solidarity and unity.

NEW ELECTORAL DIRECTIONS AND POLITICAL CAPITAL IN MULTIPLE REGIONS IN MEGHALAYA

Meghalaya, with its usual voting characteristics that is often determined by various regions in the state, has shown a complete departure this time from previous patterns. There is a common claim that the 'people in the state are not bothered about ideology or political parties....They vote individuals for their personal appeal and for personal help they are able to render in times of domestic exigencies' (Mukhim, 2018). However, historical analysis of elections in Meghalaya draws one to the fact that different regions in Meghalaya have different patterns of voting behaviour. For instance, West Khasi Hills districts have very often shown that they have priorities that are different from other regions in Meghalaya. From the time of attainment of statehood, the region has shown inclination towards ethnic and identity politics by favouring a set of political parties that set their priorities on this parameter. The election of 2013 especially was very clear when people cast their vote against uranium mining for the establishment of Khasi-Jaintia state and settling of border disputes. This is indicated by the fact that HSPDP won four out of

seven seats. The region being the most backward area of the state had never been an issue in the past. But this time, people indicated their priorities towards development and not anymore being stuck to the earlier emotional issues of electoral debates. In Jaintia Hills, the voting behaviour has been determined by the economic factor which is focused on coal mining as the population of this region mainly depends on this activity. This time also, the same factor swerved the people from the Congress party as the government could not reverse the NGT ban on coal mining. This time, the party could win only one out of the seven seats. Garo Hills, on the other hand, has often voted en masse in favour of leadership. The previous elections saw the region voting in favour of Mukul Sangma in the absence of P. A. Sangma. This time around, the people of the region voted in favour of Conrad Sangma, the son of Late P. A. Sangma. Table 24.3 indicates that NPP succeeded to get 13 seats in the entire Garo Hills where it had only two MLAs in the previous assembly. The party gained seven seats from the Congress and another four from the previously independent MLAs.

The analysis of the 2018 assembly election indicates that the usual pattern has completely changed. Parties have changed their base. The place of regional parties, identity politics and internal divide has been reduced to a great extent.

The growth of a different political atmosphere has made different political parties, except NPP, to struggle for their survival. In the case of the Congress party, it has still succeeded to get representation from almost all regions of the state. Despite its anti-incumbent factor, the powerful campaign strategies by the BJP to uproot the Congress party from Meghalaya, the party performed quite well in East Khasi Hills, although it faced major challenge from the BJP which dented some of its prospects. The Congress managed to get six seats as compared to eight seats it had earlier, losing only two in the district. However, the party failed to perform in Garo Hills where it won only 9 seats out of 14 it had earlier. In Jaintia Hills also, the party had four seats but could retain only one seat in 2018 assembly election. The party could retain two seats it had in Ri Bhoi and won another two seats in West Khasi Hills, gaining only one seat more in the latter.

The consistent endeavour of the Congress party to campaign against the NPP, painting it with the same brush as it did to the BJP failed to bear results. The Congress equated the NPP as the team B of the BJP in the state and working towards enhancing the prospect of the latter. The Congress party also made allegations that NPP was taking the help of RSS volunteers, but this did not pay dividend as the NPP emerged as the second most dominant force in the 2018 election—winning 20 seats out of the 52 it had contested in—with only one seat less than the Congress. Moreover, NPP saw an increase in seats from 2 to 19 from the 2013 assembly election. The focus of NPP on the agenda of change and transformation through inclusive governance fascinated the imagination of the voters.

Another indicator of the unprecedented trend in the 2018 election is the declining appeal of identity politics and region-specific agenda. As Table 24.2 indicates, the once dominant party—HSPDP, roaring like a lion in West Khasi Hills districts has been diffused. In many places, the party due to infighting could not even retain second position. It lost three prestigious seats in the district despite its well-known strong protest against uranium mining, demand for Khasi-Jaintia state and making strong call for solving border disputes, which had always been the winning point of the party in this region. This shows that the rural populace has gradually shifted their priorities from identity politics to development. The West Khasi Hills districts are the least developed areas of the whole state and this time, the loyalty of people towards regional parties has been considered by electorates as the reason

for their backwardness. Similarly, UDP, which had its base in East Khasi Hills and some areas in West Khasi Hills districts, now shifted its base to Jaintia Hills which gave the party three seats of the six seats it won in the entire state.

CONCLUSION

The newly sworn-in government in the state of Meghalaya is christened the Meghalaya Democratic Alliance with NPP as the leading party along with UDP, HSPDP, PDF and an independent MLA. As mentioned earlier, the formation of a government which ensured that the Congress party is kept away was expected. Moreover, with NPP being the NDA ally at the centre and other parties already in NEDA, it was only easy to predict such a government which will have the confidence of the ruling party in the national capital. The ailment of small states in the region is always common and that is the heavy dependence on the centre for financial assistance. This stark reality remained even in 2018. If Meghalaya has to remain economically sustainable, it needs a friendly government at the centre and as mentioned, NPP being an ally of NDA at the centre made it easier to form such a government with the support of BJP along with other regional parties that are also convenient for such an alliance.

The actual trend of the election results indicated the desire for change and transformation. The election held in 2018 indicated that regional parties without the patronage of parties of national significance can no longer have major impact on the state. The emergence of NPP as a party that had the ability to snatch the authority from the Congress which has ruled the state almost in all period of its statehood except on few occasions shows that this party, which has the patronage of BJP at the centre, can actually shift the narrative of politics in the state of Meghalaya. This is the first time that a regional party emerging from the state can equal the number of representatives as that of the congress party in the state.

The reluctance of other regional parties to work again with the Congress party also shows that these parties are aware about the importance of friendly relations that the state of Meghalaya has to maintain with the parties at the helm of affairs in the centre. Voters in the state, although they may have not voted BJP to power this time, however, indicated their desire for change and through the maturity of voting behaviour in which they voted for the NPP, they have indicated their understanding about the need for the state to have a good relationship with the centre. They see NPP as a reliable force to have a conditional relationship with the BJP government at the centre, which is a factor that is important for the development of the state.

However, at the root of all trends in the Meghalaya election of 2018 is the desire from within various regions for change and also the need for stability. The confidence that people of Meghalaya have put in the NPP as a party to lead the state is derived from the fact that the people having seen infightings and power tussle in the Congress party even in the last tenure, they were determined to elect a government that would provide stability while ensuring uniform development across regions in the state.

REFERENCES

Brady, H. E., Johnston, R., & Sides, J. (2006). The study of political campaigns. In H. E. Brady & R. Johnston (Eds.), *Capturing campaign effects.* Ann Arbor, MI: The University of Michigan Press.

Dash, B. B., & Mukherjee, S. (2015). Political competition and human development: Evidence from the Indian states. *Journal of Development Studies, 51*(1), 1–14.

Election Commission of India, Meghalaya State Assembly Election, 2018. Retrieved from https://eci.gov.in/files/file/3694-meghalaya-general-legislative-election-2018/

Guenauer, C. (2016). Tribal politics, suits and rock music: Electioneering in Meghalaya. *South Asia: Journal of South Asian Studies, 39(2)*, 430–443.

Mukhim, P. (2013, 24 April). Where elections equal money, music and booze. *The Statesman.* 24 April. Retrieved from http://www.thestatesman.net/index.php?optionDcom_content&viewDarticle&idD445072&catidD52&showDarchive&yearD2013&monthD2&dayD25&ItemidD66.

Mukhim, P. (2018). Meghalaya elections 2018: A repeat of 2008. *Economic and Political Weekly, 53*(11), 12–14.

PTI. (2018, 28 February). Political parties take the music route to woo voters in Meghalaya. *Indian Express.*

https://www.census2011.co.in/census/state/meghalaya.html

https://www.census2011.co.in/data/religion/state/17-meghalaya.html

https://www.electionsinindia.com/meghalaya/north-shillong-assembly-vidhan-sabha-constituency-elections

https://www.hindustantimes.com/india-news/two-meghalaya-churches-say-no-to-tourism-ministry-package/story-bZVCWKKjHbVPLM8ZIjoFZK.html

Tribal Politics and Non-state Actors in Mizoram

P. Lalpekhlui

INTRODUCTION

For the last couple of decades, liberal democracy, founded on reasons and freedom of choice, has become a new development of agenda. Theoretically, democracy is a process where individuals can freely participate and have a say in governance, a precondition for development and a strive towards inclusiveness. Since India is constituted with several categories of social groups with a complex history, positive discrimination was introduced as a mechanism to accommodate several sections of society throughout British India. Positive discrimination was a form of providing a platform for the socially, economically backward classes in the form of political reservation, separate electorates, jobs, etc. For that matter, the colonial rule in India introduced communal representation in the form of Morley–Minto Reforms. The Morley–Minto Reforms introduced communal representation through separate electorates for Muslim. Communal representation was also extended to other minorities, such as the Sikhs, the Anglo-Indians and the Indian Christians, the Depressed Classes and the backward tribes.

With regard to the Scheduled Tribes (STs) and the Scheduled Caste (SCs), it was in 1950 that the Indian Constitution provided a mechanism of compensatory discrimination to historically discriminated groups such as the STs and SCs. Their interests are articulated in the form of Articles 330 and 332 of the Constitution. These articles assured the reservation of seats for these social groups in the Lok Sabha and state assemblies, in which only the members of these groups could stand for election to guarantee the representation of these groups in decision-making bodies. The political reservation was given to the SCs as a result of the agitation led by Dr Ambedkar. However, the STs were given political reservation to accommodate the political dissent or to integrate them into the nation-building process. Hence, political reservation was used as a tool to integrate the Depressed Classes for smoothening the process of nation-building and to legitimizing their social control.

The electoral reservation was considered a much-needed initiation to ensure adequate representation of the SCs and the STs. The idea of representing the interests of the community by their own members was strongly advocated by multiculturalists such as Will Kymlicka, Charles Beitz and Melissa Williams, among others (McMillan, 2005). The electoral reservation was, however, made with the hope that it would open a way for disadvantaged groups to enter into the political institutions. In addition to political reservation, the Constitution of India made numerous special provisions for the STs, including the Fifth and Sixth Schedules. The scheduled areas are defined in the Indian Constitution as 'such areas as the President may by order declared to Scheduled Areas'. The Fifth Schedule applies to 'tribal-dominated areas' and includes areas located in 10 states, stretching from Gujarat to Odisha (Fernandes, 2005). The Fifth Schedule areas are endowed with provisions such as special administrative arrangements to safeguard and preserve the traditions and customs of the people. In this regard, the governor is vested with power for administering tribal areas in consultation with the Tribal Advisory Council (TAC). The TAC is an independent constitutional body that aims to protect the land rights of tribals residing in the scheduled area.

The Sixth Schedule applies to the tribes living in the states of Assam, Meghalaya, Mizoram and Tripura. The Sixth Schedule provision was given to meet the aspirations of the minorities. The philosophy behind the Sixth Schedule provision is to safeguard and develop tribal customs, traditions, language and cultural practices. The tribes inhabiting the scheduled areas are promised to benefit from this arrangement. Hence, the idea of self-determination and autonomy is considered as entitlement.

The adoption of reservations has been an important mechanism to accommodate the voices of tribal communities in India. The political reservation, though it might have been used as a tool to integrate the political dissent of the STs, gives a platform for the marginalized section of society to raise their interest in electoral politics.

In modern representative democracy, electoral politics has become a site where political leaders articulate their interests and mobilize the masses. It also provides an equal opportunity to the electorates (voters) to present their demands and thereby to draw the attention of the political leaders and the government. Although electoral politics is one of the most important components of democracy, it can be manipulated as well as used for personal gratification. In fact, it has been pointed out that the majority of the so-called democratic countries have suffered from a trust deficit and have left their citizens dissatisfied, leaving decisions to be taken by elites on many occasions (Warren, 2011). However, institutional mechanisms have been developed to counter such issues. In addition, non-state actors also play a significant role in ensuring free and fair elections and thereby strengthen democracy.

Non-state actors imply those associations that are not formed by the state; associations that are external and independent from the state, yet play a crucial role in the sociopolitical sphere. Both non-state actors and civil society are closely related to each other. Both terms include associations and organizations ranging from philanthropic based to church based, student union, women's associations, covering issues such as the environment, gender and human rights (McDuie-Ra, 2009). They cover a broad range of actors/institutions that provide a platform for citizens to articulate their interests and serve as an alternative to the state. This chapter focuses on non-state actors such as the Young Mizo Association (YMA), the Peoples Right to Information and Development Implementing Society of Mizoram (PRISM) and the Mizoram Peoples Forum (MPF), a conglomeration of different denominations and NGOs that have been important vehicles for sustaining democracy in the context of Mizoram. Against this backdrop, this chapter looks at the YMA, the PRISM and the MPF as non-state actors under the broad framework of civil society, and highlights their role in electoral politics. The role of non-state actors is highlighted as a way of strengthening democracy.

INTRODUCING MIZORAM

Mizoram is the 23rd state in the Indian Union. It was incorporated into the Indian Union in February 1987. Mizoram was formed out of a political dissent that manifested itself in the form of a secessionist movement in the 1960s. The region was incorporated as the Lushai Hills District in the state of Assam and acquired the status of a Union Territory in 1972. According to Pachuau (2014), the creation of the political identity of Mizo started with the arrival of the British in the region in the 19th century and the subsequent disruption of the status quo.

Before the arrival of the British in the region, the Mizo society was governed by the chiefs. Every village was ruled by an independent chief called *lal*. The institution of chieftainship emerged out of the collective needs of society. The genesis of the chieftainship is believed to have evolved back in 1550 AD, or it can be traced back to the early 18th century (Darchungnunga, 2017; Zorema, 2007). Chieftainship is a hereditary system. The chief was the supreme authority in his village. However, the institution of chieftainship was dismantled with the emergence of a political party known as the Mizo Union (MU) in 1946. The MU challenged the institution of chieftainship because it believes that such practises suppress one's freedom and rights.

The process of political awakening was already underway among the Mizos during the British administration. The introduction of education and Christianity played essential roles in creating sociopolitical consciousness among people. Political awareness among the Mizos, particularly among the educated Lushai, led to the discussion on political failure in the region, and subsequently led to the formation of the first political party known as the MU.

The political party was formed as the existing social organizations, such as the YMA, did not materialize the political objectives of the region. Discontent and aspirations among educated Lushai grew stronger to participate in political activities with the introduction of education in the Lushai Hills. Since there were no other social organizations to take up the political issue, the YMA was often used as a platform to address political problems. With the permission from the then superintendent of the Lushai Hills, the MU was formed on 9 April 1946. The activities of the political parties and the democratic form of government (based on the electoral system) began with the formation of the MU. From the discussion, we can see that non-state actors, such as the YMA, played a vital role in the creation of the MU. Hence, non-state actors have always been vibrant in Mizoram. The formation of the Mizo National Famine Front (MNFF), formed as a civil society organization in the backdrop of the deplorable economic condition of Mizoram in the 1960s, can be demonstrated in this context. The MNFF was converted into a political party known as the Mizo National Front (MNF) in 1961. Civil society organizations not only provide a platform for the formation of a political party but also challenge the sovereignty of the Indian state. As a result, Mizoram was incorporated as the state of the Indian Union in February 1987.

DEMOGRAPHY

As far as demography is concerned, the Northeast is a heterogeneous region occupied by several ethnic groups with distinct cultures and traditions. It is situated at the periphery and presents a composite picture of different realities. It is a land of diverse elements. The complex state formation was exemplary in terms of the underlying facts or differences of the region from mainland India. According to the 2011 census, the tribal population is 10.43

crores, consisting 8.6 per cent of the total population. Around 12 per cent of India's tribal population was inhabited in the north-eastern region. The 2011 census further provides the state-wise tribal population in proportion to the total state population, where 94.43, 86.5, 86.1, 68.8, 35.1, 31.8 and 12.4 per cent of the tribal population lives in Mizoram, Nagaland, Meghalaya, Arunachal Pradesh, Manipur, Tripura and Assam, respectively. Among all the north-eastern states, Mizoram has the highest tribal population in proportion to the state population. Mizoram lies in the southern corner of Northeast India. It is surrounded by the Cachar district of Assam in the north, Myanmar in the east and south-east, and Tripura and Bangladesh in the west. It shares an interstate border with Assam, Manipur and Tripura.

Mizoram is one of the most ethnically and linguistically diverse regions in India. It is inhabited by various tribes such as Lushai, Pawi (Lai), Lakher (Mara), Hmar and Ralte. After independence, except a few immigrants, the whole population of Mizoram can be said to consist of one single tribe, that is, Mizo. The term 'Mizo' is a generic term used to identify the tribes living in Mizoram. However, according to some historian, the term 'Mizo' is a relative one. It may not include all tribes who are now permanent residents of Mizoram, and it depends on the contextual situation (Nunthara, 1996). For instance, the Chakma are now regarded as the formal residents of Mizoram as far as the political structure is concerned. However, they are socially distinct tribes, having no common culture and normative pattern with the Mizos.

Mizoram is a state that has several peculiarities. It is a Christian majority state where the church has an immense say in everyday life and politics. Since the formation, state politics is inextricably associated with identity, and electoral politics in Mizoram cannot be studied without referring to ethnic-religious identity. The peculiarity of electoral politics in Mizoram lies in the constructive or direct involvement of non-state actors who have

contributed a lot for the peaceful conduct of elections in the state.

TRIBAL POPULATION IN ST-RESERVED CONSTITUENCIES

Table 25.1 shows the reserved constituency of the State Assembly. Since the Mizos are recognized as STs, they get the benefits of reserved constituencies both at the state and union levels. Out of the 40 assembly seats, 39 are tribal-reserved constituencies in which only the tribes of Mizoram can contest for the election. It can be seen that 31 constituencies have more than 90 per cent of the tribal population and that other reserved constituencies have more than 80 per cent of the tribal population. The state of Mizoram has one parliamentary constituency which is reserved for tribal communities. This, on the other way, makes it more easier for non-state actors such as the YMA, the MPF and the PRISM to mobilize the population along the lines of ethnic-religious identity.

NON-STATE ACTORS AND DEMOCRACY

Democracy, mainly understood as a rule by the representatives or the consent of the people, requires elections. Hence, election is considered as crucial in promoting democracy, as it provides an opportunity for citizens to participate in public affairs. Elections provide a starting point for a democratic transition. Since the elections are the initial stage of democratic transition, they need to be free and fair, and capable of producing an elected government. The individual should be in a position to exercise their rights. Recent years' experiences have shown that elections alone do not ensure democratic rule. The political system has become highly corrupted over the period where, in many cases, proxy voting,

Table 25.1   Mizoram Assembly Constituencies and Percentage of ST Population

No. and Name of Assembly Constituency	2001 Census Population		
	Total	STs	% of STs
Champhai North (ST)	22,078	21,884	99.12
Chalfilh (ST)	22,408	22,205	99.09
Tuivawl (ST)	20,152	19,958	99.04
Tuikum (ST)	19,669	19,419	98.73
Thorang (ST)	18,373	18,117	98.61
Tuichawng (ST)	34,529	34,019	98.52
Aizawl South III (ST)	22,171	21,763	98.16
Serchhip (ST)	19,501	19,139	98.14
Lengteng (ST)	21,315	20,912	98.11
Hrangturzo (ST)	20,155	19,711	97.80
East Tuipui (ST)	19,598	19,152	97.72
Champhai South (ST)	20,683	20,095	97.16
Lunglei East (ST)	19,346	18,740	96.87
South Tuipui (ST)	19,181	18,513	96.52
Aizawl North II (ST)	23,742	22,871	96.33
Dampa (ST)	21,606	20,746	96.02
39 - Saiha (ST)	24,614	23,602	95.89
38 - Lawngtlai East (ST)	24,748	23,702	95.77
40 - Palak (ST)	22,470	21,488	95.63
33 - Lunglei South (ST)	20,358	19,290	94.75
19 - Aizawl South II (ST)	24,550	23,194	94.48
16 - Aizawl West II (ST)	23,676	22,363	94.45
3 - Mamit (ST)	20,338	19,160	94.21
30 - Lunglei North (ST)	19,598	18,434	94.06
Aizawl North III (ST)	22,492	21,067	93.66
Lunglei West (ST)	18,891	17,682	93.60
West Tuipui (ST)	21,476	19,992	93.09
Tuirial (ST)	20,782	19,248	92.62
Aizawl North I (ST)	24,871	23,018	92.55
Lawngtlai West (ST)	28,315	26,165	92.41
Tuichang (ST)	22,491	20,655	91.84
Hachhek (ST)	20,841	19,044	91.38
Aizawl South I (ST)	23,966	21,423	89.39
Aizawl West III (ST)	23,966	21,423	89.39
Kolasib (ST)	23,190	20,723	89.36
Aizawl West I (ST)	24,080	21,492	89.25
Tawi (ST)	21,103	18,557	87.94
Serlui (ST)	21,988	19,250	87.55
Aizawl East II (ST)	22,734	19,898	87.53
Aizawl East I	22,531	19,662	87.27

Source: Final Papers, Paper no. 4, Delimitation Commission of India.

poll-related violence, low voter turnout and the involvement of insurgent armed groups have been seen. In many cases, the voters are threatened to vote for a particular candidate. Such incidents lead to the deterioration of democratic principles. If negative developments proceed without a positive check, this could result in the breakdown of the electoral system.

In this regard, the intervention of non-state actors is much needed. It has been argued that strong non-state actors strengthen democracy. They provide a context in which citizens can perform their role in elections in a democratic manner. Although the formation of non-state actors such as the YMA, the MPF and the PRISM might be different with its aims and objectives, it is a domain of purpose-built, normatively justified association. Non-state actors are as much as core feature of democracy as is the electoral system, and it is through non-state actors that people organize their interests, share their values, ideas and opinions, and act upon them (Warren, 2011). One can say that non-state actors and democracy are mutually reinforcing each other, and elections form the bedrock of democracy. It is the key activity around which representative democracy evolves.

Indian democracy rests on the concept of representative government. In such government, all citizens have the right to be equally and fairly represented. However, there is a great deal of divergence between theory and practice. Structural biases such as inclination towards the party system, money driving the process and wealthy contributors' exercised manipulation over candidates affect the representative character of the Mizoram political system. In principle, democracy ought to be inclusive, strive for the welfare of the people, but in Mizoram, just like the rest of the Indian states, the gap has widened. It failed to address the needs and aspirants of its citizens. In that regard, the leaders of non-state actors elaborated on the need to intervene in electoral politics. Leaders of the non-state actors feel the need to create public awareness and sensitize voters to the value of having free, fair and peaceful polls in Mizoram.

ELECTORAL POLITICS AND NON-STATE ACTORS

The democratic upsurge with the downfall of authoritarian regimes has resulted in the equation of non-state actors with democracy. Hence, non-state actors are often seen as a harbinger of change from authoritarian regimes to a democratic one. In the same way, non-state actors also play a key role in ensuring the functioning and deepening of democracy. The role of non-state actors as a way of strengthening democracy can be traced back to the writing of the 18th-century thinkers such as Montesquieu and Tocqueville. Both talk about non-state actors as a form of associational life in their writings. They see non-state actors and their role as a way of limiting the absolutist state. Therefore, non-state actors have been seen as protectors of the rights of the individual from the arbitrary power of the state. Non-state actors are seen as an essential prerequisite for democratization. They provide a platform where people discuss and debate on equity, participation and public fairness. In Southeast Asia, civil society has been used to discuss democracy and civil rights (Elliot, 2003).

In reference to Mizoram, major changes have taken place since 1952, and analysing various phases of electoral politics can be good way of capturing reality. The emergence of a political party since 1946 and the mushrooming of non-state actors determined the nature of politics in Mizoram. With the abolition of the institution of chieftainship, the democratic form of government was introduced in Mizoram. Subsequently, the first election was held on 5 April 1952. However, the intervention of civil society organizations in electoral politics became visible from 1972 onwards. In the 1972 State Assembly election, political appeals were issued by the church urging political parties, candidates and electorates to ensure free and fair election.

The intervention of non-state actors such as the church in electoral politics became more visible in the 1989 State Assembly election. The election was held on 21 January 1989. In this election, the church issued two pamphlets providing guidelines to the electorates, the political parties and the candidates. Although these guidelines neither supported nor criticized any political party, they were drafted in a moralistic language to guide the code of elections in the state. Since then, non-state actors became vibrant in electoral politics. For instance, the contradiction between the church and the MNF leader, Laldenga, had a great impact on the party's performance in the second legislative assembly election. In the first legislative assembly election in 1987, it secured 24 seats of the 40 seats. There was a great disparity in the second legislative assembly election. The party was in a position to secure only 15 seats.

There has been a lot of interpretation on the decline in MNF popularity in the state. Political analysts have argued that the difference in ideology between the church leaders and the party leader, Laldenga, was the main cause. When the church wanted to prohibit alcohol, Laldenga opposed such a move and emphasized that the church should not indulge in the affairs of the state. The decline of the MNF due to ideological differences with the church indicated the role of religious institutions in the process of mobilization and the political outcome (Hermana, 1999). Lund (2006) argued in the context of Africa that public authority does not fall exclusively in the realm of government. There is a dispersion of power as organizations enter the field at multiple layers and exercise some form of public authority that can also be seen in the context of Mizoram electoral politics.

Platform for Intervention

Non-state actors in Mizoram have their own way of intervention in electoral politics. These three non-state actors, such as the YMA, the MPF and the PRISM, have distinct but interrelated broader objectives of democratizing the process and strengthening the value of democracy. They have been intervening at various levels and platforms of electoral politics. Several platforms, such as *mitthi in* (house of the deceased), church, seminar, political education, signing of memorandum with political parties and common platform, have been used by non-state actors to intervene in electoral politics in Mizoram.

The signing of a memorandum with political parties restricted the use of force by political parties, the support of underground armed forces and other undue activities that could influence the voters. The use of banners, flags, microphone, posters, etc., is restricted. Altering of voters through money is strictly prohibited. Politicians or political parties caught indulged in 'illegal' activities were announced over by the MPF, which could hamper the status of both the candidate and the political parties. The criteria of candidate were also set out by the MPF, stating that the party must ensure that its candidates are honest and hard-working with high integrity and free from the influence of alcohol and other intoxications. The nature of the intervention of non-state actors in electoral politics and the strategies employed by them towards ensuring their aims and objectives were very much dominated by Christian values and the code of ethics. It is yet another platform where the church maintains its hegemonic power to moralize the voter. Electoral politics has also been an important means for non-state actors to protect the 'Mizo identity'.

Role of Non-state Actors

Earlier, political reservations were an important site of articulating tribal interests and voices. Today, it is the non-state actors who provide a platform to negotiate with the state on issues concerning tribal politics. For instance, non-state actors in Mizoram play a significant role in the process of democratization by intervening in electoral politics. They provide a platform to articulate tribal interests and often take an advantage to mobilize people in respect of their identity.

Non-state actors such as the YMA, the MPF and the PRISM emerged out of the social needs of society. In pre-colonial society, associational life was practised in the form of *Zawlbuk* (boy's dormitory) which brought cohesion and solidarity in society. It was in the colonial period that the emergence of the YMA (one of the largest social associations) in Mizoram provided a platform for the formation of the first political party. In post-colonial society, it was again non-state actors, such as church, who acted as mediator and brought normalcy when the state was in turmoil.

The YMA emerged to bridge the gap under the guidance of Christian missionaries as they felt the necessity to establish a social organization that could replace *Zawlbuk* (Sangkima, 2004; Zorema, 2007). It was formed on 15 June 1935 as Young Lushai Association and the association acquired a new nomenclature on 17 October 1947 as the YMA, as the latter had more general coverage. Since its inception, the YMA has been used as a platform to discuss matters related to politics, as there was no social organization apart from the church and the YMA in the 1940s. The YMA addresses the issues and concerns of sociopolitical needs. It has extensively played an important role in electoral politics by intervening in the electoral process (inclusion and deletion) and preventing political parties from including 'outsiders' as a means of protecting the Mizo identity. Although the political parties are not the official authority dealing with the electoral roll revision, they have the power to influence it. So it was non-state actors, such as the YMA, who often urged political parties not to push cases of 'outsider' in the electoral roll.

The MPF, a church-based association that assists the Election Commission, was formed to ensure a smooth, free and fair election in the state. In that regard, the YMA became a constituent body of the MPF as the leader believed that their objective remained in tune with the MPF. The MPF is an association constituted by a conglomeration of churches and NGOs in Mizoram, set up to reform politics and election in the state. However, due to differences in ideology, churches such as the Baptist Church of Mizoram, the Salvation Army, the Seventh-day Adventist Church, the United Pentecostal Church International and the Isua Krista Kohhran did not join the MPF.

The MPF was formed on 21 June 2006 as a result of the events and incidents associated with the 2003 Mizoram state legislative election. In the 2003 state assembly election, poll-related violence, high expenses and involvement of armed groups were detected; and if this adverse development continued, it was likely to disrupt the status quo of 'peaceful state'/Christian state. Against this backdrop, the MPF was formed to 'reform' politics and the electoral process. The MPF believes that the religious mission is not limited to the spreading of Gospel alone, but it should also strive towards the social aspects of renewal and improvement of the people. Since the Mizos understand that their identity is inextricably linked with Christianity. So in that case, tribal communities are easily mobilized by non-state actors such as the MPF.

Non-state actors and democracy complement each other. Walzer (2003) focuses on the genuine relationship between non-state actors and democracy. Democracy provides a space for citizens to dissent and struggle for their rights and freedom. And it is the non-state actors who mobilized citizens and made the government accountable. In this regard, the intervention of non-state actors with regard to tribal issues can be drawn. A non-state actor such as the PRISM was established in 2006 with the sole objective to strengthen democracy. The PRISM critically looks at the activities of the ruling government or state administration to hold the government accountable. However, in 2017, the PRISM was converted into a political party called 'Peoples Representation for Identity and Status of Mizoram', retaining the abbreviated form of PRISM. The PRISM, as a political party, contested for the 2018 state assembly election. The critical evaluation of the PRISM manifesto shows that the party aims not only to reform the political system but also to deal with tribal issues such as safeguarding and upholding the culture of Mizos, which should go in accordance with Christianity.

Voter Turnout

The intervention of non-state actors has a significant impact on voter turnout in different parliamentary and assembly elections. The intervention of the YMA, the MPF and the PRISM in electoral politics not only deals with tribal issues such as protecting the ethnic-religious identity, but it also results in an increase in voter turnout over a period of time. Table 25.2 indicates that, before the emergence of non-state actors such as the MPF, normal voter turnout was about 60–70 per cent in the case of state assembly elections. Table 25.2 shows the voter turnout of 72.55, 62.99, 68.33, 75.13, 72.63, 81.23, 80.67, 76.32, 78.59, 82.35, 83.41 and 80.03 per cent in 1972, 1978, 1979, 1984, 1987, 1989, 1993, 1998, 2003, 2008, 2013 and 2018, respectively. The voter turnout in 1989 and 1993 increased as compared to the previous elections, with a slight decrease in voter turnout in 1998 and 2003 by 4.35 and 2.08 per cent, respectively.

As has been mentioned earlier, the 2003 state assembly election formed the backdrop of the formation of the MPF. The intervention of the MPF was much visible in the 2008, 2013 and 2018 assembly elections, with high voter turnout. The voter turnout in 2008 increased by 3.37 and 4.82 per cent. However, the voter turnout in 2018 decreased by 3.38 per cent from 2013 election. From 2008 onwards, the normal voter turnout for the past three elections, that is, 2008, 2013 and 2018, increased to 80 per cent. This shows the successful mobilization carried out by non-state actors in state assembly elections.

There is disparity looking at the voter turnout at the national and state elections. The normal voter turnout in state assembly elections was 70–80 per cent over a period of time, while in the national elections it was 50–60 per cent. There could be different reasons

Table 25.2 Comparison of Voter Turnout in Parliamentary and Assembly Elections in Mizoram

Parliamentary Election		Assembly Election	
Year of Elections (%)	Voter Turnout (in %)	Year	Voter Turnout (in %)
1972	72.54	1972	72.55
1977	49.92	1978	62.99
1980	56.12	1979	68.33
1984	NA	1984	75.13
1991	58.06	1987	72.63
1996	73.41	1989	81.23
1998	69.06	1993	80.67
1999	65.31	1998	76.32
2004	63.60	2003	78.59
2009	50.93	2008	82.35
2014	61.69	2013	83.41
2019	63.14	2018	80.03

Source: Election Commission of India.

concerning the low voter turnout in national elections. First, there may be apathy, which would mean the individual's indifference towards or abstention from electoral affairs. Second, there may be a certain scepticism rooted in suspicion towards the contesting candidates and the political parties. Third, there is a degree of alienation or antagonism towards politics and in many cases names of the voters are not included in the list (Mishra, 2014).

There is also a sense of anomie, a feeling of personal ineffectiveness and a sense of divorce from society. It is because of these reasons that some people keep themselves away from the centre of affairs. It appears that the nature of the issues addressed in the national elections failed to appeal the masses. People also in many cases voted to maximize their interest or improve their lives, and the manifesto failed to address the needs of individuals (Banerjee, 2007).

Vote Share

Table 25.3 indicates the vote share of the various political parties in the state assembly elections. The MNF, as a political party, emerged out of the Mizo National Movement, which was fighting for independence from the Indian Union. The emergence of the MNF as a political party has been attributed to the popularity of the MNF among the masses, which can also be seen in the vote share of the political party from 1987 to 1993. The MNF was also successful in bringing forth the protection of the Mizo identity and Christianity to popularize their party. However, their vote share

decreased in the 1998 election, but increased in 2003 and the last assembly election, that is, 2018. The decline in popularity of the MNF in the 1998, 2009 and 2013 elections was mainly attributed to corruption, nepotism and maladministration of the party (Lallianchhunga, 2009). Table 25.3 also indicates that Mizoram state assembly elections are mainly a tussle between two political parties, such as the Congress and the MNF, though there are political parties such as Zoram Nationalist Party, Mizoram People's Conference and Bharatiya Janata Party (BJP). It is the MNF and the Congress that play a dominant role in state assembly elections.

The Congress, on the other hand, is a national political party that brings forth the idea of secularism to mobilize the people. The dominance of the Congress party in the state can also be attributed to the role of Lal Thanhawla in the aftermath of the Mizo National Movement. The fourth election to the legislative assembly of Mizoram was formed by the Congress, headed by Lal Thanhawla in 1984. However, in order to ensure a smooth transition of the agreement between the MNF and the Indian government, Lal Thanhawla stepped down as chief minister and Laldenga sworn in as the chief minister of Mizoram. On the other hand, this built the ground for the Congress to emerge as the dominant party in the state.

The Congress witnessed the highest vote share in the 2013 election, with a percentage of 44.63, the highest vote share in the state assembly elections. However, it was able to retain only 29.98 per cent in the 2018 election. In this regard, the church plays a very important role. The Congress, during it regime,

Table 25.3   Vote Share of the Congress, the MNF and the BJP in Mizoram Assembly (in %)

Political Parties	1987	1989	1993	1998	2003	2009	2013	2018
Congress	32.98	34.84	33.11	29.77	30.06	38.89	44.63	29.98
MNF	36.62	35.29	40.40	24.99	31.69	30.63	28.65	37.0
BJP	NA	NA	3.12	2.50	1.87	0.44	0.37	8.09

Source: Election Commission of India.

introduced the Mizoram Liquor (Prohibition and Control) Act, 2014, known as MLPC Act of 2014, which allowed the opening of liquor shops in the state. This Act was highly criticized not only by the opposition parties but also by the church, stating that it goes against the ethos and teaching of Christianity. The MLPC Act, along with structural biases such as the inclination towards own political party in disbursing development schemes such as the New Land Use Policy and the blooming of a national party such as the BJP in the state, is attributed to the decline of Congress in the 2018 state assembly election.

The comparison of the vote share in the state assembly elections showed that Mizoram was largely unaffected by national politics or the outcome of national politics did not have much impact on the state assembly elections. Rather, it was the interests of tribal communities, such as protecting identity, culture and tradition, the role of church, that determined the outcome of the elections. However, on the other hand, it is interesting to note that the national party, such as the BJP, which was considered as a saffron party, shows an increase in the vote share over a period of time.

The BJP contested the election for the first time in 1993 with a vote share of 3.12 per cent. The difference in the vote share between two national parties, such as the BJP and the Congress, in the 1993 election was 29.99 per cent. The vote difference between the MNF and the BJP was 37.28 per cent. Although BJP's vote share declined in the 2003, 2009 and 2013 elections, it shows a massive increase in 2018 election with 8.09 per cent, with an increase of 7.72 per cent from the 2013 election. It was an achievement for the BJP. From the BJP seat, Buddha Dhan Chakma was elected from the Tuichawng constituency, which is mainly the habitat of the Chakmas. Buddha Dhan Chakma won the seat for the Congress in the 2013 assembly polls. He quit the Congress party as a result of the controversy that arose between him and Congress leader Lal Thanhawla.

Subsequently, this paved the way for the BJP to enter the Mizoram state assembly election. In Mizoram, there was absence of caste-based politics, which is prevalent in other parts of the country. But it was community-based politics, local issues such as the development, accessibility and personality of candidates and the role of church played an important role when it came to state assembly elections.

CONCLUSION

To conclude, Mizoram is known for its peaceful election and high voter turnout, as any other state is not free from identity politics. The intervention of non-state actors in electoral politics shows the political development of the state. Although the credibility of non-state actors has been questioned, they are not free from partiality. In Mizoram, it has been observed that members of non-state actors are often mobilized along ethnic-religious lines. Theoretically, democracy is a process where individuals can freely participate and have a say in governance. Democracy also respects differences and diversity. In this context, democracy leads to power, position and opens up space for discussion and dissension. In a democracy, non-state actors have provided a platform for citizens to dissent. It provides a mechanism for citizens to openly criticize administration policies and other issues. In democracy, the notion of security, stability and unity to pursue patterns of governance is used (Kothari, 2005). This clearly manifests with the involvement of non-state actors in tribal politics of Mizoram. It is crucial to point out that non-state actors who intervene in tribal politics, often on the basis of ethnic religious identity, should not to be criticized as non-democratic. Rather their take on the ethnic-religious lines further enhanced democracy by achieving high voter turnout, ensuring free and fair elections and democratizing the political system in Mizoram. It can be seen that ethnic identity has been an instrument for political mobilization of tribal communities during elections in Mizoram.

REFERENCES

Banerjee, M. (2007). Sacred elections. Economic & Political Weekly, 42(17), 1556–1562.

Darchungnunga, R. (2017). *Kohran leh Mizoram politics* (*Church and Mizoram politics*). Aizawl: Synod Literature and Publication Board.

Elliot, C. (2003). Civil society and democracy: A comparative review essay. In C. Elliot (Ed.), *Civil society and democracy: A reader* (pp. 1–39). New Delhi: Oxford University Press.

Fernandes, W. (2005). Reservation and social change: The case of the northeast. In S. T. Lama-Rewal (Ed.), *Electoral reservations, political representation and social change in India: A comparative perspective* (pp. 83–102). New Delhi: Manohar Publisher.

Hermana, C. (1999). *Zoram politics thli tleh dan* (vol. 1). Aizawl: Presscom.

Kothari, R. (2005). *Rethinking democracy.* Hyderabad: Orient Longman.

Lallianchhunga. (2009). Mizoram: The congress holds its ground. *Economic & Political Weekly, 44*(39), 168–169.

Lund, C. (2006). Twilight institutions: Public authority and local politics in Africa. UK: Blackwell Publishing.

McDuie-Ra, D. (2009). Civil Society, democratization and the search for human security: The politics of the environment, gender and identity in Northeast India. New York: Nova Science.

McMillan, A. (2005). *Standing at the margins: Representation and electoral reservation in India.* New Delhi: Oxford University Press.

Mishra, J. (2014). Interest in politics and political participation. In S. Kumar (Ed.), Indian Youth and Electoral Politics: An Emerging Engagement (pp. 66–77). New Delhi: SAGE Publications.

Nunthara, C. (1996). *Mizoram: Society and polity.* New Delhi: Indus Publishing.

Pachuau, J. L. K. (2014). *Being Mizo: Identity and belonging in northeast India.* New Delhi: Oxford University Press.

Pallas, C. (2013). *Transnational civil society and world bank: Investigating civil society's potential to democratize global governance.* London: Palgrave Macmillan.

Sangkima. (2004). *Essays on the history of the Mizos.* Guwahati: Spectrum.

Walzer, M. (2003). The idea of civil society: A path to social reconstruction. In C. Elliot (Ed.), *Civil society and democracy: A reader* (pp. 63–87). New Delhi: Oxford University Press, 2003.

Warren, E. (2011). Civil society and democracy. In M. Edwards (Ed.), *The Oxford handbook of civil society* (pp. 377–390). New York, NY: Oxford University Press.

Zorema, J. (2007). *Indirect rule in Mizoram (1890–1954).* New Delhi: Mittal Publications.

26

The Debris of Democracy in Nagaland

Jelle J. P. Wouters

Among Nagas, the winds of democratic politics and elections carry debris—the debris of democratic waste; the afterlives of political competition and divisions that show themselves in damaged relationships, lingering resentments, festering wounds of broken promises, compromised moralities and the corrosion of community. 'The devastating tentacles of state elections have spread to all aspects of Naga life: individuals, families, villages, churches, tribes, traditional and government institutions. Elections are the biggest force that is eroding the moral foundations as well as the future of the Naga people, the spiritual and moral authority of the Nagaland Baptist Church Council (NBCC, 2012) warns. The same winds, however, also carry vestiges and signs of past ways of political life still charged in the present. Some pre/anti/extra democratic, non-state political practices and principles are repurposed to operate in the interior of the modern democratic Naga polity, including a resurgence of 'primordial' forms of village, clan and tribal allegiances, and customary law and authority in the adjudicating and allocating of collective votes (Wouters, 2014). What is defied, in this process, is the persuasion of many theorists of modernity that liberal democracy, as the highest expression of political modernity, would overpaint all things premodern, parochial, patriarchal, traditional and customary. Other putatively ancient expressions of 'the customary' no doubt lie discarded, dumped in the recesses of traditions now deemed either obsolete or wrecked beyond repair by the onslaught of India's liberal secular democracy.

Then there is the historical affinity, or growing apace, of democracy and violence in Nagaland; the observation that the arrival of formal democratic institutions and elections coincide with the Naga armed and blood-soaked struggle for the right to self-determination, the dense militarization of the hills, massive state violence and the suspension of the rule of law. Right from the beginning, the democracy process in Nagaland had to stave off rebellion, subversion and insurgent politics pursued by, first, the Naga National Council (NNC) and later by its 'successor' the National Socialist Council of Nagalim (NSCN), in its now rivalling factions, which both advocate the political refusal of the Indian state. To that end, they variously orchestrate election boycotts, threats and intimidation, and physical violence to dissuade Nagas from engaging in India's democracy process (more below). On the other hand, ordinary Naga men and women long wondered, especially in the decades immediately following India's Independence, about the purpose and meaning of the democracy process when the Indian state, in many cases, reveals itself to them as an oppressor and dispenser of violence, rather than as a benign protector. The Indo-Naga war is in a complex ceasefire since 1997, but, at the time of writing, still *sans* political settlement. Well over seven decades (and over five decades of Nagaland statehood) of confluence between democracy and insurgency now raises the question how, and at what cost, the democracy process takes root and operates in a society saturated in political conflict, lawlessness and violence.

This chapter asks what the winds of liberal democracy, and elections in particular, have done to Naga society? What has it turned Naga society into? But equally: what happens in the meeting between liberal democracy and homegrown Naga political theory and praxis. What hybrids are produced by the collusion of divergent sets of political practices and principles, ethics and mores, ethos and telos? And what, in this process, have Nagas done to Indian democracy by applying their agency and cultural creativity to retailor it to their own uses and life worlds? Further, what transpires in the co-existence, or co-becoming as I shall argue, of 'national workers', as cadres of rivalling Naga underground groups are referred to locally, and elected politicians. It is this triple investigation of how democracy changes community, of how community changes democracy and of how the democracy process and protracted armed conflict mix and mingle which leads to a number of insights into the contemporary character of the democratic domain in Nagaland.

What follows is a set of reflections; a broad overview of some of the conundrums, complications and convolutions central to the democracy process of the contemporary historical moment in Nagaland. A caveat before proceeding. Constraints of space in conjunction with the large theme at hand—democracy in Nagaland—make this chapter of necessity selective in its approach and scope. I offer a few impressions, some vignettes and large summations, and in doing so I privilege particular (and no doubt debatable) readings of the democracy process locally. I do, however, provide references to places where my arguments are either elaborated with historical and ethnographic detail or complicated by other perspectives.

CONTOURS AND CONTEXT

Liberal democracy, the way applied here, is the name for a political epoch in which democratic representation, party-based elections, majority votes, individual autonomy and choice, and equal voting rights have become the major forces that determine the form and substance of political life. Its 'imposition' among the Naga (and tribal communities more widely) tells of a big transformation: indigenous political arrangements and values that took hundreds of years of adapting and nourishing are to be replaced by the institutions and ideology of liberal democracy, most notably by its hallmark principle of elections as the prime mover of political life.

In the contemporary historical moment, liberal democracy in Nagaland, though, confronts both a traditional-cultural sentience that was alternatively democratic (more below) and a state-sanctioned protective and distinctly non-liberal regime of 'ethno-territoriality' (Baruah, 2013). The enactment of Nagaland state, in 1963, is an envisaged (but failed) political compromise to the Naga demand for sovereignty. It comes with a constitutional amendment, namely Article 371A which grants political autonomy and institutionalizes a regime of ethno-territoriality—a form of governmentality, or ethno-governmentality, and politics that essentialises the ties between Naga ethnic tribal belonging and exclusive territorial rights.[1] It promotes variegated citizenship that locally separates those deemed autochthonous from non-local 'strangers' (even if they carry the same nationality yet do not belong locally). In Nagaland, thence, autochthony, not Indian citizenship, serves as the basic criterion for entitlements to rights, employment reservation, access to state resources and benefits and, crucially here, eligibility to stand for political office. As it stands, 59 out of 60 electoral seats that make up the Nagaland Assembly are reserved for Scheduled Tribes, which in Nagaland means *de facto* Nagas. This electoral reservation is divorced from demographic changes and complex political economies that increasingly upset, certainly in Nagaland's urban areas, any simple conflation between Naga ethnic tribal identity and territory, and thus guarantees the perpetuation of a Naga political class.

Critics see in ethno-territoriality (also characteristic, in varying manifestations, of other hill states in Northeast India) an affront to liberal statecraft and universal citizenship. In Nagaland, after all, only those who 'belong' enjoy rights. For those who reside there, even if for the longest time, but do not ethnically originate from Nagaland, these are regimes of bio-political neglect and disenfranchisement. Defenders of this constitutional amendment, however, point to the threat of Nagas' demographic and cultural devouring by much larger populations from neighbouring states. They see in the current existence of exclusive ethnic tribal and territorial rights, and the reservation of nearly all electoral seats, the last line of defence for Naga culture, identity and political autonomy to survive.

The reservation of 59 out of 60 seats precludes elections in Nagaland from unfolding along a volatile tribal versus non-tribal fault line. In Nagaland, unmistakably, it is the tribes that rule. What it does not prevent, however, is the democracy process from descending into an intra-Naga and inter-tribal contest. This reveals itself most forcibly in the politics of delimitation. By the time the British Raj withdrew from the (then) Naga Hills District, the structure of Naga society had already become such that there was a power struggle among the tribes (Wouters, 2017). It is during the post-statehood, new democratic era that the political significance of tribal identification and belonging augment further: most constituencies are delimited and divided tribe wise, as are development allocations, government jobs and other state projects. In this process, one tribe is pitched against another in a near permanent struggle over access to, and ownership of, the state as well as, crucially here, in the number of electoral seats assigned to each tribal district. And while post-statehood governance in Nagaland becomes soon mired in narratives of corruption, Naga politicians are simultaneously known, and praised by their constituents, for appropriating, accumulating and redirecting government employment and state resources to their respective clans, villages and tribes, indicating, for one thing, that most in Nagaland maintain a very sectional sighting of the state (Wouters, 2018a). Consequently, a Naga tribe that 'owns' a larger number of electoral seats, through their numerical preponderance in multiple constituencies, is anticipated to experience higher levels of material development compared to those Naga tribes with fewer electoral seats within their broad control.

---

[1] Article 371A reads: 'Notwithstanding anything in this Constitution, no act of parliament in respect of (i) religious or social practices of the Nagas, (ii) Naga customary law and procedure, (iii) administration of civil and criminal justice involving decisions according to Naga customary law, (iv) ownership and transfer of land and its resources, shall apply to the State of Nagaland unless the Legislative Assembly of Nagaland by a resolution so decides'.

The upshot of this is intra-Naga competition of tribe-wise electoral representation. And this has wide ramifications. Agrawal and Kumar (2018) show convincingly how vastly inflated population censuses in Nagaland, especially the 2001 census, result from Naga tribes deliberately exaggerating their population numbers in view of the impending delimitation exercise, and so in pursuit of either protecting or expanding 'their' electoral seats. Taking cognisance of this, and in a legislative order, the Ministry of Law & Justice decreed in 2008 that the scheduled delimitation exercise in Nagaland is 'likely to arouse the sentiments of the hilly and tribal people'. It explains: 'The State of Nagaland is inhabited by various tribes, each having their own distinct traditional boundaries, on the basis of which the existing district and assembly constituency boundaries were largely demarcated, thereby making the fresh delimitation exercise involving transfer of assembly seats from some tribal/linguistic to another unacceptable', as this would disrupt the 'tribal equilibrium and peace and public order.' The legislative order concludes by deferring the delimitation exercise in Nagaland 'until further orders'. In deliberating this decision, the centre also considers 'the delicate law and order situation in the State and the ongoing cease fire and the peace talks', and it is to the insurgency–democracy complex that the next section turns.

THE DOUBLE LIVES OF NAGA INSURGENCY AND DEMOCRACY

What I pose, in this section, is that threads of Naga insurgency sheathe or at least penetrate the democracy process in Nagaland. This penetration is then forced ('NSCN-IM accused of hindering elections', the *Indian Express* (2008) reports), then by connivance (an underground leader 'called a meeting with Waromung Village Council where he demanded 500 votes from the village for a particular candidate' (*Morung Express*, 2013)) and then by consensus, as happened in 1998 when the Naga public by and large abstained from casting their votes in support and solidarity with the NSCN-IM after it entered into a ceasefire with the Indian state. Rather than constituting distinct and antagonistic political domains, Naga insurgency and democratic politics and governance imbricate into each other's politics, to the point where they nearly everywhere fuse into a single political field. For many Nagas, this is part of the tragedy of the Naga Movement. A struggle that once began with the near collective aim of securing Naga independence has over the past decades not only factionalized (Panwar, 2017) and 'turned internal' (McDuie-Ra & Kikon, 2016, p. 3) but lost focus with 'national workers' involving themselves with the micro-politics of elections. National workers at different levels do so despite the Naga rebel vanguard formally condemning both assembly and parliamentary elections as 'Indian elections imposed on Naga soil' and for waylaying Nagas' right to self-determination. The NBCC (2012), which presents itself as the spiritual and moral compass of Naga society, publicly disapproves of these 'unholy' allegiances:

> National workers should not be made, to be used as tools or puppets by some selfish politicians as their aspiration and pursuit is different from the constitutional impetus. Their involvement has been very annoying because by using arms, threats with dire consequences etc. they have been stealing the rights of the general public. National workers should oppose any vested politician/s who solicits their support to scare away the public and disrupt the democratic election.

In defiance of such (and other) statements, across Nagaland, and so for several decades, the electoral landscape is layered with state and non-state actors coexisting and co-feeding on development resources—a dyadic I have elsewhere captured as 'the insurgency complex' and the 'underground effect' (Wouters, 2018b). These mutualities shape the electoral domain where overground/underground link-ages are many and varied. They also fluctu-ate with local allegiances between national workers and politicians changing from one constituency and elections to the next. At the grassroots, the power and influence national workers hold are everywhere tangible (all the more so after the 1997 ceasefire, which ena-bles national workers to change their jungle hide-outs for public lives), to the extent that few, if any, Nagaland politicians can dream of capturing a constituency without engaging them, either directly (with national workers influencing electoral outcomes) or indirectly (with national workers agreeing not to inter-fere); both these options, in Nagaland, are not the natural condition of democracy and elections but represent hard-worked and hard-bargained political accomplishments.

Politicians cultivate relations with national workers allegedly 'for their own [political] survival and selfish gain' (Ao, 2013, p. 3). More often than not, these 'deals' consist of monetary donations and impunity in exchange for national workers' support during elections, with the latter exerting 'muscle power' to secure particular voting patterns if they must (Dev, 2006). We find, for instance, a particular Naga faction intimidating a non-Naga can-didate in the multi-ethnic town of Dimapur in favour of a Naga politician (Kuotsu & Walling, 2018, p. 116) or national workers ordering villagers to not vote for a particular party (Wouters, 2018b, p. 246). At other times, national workers seize the initiative and sup-port 'inefficient candidates who often become their puppets and together they siphon off development funds' (Ezung, 2012: 2).

Not, however, always spurred by a politics of pure material interest, overground/under-ground interlinkages may also be formed by ideological congruity as several Naga politi-cians are known to harbour sympathy for the Naga struggle or for a particular Naga faction. Affective kinship ties and social bonds of clan, village and tribe too readily cut across any

overground/underground divide, so making the Nagaland state, including its democracy process, and Naga insurgency function within a single social network. But regardless of what cements the relationship, all across Nagaland 'the underground factor' is an intricate part of 'election talk' and 'reports of insurgent groups having influenced the outcome of electoral politics have dominated popular discourse in the state' (Amer, 2014, p. 10). The concept of 'symbiosis'—mutually beneficial political living—aptly captures the recent genealogy and (often murky) character of the democ-racy process in Nagaland (on the 'under-ground factor' in Nagaland more widely, see Bhaumik, 2009, p. 210; Dev, 2006; Misra, 1987; Ngaithe, 2014; Singh, 2004; Wouters, 2018b, p. 238–276).

We now have a picture emerging of a democratic playing field that is worked and reworked by both constitutional and 'un' or 'extra'-constitutional forces that variously compete, conflict and connive. Added to this is the notorious Armed Forces Special Powers Act (AFSPA), that pitch-dark piece of leg-islation which, following the declaration of an area as 'disturbed', by a stroke of the governor's pen, drives a wedge between the law and justice by reducing selected people from right-bearing citizens into suspicious subjects (see Mamdani, 1996), even to bare life (Agamben, 2005). It assigns military and paramilitary forces with the lethal labour of shooting to kill, not just in an encounter or insurgency operation, but anywhere, anytime and anyone on the mere grounds of suspicion. Further add near absolutely legal impunity for the armed forces and we find ourselves in the dark underbelly of state power and violence. First promulgated in 1958, the AFSPA con-tinues to blanket Nagaland in legal darkness. The AFSPA's inner logic, Dolly Kikon (2009, p. 272) remarks, aptly, revolves around the categories of 'disturbed area' and 'suspicious people', categories that are deeply entangled, even mutually constitutive: 'the area inhabited by suspicious persons will eventually become a disturbed area, and those inhabiting a disturbed area fall under suspicion', thus fuelling a seemingly endless cycle of legal exceptionalism and state violence, but in which democratic institutions nevertheless exist and elections take place.

While some see the politics of pain, torture and trauma the AFSPA produces and institutionalizes as an unfortunate yet 'necessary force to avert the pain that "tortures the nation"', a pain caused by the anti-state rebellions and 'terror' in the region (Ningthouja, 2016, p. 239), critics, of which there are many more, emphasize the law's deeply undemocratic character. 'Can democracy function in militarized societies?', Dolly Kikon (2015, p. 2834) asks as she stresses the 'extremely undemocratic and militarized conditions under which electoral systems are introduced [in Nagaland]'. Her answer is a resounding 'no', which she accompanies by a devastating critique of the Indian state's inability to engage ethno-national movements and demands within a democratic framework.

Besides ardent activism that seeks AFSPA's removal, this law, or more accurately the suspension of the law, draws substantial and sophisticated scholarship that invites Derrida's distinction between law and justice, Agamben's state of exception, Benjamin's notion of sovereign violence and Foucauldian insights into discussing the peculiar relation between law, democracy and violence the AFSPA creates in Nagaland and in other parts of Northeast India (Farrelley, 2009; Gaikwad, 2009; Kikon, 2009; McDuie-Ra, 2009). What the AFSPA compromises, this body of scholarship agrees, is the very existence of democracy—both in its institutions and spirit—in the region; what, after all, is democracy's worth, they protest, when lawlessness is legitimized, civil society curtailed and the rule of law suspended; and what is left of the popular, if simplistic, equation between the right to vote and freedom when elections ensue within a permanent state of exception in which the law is far removed from justice.

To trace and place how this muddled and volatile political morass—both in the symbiosis of electoral and insurgent politics, and in the law's suspension—we need to account for the origins and evolution of the Naga uprising and the contested creation of Nagaland state in 1963. In the beginning, the fault lines were more clearly drawn. Seeing India as an invading and colonizing force, the NNC, which spearheads the Naga armed uprising from the 1950s onwards, resisted and rebelled Nagas' enclosure into postcolonial India and in an act of political refusal boycotted India's first general elections in 1952. Despite the NNC boycott, the Naga historian Horam (1988, p. 50) recalls:

> The government went ahead with the election arrangements and the entire election paraphernalia was made ready, electoral rolls were prepared, polling booths were set up, ballot boxes were made and Returning Officers were stationed. Nagas, on the other hand, were indifferent to the goings on and went about their daily work with studied calm and the whole election show proved to be a mockery as a result of an election that never was.

The NNC similarly boycotted India's second general elections in 1957. This time, however, the boycott was less definite. Three aspirant Naga politicians filed their nominations and were subsequently elected unopposed into the Assam assembly. Polling was limited, however.

Violence now escalates and turns the Naga highlands into a swathe of death and despair. Despite being outnumbered many times over, the NNC's Naga army fights Indian military and paramilitary forces to a standstill. India's central government shifted gear and in 1963 enacted Nagaland state. In creating Nagaland state, the centre empowered an assemblage of the so-called 'moderate' or 'liberal' Nagas who organized themselves as the Naga People's Convention and distanced themselves from the NNC-led Naga struggle. They became the first generation of Nagaland politicians within the Indian dispensation (Sema, 1986; Wouters, 2019).

In modern Naga political history, few events are as controversial and contested as the enactment of Nagaland state. It divides Nagas politically into two—the people of the new state and the people supporting Naga self-determination—although from the beginning, this boundary has many crossings (Wouters, 2018d).[2] The NNC, on its part, rejected the new state's legitimacy to govern: 'They are traitors. Every one of them', as A. Z. Phizo, the NNC president, condemned the Naga leaders who bring statehood. Contrary to expectations by the centre, the making of Nagaland state only intensifies Naga insurgency: 'All those wishfully expecting the collapse of the Underground after the granting of statehood', Horam (1988, p. 12) writes, 'found themselves to be wrong... On the contrary there was an ever greater explosion of Naga nationalist sentiment.'

The first election was announced in 1964. The NNC staunchly opposed these and threatened both politicians and prospective voters. Consequently, elections were held under heavy security arrangements, as are all subsequent Nagaland elections. So dense is the militarization of polling booths that Sen (1974) dubs elections in Nagaland as 'operation election.' Divergent political positions on Nagaland state and elections reveal themselves not just between 'overground' and 'underground' Nagas, however. Political

parties, too, articulate different perspectives. For the Nagaland Nationalist Organisation (NNO), the party that won the 1964 elections, the 'achievement of Statehood was a triumph of the people's will' (cited in Jimomi, 2009, p. 49). Its later political adversary, the United Democratic Front (UDF) took a different view: 'People of no other state in India have made sacrifices like the Naga, so much so that the state of Nagaland is not considered by the Nagas as a gift, but as a state created for a price dearly paid; a sacrifice of over ten thousands lives' (cited in Nibedon, 1978, p. 282). The UDF won the 1974 state elections, but was soon dismissed by the centre which imposed presidential rule, accusing the UDF of 'indirectly encouraging the secessionist activities of the Federal Government of Nagaland [the NNC's political wing]' (Horam, 1988, p. 149).

As Naga insurgency continuous, complicates and increasingly turns into an interfactional struggle over historical legitimacy, ideological differences and territorial (and tribal and taxation) domination within Naga lands (as opposed to an earlier collective struggle against the Indian state) (Wouters, 2018b), the dynamics between Nagaland politicians and national workers begin to change. No longer are national workers merely opposing 'Indian elections.' Per contra, they increasingly intervene in it. Murry (2007, 138) writes: 'the political scenario in the state of Nagaland began to change rapidly after 1975 when some more dashing political parties having the support of the underground Nagas emerged and began to take more interest in party politics.'

---

[2] The making of Nagaland state divided the Nagas also in other ways as the boundaries of Nagaland were drawn to the exclusion of Naga communities in Manipur, Assam and Arunachal Pradesh. Naga politicians, underground groups and civil society organizations have long insisted on the political integration of ancestral Naga territories within India. For instance, a resolution unanimously adopted by the Nagaland assembly in 1994 goes: 'Whereas, by quirk of history, the Naga-inhabited areas have been disintegrated and scattered under different administrative units without the knowledge and consent of the Nagas ... Whereas, the Nagas irrespective of territorial barriers have strong desire to come together under one administrative roof ... the Assembly, therefore resolves to urge upon the Government of India and all concerned to help the Nagas achieves this desired goal (cited in Chasie, 2005, 61).

Pivotal to this process is the fissuring of the Naga Movement into a myriad of factions and parallel governments—often identifying themselves with a confusing, near identical set of abbreviations: NSCN-IM, NSCN-K, NSCN-KK, NSCN-U, NSCN-R, NNC-NA, NNC-A, GPRN, FGN-A, FGN-NA and so on. What follows from this is an ever more complicating political terrain with different parties, politicians and ruling governments cultivating different relations with different underground factions and national workers.

To illustrate: during the 2003 state elections, NSCN-IM functionaries demanded Naga electors to 'vote for the Democratic Alliance of Nagaland (DAN) and oust the Congress from power'. The NSCN insisted that voting the DAN into power would be 'in the interest of peace and permanent settlement of the Naga problem', unlike the S. C. Jamir led Congress Party, which is 'subverting the negotiations' (Bhaumik, 2009, p. 210). The Congress with S. C. Jamir as its chief minister, meanwhile, had the 'backing of the other major faction of the NSCN-led by Khaplang' (*India Today*, 1998). Thus, the post-statehood democratic arena in Nagaland became complicated by the remapping of Naga factionalism unto it. These overground/underground linkages are well known locally. Ask any Naga voter about the specific underground affiliations of a particular politician or party in his or her constituency and most will offer a detailed account.

But even as the 'underground factor' becomes a sophisticated part of democracy and elections in Nagaland, it is simultaneously emphasized that Nagas need a political solution, more than they require recurrent elections. In 1998, a year into the ceasefire, this sentiment revealed itself in the popular slogan: 'No election, but solution', and a call for the deferment of Nagaland elections. The centre refused to heed and elections progressed regardless, even as all Nagaland parties, except for the Congress party, abstained from filing candidates. 'We will ignore the state government', a spokesperson of the Naga People's Movement for Democracy stated, then continued: 'We have never really recognised it [Nagaland government]. We are in the process of discussing a solution to the Naga problem with the Centre, and the chances are that if the talks succeed, the government will be dismissed anyway' (cited in *India Today*, 1998). This sentiment of present-day Nagaland institutions possibly dissolving is widespread. A. Jamir (2002, p. 3) writes: 'Nagaland state is viewed to be a temporary arrangement, pending a final political settlement'. Needless to say, this sentiment greatly complicates Nagas' sense of belonging to Nagaland state, and the validity of the democratic process locally.

In elections following the 1998 deferment call, similar boycotts were deliberated by Naga tribal and civil society bodies (*Assam Tribune*, 2013), but none of these came about in definite form, and in most constituencies a complex overground/underground connectivity remained a composite part of elections.

'SATANIC' ELECTIONS AND A CHRISTIAN CRITIQUE

Can Naga society survive liberal democracy and elections? If this question sounds incongruous (the act of voting, after all, is branded as a liberating, transformative force and democratic institutions are supposedly nurturing individual freedoms), ask anyone in Nagaland about the democracy process, and about elections in particular, and their replies are usually suffused with frustration, anguish, even despair, and not just because of the 'underground factor' discussed in the previous section.

This frustration with liberal democracy, in its contemporary sense, is expressed at two levels. First, there is the acute self-confession that Nagas—the elected and electors alike—have abused democratic institutions and elections, turning them into a free-for-all contest over power and influence spurred by greed and gluttony. Agonized over, here, is the ubiquitous role of money, gifts and favours that are used to secure voters' exclusive political loyalties; a flourishing, that is, of corruption and clientelism (and its cognates) (see Chasie, 2005; Ezung, 2012; Singh, 2004, p. 162; Tinyi & Nienu, 2018; Wouters, 2018a). The work of Arild Ruud (2001) in West Bengal comes to mind here. Ruud tells us how villagers use terms such as 'dirty' (*nungra*), 'disturbance' (*gandagol*) and 'poison' (*bish*) to describe politics and politicians whose actions they evaluate as 'something unsavoury that morally upright people would not touch' (2001, p. 116). But it is not just politicians who prove to be crooked, unprincipled and untrustworthy, rural villagers perceive the game itself as dirty: 'it was inherently so and sullying to those that participated in it' (Ruud, 2001, p. 117). This experience that politics, in its contemporary democratic sense, is 'dirty' is also widespread in Nagaland. This moral evaluation, though, does not prevent many from enthusiastically participating in it.

The second frustration is not primarily with the misuse of democratic institutions and principles but whirls around the particularistic moral logic and vision of the liberal democratic system itself. Naga elders, in particular, question the underlying ideas of equal voting rights, individual autonomy and party-based elections, which they see as undermining kinship hierarchies and moral values of consensus building they hold dear (Wouters, 2018c, 2015b). Both these frustrations are accompanied by a local rejoinder in the form of a Christian and culturalist critique, respectively. This section engages the first frustration and the envisaged 'Christian healing' of a now wounded electoral process.

'Our villagers don't know how to do elections', a pastor in the Chakhesang Naga village where I carried out prolonged fieldwork and which I call Phugwumi told me. Elucidating his point, the pastor compared the election season to a time of 'spiritual darkness'. 'It is hard to explain', he said, 'but as soon as elections are announced, most villagers metamorphose into something else, almost magically, and forget all about Christ. In the election season only money speaks'.[3]

'I don't have small change anymore', a village shopkeeper had told me the previous day as I tried to break a 500-rupee note at his counter. 'During election time everyone pays with big notes', thus substantiating the pastor's assertion.

Were Nagaland elections computed, Misra (1987, p. 2193) analysed in the 1980s, they might well be the nation's 'costliest'. Pundits and commentators on Nagaland elections subscribe to this view and routinely accuse Nagaland politicians of abusing democracy into 'an industry to earn through malpractice' (Kiewhuo, 2002, p. 61). They equally berate Naga voters for transforming 'campaign inducements [into] a sort of industry' (Amer, 2014, p. 4), thus resulting in a politics of reciprocal deceit. 'Issues are often subdued by money and the dispensation of favours by the candidate during election campaigns', Amer (2014, p. 19) writes. She concludes: 'The pervasiveness of these abuses have [*sic*] created widespread public scepticism about all electoral exercises'.

That scepticism is indeed widespread may be deduced from a series of opinion polls the popular Nagaland daily *The Morung Express* conducts. Just 17 per cent of the respondents, for instance, think 'yes' to the question: 'Do you think the Nagaland electorate is ready to vote for honest, sincere and

---

[3] In the colloquial Nagaland is habitually referred to as a 'Christian state' in view of the vast majority of its inhabitants professing the Christian faith. The arrival and spread of Christianity have been extensively documented and theorized (Joshi, 2012; Thomas, 2016).

visionary candidates in the 2018 elections?'. One respondent explained: '80 percent can be bought (money and jobs), 5 percent are just ignorant, 5 percent are apathetic, and only 10 percent are conscientious voters' (*Morung Express*, 2017a). To the question: 'Are you convinced by the Chief Minister's statement that his government is keen on changing the system to check corruption', 85 percent answer with a resounding 'no.' 'Neither him nor any politician, ruling or opposition', one respondent said. Another added: 'Election round the corner, need more money to buy votes' (*Morung Express*, 2017b). And to the question: 'Do you agree the present legislators are so blinded by political power and vested interests that they have lost the moral authority to lead?', as many as 92 per cent of the respondents said 'yes'. One of them told: 'They have fallen to the lowest pit. Lack of principles, no vision for better Nagaland, greed and thirst for their selfish needs have blinded them all beyond repair' (*Morung Express*, 2017c). These are of course perceptions, not necessarily facts, but they do illustrate, with crystal clarity, the widespread disillusionment.

'Take our church', a village deacon weighs in the conversation I had with the Phugwumi pastor. 'The closer to polling day the fewer villagers attend Sunday services. Deep down villagers know that they are engaging in selfish and immoral behaviour. They become afraid to show their face before God'. The deacon's forecast is correct and as polling day draws closer, church attendance dwindles, and in the service immediately preceding election day, the congregation fits into the first few rows of an otherwise packed church.

The exchange of money for votes and election-induced immoralities, or notions that politics is inherently 'dirty', are of course not exclusive to Nagaland. This is reported across the country (Hansen, 1999; Ruud, 2001). Where in India are the voters not paid, fed and clothed by aspirant politicians (Piliavsky, 2014), and where are election seasons not accompanied by heightened tension, volatility and sporadic violence? What is different in Nagaland is the existence of a vocal Christian critique against such practices, and the framing, as we will see, of elections as a spiritual issue.

An experienced dissonance between Christian teachings and electoral practices is frequently invoked in Phugwumi (and across Nagaland), particularly by church and village elders who question the moral and spiritual standards of particularly younger generations during election seasons. Well into his eighties, *Athe* (a Chokri classificatory term for grandfather) participated in all Nagaland's post-statehood elections and, in his judgement, electoral politics has already moved beyond redemption: 'even if Jesus Christ will descend from Heaven and contest an election in Nagaland, he will not be voted in'. Several other village elders describe elections as 'Satan's game' because, they say, it seduces otherwise upright villagers into sins, falsehoods and immoralities. In a society where Christian teaching, rhetoric, and ritual structure inundate social life, and where the figure of the devil is frequently invoked as a force of destruction, temptation and evil, this local reading of elections as Satanic in its societal effects demands careful attention.

In Taussig's (1980) classic treatise of the 'devil pact', we find plantation-labourers in Colombia bartering their soul in order to increase their productivity and wages. The money they so earn is, however, barren and cannot be used to buy land or to nourish one's family, for that will bring the devil into one's intimate orbit. It can, therefore, only be spent immediately and on luxury goods and indulgences. Taussig sees this 'devil-pact' as a parable for the transformation of a previous peasant economy based on 'value' to a capitalist economy based on 'exchange value', and the alienation that results from this. I postulate, suggestively so, that it is not too far a stretch to adapt certain features of Taussig's 'devil pact' to capture how elections cause

Naga villagers to become alienated from the village as a reciprocal community with shared concerns and ends, and the resultant local evaluation of election seasons as a period of spiritual eclipse.

When village and church elders call elections satanic and devilish, and see them as shrouding the village in temporary darkness, they apprehend as Satan's influence an experienced transition from an earlier non-state and 'pre-liberal' politics of consensus-making, virtue and community reciprocity to a contemporary electoral politics based on exaggerated individualism, deceit and competitive self-advancement, which threatens the contours of community and Christian life. It is in this domain, of societal disintegration, that dark and devilish forces not just reveal themselves but are experienced as gaining the upper hand during election seasons, temporarily suspending the desired reign of Christ. And if Taussig's plantation workers are afraid to spend their wages earned through the 'devil pact' on family sustenance, for Naga villagers the devil's prerogative of individualism, greed and dishonesty become embodied, temporarily altering the quality of a person's soul and moral substance, and in whose condition they fear to face the divine, as revealed by the deacon's observation and explanation of dwindling church attendance during election seasons.

That Nagaland elections have become a 'spiritual issue' is indeed the stance of the NBCC, which professes as its 'prophetic moral duty' to 'fight the ugly face of the election'. It states: 'It is the responsibility of [Christian] believers to work in building a democratic and ethnically acceptable process of election in Naga society'. In the wake of the 2013 state assembly elections, the NBCC launched a clean election campaign (as it had done during previous elections with varying degrees of success). The campaign began with the publication and distribution of a booklet titled: *Engaging the Powers:*

Elections—a Spiritual Issue for Christians. It reads:

> We know that the Election Code of Conduct laid down by the Government of India itself is good enough to conduct a clean and fair election. More so, as [a] Christian dominated State, Nagaland could have shown to the world the conduct of election in a much better way based on Biblical principles. The Church has raised this issue during every election in the state but we have gone against God whom we worship. Should we continue to invite the wrath of God?

For the NBCC, the buying and selling of votes, as well as proxy voting and booth capturing, are not just evidence of a perverse and dissolute democratic politics but, more significantly, constitute an abomination before God. The booklet decries: 'In the past elections, we have seen that money has been placed at the top, and God at the bottom'. It then continues:

> Candidates have used money to woe voters, while on the other hand, voters demand money from the candidates for their votes... Voters should also realise that demanding money for votes is wrong as God desires His people to choose the right leader without resorting to any unfair practices.

To achieve clean elections, the NBCC framed a set of guidelines, which pastors and deacons across the state were instructed to impress upon their congregations. In Phugwumi's church premises, a banner with the following text appears:

> Clean Election Campaign—Buying Votes, Selling Votes, Booth Capturing, Proxy Voting, Etc, are against the law and against moral and spiritual ethics. *Dzieyha ze mu khrü cuha kephouma zo* [selling and buying of votes is a sin].

Other NBBC instructions include:

> Establishment of Camps in colonies, town and villages encourages and often becomes a breeding ground of all kinds of malpractices such as,

use of alcohol, drugs, gambling, sexual immoralities, violence, etc. It disturbs the already fragile social fabric of towns and villages, and further endangers the society and the future of the youth. Therefore, the practice of establishing camps should be stopped....

While the NBBC voice is loud, their instructions often fall on deaf ears. The following is a description, more or less taken directly from my fieldnotes, about one such political camp enacted in Phugwumi in the wake of polling day, and which I visit several times.

Every evening village youth congregate in the political camp that belongs to [name redacted]. They spend their time gambling and playing carom board. They play against money, while drinking beer or rum. Both the liquor and the money they receive from their politician, who also pays them for each evening/night they spend in his camp [as a show of his strength]. The youths call themselves the politician's 'back-up force', just in case something untoward happens and muscle-power is needed. During election seasons bouts of violence are, after all, always a real possibility. Both gambling and liquor are prohibited by the village council (while Nagaland itself is a 'dry state'), as well as condemned as sinful by the village church. 'This is election time', one village youth replies as I carefully inquire into their activities. 'Usual rules don't apply'.

THE VOICE OF THE ELDERS AND CONSENSUS CANDIDATES

Democratic theory of the normative kind has difficulty viewing cultural variations in democratic life worlds as possibly democratic, and something able to be theorized. Rather, modern democracy, especially its liberal variant, is projected as a larger good and a good everyone should treasure and defend. From this vantage, elements of culture that do not contribute to the 'proper' functioning of democratic institutions and elections are seen as defective and in need of remodelling. In its extreme version, this argument holds that

'politics change a culture and save it from itself' (Daniel Patrick Moynihan, cited in Huntington, 2000, p. xiv).

This final section shows for the Naga how such perspectives are ahistorical and unresponsive to genuine differences in political sentience and morality. It does so by invoking the concept and praxis of village and clan consensus candidates, ubiquitous in places across Nagaland. Prior to elections, Along Longkumer writes, a 'pre-arranged agreement' is regularly concluded between 'village elders and political parties to select the consensus-candidate to be supported by the entire village' (cited in Amer, 2014, p. 10). At other times, it is not the village but the clan that turns into the unit of voting (Wouters, 2014). Either way, individual and autonomous balloting is regularly substituted with consensus making and the *selection* of a particular candidate, to whom subsequently all votes are cast. But rather than an electoral malpractice, plain and simple, I argue that this practice can also be read as a Naga culturalist critique and adaptation of the liberal democratic framework.

Before I proceed any further, I must stress that traditional Naga 'village republics' (Wouters, 2017) were diverse in their political systems and sentiments. Prevailing (colonial) descriptions about their form and functioning are one of nobles and commoners (Fürer-Haimendorf, 1973), bodies of elders (Mills, 1926), autocratic chiefs (Fürer-Haimendorf, 1939), the absence of chiefs (Hutton, 1921) and extreme egalitarianism (Woodthorpe, 1881). On the whole, they represent a continuum with hereditary autocracy, if not near dictatorship, and radical democracy at its opposite ends, with (a section of) the Konyak Naga usually associated with the former and the Angami and Chakhesang Nagas as the most obvious example of the latter. My engagement here pertains to Phugwumi village and the Chakhesang Naga and is, therefore, not necessarily equally applicable to all other Naga tribes.

In Phugwumi, the traditional figuration of 'the political' was deeply immersed in an archive of social knowledge and beliefs. It functioned within a wider matrix of relatedness based on genealogical and affective networks of clan and territory, and presided over a moral economy that, in principle, guaranteed protection and subsistence to all villagers. Of course, it is easy to romanticize the past, especially as it recedes deeper into the chambers of history. This impulse should be guarded against. Conflicts between clans and villages were frequent and fierce, and episodes of gruesome headhunting are impossible to ignore in the reading and reconstruction of Naga political history. On another level, however, Phugwumi, and most Naga villages, were intensely communal in nature.

This community ideology was not based on the value of equality, however. It also had many drawers and compartments and does not allow for simple generalizations. Here, I focus on two of its structuring principles, namely differentiation in the sonority of individuals' political voice and, what I will call, 'community think'. In Phugwumi, the wisdom and virtue accumulated by the elderly and meritorious were acknowledged and highly valued, and the sonority of their political voice often muffled the viewpoints of the young, the 'ordinary' and, alas, women. In this type of power relations, villagers knew when to listen and to conform or to speak and to 'command' depending on their status in the kinship and social hierarchy, which of course changed throughout a person's life. Ultimately, during the non-state epoch, Phugwumi was a sovereign order and the political form, positioning and strategies followed by the villagers were to secure protection and welfare for the village community. To this end, the Phugwumi villagers simply found no rationality in giving all villagers equal say in political affairs as there was ample evidence that some villagers were far more experienced and knowledgeable than others.

But before I explain this further, first a few remarks about the marginalization of Naga women in the political domain—both past and present. Village political space was hyper-masculine in nature and disenfranchised women. Such disenfranchisement reproduced itself in the contemporary democratic domain and Nagaland now has a 'patriarchal democracy', including the dubious distinction of being the only state in India that never elected a woman into its assembly. One of the most common misconceptions about Naga (and tribal) society, Hausing (2017, p. 245) writes, is their 'egalitarianism'. Hausing invokes the controversy, which erupted in 2017, over attempts by the Nagaland government to allocate 33 per cent reservation to women in urban local bodies, which is in compliance with the Indian Constitution. What followed was an upsurge of societal protest, led by Naga tribal and civil society bodies, each of them patriarchal in their form and functioning, and each of them insisting that women reservation goes against the grain of Naga traditional and cultural values. While Naga women have long been thought of as 'emancipated' compared to their 'mainland' counterparts, their exclusion in the political and public domain is now recognized as an urgent concern (on the marginalization of women in the political domain; Amer, 2013; Jamir, 2012; Khiamniungan, 2018; Kikon, 2002; Kuotsu & Walling, 2018).

Besides female exclusion, homespun Naga political theory and praxis were also structured by kinship and social hierarchies, and on purpose. Wealth, derived from agriculture, communicated virtue and amplified the sonority of the rich man's voice, provided, he turns himself into a feast giver and serviced the poor; a ritualized social institution known in anthropological annals as the Naga 'feast of merit' (*zhotho müza* in Chokri). Elsewhere, I argue how contemporary election feasts, invariably and lavishly hosted by Nagaland politicians in villages, are a (contested) remapping of this past moral economy (Wouters, 2015b). Brave warriors, too, were revered. 'Headhunters', Venusa Tinyi (2017, p. 126) says, 'were highly respected and honoured by all... Among the Chakhesang, only a warrior had the privilege of standing on the monolith stone when it was being pulled in honour of the couple performing the *Feast of Merit*'. Akin to the wealthy and generous, the voices of successful and courageous warriors thus could rely on a respectful audience.

But perhaps most importantly, it was the wisdom and acumen associated with ageing that demanded listening ears within the village. Horam (1988, p. 18) writes thus: 'Age, among the Nagas, has both prestige and power because it is the older people who know and pass on to younger persons the ways of society to which they are expected to conform.' While this never connoted the complete sinking of individual autonomy in collective conformity, traditional Naga politics relied on a generational asymmetry; an asymmetry which linked the prerogative of overseeing political affairs to clan and village elders. Their views, often wrapped in fine speeches and oratorical skills, were respected. Liberal democracy is averse to any such kinship and social hierarchies, and instead glorifies the values of equal say, individual rationality and autonomy. From the vantage of homespun Naga political theory and praxis, this is where the apprehension lies.

'It is because nowadays the village is ruled by the youth', Phugwumi elders often explain contemporary problems and predicaments in the village. 'They lack maturity, foresight, and wisdom that comes with old age, and instead of thinking about what is best for the community they think about what is best for themselves'. Phugwumi elders are often explicit about the exaggerated individualism and competitive self-advancement liberal democracy effectuates, and they blame it on its 'naïve'

principles of individual balloting and equal voting rights. 'Whereas in the past our youth would whisper, and were eager to listen and learn from elders', Athe told me, 'nowadays they shout and will not listen'. As opposed to village youth, whose naiveties and inexperience had to be kept in check, village elders were traditionally ascribed with the necessary acumen and wisdom, accumulated over a lifetime, to transcend both the mundane and their purely personal interests to deliberate the wider community good. In the cultural etiquette of the past, village youth, while never silenced, were expected to show deference by acknowledging, before speaking in public, the incomplete understanding and limited knowledge that came with being young and unmarried, the absence of fields and cattle in one's possession and their overall still limited experience of the perils and complications of life (Wouters, 2018c).

Besides the flattening of kinship and social hierarchies, what is lamented, too, is the open contests and competition elections invariably bring, and which sow division within the community. 'We never vote', Phugwumi's village council chairperson told me. 'Voting would only lead to more politics, more competition, and more rivalries. And this would not benefit our village'. Phugwumi's village council, which arbitrates on customary law, functions on the basis of deliberation and consensus making, even if this means council meetings often become lengthy affairs. In instances where consensus building proves impossible, the council declares an issue as unresolved or pending, which is preferred over forcing a decision through the divisive practice of voting (Wouters, 2015a, p. 141). As such, decisions made by the village council today, and in line with Naga political values and practices, represent 'community think', rather than through majority votes. In the vernacular lexicography of social and political life in Phugwumi, this principle is known as *müthidzü* or *müthiküdü*, which translate as 'the community's voice' or 'the community's thought'. In the context of the neighbouring Angami Naga, A. Z. Phizo (1951) refers to this principle as *mechü medo zotuo*, or 'the binding will of the community'.

This tradition of 'community think' is now threatened by the advance of liberal democracy, and its elevation of individual autonomy and choice. At the same time, however, Naga villagers are not the passive recipients of liberal democratic doctrines and dogmas. Per contra, they possess the agency, political imagination and cultural creativity to adapt democratic institutions and elections to their own political consciousness and uses. One way in which they adapt liberal democracy is through bypassing the principle of individual and equal vote through the method of selection consensus candidates. In the wake of the 2013 state election, the Phugwumi villagers attempted to pre-select a village consensus candidate through public deliberation, and which would then see the substituting of individual voting for a collective village vote on polling day. Alas, the Phugwumi villagers failed to unite; a failure which, in the view of many, only proved that electoral politics has already moved beyond redemption (see Wouters, 2018c).

Not a few other Naga villages, however, succeeded in selecting a consensus candidate after a social process of public deliberation presided over by clan and village elders. One village, for instance, declared in a local daily, in the run up to the 2013 election: '…in a general meeting… [the village] unanimously resolved to extend full support to the Independent Candidate for the forthcoming legislative assembly election' (cited in Wouters, 2014, p. 61). 'Unanimously', here, does not imply the absence of opposing views, but is communicative of the value of 'conformity' and 'community think' that results from this. Undoubtedly, there is an instrumental angle to this practice, resembling, as it does, what elsewhere in the country is called

'vote-bank politics'. However, this section shows that more than a straightforward assault on democratic values and principles, this social process through which village and clan elders convene, deliberate, build consensus and subsequently select a political candidate can also be interpreted as the reconstitution of a general asymmetry and 'community think' unto the new democratic domain.

The practice of consensus candidates is increasingly a contentious issue within contemporary Naga society (the NBCC, among others, condemns it). What is clear is that liberal democracy locally leads to the diminishing sonority of the voice of the elderly and wise, and the substitution of 'community think' with individual autonomy. For Phugwumi elders, and many others in Nagaland, this is where the structural problem and immoralities of liberal democracy lie.

CONCLUDING REMARKS

The Christian and culturalist critique of the democracy process in Nagaland combined make not only a few Naga voices, particularly those of village and tribal elders (also several career politicians), but also now publicly advocate the abolishment of elections in Nagaland altogether, insisting that these are detrimental to Naga conceptions of 'moral society'. Akio Tanabe (2007, p. 560) captures such a 'moral society' as a vernacular space 'in which morally desirable human relationships rather than individual rights of political gains are at issue'. On the floor of the state assembly, a prominent Nagaland minister thus argues that the Indian election system be 'reformed' for Nagaland, since it undermines 'the Naga way of life' (cited in Ao, 1993, p. 211), which is protected by Article 371A of the Indian Constitution, specifically tailored for Nagaland state. Hokishe Sema (1986), a former chief minister, also suggests that elections be replaced by community consensus making and the *selection* of representatives at village, regional and state levels. The present chief minister, too, goes on record saying: 'election is not suited for Nagas' and that 'selection of leader[s] would best suit Nagas' (cited in Solo, 2011, p. 67).

The Naga rebel vanguard, on their part, has long been critical of the ways in which the institutional machinations of India's democracy process create and co-opt a Naga political class tied to Delhi. Their political refusal to participate in 'Indian elections', at least when the Naga armed uprising first began, was not only an act of resistance, however. It was *also* expressive of cultural incongruity and ideological difference and Naga underground leaders, old and new, have long mused about the implications of constitutional democracy on the Naga political and cultural traditions they wish to preserve and perpetuate in the future. 'There is no political party in Nagaland. We don't need it', says A. Z. Phizo (1951). He continues: 'Nagaland need not imitate or adopt foreign institutions in matters of political organisation'. In Phizo's view, Nagaland was democratic by traditional design: '[it] is the very spirit of our country'. Instead, Phizo envisages a multi-tier selection system. 'We don't election leaders, we select them', he elucidates, then explains:

> The selection process goes on for several years beginning from the village level where people know each other thoroughly and only people with virtue of integrity and character are accepted to become leaders. Then on the basis of these observations the leaders of the various villages select the most competent person to be the leader. The same is followed through to the national level. Thus a national leader emerges after so many years. (cited in Mishra, 2004, p. 4)

The later NSCN agrees in the rejection of party politics, and its manifesto laments: 'The damage done to the healthy body politic and the upright characteristics of the Naga people as a whole, through the practice of Indian party

system by the traitors [Nagaland overground politicians], is beyond easy description.' In classic socialist vein, the NSCN advocates a party-less 'dictatorship of the people... through a single political organisation and the active practice of democracy within the organisation'. This document reads further: 'In a country like Nagaland, particularly at the present time, party system could never accomplish anything except leading to ruination' (cited in Horam, 1988, pp. 321–322).

That party politics has led to considerable 'ruination' locally is a conclusion even staunch opponents of the Naga Movement find difficult to deny. Concludes the Naga Reverend and intellectual V. K. Nuh (1986, p. 184): 'Unless the present election system is changed, it will not serve the [Naga] people well', and this change, he posits, must be in accordance with 'traditional and customary practices'. In Nagaland's democratic domain, traces of past, present and future mix in a bewildering political garden of the contemporary moment.

REFERENCES

Agamben, G. (2005) *State of exception* (K. Attell, Tans.). Chicago, IL: Chicago University Press.
Agrawal, A., & Kumar, V. (2018). Community, numbers and politics in Nagaland. In J. J. P. Wouters & Z. Tunyi (Eds.), *Democracy in Nagaland: Tribes, traditions, tensions* (pp. 57–86). Kohima and Edinburgh: The Highlander Books.
Amer, M. (2013). Political status of women in Nagaland. *Journal of Business Management & Social Sciences Research, 2*(4), 91–95.
Amer, M. (2014). Electoral dynamics in India: A study of Nagaland. *Journal of Business Management & Social Science Research, 3*(4), 6–11.
Ao, L. (1993). *Rural development in Nagaland.* New Delhi: Har-Anand Publications.
Ao, L. (2013). Indo-Naga political conflict, resolution and peace-process: A critical review. Delhi: Delhi Naga Students Union.

Assam Tribune. (2013, January 19). Naga hoho seeks deferment of Nagaland polls. Author.

Baruah, S. (2013). Politics of territoriality: Indigeneity, itinerancy and rights in north-east India. In J. Smajda (Ed.), *Territorial changes and territorial restructurings in the Himalayas* (pp. 69–83). Delhi: CNRS and Adroit Publishers.

Bhaumik, S. (2009). *Troubled periphery: Crisis of India's northeast.* New Delhi: SAGE Publications.

Chasie, C. (2005). *The Naga imbroglio: A personal perspective.* Kohima: City Press.

Dev, R. (2006). Ethnic self-determination and electoral politics in Nagaland. In A. Baruah & R. Dev (Eds.), *Ethnic identities: Electoral politics in India's north east India* (pp. 68–92). New Delhi: Regency Publications.

Ezung, Z. (2012). Corruption and its impact on Nagaland: A case study of Nagaland. *International Journal of Rural Studies, 19*(1), 1–7.

Farrelly, N. 2009. 'AK47/M16 Rifle – ₹15,000 each': What price peace on the Indo-Burmese frontier? *Contemporary South Asia, 17*(3), 283–297.

Fürer-Haimendorf, C. V. (1939). *The naked Nagas.* London: Methuen & Company.

Fürer-Haimendorf, C. V. (1973). Social and cultural change among the Konyak Naga. *Highlander, 1*(1), 3–12.

Gaikwad, N. 2009. Revolting bodies, hysterical state: Women protesting the armed forces special powers act (1958). *Contemporary South Asia, 17*(3), 299–311.

Hansen, T. B. (1999). *The saffron wave: Democracy and Hindu nationalism in modern India.* Princeton, NJ: Princeton University Press.

Hausing, K. K. S. (2017). 'Equality of tradition' and women's reservation in Nagaland. *Economic & Political Weekly, 52*(45), 36–43.

Horam, M. (1988). *The Naga insurgency: The last thirty years.* New Delhi: Cosmo Publications.

Huntington, S. (2000). Foreword: Cultures count. In L. E. Harrison & S. Huntington (Eds.), *Culture matters: How values shape human progress* (pp. xii–xvi). Oklahoma, OK: University of Oklahoma Press.

Hutton, J. H. (1921). *The Angami Nagas: With some notes on neighbouring tribes.* London: Macmillan.

India Today. (1998, February 16). No sign of election. Author.

Indian Express. (2008, February 29). NSCN-IM accused of hindering elections. Author.

Jamir, A. (2002). Keynote address. In C. J. Thomas & G. Das (Eds.), *Dimensions of development in Nagaland* (pp. 1–8). New Delhi: Regency Publications.

Jamir, T. (2012). *Women and politics in Nagaland: Challenges and imperatives.* New Delhi: Concept Publishing Company.

Jimomi, V. H. (2009). *Political parties in Nagaland.* Kohima: Graphic Printers.

Joshi, V. (2012). *A matter of belief: Christian conversion and healing in north-east India.* Oxford: Berghahn Books.

Khiamniungan, T. L. (2018). Patriarchy as structural violence: Resistance against women reservation in Nagaland. In J. J. P. Wouters & Z. Tunyi (Eds.), *Democracy in Nagaland: Tribes, traditions, tensions* (pp. 181–198). Kohima and Edinburg: The Highlander Books.

Kiewhuo, K. (2002). Constructive political agreement and development. In J. C. Thomas & G. Das (Eds.), *Dimensions of development in Nagaland* (pp. 59–65). New Delhi: Regency Publications.

Kikon, D. (2002). Political mobilization of women in Nagaland: A sociological background. In W. Fernandes & S. Barbora (Eds.), *Changing women's status in India: Focus on the northeast* (pp. 174–182). Guwahati: North-Eastern Social Research Centre.

Kikon, D. (2005). Engaging Naga nationalism. Can democracy function in militarized societies? *Economic & Political Weekly, 40*(26), 2833–2837.

Kikon, D. (2009). The predicament of justice: 50 years of armed forces special powers act. *Journal of Contemporary South Asia, 17*(3), 271–282.

Kuotsu, R. K., & Walling, A. W. (2018). Democratic values and traditional practices: Gendering electoral politics in Nagaland. In J. J. P. Wouters & Z. Tunyi (Eds.), *Democracy in Nagaland: Tribes, traditions, tensions* (pp. 101–122). Kohima and Edinburgh: The Highlander Books.

Mamdani, M. (1996). *Citizens and subject: Contemporary Africa and the legacy of late colonialism.* Princeton: Princeton University Press.

Mc-Duie-Ra, D. (2009). Fifty-year disturbance: The armed forces special powers act and exceptionalism in a South Asian periphery. *Journal of Contemporary South Asia, 17*(3), 255–270.

McDuie-Ra, D., & Kikon, D. (2016). Tribal communities and coal in northeast India: The politics of imposing and resisting mining bans. *Energy Policy, 99*, 261–269.

Mills, J. P. (1926). *The Ao Nagas.* London: Macmillan.

Mishra, J. P. 2004. A. Z. Phizo: As I knew him. Retrieved from http://nagaland.faithweb.com/articles/phizo.html

Misra, U. (1987). Nagaland elections. *Economic & Political Weekly*, *22*(51), 2193–2195.

Morung Express. (2013, February 7). Involved of NSC-N(IM) in election condemned. Author.

Morung Express. (2017a). Opinion poll. Retrieved from http://morungexpress.com/think-nagaland-electorate-ready-vote-honest-sincere-visionary-candidates-2018-elections/

Morung Express. (2017b). Opinion poll. Retrieved from http://morungexpress.com/convinced-chief-minsters-statement-government-keen-changing-system-check-corruption/

Morung Express. (2017c). Opinion poll. Retrieved from http://morungexpress.com/agree-present-legislators-blinded-political-power-vested-interests-lost-moral-authority-lead/

Murry, K. C. (2007). *Naga legislative assembly and its speakers*. New Delhi: Mittal Publications.

NBCC. (2012). *Clean election campaign. Engaging the powers: Elections—a spiritual issue for Christians*. Kohima: Author.

Ngaithe, T. S. (2014). The battle for ballot in north-east India. *Economic & Political Weekly*, *49*(17). Retrieved from https://www.epw.in/journal/2014/17/election-specials-web-exclusives/battle-ballot-north-east-india.html

Nibedon, N. (1978). *North-east India: The ethnic explosion*. New Delhi: Lancers Publishing.

Ningthouja, M. (2016). AFSPA and the tortured bodies: The politics of pain in Manipur. In S. K. George & P. G. Jung (Eds.), *Cultural ontology of the self in pain* (pp. 249–268). New Delhi: Springer.

Nuh, V. K. (1986). *Nagaland church and politics*. Kohima: Vision Press.

Panwar, N. (2017). From nationalism to factionalism: Faultlines in the Naga insurgency. *Small Wars and Insurgencies*, *28*(1), 233–258.

Phizo, A. Z. (1951). Plebiscite speech. Retrieved from http://www.neuenhofer.de/guenter/nagaland/phizo.html

Piliavsky, A. (2014). Introduction. In A. Piliavsky (Ed.), *Patronage as politics* (pp. 1–38). Cambridge: Cambridge University Press.

Ruud, A. E. (2001). Talking dirty about politics: A view from a Bengali village. In C. J. Fuller & V. Benei (Eds.), *The everyday state and society in modern India* (pp. 115–136). London: Hurst & Company.

Sema, H. (1986). *Emergence of Nagaland*. New Delhi: Vikas Publishing House.

Sen, A. N. (1974). Operation election. *Economic & Political Weekly*, *9*(11), 424.

Singh, C. (2004). *Nagaland politics: A critical account*. New Delhi: Mittal Publications.

Solo, T. (2011). *From violence to peace and prosperity: Nagaland*. Kohima: NV Press.

Tanabe, A. (2007). Towards vernacular democracy: Moral society and post-postcolonial transformations in rural Orissa, India. *American Ethnologist*, *34*(3), 558–574.

Taussig, M. T. (1980). *The devil and commodity fetishism in south America*. Chapel Hill: The University of North Carolina Press.

Thomas, J. (2016). *Evangelizing the nation: Religion and the formation of Naga political identity*. New Delhi: Routledge.

Tinyi, V. (2017). The headhunting culture of the Nagas: Reinterpreting the self. *The South Asianist*, *5*(1), 83–98.

Tinyi, V., & Nienu, C. (2018). Making sense of corruption in Nagaland: A culturalist interpretation. In J. J. P. Wouters & Z. Tunyi (Eds.), *Democracy in Nagaland: Tribes, traditions, tensions* (pp. 159–180). Kohima: The Highlander Press.

Woodthorpe, R. G. (1881). Notes on the wild tribes inhabiting the so-called Naga hills, on our north-east frontier of India. *The Journal of the Anthropological Institute of Great Britain and Ireland*, *11*, 56–73.

Wouters, J. J. P. (2014). Performing democracy in Nagaland: Past polities and present politics. *Economic & Political Weekly*, *49*(16), 59–66.

Wouters, J. J. P. (2015a). Polythetic democracy: Tribal elections, bogus votes, and the political imagination in the Naga uplands. *Hau: Journal of Ethnographic Theory*, *5*(2), 121–151.

Wouters, J. J. P. (2015b). Feasts of merit, election feasts, or no feasts? On the politics of wining and dining in Nagaland, Northeast India. *The South Asianist*, *3*(2), 5–23.

Wouters, J. J. P. (2017). Who is a Naga village? The Naga 'village republic' through the ages. *The South Asianist*, *5*(1), 99–120.

Wouters, J. J. P. (2018a). What makes a good politician? Democratic representation, 'vote-buying' and the MLA handbook in Nagaland, Northeast India. *Journal of South Asian Studies*, *41*(4), 806–826.

Wouters, J. J. P. (2018b). *In the shadows of Naga insurgency: Tribes, state and violence in northeast India*. New Delhi: Oxford University Press.

Wouters, J. J. P. (2018c). Nagas as a society against voting: Consensus-building, party-less politics and a culturalist critique of elections in northeast India. *The Journal of Cambridge Anthropology*, *36*(2), 113–132.

Wouters, J. J. P. (2018d). Introduction: Exploring democracy in Nagaland. In J. J. P. Wouters & Z. Tunyi (Eds.), *Democracy in Nagaland: Tribes, traditions and ten-sions* (pp. 1–42). Kohima and Edinburgh: The Highlander Books.

Wouters, J. J. P. (2019). Difficult decolonization: Debates, divisions and deaths within the Naga movement, 1944–1963. *Journal of North-East India Studies*, *9*(1), 1–28.

27

Tribes and Electoral Politics in Odisha*

Jagannath Ambagudia

INTRODUCTION

Electoral system of a country is based on the changing relationship between representative democracy and diversity that reinforces the nature and dynamics of a particular society. Indian electoral system has rich experiences of accommodating diversity across caste, gender, religion, ethnicity, etc., both at the national- and state-level politics. These variables act as the means of determining political behaviour both at the individual and community levels, and thus determine the outcome of electoral processes. The role of these variables in an electoral system is not only confined to decisively influence the outcome of various elections, but also, in a way, create political awareness among various communities belonging to different sociocultural and political identities. Politics at the national level creates pan-Indian community identities and facilitates the process of continuous interaction and interface between various

communities and politics. Such interaction leads to the emergence of identity politics, especially tribal politics in India.

The credibility of capturing the real essence of social and political differences in the process of interface between identity and politics at the national level seems to be remote indeed. This can perhaps be explained by acknowledging the fact that various sub-community/ethnic identities get subverted when they appear to function at the national level. However, the consciousness of various sub-ethnic communities appears more pronounced at the state-level politics. Considering the community dynamics of politics, the existing literature pays little attention to tribal politics at the national level, in general, and at the state level, in particular. Against this backdrop, this chapter focuses on various dynamics of tribal politics in the context of Odisha. Section I deals with the demographic picture of the reserved constituencies and its implications over determining

* I would like to thank my PhD scholar, Medusmita Borthakur, for helping me in compiling the data on tribal assembly constituencies of Odisha.

the number of tribal reserved constituencies. Section II deals with the election data in relation to the Scheduled Tribe (ST) reserved parliamentary and assembly constituencies of Odisha. Section III explains why a particular trend is taking place in the context of tribal politics in Odisha. Section IV discusses various issues that are directly or indirectly affecting the different aspects of tribal politics in Odisha, followed by conclusion.

I

TRIBAL SITUATION IN RESERVED CONSTITUENCIES

The 2011 state-wise census data on demographic picture suggests that Odisha occupies third position in terms of tribal concentration, only after Madhya Pradesh (14.69%) and Maharashtra (10.08%). According to 2011 census, Odisha has become the home of 9,590,756 tribal population, constituting 22.85 per cent of the total state population and 9.2 per cent of the total tribal population of the country. There are 62 tribal communities in Odisha, highest in terms of number in the country. Out of 62 communities, 13 are declared as particularly vulnerable tribal groups (PVTGs), earlier known as primitive tribal groups.[1] The 2011 census also shows that the tribal communities of Odisha have attained 52.24 per cent literacy rate. The 62 tribal communities of Odisha are at various stages of social, economic and political developments. The demographic picture of tribal communities is critical because the allocation of electoral seats to tribal communities depends on their share in the total population both at the state and national levels.

Table 27.1 deals with the number and types of parliamentary constituencies in Odisha. It reflects that out of 20 parliamentary constituencies allocated to the state of Odisha, 3, 2 and 4 were reserved for the tribal communities during the 1951, 1957 and 1962 elections, respectively. The ST parliamentary seats were increased to five during the 1967 election. Although the total number of seats allocated to Odisha increased by one in 1977 election, the tribal parliamentary constituencies remained unchanged. Even the implementation of the Delimitation of Parliamentary and Assembly Constituencies Order, 2008, did not alter the number of ST parliamentary constituencies (Figure 27.1), perhaps because the total parliamentary constituencies allocated to Odisha remained same though it had some effects at the level of assembly election.

Table 27.2 shows that out of 107 assembly seats, 16 seats were allocated to the tribal communities in the 1951 election, which were increased to 18 in the 1957 election. A total of 29 seats in a 140-member assembly were allocated to tribes during the 1961 election, which was the first election to be affected by the abolition of double/multi-member constituencies. The number of ST assembly seats was increased to 34 in the 1967 assembly election, and the same number also governed the 1971 election. However, during the 1974 election, the number of ST seats was reduced by 1. From 1977 to 2004 elections, 34 seats were allocated to tribes in a 147-member state assembly. The number of ST assembly seats reduced to 33 during the 2009 assembly elections and the same number continues to govern the subsequent assembly elections probably until the next Delimitation of Parliamentary and Assembly Constituencies Order comes into effect, perhaps in 2031.[2] It is crucial to point out here that the number

---

[1] Birhor, Bonda, Didayi, Dongria Kondh, Juang, Kharia, Kutia Kondh, Lanjia Saora, Lodha, Mankirdia, Paudi Bhuyan, Saora and Chuktia Bhunjia are declared as PVTGs in Odisha.
[2] It is worthwhile to mention that the Parliament has frozen the equalization of constituency population since 1971, which has further been extended up to 2026 under the 84th Constitutional Amendment Act, 2002, and will be effective only after the 2031 Census (Ambagudia, 2019b, p. 50).

Table 27.1   Number and Types of Parliamentary Constituencies in Odisha

Year	Unreserved	SC	ST	Total
1951	17	0	3	20
1957	18	0	2	20
1962	12	4	4	20
1967	12	3	5	20
1971	12	3	5	20
1977	13	3	5	21
1980	13	3	5	21
1984	13	3	5	21
1989	13	3	5	21
1991	13	3	5	21
1996	13	3	5	21
1998	13	3	5	21
1999	13	3	5	21
2004	13	3	5	21
2009	13	3	5	21
2014	13	3	5	21
2019	13	3	5	21

Source: Compiled from various reports of the Election Commission of India.

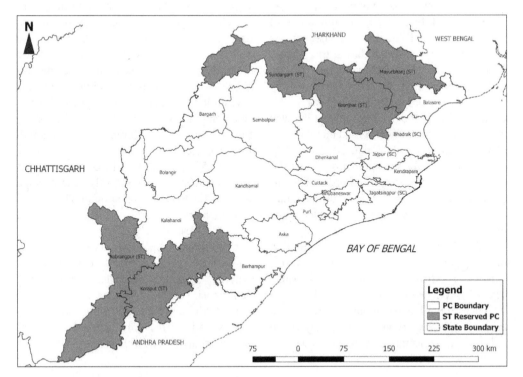

Figure 27.1   ST Parliamentary Constituencies of Odisha
Source: Adapted and redrawn by Kamal Azad. Map not to scale.

Table 27.2   Number and Types of Assembly Constituencies in Odisha

Year	Unreserved	SC	ST	Total
1951	91	0	16	107
1957	58	25	18	101
1961	86	25	29	140
1967	84	22	34	140
1971	84	22	34	140
1974	91	22	33	146
1977	91	22	34	147
1980	91	22	34	147
1985	91	22	34	147
1990	91	22	34	147
1995	91	22	34	147
2000	91	22	34	147
2004	91	22	34	147
2009	90	24	33	147
2014	90	24	33	147
2019	90	24	33	147

Source: Compiled from various reports of the Election Commission of India.

of ST assembly seats remained same from 1977 to 2004 because the Delimitation of Parliamentary and Assembly Constituencies Order, 1976, was in force during this period. Similarly, with the implementation of the Delimitation of Parliamentary and Assembly Constituencies Order, 2008, there was a real-location of seats to social groups, which also affected their entitled seats based on their population strength (Ambagudia, 2019b, p. 54). To put it differently, the number of ST assembly constituencies experienced ups and downs because various Delimitation of Parliamentary and Assembly Constituencies Orders came into effect over the period.

Table 27.3 dwells upon the concentration of tribal population in parliamentary constituencies in Odisha as per the 2001 census.[3] The tribal concentration ranges from lowest of 0.68 per cent in Jagatsinghpur constituency to the highest in Mayurbhanj constituency. Since only five parliamentary constituencies were to be reserved for the tribes based on their population strength, Mayurbhanj, Nabarangpur, Koraput, Sundargarh and Keonjhar are declared as ST-reserved constituencies. Mayurbhanj constituency has the highest (57.58%) and Keonjhar constituency has the lowest (46.98%) concentration of tribal population among the five tribal reserved constituencies. Nabarangpur, Koraput and Sundargarh constituencies have 55.58 per cent, 51.88 per cent and 50.19 per cent of tribal population of the constituencies, respectively. The average size of total and ST population in ST-reserved parliamentary constituencies is 1,786,334 and 936,242.8, respectively.

Mayurbhanj ST parliamentary constituency consists of seven assembly constituencies, that is, Jashipur, Saraskana, Rairangpur, Bangriposi, Udala, Marada and Baripada. Out of these seven assembly constituencies, Marada is the only unreserved assembly constituency and others are ST-reserved

---

[3] The demographic composition of the assembly and parliamentary constituencies is cited as per the 2001 census because the Delimitation of Parliamentary and Assembly Constituencies Order 2008, which is still in force, used the population figure as per 2001 census while declaring reserved constituencies in India.

Table 27.3   ST Population in Parliamentary Constituencies of Odisha in Descending Order (2001 Census)

S. No.	Name of the Constituency	Nature of Constituency	Total Population	ST Population	% of ST Population
1	Mayurbhanj	ST	1,762,803	1,015,042	57.58
2	Nabarangpur	ST	1,777,950	988,218	55.58
3	Koraput	ST	1,763,760	915,048	51.88
4	Sundargarh	ST	1,830,673	918,903	50.19
5	Keonjhar	ST	1,796,484	844,003	46.98
6	Kalahandi	Unreserved	1,866,184	566,794	30.37
7	Kandhamal	Unreserved	1,493,060	430,549	28.84
8	Sambalpur	Unreserved	1,668,605	467,686	28.03
9	Bargarh	Unreserved	1,861,189	423,123	22.73
10	Bolangir	Unreserved	1,879,029	328,800	17.50
11	Berhampur	Unreserved	1,718,783	297,593	17.31
12	Balasore	Unreserved	1,749,013	301,497	17.24
13	Dhenkanal	Unreserved	1,742,860	214,007	12.28
14	Jajpur	SC	1,624,341	125,989	7.76
15	Bhubaneswar	Unreserved	1,631,083	88,313	5.41
16	Cuttack	Unreserved	1,750,420	70,851	4.05
17	Bhadrak	Unreserved	1,835,403	46,653	2.54
18	Aska	Unreserved	1,700,598	42,925	2.52
19	Puri	Unreserved	1,670,195	23,829	1.43
20	Kendrapara	Unreserved	1,835,826	22,762	1.24
21	Jagatsinghpur	SC	1,846,401	12,496	0.68

Source: Final Papers, Paper No. 7, Delimitation Commission of India.

assembly constituencies. Nabarangpur parliamentary constituency is also spread over seven assembly constituencies, which are Umerkote, Jharigam, Nabarangpur, Dabugam, Kotpad, Malkangiri and Chitrakonda. Interestingly, all these assembly constituencies are reserved for the STs in Odisha. Another seven constituencies—Gunupur, Bissam-Cuttack, Rayagada, Lakshmipur, Jeypore, Koraput and Pottangi—come under the Koraput parliamentary constituency. Out of seven assembly constituencies, Gunupur, Bissam-Cuttack, Rayagada, Lakshmipur and Pottangi are reserved for the tribes. Sundargarh parliamentary constituency has seven assembly constituencies as well—Talsara, Sundargarh, Biramitrapur, Raghunathpali, Rourkela, Rajgangpur and Bonai. Out of these assembly constituencies, five constituencies—Talsara, Sundargarh, Biramitrapur, Rajgangpur

and Bonai—are reserved for the tribal communities.

The geographical boundary of Keonjhar parliamentary constituency is spread over the assembly constituencies of Telkoi, Ghasipura, Anandapur, Patna, Keonjhar, Champua and Karanjia. Out of which, Telkoi, Patna, Keonjhar and Karanjia are reserved for the STs in Odisha. In short, out of 33 ST assembly constituencies in Odisha (Table 27.4), 27 are located in five ST parliamentary constituencies of Odisha. Rest six ST assembly constituencies—Mohana, Kuchinda, Lanjigarh, Baliguda, G. Udayagiri and Phulbani—are located in Berhampur, Sambalpur, Kalahandi and Kandhamal parliamentary constituencies, respectively. Baliguda, G. Udayagiri and Phulbani ST assembly constituencies are part of Kandhamal parliamentary constituencies. The existing data suggests

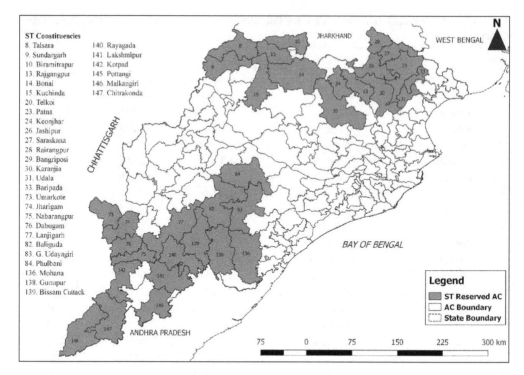

Figure 27.2   ST Assembly Constituencies of Odisha
Source: Adapted and redrawn by Kamal Azad. Map not to scale.

that the highest concentration of tribal population in Mayurbhanj, Nabarangpur, Keonjhar,
Koraput and Sundargarh parliamentary
constituencies is due to the presence of the
ST-reserved assembly constituencies.

Based on the formula for determining
the entitlement of ST assembly seats in
Odisha (see Ambagudia, 2019b), 33 seats are
reserved for the tribes based on their population strength as per 2001 census (Figure 27.2).
Final Paper 4 of the Delimitation Commission
deals with concentration of ST population
in ST-reserved assembly constituencies,
which has been presented in Table 27.4.
Table 27.4 reflects that Lakshmipur assembly constituency has the highest (68.90%)
and Sundargarh assembly constituency has
the lowest (45.54%) concentration of ST population among the assembly constituencies
reserved for the tribal communities in Odisha.
Out of 33 ST assembly constituencies, 11 of
them have more than 60 per cent of the tribal

population to the total population of the constituency. Similarly, 17 assembly constituencies have more than 50 per cent but less 60
per cent of tribal population and five constituencies have more than 45 per cent but less
than 50 per cent of the tribal population. The
tribal population of remaining assembly constituencies ranges from 0.05 per cent in Aul
constituency to 45.03 per cent in Champua
constituency. The average size of total and ST
population in ST-reserved assembly constituencies is 252,277.93 and 145,331.18, respectively (Government of India, 2008, p. 1111).

II

DEALING WITH ELECTION DATA

The electoral processes of a country are
affected by a number of variables that directly

Table 27.4 ST Population in ST-reserved Assembly Constituencies of Odisha in Descending Order (2001 Census)

S. No.	Name of the Constituency	Total Population	ST Population	% of ST Population
1	Lakshmipur	214,530	147,813	68.90
2	Bonai	277,001	188,613	68.09
3	Mohana	281,545	188,759	67.04
4	Talsara	238,920	159,558	66.78
5	Bangriposi	250,784	165,981	66.18
6	Rajgangpur	274,281	180,178	65.69
7	Chitrakonda	231,524	151,300	65.35
8	Biramitrapur	267,924	174,709	65.21
9	Saraskana	239,629	154,792	64.60
10	Karanjia	234,494	148,862	63.48
11	Jashipur	254,935	154,586	60.64
12	Telkoi	271,769	161,819	59.54
13	Rairangpur	259,590	154,360	59.46
14	Umarkote	241,030	142,571	59.15
15	Dabugam	241,525	142,182	58.87
16	Gunupur	256,827	151,176	58.86
17	Udala	229,091	131,624	57.45
18	G. Udayagiri	228,827	129,339	56.52
19	Pottangi	224,432	125,968	56.13
20	Bissam-Cuttack	283,180	158,599	56.01
21	Kuchinda	255,359	142,893	55.96
22	Jharigam	262,850	145,117	55.21
23	Kotpad	247,986	134,200	54.12
24	Rayagada	291,102	153,643	52.78
25	Baliguda	190,742	99,023	51.91
26	Patna	236,554	121,978	51.56
27	Baripada	259,019	132,395	51.11
28	Malkangiri	272,674	138,238	50.70
29	Nabarangpur	280,361	134,610	48.01
30	Lanjigarh	267,225	127,304	47.64
31	Phulbani	228,632	108,447	47.43
32	Keonjhar	263,034	123,341	46.89
33	Sundargarh	267,796	121,951	45.54

Source: Final Papers, Paper No. 4, Delimitation Commission of India, Government of India (2008, p. 1111).

or indirectly determine the community dynamics of politics. In this backdrop, this section discusses involvement and participation of tribal communities of Odisha in state politics, especially in the context of voter turnout, their relationship with invisible votes, engaging with competitive electoral politics, relationship between gender and tribal politics, contesting in unreserved constituencies, supporting political parties, etc.

Voter Turnout

The Election Commission of India uses unique criterion to calculate the voter turnout

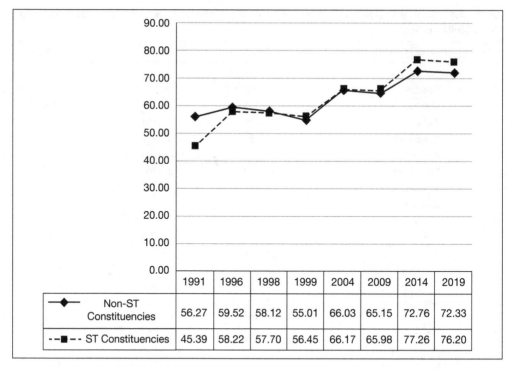

Figure 27.3   Voter Turnout in Non-ST and ST Parliamentary Constituencies, 1991–2019, Odisha (in %)
Source: Author's calculations from Government of India (1991, 1996, 1998, 1999, 2004b, 2009b, 2014d, 2019a).

in parliamentary and assembly elections. The percentage of voter turnout can be calculated by considering the number of voters cast their votes in a particular election divided by the total registered voters and multiplied by 100.

Figure 27.3 compares the voter turnout in non-ST and ST parliamentary constituencies of Odisha between 1991 and 2019 elections. It indicates that the non-ST constituencies witnessed a voter turnout of 56.27 per cent, 59.52 per cent, 58.12 per cent, 55.01 per cent, 66.03 per cent, 65.15 per cent, 72.76 per cent and 72.33 per cent in 1991, 1996, 1998, 1999, 2004, 2009, 2014 and 2019 parliamentary elections in Odisha, respectively. The ST constituencies experienced the voter turnout of 45.39 per cent in 1991 election, which was increased by an impressive 12.83 per cent in 1996 election. However, the 1998 election witnessed decline in voter turnout by 0.52 per cent. The voter turnout was further declined

by 1.25 per cent during the 1999 election in comparison to the turnout of 1998 election.

The voter turnout was increased by 9.72 per cent in 2004 election. There was a slight decline in voter turnout (0.19%) during the 2009 election. However, there was a phenomenal increase (11.28%) in voter turnout in 2014 election in tribal constituencies. The voter turnout was declined by 1.06 per cent during the 2019 parliamentary election in tribal constituencies of Odisha. To put it differently, despite myriad efforts of the Election Commission to create awareness among the voters concerning exercising their political rights and encouraging them to actively participate in elections, and the impact of modern education, the tribal parliamentary constituencies could not maintain secular increase in voter turnout, and thus experienced ups and downs in terms of voter turnout. The similar state of affairs can be seen in relation to voter

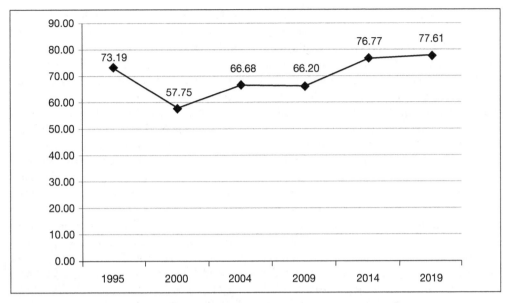

Figure 27.4   Voter Turnout in ST Assembly Constituencies, 1995–2019, Odisha (in %)
Source: Author's calculation from Government of India (1995, 2000, 2004a, 2009a, 2014c, 2019b).

turnout in non-tribal parliamentary constituencies as well.

The comparison of voter turnout in parliamentary constituencies of Odisha suggests that the non-tribal parliamentary constituencies recorded higher voter turnout of 10.88 per cent, 1.30 per cent and 0.42 per cent during 1991, 1996 and 1998 elections, respectively, in comparison to the tribal constituencies. However, this trend has begun to change since 1999, where the tribal parliamentary constituencies have recorded 1.44 per cent, 0.14 per cent, 0.83 per cent, 4.50 per cent and 3.87 per cent of higher voter turnout in 1999, 2004, 2009, 2014 and 2019 elections, respectively than the non-tribal constituencies.

Figure 27.4 demonstrates that since 1995, every alternative election year has witnessed decline in voter turnout, barring the most recent election year (2019). For instance, there was a decline of 15.44 per cent and 0.48 per cent during 2000 and 2009 elections than the elections of 1995 and 2004, respectively. However, the recent assembly election (2019) registered little higher (0.84%) voter turnout than the previous election (2014).

The comparison of the parliamentary and assembly elections in Odisha suggests that the ST assembly constituencies recorded 0.51 per cent, 0.22 per cent and 1.41 per cent higher voter turnout than the ST parliamentary constituencies during the 2004, 2009 and 2019 assembly and ST parliamentary elections, respectively. However, the ST parliamentary constituencies recorded 0.49 per cent higher voter turnout than the ST assembly constituencies in the 2014 election. The differences of voter turnout can perhaps be understood by the demographic composition of both the assembly and parliamentary constituencies, where the total population of the parliamentary constituencies range between 1,762,803 and 1,830,673 (Table 27.3), and in the assembly constituencies, it is between 190,742 and 291,102 (Table 27.4), according to 2001 census. The higher concentration of population in parliamentary constituencies has negatively affected the final percentage of the voter turnout, where the ST-reserved parliamentary constituencies, as per 2001 census, have 606,498 higher total population than the ST-reserved assembly constituencies (Tables 27.3 and 27.4).

Based on the practice of reserved constituencies in India, one may argue that the entire credit of higher voter turnout in tribal assembly constituencies shall not be given to tribal electorates alone. This argument, however, seems to be less receptive when the demographic figures of tribal-reserved constituencies are considered. Although we do not practice separate electorate consisting *only* the tribal voters,[4] the significant demographic presence of tribal communities has become the basis of declaring certain constituencies as tribal constituencies, where tribal voters have much to contribute to the higher percentage of voter turnout. The recorded statistical evidences enable to encounter the conventional understanding of the relationship between the tribes and politics in India that considers tribal communities as 'passive actors' in a political set-up. This might have been true during the colonial period because the tribals were forcefully integrated into the mainstream political system or the initial phase of the functioning of political system in the post-colonial India. The tribal communities no more remain as merely 'passive actors', they think, introspect, choose and respond to political developments that are critical to tribal communities in the contemporary period.

Invisible Votes

As it has been already stated earlier that the Election Commission of India has its own methodology to calculate the voter turnout. However, all the votes may not necessarily be visible when they come to the final tally of votes secured by the contested candidates and political parties. A small percentage of votes, mainly in the form of invalid and/or more recently none of the above (NOTA)[5] votes remain invisible in the final tally.

Figure 27.5 deals with the percentage of invalid and/or NOTA votes in non-tribal and tribal parliamentary constituencies. The comparison indicates that except 2004 parliamentary election, the tribal constituencies have polled higher percentage of invalid and NOTA votes than the non-tribal constituencies. For instance, the tribal constituencies have recorded 0.99 per cent, 1.46 per cent, 1.70 per cent, 1.30 per cent, 0.11 per cent, 1.61 per cent and 1.42 per cent of higher invalid and/or NOTA votes in 1991, 1996, 1998, 1999, 2009, 2014 and 2019 elections, respectively. However, non-tribal constituencies recorded 0.03 per cent higher invalid and/or NOTA votes than tribal constituencies in 2004 parliamentary election of Odisha.

Figure 27.6 indicates that the 1995, 2000, 2004, 2009, 2014 and 2019 assembly elections polled 4.62 per cent, 2.06 per cent, 0.03 per cent, 0.10 per cent, 2.36 per cent and 1.94 per cent of invalid and/or NOTA votes, respectively. The comparison of the parliamentary and assembly elections suggest that the ST parliamentary elections polled relatively higher percentage of invalid and/or NOTA votes than the ST assembly constituencies of Odisha. For instance, election data of 2004, 2009, 2014 and 2019 shows that the parliamentary constituencies witnessed 0.01 per cent, 0.04 per cent, 0.47 per cent and 0.45 per cent higher

---

[4] During the colonial period, B. R. Ambedkar had demanded the need of a separate electorate for the Dalits. However, he had to compromise with his demand to save Mahatma Gandhi, when the later sat on a fast unto death opposing the adoption of separate electorate system.

[5] In a response to a petition filed by the People's Union for Civil Liberty, the Supreme Court of India, in its judgment on 27 September 2013, directed the Election Commission to provide the option of NOTA to the voters by providing a button for it in the electronic voting machines. NOTA provides the political opportunity to voters disapproving the contested candidates by officially registering the vote of rejection without violating the secrecy of their decision. Vachana and Roy (2018) explore the changing relationship between NOTA and Indian voters between 2013 and 2016 and argue that Indian voters use NOTA not only to disapprove the contested candidates but also to register their disenchantment towards the existing political system.

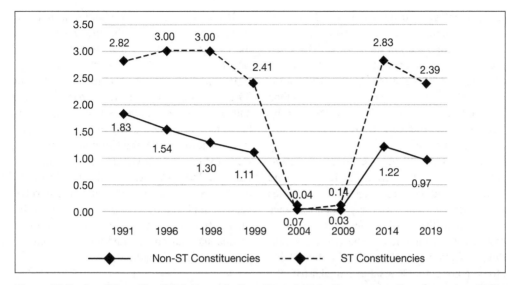

Figure 27.5 Invalid and/or NOTA Votes in Non-ST and ST Parliamentary Constituencies, 1991–2019, Odisha (in %)
Source: Author's calculations from Government of India (1991, 1996, 1998, 1999, 2004b, 2009b, 2014d, 2019a).

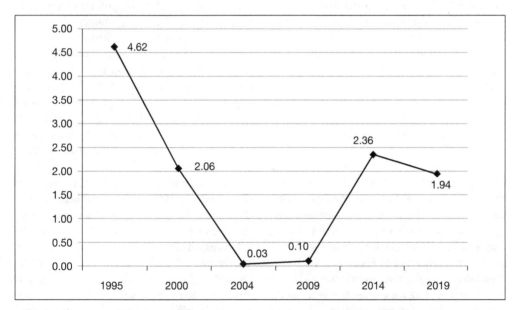

Figure 27.6 Invalid and/or NOTA Votes in ST Assembly Constituencies 1995–2019, Odisha (in%)
Source: Author's Calculation from Government of India (1995, 2000, 2004a, 2009a, 2014c, 2019b).

invalid and/or NOTA votes than the assembly constituencies.

Considering the available statistics, some of the critical questions can be asked: What is the importance of invalid and/or NOTA votes in political processes? Do they matter to the state politics, in general, and to the political parties that are having presence in Odisha, in particular? What do they mean to the contested party and independent candidates? The low percentage of invalid and/or NOTA votes may not matter much in constituencies that witnessed high margin of victories. However, they proved to be critical for political parties as well as independent candidates in constituencies where the margin of victory is less than the total invalid and/or NOTA votes, thereby having larger implications over state politics and public policy.[6]

For instance, during the 2019 parliamentary and assembly elections, at least one and eight ST candidates registered their victories in Parliament and assembly constituencies by less than the NOTA votes polled in their respective constituencies. The Congress candidate Saptagiri Sankar Ulaka defeated his close competitor Kausalya Hikaka of the Biju Janata Dal (BJD) by a margin of 3,613 votes in Koraput parliamentary constituency that recorded 36,561 NOTA votes, the second highest NOTA votes in Odisha parliamentary election after Nabarangpur ST parliamentary constituency (44,582 votes). The margins of victory were 946, 1,124, 1,433, 4,870, 2,631, 4,255, 2,545 and 229 votes in Rajgangapur, Keonjhar, Udala, Rayagada, Kotpad, Pottangi, Chitrakonda and Lakshmipur constituencies that recorded 995, 2,160, 2,271, 5,965, 3,564, 5,715, 4,158 and 7,026 NOTA votes, respectively.

The victory margin of an independent candidate, Markanda Muduli, was less than the NOTA votes polled in Rayadaga constituency. Out of these nine ST parliamentary and assembly constituencies, except Keonjhar and Udala, all the constituencies witnessed the first-time member of Parliament (MP) and members of legislative assemblies (MLAs). The Congress lost four assembly seats to the BJD where the margin of victory was less than the NOTA votes. Similarly, the BJD lost one

parliamentary seat to the Congress, and one each assembly seat to the independent and the Congress, and two seats to the Bharatiya Janata Party (BJP). Similarly, during the 2019 elections, NOTA polled 93,438 and 33,125 more votes in tribal parliamentary and assembly constituencies than the combined left parties consisting of the Communist Party of India (CPI), the Communist Party of India (Marxist, CPI(M)) and the Communist Party of India (Marxist–Leninist) Liberation in Odisha.[7] To put it differently, these votes become *invisible* as they do not figure in the final tally of either the candidates or political parties and can prove to be fatal for political parties as well as candidates.

Competitive Electoral Politics

The competitive electoral politics of a particular country depends on a number of electoral variables. The competitive nature of electoral politics can be understood by considering the level of political awareness, political education, availability of various facilities and opportunities, etc. Although these variables are critical, however, the competitive nature of electoral politics is the reflection of a number of candidates contesting the parliamentary and assembly constituencies.

The computed aggregate data suggests that, except in 1998 election, the average candidates in the non-tribal parliamentary constituencies have always been higher than the tribal constituencies and the highest difference was in the 1996 election (3.83), followed by the 1991 election (2.88) (Figure 27.7). The 1998 election experienced 0.75 higher competition in tribal constituencies than the non-tribal constituencies. However, the difference

---

[6] The larger perception of the contemporary political environment is that the tribal candidates have failed to represent the interests of their communities in true sense. However, they have played a pertinent role in a number of occasions.

[7] During 2019 elections, left parties polled 41,944 and 69,992 votes in tribal parliamentary and assembly constituencies. On the other hand, NOTA recorded 135,382 and 102,117 votes in tribal parliamentary and assembly constituencies.

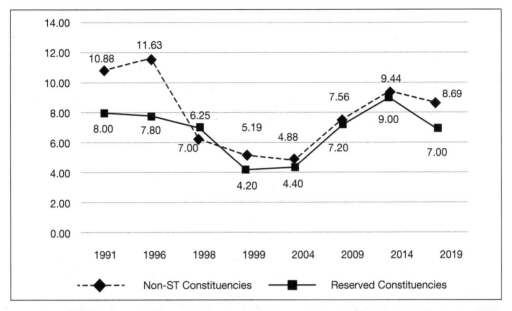

Figure 27.7 Average Candidates in Non-ST and ST Parliamentary Constituencies 1991–2019, Odisha
Source: Author's calculations from Government of India (1991, 1996, 1998, 1999, 2004b, 2009b, 2014d, 2019a).

of average candidates between the non-tribal and tribal constituencies is not significant, especially after 1998 until 2014, where it is less than one. Such figure prompted McMillan (2005, p. 252) to emphasize that the practice of reservation does not appear to negatively affect the competition in tribal constituencies.

Figure 27.8 demonstrates that the curve of the average candidates in tribal assembly constituencies of Odisha has moved upward since the 2000 election except the most recent election (2019). The average candidate of the ST assembly constituencies has decreased by 2.61 in the 2000 election and by 2.64 in the 2019 election. However, there was an impressive increase of 3.3 in the average of the contested candidates between 2004 and 2009 assembly elections.

The comparison of the parliamentary and assembly elections indicates that the ST assembly constituencies witnessed higher competition than the ST parliamentary constituencies. For instance, the ST assembly constituencies witnessed 1.45, 1.95, 0.76 and 0.12 higher competition than the ST parliamentary

constituencies in 2004, 2009, 2014 and 2019 elections, respectively. Such scenario can perhaps be explained by the degree of political assertion of tribals, which suggests that the tribal communities are becoming more assertive at the local level than the issues that affect the national politics. The relatively less competition in ST parliamentary constituencies can also be understood by considering the size of the constituencies, where each ST parliamentary constituency consists of seven assembly constituencies. Considering the large size of the parliamentary constituencies, the tribal contestants may not have requisite resources and manpower to manage the electoral engineering due to their marginal economic position.

Women Candidates in Elections

The parliamentary and assembly constituencies are gender neutral. Gender is not used as the criterion for contesting elections. Similarly, the practice of political reservation

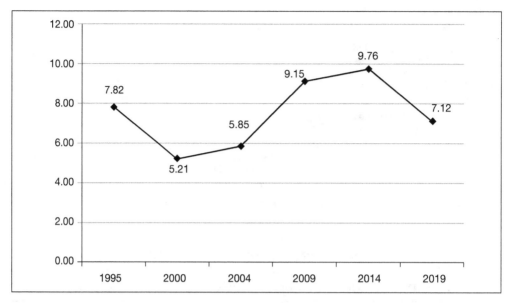

Figure 27.8   Average Candidates in ST Assembly Constituencies, 1995–2019, Odisha
Source: Author's calculation from Government of India (1995, 2000, 2004a, 2009a, 2014c, 2019b).

at the state and national levels is also gender neutral and women from tribal communities can also be the candidates in tribal and non-tribal parliamentary and assembly constituencies in India.

Figure 27.9 demonstrates the percentage of women candidates to total contested candidates in the parliamentary elections of Odisha. It shows that 7.50 per cent of women contested from the tribal constituencies in 1991 parliamentary election in Odisha, which was increased by 4.13 per cent in the 1996 election. There was a decrease by 3.06 per cent in 1998. However, there was a phenomenal increase by 10.48 per cent in 1999. It decreased to 13.64 per cent in 2004, and further to 8.33 per cent in 2009, followed by the upward curve in the 2014 and 2019 elections. Figure 27.9 depicts that more women candidates contested the tribal parliamentary constituencies than the non-tribal constituencies. For instance, 5.78 per cent, 9.48 per cent, 1.57 per cent, 14.23 per cent, 5.95 per cent, 3.37 per cent, 3.16 per cent and 3.47 per cent more

women candidates can be visible in tribal parliamentary constituencies than the non-tribal constituencies during the 1991, 1996, 1998, 1999, 2004, 2009, 2014 and 2019 elections, respectively. The wider gap between women in non-tribal and tribal constituencies was in the 1999 election and the narrow gap was in the 1998 election.

Figure 27.10 shows that 6.77 per cent, 6.21 per cent, 10.55 per cent, 10.93 per cent, 8.43 per cent and 11.06 per cent of women candidates contested from the ST assembly constituencies during 1995, 2000, 2004, 2009, 2014 and 2019 elections, respectively. During the 2004 assembly election, 4.34 per cent more women contested from the ST constituencies than the previous election, and the 2009 election experienced relatively higher percentage of ST women who contested the election. However, the percentage went down by 2.5 per cent during the 2014 assembly election. The higher percentage of women candidates in tribal assembly election was recorded in the 2019 election (11.06%).

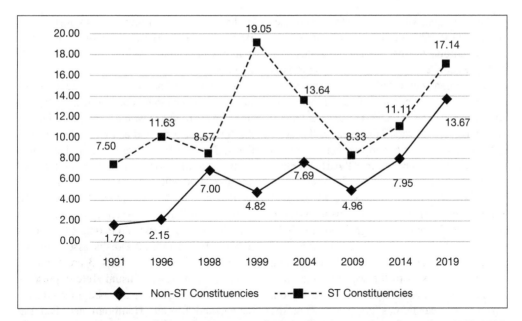

Figure 27.9   Women Candidates in Non-ST and ST Parliamentary Constituencies, 1991–2019, Odisha (in %)
Source: Author's calculations from Government of India (1991, 1996, 1998, 1999, 2004b, 2009b, 2014d, 2019a).

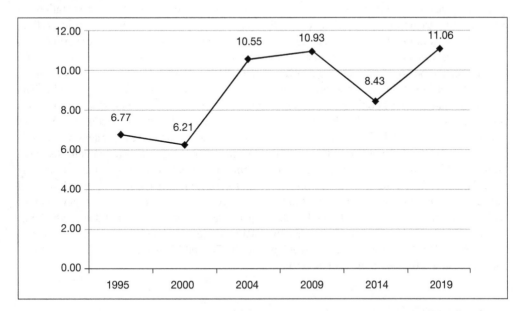

Figure 27.10   Women Candidates in ST Assembly Constituencies, 1995–2019, Odisha (in %)
Source: Author's calculation from Government of India (1995, 2000, 2004a, 2009a, 2014c, 2019b).

The comparison of women candidates contested the tribal parliamentary and assembly constituencies of Odisha indicates that 3.09 per cent, 2.68 per cent and 6.08 per cent more women contested the parliamentary constituencies than the ST assembly constituencies during the 2004, 2014 and 2019 elections, respectively. However, in the 2009 election, 2.6 per cent more women contested from the ST assembly than ST parliamentary constituencies.

Out of 51 ST women elected to the Lok Sabha since 1951, 8 are from Odisha that consisted 6 and 2 from the Congress and the BJD, respectively.[8] During the 2019 parliamentary election, the BJD was the only party that issued party tickets to the women candidates in ST-reserved constituencies. In addition, two women candidates contested from the Mayurbhanj (Parbati Purty) and Sundargarh (Juspin Lakra) constituencies as independent candidates, securing only 0.80 per cent and 1.34 per cent of votes, respectively.[9] In a way of fulfilling BJD's announcement to reserve 33 per cent tickets to women candidates, three ST-reserved parliamentary constituencies fell fray to the commitment, out of which the BJD registered its victory in one constituency and secured second position in other two constituencies. The BJD nominated Chadrani Murmu as its candidate for the Keonjhar constituency. She secured 44.74 per cent of the votes and defeated the two-time BJP MP Anant Nayak by a margin of 66,203 votes and became the youngest MP in India. During the 2019 election, the BJD offered the Koraput parliamentary constituency ticket to Kausalya Hikaka, wife of the sitting BJD MP, Jhina Hikaka. However, she lost to the Congress candidate by 3,613 votes. The BJD nominated the woman candidate Sunita Biswal to the Sundargarh ST

parliamentary constituency, who lost to the BJP's four-time MP and Union Minister of Tribal Affairs, Jual Oram, by a huge margin of 223,065 votes.

Turning to ST assembly constituencies, out of 235 contested candidates in the 2019 election, 26 were from women category. Out of 26, 6 women contested as independent candidates, 5 as the BJD, 4 as the Bahujan Samaj Party, 3 as the Congress, 2 each as the BJP and the Hindusthan Nirman Dal and 1 each as the All India Trinamool Congress, the Aam Aadmi Party, the Rashtriya Independent Morcha and the Jharkhand People's Party candidates. In the present Odisha assembly, out of 15 elected women MLAs, 3 are from the tribal communities. Kusum Tete represents the BJP from Sundargarh assembly constituency, and Basanti Hembram and Padmini Dian of the BJD represent the Karanjia and Kotpad ST-reserved assembly constituencies, respectively.

The increasing number of tribal women candidates in elections also open up the scope to have relatively better representation of women in the Parliament. Jensenius (2016, 2017) and Vaishnav (2018) underline that more women from the Scheduled Caste (SC) and ST categories are contesting elections at the cost of the SC and ST men in India. The increasing number of tribal women candidates in elections is also the product of the response that political parties have generated towards women by issuing tickets to women. Recently, some of the political parties such as the BJD and All India Trinamool Congress developed the orientation of reserving 33 per cent of party tickets for women candidates, which has largely been reflected through issuing tickets to the SC and ST women.

---

[8] Compiled from the Lok Sabha website: http://164.100.47.194/Loksabha/Members/statear.aspx?lsno
[9] This is interesting to note that both the independent women candidates were in their late 40s. Considering the vote secured by these candidates, which is marginal in comparison to the winning candidates, it reinforces the importance of party affiliation, which would help them to avail numerous benefits of being party candidate.

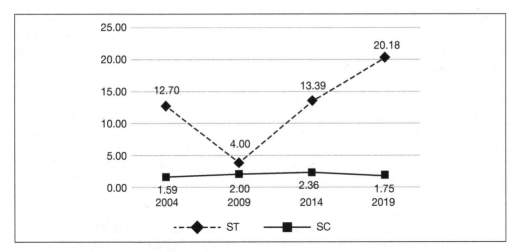

Figure 27.11   SC and ST Candidates in Non-ST and ST Parliamentary Constituencies, 1991–2019, Odisha (in %)
Source: Author's calculations from Government of India (1991, 1996, 1998, 1999, 2004b, 2009b, 2014d, 2019a).

Reserved Candidates in Unreserved Constituencies

The practice of reservation in India has been used as one of the important means of empowering the marginalized communities, such as the SCs and the STs. Hence, the practice of political reservation does not deprive the candidates from the reserved categories to contest in the unreserved constituencies. Hence, candidates from SC and ST categories are contesting in various unreserved parliamentary and assembly constituencies, sometimes as party candidates and more often as independent candidates.

Figure 27.11 reflects the percentage of SC and ST candidates who contested the elections from unreserved parliamentary constituencies in Odisha between 2004 and 2019. As per Figure 27.11, 12.70 per cent, 4.00 per cent, 13.39 per cent and 20.18 per cent of the contested candidates in unreserved constituencies were SCs in 2004, 2009, 2014 and 2019 elections, respectively. Similarly, 1.59 per cent, 2.00 per cent, 2.36 per cent and 1.75 per cent of the candidates in unreserved constituencies were tribals in 2004, 2009, 2014 and 2019 elections, respectively.

The participation rate of SCs as candidates in unreserved parliamentary constituencies was 11.11 per cent, 2.00 per cent, 11.03 per cent and 18.43 per cent higher than the STs in the 2004, 2009, 2014 and 2019 elections, respectively. These statistics suggest that the SCs are somehow in a better position to articulate themselves politically. Xaxa (2008, pp. 93–94) offers organic view of caste system to understand the relatively better political articulation of SCs than STs, suggesting that even though the SCs were subjected to untouchability and inhuman treatment, they, however, shared the language, culture and tradition of mainstream society, which eventually helped them to represent in political sphere. On the contrary, the forceful integration of tribes into the dominant political system became counterproductive, and thus dismantled their indigenous political system.

Vote Share

Different political parties make myriad competitive promises in a document called election manifesto. In addition to putting them in the document, contesting candidates and party leaders also mobilize voters on the basis of these promises. More often, voters use this document and promises as the bases of supporting candidates from different political parties. The support of the voters helps the political parties to secure competitive votes, ultimately leading to win or lose a parliamentary or assembly constituency. As political parties make competitive promises, the votes have been distributed among various political parties during various parliamentary and assembly elections.

Figure 27.12 indicates that the curve of vote share of the Congress in ST parliamentary constituencies has experienced downward movement over the period except the 2004 election, which recorded slight increase of vote share (1.51%) than the preceding election. The vote share of the Congress party over the period reflects that the Congress has been unable to retain its social support base and retain its tribal vote bank intact. The BJP has mixed experiences in terms of securing votes in tribal constituencies over the period. It secured highest votes of 44.64 per cent (highest ever secured by any political party between 1991 and 2019) in the 1999 election, when it had entered into pre-poll alliance with the BJD. Such alliance also benefitted the BJP in terms of vote share during the 1998 and 2004 elections. However, the BJP and the BJD moved away from the alliance and contested the election of 2009 on their own. As a result, the vote share of the BJP in ST parliamentary constituencies of Odisha was reduced by 13.60 per cent in the 2009 election. It managed to revive itself until recently by securing 35.20 per cent votes in the 2019 election, and this can perhaps be explained in terms of 'Modi wave' that the whole country was attracted to. The fragmentation of pre-poll alliance has strengthened BJD's position to garner highest percentage of votes in tribal constituencies among political parties, where it secured 30.63 per cent, 37.17 per cent and 35.67 per cent in 2009, 2014 and 2019 elections, respectively. The left parties have left

behind the Congress, the BJP and the BJD concerning vote share in tribal parliamentary constituencies of Odisha between 1996 and 2019.

The comparison of vote share of the Congress with the BJP suggests that the former continued to grasp more votes in ST-reserved parliamentary constituencies than the latter barring two election years. For instance, the Congress secured 30.60 per cent, 25.10 per cent, 1.80 per cent, 2.97 per cent, 8.83 per cent and 4.51 per cent higher votes than the BJP in 1991, 1996, 1998, 2004, 2009 and 2014, respectively. However, the BJP outpolled the Congress during the 1999 and 2019 elections by securing 8.49 per cent and 15.45 per cent higher votes. The Congress secured 32.47 per cent, 27.54 per cent and 29.91 per cent higher votes than the BJD during the 1998, 1999 and 2004 elections. However, this trend has begun to change since the last three general elections, where the BJD garnered 0.71 per cent, 11.03 per cent and 15.92 per cent higher votes in tribal parliamentary constituencies in the 2009, 2014 and 2019 elections. Considering the BJP and the BJD, the BJD secured 9.54 per cent, 15.54 per cent and 0.47 per cent higher votes than the BJP in the 2009, 2014 and 2019 elections. The unpleasant vote share curve of the BJD during the 1998, 1999 and 2004 elections is due to the fact that the BJD contested fewer seats because of its pre-poll alliances with the BJP. The left parties secured less than 1 per cent of votes in the 1996, 1998, 1999, 2014 and 2019 elections. However, it secured 1.29 per cent and 3.02 per cent of votes in ST parliamentary constituencies in the 2004 and 2009 elections, respectively.

Interestingly, the seat arrangement in ST constituencies was made so strategically that provided numerical edge to the BJP over the BJD. For instance, out of the five ST parliamentary constituencies, Koraput was the only constituency where the BJD contested during the alliance period. The other four constituencies, namely Sundargarh, Keonjhar, Mayurbhang and Nabarangpur, witnessed the

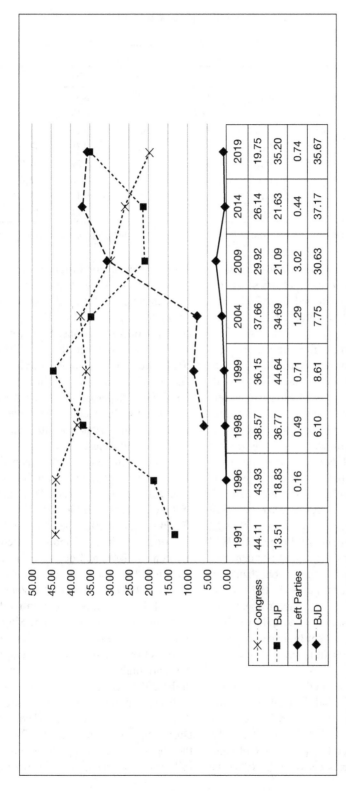

	1991	1996	1998	1999	2004	2009	2014	2019
--✕-- Congress	44.11	43.93	38.57	36.15	37.66	29.92	26.14	19.75
--■-- BJP	13.51	18.83	36.77	44.64	34.69	21.09	21.63	35.20
--◆-- Left Parties		0.16	0.49	0.71	1.29	3.02	0.44	0.74
--◆-- BJD			6.10	8.61	7.75	30.63	37.17	35.67

Figure 27.12 Vote Share of Political Parties in ST Parliamentary Constituencies, 1991–2019, Odisha (in %)

Source: Author's calculations from Government of India (1991, 1996, 1998, 1999, 2004b, 2009b, 2014d, 2019a).

Table 27.5   Vote Share of Political Parties in Non-ST and ST Parliamentary Constituencies, Odisha, 1991–2019

	Congress		BJP		Left Parties		BJD	
Year	Non-ST	ST	Non-ST	ST	Non-ST	ST	Non-ST	ST
1991	43.73	44.11	8.47	13.51	6.33	NA	NA	NA
1996	44.79	43.93	11.74	18.83	2.60	0.16	NA	NA
1998	41.41	38.57	16.44	36.77	1.82	0.49	33.52	6.10
1999	36.85	36.15	18.60	44.64	1.70	0.71	39.98	8.61
2004	41.21	37.66	14.90	34.69	0.19	1.29	36.37	7.75
2009	33.58	29.92	15.65	21.09	3.48	3.02	39.17	30.63
2014	26.22	26.14	21.77	21.63	0.75	0.44	46.79	37.17
2019	12.07	19.75	39.74	35.20	0.58	0.74	45.40	35.67

Source: Author's calculation from Government of India (1991, 1996, 1998, 1999, 2004b, 2009b, 2014d, 2019a).

BJP candidates. However, in non-ST parliamentary constituencies, out of 16 seats, the BJP and the BJD contested 5 and 11 seats during the 1998, 1999 and 2004 elections, respectively.

Table 27.5 provides the comparative figures of political parties' vote share in non-tribal and tribal constituencies, which reveals that the Congress secured 0.38 per cent and 7.68 per cent higher votes in tribal constituencies than non-tribal constituencies in the 1991 and 2019 elections. However, it secured 0.86 per cent, 2.84 per cent, 0.70 per cent, 3.55 per cent, 3.66 per cent and 0.08 per cent higher votes in non-tribal constituencies in the 1996, 1998, 1999, 2004, 2009 and 2014 elections, respectively. Considering the BJP, it secured 5.04 per cent, 7.09 per cent, 20.33 per cent, 26.04 per cent, 19.79 per cent and 5.44 per cent higher votes in tribal than non-tribal constituencies in the 1991, 1996, 1998, 1999, 2004 and 2009 elections, respectively. However, the vote share of the BJP was 0.14 per cent and 4.54 per cent higher in the non-tribal than tribal constituencies in the 2014 and 2019 elections.

The left parties secured higher percentage of votes in the non-tribal than tribal constituencies between the 1996 and 2019 elections, except the 2004 and 2019 elections. The BJD, however, experienced less percentage of votes in tribal constituencies between the 1998 and

2019 elections. For instance, the differences of vote share between tribal and non-tribal constituencies for the BJD were significant during the 1998 (27.42%), 1999 (31.37%) and 2004 (28.62%) elections. However, such differences were reduced during 2009 (8.54%), 2014 (9.62%) and 2019 (9.73%) elections. The significant differences during 1998, 1999 and 2004 can perhaps be understood by the fact that the BJD contested higher number of seats in non-tribal constituencies than the tribal constituencies.

Consider the ST assembly constituencies, the vote share of the Congress in Odisha has drastically decreased from 38.82 per cent in 1995 to 20.06 per cent in 2019 (Figure 27.13). The BJP gained 10.13 per cent votes in tribal constituencies in 1995 and increased to 26.81 per cent in 2000 and decreased to 23.86 per cent in 2004, where the BJP was in alliance with the BJD. However, the vote share of the BJP impressively increased by 11.80 per cent during the 2019 election. Similarly, the BJD has registered an upward curve of vote share between 2004 and 2019 and continued to secure highest votes in tribal constituencies in the 2019 election. The left parties continue to disappoint their supporters by securing less than 2 per cent of votes in tribal constituencies. During the 2019 election, the BJD occupied the top position among the political parties in terms of securing votes in tribal assembly

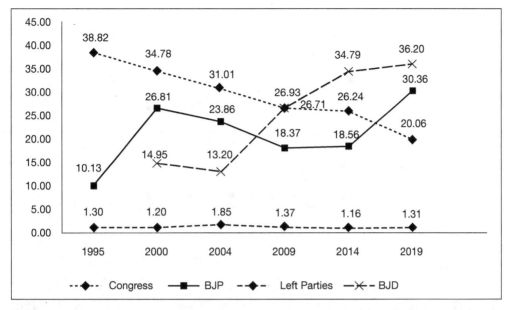

Figure 27.13   Vote Share of Political Parties in ST Assembly Constituencies, 1995–2019, Odisha (in %)

Source: Author's calculation from Government of India (1995, 2000, 2004a, 2009a, 2014c, 2019b).

constituencies, followed by the BJP and the Congress. The left parties, however, continue to be in fourth position in garnering votes in tribal constituencies both in Parliament and assembly constituencies over the period.

During the 2019 election, the Congress party occupied second position in terms of vote share in 12 assembly constituencies, third in 14 constituencies and fourth in 1 constituency. Similarly, the BJP was second in 7, third in 13 and fourth in 2 constituencies. The BJD came second in 14 constituencies and third in 1 constituency. However, the CPI(M) secured highest vote share in Bonai tribal assembly constituency. To put it differently, the performance of the BJD was impressive in terms of vote sharing in the 2019 election.

Seat Share

There is a close relationship between vote share and seat share in different parliamentary and assembly elections. Vote share of political parties would help them to gain seat share.

The close analysis of electoral statistics suggests that political parties with highest vote share usually secure the maximum number of seats in the final electoral outcome tally in India.

Turning to seat share among the political parties in tribal parliamentary constituencies, Figure 27.14 shows that the Congress has performed well by securing four and five out of five seats during the 1991 and 1996 elections. Nonetheless, the performance of the Congress went down after the 1996 election, and it did not even register a victory in the 2014 parliamentary election in tribal constituencies of Odisha. However, it managed to win the Koraput tribal constituency by defeating the BJD candidate by 3,613 votes in the 2019 parliamentary election. The pre-poll alliance between the BJP and the BJD helped the former to win three, four and three out of five tribal seats during the 1998, 1999 and 2004 elections, respectively. The dismantling of the alliance affected the performance of the BJP in terms of seat share and benefitted the BJD, where it won three and four seats in the 2009

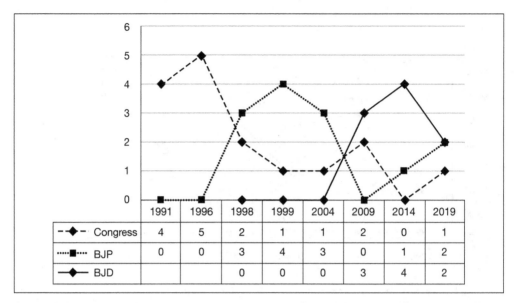

	1991	1996	1998	1999	2004	2009	2014	2019
Congress	4	5	2	1	1	2	0	1
BJP	0	0	3	4	3	0	1	2
BJD			0	0	0	3	4	2

Figure 27.14   Seat Share of Political Parties in ST Parliamentary Constituencies, 1991–2019, Odisha (in %)
Source: Author's calculations from Government of India (1991, 1996, 1998, 1999, 2004b, 2009b, 2014d, 2019a).

and 2014 elections. However, both the BJP and the BJD secured two tribal parliamentary seats each in the 2019 election, leaving one to the Congress. The left parties did not win even a single tribal parliamentary constituency of Odisha between the 1991 and 2019 elections.

During the 2019 parliamentary election, out of five ST-reserved constituencies, the Congress party contested from the Nabarangpur, Koraput, Sundargarh and Keonjhar constituencies, and it did not contest from the Mayurbhanj constituency. Out of four contested constituencies, it won only the Koraput constituency, secured second position in Nabarangpur constituency and third position in Sundargarh and Keonjhar constituencies in terms of polled votes. Similarly, the BJP and the BJD contested all the five seats in Odisha. The BJP won the Mayurbhanj and Sundargarh constituencies and secured second position in Keonjhar and third position in Nabarangpur and Koraput constituencies. It is important to mention that the BJP had issued party ticket to the parachuted candidate, Balabhadra Majhi, who had represented the Nabarangpur seat in

the Parliament from the BJD during the 2014 election. The BJD contested the Nabarangpur and Keonjhar constituencies successfully and secured second position in Koraput, Mayurbhanj and Sundargarh constituencies. The party-level analysis in ST parliamentary constituencies appears to suggest that the BJD has been successful in garnering the tribal votes in Odisha. In short, there is a proportionate relationship between vote share and seat share in tribal parliamentary constituencies in Odisha (Figures 27.12 and 27.14).

Turning to tribal assembly constituencies in Odisha, Figure 27.15 indicates that between 1995 and 2019, the best performance of the Congress was in 1995, where it won 22 out of 34 seats. Since then, the number of winning seats has gone down, leading to the worst performance in the recent election (2019), where it secured 2 out of 33 tribal constituencies in Odisha. Considering the performance of the BJP, it won 13 seats each during the period when it had entered into pre-poll alliance during the 2000 and 2004 elections. During the 2019 election, it secured 11 seats. The left

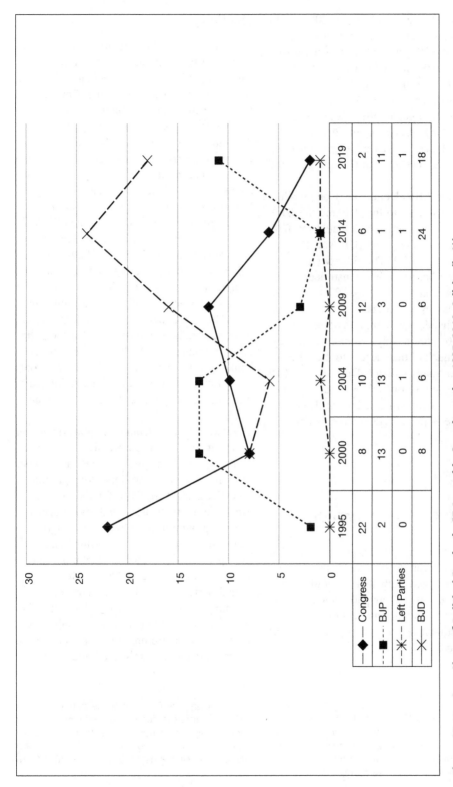

	1995	2000	2004	2009	2014	2019
Congress	22	8	10	12	6	2
BJP	2	13	13	3	1	11
Left Parties	0	0	1	0	1	1
BJD		8	6	6	24	18

Figure 27.15   Seat Share of Political Parties in ST Assembly Constituencies, 1995–2019, Odisha (in %)

Source: Author's calculation from Government of India (1995, 2000, 2004a, 2009a, 2014c, 2019b).

parties won one seat each in the 2004, 2014 and 2019 elections. The BJD won 16 out of 33 seats in the 2009 assembly election. It won 18 seats in 2019, down from 24 in 2014, but increased its vote share from 34.79 per cent in 2014 to 36.20 per cent in 2019. To put it differently, the BJD gained the tribal seats at the cost of the Congress. During the 2019 election, the BJP seat share increased, thereby leading to decrease the seat share of the Congress and the BJD.

During the 2019 election, the Congress lost 1 and 12 tribal seats to the BJP and the BJD, respectively. The Congress defeated the BJD in two seats. Similarly, the BJP won 10 seats by defeating the BJD. The BJD defeated the BJP in six tribal assembly constituencies. In Lakshmipur constituency, the BJD defeated the Congress by a meagre of 229 votes. On the other hand, the Congress defeated the BJD by 946 votes in Rajgangpur constituency. However, much of the success to the BJD has come from south Odisha. During the 2019 assembly election, out of 33 tribal constituencies, 27 of them witnessed tripartite contest between the BJD, the BJP and the Congress.

III

EXPLAINING THE PHENOMENON

The performance of political parties in tribal constituencies cannot be looked in isolation and is intertwined with their overall performance in the state. Their performance in the state also has critical implications over tribal constituencies both at the national and state politics.

The Congress

Over the period, the electoral statistics indicated that the Congress has begun to lose its support base in tribal constituencies of Odisha. Since the performance of the Congress in tribal constituencies is intertwined with the trend that the party has been witnessing at the national and state levels, the immediate explanation appears to suggest that the dismal performance of the party in tribal constituencies is due to the trend that the Congress has lost national and state elections recently. The internal faction of the party and the leadership crisis in Odisha has led to the dismal performance of the Congress.[10] Due to internal factions and incompetent leadership, the Congress could not mobilize voters at the grassroots level, including tribal constituencies. The dismal performance of the Congress is also partially due to the fact that the political entrepreneurs at the lower level who once helped the Congress to reach the grassroots shifted from the Congress to the ruling party, the BJD, during the 2014 election (Manor, 2015, p. 201).

However, the Congress' enactment of some of the most progressive legislations such as the Scheduled Tribes and Other Traditional Forest Dwellers (Recognition of Forest Rights) Act, 2006, for the benefits of tribal communities along with over dozens of welfare programmes helped the Congress to secure tribal seats at least in immediate following elections. However, the trend seems to have derailed since 2009, resulting in the dismal performance of the Congress in tribal assembly constituencies in Odisha. It failed to sustain support among the tribes in subsequent elections and, therefore, could not succeed in interpreting the legislative measures along the

---

[10] The former leader of opposition (27 May 2009 to 7 March 2014) and the President of the state unit of the Congress, Bhupinder Singh, joined the BJD in March 2014 allegedly after the Congress denied him Lok Sabha tickets from Kalahandi constituency. The BJD rewarded him with a Rajya Sabha ticket. It has also been reported that two former Congress leaders Narasingh Mishra, the former leader of opposition (11 June 2014 to 29 May 2019) and Prasad Harichandan, the former Pradesh Congress Committee president (15 December 2014 to 18 April 2018), are opposed to each other (Swain, 2019, p. 25).

line of, what Ahmed and Swain (2019, p. 13) call in the context of the BJD, the vocabulary of a state-specific language of politics.

The BJP

During the coalition government between the BJD and the BJP, the declining political fortune of the Congress in the state, in general, and the tribal constituencies, in particular, benefitted the coalition partner between 2004 and 2009. The continuous political decline of the Congress over the successive elections continued to benefit both these parties even after they parted out of the alliance. The BJP also did not succeed much in terms of polling the votes as well as seat share in tribal constituencies of Odisha. Manor (2015) accounted the failure of the BJP in Odisha during the 2014 election to the organizational weakness of the party and the crisis of the leadership. It has also been pointed out that the credibility of the party chief was so limited that there was hardly any respect of the party chief at the state level outside his home turf Bolangir. As a consequence, the prime ministerial candidate, Narendra Modi, decided to not return to the state for further campaigning after his first round of 2014 election campaign in Odisha (Manor, 2015, p. 200).

The BJP has always given importance to tribal constituencies in Odisha. Drawing lessons from the central Indian experiences where the auxiliary organizations such as the Rashtriya Swayamsevak Sangh (RSS), Vishwa Hindu Parishad and Bajrang Dal helped the BJP to gain tribal support, it had successfully bargained with its coalition partner in the 2000 and 2004 elections. Out of 5 and 34 parliamentary and assembly tribal constituencies, it contested four and 23 seats, respectively. As a result, it increased its performance from securing two seats in 1995 to 13 each in the 2000 and 2004 elections, pushing the Congress to reduce its seat share from 22 in 1995 to 8 and 10 in 2000 and 2004, respectively. Alam (2007) partially accounted

the success of the BJP to its various organizational wings. The performance was, however, not up to satisfaction when it contested the 2009 and 2014 elections solely, where it won only three and one assembly tribal constituencies. Although the BJP secured 18.37 per cent and 18.59 per cent of the votes in tribal assembly constituencies in 2009 and 2014, it failed to convert the vote share into seat share. The right-wing organizations also did not help much the BJP in this context.

Kanungo (2014) suggests that there was a remote presence of auxiliary organizations in Odisha. They were unable to make much inroads into the tribal lifeworld in terms of political mobilization, and much success was inexperienced in terms of translating the tribal support into electoral outcomes. The right-wing organization, the RSS, was earlier projecting itself as a cultural organization with a commitment to protect and promote the interests of the Hindus (Kanungo, 2003), thereby providing indirect support to the BJP. However, in recent time, there is a direct involvement of the RSS in mobilizing voters in supporting the BJP, which seems to have resulted counterproductive in Odisha (Ahmed & Swain, 2009, p. 14). In contrast, Thachil (2014) argues that the right-wing forces played a critical role in converting the tribal support into electoral outcomes for the BJP in central India.

The BJP, however, learnt lessons from its dismal electoral performance in the state in 2014, and redesigned its strategies and increased its performance during the most recent election in 2019. This is in continuation of its performance at the panchayat-level election in February 2019, where the BJP won 88 seats in comparison to its tally of 16 in 2012 panchayat election. It has been presumed that there was a shift of support from the Congress to the BJP in order to check the BJD (Swain, 2019, p. 25). Such performance of the BJP at the local level indicated the possibility of increasing both the vote and seat shares in 2019 parliamentary and assembly elections of Odisha. BJP's vote and seat shares in 2019 parliamentary and assembly elections in tribal constituencies are partially accounted to the 'Modi wave' that the whole country experienced.

The BJD

As mentioned earlier, the BJD contested the 1998, 1999 and 2004 parliamentary elections and 2000 and 2004 assembly elections in alliance with the BJP. The BJD, however, did not give much emphasis to the parliamentary and assembly constituencies reserved for the tribes on the bargaining table, ending up contesting 1 out 5 and 11 out of 34 tribal seats in parliamentary and assembly elections. The existing electoral statistics suggest that the BJD did not win any parliamentary tribal constituencies until it decided to contest the election on its own. Similarly, the success rate of the BJD in terms of vote and seat shares was relatively lower even in the tribal assembly constituencies during the alliance period. The performance of the BJD, however, was impressive when it contested the election without an alliance with the BJP.

Roy (2011, p. 33) explores the context of BJD's decision to move away with its alliance. The municipality elections in Cuttack and Baripada in the first week of 2009 provided enough indication that the BJD can contest the 2009 election without its coalition partner.[11] During this election, the BJP which had won majority of the municipality seats in the 2007 election managed to win only 2 seats and the BJD mustered 37 seats. Manor (2015) and Roy (2011) emphasize that the communal riots in Kandhamal and the involvement of the right-wing forces also enabled the BJD to

move out of the alliance. Kanungo (2014, p. 55) was, however, sceptical to such position and emphasized that during the Kandhamal violence in 2007 and 2008, Naveen Patnaik was uncertain about breaking away from the alliance.[12] The BJD opted out of the ties with the BJP when it became confident of winning subsequent elections on its own, which has probably generated with the electoral outcomes of the municipality elections in 2009. The fracture of the alliance considerably helped the BJD to win 103 out 147 assembly constituencies, and 16 out of 33 tribal assembly constituencies in 2009.

The BJD's initial success in Odisha politics is largely due to the political declining of the Congress. The popularity of Naveen Patnaik also helped the BJD to gain support from the masses in the state and across the constituencies. Manor (2015, p. 201) emphasized that BJD's success in 2014 election was linked with the poll promises such as reduction of farmer's loan to 1 per cent, creation of irrigation facilities, high-quality seeds, fertilizers, pesticides and technical assistance to gram panchayats, and electricity to villages, among others though most of them remained unfulfilled. He further summarized that tripartite contests between the BJD, the BJP and the Congress; inefficient leadership and organizational weakness of the Congress and the BJP; ability to outspend both the rival parties; the achievements in some sectors and the chief minister's image as a strong leader were responsible for BJD's win in the 2014 election (Manor, 2015, p. 202). Similarly, Ahmed and Swain (2019) give much credit to BJD's positive response to the idea of welfarism, good governance and women empowerment. They

---

[11] Although the BJD and the BJP had formed the coalition government at the state, they fought the municipality election in Cuttack and Baripada separately. The BJD moved away from the alliance on 7 March 2019.

[12] Ziegfeld (2016a) argues that pre-poll alliances may bring short-term benefits, however, they pose long-term risks of being absent in constituencies, thereby alienating voters from the political party. The BJP was the victim of such risks in the aftermath of pre-poll alliance with the BJD. For instance, consider the 10 assembly tribal constituencies that the BJP did not contested as a part of the alliance, it won only the Udayagiri constituency and secured second position in one constituency and third position in eight constituencies in terms of vote sharing during the immediate aftermath election of 2009.

did not, however, rule out the possibility that the decline of the Congress helped the BJD.

In addition, the BJD also has a good record of managing and implementing welfare programmes, which has shifted the tribal support base of the Congress to the BJD over the period. The implementation of welfare programmes through bureaucrats has provided marginal involvement for the political leaders, which has been seen by the tribals/voters in a positive light. Such style of governance through institutional approaches has proved to be productive for the BJD. However, such orientation towards governance and implementation of welfare programmes through bureaucratic means may not always produce positive results for the ruling party. It may sometimes distance the voters from the political leaders/party workers of the ruling party as it has been happening with the Trinamool Congress in West Bengal, and the opposition may take advantage of such circumstances.

The BJD has been following the notion of 'pick and choose' while implementing the welfare programmes and legislations enacted by the central government. It has a poor record in implementing the employment generation programme like the Mahatma Gandhi National Rural Employment Guarantee Act, 2005, in Odisha. However, the BJD has an impressive record of implementing the tribal targeted legislations like the Forest Rights Act 2006, and occupies first position in terms of its implementation in India.[13] Such implementation through centralized governance system has turned out to be positive for the

BJD during elections in tribal constituencies. The state also improved the public distribution system (PDS) and maintained a record of the impact of PDS on rural poverty higher than the national average. To put it differently, the BJD appropriated the central legislation when it came down to the state of Odisha.

The voter may consider the move of the central government as beneficial for the whole country (Ziegfeld, 2016b, p. 62) and the regional dimension of a specific region may not come to the limelight. The success of the BJD in Odisha in reference to the initiatives of the central government echoes the findings of Chidambaram (2014, pp. 22–14), where the state government has appropriated the benefits of central legislation (Forest Rights Act). In tribal areas, the BJD consolidated its position by implementing financial aid (popular) scheme to the farmers such as the Krushak Assistance for Livelihood and Income Augmentation, popularly known as the KALIA scheme. To suffix, the interaction of Naveen Patnaik with the (tribal) people via video conference as a part of the *Ama Gaon Ama Bikash* (Our Village Our Development) programme and assuring tribals to increase financial assistance, among others, appeared to keep the tribal support base intact and signalled that the party is committed for the development and welfare of the tribals, at a time when most of the parties endured anti-incumbency.[14] Hence, Ahmed and Swain (2019, p. 15) argue that welfarism has become the instrument of expressing political sentiment towards the marginalized sections of Odisha like the tribal communities.

---

[13] Odisha has issued the highest number of land titles under the Forest Rights Act. Odisha has a record of issuing 300,321 individual and 879 community titles as on 31 December 2012, 328,808 individual and 3,131 community titles as on 31 March 2014 (GOI, 2014a, p. 210), 340,594 individual and 3,474 community titles as on 31 December 2014 (GOI, 2015, p. 206), 349,400 individual and 5,004 community titles as on 31 December 2015 (GOI, 2016, p. 54) and 399,996 individual and 5,513 community titles as on 30 November 2016 (GOI, 2017, p. 62).

[14] When Naveen Patnaik was interacting with the people of Malkangiri district on 27 June 2018, a 25-year-old tribal woman, Mamta Padiami, requested him to enhance the amount of health insurance. Ms Padiami said, 'Health issues of women are more. While 50 percent reservation for women in PRIs has empowered them by contributing significantly in the decision-making process, you have done a lot for women under Mission Shakti programme. I request you to enhance the health coverage which will benefit the women' (Singha, 2018). As a result, Mr Patnaik increased health assistance for women from ₹5 lakh to ₹7 lakh under the Biju Swasthya Kalyan Yojana.

The regional analysis of tribal politics of Odisha suggests that much support for the BJD came from the southern part of the state, where 12 out of 33 seats are located. The BJD secured 7 out of 12 seats in 2009 election. The BJD increased its performance in the 2004 and 2019 elections, where it secured 9 out of 12 seats located in the region. Ambagudia's (2019a) empirical research explains the much success of the BJD in tribal constituencies of southern Odisha. He argues that the BJD was compelled to respond positively to issues and concerns that were grappling the tribal communities of south Odisha. For instance, when there was a conflict between tribals and the Bengali migrants over land and forest resources in Nabarangpur district in 2001, tribals demanded the identification and deportation of Bengali infiltrators. As a consequence, the BJD initiated the process of identification, detection and deportation from the state (Ambagudia, 2019a, p. 148) even though the BJP, which was then functioning as the junior partner of the coalition government, opposed the move of the BJD. The BJD also withdrew cases that were filed against the tribals during the conflicts. The BJD also performed impressively in tribal constituencies located in another migrant-receiving Malkangiri district of south Odisha. However, the BJD has begun to experience decline in the most recent election. This may be partially because of the fact that the BJD is being seen as friendly to business interests (Ziegfeld, 2016b, p. 199).

IV

ISSUES OF TRIBAL POLITICS IN ODISHA

The contemporary tribal politics in Odisha is being grappling with myriad issues. Some of the critical issues are briefly discussed below.

Migration

Ambagudia (2019a) has extensively dealt with the impact of the issue of migration on tribal politics of Odisha. Migration has become so critical, at least in the southern part of the state where most of the tribal assembly constituencies are located. The rehabilitation of Bengali migrants to whom the state granted the SC status has not only seriously affected the demographic picture of south Odisha but also cornered much of the benefits meant for general accessibility. Since the reservation of seats is based on their numerical strength, demographic change due to the accommodation of the migrants in the early 1960s has affected the total number of seats that were available earlier to the local tribal communities.

Land Alienation

The legislative measure, the Orissa Scheduled Areas Transfer of Immovable Property (by Scheduled Tribes) (OSATIP) Regulation, 1956, amended from time to time, has not proved to be successful in regulating the alienation of tribal land in Odisha. Meanwhile, the state government has made an attempt to dilute the provisions of OSATIP Regulation in 2010, allowing the transfer of tribal land to the non-tribals and this was also approved by the governor and sent for the president's assent. The president, however, did not give the assent. As a result, the state government has reconstituted an inter-ministerial committee to relook at the matter (Barik, 2015). Meanwhile, the tribals of Odisha have been experiencing high degree of tribal land alienation. Tribal lands are being alienated in various means, leading to dispossession and deprivation of tribal communities in Odisha (Mohanty, 2014; Ambagudia, 2010, 2017).

Demand for Tribal Autonomous District Council

Alam (2007, p. 272) reflects that the Orissa Nari Samaj, an apex body of 53 tribal organizations, organized a 'human chain' in Bhubaneswar on 10 March 2004. The Orissa Nari Samaj demanded the establishment of Tribal Autonomous District Council in Odisha to have a greater say of tribes in governance of the area and the management of natural resources such as land, water and forest. Such demands are emerging time and again in different parts of the state due to their increasing experiences of incompatibilities with the state in relation to resources.

Alliances between Tribes and Political Parties

Over the period, various tribal communities are forming alliances with either political parties or deciding to support a candidate filled by political parties with a hope that the elected candidates would work towards protecting and promoting tribal interests. Alam (2007, pp. 273–274) explores such alliances between tribes and political parties. For instance, the Adivasi Kranti Sangathan of Dhenkanal district decided to support Tathagat Satpathy, the BJD candidate. He was vocal on tribal issues in the Parliament until his retirement from politics recently. In 2004, the tribals backed Jharkhand Mukti Morcha candidate, Sudam Marandi, who won the election and the party increased its vote share from 16.33 per cent in 1999 to 37.43 per cent in 2004. The credit to the victory of the BJD in Phulbani Lok Sabha constituency in 2004 has been given to the Kondh tribal communities of Kandhamal district.

Tribal Movement

The state of Odisha is experiencing a series of tribal movements in relation to control over and access to resources. Tribal communities spearheaded such movements in relation to development-induced displacement, where they share more than 40 per cent of the total displacees and against the increasing interventionist role of the state in the 1990s. In the 1990s, the state entered into a number of memorandum of understandings with the multinational corporations, facilitating them to extract mineral and forest resources from tribal areas, thereby alienating the rights of the tribals over resources. Some of the prominent tribal movements are Kashipur struggle, Niyamgiri Movement, etc. (Ambgudia, 2017).

Role of Insurgent Groups

Ambagudia (2019) explores the relationship between insurgent group (Naxalites) and tribal politics in Odisha. Naxalites have made inroads into the tribal areas of Odisha. They have made frequent attempts to derail the election process in Odisha by scribing posters carrying dire consequences in tribal areas, in particular. However, their repeated attempts of creating fear among the voters in tribal constituencies and dismantling the process of exercising their political rights did not have any significant impact on electoral outcomes. The tribal constituencies located in the 'red corridors' area of south Odisha continue to experience high voter turnout despite the Naxalites' warning with dire consequences. Left parties, ideologically synchronized with the insurgent groups, have not experienced much success in tribal constituencies of Odisha. To put it differently, though there is a general perception that the insurgent groups get support from the tribes, they are, however, unable to influence the electoral outcomes in tribal areas.

Identity

The (de)scheduling of communities has become a regular phenomenon in India. The Xaxa Commission has pointed out that a total of 272 modifications have been made in the list of STs in India since 2001 (GOI, 2014b, p. 47). In Odisha, this has become a trend since the colonial period (Ambagudia, 2019a, pp. 239–242). Odisha has experienced 115 modifications in ST list since 2001 (GOI, 2013, p. 120). Although the Jhodia community of Odisha availed the ST status, the Parliament modified the ST list of Odisha and excluded them from the list. Needless to mention that a Jhodia candidate was elected in the first assembly election of the state (1951) and handful of Jhodia people were elected to the Panchayati Raj Institutions as STs. Despite the state government's recommendation, they are still struggling to get included in the central government list (Ambagudia, 2011, p. 41).

CONCLUSION

The chapter provided an overview and explored the trend of tribal politics in Odisha. In Odisha, the Congress used to garner the support of the social groups. Considering the above analysis, the tribal social support base has become unreliable for a longer period. For instance, the Congress was dominated vote share and seat share in tribal constituencies. However, the Congress party is experiencing decline at both fronts of vote and seat shares. The BJD has been able to gain much from the tribal constituencies (2009–2014). Nonetheless, the trend also seems to have begun to change. The 2019 election witnessed the slight decline of vote as well as seat shares of the BJD, and the BJP has taken the advantage of such decline of the BJD. To put it differently, the decline of the Congress benefitted the BJD and the BJP. However, such trend has not reversed where the relative decline of the BJD in the most recent times has benefitted the BJP and not the Congress. In short, the analysis of tribal politics in Odisha suggests that the national political parties used to dominate the tribal constituencies in terms of vote and seat shares, and this has changed over the period and the regional party, the BJD, is drawing more support base from social groups than the national parties such as the Congress, the BJP and the CPI.

REFERENCES

Ahmed, H., & Swain, G. (2019). Election results in Odisha: Welfarism versus Hindutva. *Economic & Political Weekly, 54*(33), 13–15.

Alam, M. B. (2007). Validating status quo and local narratives in Orissa. In R. Roy, & P. Wallace (Eds.), *India's 2004 elections: Grass-roots and national perspectives* (pp. 267–290). New Delhi: SAGE Publications.

Ambagudia, J. (2010). Tribal rights, dispossession and the state in Orissa. *Economic & Political Weekly, 45*(33), 60–67.

Ambagudia, J. (2011). Scheduled tribes and the politics of inclusion in India. *Asian Social Work and Policy Review, 5*, 33–43.

Ambagudia, J. (2017). Regime of marginalisation and sites of protest: Understanding the adivasi movement in Odisha, India. In H. Devere, K. T. Maiharoa, & J. P. Synott (Eds.), *Peacebuilding and the rights of indigenous peoples: Experiences and the strategies for the 21st century* (pp. 155–165). Cham: Springer.

Ambagudia, J. (2019a). *Adivasis, migrants and the state in India*. London and New York, NY: Routledge.

Ambagudia, J. (2019b). Scheduled tribes, reserved constituencies and political reservation in India. *Journal of Social Inclusion Studies, 5*(1), 44–58.

Barik, S. (2015, 9 November). Odisha may allow tribals to sell their land to non-tribals. *The Hindu*.

Chidambaram, S. (2014). Play in the states: The Indian voter's 2014 mandate. *Economic & Political Weekly, 49*(30), 22–24.

Government of India. (1991). *Statistical report on general elections, 1991 to the tenth Lok Sabha*. New Delhi: Election Commission of India.

Government of India. (1995). *Statistical report on general election, 1995 to legislative assembly of Orissa.* New Delhi: Election Commission of India.

Government of India. (1996). *Statistical report on general elections, 1996 to the eleventh Lok Sabha.* New Delhi: Election Commission of India.

Government of India. (1998). *Statistical report on general elections, 1998 to the 12th Lok Sabha.* New Delhi: Election Commission of India.

Government of India. (1999). *Statistical report on general elections, 1999 to the thirteenth Lok Sabha.* New Delhi: Election Commission of India.

Government of India. (2000). *Statistical report on general election, 2000 to legislative assembly of Orissa.* New Delhi: Election Commission of India.

Government of India. (2004a). *Statistical report on general election, 2004 to legislative assembly of Orissa.* New Delhi: Election Commission of India.

Government of India. (2004b). *Statistical report on general elections, 2004 to the 14th Lok Sabha.* New Delhi: Election Commission of India.

Government of India. (2008). *Changing face of electoral India: Delimitation 2008* (Vol. II). New Delhi: Delimitation Commission of India.

Government of India. (2009a). *Statistical report on general election, 2009 to legislative assembly of Orissa.* New Delhi: Election Commission of India.

Government of India. (2009b). *Statistical report on general elections, 2009 to the 15th Lok Sabha.* New Delhi: Election Commission of India.

Government of India. (2013). *Statistical profile of scheduled tribes in India, 2013.* New Delhi: Ministry of Tribal Affairs.

Government of India. (2014a). *Annual report, 2013–2014.* New Delhi: Ministry of Tribal Affairs.

Government of India. (2014b). *Report of the high level committee on socio-economic, health and educational status of tribal communities of India* (Chairman: Professor Virginius Xaxa). New Delhi: Ministry of Tribal Affairs.

Government of India. (2014c). *Statistical report on general election, 2014 to legislative assembly of Orissa.* New Delhi: Election Commission of India.

Government of India. (2014d). *Statistical report on general elections, 2014 to the 16th Lok Sabha.* New Delhi: Election Commission of India.

Government of India. (2015). *Tribal welfare & development.* New Delhi: Ministry of Tribal Affairs.

Government of India. (2016). *Annual report, 2015–2016.* New Delhi: Ministry of Tribal Affairs.

Government of India. (2017). *Annual report, 2016–2017.* New Delhi: Ministry of Tribal Affairs.

Government of India. (2019a). *General election, 2019.* New Delhi: Election Commission of India. Retrieved from https://eci.gov.in/files/category/1359-general-election-2019/

Government of India. (2019b). *Odisha legislative assembly election, 2019.* New Delhi: Election Commission of India. Retrieved from https://eci.gov.in/files/file/11679-odisha-legislative-assembly-election-2019/

Jensenius, F. R. (2016). Competing inequalities? On the intersection of gender and ethnicity in candidate nominations in Indian elections. *Government and Opposition, 51*(3), 440–463.

Jensenius, F. R. (2017). *Social justice through inclusion: Consequences of electoral quotas in India.* Oxford: Oxford University Press.

Kanungo, P. (2003). Hindutva's entry into a 'Hindu province': Early years of RSS in Orissa. *Economic & Political Weekly, 38*(31), 3293–3303.

Kanungo, P. (2014). Shift from syncretism to communalism. *Economic & Political Weekly, 49*(14), 48–55.

Manor, J. (2015). An Odisha landslide buries both national parties: Assessing the state and parliamentary elections of 2014. *Contemporary South Asia, 23*(2), 198–210.

McMillan, A. (2005). *Standing at the margins: Representation and electoral reservation in India.* New Delhi: Oxford University Press.

Mohanty, M. (2014). Persisting dominance: Crisis of democracy in a resource-rich region. *Economic & Political Weekly, 49*(14), 39–47.

Roy, R. (2011). Regional base and national dream: Alliance formation, 2009 national elections. In P. Wallace, & R. Roy (Eds.), *India's 2009 elections: Coalition politics, party competition and Congress continuity* (pp. 21–41). New Delhi: SAGE Publications.

Singha, M. (2018). Naveen keeps request of tribal lady, enhances health insurance amount up to 7 lakh for women. Retrieved from https://timesofindia.indiatimes.com/city/bhubaneswar/naveen-keeps-request-of-tribal-lady-enhances-health-assurance-amount-up-to-7-lakh-for-women/articleshow/64765643.cms

Swain, G. (2019). Odisha panchayat elections: Questioning the BJP swing. *Economic & Political Weekly, 52*(22), 23–26.

Thachil, T. (2014). *Elite parties, poor voters: How social services win votes in India.* Cambridge: Cambridge University Press.

Vachana, V. R., & Roy, M. (2018). NOTA and the Indian voter. *Economic & Political Weekly, 53*(6), 28–31.

Vaishnav, M. (2018). Will women decide India's 2019 election? Carnegie Endowment for International Peace.

Xaxa, V. (2008). *State, society and tribes: Issues in post-colonial India.* New Delhi: Pearson.

Ziegfeld, A. (2016a, 1 August). The politics of pre-election alliances in India. *India in Transition.* Retrieved from https://casi.sas.upenn.edu/iit/adamziegfeld

Ziegfeld, A. (2016b). *Why regional parties? Clientelism, elites and the Indian party system.* Cambridge: Cambridge University Press.

28

Politics of Tribalization and Contested Space in Sikkim

Tikendra K. Chhetry and
Sanghamitra Choudhury

LEGACY OF PEOPLE'S REPRESENTATION

The politics of representation for contested space within Sikkim started much before it became a federal unit of India in 1975. Even in the monarchical era, attempts were made to accommodate various ethnic groups in the State Council with a focus on balanced policy formulation. This chapter focuses on the politics of tribalization and conflict for the contested space. The demand for the inclusion of 11 communities has been raised once again in recent times under Article 342 of the Constitution. This chapter also highlights the political dynamics of the state, the much-debated historic blunder in the decisions of the state categorizing 60 per cent of the population (11 communities) as OBCs or in the General category. In other words, there is no uniformity in this categorization if we look at the overall picture of tribalization in the state of Sikkim.

The monarchical politico-administrative assortment witnessed a further evolutionary modification with the arrival of J. C. White in 1890, the first political officer of Sikkim appointed by the British colonial administration of India (Gurung, 2019a). J. C. White made several mechanisms to seize the authority of the monarch to bring the administration of state under the control of the office of colonial political officer in the state. This office became the virtual controller of Sikkim, implementing power in both the internal and external affairs of the state.

J. C. White introduced the Advisory Council, later renamed as the State Council. The first State Council that was constituted by White had four members and in the later years the number of members was raised to nine (Kazi, 2009). These members of the State Council consisted of senior and experienced men nominated by ruler from all parts of Sikkim in the name of interest of Sikkimese people across the county (Gurung, 2019a). The introduction of the State Council in an era of representation of people was hovered on the politico-administrative sphere of Sikkim. However, the initial State Councils were composed of Kazis and landlords dominantly from the Bhutia community who were considered to be faithful allies of the British colonial administration (Gurung, 2011, p. 47). Gradually, the State Council started to grow as the realm of peoples' representation in governing and administrative system with the share of three major communities, that is, Bhutia, Lepcha and Nepali/Gorkha.[1] With some minor changes and shuffles, in course of time, this combination continued in the seat reservation and representation in the State Legislative Assembly (SLA) of Sikkim and its other administrative circles.

PARITY PRAXIS: A (DIS)PROPORTIONATE REPRESENTATION?

The Indian freedom struggle and its independence was found to emerge as a source of inspiration among the aficionados of representative government form the political emancipation in neighbouring counterparts. Sikkim, the monarchical regime also could not remain within the curtain to avoid such waves. Being aware of the political objectives with democratic transition and development in the neighbouring country, leaders started to emerge and strive in Sikkim advocating the space for mass political participation and emancipation. Consequently, a popular government was constituted under the leadership of Tashi Tshering in 1949. It lasted only for 29 days but it manufactured a newer development in the Sikkimese political continuum (Gurung, 2018). The resignation of the ministry unleashed a fresh contention which resulted in the appointment of an Indian

officer as dewan with effect from 11 August 1949. With this development, the monarch and dewan became the joint authorities of the political–administrative power of the state with the divided State Council in the middle to act as pawns in the hands of either of them (Gurung, 2011, p. 49).

Voice of mass resentment started to surface in relation to the status of the State Council. The issue of a suitable framework for the satisfactory representation of major ethnic communities in the Council slowly created an uproar in the state. A Tripartite Agreement among the monarch, the Sikkim National Party and the Sikkim State Congress was convened in 1951 and resulted in the evolution of the 'parity system' as a formula for the reservation of seats in the Council (Government of Sikkim, 1962, p. 28). It juxtaposed the prerequisites of the approach to restructure the hitherto governing system with a new dimension to provide a space of representation for people from different ethnic backgrounds and belongings (Gurung, 2018, p. 13). Accordingly, a system of parity was developed to maintain a representative equilibrium of the major communities, that is, Bhutia, Lepcha and Gorkha/Nepali in the State Council (Sengupta, 1985, p. 197). Lepchas were denied the separate representation bringing them in Bhutia-Lepcha into a single fold (Government of Sikkim, 1962, p. 28). Codes of election to the State Council appeared in the proclamation of January 1952, whereas the set of the rules of governance of the State Council and its power and functions emerged through the constitutional proclamation of March 1953.[2] In 1953, the members of the Council were raised to 17, in which, as earlier, six were reserved for Bhutia-Lepcha,

---

[1] The terms 'Nepali' and 'Nepalese' have been found to be used substantially in the sources used in the chapter. The term 'Gorkha' is largely accepted and applied to address the Nepali language-speaking community in most parts of the country, but, unlike it, the term 'Nepali' is used dominantly to address the large Nepali community in Sikkim. However, debates and overarching arguments float in the sociopolitical surface of the state over the synonymous use of terms 'Gorkha' and 'Nepali'. There are several organizations and political parties in the state with Gorkha prefixes. Hence, the terms 'Gorkha' and 'Nepali' have been used synonymously or together in this chapter to avoid any form of dispute.
[2] Proclamation of H. H. Maharaja of Sikkim, dated 23 March 1953 (Government of Sikkim, 1953).

Table 28.1   Ethnic and Constituency-wise Distribution of Seats in State Council, 1953, Sikkim

Sl. No.	Name of Constituency	No. of Seats	Nepali/Gorkha	B-L
1.	Gangtok	3	1	2
2.	North Central	3	1	2
3.	Namchi	3	2	1
4.	Pemayangtse	3	2	1

Source: Gurung (2019a).

six for Nepali/Gorkha (Table 28.1) and a new provision was given for five nominated members by the monarch. The provision of five nominated members showed the monarch's intention to maintain his domination with the presence of his supporters in the legislative institution (Gurung, 2011, p. 50).

The State Council was enlarged up to 20 members in 1958 without bringing changes in the nature and number of constituencies. In enlarged council also, six seats were reserved for Bhutia-Lepcha and an equal number of seats for Gorkha/Nepali. As a newer provision, one seat each for general and *sangha* (monasteries) was introduced. The number of nominated members was raised to six (Government of Sikkim, 1958). In order to contest the general seat, a person was required to have permanent habitation in Sikkim and such other qualifications necessary for becoming a member of the council. Indians settled in Sikkim were not eligible to participate in the election (Gurung, 2011, p. 50). The *sangha* seat was reserved for Buddhist Lamas (priests) of the Buddhist monasteries.

The next election for the Council was due in 1961, but it was held later in 1967. The State Council as constituted was allowed to continue in office till the next election (Gurung, 2019a). The floor of council was again extended in 1967, increasing its total number up to 24 of which 7 seats each were reserved for Bhutia-Lepcha and Nepali/Gorkha (Table 28.2), and one each for general, Tsong, Scheduled Caste (SC) and six for nominated members. Until then, the Limboo community was eligible to contest for the seats reserved for the Nepali/Gorkha community, but with provision of one seat reserved for Tsong, Limboos were provided a separate reservation. Along with the newer ethnic composition, the number of constituencies was increased to five.

The fourth State Council was constituted in April 1970. Without summoning any new changes, the pattern of 1967 was continued. The next election for the Council was held in 1973. The State Council election witnessed resentment over the rift between candidates from two different ethnic affiliates. Worsening the situation, an agitation appeared on fore (Government of Sikkim, 1972; Gurung, 2011).

The election of 1973 grew as a turning point in the political history of Sikkim. The declaration of the result of the election emerged as a source of agitation accusing the royal palace. The palace was accused of

Table 28.2   Ethnic and Constituency-wise Distribution of Seats in State Council, 1967, Sikkim

Sl. No.	Name of Constituency	No. of Seats	Nepali/Gorkha	Bhutia-Lepcha
1.	Gangtok town constituency	2	1	1
2.	East constituency	3	1	2
3.	South constituency	3	2	1
4.	West constituency	3	2	1
5.	North constituency	3	1	2

Source: Gurung (2019a).

having rigged the poll of 1973 to the advantage of the Sikkim National Party.[3] The boiling political turmoil attempted to resolve the execution of a Tripartite Agreement on 8 May 1973 (Gurung, 2019a). The agreement among *Chogyal*, the Government of India and the political parties of India designed a larger legislative and executive power framework for elected representatives (Government of Sikkim, 1972; Gurung, 2011). Under Clause 1, the agreement installed the provision of adult suffrage to give effect to the principle of *one man one vote* as the basis of the election (Kiran, 2015, p. 69) to be conducted under the supervision of the Election Commission of India and the constitution of the assembly in a four-year interval in place of the State Council (Gurung, 2011, p. 54). The agreement under Clause 2 attracted to constitute an assembly in Sikkim with the provision to be elected every four years (Kiran, 2015, p. 70). Through the agreement, the court of monarch was to compromise its power to a large extent, despite the fact that monarch was maintained as the 'head of state'. The agreement shook the superiority of the ethnic community that the monarch belonged to. Further, the agreement assured fair dealing with the Gorkha/Nepali people of Sikkim in the years to come. (Basnet cited in Gurung, 2011, p. 54). The internal administration of Sikkim had, to all intents and purpose, been taken over by India (Government of Sikkim, 1972; Gurung, 2011). The Tripartite Agreement eased the transformation of a protectorate state into an associated state of India (Ray cited in Gurung, 2011, p. 54).

Within a span of one year after the agreement of 8 May 1873, the representation of the Sikkim Subjects Act, 1974, came into appearance with the prescribed numerical strength of the representatives in the Sikkimese Assembly. The representation of the Sikkim Subjects Act, 1974, constituted an assembly of total 32 members with ethnic representation as follows:

1. a. 16 seats shall be reserved for Sikkimese Bhutia-Lepcha origin.
   b. Out of these 16 seats, 1 shall be reserved for the *sangha*.
2. a. The remaining 16 seats shall be reserved for Sikkimese Gorkha/Nepali, including Tsong and SCs.
   b. Out of the aforementioned 16 constituencies reserved for Sikkimese of Gorkha/Nepali origin, 1 constituency shall be reserved for persons belonging to SCs (Kiran, 2015, p. 73).

The first inaugural session of the Sikkim Assembly was held on 10–11 May 1974. Kazi Lhendup Dorji was appointed as leader of the assembly. Under the leadership of Kazi as the first chief minister (CM) of Sikkim, the kingdom (though, at that point of time, it was not enjoying a full-fledged sovereignty but a protectorate state of India) became an associated state of India in September 1974. It became a federal unit of India on 16 May 1975 as the 22nd state of the Indian union. The original assembly of the erstwhile kingdom started to function as an SLA under the Constitution of India (Gurung, 2019a) more or less with the perpetuation of the hitherto parity system.

The enabled parity system was justified on the principle that it would be unfair to deny the political safeguard of the Bhutia-Lepcha minority. The arrangement was formulated with the view to satisfy the majority, on the one hand, and to safeguard the interests of the minority, on the other, so as to avoid ethnic conflicts in the Sikkimese multi-ethnic space (Gurung, 2018, p. 13). It was to serve the political rights of people in a larger framework, but the result appeared to be meagre. The system of peculiar kind where the Gorkha/Nepali

---

[3] The Sikkim National Party was tallied as a pro-palace party since its origin. Since the first election in 1953, the party had been winning almost all Bhutia-Lepcha seats, but not a single Nepali seat. But, for the first time in 1973 election, the party secured two Nepali seats also. This made people suspicious about rigging of the poll (Gurung, 2019a).

constituted a majority group was equated with Minority Bhutia-Lepcha fold (Gurung, 2018, p. 13). Thus, ethnic considerations continued to receive major attention at the political decision-making process (Gurung, 2011, p. 50). The parity formula continued as the principal basis for the distribution of seats in the assembly among the Bhutia, Lepcha and Gorkha/Nepali population, including the old rules favouring the erstwhile ruling section of the Sikkimese population. Much of the schemes designed by the monarch have been kept in continuation despite the fact that his office had been abolished. The monarchical idea of government should be carried on equally by the Bhutia-Lepcha and Gorkha/Nepali, as it had been cherished shadowing the fact that the Constitution of India justifies the rule of majority with undeniable necessary justice of minority (emphasis added, Gurung, 2011, p. 59).

POST-MERGER MECHANISM OF SLA SEATS DISTRIBUTION: A MANHANDLED PUZZLE

On 23 April 1975, the Lok Sabha, the lower house of the Parliament of India, passed the Constitution (Thirty-Sixth Amendment).[4] Under Clause 3 of the bill, with the insertion of new Article 371(F),[5] special provisions were made with respect to the state of Sikkim. Under Clause 3(a) of the bill, the number of the seats in SLA shall not be less than 30. Clause 3(b)(i) of the bill indicates that the assembly for Sikkim formed as a result of the elections held in Sikkim in April 1974 with 32 members elected in the said election

(hereafter referred to as sitting members) shall be deemed to be the SLA duly constituted under this constitution (Kiran, 2015). Rajya Sabha, the upper house of the Parliament of India, passed the bill on 26 April. Fakhruddin Ali Ahmed assented the bill on 16 May 1975 to bring Sikkim into India as a sovereign state with a constitutional assurance of the preservation of the political, social and cultural uniqueness of the state under Article 371(F) of the Constitution (Gurung, 2011, p. 58).

In post-merger space, the first election of the SLA was held in 1979. With the approach for election, the matter of the distribution and reservation of assembly seats among the different communities caused deeper worries among the different communities in the state, which was already in a politically turbulent condition. The Government of India deliberated on the omission of the parity system hitherto (Gurung, 2018, p. 45). Before the election, the president of India issued an ordinance called the Representation of the People (Amendment) Ordinance, 1979, deciding the seats in the SLA. In accordance to the Ordinance, out of the 32 seats of the assembly, 12 seats have been reserved for Bhutia-Lepcha, 2 for SC, 1 for *sangha*. The seats reserved for Gorkha/Nepali hitherto under the parity system have been omitted. The abolition of reserved seats for Gorkha/Nepali evoked criticism from different sociopolitical walks (Gurung, 2019b). The ordinance caused a political turmoil and a feeling of ambiguity in the state. The majority of the leaders of Gorkha/Nepali and its sub-ethnic groups, irrespective of the ruling opposition parties, became assertive and apprehensive of the future of the community that they had a sense of belonging (Gurung, 2018). The

---

[4] Clause 2 of the bill reads the amendment to the First Schedule. In the First Schedule to the Constitution, under the heading 'I, The States', after entry 21, the following entry shall be inserted, namely 22, Sikkim, the territories which were included in Sikkim immediately before the commencement of the Constitution (Thirty-Sixth Amendment) Act, 1975 (Kiran, 2015).

[5] Clause 3. Insertion of new Article 371F. After Article 371E of the Constitution, the following article shall be inserted, namely 371F. Special provisions with respect to the state of Sikkim, notwithstanding anything in this Constitution.

opinion started to appear on the public surface that the reservation of seats for Bhutia-Lepcha should have been proportionate to their share of 22 per cent of the total population vis-à-vis the remaining population of the state. Disgruntled section made the arguments that at par the share of the population, Bhutia-Lepcha should have been allocated 6 or 7 seats at best instead of disproportionately provided 12 seats (Gurung, 2018, p. 46). Pahalman Subba, Sikkim's lone Rajya Sabha member, acquitted the House that the state government was in favour of reserving 12 seats for Bhutia-Lepcha, 15 for Gorkha/Nepali, 2 for general, 2 for the SCs and 1 for *sangha* (Table 28.3).

CM Nar Bahadur Bhandari placed his proposal to the then Prime Minister of India, Rajiv Gandhi, which contained a different distributive mechanism. In 1987, Bhandari suggested to the prime minister that 13 seats should be reserved for Bhutia, Lepcha and Sherpa of Sikkimese origin, including *sangha*. Similarly, he suggested that 13 seats should be

Table 28.3 Distribution of Seats as Pahalman Subba Acquitted to Rajya Sabha

Bhutia-Lepcha	12 seats
Gorkha/Nepali	15 seats
General	2 seats
SC	2 seats
Sangha	1 seat

Source: Prajashakti (2000; cited in Gurung, 2011, p. 277).

Table 28.4 Bhandari's Proposal on Seat Distribution for the SLA

Bhutia, Lepcha and Sherpa of Sikkimese origin including Monasteries	13 seats
Gorkha/Nepali	13 seats
General	4 seats
SC	2 seats
Tsong (Limboos)	2 seats
Total number of seats	34

Source: Government of Sikkim Publication (1987; cited in Gurung, 2011, p. 280).

Table 28.5 Vardhan Committee's Suggestion on Distribution of Seats in the SLA

Caste/Communities	Seats
Lepcha	6
Bhutia	6
Sherpa	1
Limboo (Tsong)	3
Tamang	2
Sangha	1
Gorkha/Nepali	17
SC	2
General	2

Source: Vardhan Committee Report, Government of Sikkim (Gurung, 2011).

reserved for Gorkha/Nepali, 2 for the SCs, 2 for Tsong (Limboo) and 4 for general.

In 1995, the Government of Sikkim constituted a six-member committee under the chairpersonship of K. A. Vardhan, the former chief secretary of Sikkim, to observe the rights of various major ethnic groups and their sub-ethnic communities of Sikkim. The committee suggested a separate reservation of seats for Lepchas and Sherpas, which were kept regularly in club and shared with the seats reserved for Bhutias (Vardhan Report, cited in Gurung, 2011, p. 283).

Ensuring no dominant position for any community, the Vardhan Committee recommended for an increase in the number of assembly seats to 40 from the erstwhile 32, with the distribution shown in Table 28.5, unlike the suggestion and recommendation of former Rajya Sabha MP, Pahalman Subba, and former CM Nar Bahadur Bhandari.

POLITICS OF ST STATUS AND SEAT RESERVATION IN THE SLA FOR LIMBOOS AND TAMANGS

Politics over the issue of seat reservation for Gorkha/Nepali sub-ethnic groups Limboo and Tamang has been occupying a major space in the larger politics in Sikkim. In the name of accomplishing the political rights of these communities, time and again, many political parties and other associated organizations have been brewing their hot cups of tea in the political atmosphere of Sikkim. The politics over tribal status and the seat reservation in the highest decision-making body of the state was not new. However, the politics of reservation took on a different trajectory once the ST status was granted to the Bhutia and Lepcha communities in 1978, cornering all other remaining communities of Sikkim. The CM, Shri Nar Bahadur Bhandari, in 1981, strongly advocated for the due recognition of the Limboo and Tamang communities as per Article 332 of the Constitution of the country (Gurung, 2011, p. 394). However, in a note on the report submitted by the secretary of the SC/ST welfare department, Government of Sikkim, Bhandari declined his own recommendation for the same in 1987 to avoid fear of further division of society. Bhandari suggested the revival of Tsong seat in the legislative assembly, which was abolished in 1974. For a period of time, one seat was reserved for Tsong in the assembly, but with the proclamation of the representation of the Sikkim Subjects Act, 1974, the said seat was removed. Bhandari initiated to increase the seats in the assembly from 32 to 34 with 2 seats reserved for the Tsongs (Table 28.4), but that could not be materialized in the law.

Akhil Sikkim Kirat Limbu Chumlung, a pioneering organization that was formed on 19 May 1973, submitted a memorandum to the prime minister of India on 19 July 1990 in the presence of Shri Sanchaman Limboo, the former CM of the state (Gurung, 2011, p. 394). The Sikkim Democratic Front (SDF) headed by Shri Pawan Kumar Chamling, in 1994, was compassionate towards the concerns of Limboos and Shri Chamling placed a demand for the ST status of Limboos of the state. In 1995, the Vardhan Committee, as discussed earlier, proposed the reservation of three seats for Limboos (Tsongs) and two seats for Tamangs. In the post-merger political

epoch dominantly, the reservation of the seats in the assembly was advocated for Limboos (Tsongs), while the Vardhan Committee recommended the reservation for Tamangs too with a specific mention (Table 28.5).

After perpetually a long struggle for the ST status, the Limboo and Tamang masses could celebrate the day they desired and struggled for, when the Parliament of India granted their inclusion in the fold of the STs. In January 2003, the twin communities were declared as ST communities of the state, but without specifying the number of seats in the assembly to be reserved under Clauses 1 and 3 of Article 332 of the Constitution. With it, the political uproar received an added elevation in the political ambience in Sikkim, especially in relation to politics of tribal and ethnic reservation in the assembly. The Gorkha Apex Committee (GAC) formed in May 2003 advocated a newer mechanism of reservation policy in the assembly. The GAC demanded reservation for 13 seats out of a total of 32 seats and urged that the pattern of the reservation shouldn't be a conventional pattern for seat reservation for STs. At a crucial conference in Marwari Dharmshala, Singtam, east district of Sikkim, the GAC echoed that 'with the inclusion of the Limboos and Tamangs the reservation may shoot up to more than fifty percent from the existing forty seven percent, therefore, the remaining sixty five percent of population, besides being majority might become minority and would be unconstitutional and undemocratic.' The apex body, in a memorandum submitted to the CM, Shri P. K. Chamling, in August 2003, suggested that seven seats should be reserved for Limboos and Tamangs in the hitherto 13 seats reserved for the Bhutia-Lepcha community and the conversion of Bhutia-Lepcha seats into ST seats (Gurung, 2011, pp. 391–92).

Sikkim Limboo Tamang Tribal Joint Action Committee (SLTTJAC), formed in 2003, raised the issue of the reservation of seats in the assembly without reorganizing the numerical position of the House. The Committee submitted a memorandum to the central government and the State Delimitation Committee demanding a special census of the Limboos and Tamangs, and the allocation of seats by following similar criteria, which were maintained to reserve seats for the other STs. The Government of Sikkim vide notification no. 73/Home/2005 in December 2005 constituted a Commission for Review of Social and Environmental Sector Policies, Plans and Programmes (hereafter CRESP; Gurung, 2011, p. 287). The Commission submitted the report on 31 March 2008 with the recommendation to (a) enhance the number of seats in the assembly to 40 from existing 32; (b) reserve 20 seats for the ST, including Tamang, Limboo and any other communities which would be notified as ST in the future; (c) continue the reservation of 12 seats for the Bhutia-Lepcha communities; (d) 4 seats to be reserved for the general/open category and (e) increase the seats of *sangha* to 2 in view of growing monasteries and monks belonging to Gurung and Tamang Buddhists and 2 seats to be reserved for the SCs (Table 28.6).

In reference to the recommendation of the Commission, the state government headed by Pawan Kumar Chamling demanded for the increase of the total number of seats in the assembly to 40. After the recognition of ST status accorded to Limboos and Tamangs in 2003, the SDF government made more than 18 representations to the offices of the president, prime minister and home minister of India for the allocation of seats to the communities in the assembly under Clauses 1

Table 28.6   Recommendation of the CRESP, Sikkim

Communities/Categories	Proposed Reservation of Seats
ST	20
Bhutia-Lepcha	12
General/Open	4
SC	2
Sangha	2
Proposed total seats	40

Source: Report submitted by the Commission (2008).

and 3 of Article 332 of the Constitution. The Chamling government made several efforts to materialize the demand into a reality and one of the objectives of constituting the CRESP was to find a solution to the same (Barnes & Rai, 2018, p. 153). Shri Chamling had assured that the reservation of seats for these two communities in the assembly would be resolved before the general election of 2019, but he did not succeed in turning his assurance into a reality. The SDF's 25-year-old government led by him witnessed the opposition berth, a new political outfit, Sikkim Krantikari Morcha (SKM), which defeated the SDF regime in May 2019.

Maintaining the pace of sensitivity of the issue, Prem Singh Tamang (Golay), the newly elected Sikkim CM, reminded the central government in June 2019 to reserve seats in the assembly for the Limboo-Tamang communities. He advocated that the demand for the reservation of seats in the assembly for Limboos and Tamangs has been pending for the last several years, as a result of which the communities have remained deprived of their political rights (Chhetri, 2019). The SLTTJAC filed a petition to the Supreme Court seeking the reservation for these two STs in the assembly. In filing the petition, the members of the organization sought direction from the centre to take appropriate action (Tamang, 2019).

POLITICS OF THE ST STATUS OF THE 11 LEFT-OUT COMMUNITIES

Noticeably, politics over the issue of granting ST status to 11 left-out communities is in the political domain of Sikkim. The Khas, Rai, Gurung, Magar, Sunwar, Bhujel, Thami, Jogi, Newar, Dewan and Sanyasi are still not enlisted as STs. The genesis of the demand for the ST status of these left-out communities, more or less, can be traced back to the parity system that prevailed during the pre-merger political regime. In fact, the politics of the pre-merger sociopolitical spectrum has even been the reference point in the explosion of present-day sociopolitical and identity deliberation, though the merger of the state with India reframed the political canvas of Sikkim and the sociopolitical identity of its people. Still, the pre-merger sociopolitical scale appears to measure and redefine the 'distinct Sikkimese identity' and the sociopolitical upheaval (Barnes & Rai, 2018, p. 163). Virtually all three ethnic communities, that is, Bhutia, Lepcha and Gorkha/Nepali, were considered to be somewhat under the equal status of tribes, though the seats distributed under hitherto parity system was not proportionate to their size of the population. During the parity penalization, though Gorkha/Nepali constituted approximately 80 per cent of the total population, the seats reserved for them were not in proportion with the population size and were fixed with the other 20 percent of the population till 1978.

Till 1978, the designed Gorkha/Nepali umbrella under the monarch regime, including the Khas, Rai, Gurung, Magar, Sunwar, Bhujel, Thami, Jogi, Newar, Dewan, Sanyasi, Limboo and Tamang, was considered equal to the status of tribes, though the seats distributed under the hitherto parity system were not proportionate to the size of the population of Bhutias and Lepchas. The reservation of seats for the Gorkha/Nepali community was in operation for some years after the merger. The situation, more or less, took a dissimilar twist when the union government enlisted only Lepchas and Bhutia as STs in 1978. The move of the union government appeared as the virtual delisting of Gorkha/Nepali sub-ethnic groups from pre-merger privileges leading to unbroken deprivation. For this, not only the policies of the union government are to be brought to the scanner of (in)justice but also the post-merger initial government of the state is to be found responsible and irrational for its short-sightedness and ethnic partiality. The concerns expressed by the union government towards the safeguarding of Gorkha/Nepali

ethnic groups were sidelined, left unaddressed from the side of the state government, without necessarily accountably replying to the queries and interest of the union government to enlist, more or less, all the Gorkha/Nepali sub-ethnic groups to the status of STs. The Director-General of the Union Ministry of Home Affairs sent a letter to the Government of Sikkim a year after the merger (Barnes & Rai, 2018, p. 153).

The letter vide D.O. letter no. BC 12016/24/75-SCT V dated 21 July 1979, in its paragraphs 5 and 6, reads as follows:

> It would also appear that there is another primitive tribe namely the Limboos who have social affinity with the Lepchas and some of them are animists. The Limboos have been mentioned as autochthonous inhabitants of Sikkim and are sometimes considered as Limboo and Lepchas as is the case of Muglan Lepcha from Darjeeling District.
>
> The status of the Limboos will have to be spelt out clearly and if necessary they may be grouped with Lepcha and their entry could be 'Lepcha, Limboo'.
>
> There are other tribal communities for example, Magar, Gurung, Tamang, Tsong, Subba and Rai. The Sikkim government may kindly review the case of these communities and also any other communities have been left out.

The interest of the union government towards listing the entire groups of Gorkha/Nepali in the ST list was reflected in the letter. Despite the eagerness of the union government to include, more or less, all left-out communities in the list, the state government was found apparently disinterested without displaying the reason in this relation. Had the L. D. Kazi government been a little more alert and wedded to the issue, the matter would have been sorted out long ago (Barnes & Rai, 2018, p. 153). After a long struggle, Limboos and Tamangs were included in the list in 2003 but others were left out from the list.

In February 2005, under the chairpersonship of Professor A. C. Sinha, Pawan Chamling led the state government to set up

a four-member commission to prepare an ethnological account for the inclusion of left-out
communities in the ST list. The commission
submitted a report in May 2005, presenting an
impressive account of the ethno-genesis and
diagnostic ethnic traits of the aforementioned
communities (Government of Sikkim, 2005).
The state government also constituted a commission for the CRESP in December 2005
and the commission submitted its report on 31
March 2008 (Gurung, 2011, p. 286). The commission strongly recommended the granting
of ST status to all Sikkimese ethnic communities. The Commission placed the justification
that the Sikkimese communities should be
regarded as a single entity through the enactment of the Sikkim Subject Regulation, 1961,
which was later validated by the Government
of India in the 1973 Tripartite Agreement.
Needless to mention, the Sikkimese communities are defined by the Sikkim Subject
Regulation, 1961 (Barnes & Rai, 2018, p.
167). The commission's report appeared at par
that the regulation of 1961 encompassed all
the people and communities of Sikkim living
in the state at that point of time considered as
a single sociopolitical entity, now generally
called Sikkimese. The state assembly already
endorsed thrice the report of the CRESP 2008
(Barnes & Rai, 2018, p. 168). CM Chamling,
along with MPs, MLAs and minister of
Sikkim, visited New Delhi in 2016 and had
an audience with Prime Minister Narendra
Modi and the concerned union minister in
connection with the demand. The stand of the
Government of Sikkim was made clear with
the submission of a memorandum (Barnes &
Rai, 2018, p. 166).

Sikkim witnessed a power shift after the
defeat of 25 years only by a marathon government led by Pawan Chamling. The issue of
granting ST status to 11 left-out communities
played a vital role during the 2019 election
campaign in the state. The SKM party, led by
the newly elected CM, P. S. Golay, was able
to convince the masses of the state through its
election manifesto. In June 2019, the new CM
reiterated the demand before the union minister for the inclusion of the 11 left-out communities in the ST list envisioning the equality
among all Sikkimese.

CONCLUSION

The major part of the politics in the Himalayan
state of Sikkim spins on the axis of ethnic and
tribal issues. Sikkim is more or less still a state
based on sociocultural interaction in the guise
of traditional society and is also reflected in
the large politics of state. Unlike the larger
ideological affiliation, the very local issues
of the tribes and their sociopolitical and economic share over resources occupy a major
space of politics and political manipulation.
The state has already been sharing the sociopolitical and representative mechanism since
the last four decades. The distinctiveness of
the state remains with its own sociopolitical
and ethnic representation within the Indian
constitutional framework, celebrating the provisions guaranteed through the merger agreement and the safeguards under Article 371(f)
of the Constitution. Hence, the sociopolitical
environment of the state revolves around the
pre-merger sociopolitical helm. Despite the
fact that the merger agreement brought the
Himalayan kingdom to Indian sovereignty in
1975, the policy of ethnic representation was
introduced into its practice long before the
merger. However, the pre-merger representative mechanisms were always in question as
a bone of contention among ethnic communities and accused for being disproportionate
and unequally represented in decision-making
bodies. The representation of three major
ethnic communities, that is, Bhutia, Lepcha
and Gorkha/Nepali in decision-making bodies
was mostly considered as hostile and suppres-
sive as the Gorkha/Nepali community, with
about 80 per cent of the total population of the

state, was equated with Bhutia-Lepcha into a single fold of about 20 per cent population of the state in decision-making bodies through a parity system. Against this backdrop, the politics of the state was spinning on the axis of ethnic representation for proportionate justice.

Merger was expected to resolve a perpetually pending issue and disgruntlement over disproportionate justice. In the post-merger space, 12 seats were reserved for Bhutia-Lepcha, one for *sangha* and two for SC and 17 for all. The Gorkha/Nepali community, time and again, placed displeasure that it had been reduced to only 17 open seats in the assembly, leaving Gorkha/Nepali in a deprived sense even in the post-merger space. Moreover, granting ST status only to the Bhutia-Lepcha communities added newer contention in politics, as all the sub-ethnic groups of Gorkha/Nepali fold felt that they were categorically excluded, which was not the practice in the pre-merger space. After a long constitutional battle, Limboo and Tamang were declared STs in 2002. But this time too, the move added newer dynamics in the politics of the state as the other 11 sub-ethnic groups of the same larger Gorkha/Nepali ethnic fold were excluded from equal status under a historic single entity called Sikkimese.

The insensitivity and short-sightedness in engaging with the necessary concerns of the plural society and the escapist nature of people in power still cause several movements related to different ethnic communities in the state. The demand for the reservation of seats in the assembly for Limboo and Tamang, and the movement to grant ST status to 11 left-out sub-ethnic groups of the larger Gorkha/Nepali community and the political manipulation are in proactive run with diverse arguments and counterarguments. Now the ball is in the hands of the state and the centre that how respective governments handle these issues delivering the justice equally or proportionately. The movement of governments of the state and the centre will definitely decide tribal politics or politics related to tribal status in the near future.

NB: The terms 'Nepali' and 'Nepalese' have been found to be used substantially in the sources used in the chapter. The term 'Gorkha' is largely accepted and applied to address the Nepali language-speaking community in most parts of the country, but, unlike it, the term 'Nepali' is used dominantly to address the large Nepali community in Sikkim. However, debates and overarching arguments float in the sociopolitical surface of the state over the synonymous use of terms 'Gorkha' and 'Nepali'. There are several organizations and political parties in the state with Gorkha prefixes. Hence, the terms 'Gorkha' and 'Nepali' have been used synonymously or together in this chapter to avoid any form of dispute.

REFERENCES

Barnes, H. A., & Rai, J. (2018). *Pawan Chamling: Champion of social justice*. New Delhi: Penguin Random House.

Chhetri, S. (2019). Sikkim CM urges centre to reserve seats in assembly for Limboo-Tamang. *Northeast Now*, 29 June 2019. Retrieved from https://nenow.in/north-east-news/sikkim-cm-urges-centre-to-reserve-seats-in-assembly-for-limboo-tamang.html

Government of Sikkim. (1953). *Proclamation of H. H. Maharaja of Sikkim*. Gangtok: Government of Sikkim.

Government of Sikkim. (1958). *Sikkim Darbar Gazette, Extraordinary Gazette*, 7(5).

Government of Sikkim. (1962). *Sikkim: A concise chronicles*. Gangtok: Government of Sikkim Publication.

Government of Sikkim. (1972). *Sikkim government gazette, ex. Gazette* (vol. 22). Gangtok: Government of Sikkim Publication.

Government of Sikkim. (2005). *Sinha Committee report*. Gangtok: The author.

Gurung, S. (2018). *Sikkim's democratic experience: Political and social aspects*. Kolkata: Levant Books.

Gurung, S. (2019a). Elections in Sikkim: An overview Part-I. *Sikkim Express*, 20 May. Gangtok.

Gurung, S. (2019b). Elections in Sikkim: An overview Part-II. *Sikkim Express*, 20 May. Gangtok.

Gurung, S. K. (2011). *Sikkim: Ethnicity and political dynamics*. New Delhi: Kunal Books.

Kazi, J. N. (2009). *Sikkim for Sikkimese: Distinct identity within the union*. Gangtok: Hill Media Publication.

Kiran, N. (2015). *Rights of the Sikkimese*. Gangtok: Prime Printers.

Sengupta, N. (1985). *State government and politics in Sikkim*. New Delhi: Sterling Publication.

Tamang, Y. (2019). Sikkim Limboo Tamang tribal joint committee files plea in supreme court for LT seat reservation. *Sikkim Chronicles*, 17 January. Retrieved from https://www.thesikkimchronicle.com/sikkim-limboo-tamang-tribal-joint-committee-files-plea-in-supreme-court-for-lt-seat-reservation/

29

Tribal Politics in Tripura:
A Spatial Perspective*

R. K. Debbarma

What can constitute a category called tribal politics in Tripura? What does it mean to name particular kinds of politics as 'tribal politics' and not by other names? These questions are rendered thinkable only when we pose the unthinkable question: is there a non-tribal politics in Tripura? The absence of a category called non-tribal politics, because this politics can claim for itself politics proper, is the product of a certain history. Conversely, the category of tribal politics is the product of denial—that politics is politics proper. As such, framing an aspect of politics as 'tribal' is not only historical but also ideological. This chapter will shed light on this history and ideology and, in doing so, provide an account of tribal politics in Tripura.

This chapter is divided into three sections. In the first section, I outline and criticize the prevailing ways of framing tribal politics in the state. I consider two interrelated themes—demographic transformation and land alienation—as the dominant frameworks for explaining tribal politics. In the second section, I outline the historical–geographical context for the understanding of politics in Tripura. I do this by analysing three historical events that are interpreted as opposition to the Manikya rule. These events were the Jamatia rebellion in 1862–1863, the Reang insurrection in 1941–1942 and the mass literacy and armed movement spearheaded by Janashiksha Samiti-Gana Mukti Parishad (JSS-GMP) between 1944 and 1949. I pay close attention to the JSS-GMP because it embodied the transformation from politics proper to tribal politics.

In the third section, I trace the emergence of what came to be categorized as tribal politics to show how politics proper came to be delimited and configured as tribal politics. I trace the shape and contours of this politics by

* Much of the discussion on the historical and geographical context of Tripura is taken from my PhD thesis titled 'A Genealogy of Place and Articulation of Political Identity: A Study of the Emergence of Tripura as a Homeland' (2012), Department of Political Science, University of Hyderabad. The discussion on tribal movements and their political parties have been taken from some of my recent publications. I am grateful to my colleague Rajdeep Singha for his help with the census and election data.

analysing the emergence of Tripura Upajati
Juba Samiti (TUJS) in 1967 to the birth and
rebirth of the Indigenous Peoples Front of
Tripura, 2000–2018 (IPFT), which is demanding a separate state, Tipraland. What distinguished this politics from the JSS-GMP was
its use of history and geography. While the
JSS-GMP opposed the Manikya rule as feudalistic and oppressive, the new identity politics celebrated the Manikya rule.

I

THE TRIBAL AS A SITE OF POLITICS

Tribal politics in Tripura is usually framed
through two interrelated themes—the demographic transformation of the state after 1947
(Bhaumik, 2002; Hrangkhawl, 2002) and
the subsequent land alienation of the indigenous by the Bengali settlers. Those who
used demography as a starting point for their
analysis of tribal politics, depending on their
political persuasion, proceed from a very different reading of the pre-colonial and colonial Tripura. For some, Tripura has always
been part of the geography of 'Bengal', and
that this historical connection legitimates the
settlement of Bengalis after the partition of
Bengal (Bhaumik, 2003; Paul, 2009). What
follows from this reading of historical geography is this: the Bengalis who settled in Tripura
after the partition of Bengal were subjects of
the former Manikya rulers of Tripura. On the
other hand, there are those who view Tripura
as a place outside Bengal and that it was an
independent state during British-India colonialism (Debbarma, 2008). The latter view
animates politics of self-determination and
indigeneity.

Both proponents are obsessed with demography and use census data uncritically. For
example, Bijoy Kumar Hrangkhawl—who led
the first armed movement in Tripura, the Tripura
National Volunteer (TNV), and now a prominent leader of the Indigenous Nationalist Party
of Twipra (INPT)—uses census data of 1901
and then data from 1951 to 1981 to show how
the indigenous population became a minority
in Tripura (Table 29.1). He also cites government data on refugees from 1950 to 1957 to
further highlight the point that the indigenous
population is outnumbered by immigrants in
the post-independence period (Table 29.2).
On the other hand, Subir Bhaumik employs
census data from 1874 to 1981 to assert that
tribals were never a dominant majority in
Tripura (Table 29.3). Both of them arrive at
a very different conclusion about Tripura by
looking at the census data. What this tells us
is that we need to approach the census data of
Tripura, especially the census carried out by
the Manikya state, with some incredulity for
three reasons, which are based on my reading of Debbarma's (1997) work on census in
Tripura. One, it would be a mistake to assign
methodological rigour to census data prior to
1951. It is unclear how data were collected.

Table 29.1 Tribal Population of Tripura, 1901–2001

Year	Total Population	Indigenous/Tribal Population	Other Population
1901	173,325	92,477	80,848
1951	645,707	237,953	407,754
1961	1,142,005	360,070	781,935
1971	1,556,342	450,544	1,105,798
1981	2,053,058	583,920	1,469,138
1991	2,757,205	853,345	1,900,560
2001	3,197,000	NA	NA

Source: Hrangkhawl (2002).

Table 29.2   Presence of Infiltrators in Tripura, 1950–1957

Year	Number of Infiltrators
1950	67,151
1951	2,016
1952	80,000
1953	32,000
1954	4,700
1955	37,500
1956	50,700
1957	3,600

Source: Hrangkhawl (2002).

Most likely, the data were collected from Dewans, Choudhuris and Sardars, who were responsible for tax collection for the Tripura state, who in turn depended on the village chiefs to provide the data. At both levels, it was in their interest to undercount the number of households and their members within their jurisdiction. Two, enumeration of population prior to 1951 census was limited by the state's inability to classify a large number of communities. The classification of the population into various tribes is the product of a later census. Three, many of the hill communities were mobile, escaping the oppressive tax regime of the state.

Census data are useful for state and academic analysis. But one should be cautious when they are deployed for political objectives. It can feed into exclusionary policies, such as the National Register of Citizens, which is currently demanded by various regional parties in the state. However, my concern here is rather a different one. The premise for engaging in demographic transformation is not merely to evidence the fact that tribals are becoming a minority in Tripura but to argue that, being a minority, they are politically disabling. What follows from such a premise, then, is that no one should be a minority within a political community. This is a politically dangerous notion, one that pervades across Northeast India today—Tripura as an example of what they should not become. I agree that being a minority can be politically disabling, a point well noted by Xaxa (2005 and 2017) that demographics matter when political decision-making is heavily invested in dispossessing tribals. What should follow from this is that minorities are facts of any political life, whereas dispossession is artefact of politics.

Demographic transformation as a dominant framework for understanding tribal politics in Tripura has given rise to two modes of political action. First, the long history of armed

Table 29.3   Decadal Growth of Population in Tripura, 1874–1981

Year	Total Population	Percentage Variation	Total Tribal Population	Percentage of Tribals
1874–1875	74,523	NA	47,523	63.77
1881	95,637	28.33	49,915	52.19
1891	137,575	43.85	70,292	51.09
1901	173,325	25.99	91,679	52.89
1911	229,613	32.48	111,303	48.47
1921	304,347	32.59	171,610	56.37
1931	382,450	25.63	203,327	52.00
1941	513,010	34.14	256,991	53.16
1951	639,028	24.56	237,953	37.23
1961	1,142,005	28.71	360,070	31.50
1971	1,156,342	36.28	450,554	28.95
1981	2,053,058	31.92	583,920	28.44

Source: Bhaumik (2002).

Table 29.4   Vote Share of Political Parties in ST Assembly Constituencies, Tripura, 2003–2018

	2003	2008	2013	2018
AITC		0.36		0.06
AMB	0.81	0.20	0.82	0.13
BJP	1.88	1.26	1.90	30.04
CPI	3.65	3.31	3.69	2.67
CPI(M)	45.45	47.81	45.31	38.58
CPI(ML)(L)		0.10		
INC	2.71	20.41	5.30	1.48
IND	0.22	5.00	0.22	0.43
INPT	44.18	21.08	41.48	2.32
IPFT				23.56
NEINDP				0.02
TLSP				0.44
TRIPP				0.27
LJNSP	0.42		0.57	
LJP		0.32		
NCP	0.68	0.16	0.69	

Source: Election Commission of India.

insurgency which demands the deportation of Bengali settlers, and second, the recent demand for the creation of a separate state for indigenous communities. Both involve invoking a particular nostalgia about Tripura's past and a potentially radical interpretation of Tripura as a place. It is this interpretation of Tripura that (Debbarma, 2017) the CPI(M) government under Manik Sarkar sought to counter by enacting memorials of Tripura-Bengal connections and, in the process, exacerbating the Bengali communalism that catapulted the BJP to power in 2018. Table 29.4 shows the data from the last four assembly elections indicating the rise of the BJP among Bengali voters and the IPFT among tribal voters. This brings me to the second theme, land alienation, which is closely tied to the CPI(M)'s understanding of tribal politics or, more precisely, the role of tribals in their scheme of politics.

Land alienation as a framework to understand tribal politics is largely associated with the Indian Left, especially the CPI(M) that posed 'the tribal question in India'. The question underlies their interpretation of the tribal situation—backward, behind time and outside of modernity. Modernity is inhabited or occupied by those who pose such a question. For the Indian Left, the tribal has been the 'other', requiring interpretation, leadership, radicalization and mobilization against capitalism. Those who pose the tribal question diagnose tribals as dispossessed and alienated, but refuse to examine how these are the consequences of the social, economic and political institutions and structures from which they benefit. The problem of land alienation is then associated with the inability of tribals to catch up with the modern mainstream. Such a perspective has been challenged by Xaxa (2005, 2019) who locates land alienation of tribals to the exploitative relationship between tribals and non-tribals. In this chapter, I will try to push Xaxa's argument further by showing that what constitutes as well as perpetuates that exploitative relationship is the fiction of a separation between politics proper and politics by other name. For the Indian Left, tribal societies are sites for their political actions, not the social structure which they inhabit. At least in Tripura, what emerged from such a position is a feudalistic and paternalistic politics in which non-tribals are subjects of politics proper, and tribals are subjects of politics by other name. Almost in all other north-eastern states, tribal question is no longer relevant, but in Tripura it continues to do so, forming a separate domain as a 'tribal wing' within politics proper. What I plan to do in the rest of this chapter is to show how what is now thought of as 'tribal politics' coincide with settler society's claim to politics proper. This fiction is the basis for legitimizing exploitative relationship and perpetuates the continuing dispossession of tribals or indigenous communities.

II

REBELLION MAKES THE TRIBE

In 1862–1863, a rebellion against the Manikya ruler broke out around the then capital of Tripura. The Manikya ruler had to raise a mercenary force to quell the rebellion. Rebellion came to be recorded as Jamatia rebellion. It was as if the rebellion created a new identity in the state-making apparatus of Manikya. The popular story in Tripura is that those who took part in the rebellion against increased taxation came to acquire a new identity, Jamatia, recorded, described and sanctioned by the *Sri Rajmala*. Although the available record of rebellion is sketchy, much of which is dedicated to the then ruler's ability to successfully crush it, we can reconstruct the events that precipitated it and the ruptures it forced on the spatial and social organization of political power. Rebellion disrupted the spatial strategies of power and state-making. However, the rebellion was also the product of the spatial disruptions inflicted by British-India in 1761. Understanding pre-colonial space is essential to understanding contemporary politics in Tripura.

Pre-colonial Tripura emerged as a stable political centre in the 15th century under Ratna Fa, who adopted the title Manikya (Nath,

1999). This political stability was contingent upon the strategic bound-up of three spaces: mobile hill space, state space and contested extractive space. These three spaces were connected through multiple plexus and made possible for the existence of tiny mimetic states in the hills. This spatial arrangement, upon which state-making was contingent, may be termed as Manikyan spatial ideologies (Debbarma, 2011). State space was the core of the state on the foothills from where the religious and political elites controlled the extractive space. The hilly terrains adjacent to the state space constituted the mobile hill space; and the extractive space was the vast alluvial plain that produced the surplus paddy absorbed by the state core.

The state centre was a fortified town from where the ruling religious–political elites controlled grain production in the alluvial plains of present-day Bangladesh. By locating the state centre at the foothills, it could strategically thwart superior invading powers by escaping into the hills. Therefore, the state centre should be seen as a space which connected the mobile hill space and the contested plains. The state core was located on the interstices of hills and plains. It can be conceptualized as a space where hill-ness and plainness merged, melted and conflicted, yet produced and precariously sustained the state. The mobile hill space and the contested plains were not disconnected spaces. These two spatial realities facilitated mimetic state formation in the hills. By locating strategically, in between these two spaces, the former Tripura rulers were able to structure a surplus grain absorbing religious–political elites.

The alluvial plains were, then, the contested agricultural space between the rulers in Bengal and Tripura. The contest was struggle for control over sedentarized population and surplus grain. As long as Tripura recognized Bengal's sovereignty through the payment of tributes, the religious and political establishment of Tripura were secure. Any act of insubordination on the part of the Tripura ruler would be treated as defiance to the Mughal authority and a case for invasion, ouster and replacement. Bengalis (Hindus and Muslims) constituted the permanent surplus producing (wet or valley agriculture) subjects. The sedentarized population (in state space) was connected to the undivided Bengal by means of culture, language and religion (Sen, 1998). These valley places were legible state spaces for appropriation and state-making function. These were the spaces of contention between the Tripura and the Mughals and later the British-India.

This spatial arrangement was snapped in 1761, when the combined power of British-India and the ruler of Bengal forced Tripura to accept the authority of British-India over the alluvial plains. The hills which constitute the modern Tripura came to be designated as independent Tripura; and the alluvial plains came to be designated as British Tripura, for which Tripura rulers became a zamindari to the Raj (Mackenzie, [1884]1999). Divested of its control over plain land, Tripura's political and religious elites needed to convert the hill tracts into new extractive space. This project had two objectives: one, to take control over the lowlands and outlaying the mid-slopes that protruded into the newly named 'British Tipperah' or 'Plain Tipperah' and transform the tiny valleys, the river banks into cultivable fields. Second, the need to reproduce, even at the point of sword, a Hinduized hill society. The latter objective assumed urgency owing to the initial unsuccessful attempts by the state to lure the Bengali peasants (who were now categorized as British subjects by default) into the newly marked state. The Jamatia rebellion was a resistance to these state-making enterprise by Manikya ruler.

Hill people who resisted these state enterprises were captured, brought to the capital and were either hanged (as an example to those who resist) or forcibly converted to Hinduism—their head shaven, body purified by sacred thread and given Hindu names. They were also prohibited from eating pork,

she-goat and fowl. The body becomes the object of appropriation, imposition and control in the project of alchemizing the hills as extractive space. The history of the entire 19th century and the first half of the 20th century can be described as a history of state-making on the hills—map making, census taking, cadastral survey, geological explorations, the introduction of modern administrators (borrowed from Indian Civil Services), the introduction of foreign seeds into the hills, campaign for cow (instead of buffalo) and plough cultivation.

This period was also a period of Hinduization of hills—the induction of paid Bengali Brahmins into the hills, the imposition/introduction of sacred thread, prohibition of beef, pork, she-got and fowl. To produce a state, in the hills, it must simultaneously produce a Hinduized hill society, a society amenable to state-making. These enterprises pushed people into the periphery, on the newly produced borderland. In 1941, another insurrection broke out all over its southern areas owing to the aforementioned invigorated state-making enterprise. This rebellion came to be called the Reang uprising. The uprising was led by Ratnamani.

Around the time, Ratnamani was preaching rebellion in the far-flung areas of Tripura, young students from around Agartala were beginning to assert politically. These young students were starting to question the policies of Manikya rulers towards their subjects, especially the dominance of Bengali bureaucrats in the administration (Debbarma, 1997). These young students soon formed the Janashiksha Samiti (JSS) in 1944 and launched a movement to educate the masses. The organization spearheaded the movement for mass education. Its manifesto envisioned itself as a champion of 'tribal' emancipation—a task in which 'educated and half-educated' were commanded compulsory participation in order to raise their society from the 'curse of illiteracy and poverty that have descended on the tribal society of Tripura during the thirteen hundred and fifty years of princely regime in the state'. After the death of Bir Bikram Manikya in 1947, JSS's opposition to the large-scale settlement of Bengali-Hindus from East Pakistan and the new government, the leaders of JSS were proscribed by the state along with the communists.

In 1948, after the infamous Golaghati massacre, the leaders went underground and founded the Tripur Jatiyo Mukti Parishad and carried out armed struggles against the state. The state responded by declaring martial law in the entire hills in order to stump out opposition. The leaders of this organization drew upon its already established mass support (Debbarma, 2003). They had to go underground, and some of them formed the Tripura Rajya Upajati Ganamukti Parishad. This underground armed organization became the backbone of the communist mobilization in Tripura. The period also saw the proliferation of numerous other organizations wedded to the ideological opposition of Bengali-Hindu dominance in the state administration and their rehabilitation in the state—Sengrak, Paharia Union and Adivasi Sangh. Although the mass base of these organizations is questionable, they, along with the JSS and the Ganamukti Parishad (GMP), constituted the politics proper. In the next section, I will begin by delineating how the political questions articulated by the JSS-GMP were reduced as a 'tribal question' and therefore marked the emergence of tribal politics in Tripura.

III

SETTLER SOCIETY MAKES THE TRIBAL POLITICS

When the JSS was formed in 1944, their pamphlet created a political uproar in and around Agartala. The exact content of the pamphlet is not known, but it must have reflected the discussion that transpired in the meeting that led to the formation of the JSS. The political elites in Agartala, the Kartas and the Thakurs, felt threatened and secretly met to form their own organization, Seva Samiti. Bir Bikram Manikya, the then King of Tripura, rushed back from Shillong and summoned the leaders of both organizations. The idea of Seva Samiti was abandoned and, with the nod from Bir Bikram, Tripura Sangha was formed as a counter to the JSS. Tripura Sangha collapsed when Bir Bikram suddenly passed away in 1946 (Debbarma, 1997b). The JSS became the most important political organization in Tripura. No doubt, there were other political groups in Agartala, such as Praja Mandal and Praja Sangha. But they were all confined to Agartala. The JSS had the support of the masses and was poised to form the government. They demanded a representative government in place of Dewanship, which was installed after the death of Bir Bikram. But the partition of British-India in 1947 and the subsequent settlement of refugees from East Pakistan changed the contours of political trajectory in Tripura. In 1948, the JSS was proscribed, its leaders went underground and formed the Tripura Jatiyo Mukti Parishad (TJMK) and carried out an armed revolution. The leaders of Praja Sangha transformed their association into the Indian National Congress (INC) and became prominent members in the new political dispensation. After Tripura merged with India, the TJMK rechristened itself as GMP and later became a tribal wing of the communist party in Tripura. The politics articulated by the GMP was subsumed as a 'tribal question' within the communist party. It would no longer represent the politics proper in Tripura.

The Jamatia rebellion, the Reang insurrection and the JSS-GMP represented the politics proper in Tripura, in that they played a transformative role in Tripura's politics. But in the contemporary politics of knowledge formation, these historical events are configured as tribal politics. We cannot understand this transformation of politics proper to tribal politics outside the ideological structure of producing Tripura as a settler society. We can note at least three spatial props for this ideological structure. One, imagining the past as a blooming together of tribals and non-tribals under the benevolent rule of Manikya kings. Two, inscribing the Indic presence on the geography of the modern Tripura. Three, Tripura's historical connection with Bengal as the premise of the historical geography of Tripura. These three props formed the discursive strategies of memorials, research and archives in contemporary Tripura. Together, these strategies functioned to produce the settler as a subject of history and law—the subjects proper. The tribal was the subject of culture and custom, within which they could be a distinct unit of analysis. This binary framed and rendered boundary and meaning to tribal politics. Within this binary, the tribals invited intervention and awaited a new consciousness. Outside this binary, 'tribal politics' in Tripura did not constitute a meaningful category.

If the settler colony rendered politics proper as tribal politics, the identity politics that emerged in Tripura in the late 1960s—and which are usually studied as tribal politics—exposed Tripura for what it had become a settler colony. Tripura identity politics framed the settler question in Tripura. They did this by appropriating the past and laying claim as subjects of history, and thereby inciting politics that unsettled the binary and upset the ideological structures of the settler colony. In the following text, I provide a trajectory of this identity politics.

A new kind of identity politics emerged in the late 1960s that would transform the political landscape of Tripura. This new identity politics was represented by three new political formations: the TUJS, the Tribal Students Federation (now Twipra Students' Federation) and the TNV. These groups were particularly responsible for their ideological investment in what can be described as reinvention of Tripura's past and how the present should be imagined. Unlike the previous narrative of

the Manikyan rule as 'feudalistic' by the JSS-GMP, the past (prior to the merger with India) is reimagined as 'glorious'. The post-merger is narrated as settler colony.

These departures informed their political rhetoric and struggles. Throughout the 1970s, identity politics in Tripura was marked by radically polarized confrontations between the ethno-nationalist fronts and the state. Their demands for the deportation of foreigners and the implementation of the Sixth Schedule (District Council) eventually led to ethnic riots between Bengalis and Tribals in 1980. The riots, now popularly known as *danga*, became an important point of reference, a marker of time, especially in the last century, in everyday social discourse. Events came to be plotted and understood as pre-*danga* or after *danga*. The ugliness and intensity of the conflict was well portrayed by Jagadish Gan-Choudhury (2004, p. 64).

In the succeeding decades, after the 1980 ethnic riot, Tripura has been converted into a killing field: intermittent communalized killings between Tripuris and Bengalis. After 1980, ethnic violence of that scale and magnitude did not take place. Nevertheless, the period between 1998 and 2001 was marked by another phase of ethnic violence. Many believed that the violence was engineered by the proscribed Tripuri armed group, the National Liberation Front of Tripura (NLFT). There were other political events within which this phase of violence may be located.

In 1982, TUJS's brief stint in power as a coalition partner of the INC in many ways discredited the leaders. The party suffered a vertical split, with more extremists among them breaking away to form their own parties, with claims to pursue the unachieved abandoned goals of the parent organization. Debabrata Koloi formed the Tripura Hills People's Party and Harinath Debbarma, the former chief of TUJS, formed the Tripura Tribal National Conference. However, these parties failed to make any impact on the state politics. The parent organization was able to retain some visibility, but lost its credibility and standing among the Tripuris.

The ensuing political sterility disenchanted and disillusioned many radical youths (with mainstream politics) who had taken an active part in the articulation and mobilization of Tripuris during the period 1970–1980. As a result, the beginning of the 1990s saw a proliferation of several insurgent groups, of which the All Tripura Tiger Force (ATTF) and the NLFT emerged as the leading fronts in extremism. These two organizations carried out eviction (of Bengalis) programmes from Tripuri-inhabited areas since 1994 and, by 1999, certain areas came to be designated as 'liberated zones'. There is a widely held belief that the NLFT was the intellectual author behind the formation of the IPFT–comprising all the splintered factions of the TUJS. The IPFT carried out campaign for ousting of 'foreigners' and toppling of 'refugee government'. The IPFT came to power in the District Council election in 2000 and introduced hugely controversial policies such as rewriting of *kokborok* in Roman script instead of Bengali (Devanagari) script; invention or as they called it 'revival' of Tripuri new year 'Tring' and reuse of Tripura Era as the official calendar.

Presently, Tring has become an important symbol of Tripuri nationalism. It historicizes a possible event and collectively recollects a different history and geography in order to produce modern Tripuri's 'Other'. As evident from the preceding text, Tripuri identity politics is constituted by the production of spatial differentiation—Tripuris and Bengalis occupying separate geography, distinct discontinuous places. Tring isolates a (possible) event in history in order to remark that boundary and thereby to frame a settler colonial. Settler colonialism is made real in their everyday imaginaries and experiences of displacements from imagined history and geography. These new identity politics is dependent on two spatial strategies: indigenous topographies and contesting memory.

One, after the partition of British-India and the disruption of the erstwhile ruling house of Tripura, a new idea of place needed production. This became critical for two reasons: integration into the Indian union and rehabilitation of large-scale Bengali refugees from East Pakistan. The new political elites aspired to solve these two problems through appropriating Tripura's past: one, the invention of Hindu sacred toponymies, and thereby imagining Tripura as a place within Indic cosmography; two, the Bengali-Hindus, as originally subjects of Manikyan past (the proofs being that the Manikya rulers controlled a large swathe of Bengal) and thereby making them legitimate citizens in the new spatial formation. What emerged from this appropriated past is the central idea of Tripura as the historical place of harmonious 'hill-man and plain-man', reproduced in school textbooks. This idea of the past is the absence from the politics of memory making in contemporary Tripura. What I will demonstrate, in the following three sections, is that 'absence' marks a contradiction and announces a problematic space.

The Memorandum of Settlement, signed between the Government of Tripura and the ATTF in 1993, among other things, includes two interesting points: one, places to be renamed in their original indigenous names; and two, the conversion of Ujjayanta Palace (the seat of the former ruling house of Tripura and the present Tripura Legislative Assembly) into a historical monument. This urge by Tripuri armed nationalists to reinstate indigenous toponymies flags off a spatial strategy sculpted as a struggle over the loss of geographies. This sets off uncompromisable politics, where the erasure of new place names constitutes a refusal of the dominant, state-promoted idea of Tripura. It unsettles signs and memories that legitimate 'non-tribal' in the state-promoted vision of 'tribal and non-tribal' Tripura.

The state, in order to produce Tripura as a home for Bengalis who migrated after partition of British-India, drew upon a considerable amount of existing Indic place names. These names were believed to be connected to Indic cosmography and, therefore, these sacred Hindu geographies made it possible for the home to be retrofitted into an unknowable past. The fact that these places were conferred sacredness by the post-colonial state did not prevent the invention of Bengali's presence since antiquity. Nevertheless, what I wish to emphasize is that place names can be viewed as sites for the investment of certain kinds of memories, carries a particular identity and makes real different geographies. In Tripura, these place names are deeply embroiled in the struggle for identity and place.

In the post-colonial Tripura, within the political ideology of the new state, indigenous toponymy not only symbolized rival geographies but they were also viewed as a threat to the new history and geography of the place. Therefore, simultaneous to the reinvention of Hindu sacred sites, indigenous place names were erased by ossifying new names, written and made official. Rabindra Kishore Debbarma, a writer, noted that Bengali surveyors would come to the village, enquire the name of the place, then translate the name to Bengali and record it (Debbarma, 1998). These acts have to be understood within that political ideology of producing a discourse of right over a territory—a moral right to own and inhabit a territory.

These new place names disrupt old topographies of identity—the connection between identity (not necessarily modern identity) and place—allowing new connections and linkages to appear as natural and given. However, indigenous names continue to exist in the everyday discourse of the other inhabitants, as an oral memory, always as a potent source of rival imaginings of the place. Tripuri ethno-nationalist struggle to reclaim the indigenous toponymy converts these surfaces into sites of different memory production and circulation.

Place names, as important markers of territorial identity, are sites of contested memory and of the construction of a particular identity of the place. The identity of the post-colonial Tripura, as a specific type of place, was produced via the appropriation and invention of sacred spaces (drawing on connection between place names and their connection to Hindu cosmographies), as well as the conscious transformation (read erasure) of the existing indigenous toponymy. Therefore, the demand for the restitution of indigenous toponymy, which asserted a different reading of modern landscapes of Tripura, flagged off politics of uncompromising spaces.

Two, the politics of memory making enacts post-colonial Tripura as a specific place. The city landscape is filled with statues, memorials and monuments of historical figures drawn from Indian national struggle, largely from Bengal. The visual of a youthful statue of Khudiram Bose, at the entrance of Ujjayanta Palace (former legislative assembly of the state), and Rabindranath Tagore and Ambedkar, on the precinct of the palace signals, points to two ideological agendas— the appropriation of the historical site to the Indian national imagination; and, in the eyes of Tripuri nationalists, the 'Bengalinization' of the indigenous historical sites. The (almost) absence of erstwhile Manikya rulers (appropriated as heroes by Tripuri nationalists) from the memorial landscape of the city tells a different story. What is the difference that this absence makes in 'thinking' space? What does it say about the relationship between place and identity?

Monuments and memorials create and maintain a particular view of a place—they impress that conception on the public landscape or inscribe a particular view of the history on the landscape. The politics of 'memorials' work within the ideology of producing place and identity, and as 'a marker of memory and history. Places of memory provides ideal way to trace the underlying continuities and discontinuities in (national) identity politics'. The underlying assumption is that a place of memory (memorials) makes real, in the everyday lived experiences of given population, the invented idea of place and identity. These sites symbolize a connection with a particular idea of the history of the place, entomb a specific memory and perform rituals of commonality. I wish to flesh out, notwithstanding these connections, a different reading of these sites and to arrive at a radical take on the idea of Tripura.

In 2010, a controversy over memory making erupted in Tripura, which contained the seeds of the historic defeat of the CPI(M) in the 2018 assembly election. The Left Front government had proposed a bill in the assembly to rename Agartala Airport after the poet Rabindranath Tagore. The airport was built by Bir Bikram Kishore Manikya during the 1940s and was used by the allied forces in the Second World War. The very idea of commemorating and memorializing Tagore by naming the airport after him, instead of Bir Bikram Manikya, who commissioned it, sparked unprecedented opposition from the ethno-nationalist Tripuris. Between the state's choice of Tagore and Tripuri nationalists, open espousal of Bir Bikram to be commemorated and memorialized as a name of the significant site, lies the troubling politics of identity and place. Despite the conscious appropriation of the past spaces of Manikyan rule by the new state, its inability to commemorate and to memorialize that history subverts that produced connection. Consequently, this calls for the rethinking of these sites, not only as spaces commensurate with a particular invented place identity but also as ambivalent sites which display dissonance with the central ideology of a place.

In order to situate this dissonance, perhaps, it is necessary to look more closely at the way Tripuri nationalists imagined their identity and Tripura. First, Manikya rule and its history were disavowed by the early Tripuri

elites, especially by the members of the JSS-GMP. Second, Manikya rulers were glorified, and its history was appropriated by the new nationalist groups, such as the TUJS, the TSF and the TNV. Later, nationalists retrofitted their nation onto hoary past and produced the present as a colonial condition—the hoary past as their resource to rival geographical imagination. This brand of nationalist discourse wrought much havoc to the nascent modern state's control over Tripura's past. Rather, the past became an untouchable domain, whereby the use of it entailed allowing larger space to Tripuri nationalists in the body politics of the state.

The Manikyan period and the Manikya rulers were nationalized—an ideology (Tripuri nationalism) chastised, stigmatized and delegitimized as 'extremism', 'anti-national' and 'anti-social' since 1947. Nationalized history can no longer serve as a symbolic agenda for the state-promoted vision of a common past. The point is that the incorporation of nationalized historical figures would confer legitimacy to rival geographies—a situation where even 'common past' can no longer exist. These built environments, ironically, merely serve as markers of the Bengalis present in Tripura. They no longer tell a shared past between 'tribals' and 'non-tribals'.

The marks of identity, which interspersed the city landscape then, are non-commensurate with the state's ideology of place and identity. These marks dot the landscape, as rain-battered statues, names memorialized in public places, martyr memorials and gravesites. These do not necessarily tell only of the identity of Tripura, but they also symbolize the failure of that supposed identity.

Since the 1960s, politics in Tripura has been about how to interpret Tripura—as a place, as a home. The narrative of Tripura as a place connected to Bengal is contested by identity politics that is contingent on the rival idea of Tripura's past and present. The later notion of place incites not only radicalized everyday politics but also serves as an ideological resource for armed struggle, waged with the objective of restoration of lost geographies. Countering the ideological basis of Tripuri identity politics has been one of the most important agendas of the Left Front government under Manik Sarkar. The Left Front government has adopted two strategies: One, to crush the tribal insurgency to the point of militarizing the state; two, to reinvest in the narrative of Tripura's historical and immutable connection to Bengal by renaming places and historical sites. While tribal insurgency has been crushed to a large extent, the second strategy has been counterproductive. It led to the rise of the IPFT and the INPT, which mobilized tribals around the themes of political and economic dispossession, as well as dispossession from historical memory.

CONCLUSION

In the recently concluded state assembly election, the Left Front was defeated by the BJP–IPFT alliance. The IPFT led by N. C. Debbarma has largely benefited from mobilizing tribals against Sarkar's attempt to rename Agartala Airport (after Rabindranath Tagore and Ujjayanta Palace (as Tripura Museum) and the renaming of Stable Ground after Vivekananda. These acts were seen as an attempt to officially inscribe and promote the narrative of Tripura's connection to Bengal. These acts have made the newly invented Tripuri new year 'Tring' celebration more popular among tribals. For the past decade, every year on 21 December, the INPT, the IPFT and other nationalist groups would gather to keep vigil as the New Year approached. Beneath the celebratory veneer lies a mourning for a political present and the yearning for a glorious past and lost geographies. This what animates tribal politics in contemporary Tripura.

REFERENCES

Bhaumik, D. (2003). *Tribal religion in Tripura: A socio-religious analysis.* Agartala: Tribal Research Institute.

Bhaumik, S. (2002). Disaster in Tripura. *Seminar-India.* Retrieved from https://www.india-seminar.com/2002/510/510%20subir%20bhaumik.htm

Bhaumik, S. (2003). How Tripuris got wiped out by Bangladesh refugees. Retrieved from https://assam.org/news/how-tripuris-got-wiped-out-bangladeshi-refugees

Debbarma, A. (2003). *Upajatider proti CPI(M) pratir biswasghatak aitihasik dalil.* Agartala: The author.

Debbarma, M. (2008). *A handbook on the identity, history and life of Borok people.* Agartala: Kokborok Sahitya Sabha.

Debbarma, R. K. (2011). *Genealogy of place and articulation of political identity: A study of the emergence of Tripura as homeland* (unpublished PhD thesis). Hyderabad: University of Hyderabad.

Debbarma, R. K. (1998). *Tripurar gram.* Agartala: Tripura Darpan.

Debbarma, R. K. (2017). Where to be Left is no longer dissidence: A reading of Left politics in Tripura. *Economic & Political Weekly, 52*(21), 18–21.

Debbarma, S. (1997). *Ki kore rajnitite joriye porlam.* Agartala: Tripura Darpan.

Debbarma, S. C. (1997). *Census Bibrani.* Agartala: Tripura Tribal Research Institute.

Gan-Choudhury, J. (2004). *A constitutional history of Tripura.* Kolkata: Parul Prakashani.

Hrangkhawl, B. K. (2002). Speech delivered at the 20th meeting of working group of indigenous population (WGIP), 22–26 July. Geneva: WGIP.

Mackenzie, A. ([1884]1999). *The northeast frontier of India.* New Delhi: Mittal.

Nath, N. C. (1999). *Sri rajmala* (trans.). Agartala: Tribal Research Institute.

Paul, M. 2009. *The eye witness: Tales from Tripura's ethnic conflict.* New Delhi: Frankfurt and Lancer.

Sen, T. C. (1998). *Tripura desher katha.* Agartala: Tribal Research and Cultural Institute.

Xaxa, V. (2005). Politics of language, religion and identity: Tribes in India. *Economic & Political Weekly, 40*(13), 1363–1370.

Xaxa, V. (2017). Voiceless in Jharkhand: Freedom of religious act, 2017. *Economic & Political Weekly, 52*(40), 23–26.

Xaxa, V. (2019). Tribal politics in Jharkhand. *Economic & Political Weekly, 54*(28), 10–11.

30

Revisiting Tribal Discourse
in Uttar Pradesh

A. K. Verma

This chapter raises three concerns in respect of tribal communities in Uttar Pradesh (UP). First, it enquires into social exclusion of tribals in UP. Exclusion was triggered by the fact that the Constitution of India did not recognize tribals as a separate social category. Out of the hundreds of tribes and subtribes existing in UP before independence, the Constitution created a new tribal category of 'Scheduled Tribes' (STs) and placed only a few tribal groups in that category, leaving all other tribals outside that category. The Constitution divided tribal population into STs and non-STs, but failed to give any recognition to non-STs. The misfortune of not having a social category of non-STs created an identity crisis for tribal communities and groups excluding them from population mapping device like census. There is no count of tribes in the country that were not scheduled. The identity of such tribes that were not scheduled was completely eclipsed owing to their forcible and arbitrary placement in different 'other' social categories.

The second concern raised in the chapter is about the political deprivation of tribals in

UP as a whole. By separating the STs from non-STs and recognizing only the STs for the purposes of reservations in the Parliament and the legislative assembly, it deprived a whole lot of non-STs from political representation and consequent political empowerment. Because it was presumed that there were very few tribals in UP, they were denied their share of reservation in the Lok Sabha and the UP assembly. Later, when the SCs/STs were given reservations in government jobs and educational institutions, their share was eaten up by the Scheduled Castes (SCs). In a state like UP, the reservation share of the SCs swelled from 13.5 per cent to 21 per cent, leaving just 1 per cent for the STs.

The third concern is about the economic exploitation of the STs and non-STs. The STs suffered economic exploitation because of the lack of political clout. Their numbers were arbitrarily and artificially reduced substantially and, consequently, they could not assert themselves politically. Non-STs remained marginalized in the 'other' social categories within which they were placed. Thus, the

trinity of social exclusion, political deprivation and economic exploitation of tribals in
UP is the subject matter of this chapter.

SOCIAL EXCLUSION

The conventional wisdom is that there are
no tribals in UP. That was in spite of the fact

that scholars and census had laboriously cat-
alogued several tribal communities in UP
since their inception. Before independence,
there were hundreds of tribals in UP (Russell
& Lal, 1916). W. Crooke (1896) reported in
his work the number of tribal communities
in 1891 district-wise. That showed that every
district in UP had several tribal castes/sub-
castes in big or small numbers (Table 30.1).
Their cumulative number throughout UP was

Table 30.1   Population of Some Tribal Cases and Sub-castes in UP (1891 Census)

S. No	Tribe	Population in UP	S. No	Tribe	Population in UP
1	Agariya	938	31	Dharhi	14,294
2	Aghori	4,947	32	Dogar	339
3	Baheliya	13,754	33	Dusadh	82,913
4	Bandi	110	34	Gadariya	929,437
5	Banjara	66,828	35	Gandhila	134
6	Bari	69,700	36	Gara	51,088
7	Barwar	5,082	37	Ghasiya	198
8	Basor	25,443	38	Gond	124,504
9	Bawariya	2,729	39	Gurchha	963
10	Beldar	37,399	40	Habshi	194
11	Bilwar	6,194	41	Habura	2,596
12	Bhantu	372	42	Harjala	246
13	Bhars	417,745	43	Hurkiya	801
14	Bharbhunja	310,202	44	Kachhi	703,367
15	Bhatiyara	30,658	45	Kahar	1,191,379
16	Bhils	190	46	Kanjar	17,865
17	Bhoksa	1,907	47	Khangar	32,921
18	Bhotiyas	7,457	48	Kol	Not Counted
19	Bhuiya	839	49	Korwa	Not Counted
20	Bhurtiya	423	50	Majhwar/Manjhi/Gand Majhwar	21,305
21	Bihishti	80,147	51	Meo/Mewati/Mina	81,616
22	Biloch	13,672	52	Murao	664,916
23	Bind	76,986	53	Musahar	40,662
24	Biyars	18,821	54	Nat	63,282
25	Boriyas	26,909	55	Panka/Panika	913
26	Chero	4,881	56	Radha/Bhagat	233
27	Daflis	42,075	57	Raji	Not Counted
28	Dalera	2,233	58	Saun	256
29	Dangi	2,363	59	Taga	127,527
30	Dhanuk	146,189	60	Tharu	25,492
Total 5,596,634					

Source: Crooke (1896).

quite substantial.[1] But census data reported zero STs in UP in 1951 and 1961. How could they suddenly disappear in the state after independence?[2] The reason was that there were multiple onslaughts on tribal identity in UP as well as all over the country through political ignorance and administrative apathy or connivance. That led to the loss of identity and social exclusion of tribals in UP, as well as all over the country.

TRIBAL IDENTITY

The loss of identity and the consequent social exclusion of tribals of UP was due to the fact that they suffered a three-fold onslaught—constitutional, political and administrative.

Constitutional Assault

The first onslaught on tribal identity was made by the Constitution of India itself. The Constitution, while dealing with tribals, made a historical mistake. During the British period, some of the most undeveloped and inaccessible areas inhabited by tribals were christened as *Schedule Areas* and some special provisions were made in law to give them some kind of protection from outsiders and also to give them some concessions in tax collection, etc. (Kulkarni, 1991). When the constitution was drawn, untouchability was prevalent, and those belonging to the lowest rung of the social hierarchy were called untouchables and considered to be polluted castes. The makers of the constitution abolished that social evil through constitutional provision and renamed the then polluted (untouchable) castes as SCs, giving them reservation in legislatures at central and state levels. For identifying the SCs, pollution of castes was an objective criterion. But when the issue came up for discussion

in the constituent assembly about tribals and giving them protection, the makers of the constitution committed 'historic wrong' and chose to call the tribals living only in the Scheduled Areas as STs (Verma, 2013a). In doing so, they completely ignored the other tribals who were equally or more backward, poor and marginalized but who were living in non-Scheduled Areas (Verma, 2013a).

The constitution makers made another mistake by selectively picking up only the STs for the affirmative action benefits while completely ignoring the other tribals, namely non-STs, for any other such consideration. That was not only the case in UP, but all over the country. By selectively picking up some tribal castes and communities as backward and identifying them as STs in each and every state, the constitution did a great deal of harm to the sensibilities of other tribal communities that were banished from the tribal domain as enshrined in the constitution. The multitude of tribals were denied tribal identity because the constitution did not provide them any recognition nor gave them any protection. Thus, a very large number of non-STs lost tribal identity.

The insult to tribal identity was not complete yet. A lot of salt to their insult was put thereafter. Further assault on their identity was made when they were forcibly and arbitrarily put into 'other social categories', namely SCs, OBCs or, in some cases, general, to which they did not belong. As uninvited, unwanted and unwelcome guests in their new-found captive social categories, they felt totally out of place—subordinated or subservient to that social category as they could never compete with members in those categories because of their underdeveloped socio-economic conditions. The outcome was that they were excluded from the domain of tribal society and placed in non-tribal Hindu social order where they did not belong. Their social exclusion was complete.

---

[1] In census data 1891, there were approximately 5,596,634 tribes and subtribes reported.
[2] After independence, the census 1951 and 1961 showed zero STs in UP.

Political Assault

The second assault on tribal identity was political that came from the highest executive office, the president of India. Under Article 342 of the Constitution, the president was authorized to identify STs state-wise in consultation with the governors of the respective states. It is not clear how that consultation process was actually conceived and carried on in the first place. What criteria were formulated by governors in several states to identify and select tribal castes and communities for inclusion in STs in their respective states? Obviously, the governor must have asked the district magistrates of each district to do the identification on their behalf. The entire process is shrouded in mystery because it completely neglected the scholarly works of R. V. Russe and Hira Lal (published under the orders of the central provincial administration) and W. Crooks (published by the Office of the Superintendent of Government Printing). These were not ordinary documents, but they could be considered almost 'official'. Both had listed several tribes in UP district-wise. In addition, the government had the record of the census 1891, which also listed several tribes in UP (Table 30.1). All those tribals were extremely underdeveloped and needed protection. But in UP, it was strange that the president of India, acting on the recommendation of the governor of UP, notified only five tribes—Bhotiya, Bhoksa, Jansari, Raji and Tharu—as STs. He did not bother to raise the issue of what would happen to the remaining tribes in UP, or what would happen to them if they were excluded from the purview of the STs? It was really an assault on the tribal community as a whole that innumerable tribals were arbitrarily excluded from the domain of the STs and not even given non-STs status.

Administrative Assault

The third assault on tribal identity in UP came from the administrative agency called the Registrar General and Census Commissioner of India, which is responsible for making headcount of individuals and social groups such as the SCs and the STs. The Registrar General works under the Ministry of Home Affairs. It is very surprising that, in spite of the fact that the president of India issued a public notification in 1950 about the existence of five STs in UP, namely Bhotiya, Bhoksa, Jansari, Raji and Tharu, the Census of India showed zero STs in the state in two successive census reports in 1951 and 1961 (Verma, 2013a). How could it be that the president of India, in consultation with the governor of UP, notified the existence of five STs in UP, whereas the Census of India reported zero ST population in the state? One of them was surely wrong. Either the president made a false notification about the existence of five STs in UP or the census was wrong in not reporting their numbers (Verma, 2013a).

The said anomaly resulted in creating an incorrect initial perception that UP is a non-tribal state. From 1951 to 1971, census data showed zero STs in UP. Right from top to bottom in the political and administrative circles, they all came to believe this falsity. That in spite of the fact that the president of India, under Article 342 of the Constitution, in consultation with the governor of UP, declared that there were five STs in UP, namely Bhotiya, Bhoksa, Jansari, Raji and Tharu through Presidential Order 1950. Hence, they were denied the benefits of the affirmative policies formulated by governments. Only in 1971 census, the ST population in UP was reported in census data (Verma, 2013a). That was because the Government of UP notified the Presidential Order of 1950 recognizing these five tribes as STs only in 1969—after a long neglect of the Presidential Order for 19 years. So the Registrar General of India got a legal basis to count notified STs in UP— Bhotiya, Bhoksa, Jansari, Raji and Tharu—as STs only from the 1971 census. Since then, they have been regularly counted in UP.

The results of all these three onslaughts—constitutional, political and administrative—led to a severe identity crisis among the tribal communities in UP. Their non-count by census and reporting zero STs in two successive censuses (1951, 1961) made them almost extinct in the state. Consequently, there was a severe setback to their social and cultural identities and, consequently, loss of their economic and political empowerment. As they were not counted by census as STs, there was no idea of their strength either district-wise or in the whole of UP. Hence, no one could know how strong they were numerically in UP. Being poor, uneducated and highly backward, they could not protest their exclusion from the tribal domain and meekly accepted their arbitrary and artificial placement in the 'new social category' of the Hindu hierarchy (Verma, 2013a).

As the non-STs were merged into 'other categories' of Hindu social order, they suffered humiliation and unease in their new social environment and were not able to enter into any *roti-beti* (marriage) relationship with other castes and communities within their respective 'new' social categories. They could not compete with others so far as getting any benefits of reservation in legislatures and later in jobs and educational institutions, because they were socially, educationally and economically far-far backward than others in their 'new' social groups. Thus, they did not benefit from any reservations offered to their social category.

Wrong Census

The Census of India had a major role to play in creating a blatantly false perception of the absence of tribals in the first place, and when they started reporting STs since 1971, the data seemed utterly wrong. The first census data on STs in UP were available only in 1971; thereafter, they were regularly counted in every subsequent census (1981, 1991, 2001 and 2011). The census reported 17 per cent decadal growth rate in the ST population in UP during 1971–1981, 23 per cent during 1981–1991 and 26 per cent during 1991–2001. But

it surprised us all by reporting 2,500 per cent decadal growth rate in the ST population in UP during 2001–2011 (Verma, 2013a). How could that be? The very magnitude of the decadal growth rate of the ST population in UP, as reported in the 2011 census, is indicative of major wrongs at various levels in the political and administrative systems earlier while identifying and counting STs in UP. And this is so when Uttarakhand, a major tribal concentration area of the state, was carved out of UP and made a separate state in 2000 resulting in UP losing 256,129 STs (Table 30.2).

The messy ST picture in UP recorded by the census can be understood by an example from the 2011 data. The census data 2011 shows that the tribal population in UP was 1,134,273 (Verma, 2013a). But according to the 2011 census data on ST households for UP (HH–5 Series Tables, Census of India 2011), there were 512,649 ST households in UP; 359,499 rural and 153,150 urban. On the basis of the previous census (1991 and 2001) reporting 5.2 persons per ST household on average in UP, the ST population in UP in the 2011 census could be estimated at 26 lakhs plus (Verma, 2013a). Thus, according to the census records, there were three sharp watersheds of the ST population in UP: first, 1951–1971: zero STs in UP; second, 1971–2011: 1.07 lakhs STs (excluding Uttarakhand) and, third, 2011 census: 26 lakhs plus STs. If correctly identified and counted, the ST population in UP may be close to the ST population percentage at national level, that is, 8.6 per cent (Verma, 2013a).

This claim is founded not only on the wrong census count but also on the fact that there are not just five STs in UP, as notified by the president in 1950. How only 1 lakh STs in 2001 swelled up to 26 lakhs in 2011 in UP? Is not that fishy? After a fight for 52 years, the Parliament, by law, recognized 17 more STs wrongly placed in the SC/OBC category and made them STs in 2002. Unfortunately, these 17 tribal sub-castes were given ST status only in 13 districts of UP—12 districts of eastern UP and one district of Lalitpur in

Table 30.2   ST Population and Decadal Growth Rate in UP, 1901–2011

Census Year	Indian Population in Crores	Decadal Growth Rate %	ST Population in India	ST Decadal Growth Rate in India (%)	ST Population in UP	ST Decadal Growth Rate in UP (%)	Remarks
1901	23.83	–	–	–	–	–	
1911	25.20	5.7	–	–	–	–	
1921	25.13	(–)0.31	16,100,000	–	–	–	
1931	27.89	11	22,400,000*	39.1	–	–	
1941	31.86	14.22	24,700,000**	2.3	–	–	
1951	36.10	13.31	19,100,000***	(–)22.6	#	–	
1961	43.92	21.64	29,883,470****	57.6	#	–	
1971	54.81	24.80	38,015,162	26.2	199,000	–	After the formation
1981	68.33	24.69	51,628,638	35.8	233,000	17	of Uttarakhand
1991	84.64	23.85	67,758,380	31.2	287,901	23	in 2000, UP lost
2001	102.87	21.23	84,326,240	24.4	107,963	26	256,129 STs
2011	121.01	17.60	104,281,034	23.7	1,134,273	950	
					2,665,774##	2,500##	

Source: Compiled from various census reports of respective years.

Notes: *Hill and forest tribes, **primitive tribes, ***tribes, ****STs (as listed in census data).

\# Figures for 1951 and 1961 are not available because it was in June 1967 that five tribal castes—Bhotiya, Bhoksa Jaunsari, Raji and Tharu—were notified as STs in UP and, hence, their first census count could take place in 1971.

\#\# Although the primary census abstract (UP) shows the ST population in UP to be 1,134,273, household ST data and data on the number of married couples per household suggest that the ST population is double that number with a much higher decadal growth rate (Verma, 2013b).

Bundelkhand (Table 30.3). Thus, a blatant injustice was done to the 17 new STs because they were denied their fundamental rights, which bar any discrimination on the grounds of place of birth or residence. In 13 districts of UP, they are STs, whereas in the rest of 62 districts, they are not. Is not that bizarre? Imagine what would be the real number of these new STs if they were given recognition as STs in all 85 districts in UP? And that would have the potential to bring the percentage of the population of STs in UP at par with the national ST percentage of 8.6 per cent. Surely, that would be the ground for awarding them true identity and terminating their 'social exclusion', which had hitherto been primarily responsible for the lack of their political empowerment and economic betterment. Not only that, even the shifting of 17 OBC/SC castes to the ST list by the Parliament in 2002 suffered two major wrongs.

First, while it recognized 'Gonds' as STs in the first place, it also mentioned Dhuria, Naik, Ojha, Pathari and Raj Gond as its sub-castes. The districts in which they were recognized were all from Poorvanchal (eastern UP; Table 30.3). In that area, we know that the upper caste Brahmins use Ojha and Nayak as their surnames. Therefore, when it came to getting the ST certificate, the Brahmins using Ojha and Nayak surnames also applied for the ST status and were granted the ST status—either due to the ignorance of the local administration or by their connivance. Misusing this, the Brahmins with Ojha and Nayak surnames also got reservation benefits in jobs. This is not only an anomaly, but a great injustice to the Gonds. It also amounts to a criminal act for faking one's identity as ST while one belongs to another upper caste category. That could result in the upper caste Ojhas and Nayaks gobbling up all the advantages of the STs in

Table 30.3   Tribes Recognized as STs in Some Districts of UP by the Parliament in 2002

S. No.	Tribal Castes/Sub-castes	Residential Restriction (Districts)
1	Gond, Dhuria, Nayak, Ojha, Pathari, Raj Gond	Maharajganj, Siddharthnagar, Basti, Gorakhpur, Deoria, Mau, Azamgarh, Jaunpur, Ballia, Ghazipur, Varanasi, Mirzapur and Sonbhadra
2	Kharwar, Khairwar	Deoria, Ballia, Ghazipur, Varanasi and Sonbhadra
3	Saharya	Lalitpur
4	Parahiya	Sonbhadra
5	Baiga	Sonbhadra
6	Panka, Panika	Sonbhadra and Mirzapur
7	Agariya	Sonbhadra
8	Patari	Sonbhadra
9	Chero	Sonbhadra and Varanasi
10	Bhuiya, Bhuiyan	Sonbhadra

Source: The Scheduled Castes and Scheduled Tribes Orders (Amendment) Act, 2002.

eastern UP owing to their social, educational and economic background.

The second wrong was that the real sub-castes of 'Gonds' called Beldar, Gudia, Kahar, Kharwar, Mallah, Turha, etc., were not included in the list that detailed the 'Gond' sub-castes in 2002. That left out the real ones of the Gond sub-castes from being recognized as STs, while the other spurious castes were included without any precaution. That is why the Government of UP needs serious exercise to recommend to the central government to weed out the undeserved, unscrupulous tribal castes/sub-castes from the ST list and include those left out in 2002. If that happens, the population of the STs would rise phenomenally in UP, and their social exclusion could take a back seat.

Political Deprivation

The tribals of UP had also lagged behind politically. By being wrongly placed in other social categories and, consequently, erroneous headcounts by census, they have suffered political deprivation. Such deprivations can be seen on many counts. First, they could not become a strong primordial group with political clout so as to attract the attention of political parties as a vote bank. Second, they failed to get into political formations like political parties and their ancillary organization and could neither become members or office-bearers of any prominence. Third, they naturally had no reason to demand their entry into the list of candidates finalized by political parties for contesting various local, assembly or parliamentary elections. Fourth, as a corollary, they failed to become peoples' representatives at the panchayat, municipal, assembly or parliamentary levels.

No wonder that tribals were marginalized in state politics and suffered acute political deprivation in UP. Hence, the crucial issues of loss of tribal identity, their placement in wrong caste categories, the neglect by the Registrar General in making census headcounts, the failure of the UP government to notify the Presidential Order of 1950 granting ST status to five tribal castes (Bhotiya, Bhoksa, Jansari, Raji and Tharu) for about 19 years and, finally, the shifting of a few castes from SC to ST category after 52 years in 2002 that too in 13 districts of eastern UP only speak volumes about the plight of the tribals and their political marginalization in the state of UP. It is only after being exploited by all parties that the tribals in UP are now gearing up to show their political clout.

The Gonds were recognized as tribes as far back as the 1891 census. But see the injustice against them after independence, when our new constitution came into force. The Gonds were put in the SC category in Mirzapur and Sonbhadra districts in UP, whereas in the rest of state, they were declared to belong to the General category. After 52 years of struggle, when the Parliament woke up in 2002 to give them ST status, they were granted that status only in 13 districts, mostly in eastern UP. In the remaining districts of UP, they are still in the General category (Table 30.3).

More bizarre was the exclusion from 'Gond' category of its most numerous species, namely Kahars and Mallahs. The most eminent scholars on tribal studies in UP have categorically opined that the Kahars and Mallahs are integral to the Gond tribe. Kahar, also known as Mahar, Dhimar, Bahera, Bhoi and Machhmar (in Bundelkhand), are sub-caste of the Gonds. Gond is the main tribe of which Kahar is only an occupational derivative (Russell & Lal, 1916, pp. 291–296). Similarly, Mallahs are fishing and boating tribes and were mainly involved in transporting goods through waterways during the British reign. The term 'Mallah' is purely occupational and the Mallahs represent themselves as descendants of the Nishads, a mountain tribe of the Vindhya ranges (Crooke, 1896, pp. 460–461). It, thus, looks very clear that the Kahars and Mallahs were sub-castes of the Gonds and very much deserved to be treated as STs. In the 1891 census, the population of Gonds, Kahars and Mallahs was 1,682,981. Their projected cumulative population in the 2011 census would be 8,509,636 (Verma, 2013a).

That is just about one significant tribal group 'Gonds'. There were several such tribal groups in UP. If they all are brought within the ST category, many things will happen. First, the total ST population in UP would become very large, about 8.2 per cent of the state population (almost close to 8.6% of the ST population at national level; Verma, 2013a). Second, because of their projected numerical

strength, they would become a very significant social group and wield a political clout capable of influencing the political fortunes of several political parties and contestants in the electoral battle. Third, as a consequence, that would lead to their better presence across all political parties and at the various political positions therein. Fourth, it would enable them to have their due share of 7.5 per cent reservation in the legislature at state and national levels, as well as in jobs and educational institutions—a share which had been given to the SCs in the state. Fifth, it would mean reserving about 30 out of 403 seats in the UP assembly and 6 out of 80 Lok Sabha seats in UP for the STs. Presently, there are no seats reserved for them either in the UP assembly or in the Lok Sabha. So, whenever a correct approach to tribal identification and enumeration is taken in UP, the STs in UP will have substantial gains politically. At the next census in 2021, their real number in UP and population percentage would be known. Therefore, whenever a new delimitation commission is appointed and attempts are made for the apportionment of seats and to attend to the issues of reservation of the SCs and the STs, it would surely reserve adequate seats for them in assembly and the Lok Sabha as per their share in the population of UP that would lead to their political empowerment.

Economic Exploitation

The tribals of UP have suffered economic exploitation for a very long time. The reason is that they have been dependent on three components of nature—*jal, jungle, zameen* (water, forest, land). That had been the sole economic source of their livelihood. They had been using these sources very sparingly for a very long and using them in a very eco-friendly way that could sustain the life cycle of flora and fauna. While consuming natural resources, they also nursed nature without harming the wildlife and plant life.

But, after independence, the tribal groups in UP suffered two major setbacks; first, as most of them lost tribal identity, their traditional occupation remained unprotected; second, in the name of development, many feudal-type rural elites encroached on their economic resources either by paying them 'peanuts' or simply by using muscle and not paying at all and also displacing them from their place of residence making them homeless and workless.

KOLS IN UTTAR PRADESH

Out of the several hundred tribe castes/subcastes in UP, let us take the case of the Kols in UP to understand the economic exploitation of the tribes. Since our childhood, we have learnt of Kols and Bhils as Adivasis or aboriginal tribes throughout India. But when we look at the Kols of UP, we find a very strange situation. The Kols are found in Madhya Pradesh (MP) and adjoining areas of southern UP, namely Allahabad, Chitrakoot (part of the Banda district till 1997), Varanasi, Mirzapur and Sonbhadra. These areas are located in Bundelkhand and Baghail Khand which are divided between UP and MP. Their population in Bundelkhand (both UP and MP) is estimated to be about 3 lakhs.[3] However, the Kols were not given recognition as tribes in UP after independence. The Kols residing across the border on MP side were recognized by the president of India as STs in 1950, but the Kols living on UP side were not accorded ST status. Instead, they were declared SCs. Consequently, they got the tag of polluted caste, whereas they had not experienced any social discrimination earlier owing to their status as a tribe.

The Kols trace their lineage to the legendary Shabari of the Ramayana, who had been revered by generations of Hindus for her extreme devotion to Lord Rama during his exile. Hence, placing them in a polluted caste category in the early 1950s was an affront to the sensibilities of both Kols and Hindus.

However, the dark side of the story is that the Kols had been treated very badly by feudal lords who resorted to their economic exploitation. They tried to dispossess them of their land, their only source of livelihood, by hook or crook. In doing so, they took advantage of the fact that the Kols (tribals) did not believe in private ownership of land nor were aware of any legal requirement to establish such ownership. Therefore, when the feudal lords, with the connivance of the local administration and the goons, tried to dispossess them of their land, the Kols (tribals) could not establish their legal rights over the same.

So what options were left with the Kols/tribes in UP? Either they could move further into the deep forest or work as bonded labours of their exploiters. Owing to the stringent laws of the governments regarding the conservation of forests and, consequently, increased state control that banned human activity in forests, the Kols in Bundelkhand and Baghail Khand were left with no option except to join the bandwagon of bonded labours of their exploiters. The Kols also became victims of modern developments that regularly led to the construction of hydroelectric dams and thermal power stations, as in the Sonbhadra district or the creation of wildlife sanctuaries elsewhere.

Some organizations such as the Patha Kol Adhikar Manch (Dogra, 2009) and the Uttar Pradesh Adivasi Vikas Manch have been taking up the case of the Kols. These organizations have adopted a three-pronged strategy to ameliorate the conditions of the Kols. First, to create awareness among the Kols about their plight and rights; second, to create social awareness through media and interaction with government officials and, third, to lobby with the government for the speedy implementation of the schemes designed for tribal

---

[3] Retrieved from http://absss.in/stories-from-the-field/68-up-tribal-groups-ignored-by-policy-makers

welfare and development.[4] During the infamous Emergency period in India (1975–1977), the Indira Gandhi government allotted the Kols rights to Gaon Sabha land as per Sections 195 and 198 of the Zamindari Abolition and Land Reforms Act, 1950. That was just to win over the angry Kols who were turning to take up arms against their perpetrators.[5]

However, the entire scheme remained on paper, as the local feudal called *dadus* manipulated ownership by splitting the land in the name of their relatives and the Kol servants, without their knowledge, and persuaded them to take loans from the bank, promising to pay that back on their behalf. When they did not pay back, it was the poor Kols who lost their meagre land and landed in jail on many occasions.[6]

In several cases, where the pattas were allotted to Kols, they were unaware of the allotment, and, even if aware, faced litigation with such giants as the forest department which claimed ownership rights. One such case was the Ranipur Wildlife Sanctuary in Chitrakoot (UP) encompassing 23,000 hectares of land where the Kols lived. The NGO 'Akhil Bharatiya Samaj Sewa Sansthan' (ABSSS) working in Banda–Chitrakoot area intervened on their behalf. The effort of ABSSS was successful because after 20 years of continued struggle (1978–1997), about 2,500 Kol families in the region got back 10,000 acres of land without any bloodshed.[7]

In UP, the distribution of 'pattas' and the legal ownership of land to landless people is covered under the UP Zamindari Abolition and Land Reforms Act, 1950. However, due to the collusion of local feudal, administrative and political parties, the implementation of the same is made difficult and against the interests of the tribals. The distribution involves three steps: first, distribution of land pattas; second, entry of allottee's names in village land records and, third, actual possession of the land to the allottees. While the first two steps are fairly easy, the third one—'actual possession of land'—is a very tardy process. Hence, the Kols did not get actual possession of land in several cases.[8] Here, the intervention of the various NGOs and CSOs was quite effective, though the patta-holders had to face regular intimidation from the local feudal authorities.

Additionally, the size of 'patta-land' being just 1.2 to 1.5 hectares, and the quality of the land being poor with hardly any irrigation facilities, the yield from them was very meagre—barely sufficient for about 5–6 months. So they had to look for income from other sources. That again took them to the local feudals who would employ them with all the vengeance at their disposal. Alternatively, they could collect forest produce such as tendu leaves (used to make bidis), firewood, amla (fruit for making pickles, and having medicinal values too), honey, mahua (for making liquor) and chiraunji (a dry fruit variety). But the control of the government over forests made that steadily difficult.[9]

Obviously, there was no political support at their command to browbeat these inconveniences. This is just about the Kols. There were, and still are, hundreds of tribal castes and sub-castes who still suffer the same humiliation. Although political formations of tribal groups such as the Nishad Party of Nishads, Mallahs and Kewats, and the Suheldev Bahujan Samaj Party (SBSP) of the Rajbhars have come up in eastern UP, the problem of tribals is very widespread, deep-rooted and complex. These parties have a clout and are

[4] Retrieved from http://absss.in/land-distribution-for-kol-tribals-in-uttar-pradesh
[5] Retrieved from http://absss.in/
[6] Retrieved from http://absss.in/
[7] Retrieved from http://absss.in/
[8] Retrieved from http://absss.in/
[9] Retrieved from http://absss.in/

becoming significant in state politics. The SBSP of the Rajbhars was a great help to the BJP in securing the victories in the 2014 and 2019 Lok Sabha and the 2017 assembly elections in UP. The Nishad Party became so influential in Gorakhpur that the Samajwadi Party lured its leader Sanjay Nishad to become its candidate and win by-poll in Gorakhpur, a seat vacated by veteran Adityanath Yogi, who became the chief minister of UP in 2017. Thus, much of the problems of social exclusion, political marginalization and economic exploitation of tribals in UP are intertwined, and unless some very knowledgeable, serious and sustained efforts are made by the government first to correct the historic wrong, we cannot expect any radical change in their social, political and economic conditions.

RECOMMENDATIONS

For the convenience of further study and research on the subject, and for the government to take some futuristic policy decisions to rectify historic wrongs against the tribal community in general, and the STs of UP in particular, we are making only a few practical recommendations. First, the state government, the central government and the newly formed National Commission for Scheduled Tribes should make a fresh effort to correctly identify tribals in UP and accord them ST status. Those already identified as STs in 13 districts of UP in 2002 should be given ST status throughout the state. Second, after that, when the next census is done in 2021, the correct ST population in UP should be ascertained which is likely to be close to the national average of 8.6 per cent. On this basis, the STs in UP should be given due reservation in the state assembly and Lok Sabha by the next delimitation commission. Third, the state of UP should also constitute a full-fledged state commission for STs in UP for fresh identification of tribes and making all-out efforts to enable the

government to create a separate social category of 'non-STs' so that those tribal groups who are not able to get entry into the ST category should get, at least, recognition as tribals and get back their original identity. That Commission should also make recommendations for the betterment of the socio-economic conditions of non-STs and STs.

It is very unfortunate that various governments simply try to take cosmetic steps and attempt to shift some castes from the OBC to the SC category. For a very long time, this mistake is being repeated by all governments, beginning in 2004 with Mulayam Singh Yadav. Since then, all subsequent governments headed by Mayawati, Akhilesh Yadav and Adityanath Yogi have tried to replicate this mistake (Verma, 2019). They have represented all the three major parties in UP—the Bahujan Samaj Party, the Samajwadi Party and the Bhartiya Janata Party. Thus, it is clear that at the political and governmental levels, there is no knowledge or awareness about the real problem faced by the tribes in UP. Probably, they must know that shifting castes from one social category to another is the sole prerogative of the Parliament.

Hence, it is hoped that this academic intervention would make some dent on the current tribal discourse in UP in particular and in the country in general and would facilitate the conferment of tribal identity on several castes and sub-castes which are wrongly placed in other social groups. This could lead to the end of social exclusion, political marginalization and economic exploitation faced by tribals in general and the STs in particular in UP.

REFERENCES

Crooke, W. (1896). *The tribes and castes of the north-western provinces and Oudh* (vols. I–IV). Punjab: Office of the Superintendent of Government Printing.

Dogra, B. (2009). Kol tribals come forward to expose corruption. *Panchayat Raj Update*.

Kulkarni, S. (1991). Distortion of census data on Scheduled Tribes. *Economic & Political Weekly*, *26*(5), 205–208.

Russell, R. V., & Lal, H. (1916). *The tribes and castes of the central provinces of India* (vols. I–IV). London: MacMillan & Co Ltd.

Verma, A. K. (2013a). Tribal annihilation and upsurge in Uttar Pradesh. *Economic & Political Weekly*, *48*(51), 52–59.

Verma, A. K. (2013b). Incorrect ST data (letters). *Economic & Political Weekly*, *48*(20), 4.

Verma, A. K. (2019). Yogi Adityanath's triple faults in transferring 17 MBCs to SC category in Uttar Pradesh. *Swarajya*, 22 July. Retrieved from https://swarajyamag.com/politics/yogi-adityanaths-triple-faults-in-transferring-17-mbcs-to-sc-category-in-uttar-pradesh

31

Tribal Politics in West Bengal: Quest for Identity and Recognition

Nilamber Chhetri

It is an irony of our time that the developmental parameters adopted by the state have indeed induced displacement, exclusion, discrimination and added to vulnerabilities of tribes in many ways. The democratic processes ensued in the post-colonial Indian state have created structures of inequalities for the tribes. Their image in the public is construed through an anachronistic understanding of history; wherein they are considered as a remnant of history, therefore, out of step of modernity (Skaria, 1997, 1999). In comparison to the scheduled castes (SCs), the scheduled tribes (STs) are much less likely to take the advantage of affirmative actions as they are not a homogeneous category and differ in terms of their exposure to wider society (Xaxa, 2001, pp. 2,765–2,768). To root out these discriminatory practices, these groups have periodically engaged with the colonial and post-colonial state in India. Especially, the tribes have reacted to the state in various forms-be it revolts and rebellions in the colonial days or the violent arm struggles in the post-colonial decade.[1] The recent upsurge of Naxalite violence in remote districts of India also stands testimony to the resistance carried by tribes against the exploitative and discriminatory practices. In such struggles, they utilize their oral traditions to incite revolutionary spirit and also use their social networks based on clan and kinship to incite guerilla warfare against the state (Duyker, 1987; Samaddar, 2019).

Discursively construed as primitive aborigines in colonial canon, the label of tribe has undergone subsequent changes, indicating changed stance of the state vis-à-vis them. The administration of the tribes in the past was structured through politics of colonial

---

[1] Tribal movements such as a Santal Rebellion of 1855–1856 was a decisive moment in the history of colonial India. For detailed discussion on various tribal movements, see Singh (1983).

difference. Based on this idea of difference, tribe was segregated as discrete categories markedly distinct from castes groups. Such rendition often conflated or at times by-passed intricate differentiations between and amongst groups. The romanticized view of tribe as egalitarian and primordial communities often painted a stereotypical image and promoted an essentialized view of the group as uncivilized, wild and uncouth (Van Schendel, 2011, p. 21). Indeed this type of depiction often created a uniform image of tribal groups in India neglecting the regional, cultural, and historical variations. In this sense, tribe was a modern construction defined in contra-distinction with the modern and westernized self of the colonizers (Banerjee, 2016, p. 3).

It is within this ambit that the identity of tribe started to take a concrete shape which was inextricably related to the political and economic transformation of the state. Tribes from Indian heartland were thus uprooted from their place of origin and employed in various tea plantations of Bengal and Assam (Bhowmik, 1981, p. 55). The post-colonial Indian state often reproduced the same stereotypical understanding of tribe. The technology of governance and the classificatory regime instituted during the colonial period was re-appropriated in renewed forms thereby creating varied forms of contestations. Owing to its frequent associations with the affirmative policies of the state the category of ST in recent years have been refurbished with a social importance, it has assumed a life of its own often ensuing protracted struggles for recognition, rights, and state entitlements. At the same time the developmental model adopted by the state based on the notion of resource extraction from the mineral rich tribal belts at the cost of the tribal livelihood. Such disproportionate extractions of resources have made the tribes more vulnerable to the forces of global capitalism. The triads of resource extraction, breaking of traditional system of knowledge, and livelihood have made them one of the most vulnerable groups.

Considering these issues Sundar writes 'the language of 'protection' and 'uplift' deployed for them has negated the possibility of 'rights' (Sundar, 2016, p. 13). Inequality persists and is perpetuated owing to the restricted opportunities to avail the benefits offered by the state sponsored developmental programmes. Following Agamben, Vikas Dubey characterizes the plight of the tribes as homo-sacer wherein the structural violence perpetuated against these groups has reduced them to 'bare existence' (Dubey, 2018, p. 244). Highlighting these issues the chapter argues that the politics of tribe in West Bengal have to be understood in relation to the pan-Indian framework which have structured specific contours for state-tribal interaction.

This chapter explores varied forms of tribal politics ensuing in the state of West Bengal along three axes. First, it explores the nature of ST population in the state while providing an overview of the tribal situation with regards to their population, education, poverty and so on. Second, the chapter exclusively focuses on the changing nature of electoral politics unfolding in the tribal constituencies in the state. The third section deals with empirical account to document the recent upsurge of demands for recognition as ST by various groups in the hills of Darjeeling. Tribal politics in recent years is shaped by the opportunities offered by the existing nation-state framework of affirmative actions as well as the global upsurge for asserting rights of indigenous peoples (Karlsson, 2003, p. 405, 2018). Highlighting these issues, the chapter will chart the interphase between regional demands and aspiration of ethnic groups to attain ST status in Darjeeling.

TRIBES IN BENGAL: SOCIOECONOMIC PROFILE

Bengal is home to a large number of tribal groups, in total there are 40 groups classified as STs in the state.[2] Based on their ethnological character, original homeland, their route of migration and current distribution pattern, we can classify three broad zones in the state where tribal groups predominate. The hilly terrains and the foothills are home to groups such as Lepcha, Bhutia, Toto, Garo, Mech, Rabha and others; the Terai region of Jalpaiguri and Cooch Bihar is home to groups such as Garo, Mech, and Rabha. In the plains of Malda, Birbhum, Burdwan, Midnapur and Purulia, groups such as Oraon and Santhals predominate. As per the census report of 2011, the total tribal population of the state is 52,96,953 persons, which constitutes 5.8 per cent of the total population of the state and 5.08 per cent of the total tribal population of the country.[3] The total male population is 26, 49,974 and the females 26,46,979.[4] The decadal growth of population of ST is 20.20 per cent which is lower than the rest of India which stands at 23.66 per cent. The sex ration in West Bengal is 999 women per 1,000 men which is higher than the all India ration of 990. The literacy rate of tribes is 57.90 per cent which is, however,

lower than the all India rank of 58 per cent (Government of West Bengal, 2013–2014, p. 12). School drop pout rate amongst the tribes in the state for class I-V is 28.3 per cent, for class I-VIII is 48.2 per cent, class I-XII is 74.6 per cent.[5] More than half of the total ST population of the state is concentrated in the four districts, namely, Medinapore, Jalpaiguri, Purulia, and Bardhaman, however, none of the districts in the state have 25–50 per cent concentration of tribes.[6] Of the remaining districts, Bankura, Maldah, Uttar Dinajpur, and Dakshin Dinajpur have sizable ST population. The highest recorded population of ST can be found in the Jalpaiguri district with 18.89 per cent and Kolkata with the lowest ST population in the state.[7] Census figures reveal that predominantly the tribes in the state profess Hinduism with 3,914,473, Muslim 30,407, Christians 343,893, Sikhs 1,003, Buddhists 220963, Jains 876, Other religion 77,4450, and religion not stated 10, 888.[8] Table 31.1 shows a brief profile of the ST population of West Bengal.

---

[2] The predominant tribal groups of Bengal are- 1. Asur; 2. Baiga; 3. Badia, Bediya; 4. Bhumji; 5. Bhutia, Sherpa, Toto, Dukpa, Kagatay, Tibetan, Yolmo; 6. Birhor; 7. Birjia; 8. Chakma; 9. Chero; 10. Chik Baraik; 11. Garo; 12. Gond; 13. Gorait; 14. Hajang; 15. Ho; 16. Karmali; 17. Kharwar; 18. Khond; 19. Kisan; 20. Kora; 21. Korwa; 22. Lepcha; 23. Lodha, Kheria, Kharia; 24. Lohara, Lohra; 25. Magh; 26. Mahali; 27. Mahli; 28. Mal Pahariya; 29. Mech; 30. Mru; 31. Munda; 32. Nagesia; 33. Oraon; 34. Parhaiya; 35. Rabha; 36. Santal; 37. Sauria Paharia; 38. Savar; 39. Limbus; and 40. Tamangs. The last two groups were added to the list in 2003.

[3] The first 10 major STs in West Bengal according to the population and proportion are: Santhal (51.8%), Oraon (14%), Munda (7.8%), Bhumij (7.6%), Kora (3.2%), Lodha (1.9%), Mahali (1.7%), Bhutia (1.4%), Bedia (1.3%) and Savar (1%). Mainly in the four districts namely: Medinipur, Jalpaiguri, Purulia and Bardhaman, more than half of the total ST population is concentrated. The other districts like Bankura, Maldah, Uttar Dinajpur and Dakshin Dinajpur has sizeable ST population.

[4] As per 2001 Census report the sex ratio of total ST population in the state is 982, which is higher than the national average for STs (978). The state also has higher child sex ratio (0–6 age group) of 981 as compared to the aggregated national figure (973) for the STs. The sex ratio among Bhutia (999) is the highest among the major STs but their child sex ratio (951) is low. This is in contrast to Bedia who has recorded the lowest sex ratio of 962 but a high child sex ratio.

[5] Statistical profile of Scheduled Tribes in India 2013, Ministry of Tribal Affairs Statistics Division Government of India. http://www.indiaenvironmentportal.org.in/files/file/statistical%20profile%20of%20scheduled%20tribes %20in%20india%202013.pdf, p.180.

[6] Statistical profile of Scheduled Tribes in India 2013, Ministry of Tribal Affairs Statistics Division Government of India. http://www.indiaenvironmentportal.org.in/files/file/statistical%20profile%20of%20scheduled%20tribes% 20in%20india%202013.pdf, p. 131.

[7] See the census report 2011: http://censusindia.gov.in/2011census/dchb/1916_PART_B_DCHB_KOLKATA.pdf. Also see Government of West Bengal (2013–2014, p. 59).

[8] Source: http://www.censusindia.gov.in/2011census/population_enumeration.html.

Table 31.1 Basic Profile of ST Population in Rural and Urban Areas of West Bengal, 2011 Census[1]

	Household	Population	Literate	Illiterate	Working	Agriculture	Marginal Workers	Non-Working
Total	1,160,069	5,296,953	2,664,431	2,632,522	2,509,166	717,047	1,057,395	2,787,787
Rural	1,065,283	4,855,115	2,383,831	2,471,284	2,342,896	703,244	1,016,521	2,512,219
Urban	94,786	441,838	280,600	161,238	115,195	13,803	40,874	275,568

Source: Tabulated from the census data of 2011.

[1] Primary Census abstract data for scheduled tribes (ST) India and States/UTs-District Level. Retrieved from http://adibasikalyan.gov.in/html/state-data-2011.php.

The census figures reveal that substantial tribal population in the state is concentrated in the rural areas and are predominantly illiterate, working as marginal workers or non-workers. The presence of the tribal population in the urban areas is negligible considering their overall population. Out of the total population of 4,41,838, a significant number 2,75,568 are non-workers in urban areas (Table 31.1). The figures point to the fact that tribal groups residing in the urban areas also face marginalization like their rural counterparts. In the sample population of 4,76,579—live birth was recorded as 30,291, with maternal death of 44, the maternal mortality ratio of 145 and the maternal mortality rate of 9.2 per cent.[9]

One of the pressing concerns of tribes since the colonial period is the issue of rights over land. From the Kisan Sabha movement to the Naxalbari uprising, the issue of land has stirred political mobilization and structured political actions (Samaddar, 1998, Skaria, 1999, Karlsson, 2000). The large-scale displacement of the indigenous groups for developmental activities is inextricably linked to tribal question in West Bengal. The story of tribes in West Bengal compels us to rethink the processes through which impoverished mass are relentlessly exploited not just by the colonial forces but also by the global forces of capital. In recent years, brutal state suppression such as in Singur and Nandigram stands testimony

to the fact that tribes and Dalits have fought long battle against the state and the agents of global capitalism to safeguard their lands which were earmarked for special economic zones. Owing to the repeated onslaught of the state and the police, the tribes in various parts of the state have taken up Maoists ideology and resorted to violence to ameliorate their situation. Especially in district like Bankura, Purulia and Midnapore, the effects of Maoists activities have had drastic impact on the lives of the tribes.

The state government in accordance with the national schemes has adopted many policies for the betterment of the tribal population in the state. In order to cater to the needs of the STs, a new department, namely, Tribal Development Department was created by bifurcating the Backward Classes welfare Department. The newly instituted Tribal Development Department is headed by the Chief Minister and is assisted by the principal secretary, special secretary and deputy secretary along with assistant commissioner for reservation. The joint commissioner for reservation is entrusted with the allied task of reservation and prevention of atrocities against STs in the state. Backward classes welfare offices are instituted in places like Jhargram, Alipurduar, Kalimpong and Basirhat subdivisions. Officers and Inspectors are deployed in these regions to look into matters concerning

[9] Special Bulletin on MMR, June 2011 - Registrar General of India cited in Statistical profile of Scheduled Tribes in India 2013, Ministry of Tribal Affairs Statistics Division Government of India. http://www.indiaenvironmentportal.org.in/files/file/statistical%20profile%20of%20scheduled%20tribes%20in%20india%202013.pdf. p.131.

issuance of caste certificate.[10] The Cultural Research Institute chiefly responsible for undertaking research on tribal life in the state also comes under this department. The institute helps in conducting socio-cultural, ethnographic, economic, and educational studies of the tribal groups and guides the government in formulating developmental projects, polices and plans. This organization is headed by the director assisted by deputy directors, cultural research officers, research investigators, and other staff.[11] The department also looks after the running and management of Ekalavya Model Residential Schools (EMRS) through its Paschim Banga Adibasi Kalyan O Siksha Parishad (PBAKOSP). At present, seven EMRS are functioning in districts such as (a) Bankura, (b) Purulia, (c), Burdwan, (d) Paschim Medinipur, (e) Jalpaiguri, (f) Birbhum, (g) Dakshin Dinajpur with funds from Government of India (GOI) and the state government.[12] The department also looks after the functioning of financial institutions for the welfare of tribal groups such as the West Bengal Tribal Development and Co-operative Corporation Ltd. (WBTDCC Ltd.).

Despite being home to many tribal groups, the chief lacunae of West Bengal is the lack of any scheduled areas for STs in the state. In India, states, namely, Tamil Nadu and West Bengal have sizeable ST population but do not have any scheduled areas. Yet, in recent years, the West Bengal government has approved the formation of Tribe Advisory Councils (TACs) for the development of tribes in the state. [13] The council strives to provide old age pensions in timely fashion, engage inspectors for the state runs hostels for ST students, to undertake special drives to dispose all pending case related to caste certificates, construction of Ashrams, creating the post of tribal development officer in each district and construct Adivasi Bhawan for tribal development.[14] However, the actual functioning of this organization is unclear and the way funds are allocated through it remains fuzzy. This may be owing to the fact that most tribes in the state live in predominantly mixed villages without being concentrated in one single region of the state.

POLITICAL ENTANGLEMENTS OF TRIBES IN THE STATE

For centuries, tribes have been engaging with the state structure to ameliorate their condition. Be it in forms of violent revolt or a more reformative movement, they have either tried to evade the state or encounter the state directly (Hardiman, 1995). In the post-independent phase, tribes have also engaged the state in the political spheres. The politics of tribes in West Bengal represents unique and chequered characteristics-often driven by the one party system, party affiliations played a decisive role in the overall performance in the electoral politics. The nature of the political participation of the tribes in the state of West Bengal reflects a transformation in their overall allegiance to a political ideology. Swayed by the promise of a new and efficient administration, most of the reserved constituencies in the state voted for All India Trinamool Congress (AITC) in 2014 (Bhattacharyya,

---

[10] For details see http://adibasikalyan.gov.in/html/admin-setup.php.
[11] For details see http://adibasikalyan.gov.in/html/admin-setup.php.
[12] For details see http://adibasikalyan.gov.in/html/pbakosp.php.
[13] The West Bengal Tribes Advisory Rules, 1953 were amended vide Notification No. 820-BCW dated 06.03.2012 to make the council compact and effective. The West Bengal tribes advisory council is re-constituted in the state in terms of Sub-rule (a) of rule 4 of West Bengal Tribes Advisory Council Rules, 1953, Vide Notification No.4140-BCW/3C (MC-08/96 (Pt-I, Duplicate) dt., 10 December 2013. The council was earlier defunct and held no meetings in the past but the council is now holding meetings as per mandate.
[14] For details see http://adibasikalyan.gov.in/html/tac.php.

2016). Once a stronghold of the left fronts such as Revolutionary Socialist Party (RSP), and Communist Party of India Marxist (CPI-M), the tribal pockets in the state have adopted a new strategy as evident in the representatives elected in both the state, as well as, the central legislature from the reserved constituencies of the state. As elections masks and reinforces system of inequality, tribal groups forge their own clan based networks to secure the most from the elections (see Wouters, 2018).

A comparative analysis of the Lok Sabha and Vidhan Sabha elections in West Bengal since 1999 gives us a vivid picture of the changing nature of political affiliations of tribes in the state (Table 31.2). Out of the total of 42 Lok Sabha seats from the state, two constituencies, namely, Alipurduar and Jhargram are reserved for the STs. The Alipurduar constituency comprises of seven assembly segments, however, following the recommendations of the delimitation commission, one segment, namely, Falakata (Vidhan Sabha constituency) was converted into SC-reserved constituency. In 2009 Shri Manohar Tirkey of RSP, and in 2014 Dasrath Tirkey of AITC were elected from the constituency.[15] Lok Sabha constituency in Alipurduar was dominated by RSP (India) since 1977.[16] However, the presence of BJP in 1999 and 2004 was significant as the party secured 2,36,786 and 2,39,128 votes in Alipurduar constituency, respectively. The other parliamentary constituency reserved for the STs in the state is Jhagram which too has seven segments. Unlike Alipurduar, the presence of BJP in Jahrgram is negligible. Since 1977 till 2014 all the MP from the constituency belonged to the CPM party, this record was broken when Uma Saren of AITC was elected from the constituency with 6,74,504 votes in 2014 general elections.[17] Table 31.2 details the votes secured by the elected candidates from

Table 31.2 Vote Share of the Elected Candidates in ST-Reserved Parliamentary Constituencies in West Bengal, 2009–2019

Name of constituency	Year	Category	Winner	Party	Vote
Alipurduar	2019	ST	John Barla	BJP	750,804
Alipurduar	2014	ST	Dasrath Tirkey	AITC	362,453
Alipurduar	2009	ST	Tirkey,Shri Manohar	RSP	384,890
Alipurduar	2004	ST	Joachim Baxla	RSP	384,252
Alipurduar	1999	ST	Joachim Baxla	RSP	389,919
Jhargram	2019	ST	Kunar Hembram	BJP	626,583
Jhargram	2014	ST	Uma Saren	AITC	674,504
Jhargram	2009	ST	Baske, Dr. Pulin Bihari	CPM	545,231
Jhargram	2004	ST	Rupchand Murmu	CPM	509,045
Jhargram	1999	ST	Rupchand Murmu	CPM	402,325

Source: Data tabulated from the elections results of Alipurduar and Jhargram 1999–2019.[1]

[1] For elections results see http://www.elections.in/west-bengal/parliamentary-constituencies/alipurduar.html and http://www.elections.in/west-bengal/parliamentary-constituencies/jhargram.html.

[15] For delimitation, see An Extraordinary Issue of the Gazette of India, Part II, Section 3 (iii) dated 15 February, 2006. To be published in An Extraordinary Issue of the West Bengal State Gazette dated 15 February 2006.
[16] For elections results see http://www.elections.in/west-bengal/parliamentary-constituencies/alipurduar.html and http://www.elections.in/west-bengal/parliamentary-constituencies/jhargram.html.
[17] For elections results see http://www.elections.in/west-bengal/parliamentary-constituencies/alipurduar.html and http://www.elections.in/west-bengal/parliamentary-constituencies/jhargram.html.

Table 31.3   West Bengal State Assembly Election Results in Tribal Constituencies, 1991–2016

	Name of the Winning Party with the Number of Votes Secured in Subsequent Elections					
Constituency	2016	2011	2006	2001	1996	1991
Madarihat	BJP (66,989)	RSP (42,539)	RSP (47,331)	RSP (60,412)	RSP (57,663)	RSP (45,400)
Kumargram	AITC (77,668)	RSP (71,545)	RSP (69,540)	RSP (60,966)	RSP (59,032)	RSP (52,282)
Kalchini	AITC (62,061)	IND (46,455)	RSP (52,748)	INC (43,749)	RSP (48,141)	RSP (39,447)
Mal	AITC (84,877)	CPM (62,037)	CPI(M) (56,564)	CPM (53,683)	CPM (60,559)	CPM (51,351)
Nagrakata	AITC (57,306)	INC (46,537)	CPI(M) 62,676	CPM (60,287)	CPM (71,274)	CPM (68,331)
Phansidewa	INC (73,158)	INC (61,388)	CPI(M) (93,689)	CPM (77,507)	CPM (85,845)	CPM (62,076)
Tapan	AITC (72,511)	AITC (72,643)	RSP (74,414)	RSP (58,892)	RSP (65,142)	RSP (56,161)
Habibpur	CPM (64,095)	CPM (59,286)	CPI(M) (56,477)	CPM (43,992)	CPM (55,288)	CPM (42,781)
Sandeshkhali	AITC (96,556)	CPM (66,815)	CPI(M) (69,859)	CPM (65,214)	CPM (65,467)	CPM (58,031)
Nayagram	AITC (98,395)	AITC (75,656)	CPI(M) (65,495)	CPM (56,753)	CPM (57,954)	CPM (44,715)
Keshiari	AITC (104,890)	CPM (76,976)	CPI(M) (88,763)	CPM (76,278)	CPM (82,366)	CPM (65,497)
Binpur	AITC (95,804)	CPI(M) (60,728)	JKP(N) (54,149)	IND (37,680)	JKP(N) 50,981	IND (53,147)
Bandwan	AITC (104,323)	CPM (87,183)	CPI(M) (55,486)	CPM (48,299)	CPM (53,680)	CPM (46,007)
Manbazar	AITC (93,642)	AITC (78,520)	CPI(M) (56,739)	CPM (54,162)	CPM (53,155)	CPM (54,630)
Ranibandh	AITC (92,181)	CPM (75,388)	CPI(M) (52,827)	CPM (54,186)	CPM (58,474)	CPM (48,089)
Raipur	AITC (89,841)	CPM (69,008)	CPI(M) (72,397)	CPM (66,973)	CPM (67,754)	CPM (59,198)

Source: Data tabulated from the elections results of State Assembly election 1991–2016.[32]

---

[32] http://www.elections.in/west-bengal/assembly-constituencies/

Alipurduar and Jhargram parliamentary constituencies between 1999 and 2019.

Out of the total of 294 state assembly constituencies in the state, 16 are reserved for STs. These constituencies are namely Kumargram, Kalchini, Madarihat, Mal, Nagrakata, Phansidewa, Tapan, Habibpur, Sandeshkhali, Nayagram, Keshiary, Binpur, Bandwan, Manbazar, Ranibandh and Raipur. Most of constituencies were dominated by the left leaning political parties such as the RSP, CPI, CPI-M and in the past, the Indian National Congress.[18] Manbazar was an open constituency till 2011 after which it was reserved for the ST. Likewise Sandeshkhali was a SC reserved constituency, but from 2011 onwards it was reserved for ST (Table 31.3).

In Bengal, the CPI-M party was embodied as the government, and in the lack of other avenues of political engagement, the party affiliation played a significant role. In such a condition, the party played the role of moral guardians of social life (Bhattacharyya, 2009, p. 61; 2016, p. 126). The lack of focus on cultural identities was also a major feature of CPI-M led Left Front government in Bengal. During the CPI-M decades the ruling party saw tribes as an archaic embodiment of traditionalism and feudalism. The communists construed tribes as victims of brutal capitalist and semi-feudal exploitation.[19] Such a conception of tribe has been altered in recent years. The policies of crass industrialization through forcible land-grab endorsed by the Left Front led to dissent and resentment within the party.

---

[18] https://www.mapsofindia.com/assemblypolls/west-bengal/
[19] See CPI-M Policy document on tribal Question. Adopted by the Central Committee in its meeting held on 2–3 March 2002. https://cpim.org/content/cpim-policy-document-tribal-question.

Moreover, the prolonged marginalization of Dalits, and minorities within the party, and increasing elitism and bureaucracy led rebel CPI-M leaders like Rezzak Mollah to come up with autonomous political formations like the recently formed Social Justice Forum (Sinharay, 2014, p. 11)

The people of West Bengal voted for political change by ending thirty four years long left regime in 2011. In the 2016 assembly elections, the TMC independently secured 211 out of 294 seats, sharing about 45 per cent of the total votes to secure a second term (Battarcharya, 2011; 2016). The relentless plea of Mamata government on the indigenous '*ma, mati, manush*' (mother, soil and people) heralded the demise of what Dwaipayan Bhattacharyya calls 'party-society' (Bhattacharyya, 2010, p. 52; 2011). The overall downfall of the party system unleashed new political forces where community and culture based identities like the Matuas in the border districts, the Gorkhas in Darjeeling, the Rajbanshis and Adivasis in north Bengal, and the Muslim minorities have come to take the centrestage. Noting the importance of community based identities in the electoral politics, Sinharay writes, 'the party-identity of a candidate is no longer the only strong marker of her or his political credibility, rather the identity of the candidate as a minority has become crucial in support of the candidature' (Sinharay, 2014, p. 11). Nath, while noting the difference in the strategy adopted by the CPI-M and the TMC regarding tribes, states that CPI-M followed the strict idea of adherence to party ideologies while the TMC used the traditional tribal hierarchy to gain popularity amongst the people. Party affiliations were accepted by the tribes in rural areas as it meant gaining access to government schemes. In contrast, the TMC followed a different strategy by funding the festivals of groups such as Santhals, and was

able to muster greater support from the tribes. Following Bourdieu, Nath considers such strategies adopted by the political parties as 'cultural misrecognition' (Nath, 2018, p. 96). Emphasizing greatly on the cultural aspects over structural issues, the TMC was able to allocate mass benefitting schemes from tribal to non-tribal areas.

In recent years, one significant development recorded in West Bengal is the growing influence of Rashtriya Swayamsevak Sangh (RSS) and ascendancy of the BJP in electoral politics. In the neighbouring state of Jharkhand and Chhattisgarh, the RSS has started to influence the tribes through the Akhil Bharatiya Vanvasi Kalyan Ashram (Sundar, 2016, p. 154). The performance of the BJP in the tribal belts of the state has been significant. In the recently concluded panchayats elections of 2018, BJP scored 42 per cent and 33 per cent seats in Jhargram and Purulia. While the ruling TMC bagged 48 per cent and 43 per cent seats, respectively (Bagchi, 2018). The 2019 Lok Sabha election also indicate to the fact that BJP is gaining stronghold in tribal regions of the state. The rank and file of the TMC seems to be in disarray in the tribal pockets of the state. Whereas the BJP and its parent organization, the RSS, have been making active networks in the tribal regions of the state for a considerably longer period of time. By running its schools and by providing welfare activities amongst the tribal communities, the BJP has created a strong network amongst the tribes. The Trinamool Congress secured its dominant position in the panchayats election; the BJP too fared well and secured second position posing a serious challenge to the ruling party.[20] In the panchayats elections, the BJP made deep inroads into districts long considered as Maoist bastions in the state (Dutta Majumdar, 2018).

[20] West Bengal Panchayat elections: Trinamool leads, BJP second . https://economictimes.indiatimes.com/news/politics-and-nation/trinamool-congress-leading-in-gram-panchayat-seats/articleshow/64201136.cms.

POLITICS OF STATE CLASSIFICATION

The colonial machinery of state classification which was perpetuated in the post-colonial period has led to internal classification within the ST category. Like other states, in the state of West Bengal, area restrictions were adopted for the identification of STs for the purposes of affirmative action. Following section 14 of the Bihar and West Bengal (Transfer of Territories) Act, 1956, the SC and ST list was modified via order 1956.[21] Following this order four criterions were adopted for the identification of STs in the state namely,

1. Throughout the State: Ho, Kora, Lodha, Kheria or Kharia, Mal Pahariya, Munda, Oraon, Santal.
2. Throughout the State except the territories transferred from the Purnea district of Bihar:-Bhumij.
3. Throughout the State except in the Purulia district and the territories transferred from the Purnea district of Bihar:-Bhutia including Sherpa, Toto, Dukpa, Kagatay, Tibetan and Yolmo, Chakma, Garo Hajang, Lepcha, Magh, Mahali, Mech, Mru, Nagesia, Rabha.
4. In the Purulia district and the territories transferred from the Purnea district of Bihar:-Asur, Baiga, Banjara, Bathudi, Bedia, Binjhia, Birhor, Birjia, Chero, Chik Baraik, Gond, Gorait, Karmali, Kharwar, Khond, Kisan, Korwa, Lohara or Lohra, Mahli, Parhaiya, Sauria Paharia, Savar.

The census data regards people who returned their identities as Anuschuchit Janjatis, Girijan and Adivasi within the generic category of tribe. Along with these groups the state of West Bengal also recognizes some groups as particularly vulnerable tribal groups (PVTGs). Three groups namely Lodha, Birhor and Totos are declared as PVTGs in the state. As per the census report of 2011, the total population of these PVTG are: Birhor - 2,241, Lodha - 1,08,707, Totos - 66,627 respectively (Government of India, 2013, p. 162). These groups predominantly reside in Paschim Medinipur, Purulia, Jalpaiguri and Sagar Block of south 24 Parganas, that is, Lodhas in Paschim Medinipur and Sagar Block of south 24 Parganas, Totos in Jalpaiguri and Birhors in Purulia. The inherent classification within the category of ST has itself created rift amongst groups in recent years. Though there is a policy to provide assistance to PVTG in the forms of grants and special funds, seldom do these groups benefit from such programmes. Despite the central and the state government running specific schemes for the development of the PVTG, their condition is deplorable. While reflecting on the condition of Totos in Totopara, Daw writes that the schemes and policies of both state and the central governments have not been implemented in Totopara (Daw, 2015, p. 913). Indeed, the changes brought about in the lives of the Totos through state sponsored developmental activities have had a profound impact on their traditional ways of live, often resulting in acute crisis (Biswas, 2009, p. 102).

Along with it, the nature of state classification has in-turn created inter-tribal competition in the state. The internal classification of STs has created fervent demands by others to accesses the same nature of benefits from the state. The exclusive developmental focus on certain groups while excluding other has created a rift amongst the tribes in West Bengal. Initiation of developmental projects such as an insurance scheme called 'Janashree Bima Yojana' covering exclusively the PVTGs, alongside schemes such as Scheme of Development of Primitive Tribal Groups (PTGs) by the Ministry of Tribal Affairs, GOI, in 2008, for the socio-economic development of PTGs have created intra-group competition within the STs of the state. Such a condition of intra-tribal competition is also reflected in Nagaland where the sub-tribes of Nagas try to secure the benefits that are reserved for the groups defined as 'backward' within

---

[21] The Gazette of India EXTRAORDINARY PART II—Section 3, No. 316-A. New Delhi, Monday, October 29, 1956. http://egazette.nic.in/WriteReadData/1956/E-2188-1956-0000-100067.pdf

the state (Das, 2017, p. 67). Since 2005, the Lepchas following their recognition as PVTG in Sikkim have demanded their recognition as PVTG in West Bengal as well.[22]

TRIBALIZATION OF IDENTITIES: THE DARJEELING SAGA

'Who is a tribe?' was a major historiographical and anthropological question in India. The specific understanding of tribe was structured through its understating as a form of social groups distinct from caste. However, in subsequent decades anthropologists realized that rather than being distinct tribes and castes formed a continuum, with tribes gradually assimilating or acculturing themselves into the social structure and cultural fabric of the caste society (for debate on the issue see Bose, 1941; Sinha, 1965; Beteille, 1992; Nathan, 1997). Research has indicated that for groups such as Koch Rajbansi upward mobility following Kshatrization has pushed them further into backward position (Das, 2004, p. 562). Similarly, Chattopadhyay (2014) discusses how the changes in the government policies and the socio-religious reforms movement have impacted the Santhals of Jungle Mahal areas of Birbhum, Bankura and Midnapur. Such developments have further complicated the process of identification of tribe as a distinct social unit. With varying degree of assimilation within the caste society a clear cut distinction between caste and tribe could not be drawn. Thought of as a distinct group, the understating of tribe as a primitive group with archaic subjectivity-distinct from the modern rational self- was further accentuated in the

post-colonial period. Vicariously defined as 'the other of the modern self', tribes were seen as being outside the folds of the caste Hindu society. Such a conceptualization has structured subsequent policy framework for STs in India.

The process and practices of classification have induced new politics of recognition in recent years. In West Bengal, the hill district of Darjeeling has become the epitome of the new politics of tribalism. Structured by the host of historical and political factors, demands for recognition as ST have made deep inroads which are further accentuated by the regional politics. A host of groups in the North Bengal such as Koch and the Mech have demanded recognition as STs in recent years (Roy, 2018, pp. 19–21). Similarly, the assertion of identity amongst groups such as Rabha has taken 'latent forms' wherein identity formation is taking place implicitly rather than taking an explicit form in terms of political mobilization (Karlsson, 2000). In the process of establishing a distinct identity, Rabhas often claim affinity with the larger Koch tribe often echoed in slogan such as 'Koch is Rabha—Rabha is Koch'(Karlsson, 2001, p. 27).

Since government's decision to implement the recommendation of the Mandal Commission in 1990, many ethnic groups started to claim OBC status to reap the benefits of affirmative action.[23] In subsequent years these ethnic groups formed their associations and started applying for the ST status (Shneiderman & Turin, 2006; Shneiderman, 2009; Middleton, 2011a; 2011b; 2015; Chhetri, 2015; 2016a; 2016b; 2017). Ethnic associations thus sprang up amongst groups who were categorized as caste groups within the generic Nepali/Gorkha community (Chhetri, 2018,

[22] Kalimpong Lepchas in primitive status cry. *The Telegraph* dated 4/03/2005. https://www.telegraphindia.com/states/west-bengal/kalimpong-lepchas-in-primitive-status-cry/cid/674680
[23] Following the recommendation of Mandal Commission, groups such as Bhujel, Newars, Mangars, Nembang, Sampang, Bungchheng, Thami and Jogi were recognized as OBCs in the West Bengal in 1995. In this OBC list prepared by the West Bengal government, some groups like Sunuwars were excluded and were not recognized as OBC till 1999 and Dewan and Rai (including Chamling) till 2001. See the details: http://www.anagrasarkalyan.gov.in/htm/obc_list.html.

p. 155, 2017). The entire discourse of tribalism was given a renewed life by the then chief of the Darjeeling Gorkha Hill Council (DGHC) Subhas Ghisingh, who demanded that the entire Gorkha community be recognized as STs and the region placed under the ambit of sixth schedule.[24] The cultural renewal tactics adopted by Ghisingh to include the entire Gorkha community as STs further accentuated exclusive ethnic claims for recognition as tribes in the hills. The Department of Information and Cultural Affairs (DICA) of the DGHC under Ghisingh launched fervent programmes to showcase the tribal characteristics of the Gorkha community. Driven by the quest to register their identities as authentic tribal groups of the Himalayas many ethnic groups started to reclaim lost historical genealogies and engaged in auto-ethnographies (Middleton, 2011a, p. 251). The discourse of tribalism in hills augmented the politics of cultural differentiations and initiated a fervent discourse of authenticity. In many ways, the failure of the Gorkhaland movement and the lack of developmental parameters in the hill further escalated the demand for ST recognition.

In this entire discourse, ethnic demands are framed around the anthropological language of rights and structured around constitutional provisions. The group's rejection of OBC status and adoption of tribal identity indicate a quest to assert their belongingness as the authentic inhabitants of the region. Claiming indigeneity is the new politics of becoming authentic citizens of the nation- a strategy which Karlsson calls as 'indigenous slot' (Karlsson, 2003, p. 405). Structured around such conceptions, demands for recognition as ST has led to constant reworking of statist category through discursive practices. The

hosts of demands raised in Darjeeling show how there is a complex interplay of collective Gorkha/Nepali and exclusive ethnic identities. Within this milieu, it is significant to note that ethnic association in Darjeeling often use the term 'Janjati' to claim their primitive tribal culture and heritage. Ethnic leaders, however, make a crucial distinction between Adivasi and the janjatis. The term Adivasi is mainly used to refer to tribal groups who reside in Jalpaiguri and Dooras areas (Chhetri, 2017, p. 84). The selective use of labels also shows how ethnic identities are marked and maintained even when they claim similar identities based on the statists category of tribe. Ethnic groups, therefore, adopt the statist's definition of tribe as isolated, and backward groups to present their own identities. The growth of demands of indigenous nationalities by ethnic groups in Nepal also had a spillover effect in Darjeeling hills. Borrowing extensively from ethnic activism of Nepal groups started to reclaim their lost tradition, revive their language, grammar, and script to refurbish their ancient genealogies, and rework their cultural practices- a process which Wagner (1981) calls as 'invention of culture'. These processes also correspond to what Cohen (1985) calls the symbolic construction of the community, where cultural traits from the past are carefully and judiciously selected and reinterpreted to suit the requirements of the present (Cohen, 1985, p. 99).

The growing incidences of tribal demands in Darjeeling from early 2000 led to negotiations between the centre-state and the hill leaders regarding the inclusion of Darjeeling in the sixth schedule. A memorandum of settlement was signed which stipulated the formation of a new council under the sixth

---

[24] The demands for the regional autonomy for the Darjeeling hills was made since the turn of the 20th century. The demands ultimately culminated in the violent movement raised by Subhash Ghising in the late 1980, when his party GNLF launched an armed struggle to carve a separate state of Gorkhaland from the existing territories under the West Bengal government. The movement gained prominence from 1986 and came to a standstill in 1988 when a memorandum of agreement was signed which led to the formation of Darjeeling Gorkha Hill council (DGHC).

schedule in 2005.[25] During 2005–2006, the West Bengal government recommended inclusion of ten hill groups within the category of ST so as to increase the total tribal population in the district a required mandate for its inclusion within the ambit of sixth schedule.[26] During the course of fieldwork in 2013–2014, it was revealed that earlier the state government had twice proposed ST status for the 11 hill communities but the Registrar General of India (RGI), a body under the centre, had rejected it. In Darjeeling, the ruling party GNLF welcomed the new council within the sixth schedule but was vehemently opposed by the newly found party Gorkha Janmukti Morcha (GJM) under the leadership of Bimal Gurung. With the ascendancy of GJM in the hills, the sixth schedule issue was sidelined and the movement for the separate state of Gorkhaland was re-launched with renewed fervour in 2007. With the change of government in the state and ascendency of the Mamata Banerjee in 2011, the GJM started to negotiate for an amicable solution for the Darjeeling debacle. Significant to note in this regard is the fact that the GJM started to negotiate with many ethnic and Adivasis organizations from the adjoining plains and Terai region of Dooars for their inclusion within the newly proposed hill council. On 8 December 2011, the GJM discussed the issue of inclusion of Dooars in GTA with minority groups like Millatt-e'-Islamia. Together they decided to demand for Gorkhaland Adivasi Minority Territorial Administration (GAMTA). Along with the West Bengal government, GJM agreed to constitute a high level committee to look into the question of including Gorkha dominated areas in Dooars and Terai region. However, such an agreement between the government and the GJM was resisted by the Akhil Bharatiya Adivasi Vikas Parishad

(ABAVP). The GJM, the state and central governments finally reached an agreement on 18 July 2011 regarding the formation of the Gorkhaland Territorial Administration (GTA). Later in the year on 29 October 2011, the Gorkha Janmukti Morcha, and the ABAVP, Dooars unit signed an 18-point agreement at Mongpoo, after which these organizations jointly proposed a new administrative body called the Gorkhaland and Adivasi Territorial Administration (GATA) in place of the GTA. The ABAVP agreed to incorporate 196 mouzas of the Dooars, and 199 mouzas of the Terai region into the proposed GATA. The ABAVP had earlier demanded the creation of Adivasi Territorial Administration (ATA) on the lines of the GTA for the welfare of the tribals. Though GJM and the local ABAVP leaders reached an agreement on GATA, yet this was opposed by the state committee of the ABAVP under Birsa Tirkey. Following such a staunch opposition from the state president of the ABAVP, John Barla, president of the Terai-Dooars regional unit of the ABAVP, was expelled from the party (Chhetri, 2012, pp. 146–147).

The formation of GTA signaled a new wave of politics in the hills, demands for recognition as ST re-emerged in the changed political scenario. The tribalization of identities thus created a fertile ground for the TMC to make inroads into the hill politics. Unlike the CMI(M) which did not actively intervene in the internal working of groups in the state, the TMC started to make direct impact on the everyday working of the tribal groups in the state. The CPI-M under Jyoti Basu had adopted policy of non-interference in hill politics which was direct contradiction with the policy adopted by the TMC under Mamata Banerjee. Since her election in 2014, she started to work relentlessly to address the crisis in Darjeeling

---

[25] The memorandum of settlement for sixth schedule status for Darjeeling was signed on 6 December 2005. The salient provisions of the memorandum of settlement included formation of Gorkha Hill Council, among others, by replacing the DGHC.
[26] The 10 groups recommended for inclusion in the ST list were-Mangar, Gurung, Khambu Rai, Bhujel, Yakkha, Thami, Sunuwar, Jogis, Newars, and Khas.

by directly intervening in the internal cultural politics of the region. During the course of the fieldwork (2013–2014), some informants expressed the views that the Mamata Banerjee government is channelizing the funds meant for the TAC for the constitution of development boards in the hills. The funds meant for the development of the needy tribal was thus expended to garner political support in the hills.[27] Following such developments, the Lepchas from the district under the banner Lepcha rights movement (LRM) spearheaded a movement for the formation of a separate council for the protection and upkeep of their language, culture, and economic development. A concerted effort was made from Kalimpong by the Lepchas to retribalize themselves (Arora, 2017, p. 88). The demands of Lepchas ultimately came to fruition when Mayel Lyang Lepcha Development Board (MLLDB) was established by the state government in 2013.

Other tribal groups such as Tamangs, Bhutia, Limbus, and Sherpas followed suit and demanded development boards exclusively for their ethnic community. These hosts of demands in the hills created conducive environment for the Mamata Banerjee government to intervene in the inter-ethnic politics of Darjeeling. Taking advantage of the dissipating situation Banerjee announced formation of Tamang Development and Cultural Board (TDCB) on 27 June 2014. Similarly, Sherpa development board was announced on 23 January 2015 and a Bhutia development

board on 25 August 2015 (Chhetri, 2016b, p. 12). Till date, a total of 16 development boards have been announced by the Mamata Banerjee government.[28] The mushrooming of these development boards reflects the changing nature of ethno-politics in the hills.

The strategy of the Banerjee government to appease ethnic minorities by dolling out developmental plans and packages have worked as the newly constituted development boards have announced their support to Mamata Banerjee in the 2016 election.[29] In 2013, the Lepchas welcomed Mamata Banerjee where she was conferred the title of 'Kingchum Darmit' (goddess of fortune in Lepcha language) (Arora, 2017, p. 107). The constitutions of these development boards have instituted a paradigm of governance which Kaushik Ghosh calls 'exclusive governmentality' (Ghosh, 2006, p. 508). The formation of development boards and the race for its attainment point to the fact that unlike the previous decades where tribes and minorities struggled within an assimilationist state, today, the struggle have become more complex, it is unleashing conflicts amongst minority communities within the state for coveted status and state entitlements.

Metei reflects on a similar condition in Meghalaya where the politics of formation of autonomous councils have created a rift between various ethnic groups (Meetei, 2011, p. 167). In the hills too, the formation of development boards has ignited sectarian

---

[27] Interviews conducted with ethnic leaders from various ethnic associations in Kalimpong and Darjeeling during 2015–2016. Strict anonymity of the respondents is maintained based on their requests.

[28] The development boards constituted in hill are namely-Mayel Lyang Lecpah Development board (2013), Tamang Development and Cultural Board (2014), Sherpa Cultural Board (2015), Bhutia Development board (2015), Kahmbu Rai Development Baord (2016), Mangar Development Board (2015), Limbu Development Board (2016), Pahadia Minority Development and Cultural Board (2017), Gurung Development and Cultural Board (2017), Kami Development and Cultural Board (2016), Khas Development and Cultural Board (2017), Sarki Development and Cultural Board (2016), Bhujel Development and Cultural Board (2016), Newar Development and Cultural Board (2016), Damai Development and Cultural Board (2016), Terai, Dooars, Siliguri Development and Cultural Board (Gorkha Community (2018) (Khawas, 2018).

[29] The chairmen of six development boards of different communities in the hills today said they wanted members of their communities to support the Trinamul Congress in assembly polls as a token of gratitude for the formation of the bodies. Chamling, Sanjog. 2019. Hill development boards to support the Trinamul Congress in assembly polls. http://www.indiangorkhas.in/2016/04/hill-development-boards-to-support-tmc-assembly-election.html

and political differences. For instance, the decision of the ethnic associations to support TMC in the upcoming elections in hills was challenged by the GJM who launched a complaint with the election commission.[30] Along with this, internal cleavages have appeared within ethnic associations itself owing to the issue of allocation of developmental funds and resource distribution.[31]

The Banerjee government has adopted the development and cultural board design to appease the hill minorities, sidelining the century old demand for Gorkhaland. Along with this, the formation of Kalimpong on 14 February 2017 was a tacit strategy deployed by the state government to divide the hill population and thereby weaken the collective mobilization for Gorkhland. A popular mobilization following the proposed bill to make Bengali language mandatory in all government schools across states erupted in the hill in 2017. The forced imposition of Bengali and linguistic imperialism was resisted ultimately culminating in outburst of violence in the region (Darjeeling Collective, 2017). The ensuing conflict magnified resulting in the deaths of protestors, thus leading to a 104 days long strike in the region. One significant development after the unrest was the creation of rift within the ranks of the GJM (Chhetri & Thapa, 2017). The faction of GJM led by Binay Tamang relentless appealed to lift the strike while Bimal Gurung refused to step down from his position. Faced with rebellion within the party, the GJM chief Bimal Gurung fled the hills creating further confusion. In recent years, the Bimal Gurung faction of GJM along with GNLF supported the BJP candidate in the 2019 Lok Sabha election, whereas the estranged faction of the GJM under Binay Tamang now heading the GTA has shown allegiance to Mamata Banerjee and her party.

CONCLUSION

The chapter concludes that a provocation-tribal politics in Bengal has been taking place within and outside legal frontiers of affirmative action. For groups already scheduled, they want to be recognized as most primitive and backward to garner further state resources while others who are yet to be recognized as ST raise relentless struggle to be recognized as ST. As evident in our discussions above, groups in Darjeeling such as Lepchas have demanded primitive tribal status to safeguard their position and also formed the development board for their exclusive development in the region. Such demands highlight how in the wave of political change in the hill, the nature of contestation within the category of tribe has undergone tremendous shift in recent years.

Highlighting the nature of tribal recognition movements in India, Sunder reflects, 'some communities who really deserve ST status in order to get protection and reservation in jobs and schooling are too poor and politically marginalized to demand it' (Sundar, 2016, p. 6). Tribal politics in India, therefore, have to be located and understood within this complex admixture of legal recognition, regional development, and ever present quest to protect and preserve their traditional practices and customs. The present discourse of tribal politics in Bengal, thus, reflects the pan-Indian concerns of groups and communities who see recognition as STs as a secure ground to assert their rights and entitlements from the state. The voting pattern and the electoral qualms indicate the shift of focus from the paradigm of underdevelopment championed by the Marxists and the communists in the past decade. Today tribes are more vocal to assert their rights by voicing their concerns through major political parties such as

[30] GJM to complaint against development boards to Election Commission. http://www.indiangorkhas.in/2016/04/gjm-to-complaint-against-development-boards-ec.html.
[31] Sherpa cultural board vice-chairperson suspended. http://www.indiangorkhas.in/2016/07/sherpa-cultural-board-wb-vice-chairperson-suspended.html.

Trinamool Congress. They want to have an active say in the developmental projects initiated by the state, the relentless quest to garner developmental boards in Darjeeling by showing their allegiance to the Trinamool Congress is a tacit strategy adopted by the groups to garner rights and entitlements.

With BJP winning 18 seats from West Bengal in the 2019 Lok Sabha election, the right wing is set to make history in the state. In both the ST constituencies of the state the BJP emerged victorious. John Barla from Alipurduar and Kunar Hembram from Jhargram both from BJP won the elections. In such a surcharged political atmosphere, the state legislative assembly election in 2021 will indicate whether the planned policies of the chief minister especially the formation of development boards in the hills of Darjeeling have really paid the dividend. The politics of classification and reclassification of groups followed by the periodic and sporadic appeals for tribalization have questioned the ephemeral core of tribal identity. From symbolic to the material struggles, the tribal politics in West Bengal indicates a complex admixture of politics of recognition and redistribution. The politics of tribes in the state, therefore, indicates a quest to register their voices in the electoral and political processes, while others who have been neglected view ST status as an avenue to ascertain their identities as true citizens and denizens of the region.

REFERENCES

Arora, V. (2017). The making of the subaltern Lepcha and the Kalimpong stimulus. In V. Arora and N. Jayaram (Eds.), *Democratisation in the Himalayas: Interests, Conflicts, and Negotiations* (pp. 79–114). New Delhi: Routledge.

Bagchi, S. (2018, June 2). Why are the tribals unhappy with Trinamool Congress? *The Hindu*.

Banerjee, P. (2016). Writing the Adivasi: Some historiographical notes. *The Indian Economic and Social History Review, 53*(1), 1–23.

Beteille, A. (1986). The concept of tribe with special reference to India. *European Journal of Sociology, 27*(02), 296–318.

Bhattacharyya, D. (2009). Of control and factions: The changing 'party-society' in rural West Bengal. *Economic and Political Weekly, 44*(9), 59–69.

Bhattacharyya, D. (2010). Left in the lurch: The demise of the world's longest elected regime? *Economic and Political Weekly, 45*(3), 51–59.

Bhattacharyya, D. (2011). Party society, its consolidation and crisis: Understanding political change in rural West Bengal. In A. Ghosh, T. Guha-Thakurta, & J. Nair (Eds.), *Theorizing the present: Essays for Partha Chatterjee* (pp. 226–250). New Delhi: Oxford University Press.

Bhattacharyya, D. (2016). *Government as practice: Democratic left in a transforming India*. Delhi: Cambridge University Press.

Bhowmik, S. K. (1981). *Class formation in the plantation system*. New Delhi: People's Publishing House.

Biswas, S. K. (2009). Socio-economic crisis and its consequences on a little known tribal community in West Bengal, India. In E. Kolig, V. S. M. Angeles, & S. Wong (Eds.), *Identity in Crossroad Civilisations: Ethnicity, Nationalism and Globalism in Asia* (pp. 97–114). Amsterdam: Amsterdam University Press.

Bose. N. K. (1941). The Hindu mode of tribal absorption. *Science and Culture*, vii, 188–194.

Chattopadhyay, P. (2014). *Redefining tribal identity: The changing identity of the Santhals in South-West Bengal*. New Delhi: Primus books.

Chhetri, N. (2012). *Politics and identity: The changing contours of Gorkhaland movement* (Unpublished M. Phil dissertation). New Delhi: Jawaharlal Nehru University.

Chhetri, N. (2016a). Ethnic renewal and claims for tribal identity: An ethnographic exploration of Bhujels of Darjeeling. *The Indian Journal of Anthropology, 4*(1), 1–22.

Chhetri, N. (2016b). Restructuring the past, reimagining the future: Ethnic renewal process and claims for recognition as scheduled tribe in Darjeeling. *Asian Ethnicity, 18*(4), 470–487.

Chhetri, N. (2017). From jat-jati to janjati: Demands for recognition as scheduled tribe and claims of Indigeneity in Darjeeling. *Sociological Bulletin, 66*(1), 75–90.

Chhetri, N. (2018). The quest to belong and become: Ethnic associations and changing trajectory of ethnopolitics in Darjeeling. In T. Middleton, & S. Shneiderman (Eds.), *Darjeeling Reconsidered: Histories, Politics, Environments* (pp. 154–176). New Delhi: Oxford University Press.

Chhetri, N., & Thapa, A. (2017). One hundred and more years of solitude. *Raiot Journal*, 6 October 2017. Retrieved from http://raiot.in/gorkhaland-one-hundred-and-more-years-of-servitude/

Cohen, A. P. (1985). *The symbolic construction of community*. London: Ellis Horwood.

Dutta Majumdar, A. (2018, May 21). West Bengal Panchayat polls: Former Maoist bastions now BJP hubs. *Livemint*.

Das, J. N. (2004). The backwardness of the Rajbansis and the Rajbansi kshatriya movement (1891–1936). *Proceedings of the Indian History Congress, 65*, 559–563.

Das, D. (2017). The politics of census: Fear of numbers and competing claims for representation in Naga society. In V. Arora and N. Jayaram (Eds.), *Democratisation in the Himalayas: Interests, Conflicts, and Negotiations* (pp. 54–78). New Delhi: Routledge.

Daw, S. (2015). Survival of the endangered sub Himalayan Adivasis: Totos in contemporary India. *Proceedings of the Indian History Congress, 76*, 908–917.

Dubey, V. (2018). Asur as homo sacer: Political economy of vulnerability. In M. C. Behera (Ed.), *Revisiting Tribal Studies: A Glimpse after Hundred Years* (pp. 235–246). New Delhi: Rawat Publications.

Duyker, E. (1987). *Tribal guerrillas: The Santals of West Bengal and the Naxalite movement*. Delhi: Oxford University Press.

Ghosh, K. (2006). Between global flows and local dams: Indigenousness, locality, and the transnational sphere in Jharkhand, India. *Cultural Anthropology, 21*(4), 501–534.

Government of India. (2013). *Statistical profile of scheduled tribes in India*. New Delhi: Ministry of Tribal Affairs.

Government of West Bengal (2013–2014). *Annual administrative report*. Kolkata: Saraswati Printing Works.

Hardiman, D. (1995). *The coming of Devi: Adivasi assertion in western India*. New Delhi: Oxford University Press.

Karlsson, B. G. (2000). *Contested belonging: An indigenous people's struggle for forest and identity in sub-Himalayan Bengal*. Richmond: Curzon Press/ Routledge.

Karlsson, B. G. (2001). Indigenous politics: Community formation and indigenous peoples' struggle for self-determination in northeast India. *Identities Global Studies in Culture and Power, 8*(1), 7–45.

Karlsson, B. G. (2003). Anthropology and the 'indigenous slot' claims to and debates about indigenous peoples' status in India. *Critique of Anthropology, 23*(4), 403–423.

Karlsson, B. G. (2013). The Social life of categories: Affirmative action and trajectories of the indigenous. *Focaal—Journal of Global and Historical Anthropology, 65*, 33–41.

Khawas, V. (2018, August 23). Mamata, development boards, Darjeeling-Dooars and the Gorkhas: Apprehensions and implications. *The Darjeeling Chronicles*. Retrieved from https://thedarjeelingchronicle.com/development-board-implications/

Meetei, B. (2011). Politics of recognition: Rethinking existing institutional measures in India. In Gurpreet Mahajan (Ed.), *Accommodating Diversity: Ideas and Institutional Practices* (pp. 161–181). New Delhi: Oxford University Press.

Middleton, T. (2011a). Across the interface of state ethnography: Rethinking ethnology and its subjects in multicultural India. *American Ethnologist, 38*(2), 249–266.

Middleton, T. (2011b). Ethno-logics: paradigms of modern identity. In S. Dube (Ed.), *Modern Makeovers: Handbook of Modernity in South Asia* (pp. 200–216). Oxford: Oxford University Press.

Middleton, T. (2015). *The demands of recognition: State anthropology and ethnopolitics in Darjeeling*. California: Stanford University Press.

Nath, S. (2018). Cultural misrecognition and the sustenance of Trinamool Congress in West Bengal. *Economic and Political Weekly, 53*(28), 92–99.

Nathan, D. (1997). *From tribe to caste*. Shimla: Indian Institute of Advanced Study.

Roy, K. C. (2018). Demand for scheduled tribe status by Koch-Rajbongshi. *Economic and Political Weekly, 53*(44), 19–21.

Samaddar, R. (1998). *Memory, identity, power: Politics in the Jungle Mahals 1890–1950*. New Delhi: Orient Longman.

Samaddar, R. (2019). *From popular movements to rebellion: The Naxalite decade*. Park square, Oxon: Routledge.

Shneiderman, S. (2009). Ethnic (p)reservations: Comparing Thangmi ethnic activism in Nepal and India. In D. N. Gellner (Ed.), *Ethnic Activism and Civil Society in South Asia* (pp. 115–141). New Delhi: SAGE Publications.

Shneiderman, S. (2015). *Rituals of ethnicity: Thangmi identities between Nepal and India*. Philadelphia: University of Pennsylvania Press.

Shneiderman, S., & Turin, M. (2006). Seeking the tribe: Ethno-politics in Darjeeling and Sikkim. *Himal, 18*(5), 54–58.

Sinha, S. (1965). Tribe-caste and tribe-peasant continuum in Central India. *Man in India, 45*(1), 75–77.

Sinharay, P. (2014). The West Bengal story: The caste question in Lok Sabha elections. *Economic and Political Weekly, 49*(16), 10–12.

Skaria, A. (1997). Shades of wilderness: Tribes, caste, and gender in Western India. *The Journal of Asian Studies, 56*(3), 726–745.

Skaria, A. (1999). *Hybrid histories: Forest, frontiers and wilderness in western India*. New Delhi: Oxford University Press.

Sundar, N. (2016). Adivasi vs vanvasi: The politics of conversion in Central India. In N. Sundar (Ed.), *The Scheduled Tribes and Their India: Politics, Identities, Policies, and Work* (pp. 134–167). New Delhi: Oxford University Press.

The Darjeeling Collective. (2017, June 25). What is brewing in Darjeeling? *The Hindu*.

Van Schendel, W. (2011). The dangers of belonging: Tribes, indigenous people and homeland in South Asia. In D. J. Rycroft, & S. Dasgupta (Eds.), *Becoming Adivasi: The Politics of Belonging in India* (pp. 19–43). Oxford/New York: Routledge.

Wagner, R. (1981). *The invention of culture*. Chicago and London: University of Chicago Press.

Wouters. J. J. P. (2018). *In the shadows of Naga insurgency: Tribes, state, and violence in Northeast India*. New Delhi: Oxford University Press.

Xaxa, V. (2001). Protective discrimination: Why scheduled tribes lag behind scheduled castes. *Economic and Political Weekly, 36*(29), 2765–2772.

Index

CPSIA information can be obtained
at www.ICGtesting.com
Printed in the USA
LVHW060734300321
682906LV00007B/138